# Strategic Management and Information Systems

## An integrated approach

D0528895

SECOND EDITIO

# Wendy Robson

PITMAN
PUBLISHING

London · Hong Kong · Johannesburg · Melbourne · Singapore · Washington DC

PITMAN PUBLISHING
128 Long Acre, London WC2E 9AN
Tel: +44 (0)171 447 2000
Fax: +44 (0)171 240 5771

A Division of Pearson Professional Limited

First published in Great Britain in 1994
**Second edition 1997**

© Wendy Robson, 1994, 1997

ISBN 0273 61591 2

*British Library Cataloguing in Publication Data*
A CIP catalogue record for this book can be obtained from the British Library

10 9 8 7 6 5 4 3 2 1

Typeset by Pantek Arts, Maidstone, Kent
Printed and bound in Great Britain by Clays Ltd, St Ives plc

*The Publishers' policy is to use paper manufactured from sustainable forests.*

Learning Resources
Centre

# PLAN OF THE BOOK

## PART 1 – INTRODUCTION TO STRATEGIC MANAGEMENT

| Chapter 1 Strategic management and planning | Chapter 2 Analytical tools in strategic management |
| --- | --- |

## PART 2 – INFORMATION SYSTEMS STRATEGY FORMULATION

| Chapter 3 What *are* management information systems? | Chapter 4 Strategy planning for information systems | Chapter 5 The information systems strategic planning 'toolkit' |
| --- | --- | --- |
| Chapter 6 Frameworks for integrating IS strategies with business strategies | Chapter 7 Information value and IS investment | Chapter 8 IS, business competition and organisation |

## PART 3 – INFORMATION SYSTEMS STRATEGY CHOICES

| Chapter 9 IS resource mangement | Chapter 10 IS management and the IS profession | Chapter 11 Managing user-controlled computing |
| --- | --- | --- |
| Chapter 12 Selection and acquisition | | Chapter 13 Responsible IS management |

# CONTENTS

## PART 2 ◆ INFORMATION SYSTEMS STRATEGY FORMULATION

## 3 What *are* management information systems?

## PART 3 ◆ INFORMATION SYSTEMS STRATEGY CHOICES

# INTRODUCTION

This is a book about how to manage Information Systems *effectively*. Effectively, meaning that IS are deployed, used and managed in an organisationally beneficial way. Effective IS management must determine what support can be drawn from contemporary organisational thinking and an understanding of technological complexity. This book is therefore concerned with the intersection of strategic management and IS (and hence its title!) which is perhaps even more accurately thought of as the strategic management of IS. The main thrust throughout the text is the practical *how to* of IS management. Given the variety of IS management situations, prescriptions whilst simple are too inflexible to be of real practical help. This book therefore offers practical and usable guidance by grouping, reviewing and critiquing principles, tools and techniques by how they support a particular IS management situation. By *explaining*, rather than just describing, these tools this allows the reader to:

- appreciate the context of that situation
- gain a feel for what it is about that situation that it is important to be clear about
- appreciate how the situation influences, and is influenced by, other situations
- judge when IS management decisions and actions are appropriate to the situation
- understand where there are links to other sources of guidance

Organisational forms, competitive pressures and relationships, employment structures, social concerns and cultural norms are all continually shifting in focus. Technological capabilities create increased complexity and opportunities for increased diversity of responses. IS management for the twenty-first century will be about managing this technological risk. Those who form part of IS management, therefore, need to be equipped to understand the risks, balances and trade-offs to be made in deploying IS for organisational gain.

## Who the book is for

This book will appeal to a wide audience across the business management and technology related disciplines. I hope that it will be of use to three categories of those interested in learning about managing organisational use of IS. Firstly, this will include those studying on undergraduate and postgraduate programmes. The book addresses themes central to both IS specific or more general business and management courses; out of such courses may come the potential hybrid manager whose professional profile the book will discuss in Chapter 10. The notion of the 'reflexive practitioner' often makes the dividing line between the student and the practitioner meaningless, as does the increasing tendency to create professional development programmes as joint ventures between industry and universities. So, secondly I hope those not on formal programmes of study, but concerned to learn continually, will find the book both useful to dip into for reference and to broaden their understanding of IS management issues. Thirdly, I hope this book will be helpful for those facilitating the development in others of the capacity to manage IS in a systemic way. The structure of the text accommodates situations where the need is to develop strategic management awareness in IS students. It also supports the development of an awareness of the particular opportunities and difficulties of IS in management students. Most importantly, it also offers support to those who must do both.

This is a student (defined widely) book that integrates material that is currently indigestible by virtue of being in several, often narrowly focused or overly prescriptive texts. I hope to support the development of the increasingly wide skills profile expected of the business/IS professional. For that reason the book aims for a comprehensive coverage of themes. As an integrative volume, this can support a wide variety of developmental programmes. The student so equipped can move, when required, from this intellectual base into an *effective* consideration of the more single-dimension aspects covered in 'specialist' texts on separate aspects of the strategic management of IS. It is the comprehensive coverage of integrated themes that most distinguishes this book from those (frequently excellent) single-theme books.

Throughout the text the only assumed prior knowledge is of a general awareness of business/commerce and some degree of IT literacy. Typically this level of understanding will have been developed by the foundation levels of any general business or IS undergraduate or postgraduate programme of study or, of course, by personal exposure to the use of IS in a business context.

## The structure of the book

IS management is the complex inter-relationship of a large number of issues. In any particular IS situation they will all have some influence. That means that, ideally, all would be presented to the reader simultaneously. This is not possible in a linear sequential form such as a book, or very helpful to a human! Therefore the *logical* elements of IS management are grouped together by their main emphasis. This brings the danger that the reader may compartmentalise IS management concerns and miss the messy interactions that actually exist. To mitigate against this danger, extensive use is made of cross-references to point the reader towards related issues. By explicitly highlighting associations within chapters, between chapters, within parts and between parts of this text I hope that the reader will recognise the *actual* messy connections between tidily presented elements. Figure I illustrates what the logical elements of IS management are, these are then used to form the major parts of the book.

To reflect the logical elements of IS management, the text is separated into parts whose chapters discuss those concerns, situations, models, tools, and techniques that address the main emphasis of that element.

- *Part 1: Strategic Management*, provides the reader with an introduction to the notion of managing strategically. This relatively brief part gives a broad overview of what is meant by *strategy* and how, in general, it is believed to be created and used. This overview serves as a backdrop to the consideration of how this notion of strategy and the associated matters of strategy formulation and action are used in an IS context. The emphasis in Chapter 2 is to provide the reader with a box of tools. This 'tool-box' approach reflects my intention to make

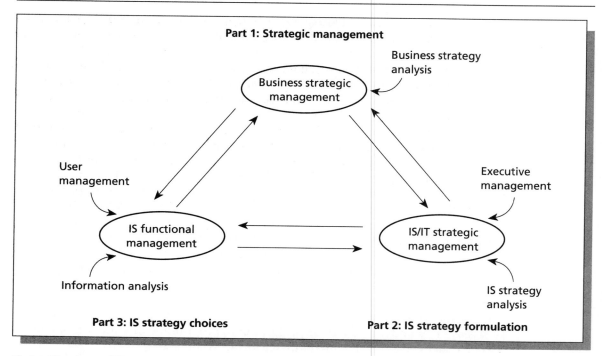

**Fig I ◆ Elements of IS management**

the book *practically* useful. As with all subsequent parts these introductory chapters provide extensive direct references for further reading.

- *Part 2* : *IS Strategy Formulation*, is in essence about the application, in the IS-specific arena, of the notion of strategic management first introduced in Part 1. Collectively the six chapters of this part consider how the different perceptions of strategy have particular implications to IS strategic management. The tool-box approach continues so that the reader is presented with explanations of a variety of ideas, models, and techniques relevant to the process of IS strategy formulation.
- *Part 3*: *IS Strategy Choices*, contains five chapters that look at specific IS management activities through which IS strategy is made *real*. In essence these chapters address different aspects of the trade-offs that organisational IS must make. These are the resource allocation choices made and the collective pattern of these resource allocations is the IS strategy. So the nature of an organisation's IS strategic management is *visible* through such resource allocations. This part discusses how IS management has evolved towards the rich range of methods of sourcing, organising, managing and controlling IS that are currently possible.

It is outside the scope of this book to address the technical IS processes of systems development and operation. How to perform these technically complex processes falls beyond the book's intent to support IS *managerial* decision making. Those concerned with technical delivery will find many excellent books about software analysis, design, coding, hardware installation and cabling and so on. Chapter 3 offers some pointers for those who wish to pursue any of these areas. In fact the vast bulk of IS attention has been directed at such technical aspects. There is also extensive attention given to the general concerns of manging an enterprise. This book is positioned for the much more sparsely supported area of *using* strategic management skills in technologically complex issues.

I hope those who either 'dip into' this text for reference, or read complete parts, will find it improves their ability to understand the complexities of a given IS management situation. I hope that this will lead to improved IS management choices. No *text* alone can improve IS management. However, this book, and the direct references and further reading it points the curious towards, will help equip the reader with improved analytical and critical thinking skills that can then be applied to the diverse IS situations they must manage in contemporary business.

Every effort has been made to trace and acknowledge ownership of copyright. The publishers will be glad to make suitable arrangements with any copyright holders whom it has not been possible to contact.

# ACKNOWLEDGEMENTS

No compendium text of this type starts from nowhere, it collates and builds upon the excellent material already available. I would therefore like to acknowledge the foundation that the work of others has given me.

On a personal note I would like to thank Dr Richard Rolfe for his extraordinarily thorough review of the first edition.

Nothing would have got done without Ian and Zöe, it is not possible to thank them enough for their long-term support, direct help and last minute patience.

Thanks Guys!

# PART 1

# Introduction to strategic management

This Part provides a very brief summary of what is meant by strategy, strategic management and strategic planning. Having provided this brief summary in Chapter 1, Chapter 2 moves into explaining a number of the models, tools and techniques used to support the process of strategy formulation and implementation. This introduction to the *general principles* and tools of strategic management forms an essential platform from which to consider their implications in the management arena. The strategic management of IS must draw extensively upon general strategic management principles; Parts 2 and 3 therefore lean upon, and often refer back to, the material first covered here.

# CHAPTER 1

# Strategic management and planning

Whilst determining the strategy of an organisation is only one of the functions of management it may be the most significant form of management decision making. The complexity of modern business ensures that strategic management is, at least partially, the responsibility of all managers and hence all managers require an awareness of the business direction of the whole organisation: that is, its corporate strategy. 'I am interested in the future because I will spend the rest of my life there.' What we are interested in we seek to manage and control. We manage and control by planning for.

Management thinking in this context is not simply what Ball (1991, p. 1) calls management:

> the control of management activities which are undertaken to achieve the objectives of the organisation.

Rather we are concerned with the determining/interpreting of the objectives themselves. In thinking about this we concern ourselves with a decision making process (often called planning – *see* Section 1.6) and a product (often called a strategy – *see* Section 1.7). There are many ways of thinking about both the product and the process. The thinking about both is often called strategic management and what Strategic Management might mean is the focus of this chapter. This chapter gives some overview discussion and attempts to introduce some of the notions of what is meant by performing the act of strategic management, by being a strategic manager and thinking strategically.

IS strategic planning is considered separately in Chapter 4 but is obviously closely related to the issues considered in this chapter.

## 1.1 ◆ WHAT IS STRATEGIC MANAGEMENT?

It is certainly not an exact science. No organisation can apply strict rules, the 'best' strategy does not emerge from cookbook approaches, and there certainly are no formulae for *calculating* the strategy. Rather, strategic management is about the reading of signs and portents of the future and interpreting them in order to choose an appropriate direction for the future development of the organisation. Whilst this art does not lend itself to rigid mathematical or logical rules it is by no means impossible. John Argenti (1989) calls changes in the environment 'strategic elephants' so any competent manager should have no trouble spotting them if they stop to look!

If it is not an exact science, what is it? Here are some definitions of strategy since they underpin the subsequent definitions of strategic management:

### 1.1.1 ◆ Definitions of strategy

A number of definitions of strategy have been offered. There is no absolute consensus on what the term means since every definition contains implications of how strategy should be created (and so subject to methodological preference). The example definitions are given in date order and so could be interpreted to indicate something about methodological development but should not be interpreted to indicate any implied order of importance.

*Strategy is a rule for making decisions under conditions of partial ignorance, whereas policy is a contingent decision.*

*Business strategy is the broad collection of decision rules and guidelines that define a business' scope and growth direction.*

**Ansoff** (1965) *Corporate Strategy.*

*Strategy refers to the formulation of basic organisational missions, purposes and objectives; policies and program strategies to achieve them; and the methods needed to ensure that strategies are implemented to achieve organisational ends.*

**Steiner and Miner** (1977) *Management Policy and Strategy.*

*Strategy formulation involves the interpretation of the environment and the development of consistent patterns in streams of organisational decisions.*

**Mintzberg** (1979) *The Structuring of Organisations.*

*Strategy is a broad based formula for how business is going to compete, what its goals should be, and what policies will be needed to carry out those goals. The essence of formulating competitive strategy is relating a company to its environment.*

**Porter** (1980) *Competitive Strategy.*

*Strategy is the pattern or plan that integrates an organisation's major goals, policies and action sequences into a cohesive whole.*

*A well-formulated strategy helps to marshal and allocate an organisation's resources into a unique and viable posture based on its internal competencies and shortcomings, anticipated changes in the environment, and contingent moves by intelligent opponents.*

*Goals (objectives) state what is to be achieved and when results are to be accomplished, but they do not state how the results are to be achieved.*

*Policies are rules or guidelines that express the limits within which an action should occur. Major policies that guide the entity's overall direction and posture or that determine its viability – are called strategic policies.*

*Programs specify the step-by-step sequence of actions necessary to achieve major objectives within the limits set by the policy.*

*Strategic Decisions are those that determine the overall direction of an enterprise and its ultimate viability in light of the predictable and unpredictable and the unknowable changes that may occur in its most important surrounding environment.*

**Quinn** (1980) *Strategies For Change: Logical Incrementalism.*

*The essence of strategy is for a firm to achieve a long-term sustainable advantage over its competitors in every business in which it participates. A firm's strategic management has, as its ultimate objective, the development of its corporate values, managerial capabilities, organisational responsibilities, and operational decision-making, at all hierarchical levels and across all business and functional lines of authority.*

**Hax** (Ed.) (1987) *Planning Strategies That Work.*

*There is no single, universally accepted definition of strategy.*

   *There is no one best way to create strategy, nor is there one best form of organisation. The world is full of contradictions and the effective strategist is one who can live with contradictions, learn to appreciate their causes and effects and reconcile them sufficiently for effective action.*

   *No single model or theory can incorporate all the factors that influence major business decisions or all the possible combinations of these factors that could be faced. Nor can any anticipate the bizarre changes that occur in real world environments, or, even more important, the impacts of your own or others' creative innovations.*

**Quinn** and **Mintzberg** (1991) *The Strategy Process.*

*Strategic decisions are concerned with:*

- *The scope of an organisation's activities*
- *The matching of an organisation's activities to its environment*
- *The matching of an organisation's activities to its resource capability*
- *The allocation and reallocation of major resources in an organisation*
- *The values, expectations and goals of those influencing strategy*
- *The direction in which an organisation will move in the long term*
- *Implications for change throughout the organisation.*

**Johnson** and **Scholes** (1993) *Exploring Corporate Strategy.*

The definition of strategy that will be used throughout this text is that:

**Strategy is the pattern of resource allocation decisions made throughout an organisation. These encapsulate both desired goals and beliefs about what are acceptable and, most critically, unacceptable means for achieving them.**

From this definition it follows that it is always possible to *see* what an organisation's strategy is by inspection of the whole of what it *does*. This inspection/deduction process of 'seeing' the strategy is a social process of interpretation so different groups 'see' a different pattern. Stacey (1993) offers a particularly refreshing discussion of what strategy is with a focus on strategy as a game and a pattern both offered as useful notions.

Strategy may be articulated or unarticulated. If unarticulated it shapes actions but can only be directed at the point of those actions. If articulated (through documents or processes) it will tend to be future oriented but for that reason the articulation is of a *forecast* and will probably differ from the *actual* pattern of resource allocations when they happen. Whether articulated or unarticulated, strategy can be detected and will be interpreted.

## 1.1.2 ◆ Definitions of strategic management

Definitions of strategic management do show rather more consistency:

*Strategic Management is a systematic approach to a major and increasingly important responsibility of general management to position and relate the firm to its environment in a way which will assure its continued success and make it secure from surprises.*

**Ansoff** (1990) *Implanting Strategic Management.*

*Strategic Management is a stream of decisions and actions which leads to the development of an effective strategy or strategies to help achieve corporate objectives.*

**Gleck** and **Jaunch** (1984) *Business Policy and Strategic Management.*

*Strategic Management is the decision process that aligns the organisation's internal capability with the opportunities and threats it faces in its environment.*

**Rowe** *et al.* (1994) *Strategic Management.*

*Strategic Management is concerned with the overall long-range direction of organisations . . . and consequently also provides a framework for operational management.*

**Greenley** (1989) *Strategic Management.*

*Strategic Management is concerned with deciding on strategy and planning how that strategy is to be put into effect via:*

- *Strategic analysis*
- *Strategic choice*
- *Strategic implementation.*

**Johnson** and **Scholes** (1993) *Exploring Corporate Strategy.*

So exact opinions differ! Essentially, strategic management is going to be something to do with deriving and describing the *strategy*. This is something that is applicable to all organisations whether large or small, public or private, profit or non-profit making. So strategic management encompasses the entire enterprise and looks beyond day-to-day operating concerns in order to focus upon the organisation's long-term prospects and development. The responsibility for doing this will lie with different people depending upon the size and type of the organisation. In a small business a single owner may do everything, including the strategic management. The owner may not formalise this but since they, at least sometimes, consider their firm as a whole and try to ensure consistency of action by directing all the activities towards the same end they are taking responsibility for the strategic process. At the other extreme very large multinationals may employ an entire level of senior management with this sole responsibility.

Additionally, in such very large organisations there may be a number of *interdependent areas* of strategy. It is convenient to define these as corporate strategy for the entire corporate group, business strategy for that unit of the group – usually called a strategic business unit (SBU), and a functional strategy for each part of the single business unit. All of these levels must be consistent with each other in order for the entire corporation to be successful since they are all aspects of a single whole. Consistency may take many forms and it is the consideration of various interpretations of consistency between interdependent areas as relates to the IS functional strategy that is the focus of much of Part 2 of this book. This chapter will not address who will determine (consciously or unconsciously) what each strategy will be. The tools used and the way of connecting each aspect as well as organisational shape will alter that.

## 1.1.3 ◆ Corporate strategy

This is the sense of direction for the *entire* organisational group, and so it identifies those businesses that the organisation will engage in. At this level, only the global objectives, and the general orientation in order to achieve them, are defined. These are likely to be either growth, stability or defence (retrenchment). Chapter 2 discusses models of these three corporate postures. Corporate strategy is frequently expressed as the answer to the question 'what business(es) are we in?' Therefore corporate strategy provides the framework for the business style that reflects the business strategy and, in turn, does so much to influence the business strategy, particularly the extent of outsourcing, diversification, scale and scope.

## 1.1.4 ◆ Business strategy

This deals with the single SBU and how, by coping with its industry environment, it can successfully contribute to the corporate strategy. By definition, it should have an identifiable and definable product range, market segment and competitor set. Porter (1985) provides a useful way of classifying business strategies; he suggests they are either cost leadership or differentiation of products and may encompass an entire market or be focused upon a particular segment of it. Each SBU will have its own coherent business strategy. Chapter 2 discusses the models of these business strategies.

The business' strategy is that business' 'intent', that is, the strategy is the way in which it wishes to proceed. Many western organisations, as distinct from Japanese ones, fall into the trap of producing rigid definitions that go into far too much detail of future actions. This is a trap because, as chaos theory if not common sense has shown us, the future is inherently unknowable and attempting to identify every contingency tends to create a 'paralysis by analysis'. Quinn's (1982) incrementalism is one way of responding to this trap and is closely allied to the 1990s notion of the 'learning organisation' (*see* Chapter 8). What the organisation requires is the broad *direction* and not the detail of how to get there. The necessary detail is more correctly provided, and the strategy 'fleshed out', via functional strategies and sub-strategies developed throughout the management structure and over time. *See* Chapter 4 for a discussion of the 'system of strategies'.

### 1.1.5 ◆ Functional strategy

There will be a set of these for each SBU. Each will aim to make the best use of the resources available in order to contribute to the business strategy. In order to improve performance functional strategies harness the activities, skills and resources available. Parts 2 and 3 of this text consider *one* functional strategy (that for IS) in some considerable detail and clearly show the interdependencies since corporate and business strategies shape IS strategies but IS strategies shape business and corporate strategies both directly and indirectly through each other. Of course IS is not the only functional strategy; for example, McDonald (1989) sets marketing strategy in just that context.

These areas represent only a *logical* separation of purpose and many, especially smaller, organisations may not formally separate the strategic areas. It should also be noted that there is a great deal of interaction and interdependency among these three strategy elements. They must integrate into a *whole* for the organisation to be successful. The determination of a strategy may reflect these three levels via a top-down development, where each level is 'given' the constraints within which it must develop its strategic direction. Conversely there may be a bottom-up emergence, where the higher level's strategy is the aggregation of those below.

### 1.1.6 ◆ Strategic process

The strategic management *process* is that of making strategic decisions. The model of the strategic decision making process offered by Johnson and Scholes is of three interacting elements: strategic analysis, strategic choice and strategic implementation. This representation is convenient to use because it is well known and used by many authors, for example Dess and Miller (1993) and Rowe, Mason, Dickel, Mann and Mockler (1994) so will be met in much literature. It is a powerful model primarily because it allows us to organise our thoughts without losing sight of the interacting nature of the elements. Similar ideas of three areas existing within an iterative relationship appear in many other works. For example, the model used in the far less well known Smith (1994) names the areas as 'Preparing the Planning Base' (equivalent to Johnson and Scholes' Strategic Analysis); 'Establishing Strategies' (equivalent to Johnson and Scholes' Strategic Choice); and 'Implementing the Plan' (equivalent to Johnson and Scholes' Strategic Implementation). The purpose is the same in every case, to provide a vehicle through which to explain something complex, even though the preference as to names may differ. The strategic decision making process produces the strategy itself and, as already shown, it is sometimes convenient to also view the strategy as made up of three interacting elements.

Strategic management is therefore the process by which an organisation establishes some answers to questions such as:

- What business is it in, exactly?
- Who is it competing with?
- How is it performing?
- How are the business and its markets changing?
- Where, within the industry, does it need, or want, to be?

- What must be done to achieve its objectives?
- How can it set about doing what is necessary?

There are a number of schools of thought as to how an organisation may go about asking, never mind answering, these and other questions. These include the Design School, Planning School and Positioning School to name but a few. Strategy, whether it is explicitly designed or emerging as a pattern of decisions that reveals objectives, goals and plans for achieving them, is important for the long-term survival of the organisation. For any strategy to be relevant and applicable it needs to:

- Be used proactively
- Recognise that there are severe limits to the predictability of the future
- Take account of the organisational, political and psychological dimensions of corporate life
- Be accepted by the majority of those concerned with strategy to be a realistic relevant tool for more effectively coping with the future

## 1.2 ◆ THE MAJOR ELEMENTS OF STRATEGIC MANAGEMENT

Just as strategy has three interdependent elements, so too does strategic management. Johnson and Scholes presented a model of the interlocking elements that they suggest make up the aggregate that is strategic management and this is shown in Figure 1.1. While they themselves are very careful to disclaim any intention of specifying exactly *how* the process that is strategic management must take place it is an extremely useful device to model the enormous complexities of strategic problems. For this reason this model of interlocking elements is the one used in the next chapter in order to group the included tools and techniques.

While Chapter 2 will address each element in turn there is no implication that this process is a simple sequential one in which the organisation deals with each element in turn. Rather, as shown by Quinn (1980):

> The total strategic process is anything but linear. Integrating all the subsystem strategies is a groping, cyclical process that often circles back on itself, encountering interruptions and delays, and rarely arrives at clear-cut decisions at any one time... The strategy's ultimate development involves a series of nested, partial decisions interacting with other partial decisions, like fermentation in biochemistry, rather than an industrial assembly line

However, by having some way to represent complexity we are able to study it. The strategic analysis element represents what should be a continuous, automatic process, though formal outputs may only appear annually. 'Good' managers must be constantly aware of what is happening in their organisation's environment and how any changes may affect the organisation; their organisation's available resources, including the strengths and weaknesses that these equate to; the culture of their organisation, including the management style and the relative power of stakeholder groups. The first part of Chapter 2 covers some techniques appropriate to the formal aspects of this strategic analysis.

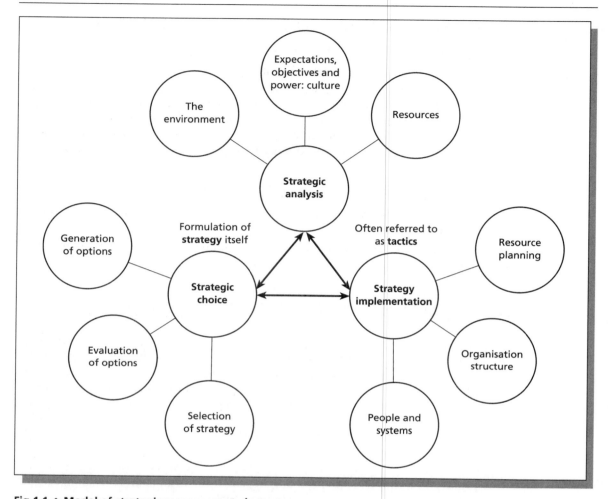

**Fig 1.1 ◆ Model of strategic management elements**
(adapted from Johnson and Scholes, *Exploring Corporate Strategy: Texts and Cases* (1993) by permission of Prentice Hall)

The 'good' manager must also be able to generate and evaluate possible strategies taking into account the nature of the organisation and its industry. Risk, structure and culture are just three of the issues of concern here. Techniques for performing the formal aspects of generating, evaluating and selecting strategic options form the second part of Chapter 2. Finally, the 'good' manager implements the chosen strategy by way of making any necessary adaptations to the structure, systems and people of the organisation and manages the required acquisition and deployment of resources. Techniques that support the formal aspects of strategic implementation form the third, and final, part of Chapter 2.

The strategic management process is not just an 'empty box' that contains only those elements modelled by Johnson and Scholes. Ansoff, writing in his welcome to the *Journal of Strategic Change* (1992), notes that the additional, non-modelled element is the strategic manager's appreciation of the *interdependence* of the elements. However, as long ago as 1984, McGinnis was suggesting that the integration of analysis and intuition was the key to successful strategic management.

## 1.3 ◆ THE DIVERSITY OF STRATEGIC PROBLEMS AND DECISIONS

Since, by definition, strategic decisions are those that are broad in their scope, enduring in their effects and difficult in their reversal, they must also, by implication, be worth devoting time and resources to in an attempt to make the 'right' decision. Examples of these strategic decisions might be the decision by Ford to launch a new model; by ASDA to diversify into non-food products; by BP to divest itself of filling stations; by SHELTER to establish a chain of shared ownership schemes; or by an unemployed craftsman to establish his own business. These decisions have much in common, they are all significantly important, but equally they have many differences. Some involve business start-ups, some major structural changes, others very major capital investments. Strategic decisions are made by profit and non-profit making organisations and by large ones and small ones. Similarly strategic problems can be very diverse.

The factors that determine the nature of the strategic problems facing an organisation fall into four groups.

### 1.3.1 ◆ The nature of the industry

The key industry factors include: the type of products produced, the markets served, the technology of production, and the access to, or the nature of, the materials required. For example, developing new products may require expensive investment in R&D or, conversely, as with the cosmetics industry, may be primarily a matter of market development and promotions. Closely related to the nature of the product is the nature of the market. For example, the markets for standard products will ensure that there is little scope for strategic initiatives in marketing. In the case of monopoly or near-monopoly situations any strategy may revolve around how to maintain this position by keeping out new entrants. The technology of production affects the strategy in a variety of ways. Capital intensive industries such as steel and chemical production tend to revolve around plant requirements or investment in new equipment. Assembly industries, such as the car industry, are primarily concerned with component supplies and manning levels. The access to materials may be a major strategic factor in industries such as oil, gas, coal, iron ore, etc. In these industries mining and drilling rights, for instance, will be critical to an organisation's strategic future.

Every type of organisation has its own distinctive and diverse strategic problems and a true appreciation of the nature of the problems of the industry itself is essential for any successful strategy.

### 1.3.2 ◆ The nature of the enterprise

The size of the organisation affects the nature of its strategic problems and the means available to the organisation to deal with them. The need for a generally agreed strategy is often more apparent in a large firm than in small ones, because of the complexity and diversity of their activities. To balance this greater demand there can be a greater supply of senior management and planning staff support since large firms also have more resources to devote to the determination of strategy. *Strategy*, however, is equally important in small- and medium-sized organisations.

The ownership of the organisation is another important influence upon strategic problems. In small family-sized firms personal aims are closely integrated with strategy determination. However, in public shareholder organisations there may be more diversity of aims, although one powerful stakeholder group may still dominate the strategy development process and the resultant strategy. If the organisation is state-owned, its strategy will be subject to a number of additional constraints. Public corporations may find that the law and statutory obligations define their scope of activities. Public pressures may also figure from trade unions, local authorities and other public bodies and they may also be subject to tight control of their finances.

The degree of maturity of the organisation is also an important factor, as is the extent to which it operates across national boundaries. When an organisation operates internationally, its problems become a step function more complex. Making international product and market choices is extremely difficult. Single-industry companies face a quite different set of strategic issues from conglomerates producing and selling a range of largely unrelated products. The degree of diversification, particularly in large organisations, has a major impact upon both the organisation and its approach to strategic planning.

### 1.3.3 ◆ The current circumstances

The circumstances under which the firm is operating at any given time, and, in particular, the state of the economy in which it is operating, will be major influences on the organisation. The perception of strategic managers, the nature of the strategic planning process and the objectives of the chosen strategy will all reflect the state of that economy. Strategy in times of depression will obviously be quite different to strategy during times of economic expansion. During recessionary times there are financial difficulties, pressures for closures and divestment, and generally a greater sense of 'crisis' and uncertainty typically driving shorter planning horizons than those prevailing during economic buoyancy.

### 1.3.4 ◆ The organisation's environment

Different strategies are needed to operate successfully within different economies. For instance, in *developing* countries far less can be taken for granted. In such countries, necessary components, the industrial and social infrastructure and skilled manpower may all be in limited or unpredictable supply. The government policy is also an important strategic issue, having either a positive or negative, that is restrictive, impact upon the organisation's environment. There may be strong or weak state control, greater or lesser market orientation, and significant cultural differences and all of these will alter the nature of the organisation's strategic problems and decisions.

## 1.4 ◆ THE DEVELOPMENT OF STRATEGIC MANAGEMENT

Strategic management, as a sub-set of management, concerns itself with the general direction and long-term policy of a business, as distinct from its day-to-day operations. Determining the strategy of an organisation is only one of the functions of management but it is probably the most significant area of management decision making. Although the systematic *study* of business strategy, strategic decision making and strategic management process is a relatively recent phenomenon their *existence* dates back to the earliest commercial and industrial ventures. Study does not generate strategy, and many successful businesses are led by strategies derived from experience or intuition rather than analysis. Indeed, these organisations may have achieved their success without an *explicitly* stated strategy at all! However, emergent strategies, that is, those that can be *implied* from actions rather than explicitly stated, are still subject to the same discriminators of success: namely, that whether a strategy is a success or not depends upon whether it exploited the opportunities and fitted the circumstances at the time. Business life has steadily become more complex and increasingly fast changing. Organisations have, therefore, come to realise that their chances of success increasingly depend upon the systematic, skilful, accurate and realistic assessment of their *position* with respect to their *opportunities* and to re-evaluate them constantly in real-time. Chapter 2 looks at some of the tools for doing just that.

As with any other management activity, there is some element of 'fashion' associated with the study of strategic management. Indeed until the 1980s the study discipline would have been referred to as 'Business Policy'! The strategic emphasis has shifted over time; from the *formulation* of strategy to its *implementation*. What this means is that analytical skills are no longer the entire focus; what the study of strategic management now recognises is that the ability to analyse and also the ability to synthesise the analytical with the behavioural are required. In other words, strategic management is recognised to be about *combining* the perspectives of the analytic, psychological, sociological and political domains.

After two decades of significant growth in organisational strategic management teams, the late 1980s' cut-back of such teams seemed to imply a decline in the value placed upon strategic management and planning. In reality, it probably reflected the fact that strategic management and strategic planning are now acknowledged as a line, and not a staff, activity. *Every* manager is involved with the tools and techniques of strategic planning since strategic planning is embedded within management. Mintzberg (1994) offers some discussion of the (remaining) roles for Strategic Planners as distinct from line managers.

Strategic management certainly encompasses strategic planning (though Taylor (1984) would, in fact, place strategic management as one *style* of strategic planning) but it goes much further than that. Strategic planning is now valued and, at least partially, undertaken by all senior managers, but strategic *management* also includes creative, leadership, entrepreneurial and innovative dimensions. Strategic management aims to create the future as well as reacting to changing times. Analytical tools certainly help in the process of strategic planning (*see* Chapter 2) but strategic management, the concern of the 1990s, must also encompass innovation and leadership and neither of these are well supported by such tools.

## 1.5 ◆ THE HISTORY OF STRATEGIC PLANNING AND MANAGEMENT

Fayol in 1916 presented an early attempt at formalising the manner in which to deal with the future. Although Dupont and General Motors used his approach, it was not until the 1950s and 1960s that the expansion of both organisation size and business opportunities demanded a systematic way of looking at the future. Prior to that there had been an almost total reliance upon the entrepreneurial skills of the organisation's owner (or senior manager).

Out of this need long-range planning was born, for the purpose of defining the organisations' objectives and allocating resources to the achieving of them. A key activity was the identifying and plugging of any gaps between the demands assumed by the extrapolation of existing trends, and the organisation's perceived current abilities. It became obvious, however, that extrapolation of trends into forecasts was not accurate, that growth, as experienced in the 1950s and 1960s, could be interrupted and, in any case, new opportunities that no one had forecast were possible. So, it became recognised that closing the 'planning gap' (the difference between forecast demands and forecast abilities) was not the most critical aspect of strategy formulation. So during the 1970s, *strategic* planning replaced long-range planning; this incorporated the recognition that trends had the potential for change, and did not incorporate the assumption that adequate growth could be assured. Strategic planning was much more closely concerned with market competition since the more limited expansion of markets and products could not support the growth aspirations of all the industry players.

Despite the differences between long-range planning and strategic planning, they were both based upon three key assumptions:

- Environmental forecasting is sufficiently accurate to predict the future
- Strategy formulation is a rational process; objectives can be formulated and alternatives can be identified and optimised
- Behavioural dimensions can be ignored

But, forecasting, especially long-term forecasting:

- Is inevitably very inaccurate
- Important factors such as product life cycles cannot be predicted
- Behavioural and cultural aspects are hugely significant to the formulation and implementation of strategy

Perhaps most importantly, an involvement in survival-critical decisions does not make someone superhuman or able to make perfectly rational decisions. In reality, under the stress of making such organisationally vital decisions the quality of decision making will degrade.

During the 1970s it became increasingly apparent that formal planning often lacked relevance, its resultant plans were often 'buried' and critical decisions were often taken *outside* the formal, strategic planning process. To respond to these problems, uncertainty analysis became the new focus. The discovery of competitive rules and principles through industry analysis and scenario management, contingency planning and weak-signal monitoring helped managers better understand future uncertainty. However, to actually identify which of these uncertainties will be critical to the organisation needs considerable skill. Which brings us back to a heavy reliance upon the entrepreneurial skills of the organisation's owner or manager!

Currently strategic management focuses upon understanding the general principles that govern competition. The widespread use of concepts such as experience curves and generic strategies are attempts to do just that. There have been two, broadly parallel, developments in the field of strategic management. More recently developments in strategic management have de-emphasised planning and emphasised learning and adaptability, drawing upon, for example, systems thinking and chaos theory (Stacey (1993) gives an analysis of chaos theory applied to strategic planning). So attention shifts from how to develop long-term set piece plans to how to enable light-footed incrementalism and chaos theory based short-term interpretations within adaptive learning based organisations.

In the development of thinking about strategic management the value of historical data has shifted from a direct forecasting role to one in which it is primarily to enable the search for patterns which alert us to the arrival of the inevitable disconti-nuities. Increasing sophistication of measurement is recognisably futile and increased value comes from very good quality short-term estimates within broader 'guestimate' frameworks. Adaptability to emergent chaos must be preferred over long-term 'mapped out' blueprint plans though when the situation is likely to be prior to the onset of chaos breakpoints then short-term forecasts can be very accu-rate. There is a need for organisational-wide abilities to identify when that pre-chaos situation ends whilst recognising the impossibility of precise predictions of what will follow. People and organisations need to be ready for anything. This need favours contingency planning and indicates that competitive health is best achieved from shorter-term strategic planning, structural flexibility that allows maximum variety, and processes that store and amplify local judgement capabilities.

### 1.5.1 ◆ The analytical school

This school assumes that strategists can be trained to anticipate and respond to complexity in a controlled manner. It also assumes that strategy can be *designed* using a range of models that are based upon *normative* principles. That is, concep-tual reasoning and/or empirical evidence have been used to produce a picture of generalised circumstances so that the general picture can then be used by others deemed to be in similar circumstances. The aim of all these models is to provide an indication of what should normally occur. These models include techniques such as business portfolio analysis, for instance the BCG box, and they all aim to clarify strategic choice in an attempt to introduce greater discipline in strategic thinking by highlighting the 'best' actions to take to improve the organisation's competitive position. The conceptual simplicity of the tools used is their main strength but also their main weakness. In addition, many of the models are based upon somewhat dubious assumptions, that is, they assume a fairly predictable environment; ignore the interdependence of activities; and do not take into account behavioural aspects. The analytical view has been challenged a number of times, for instance by Pascale and Athos (1982):

> The principal fallacy of the portfolio concept is that all that frequently stands between a division being viewed as a cash cow or a star is management creativity in seeing how to reposition their products in tune with the marketplace.

This school does, however, offer a range of techniques that can be *learnt*, and therefore it is appealing to those who seek to discipline the complexity of manage-ment skills.

### 1.5.2 ◆ The pattern school

Since the 1960s there has been a parallel development of a different school that believes that the raison d'être of firms is to allocate resources. The *pattern* of this resource allocation – whether done explicitly or implicitly – *is* the strategy of the organisation. If this notion is accepted then all firms have a strategy that can be inferred, after the fact, by analysing and observing how they have allocated the resources within the organisation.

Empirical studies suggest that fully fledged strategies rarely exist at the onset and so strategic decisions are rarely the result of planned moves. Rather, the allocation-of-resource process evolves, on a trial-and-error basis. Successful actions are pursued; unsuccessful ones avoided; in a behaviour pattern that is typical of Japanese managers. The end result of this process of trial and reaction is a set of resource commitments that reflects the competitive force upon the organisation and the needs and aspirations of those within it who have the power to commit resources.

The value in such a process-based approach to strategy is in gaining an understanding of *how* the resources are being committed. Since the resource allocation *is* the strategy of the firm, understanding allows the process to be influenced in order to align the *de facto*, emergent, strategy with the intended one. One question obviously emerges: how can understanding that a strategy *evolves* over time, and understanding how it does so, help managers make better decisions and take more appropriate actions, now for *future* events. Understanding history is always interesting since it certainly influences the present, and the future, but the past never repeats itself *exactly*. There is also a danger that recent history will be used to justify or rationalise decisions, or mistakes. So for this school, the driving need is for *objective* ways to analyse the strategy history, that is, the pattern of resource allocations in order to adjust it more skilfully.

## 1.6 ◆ A MODEL OF THE STRATEGIC PLANNING PROCESS

Whilst acknowledging that the three elements of strategic management interact and that therefore strategic planning is not a linear activity, it is still valuable to have some model of the planning process. The model given here obviously relates primarily to the design school of strategic management since the pattern school would suggest that whatever is documented or articulated as the strategy is largely irrelevant – assessment of *actions* defines strategy rather than statements of *intent*. It is possible to take a number of rather different interpretations of what the strategic planning process is. Indeed Mintzberg (1990) identified 10 different such interpretations, where three schools of thought aim to prescribe how strategies could/should be formulated whilst seven simply describe what goes on.

|  |  |
|---|---|
| *Prescriptive interpretations* | *Descriptive interpretations* |
| • Design School | • Entrepreneurial School |
| • Planning School | • Cognitive School |
| • Positioning School | • Learning School |
| | • Political School |
| | • Cultural School |
| | • Environmental School |

Strategic planning can be defined as the process of developing and maintaining consistency between the organisation's objectives and resources and its changing opportunities. Hence strategic planning aims to define and document an *approach* to doing business that leads to satisfactory profits and growth. This approach, or strategy, sets the general direction for the use and management of all resources, including, of course, information, throughout the organisation, and generally this direction will remain valid for an extended time period. Noorderhaven (1995) provides a good discussion of the theoretical underpinnings of this as a decision making process.

Strategic planning turns an organisation's vision (usually as expressed by its senior board), more commonly referred to as its mission, into concrete achievables. Although Cummings and Davies (1994) argue that the two are very different (essentially that mission is about stating the purpose whilst vision is about stating the imagined future) many writers and practitioners use the terms interchangeably. If we were to take up this distinction then the labels in Figure 1.2 would be altered with Vision being substituted for the Mission element whilst the existing Goals element would be renamed as Mission. Whatever it is called, the mission statement does not schedule responsibilities or operating details. It describes the initiatives that will achieve the vision in ways deemed consistent with the organisation, its

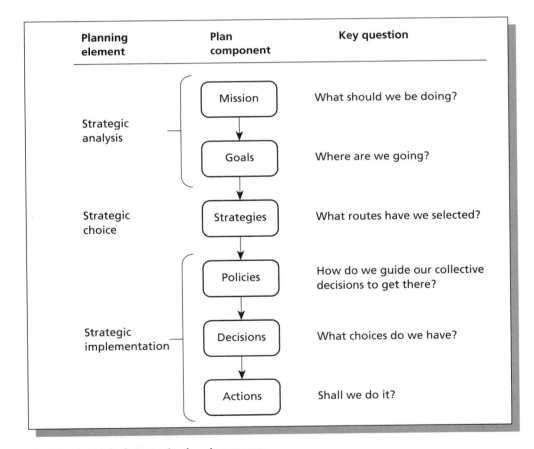

**Fig 1.2 ◆ Model of strategic planning process**

assumed market and the competitive, regulatory, social and technological environment. Jennings and Wattam (1994, p. 217) define mission as a statement that:

*defines the basic reasons for the existence of an organisation and helps legitimise its function in society.*

The initiatives that form the strategic plan are likely to create the future of the organisation.

Once the organisation's vision has been defined in achievable terms then an outline plan must be created which will indicate (again in outline) what actions need to be taken, and when, in order to achieve that vision. Typically these tactics form the medium-term aims and cover the portfolio of projects that will be implemented over a two to four year horizon. This outline plan creates a framework of priorities and budget constraints and establishes specific and measurable objectives whilst seeking to leave as much freedom as possible to respond to a specific alternative since flexibility within some overall strategic intent is sought. In many organisations the vision and objectives and the master plan for achieving them are combined into a single deliverable 'the strategy plan' but actually in such instances, both strategy and *policy* are being covered, with the policy element specifying responsibilities plus the general estimates of costs and benefits.

In addition to the strategy and policy elements, the planning process may also make provision for the short-term directing of actions with an inclusion of specific details, including people and dates, for a one to two year horizon. This action element once set off is, obviously, far less flexible than the strategy and policy elements. So the process of strategic planning is an ongoing activity of assessment, selection and implementation. This process requires a framework for evaluating alternatives that acknowledges all influences. Chapter 2 covers some of the tools available to do this.

The example in Figure 1.3 illustrates the cascade effect of the planning process' elements. Each level determines the small set of items that are appropriate at the next stage. Remember, this model is of the planning process and not of the plan itself. If the intention is to generate a strategy plan then this should remain firmly in focus; there is a danger of an organisation constantly 'planning to plan' and never defining a strategy.

The decisions in each area are important for what they constrain the organisation not to do as well as to actually do. For instance, it might be possible to achieve staff productivity gains by forbidding tea breaks, however for very few organisations would this be an acceptable means to the end, though it certainly is *possible*, and it could have the desired effect. Nor, for most organisations, would it be *consistent* with the culture and power environment.

Strategic planning is a management *process* and we can, therefore, conceptually view it as being like any other process; that is, it takes inputs, performs some transformation, in order to generate some outputs. We can view the inputs as being the available understanding of the organisation, its environment and its management; the process of strategic planning to be the transformation; and the output to be the defined strategy. Forecasting is needed for any business process since there will usually be a lag between a demand being expressed for the outputs and the supply being available. During this lag time things go wrong, or at least alter, in other words the environment causes disturbances. Since the longer the duration of the

| | |
|---|---|
| **Mission:** | To be the industry cost leader |
| **Goal:** | Achieve staff productivity gain of 5 per cent within three years (This will be one of a small set of goals intended to achieve the 'vision' that is defined as the mission) |
| **Strategy:** | Reduce time lost due to ill health (Again, this will be one of a small set that the organisation selects as leading along the road to achieving the goal) |
| **Policy:** | Maintain a healthy work place (Again, one of a set) |
| **Decision:** | Ban smoking (As always, part of a set) |
| **Action:** | Put up the signs and police the decision!! |

**Fig 1.3 ◆ Simplified example of planning stages**

lag the greater the chance of the forecast being inaccurate, the process needs a *strategy* to deal with the future.

There are two simultaneous and seemingly contradictory types of behaviour that enable biological and human cultures, or systems, to survive:

- Dominance over competitors; which is achieved through specialisation
- Ability to deal with environmental change; requiring adjustments and adaptation over time, which is inhibited by specialisation

The business strategy is how the organisation defines its balance between these contradictory forces.

It is very difficult to judge the effectiveness of an organisation's strategic planning. If we take a simple definition of effectiveness as being the achievement of goals we would assess strategic planning as effective if it achieved the organisational *goals*. The problem with this simple way of judging strategic planning is that strategic planning, like any other process, is subject to environmental disturbances particularly so with a very fast changing or uncertain environment. Such disturbances bring unanswerable questions: has this planning process actually ensured the organisation's survival even if not achieving the intended goals; would an alternative planning process have led to an improved situation? In addition, this would place the organisational goal setting outside the strict view of the planning process and yet, in most organisations, the goal setting is central in the planning process!

So it is not appropriate to use that simple definition of effectiveness, instead it is only appropriate to assess the effectiveness of the strategic planning process in relation to itself. An effective planning process is one which generates a sufficient flow of worthwhile strategic options which the effective planning process is then able to assess and evaluate with respect to possible futures.

Clarke-Hill (1991) re-jigs Johnson and Scholes' model of strategic management into a model of strategic planning. They effectively re-name the key elements and structure them in order to define a sequence. This redefining of a model of interacting elements into a model of the process has both good and bad aspects. To have a prescriptive 'model of' sequential actions usefully provides guidance on *how* and in *what order* to tackle the complexity of three interdependent areas. However, such a linear model inaccurately implies a *separation* to the areas.

## 1.7 ◆ COMPONENTS OF THE STRATEGIC PLAN

Four major components that make up any strategic plan will now be considered. They may appear in various documentation guises, be formally or informally defined and/or disseminated and they may be consciously or unconsciously recognised as collectively representing the values and priorities of the organisation.

### 1.7.1 ◆ Mission

This component addresses the organisation's basic question of 'What business are we in?' This single, essential, sentence should include no quantification but must unambiguously state the *purpose* of the organisation and should, just as carefully, define what the organisation does not do. This mission represents the view that senior managers have for the future of the organisation; so it is what they want it to become or achieve. This view – hence one alternative name for mission is vision – is the central purpose for the existence, of the organisation. The mission gives a way to judge the appropriateness of all potential activities that the organisation might engage in. Rader (1994) suggests that published mission statements act as a 'proof of correctness' of a particular choice since any choice can be tested against this statement which defines the aspirations, values, roles and goals of a specific community (what it means to be part of it). He goes on to offer seven characteristics of powerful mission statements. These are that they should:

- engage the imagination with powerful images of target outcomes
- employ images that are clear, concise and compelling
- express strong values and beliefs about the future
- provide guidance for actions that must and must not be done
- focus discussions and shape choices about consequences
- challenge us to stretch continually beyond current performance
- apply to each and every member of the community – 'I see what it means to me'

Many organisations (mis-)use the mission statement as an external device. This tends to lead to the statement being created as a form of PR rather than as an essentially internal and internalised integral part of strategic planning. When constructed primarily for external consumption mission statements rarely reflect real values. The mission statement, to have a *real* purpose within the strategic plan, should be understandable, applicable and serve to rule out actions. Statements that cannot be seen to dismiss some choices offer no guidance.

### 1.7.2 ◆ Goals

This component defines the desired future positions of the organisation. They are selected on the basis of the defined mission. Some models of the strategic planning process separate goals from objectives. In that case goals are broad and timeless statements of the end results that the organisation considers will achieve the mission. Objectives would then 'flesh out' these goals with quantitative as well as qualitative terms since they are specific and tangible measures of the goals to achieve the mission. In other instances organisations use the terms goal, objective, and aim interchangeably.

### 1.7.3 ◆ Strategy

As said before, this element defines the general direction in which the organisation chooses to move to meet goals to achieve the mission. This strategy will include statements of the acceptable *how* to move towards the desired *what*. The strategy is therefore constrained by the nature of the organisation, including its resources, capabilities, culture, structure, etc. and by the environment within which it operates. The strategy constructs a framework which hopes to ensure that the organisation makes the *best use* of what it has to work with and adequately *compensates* for its limitations. The more highly competitive the environment is the more important the latter will be.

Just as the mission defined what the organisation did not do, so the strategy also defines how it will not achieve its aims. The rejected approaches, whether they were consciously rejected or not, allow all management decisions to be tested against the strategy as a measure of 'acceptability'. Therefore the plan that documents this component should clearly state those assumptions that formed the underlying structure to the formulation process. It could consider the threats and opportunities that were judged to be appropriate to the acknowledged strengths and weaknesses. In the light of these, the strategy plan should document *which* of the strategic opportunities are deemed most beneficial to pursue.

### 1.7.4 ◆ Policy

The strategy exists as a collective umbrella for the *policy* component. This element should give a broad assessment of the organisational structure, business system and resources inherent in the selected strategies. The policies provide a framework for the implementation of any major changes needed to be made. The policies should provide the key measurements and key ratios that summarise the expected benefits the strategy is intended to yield so that, in due course, the success, or otherwise, of it can be judged. The policies, since they structure the actual *management* of projects, are a form of delegation that hopes to allow autonomy and yet still maintain a consistency of direction.

## 1.8 ◆ EXAMPLES OF STRATEGIC PLANS

It can be difficult to obtain a copy of the strategic plan for a real organisation, since, by definition, elements of it must be competitively confidential! A hypothetical strategic plan for a bio-medical company is shown in Figure 1.4. This illustrates all the components of the plan and how they relate to the elements of the strategic planning process.

Another example, that of a private healthcare company shown in Figure 1.5, illustrates how a strategic plan can define the parameters of acceptable and unacceptable strategies. Since the company has *documented* its concern with how it is

> **Vision:**
> We are focused on research – to search for breakthroughs and innovative products. We are a company on the move with a critical mass of financial strength, of scientific research, of marketing expertise, and of existing and future products to meet the global challenges we face and to assure us significant growth.
> Mission: We are dedicated to enhancing life – from pharmaceuticals we will make and market, to the consumer, health care, and nutritional products we will continue to develop and sell.
>
> **Goals:**
>
> - To achieve global pre-eminence in our pharmaceutical, consumer, medical device, and nutritional businesses.
> - To establish the company as one of the world's truly great research-based companies with a commitment to excellence in bio-medical science that is recognised by the medical and scientific community around the world.
>
> **Objectives:**
>
> - To achieve at least 15 per cent annual compounded increase in per share earnings, along with continuing attention to margin improvement and increase or maintenance of market share.
> - To achieve product leadership in our core businesses, both in home markets and in key foreign markets.
>
> **Strategies:**
>
> - Co-ordinate sales and marketing activities and the scope and quality of the combined pharmaceutical research and development effort.
> - Improve efficiency in the administrative and manufacturing areas of our company throughout the world to produce savings that will provide additional resources to invest in our future growth.

**Fig 1.4 ◆ Elements of the strategic plan of a bio-medical company**

seen in society and since this forms part of their formal strategic plan then this concern will constrain it in its choice of strategies to achieve the objectives.

The final example, shown in Figure 1.6, illustrates how the mission and objectives define what will not be done, and how things will not be done.

This American air-conditioning company does not intend to provide entire systems, or to provide residential systems or components, nor does it intend to compete on a lowest cost basis. In a similar vein, the more detailed elements of its strategic plan would include items such as:

- We have a good reputation, great skills and experience, a viable organisation, and, in some instances, a special situation in the industry, and will:
    1 Exploit these strengths and not diversify at the present time into unrelated industries
    2 Increase US market penetration through the development of a regional manufacturing capability and the development of secondary distribution channels

---

**Objectives:**

1 The provision on a firm financial yet caring basis of provident fund schemes for the purpose of offering private medical and dental insurance to the UK, and overseas markets.
2 The development of other activities complementary to private medical insurance, both in Britain and overseas.

In providing for these various activities we shall aim to:

- Create significant growth in volume of business and profit terms by meeting market needs in:
  - Protecting and developing our care business
  - Diversifying the base of our operations into associated fields, for example, into 'health care' and into 'financial services'
- Provide for high standards and quality of service to customers, meeting all reasonable requirements at fair prices
- Develop the career paths of our staff by providing appropriate training
- Act as a responsible member of the sectors within which we operate

---

**Fig 1.5 ◆ Objectives from the strategic plan of a private healthcare company**

Matejka *et al.* (1993) provide some further examples of mission statements in their paper arguing the value and power of well constructed statements. However, Van der Weyer (1994) whilst recognising the value of senior management developing a shared vision challenges the value of the mission statement itself. In an experience typical of an organisation responding to turbulent times the University of Humberside mission statement changed frequently over a one-year period (Should it represent the University's identity as regional, national, international? Should it

---

*Mission:* We are in the business of supplying system components and services to a world-wide, non-residential, air-conditioning market. Air-conditioning is defined as heating, cooling, cleaning, humidity and air movement.

*Objectives:*

- To increase earnings per share to attain a continuing return of 14.5 per cent or more on stockholder's equity and to provide consistently increasing dividends.
- To employ the least number and highest quality of people necessary to accomplish the prime objective and to provide them with the opportunities to develop and apply their fullest abilities.
- To have the company accepted as a dynamic, responsible, professionally managed, profit oriented corporation engaged in exciting and important fields of business, with the ability to meet successfully the economic and social challenges of the future.

---

**Fig 1.6 ◆ Mission and objectives of an air conditioning company**

target research per se, or only applied research? Should it represent the University's focus as vocational or intellectual?). Varying the mission statements so frequently accurately indicated a senior management attempt to respond to continual change and their involvement in a *process* of recasting the statement served to clarify emerging values and priorities and shifting power structures. However, the notion of frequently re-publishing altered mission *statements* is something of a contradiction in terms; a broad organisational sharing of commitment cannot be so frequently varied.

## 1.9 ◆ SUMMARY AND CONCLUSIONS

This chapter has offered some tentative explanations of what is meant by key ideas such as strategic management, strategy itself, and the process and products of strategic planning. It has presented something of the diverse historical and current perspectives on these notions and has adopted a model of strategy context that informs the structure of the entire text. It has also adopted a model within this one whereby each strategy level contains three interdependent areas (strategic analysis, strategic choice, strategic implementation). These models shape the book's structure which must, unfortunately, be linear but the concept being modelled is anything but linear.

What can we conclude? That strategic management through its various decision processes and products is about *creating* a future rather than merely forecasting it. Smith (1994) describes an ocean liner captain's forecast of its position 24 hours hence as its long-range plan. In fact, since there is no creating of the future I would dispute that this is a plan at all. He goes on to describe how that same captain could *decide* where the liner should be in 24 hours and names this as the strategic plan. I would suggest that this issue of creating the future is the core of strategic management, through strategic planning in which analysis, choice and implementation all play a part alongside strategic imagination and leadership. The tools and techniques as presented throughout this text intend to help in aspects of deciding what future to create and how to create it. Discussions of IS attributes throughout the text intend to help in understanding the IS aspects of that future.

**References and further reading**

Ackoff, R. (1981) *Creating the Corporate Future*, Wiley.
Ansoff, H.I. (1965) *Corporate Strategy*, McGraw-Hill.
Ansoff, H.I. (1990) *Implanting Strategic Management*, Prentice-Hall.
Ansoff, H.I. and McDonnell, E. (1990) *Implanting Strategic Management* (2nd edn), Prentice-Hall.
Argenti, J. (1989) *Practical Corporate Planning*, Unwin Hyman.
Ball, R. (1991) *Quantitative Approaches to Management*, Butterworth-Heinemann.
Christensen, C.R. *et al.* (1973) *Business Policy: Text and Cases*, Irwin.
Clarke-Hill, C. and Glaister, K. (1991) *Cases in Strategic Management*, Pitman Publishing.
Cummings, S. and Davies, J. (1994) Mission, Vision, Fusion, *Long Range Planning*, Vol 27 No 6 pp. 147–50.
David, F.R. (1989) How Companies Define Their Mission, *Long Range Planning*, Vol 22 No 1 pp. 90–7.
Dess, G.G. and Miller, A. (1993) *Strategic Management*, McGraw-Hill.
Dyson, R.G. (1990) *Strategic Planning: Models and Analytical Techniques*, Wiley.

Economist (1991) Management Focus: The Vision Thing, *The Economist*, 9 Nov p. 75.

Fayol, H. (1949) *General and Industrial Management*, Pitman Publishing.

Glaister, K. and Thwaites, D. (1993) Managerial Perception and Organisational Strategy, *Journal of General Management*, Vol 18 No 4 Summer pp. 15–33.

Gleck, W.F. and Jaunch, L.R. (1984) *Business Policy and Strategic Management*, Butterworth-Heinemann.

Goold, M. and Campbell, A. (1987) Many Best Ways to Make Strategy, *Harvard Business Review*, Nov-Dec pp. 70–6.

Gore, C., Murray, K. and Richardson, B. (1992) *Strategic Decision Making*, Cassell.

Greenley, G. (1989) *Strategic Management*, Prentice-Hall.

Hax, A. (Ed.) (1987) *Planning Strategies That Work*, Oxford University Press.

Jennings, D. and Wattam, S. (1994) *Decision Making: An Integrated Approach*, Pitman Publishing.

Johnson, G. and Scholes, K. (1993) *Exploring Corporate Strategy; Texts and Cases* (3rd edn), Prentice-Hall.

Kenyon, A. (1993) The Meaning of 'Strategy': The 'Design' versus 'Emergent' Dispute, *European Management Journal*, Vol 11 No 3 Sept pp. 357–60.

King, W.R. and Cleland, D.I. (1987) *Strategic Planning and Management Handbook*, Van Nostrand Reinhold.

Matejka, K., Kurke, L. and Gregory, B. (1993) Mission Impossible? Designing a Great Mission Statement to Ignite Your Plans, *Management Decision*, Vol 31 No 4 pp. 34–7.

McDonald, M.H.B. (1989) *Marketing Plans*, Butterworth-Heinemann.

McGinnis, M.A. (1984) The Key to Strategic Planning: Integrating Analysis and Intuition, *Sloan Management Review*, 26 pp. 45–52.

Mintzberg, H. (1978) Patterns in Strategy Formulation, *Management Science*, 24 pp. 937–48.

Mintzberg, H. (1979) *The Structuring of Organisations: a synthesis of research*, Prentice-Hall.

Mintzberg, H. (1990) Strategy Formulation: Schools of Thought, in *Perspectives on Strategic Management*, (Ed. Fredrickson, J.W.), Harper Business.

Mintzberg, H. (1994) *The Rise and Fall of Strategic Planning*, Prentice-Hall.

Mintzberg, H, and Quinn, J. (1991) *The Strategy Process*, Prentice-Hall.

Mintzberg, H., Quinn, J. and Ghoshal, S. (1995) *The Strategy Process: Concepts, Contexts and Cases* (European Edn). Prentice-Hall.

Noorderhaven, N. (1995) *Strategic Decision Making*, Addison-Wesley.

Pascale, R. and Athos, A. (1982) *The Art of Japanese Management*, Warner Books

Porter, M.E. (1980) *Competitive Strategy: Techniques for Analysing Industries and Competitors*, Free Press.

Porter, M. E. (1985) *Competitive Advantage: Creating and Sustaining Superior Performance*, Free Press.

Quinn, J. (1980) *Strategies For Change: Logical Incrementalism*, Irwin.

Quinn, J. (1982) Managing Strategies Incrementally, *Omega*, Vol 10 No 6 pp. 613–27.

Rader, D.A. (1994) *What Constitutes Well-Defined Missions and Visions?* BPR-@ duticai.twi.tudelft., 19 Oct.

Richardson, W. (1992) *Business Planning: an Approach to Strategic Management*, Unwin.

Rowe, A.J., Mason, R.O., Dickel, K.E., Mann, R.B. and Mockler, R.J. (1994) *Strategic Management: A Methodological Approach*, Addison-Wesley.

Smith, N.I. (1994) *Down-to-Earth Strategic Planning*, Prentice-Hall.

Stacey, R.D. (1993) *Strategic Management and Organisational Dynamics*, Pitman Publishing.

Steiner, A. and Miner, J.B. (1977) *Management Policy and Strategy*, Macmillan.

Taylor, B. (1984) Strategic Planning: Which Style do you Need?, in Smith J. G. (Ed.) *Strategic Planning in Nationalised Industries*, Macmillan.

Taylor, B. (1991) *The Manager's Casebook of Business Strategy*, Butterworth-Heinemann.

Thompson, J.L. (1990) *Strategic Management: Awareness and Change*, Chapman and Hall.

Thompson, J.L. (1995) *Strategy in Action*, Chapman and Hall.

Van der Weyer, M. (1994) Mission Improbable, *Management Today*, Sept pp. 66–8.

# CHAPTER 2

# Analytical tools in strategic management

This chapter presents a toolkit of techniques that can be used to inform strategic management, along with some discussion of the value in application of particular tools in order to develop in the reader some skill in judging the appropriateness of a given tool set to a given organisation operating within a given environment. Since, as was explained in Chapter 1, the process of strategic planning can be modelled as strategic analysis, strategic choice and strategic implementation, the included techniques are placed under these three broad headings (despite the overlapping nature of the areas and therefore the likely application overlap of a specific tool). This chapter is, therefore, structured around the convenient model for studying and understanding the complexity of the strategic management process as three interacting elements that Johnson and Scholes (1993) present. This model was given in Figure 1.1 and is repeated in Figure 2.1. Therefore Section 2.2 looks at strategic analysis, Section 2.3 looks at strategic choice and finally Section 2.4 looks at strategic implementation.

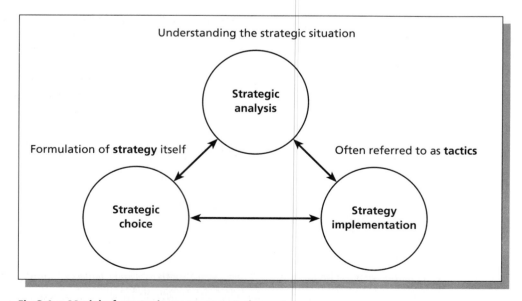

**Fig 2.1 ◆ Model of strategic management elements**
(adapted from Johnson and Scholes, *Exploring Corporate Strategy: Texts and Cases* (1993) by permission of Prentice Hall)

The fact that strategic analysis, strategic choice and strategic implementation are covered in a linear fashion in this chapter should not be interpreted as indicating that the *process* is linear. This one view of strategic management (*see* Chapter 1 for others) sees strategic management as being about reaching an understanding of the organisation and its situation in order to make choices about its future direction and so assumes that strategic *management* is significantly about strategic *planning*. From this perspective tools are needed to help reach that understanding, to help make the choices and to help put in place those choices. The chapter structure follows that line of reasoning and presents a range of tools that might offer that help. It must be stressed that it is the whole that must be interpreted, just as strategic management is something holistic of which strategic analysis forms a part.

This chapter could have presented the selected tools under many different headings, For instance, Chalak's (1993) translation of Sun Tzu's *The Art of War* suggests that there are five basic factors which must be understood in order to conduct business planning (*see* Figure 2.2 for the five basic factors). These five could have been used to structure the chapter sections. However, these five (as listed in translation) broadly equate to the three areas indicated by Johnson and Scholes (Figure 2.2 indicates the equivalence) and the familiarity of the Johnson and Scholes model makes it particularly useful as a road map for this chapter.

In noting the usefulness of familiar models it is worth commenting that familiar tools may acquire a usefulness from their very familiarity. In fact the most significant usefulness of the tools may be not so much in helping *formulate* strategy in the sense of making a decision (where familiarity might lead to increased skill) as helping to *develop* strategy in the broadest sense of gaining organisational consistency where familiarity makes them attractive as a shared language. As noted by Eden (1992), familiar, attractive and plausible *analytical* tools may serve, not so much analysis but as group identity *communication* devices. The apparent process of using analytical tools to make decisions may in fact enable an effective surfacing and testing of shared values and hence gain commitment. Therefore even those tools that can be significantly challenged with respect to their conceptual underpinnings and assumptions (for instance Porter's notion of Generic Strategies, *see* Figure 2.26 or the BCG Matrix, *see* Figure 2.19) will have a strong utility in this process sense.

Whilst detailed consideration of strategic change, the nature of profit versus non-profit making organisations and models of how strategic decisions are made would all be very important they lie outside the scope of this book.

| From *The Art of War* | From Johnson and Scholes' model |
| --- | --- |
| Economic influences | The environment |
| Company culture<br>Leadership | Expectations, objectives and power:<br>Culture |
| Logistical factors<br>Organisational structure and order | Resources |

Fig 2.2 ◆ Equivalence between Johnson and Scholes' strategic management elements and Sun Tzu's business planning factors

## 2.1 ◆ THE ROLE OF IS IN STRATEGIC PLANNING

While much of this book is concerned with the strategic management of IS and the strategic management of an organisation in the light of IS, this brief section takes a first look at IS in strategic management. Since the speed of technology change is causing the strategic planning time horizon to contract it is reasonable to consider the role of IS in allowing strategic management to cope with that contracting horizon.

A large number of physical and intellectual activities make up the process of strategic management. Some of them can be easily and effectively supported by IS: environmental scanning, internal resource analysis, the organisation structure, patterns identified, and so on. The areas permitting of automation in part are:

- Data acquisition
- Financial planning
- Expert-system-based decision analysis

There is a clear and obvious role for IS in the number crunching aspects of scenario analysis (MaxiMin, MaxiMax, Laplace, Hurwicz, Savage, etc), financial returns predictions and risk assessment. And, of course, IS permits the maintenance of the databases of strategy results (such as the PIMS database) that can then be used to test strategy options against. Again, a key aspect of strategic implementation is often to redesign business processes (BPR) and the role of IS in enabling that redesign is discussed in Chapter 8. The major limitation to the support offered by IS is that, whilst data gathering can readily be automated, the conceptual and inferential skills of doing something with the data are proving hard to automate. Automating the handling of the 'hard' data may leave more time for personal consideration of the 'soft' data and thus not presuming that hard data is more important. The difficulty is one of integrating the hard and soft aspects into a whole. Yet for a decade strategic decision support has been just 'over the horizon'.

So far support has tended to be project rather than strategy oriented and indeed the development of IS in general has primarily been concerned with internal aspects and yet (as the following tools indicate in environmental analysis) assessment of the implications of external information is critical. IS developments to manipulate such external information is only now really possible (Internet, on-line information services, etc).

Decision Support Systems do have a role to play in supporting the process of strategic planning. The essence of a 'good' strategic decision making process is one in which timely and integrated information is available to the senior manager when needed. This process will need a broad range of information and IS can successfully automate the integration of data from diverse sources and its presentation in a strategically meaningful way. The use of models, simulations and analyses in the strategic management process is an ideal candidate for automated support. IS offers tremendous support by automating the more 'tedious' aspects of strategic planning. For example, Molloy and Schwenk (1995) found that IT had had beneficial effects upon strategic decision making, primarily by enabling faster and more accurate analysis. This support becomes ever more critical as strategic planning moves from being a project-based activity undertaken intermittently to one that is firmly embedded in the process of managing strategically.

Despite this embedding, it is the major consultancy firms that have been the main drivers of automating the processes of strategic management. A number of automated tools do exist, from those that offer strategic planning as an 'add-on' to a system development automation tool to those that are specifically strategic planning tools. Many of these latter are based around expert system shells. For example, the process of Strategic Choice is one of trying to understand the implications of alternatives, a form of risk analysis. Some aspects of risk analysis can be automated, either through Monte Carlo simulations of probabilities of outcomes or through rule-based expert systems. Such systems work by modelling the organisation in order to test strategy against this model. Others work by supporting the collaborative testing of ideas. Many of the strategic planning models have a contingency nature, that is they take the form of 'if these circumstances exist, then this is the most appropriate action to take'. This contingency nature makes them natural candidates for the rule-based expert systems. The organisation can 'fill-in' details of their situation and be 'told' the strategy of the likeliest success. So far the capabilities of these expert systems only allow them to provide the start-point to a strategic debate!

There are however a growing number of group decision support tools that may have a significant impact on all areas of strategic management and Eden and Ackerman (1992) discuss how this might work. Many managers will have an 'outcome' focus on strategic planning, that is they use, consciously or otherwise, the Johnson and Scholes model of the process in order to produce a product – a strategy plan. To this school, setting aside any of its limitations, it is important to be able to gather a large variety of quantitative and qualitative data and present it in analysed form; IS plays a vital role in this. However, for those who concentrate upon the relationships between areas, the system school, the ability to automate shared communication is just as vital, so IS needs to act as a 'mind-to-mind telephone'.

## 2.2 ◆ STRATEGIC ANALYSIS

This section considers the part of the overall strategic management process which concerns itself with attempting to understand the strategic position of the organisation, to consider what is happening in the environment in order to judge how those happenings may affect the organisation, to consider the organisation's strengths and weaknesses with respect to those happenings and to assess how the organisation's groups of stakeholders feel. Strategic analysis aims to form a picture of the influences playing upon the organisation in order to be *informed* for the strategic choice element of the overall strategic management process.

Johnson and Scholes (1993) suggest that strategic analysis involves understanding three factors, as illustrated in Figure 1.1 and repeated in Figure 2.3, namely the organisation's:

- Environment
- Values and objectives
- Resources

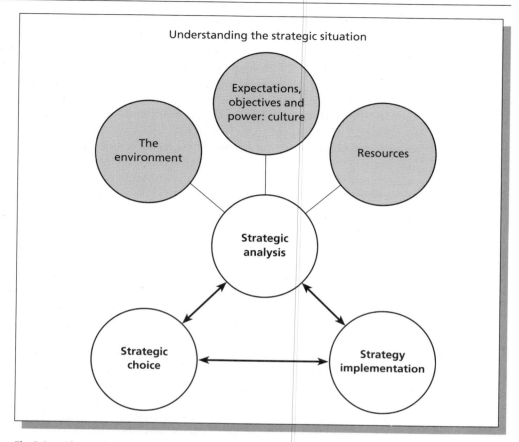

**Fig 2.3 ◆ Three elements of strategic analysis**
(adapted from Johnson and Scholes, *Exploring Corporate Strategy: Texts and Cases* (1993) by permission of Prentice Hall)

As discussed in Chapter 1, by having some way to represent complexity we are able to study it. 'Good' managers must be constantly aware of what is happening in their organisation's environment and how any changes may affect the organisation; their organisation's available resources, including the strengths and weaknesses that these equate to; the culture of their organisation, including the management style and the relative power of stakeholder groups. This part of the chapter follows the adopted Johnson and Scholes (1993) structure within which to introduce the strategic analysis tools. Therefore Section 2.2.1 presents those that might help to identify the nature of the economic operating environment, Section 2.2.2 those that help to interpret the cultural nature of the organisation, and Section 2.2.3 those that help judge its strategic capabilities in terms of business resources and competencies.

Values and objectives will influence the perceived acceptability (to each stakeholder group) of candidate strategies. It is through these perceptions that other influences are interpreted and power differentials are an important element of this. They are interpretations, because if the analysis is presented as an abstract statement of fact we don't learn anything from it. What it means to us is needed, and hence the interdependence, since conclusions of what it all means are reached as a result of who we are. This is Handy's (1991) wheel of learning. The environment is the world in which the organisation exists and so some view of the enormously complex set of variables must be forged in order to understand the impact of the environment upon the organisation. Resources provide the internal influences upon strategy choice and strategic analysis of resources aims to build a picture of them. Strategic analysis is not a static, snapshot event but a continuous process since the strategic choices and their implementation *impact* upon the environment, culture, and resources of the organisation (and indeed will be being done about an organisation as well as by them).

## 2.2.1 ◆ Environmental analysis

An analysis of the environment is important because it increases the quality of the strategic decision making by considering a range of the relevant features well before the need to make an irrevocable decision. The organisation identifies the threats and opportunities facing it and those factors that might assist in achieving objectives and those that might act as a barrier. The strategy of the organisation should be directed at exploiting the environmental opportunities and to blocking environmental threats in a way that is consistent with internal capabilities. This is Porter's concept of 'environmental fit' that allows the organisation to maximise its competitive position.

The success of an environmental analysis is largely dependant upon the characteristics of that environment: the complexity of it, that is how many variables are in the environment, the rate of change and the amount (and cost) of available information about it. Environmental analysis considers the external situation within which the organisation 'floats'. A possible process to go through in doing this is:

- Audit the environmental influences
- Assess the nature of the environment to judge whether it is simple or complex
- Identify the key environmental forces using Porter's five-forces model
- Identify the competitive position using a life cycle analysis
- Identify the key opportunities and threats using SWOT/TOWS analysis

### Nature of the environment

The organisation's environment comprises all those events, issues and facts which will influence its performance, but over which it has little influence. The environment is under the control of others as illustrated in Figure 2.4.

In Figure 2.4 the societal environment comprises those conditions that have a broad, rather than direct, impact upon the organisation. These include demographic factors, legal, political or social pressures all of which represent the world within which the organisation operates (*see* Figure 2.5).

The task environment, by contrast, is that which has a major and direct impact upon the organisation, and its strategic planning process. Among the most significant environmental variables are those relating to the nature of competition in any particular market as these will determine current profitability and the scope for strategic manoeuvring within that market (shown in Figure 2.6).

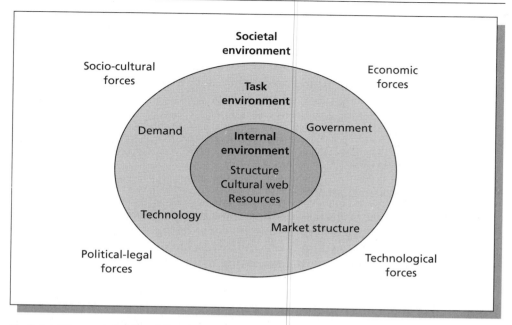

Fig 2.4 ◆ The organisational development

| Socio-cultural | Economic | Technological | Political-Legal |
|---|---|---|---|
| Life-style changes | GNP trends | Total organisational spending on R&D | Antitrust regulations |
| Career expectations | Interest rates | | Environmental protection laws |
| Consumer activism | Money supply | Total industry spending on R&D | |
| Rate of family formation | Inflation rates | | Tax laws |
| Growth rate of population | Unemployment levels | Focus of technological efforts | Special incentives |
| Age distribution of population | Wage/Price controls | Patent protection | Foreign trade regulations |
| Regional shifts in population | Devaluation/revaluation | New products | Attitudes towards foreign companies |
| Life expectancies | Energy availability and cost | New developments in technology transfer from lab to marketplace | Laws on hiring and promotion |
| Birth rates | | | Stability of government |
| | | Productivity improvements through automation | |

Fig 2.5 ◆ The key dimensions of the societal environment

| Demand | Market structure | Technology | Government |
|---|---|---|---|
| Size and growth of existing market | Number/size distribution of competitors and suppliers | Level of technology and likely change | Impact of particular legislation on the industry relating to product or consumption |
| Number/size distribution of customers | Barriers to entry or exit to market | Cost structure including economies of scale | |
| Physical distribution channels | Product characteristics | Dependence upon particular raw materials or labour | Role of government as supplier, competitor or customer |
| Nature of competition in market, eg importance of price and non-price competition | | | |

**Fig 2.6 ◆ The key dimensions of the task environment**

Assessing the effects of possible changes in the environment is an essential part of strategic analysis. There are two steps to this process (shown in Figure 2.7):

1 To consider how the societal, task, and/or internal environmental factors may change

2 To assess the strategic implications of such change for the organisation

Brannan (1992) discusses the potential major changes facing business. He calls it a 'complex web of near-chaos' where all factors interact and yet an organisation must establish a framework for understanding this chaos in order to survive. A possible framework for at least listing such changes is PEST – politics, economics,

**Fig 2.7 ◆ Assessing the changes in the business environment**

sociology and technical developments. Brannan illustrates the degree of change there can be under just some of these checklist headings. For instance, how many countries will there be in the year 2000? The USSR and Balkans are already torn apart whilst China is culturally changing, the EU staggers towards union and there are shifts in the global economic power base away from the West and towards the East. There is a radically changed view of the labour pool as the leisure society arrives in the West, and not necessarily by the choice of those at leisure. The slow-down of global consumption may not be cyclical, and consumer attitudes are permanently shifting. The primary criteria are now likely to be those related to environmental and social responsibility issues. From a business perspective, these chaotic changes bring significant opportunities as well as threats. Brannan suggests that as long as the value adding process continues to represent better satisfaction to the customer than that of the competitors then the organisation will remain competitive. To do this requires constant, effective, environment analysis to inform and allow the strategic decisions that keeps the organisation competitively healthy to be made.

Strategic change can take a number of forms, that is the strategies of an organisation can be considered under the headings of continuity/incremental/flux/global; the model of these is shown in Figure 2.8.

One way to deal with interpreting change is not to forecast the future but to consider a range of futures – scenario planning. The use of this technique has been championed by Shell since the early 1970s. Perhaps discussion of this notion would be better situated in section 2.3 under the heading 'Strategic Choice', but it is located here since, in a sense, no *choice* is being made, but rather possibilities are being imagined. The scenario planning technique requires a significant degree of skill since it melds rigorous analysis to imagination in a form of systematic synthesis. Scenarios are a way of *interpreting* the organisation's environment and can also be used as the 'filter' for making the strategic choice discussed in Section 2.3. Schoemaker (1995) describes scenario planning as capturing ranges of possibilities in rich detail. Schoemaker presents ten steps to go through when constructing scenarios.

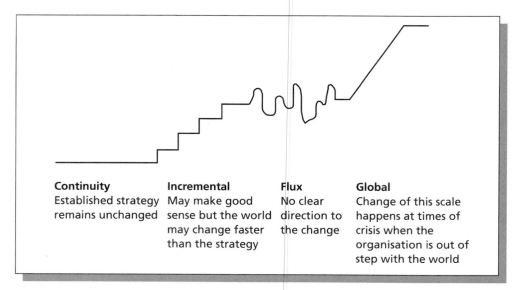

| Continuity | Incremental | Flux | Global |
|---|---|---|---|
| Established strategy remains unchanged | May make good sense but the world may change faster than the strategy | No clear direction to the change | Change of this scale happens at times of crisis when the organisation is out of step with the world |

**Fig 2.8 ◆ The nature of strategic change**

1. *Define the scope*

   Begin by determining what time scale, products, markets, geographic areas and technologies the scenarios should be addressing. Schoemaker suggests a way to do this is to look back over a similar scope to see what changes have occurred and assume at least a similar scale of change to come.

2. *Identify major stakeholders*

   And move on to ask how their roles, interests and power positions have changed.

3. *Identify basic trends*

   This step is about identifying those features that the group creating the scenarios are fairly sure will continue and which are sure to affect the aspects defined in Step 1.

4. *Identify key uncertainties*

   If Step 3 is about 'what we know' then this one is about 'what we know we don't know', that is what events would have a significant impact within the scope of concern defined in Step 1. At this stage, offer alternative outcomes for each and for combinations of each.

5. *Construct initial scenario themes*

   Schoemaker suggests a way to start is to make scenarios of extremes; the famous worst-case scenario and best-case scenario! Of course, 'best' and 'worst' are defined by the current perceptions and these may shift as a result of responses generated by the constructed scenarios. Alternatively scenarios could reflect high/low continuity on the degree of organisational preparedness or be based on issues of greatest uncertainty.

6. *Check for consistency and plausibility*

   This step takes the draft worlds of Step 5 and tests: whether trends are compatible with the time scale; whether combinations of outcomes are plausible (Schoemaker quotes full employment and zero inflation as two outcomes that cannot plausibly combine); and if stakeholder positions are plausible (strong groups like the World Bank will not plausibly be in an uncomfortable position). Perhaps what is most valuable about this stage is the necessity to really expose and challenge the assumptions made *about* plausibility.

7. *Develop learning scenarios*

   It is now possible to draw out the themes of the draft scenario into the 'stories' that will be the base for research and learning. Schoemaker claims that the name of each scenario is very important. Presumably the name Scenario 2 is not intrinsically helpful as a learning device whereas the name Global Annihilation gives us instant access to its themes.

8. *Identify research needs*

   This identification enables the organisation to flesh out the understanding of trends and of the surroundings of the key uncertainties.

9. *Develop quantitative models*

   This step moves on to formalise the relationships between many factors, for example between inflation; interest rates; employment levels. Formalising these relationships can keep imagined futures on a plausible and internally consistent footing.

10. *Evolve towards decision scenarios*

    Ultimately the scenarios are created to enable organisations to *prepare* for the outcomes presented by them, or at least to decide how far to go in ignoring

the possible outcomes. Useful scenarios are relevant to the decision community, obviously and visibly internally consistent and describe *real* alternatives
and not shades of the *same* future.

All early work on scenario planning assumed the existence of specialist planning
teams. This is no longer a valid assumption and so, as Mercer (1995) points out, the
significant skills required are diffused throughout the organisation. Therefore, to be
useful, scenario planning has to be simple in use and so make more realistic skill
demands. Despite that, and the fact that he offers just six steps, the approach he
advocates is little different to that of Schoemaker. However Mercer is specific in the
size of the scenario development teams he recommends (6–8 members) and the
number of scenarios it is useful to fully develop (2 scenarios).

## Porter's five forces model of competitive structure

This models the competitive world in which any organisation exists and the forces
that play upon it (Figure 2.9). The current competitive position of any organisation
will be the net force of these five aggregated.

In order to understand the strength of any one of these forces, an understanding
must be built up of the contributory factors to its power. Theoretically there are a
huge number of these but for any given organisation large numbers of them will
be irrelevant.

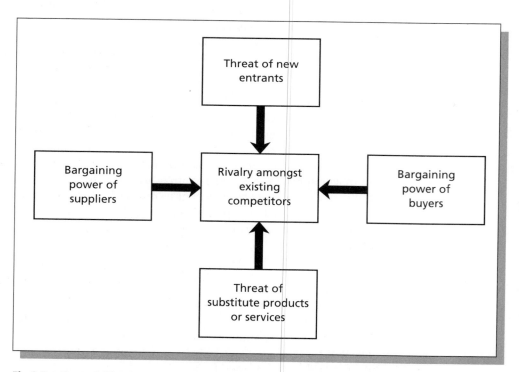

**Fig 2.9 ◆ Porter's Five Forces Model**
(adapted with the permission of The Free Press, a division of Simon & Schuster, from *Competitive Strategy:
Techniques for Analysing Industries and Competitors* by Michael E. Porter. Copyright © 1980 by The Free Press)

| Force | Contributory factors |
|---|---|

**Rivalry between competitors**

*This rivalry can range from intense in a cut-throat industry to mild in an affluent and affable one. When rivalry is high profits will tend to be low.*

- *Industry growth.* Industries that are static or in decline will have more intense rivalry than those which are rapidly growing.
- *High fixed costs or high storage costs.* When these are high the volume of sales must be maintained and so rivalry heightens.
- *Intermittent over-capacity.* Rivalry is more intense when, either because of demand fluctuations or production constraints, the industry experiences periods of over-capacity.
- *Product differences, brand identity and switching costs for customers.* Where there is no brand loyalty, ie no differentiation, then custom depends upon price and when switching costs are small this is very elastic, so rivalry will be heated. Conversely when differentiation or switching are high then demand is less elastic and rivalry is cooled.
- *The number of organisations and their size.* If there are lots of organisations of a similar size in the same pool then rivalry will be intense. Fewer firms or one of a dominant size reduces rivalry and enforces 'orderly' competition.
- *Diversity of competitors.* The greater the degree of similarity between the different organisations the lower the level of rivalry is. An industry with structurally, culturally and geographically diverse players will have intense rivalry.
- *Corporate stakes.* The rivalry of the industry will vary with the importance of it to the players. Side-line industries have low rivalry, whilst single-product industries have very intense rivalry.
- *High exit barriers.* If leaving the industry will cost a lot either physically or emotionally then the rivalry will tend to be intense. Low cost to leave means low angst and hence low rivalry.

**Threat of new entrants**

*The height of the barriers against this threat and the determination to get over them defines the industry's profitability.*

- *Government policy.* The extreme of this as a barrier is the need to acquire a licence to operate, a more subtle form is the strictness of safety rules.
- *Expected retaliation.* The threat of retaliation to a new entrant acts as a barrier, since dealing with aggressive counter-moves needs strong capabilities and significant advantages.
- *Absolute cost advantage.* If existing firms have lower costs than new entrants can have, then this is a very high barrier.
- *Access to distribution channels.* These must be established by a new entrant so the difficulties of access act as a barrier to entry.
- *Switching costs for buyers.* If buyers would have to face extra costs to change suppliers, or have a reluctance to do so, this acts as an entry barrier.
- *Economies of scale.* If scale is an important pricing factor then new entrants either need large markets straightaway or must face higher costs. Economies of scale are available in areas outside production.
- *Product differentiation and brand loyalty.* The degree of this is directly related to the height of the entry barrier.
- *Capital requirements.* Some industries involve major start-up costs and obviously in them the barriers to entry are very high.

**Threat of substitutes**

*When this threat is high the 'safe' profit margin is low as customers more readily change when prices are high.*

- *The relative price and performance of substitutes.* If a similar product or service is available at the same, or lower, price then the threat is high. If potential substitutes are more expensive, or inferior, then the threat is low.
- *Switching costs for customers.* This factor determines the threat of substitutes as well as determining the height of the entry barrier. If no extra costs are incurred then change is likely.
- *Buyers' propensity to substitutes.* Apathetic or satisfied buyers are not likely to change, militant or dissatisfied ones are. Generally the more significant the purchase is to the customer the higher is their propensity to switch.

**The power of buyers**

*This primarily depends upon their price sensitivity and their bargainning leverage.*

- *Price sensitivity.* This depends upon the purchaser's relative cost importance to the buyer. A number of things can reduce price sensitivity:
    1 brand loyalty and differentiation
    2 the impact of the product on their product
    3 customer's own profitability
    4 decision makers' incentives (eg quality, etc).
- *Bargaining leverage.* All the following factors determine the amount of leverage buyers have:
    1 buyer concentration and volume
    2 buyer switching costs
    3 buyer information
    4 threat of backward vertical integration by buyers
    5 existence of substitutes.

**The power of suppliers**

*This is the differentiation of the inputs, and matters when the organisation's process needs a rare commodity.*

- *Switching costs of changing to an alternative supplier.* When these costs are high then suppliers are relatively powerful since the organisation would face significant costs if it were to leave them. Where a supplier is effectively in a monopoly position, for example electricity supplies, their power is extremely high since changing to gas causes high switching costs.
- *Availability of substitute supplies.* When substitutes are available the power of the supplier is reduced, for example if the fuel used can be changed from electricity to gas.
- *Supplier concentration.* The more singular the supplier is the higher its power is. The extreme of this is the monopoly supplier situation. When suppliers are not concentrated their power is lowered.
- *The importance of volume to suppliers.* If the supplier has to achieve high volume sales then they hold less bargaining power. If the volume of sales represented by that customer is less significant then the supplier bargaining position is heightened.
- *Cost relative to the purchasing industry's total costs.* Supplier power is low when goods provided form a cost significant input. Bargaining power increases when their ratio to the users' total costs falls.
- *The impact of product to cost or differentiation.* Supplier power is higher when their product is significant to the buyer organisation's overall costs or chances of product differentiation. Their power is weaker if the quality or cost of the supplies is not significant to the quality or cost of the purchaser's product.

- *The threat of forward integration by suppliers*. When suppliers will find it easy to forward integrate into the purchaser's industry then they have high bargaining power. If pushed to lower prices they will themselves produce the 'finished product'. Where the barriers to such integration are high (see threat of new entrants) then the power of suppliers is weakened.

To produce a model of the competitive forces playing upon an organisation requires detailed research into its industry, but it then allows the net power of the five forces to be judged in order to concentrate attention upon those most significant. This concentration may be either to exploit a powerful position or to protect from a weak one.

### Life cycle analysis

There are a number of models that aim to relate the competitive position of an organisation to the maturity of the industry or its products. The models assume there is a basic S-curve description to the growth phenomenon of the organisation and its products. Examples of such approaches include Greiner (1972), Arthur D Little, Boston Consulting Group and Shell Directional Policy Matrix.

Four stages in the life cycle of any product or industry can be identified (*see* Figure 2.10). The exact shape of the curve will vary but each stage can always be discerned. When products are the focus, then the stages are:

- *Introduction*: the activity or product is new and there is an initial stage of experimentation and gradual acceptance
- *Growth*: there is a rapid growth of the activity or rapid increase in sales
- *Maturity*: the activity or sales remain high but there is no further increase in activity or sales
- *Decline*: the competition, product displacement, or other forces cause a decline in the activity or sales

The stage in this cycle will affect the organisation's environment and hence strategies in a number of ways. The growth phase of a business or industry is the market capture stage since any ground gained during this stage is of enduring benefit. It is relatively easier to gain market share when the total market is growing than when this market is static or in decline. The strategies during this stage will revolve around increasing the volume at the desired rate. As the industry reaches maturity a more formal approach of monitoring of costs will emerge. During this stage increased growth is usually only achieved by niche marketing. As the cycle moves into the decline stage, the strategies will be those of removal, displacement or divestment.

### Key opportunities/threats (SWOT) analysis

This is a model for assessing the Strengths, Weaknesses, Opportunities and Threats that face an organisation (*see* Figure 2.11). This, conceptually simple, model offers headings under which to classify any number of aspects of a situation. Strengths and weaknesses are ways to classify the internal circumstances of the organisation, while opportunities and threats are ways of defining the external environment.

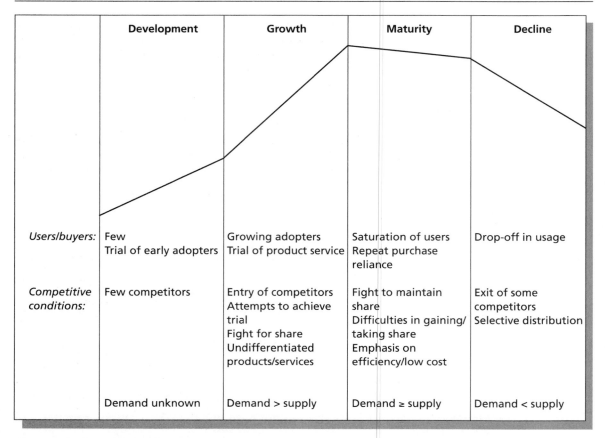

| | Development | Growth | Maturity | Decline |
|---|---|---|---|---|
| *Users/buyers:* | Few<br>Trial of early adopters | Growing adopters<br>Trial of product service | Saturation of users<br>Repeat purchase<br>reliance | Drop-off in usage |
| *Competitive conditions:* | Few competitors | Entry of competitors<br>Attempts to achieve<br>trial<br>Fight for share<br>Undifferentiated<br>products/services | Fight to maintain<br>share<br>Difficulties in gaining/<br>taking share<br>Emphasis on<br>efficiency/low cost | Exit of some<br>competitors<br>Selective distribution |
| | Demand unknown | Demand > supply | Demand ≥ supply | Demand < supply |

**Fig 2.10 ◆ Industry life cycle model**

It is important to remember that, whilst the SWOT acronym offers a fast 'pocket sized' method of conceptualising complex reality, it is more properly a matrix. It is when considering the interaction between the two axes that real support to strategic analysis and strategic choice, as an option generator, is obtained. A process to go through in order to fill out the matrix was suggested by Weihrich (1982) as follows:

Step 1    Prepare an Enterprise Profile of the kind of business, the geographic domain, the competitive situation and the top management orientation

Step 2    Identify and evaluate economic, social, political, demographic, products and technology and market and competition factors

Step 3    Prepare a forecast, make predictions and assessment of the future

Step 4    Prepare an SW audit in management and organisation, operations, finance, marketing and other

Step 5    Develop alternatives

Step 6    Make Strategic Choices by considering strategies, tactics, and action.

Steps 1–6 Test for consistency

Step 7    Prepare contingency plans

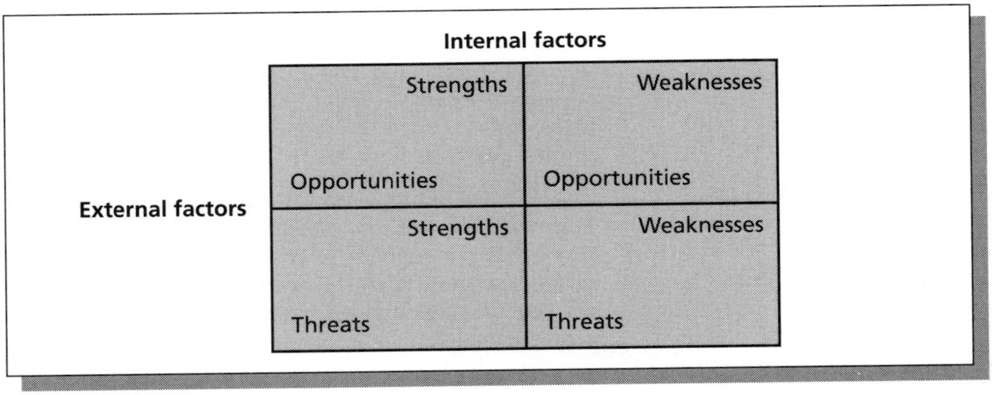

|  | Internal factors | |
| :--- | :--- | :--- |
|  | Strengths | Weaknesses |
| **External factors** | Opportunities<br><br>Strengths | Opportunities<br><br>Weaknesses |
|  | Threats | Threats |

Fig 2.11 ◆ SWOT Matrix

A SWOT analysis defines the relationship between the internal and external appraisals in strategic analysis. It is an exercise in identification and analysis. Analysing the key factors of the environment and the fundamental internal strengths and weaknesses of the organisation will help dictate the strategies appropriate to the firm. No organisation should forget to apply a SWOT analysis to competitors, supplies and customers as well as to itself in order to assess the full position within the industry and to direct the firm towards the appropriate direction. Various strategies suggested by a SWOT analysis are shown in Figure 2.12.

Whilst identifying a strategy is about tackling the future, it must be based on a realistic appraisal of the organisation's past and present performance. No organisation can develop a strategy only on the basis of identifying opportunities and threats. The organisation's strategy must take account of the resources and competitiveness of the organisation. Therefore the strategy must emerge as a result of the combined assessment of market attractiveness and business strength. So a vital part of this is the analysis of resources and capabilities. The object of the exercise is to use the strategic pointers in order to use the existing business strengths to exploit opportunities, to create new opportunities, to counteract threats and repair the weaknesses. To use strengths in this way they must be realistically identified and assessed. By using the same technique to assess competitors the organisation can capitalise upon those competitors' weaknesses and avoid going head on against their strengths.

The SWOT analysis is also referred to as the TOWS Matrix – this naming is perhaps more suitable when it forms part of an environmental analysis! Rowe, *et al.* (1994) call it a WOTS-UP analysis and offer suggested actions for each matrix segment. With either name it is a systematic method for matching environmental threats and opportunities with the organisation's strengths and weaknesses. There is a tendency when doing a SWOT analysis to be less than honest in the appraisals and to feel the need to cover up feared weaknesses by proclaiming perceived strengths. As well as analysing the environment it can be used to generate strategic options, so it also forms part of the Strategic Choice element. SWOT may offer its best service at warning of the need for avoidance and so the results may tend to the negative in bias. Although it is future oriented it does not build in any mechanisms for handling the uncertainty of the future, nor does it give any holistic model of the

| | |
|---|---|
| **Maxi-Maxi** | In this segment the organisation is playing from its strengths to an opportunity and hence the business objectives are generally to reduce internal weaknesses and overcome external threats in order to focus upon this segment. Rowe, Mason, *et al.* (1994) call this segment **exploit.** |
| **Mini-Maxi** | The strategy appropriate for this segment would be one that minimises weaknesses and maximises the opportunities. The opportunity exists but requires strength where the organisation currently has a weakness. Without strategic action to remove this weakness the opportunity must go to competitors. Rowe *et al.* (1994) call this segment **search.** |
| **Mini-Mini** | The strategy for this segment is one that will reduce both the weakness and the threat. This is the precarious segment and so organisations should adopt strategies that avoid it. Rowe *et al.* (1994) call this segment **avoid.** |
| **Maxi-Mini** | The indicated strategy for this segment is one that uses the strength of the organisation in order to deflect the threat. Care must be taken to avoid unnecessary competitive battles, and strategic options that circumvent the threat are to be preferred. Rowe *et al.* (1994) call this segment **confront.** |

**Fig 2.12 ◆ Strategies indicated by a SWOT analysis**

organisation and is not aimed at option evaluation and, hence, nor selection. However, the process of going through an internal and external appraisal may cause the objectives, and hence also the performance measures, to be reviewed.

## 2.2.2 ◆ Analysis of values and objectives

The second of the three aspects of strategic analysis is the interpretation of the complex cultural web of an organisation. That is, to interpret what the culture is and what it means for it to be that way. Models of culture and objectives are covered here. Models of power and structure which also assist in this process are covered in 2.4 Strategic Implementation.

### Strategy and culture

The organisation and the sub-units within it have a culture. This corporate culture can be defined as the pattern of basic assumptions that a given group has invented, discovered, or developed in learning to cope with its problems of external adaptation and internal integration, and that worked well enough to be considered valid and, therefore, to be taught to new members as the correct way to perceive, think, and feel in relation to those problems. Analysing the organisational culture will enable interpretations of its meaning to inform the selection of feasible and acceptable strategy options (*see* Section 2.3) and also issues of strategic implementation (*see* Section 2.4). However, the organisational culture will actually shape whether analysis in a formal sense is done at all.

The organisational culture is the element that ensures that, faced with the same set of circumstances in the environment and internal resource constraints, organisations respond in different ways. The culture of the organisation determines how they measure success. This perception can have a dampening effect upon the influence of environmental factors upon strategy since environmental factors influence the strategy *through* the perception although they *directly* affect the business performance. The organisation creates its own model of reality and every decision is seen in the light of that model.

Many writers describe culture in terms of levels distinguishing between the visible aspects of culture (all the things that can be seen and heard, including the rules, procedures, technology, etc) and the underlying aspects of culture (the unseen, unarticulated and untested values and assumptions). Different writers give different numbers of levels with different names but retain the essential distinction between what can be detected directly and what can be detected only indirectly from what people do. An organisation has a strong culture when the visible and the underlying levels are consistent with each other and shared by all. A weak organisational culture results when the cultural levels are inconsistent with each other and/or in pockets.

There are various ways to assess and categorise the culture, or set of shared beliefs, of the organisation. Many elements aggregate to make up that culture: the power, stories, history, language and dress codes, status symbols, reward structures, logos, organisation charts, etc. What Deal and Kennedy (1982) call 'the way we do things around here.' Miles and Snow (1978) classify organisations as either conservative, valuing low-risk strategies, secure markets and well-tested potential solutions, known as *defenders*, or innovative, ground breaking, valuing risk and pay off, known as *prospectors*. These two types of organisation will behave quite differently under the same circumstances. Within defender organisations 'the prevailing beliefs are essentially conservative, where low-risk strategies . . . are valued.' On the other hand, prospector organisations are those in which 'management tends to go for higher-risk strategies and new opportunities'.

This classification of culture according to an organisation's desire to take risks is analogous to the management accounting concept of attitudes towards risk in investments. Drury (1988), for example, defines two initial attitudes to risk:

> *A risk seeker is an organisation who, given a choice between more or less risky alternatives with identical expected values, prefers the riskier alternative (alternative B). Faced with the same choice, a risk averter would select the less risky alternative (alternative A).*

The alternatives A and B referred to by Drury are:

| State of economy | *Possible return on investment of £100* | |
| --- | --- | --- |
| | *Alt A* | *Alt B* |
| Recession | 90 | 0 |
| Normal | 100 | 100 |
| Boom | 110 | 200 |

So a prospector organisation is a risk seeker, whilst a defender organisation is risk averse. Drury also includes a third risk attitude, that of risk neutrality such that an organisation would be indifferent to the two possible outcome alternatives.

Assessment of the culture of the organisation is nothing new and does not depend only upon new models. For instance McGregor's (1960) Theory X/Theory Y model is a way of encapsulating the cultural attitudes the organisation has to its human resources. The main points of this theory are illustrated in Figure 2.13.

The groups within the organisation may have clashing cultures. For example a sales team may have a culture that focuses upon results whilst an accountancy group may have a culture that focuses upon accuracy. The 'tales' told reflect and reinforce this culture; clinching the sale over expensive lunches: finding the 3p error. The culture may flow from a dominant leader figure and their vision, as Henry Ford and Ford Motor Company, or from the history, stage in technology maturity, perceived reasons for past successes or failures, etc. Two contrasting cultures are modelled below:

| | |
|---|---|
| High technology | Low technology |
| Price leader | Price follower |
| High quality, high price | Low quality, low price |
| High service | Low service |
| Innovator | Follower – copier |
| Selective marketer | Mass marketer |
| Risk taker | Risk avoider |

---

**Theory X**

1  Management is responsible for organising the elements of productive enterprise – money, materials, machines, men – in the interest of economic ends.
2  With respect to people, this is a process of directing their efforts, motivating them, controlling their actions, and modifying their behaviour to fit the needs of the organisation.
3  Without this active intervention by management, people would be passive – even resistant – to organisational needs. They must therefore be persuaded, rewarded, punished, controlled – their activities must be directed. This is management's task. Management consists of getting things done through other people.

**Theory Y**

1  Management is responsible for organising the elements of productive enterprise – money, materials, machines, men – in the interest of economic ends.
2  People are not by nature passive or resistant to organisational needs. They have become so as a result of experience in organisations.
3  The motivation, the potential for development, the capacity for assuming responsibility, the readiness to direct behaviour toward organisational goals are all present in people. Management does not put them there. It is a responsibility of management to make it possible for people to recognise and develop these human characteristics for themselves.
4  The essential task of management is to arrange organisational conditions and methods of operation so that people can achieve their own goals best by directing their own efforts toward organisational objectives.

---

**Fig 2.13 ◆ McGregor's Theory X/Theory Y**

## Strategy and objectives

The objectives of the organisation perform three important functions:

- They provide a statement of the financial objectives compared with the current performance of the organisation indicating the extent and scope of the strategic decisions to be made.
- By providing a statement of the broad mission of the organisation they provide a product-market focus for the business strategy of the organisation.
- Having a set of corporate goals established at the senior level of the organisation provides objectives for individual functions or areas of responsibility within the rest of the organisation.

Objectives can be 'closed', meaning they can be *achieved*. These are usually measurable and definable in terms of their inbuilt measures of success. Objectives that can be measured, and are therefore closed, may be called targets. Conversely objectives can be 'open', meaning they can be striven for, but can *never* be achieved, so that they persist throughout the life of the organisation. The organisation-wide mission is *always* an open objective. The mission might document the objectives, but probably only one facet of them. Therefore, the business' objectives can be:

- Corporate open
- Corporate closed
- Unit open
- Unit closed

The question of analysing objectives in a strategic context is a more complex one than at first it seems. The question of 'whose objectives are they?' must be resolved by assessing the stakeholder groups. In any organisation there will be several *groups*, the stakeholders, whose interests, and hence objectives, may not only differ but be mutually exclusive. Stakeholder analysis is an increasingly important technique associated with strategic analysis.

Cyert and March (1992) argue that the organisation's objectives emerge as a result of the process of internal negotiation amongst power groups within the organisation; it is these power groups that are the stakeholders. Perhaps the conflicting objectives could be:

| *Group* | *Objective* |
|---|---|
| Shareholder | Market value of the investment |
| | Stability of dividends |
| | Size of the dividend |
| Management | Sales growth |
| | Asset growth |
| | Profitability |
| Labour force | Wage increase |
| | Numbers employed |
| | Job security |
| Society | Productivity gains |
| | Exports |
| | Profitability |
| | Social welfare. |

So the organisation's objectives represent the *current* position of the compromise between these tensions. The power structure of the organisation is one determinant of where the balance point lies since, by definition, it refers to the ability of individuals or groups to obtain and use the human and material resources available. Power is *not* evenly distributed, some units, groups and individuals are more powerful than others. While Section 2.4 will give a fuller coverage of power structures, three contributors to the power of a business unit can be identified:

- *Work flow pervasiveness*: The amount of the organisation's tasks that are dependant upon this unit's activities
- *Immediacy*: The speed and severity of the effect upon the rest of the organisation of the loss of this unit
- *Substitutability*: The ability of the other parts of the organisation to perform the activities of this unit or find others to do so.

Within any organisation, multiple, possibly mutually exclusive, objectives can exist and most organisations settle for *satisfactory* rather than *optimal* solutions for resolving them.

The objectives and goals of the organisation are talked about as if they existed *apart* from the people that make up that organisation. The goals arrived at for the coalition are the net result of the negotiations amongst the individuals. The goals, therefore, change as the coalition membership changes and as the goals of those members change. Goal displacement is a common occurrence and occurs when the goals of those *operating* the business displace the business goals as the primary goals. Examples are where office hours are chosen to suit staff rather than to meet the objective of client servicing, government bodies intended to regulate trades end up protecting them, computer centres whose primary goal becomes to provide a technologically interesting staff environment rather than providing computer *services*. The student travel service that moved from providing cheap charter flights to being a conventional travel agency to suit the goals of the operating staff is a perfect example of how goal displacement alters the *nature* of the organisation.

## 2.2.3 ◆ Analysis of resources

The third element of strategic analysis is to perform a resource analysis. The object of this is to understand the organisation's strategic capability. Johnson and Scholes (1993) suggest a process for doing this, illustrated in Figure 2.14.

This process aims to establish what strengths and weaknesses the organisation has, in other words what it does well and what it does not do well. There are a number of key areas for assessing this, shown in Figure 2.15.

During the 1980s it was 'out of fashion' to base competitive strategy on views of internal capability since it was felt that that an internally driven competitive perspective would lead to a lack of innovation and a tendency to avoid 'stretch' targets. However, with the rise of process views of organisations such as Total Quality Management, Business Process Re-engineering and so on (*see* Chapter 7 for a discussion of these and other process views of organisations), there has been a corresponding growth in interest in understanding (and changing for the better) the organisation's strategic *capability*. Much current work, for instance that of Collis and Montgomery (1995), focuses upon resource analysis but directly relates it to environmental analysis issues by considering resource analysis in relative terms

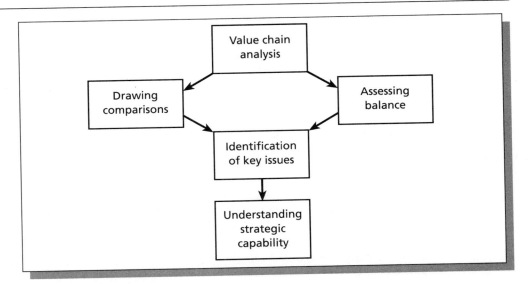

**Fig 2.14 ◆ Resource analysis process**
(after Johnson and Scholes)

| Key area | Dimensions |
|---|---|
| *Product/market* | Share of existing markets<br>Range of products<br>Position in product life cycle<br>Dependence upon key product for sales/profits/cash flow<br>Distribution network<br>Marketing and market research |
| *Production* | Number, size, location, age and capacity of plants<br>Specialisation/versatility of equipment<br>Production and cost levels<br>Cost/availability of raw materials<br>Production control systems |
| *Finance* | Present asset structure<br>Present capital structure<br>Access to additional equity and debt finance<br>Pattern of cash flow<br>Procedures for financial management |
| *Technology* | Currency of production methods and products<br>R&D spending and effectiveness |
| *Organisation and human resources* | Organisation structure<br>Management style and succession<br>Staff development policies<br>Management/labour force relationship<br>Reward structures |

**Fig 2.15 ◆ The key areas of business resources and competence**

with respect to current and potential competitors. Competing on resources, as this resource-driven view of competitive strategy is often called, is primarily about ensuring that the organisation's inherent nature, that is its resources, adds value to what it does.

## Value chain analysis

As part of the process of assessing the organisation's strategic capabilities a resource audit can provide significant insights into the competitive possibilities open to it. One of the commonest tools used to help gain some understanding of the internal nature of the organisation is to structure a picture of its capabilities by looking at it as a collection of processes that occur. Perhaps the commonest model of this notion is Porter's value chain (Figures 2.16a and 2.16b) which portrays the organisation as a connected chain of activities each of which relates in some different way to the provision of the organisation's products (including service products) to its customers. The value chain therefore models the flow of activities that add value by contributing to a customer's willingness to 'buy' the product. Since both products and customers can be defined in increasing or decreasing levels of detail the concept can be used across an entire industry (the industry value system) or to show internal customers.

By modelling the activities of an organisation it is possible to distinguish the primary activities, those that contribute to getting the goods or service one step closer to the customer, from the secondary activities, and those whose role it is to *support* primary activities. The organisation can use this model to *assess* the degree of effectiveness of resource use in this value chain. Activity by activity resource use can be judged in terms of efficiency and effectiveness. Efficiency is the measure of how well the resources are being used, and such measures could include profitability, capacity use and the yield gained from that capacity. Effectiveness, however, is the assessment of how well the resources are allocated to those activities which are the most competitively significant within the value chain. Such assessment could involve monitoring the use within the value chain of capital, people, goodwill and

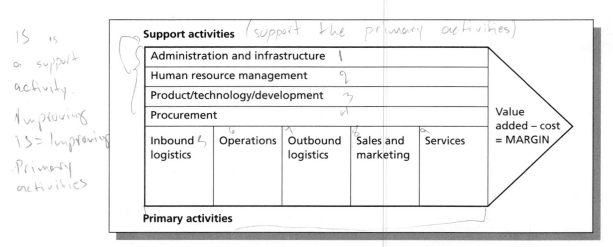

Fig 2.16a ◆ Porter's Value Chain Model
(adapted with the permission of The Free Press, a division of Simon & Schuster from *Competitive Advantage: Creating and Sustaining Superior Performance* by Michael E. Porter. Copyright © 1985 by Michael E. Porter)

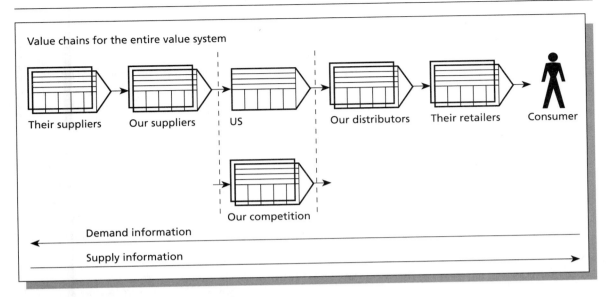

Value chains for the entire value system

Their suppliers    Our suppliers    US    Our distributors    Their retailers    Consumer

Our competition

← Demand information

Supply information →

**Fig 2.16b ◆ Porter's Value System Model**
(adapted with the permission of The Free Press, a division of Simon & Schuster from *Competitive Advantage: Creating and Sustaining Superior Performance* by Michael E. Porter. Copyright © 1985 by Michael E. Porter)

R&D. The main focus of the value chain analysis is on the links between the activities in order to highlight areas of strategic strength or weakness and competitive opportunity or threat.

There are nine activities that logically make up the business of any organisation, as shown in Figure 2.16a. Primary activities are those that have a direct relationship, potential or actual, with the organisation's customers and the five of these appear as vertical (sequenced) processes. Underpinning and easing these five primary tasks are four *support* activities that facilitate their smooth functioning and have only an indirect relationship with the process of adding value for the organisation's customers. Support activities are those shown horizontally in Figure 2.16a. Both primary and support processes are described in Figure 2.17.

So each of these nine activities is assessed in terms of its efficiency of resource use and effectiveness of resource allocation, with a view to identifying areas of potential improvements. These improvements are sought in order to enhance the organisation's competitive position – Porter suggests this improvement constitutes competitive advantage and if the improvements are wrought using IS then that competitive advantage comes about because of IS.

The intention in analysing the value chain is to develop one that is configured differently to competitors or by having a cost advantage on some of the activities within it. Figure 2.18 shows two sample value chains. The re-configuring of the value chain is a process of business re-design and increasingly such re-configuring is facilitated by the use of IS – *see* Chapter 8 for more on business re-engineering.

### Performance assessment

Value chain analysis is closely related to financial resource analysis and core competence analysis (discussed later in this section). All seek to judge along some dimension whether the organisation is being 'successful' and indeed this is at the

| **Primary activities** | |
| --- | --- |
| *Inbound logistics* | All processes associated with receiving, storing and disseminating inputs to the production process for the product or service. |
| *Operations* | All processes associated with transforming the inputs into outputs. These may be processes *other* than physical manufacturing operations since the value chain can relate to the provision of a service. |
| *Outbound logistics* | All activities concerned with distributing the products or services to the customers. This may be the physical or conceptual movement or storage of the goods or service. |
| *Sales and marketing* | Activities which provide opportunities for the potential customer to buy the product or service and offer inducements to do so. This section of the value chain includes such processes as advertising, pricing, tendering, salesforce management, selection of distribution channels, etc. |
| *Services* | All processes concerned with the provision of service as part of the deal struck with the customers. They are those activities that enhance or maintain the value of the product or service once the customer has bought it. These activities include repairs, maintenance, spare parts supply, product upgrades, follow-up services, training and installation, etc. |
| **Support activities** | |
| *Administration and Infrastructure* | Which are the tasks that comprise the general management of the organisation as a business entity, and encompass financial management, planning, legal services, quality management, office administration, etc. |
| *Human resource management* | This is all those activities associated with the recruiting, training, developing, appraising, promoting, and rewarding of the personnel of the organisation. |
| *Product/Technology development* | Whilst these activities do include those activities traditionally called R&D they actually include all activities that relate to developing the *technology* of the product or service and the *processes* that produce it and the processes that ensure the *management* of the organisation. So, as well as R&D, these activities include the development of technology in support of all the organisation's tasks – for instance IS for human resource management or accounting or internal or external telecommunications. And, of course, development of new product and service designs. |
| *Procurement* | These are the activities that support the procurement of inputs for all of the activities of the value chain. These range from raw materials and production equipment, through office and factory provision to purchase of office supplies. It also includes the procurement of IS. These activities include every aspect of acquiring the required inputs to the value adding process *except* human resource procurement. |

**Fig 2.17 ◆ Value chain activities**

| Harrods | Appeals to a service-sensitive rather than price-sensitive customer group. Buyers focus upon exclusive products and ranges. So links to suppliers and the procurement function are important. Customer contact is high. IS can be used to improve communications with customers, for instance Harrods maintain a wardrobe service, which is a database of individual customers' sizes and requirements. The support activity (technology development) is closely linked to primary activity (service) to create a competitive gain. |
|---|---|
| Argos | Focuses upon low-cost offers sustainable over the life of their catalogue. Inbound logistics and the retail operation itself must be tightly managed to keep costs down. IS based systems are important and illustrate another close link to make a competitive gain. The support activity (again technology development) links to the primary activity (inbound logistics and operations). Argos offers little in the way of service and staff need little product knowledge. |

Fig 2.18 ◆ Example value chains

heart of resource analysis where such judgements allow priorities to emerge that then allow effort to go where it will reap the 'best' results. This can only be done from a view of *relative* performance. Financial resource analysis monitors the use of funds within an organisation to give some measure of the business' performance. Monitoring performance using financial ratios can only act as a guide to strategic capability and can be misleading unless used in association with assessment of the performance of business processes and capabilities (which is where value chain analysis and core competence analysis would come in). It is the act of assessing the performance of processes that may lead to a Business Process Re-engineering initiative (*see* Chapter 8 for more discussion of BPR). So, although financial measures can be used to judge where the organisation is in terms of its performance it is important to use a number of other tools to help. Such tools, in addition to those already mentioned, might include:

1 *Experience Curve* – gives the basic message that benefits, primarily in the form of lower unit costs, can be obtained by increasing the volume of production. So the experience curve supports strategies aimed at increasing volume and market share. Its main role is as a strategic option generator. It does model a behavioural relationship.

2 *Growth-Share Matrix* – helps companies with a portfolio of businesses decide, for each business, whether to invest to increase market share, use a business as a source of finance for investment in other businesses, or whether to divest. So it contributes to the strategic planning process by supporting strategic option generation. Because it recognises that market share and industry growth are profitability indicators it also assists in option evaluation and selection, though it does not assess uncertainty or explicitly model the business.

3 *Industry Attractiveness – Business Strength Matrix* – this is a development of the growth-share matrix, though it has some features in common with the TOWS Matrix. Mainly helps strategic option generation with secondary support to evaluation and selection.

## Product portfolio analysis

The matrix produced by the Boston Consulting Group (BCG) is a tool that is so familiar to business analysts that using this technique, along with SWOT, has come to be regarded as an effective minimum standard in assessing organisations. This 'box' models the relationship between a division or product's current or future revenue potential and the appropriate management stance, *see* Figure 2.19. The two by two matrix names the divisions or products in order to chart symptoms into a diagnosis so that an 'effective' cure, or management behaviour, can be adopted. Derivatives of it have been developed that are more qualitative and more geared to developing an interpretation of the choices to be made; examples of these include the one documented in Hussey (1978).

This two by two matrix classifies businesses, divisions or products according to the present market share and the future growth of that market. A successful product which lasts from emergent to mature market goes clockwise around the matrix. To sum up, the intention of the BCG matrix is to distinguish between the cash generators and the cash consumers. The matrix segments summarise the expected profit and cash flow and also recommends (since this is another normative model) an outline strategy to follow. Crudely these are to milk the cows, divest the dogs, invest in the stars and examine the question marks; a fuller explanation of the nature of each segment is given in Figure 2.20. This model can be used as a predictive device since positioning an element of the portfolio, whatever it is, gives some advice as to how to manage that element appropriately; Figure 2.20 shows the type of advice given. One of the fundamental problems with this model is that the advice given is essentially one dimensional and no comment is made on any value added by a combination (such as within a corporate group) or in relating to a long-term strategic direction (such as linked to core competencies). In fact only immediate financial gain is being commented upon.

## Analysis of core competencies

Prahalad and Hamel (1990) suggest that the key issue facing organisations in the 1990s is to assess their 'core competencies' (*see* Figure 2.21). Core competencies are those capabilities that are vital for competitive well being and which significant

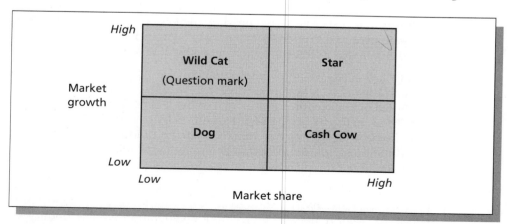

**Fig 2.19 ◆ Boston consulting group matrix**

| | |
|---|---|
| **Cash Cows** | Products or divisions in this segment are those that are the current high income earners for the organisation. They are expected to provide the major part of current profits, and form the major source of funding for future developments. However, Cash Cows are relatively short-term so they are not expected to provide significant future revenues. For business areas and products in this segment, the organisation should look to adopt measures, including the use of IS, to increase the profit, extend the life time or shift the division or product into the Star segment. These are the well-established products in mature markets. |
| **Stars** | Products or business divisions in this segment are the ones that provide significant revenue now and are expected to continue to do so in the future. In this segment, the organisation will wish to seek opportunities to increase profits and extend the life of the product or division. Again these measures may include the judicious use of IS. These are the market leader products in growth markets. Since these products or divisions require ongoing investments they do not generate as much margin as Cash Cows do. |
| **Dead Dogs** | Divisions or products in this segment provide little or no contribution to profits today and it is not expected that this situation will change. This segment should be removed, which may be achieved by divestment of the division or product, or by taking steps to reduce associated costs or to move the division or product into the Cash Cow, or even, if lucky, the Star segment. These are the products that have lost market share to competitors or are in declining markets. |
| **Wild Cats** | Divisions or products in this segment are those that the organisation is currently prepared to 'carry' since, although they make little or no contribution to revenue now, they are expected to in the future. These are usually young areas or products and are probably still being developed. Investments should be made cautiously in this segment since the risks associated with this segment are higher than with others. Clearly the organisation will seek ways to ensure that the divisions or products of this segment quickly mature into highly profitable Stars. These are the products with low market share but in fast growing markets. If successful these products or divisions will become Stars. |

**Fig 2.20 ◆ Boston matrix segments**

resources must be put into acquiring. Often decentralisation will act against the identification and acquisition of core competencies since such decentralisation tends to favour dependency upon outside agencies. Whilst short-term competitiveness derives from price/performance attributes of current products, long-term competitiveness derives from the ability to get, at lower cost than others, core competencies that will, in turn, beget new, unanticipated products.

Core competencies support *all* aspects of the business and represent the collective learning of the organisation, particularly of how to co-ordinate and integrate production skills and multiple streams of technology. A number of tests can be used to identify the *core* competencies:

- A core competency will provide potential access to a wide variety of markets. For example, the organisation which has a core competence in display systems can participate in markets for calculators, miniature TVs, monitors for lap top computers and car dashboards.

- A core competence should make a significant contribution to the perceived customer benefits of the end product.

- A core competence should be difficult for a competitor to copy. And it certainly will be difficult when it is the complex, integrated web of individual technologies and production skills.

There should be five or six such core competencies for any organisation. Those that list twenty to thirty have not listed *core* competencies. However, producing *any* list prompts the organisation to consider its capabilities in terms of building blocks towards competencies and highlights any gaps where they need to forge alliances to plug them. Competitiveness must be thought of in these terms. The *embedded* skills that breed the next generation of competitive products cannot be bought in or rented in on outsourcing deals. Organisations must be aware of the danger in cutting out 'cost centres' by replacing them with contract deals – core competencies

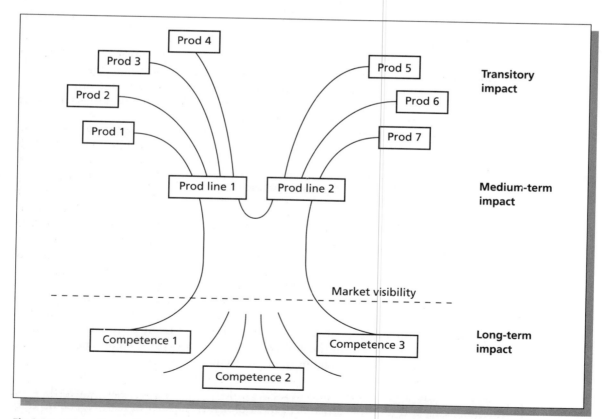

Fig 2.21 ◆ How the notions of organisational competence relate to its product lines and individual products

may go as well. Any outsourcing needs to be treated with care; it can give a short-cut access to today's competitive product – but not to tomorrow's since people skills need nurturing.

Core competencies deliver core products; these are the components that physically embody those competencies and are the components or sub-assemblies that actually add to the value of the end products. A perfect example of this is Canon's holding 84 per cent of the manufacturing share of laser printer engines whilst holding minute market share of laser *printers*. Core competencies are used to seek maximum world manufacturing share in core products, and this may be at the expense of end product market share. The core products drive the resources for further investment in core competencies. They also drive the ability to define what the end products will be and enough success with core products allows the sub-assemblies or components to be used as leverage into eventual *major* end product shares.

The organisation needs to create a strategic road map of the *desired* core competencies and *how* to get them. To judge the extent of this architecture the organisation can pose three questions:

- How long could we preserve our competitiveness in this business if we did not control this core competence?
- How central is this core competence to perceived customer benefits?
- What future opportunities would be foreclosed if we were to lose this particular competence?

This architecture gives a way to assess possible diversification. It can test any option against the goal of being the best player in the world at X. It provides a template for the allocation of resources and makes the logic for doing this obvious and explicit so lower level management can understand the priorities and so maintain consistency with them.

Like the arguments about information in the 1980s, core competencies are a *corporate* resource which suggests that SBUs should be able to bid for the people skills just like they bid for capital. The more the competence is used the stronger it gets, hence SBUs must justify their retention of skilled people by showing an effective yield on their skills. Diversified organisations need to recognise that they hold a portfolio of core competencies as well as a portfolio of businesses. If such organisations wish to make something of those portfolios then there are three domains which need to be assessed: core competencies; core products; and end products. Human skills embody the core competencies and yet organisations that devote effort to capital bidding may well have no *people* bidding equivalent. The structure of SBUs can act as a straight-jacket that makes innovation limited to only those ideas that lie close at hand (within one SBU). *Hybrid* opportunities that would combine across SBUs will go unexploited unless the core competencies are used to *widen* the domain of innovation. The organisation must alter its patterns of communication, career paths, strategy formulation and managerial rewards away from the SBU constraints. Reward systems must reflect this approach; perhaps rotation schemes might help to change the culture in which managers 'belong' to an SBU.

Recognition of the problems of the SBU approach and a recognition of the competitive value held by core competencies may reverse the trend of radical decentralisation which made top management just a layer of accounting consolidation. Senior management must add value by directing the architecture that directs core competence acquisition and development process. Nicholls (1995) and the MCC matrix offers a tool for considering the value added by overall relationships. Belonging together must be considered to add something that would not be present if each SBU were truly an independent operator (though accounting strengths can, of course, be a core competence across the group).

The concepts of organisational vision and mission, the notion that there are competencies which are core to what an organisation does and the BCG's notion that activities have a profile of value that they contribute are all individually useful concepts. Perhaps even more usefully, Nicholls (1995) offers an attractive way to consider these ideas as a coherent whole by using the Mission and Core Competencies (MCC) portfolio decision matrix. The MCC Matrix is based upon considering an organisation as a tree. It is the mission and vision that provide the nutrients that feed the tree, the core competencies serve as its roots which, through core processes, produce 'fruit' in terms of projects and products. If this is an acceptable analogy then the matrix based upon it offers a way of selecting which actual and potential 'fruit' to support since each project and product can be judged in terms of its match to the mission and to the core competencies of the organisation. Like the BCG, the MCC is also offered in an extended and rather more qualitative 3 × 3 version but at its simplest each of the four segments is given a name that captures the essence of the advice being given. This simple version of the matrix is shown in Figure 2.22.

Nicholls argues most persuasively for the use of the matrix as a tool to force the testing of assumptions about what the core competencies actually *are* and what the mission actually *is*. He further suggests that this tool can integrate issues to support making holistic decisions at any level within the organisation that has got a definable mission and definable core competencies. Clearly the 'redefine framework' 'advice' given for the matrix segment he calls 'Dilution' makes this point strongly. The redefinition of the framework so that a stubbornly attractive 'fruit' can be legitimately 'cherished' is not, as it might at first glance seem, an overthrowing of the *theory* of the matrix. It is actually an explicit recognition that, if projects

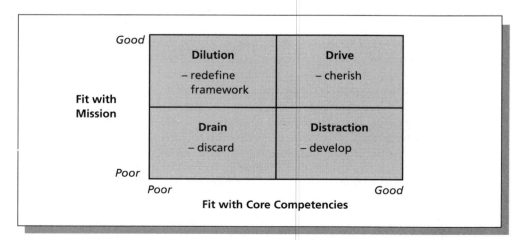

Fig 2.22 ◆ Mission core competence (MCC) decision matrix

or products *are* remaining stubbornly attractive, then the organisation has probably defined its mission or its core competencies inappropriately. Nicholls does not make it explicit but, if the framework is redefined in this way then the organisation must then re-assess all other existing and potential 'fruits' for their match to the new framework.

## 2.3 ◆ STRATEGY CHOICE

Once management has generated a picture of strategic *possibilities* then it requires techniques that assist in the evaluation of the available choices. This choice element of strategic management is concerned with choosing a strategy based upon the foundations laid by strategic analysis. The 'good' manager must be able to generate and evaluate possible strategies taking into account the nature of the organisation and its industry. Risk, structure and culture are just three of the issues of concern here. This section of the chapter presents techniques for performing the formal aspects of generating, evaluating and selecting strategic options. These techniques are presented under the headings offered by the Johnson and Scholes model of strategic management. The elements associated with making strategic choices are shown in Figure 2.23 and will involve three factors:

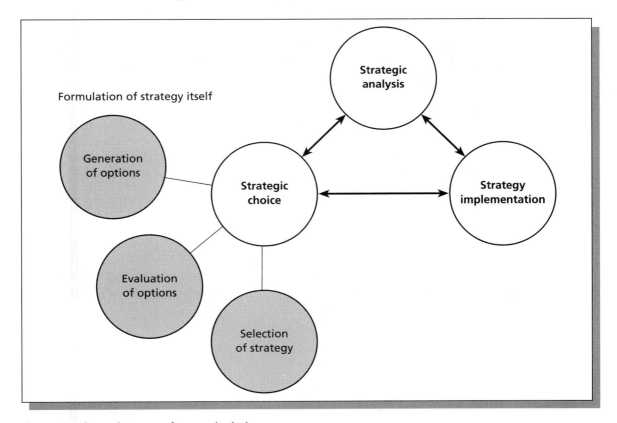

**Fig 2.23 ◆ Three elements of strategic choice**
(adapted from Johnson and Scholes, *Exploring Corporate Strategy: Texts and Cases* (1993) by permission of Prentice Hall)

- identifying the options
- evaluating those options
- selecting an option

Generation of strategic options involves identifying as many as possible of the potential courses of action. To find all is not likely to be possible but a very real danger is that only the obvious ones are spotted. Evaluation of strategic options is performed within the framework created by the strategic analysis. The alternatives listed as strategic options must be tested for suitability (strategic fit), feasibility and acceptability. These three form the evaluation criteria. Selection of strategy may result in a single strategy or a strategy set that will be the target for the strategic implementation element of the process, remembering that innovation is not made up of *obvious* choices but of the off-beat alternatives. The culture and power structure of the organisation will have a significant impact upon this selection process. Many of the tools discussed here are those introduced in the first part of this chapter but now they focus upon providing methods for formulating, evaluating and selecting options to deal with the issues identified during the strategic analysis.

## 2.3.1 ◆ Strategy formulation

This element of the strategic choice process aims to generate an adequate flow of strategic options for subsequent evaluation. There are a number of ways of perceiving this process, Johnson and Scholes (1993) suggest identifying the 'what basis/which direction/how' options illustrated in Figure 2.24.

### What basis? – alternate competitive strategies

One of the best known answers to the question of what competitive strategy to adopt is Porter's seminal classification of the three possible ways for an organisation to outperform its competitive rivals (based upon the five competitive forces acting upon an organisation). Porter presented the choice as being between three (he later expanded this to four) generic business strategies. Porter developed these

| What basis? | Which direction? | How? |
| --- | --- | --- |
| Generic strategies | Alternate directions | Alternate methods |
| Low cost | Do nothing | Internal development |
| Differentiation | Withdrawal | External development (acquisition) |
| Focus/niche | Consolidation | Joint development |
| | Market penetration | |
| | Market development | |
| | Diversification<br> – related<br> – unrelated | |

Fig 2.24 ◆ Strategic option formulation

as a picture of the possible ways to respond to the situation modelled by its industry attractiveness as captured by his five forces model discussed in Section 2.2. This concept is extended in Wiseman's strategic thrusts covered later in this chapter. At the level of a single coherent business (what that actually is will depend upon the structure of the organisation) an organisation can define the way it will compete and within what style of market.

The generic strategies are illustrated in Figure 2.25. Two paths, Product Differentiation and Overall Cost Leadership, pertain to the entire market. Both of these two strategies 'fish in the entire pond'. The third strategy, Focus/Niche, concerns itself with a distinct market segment; this strategy Porter later subdivided into Cost Focus/Niche and Differentiation Focus/Niche to give the four generic strategies mentioned above. However quite what is the entire market is increasingly blurred. Is it on a regional; national; continental; or global basis? Is it by product or product type? These are unanswerable questions and the fact that they are unanswerable is given as one significant criticism of this notion of generic strategy. In fact perhaps the useful issue is one of, does the organisation have any *sense* of niche, what does the organisation itself define as the whole industry?

The notion of generic strategies is pragmatically useful as a device to force explicit consideration of the *way* of competing by showing the alternatives as by lowest cost (giving strength from margin and ability to sustain price competition) or by most differentiation (giving strength from strong loyalties) and *where* competing, showing the alternatives as everywhere or in a segment. Beyond that the complexity of reality tends to limit the usefulness of this model and there will be

| | Uniqueness perceived by customer | Low cost position | |
|---|---|---|---|
| **Industry wide** | *Product differentiation*<br><br>By following this strategy the organisation hopes to win customers by offering 'better' products or services than its competitors. The organisation adopting this strategy must focus upon building unique products and services and publishing their existence. | *Overall cost leadership*<br><br>By following this strategy the organisation seeks to win customers upon the basis of cost, for a given level of quality and service. The organisation must focus on 'good' cost control, seeking cost reductions wherever possible. This cost leadership can be achieved throughout the value chain, from low unit cost raw materials to low unit cost distribution process. | **Strategic target** |
| **Segment only** | *Focus/niche*<br><br>By following this strategy the organisation is targeting particular parts of the market, such as certain customer groups or regional areas. This basis for competition is selective but, within the niche market, competition is either on a low cost or a differentiation basis. | | |

**Fig 2.25 ◆ Porter's generic business strategies**
(adapted with the permission of The Free Press, a division of Simon & Schuster from *Competitive Advantage: Creating and Sustaining Superior Performance* by Michael E. Porter. Copyright © 1985 by Michael E. Porter)

many instances where effective management would be to create some mixture of these and indeed Porter acknowledged this possibility.

## Which direction? – alternate directions

There are a number of strategic directions that an organisation can pusue. Possible development strategies are modelled in Figure 2.26 in which seven alternatives are suggested based upon the extent to which new markets and/or new product are sought, see Ansoff (1968). The seventh alternative, that of diversification, splits down into two option sub-types since the chosen diversification may be into related or unrelated business areas.

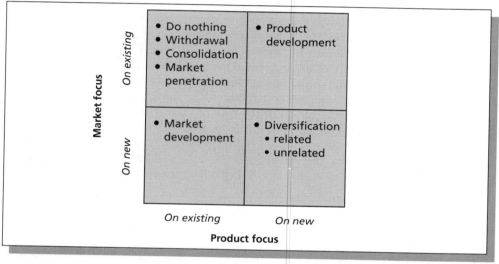

Fig 2.26 ◆ Alternative strategic directions

These strategic options are summarised in Figure 2.27.

- *Do nothing.* This is a strategy that implies the continuation of existing direction. Whilst as a long-term approach it is unlikely to be beneficial, as a short-term response to a static or highly uncertain environment it may be appropriate. The organisation carries on as before and since it 'goes with the flow' some growth may occur if the current market grows. The resource levels remain constant.

- *Withdrawal.* This strategy has the organisation removing itself from the industry because of an irreversible decline in demand, an over-extended position, adverse competitive pressures and environmental changes or opportunity costs that indicate that other business activities offer a more appropriate strategic direction. This is a strategy of asset realisation and resource deployment.

- *Consolidation.* This is when an industry dominant organisation aims for stability in order to accumulate cash reserves for some future activities. This then is done by cutting costs and/or increasing prices; the aim is to obtain a better margin. Consolidation is strictly speaking the strategy followed to maintain the existing market share; a similar strategy, when the intention is to obtain a reduction in the scale of operations, is usually called retrenchment.

| | Internal | Acquisition | Joint |
|---|---|---|---|
| Do nothing | – | – | – |
| Withdraw | Liquidate | Complete sell-out<br>Partial divestment<br>Management buyout | Licensing<br>Sub-contracting |
| Consolidation | Grow with market<br>Increase:<br>• quality<br>• productivity<br>• marketing<br>Capacity reduction/<br>rationing | Buy and shut down | Technology transfer<br>Sub-contracting |
| Market penetration | Increase:<br>• quality<br>• productivity<br>• marketing | Buy market share<br>Industry rationalisation | Collaboration |
| Product development | R&D<br>Modifications<br>Extensions | Buy-in products | Licensing<br>Franchising<br>Consortia<br>Lease facilities |
| Market development | Extend sales area<br>Export<br>New segments<br>New uses | Buy competitors | New agents<br>Licensing<br>Consortia |
| Backward integration<br>Horizontal integration<br>Forward integration<br>Unrelated diversification | Switch focus<br>New units<br>Create subsidiaries | Minority holdings<br>Buy subsidiaries | Technology sharing<br>Exclusive arrangement<br>Tied arrangement<br>Franchising<br>Consortia |

**Fig 2.27 ◆ Summary of strategic options**
(after Johnson and Scholes)

- *Market penetration.* By following this strategy the organisation seeks growth within the same market and using the same products. Growth is achieved either by the market itself growing or by grabbing the market share of others. This is the most conservative of growth strategies since it builds upon the strengths of the organisation and requires no substantial R&D effort. This strategy will meet with fierce opposition if the market is static or declining but may be relatively easy during the growth phase.
- *Product development.* A strategy that keeps the organisation operating within its current markets but competing on the basis of new products. Thus growth is obtained if these new products are successful. This is a relatively low-risk strategy and one that works well when product life cycles are short and products are the natural spin-off from the R&D process.

- *Market development*. By following this strategy the organisation takes its current product range into new markets. It is a relatively high-risk strategy given the state of ignorance of this new market. When growth is sought and existing markets have little scope this direction is taken into new geographical areas, new market segments or into new market uses. It is least risky when the organisation's main competence is product rather than market related.

- *Diversification*. This then is a strategy that takes the organisation away from both the existing markets and the existing products. This is the highest-risk strategy because of unfamiliarity but related diversification remains broadly within the same industry, either backward into the supply chain, forward into the distribution chain or horizontally into complementary activities, and so lowers the risk. Unrelated diversification is a strategy popular with holding company conglomerates.

### How? – alternate methods

It should be possible to implement such growth strategies by means of internal, organic development of growth over time, though this is slow; by external development via mergers and acquisitions which, whilst expensive, is fast in gaining access to markets; or it can be through joint ventures. The trade-offs between cost/risk/speed shape the choice between these alternatives.

### Other approaches to generating strategic options

There are a number of alternate approaches to perceiving the strategic options of the organisation. These include:

**(a)** Focusing upon the broad strategy alternatives of:

- Growth
- Stability
- Retrenchment

These broad strategies primarily relate to the existing products/existing markets segment of the growth vector matrix since in the three other segments growth is always the broad strategy. The *growth* strategies are therefore product development, diversification, market development or market penetration whilst the *stability* strategies are do nothing (also known as holding) and consolidation (or harvesting). The *retrenchment* strategy can, in turn, be considered in three sub-divisions:

- *Liquidation*: where the organisation 'calls in' its resources from that market or product in order to move them into somewhere else when a market has declined.

- *Divestment*: where the organisation 'sells off' a division because it perceives threats in the environment such that the division can no longer be effective or it feels the nature of the division no longer 'fits' the group. This strategy is often associated with returning to the 'core business' by shedding peripheral activities. (Note: this is *not* necessarily the same as core competencies, *see* section 2.2.)

- *Turnaround*: This strategy is needed to recover from *forced* liquidation of the business – bankruptcy. This must be the most complex strategy to pursue since turning a non-profitable concern into a profitable one will frequently be beyond the management skills of the organisation – or it would not be in this position! This may be a strategy resulting from new management/owning groups.

**(b)** Strategic *thrusts*

Rackoff *et al.* (1985) have expanded upon Porter's work on competitive strategies and offer a more comprehensive model of industry competition. This fuller model provides a framework for strategic opportunities. They suggest that strategic thrusts are the major moves, or actions, that an organisation takes and these can be offensive or defensive in nature. The strategic thrusts model suggests that all possible activities can be summed up as:

- *Differentiation*: to get an advantage by distinguishing products and services from competitors' or by reducing the differentiation advantage of rivals.
- *Cost*: to get an advantage by reducing own, suppliers' or customers' costs or by raising the costs of rivals.
- *Innovation*: to get an advantage by introducing a product or process change that fundamentally changes the industry's method of business.
- *Growth*: to get an advantage by volume or geographic expansion, backward or forward integration, product line or entry diversification.
- *Alliance*: to get an advantage by forging marketing agreements, forming joint ventures or making acquisitions related to the other four thrusts.

These strategies can be applied to three possible target categories:

- *Supplier targets*: those providing the organisation with materials, capital, labour, services, etc.
- *Customer targets*: those requiring the organisation's products or services; either for their own use or for subsequent re-sale.
- *Competitor targets*: those selling, or potentially selling, products seen by customers to be the same as, or tolerable substitutes for, those produced by the organisation.

This model is represented on a grid, known as a generator of strategic options and, illustrated in Figure 2.28, that permits the analysis of the three strategic targets of the organisation's industry and makes the manager aware of the main actions the organisation can take in the quest for competitive gain.

This option grid can be 'filled in' by asking a number of questions, these include:

- What is our strategic target?
  Suppliers  Customers  Competitors
- What strategic thrust can be used against the target?
  Differentiation  Cost  Innovation  Growth  Alliance
- What strategic mode can be used?
  Offensive  Defensive
- What direction of thrust can be used?
  Usage  Provision

IS can support or shape the organisation's competitive strategy by supporting or shaping the competitive thrusts.

| Strategic thrust | Strategic target | | |
|---|---|---|---|
| | Supplier | Customer | Competitor |
| Differentiation | | | |
| Low cost | | | |
| Innovation | | | |
| Growth | | | |
| Alliance | | | |

**Fig 2.28 ◆ Strategic option generator**

## 2.3.2 ◆ Strategy evaluation and selection

Once the strategic options open to the organisation have been generated there must exist a framework within which they can be evaluated for suitability, feasibility and 'fit' to the organisation. The process for doing this may involve rational, analytical techniques or be a more subjective, implicit process. In either case, Figure 2.29 illustrates why the two elements of evaluation and selection are covered together since it is going through the evaluation process that leads to the selection as an outcome. This process refers back to use of many of the tools considered under the strategic analysis section. For example, using the MCC matrix of Section 2.2.3 contributes towards evaluating an option as well as acting to model the organisation's capabilities. In general the criteria against which possibilities are evaluated are:

- Does the option take advantage of a strength the organisation possesses?
- Correspondingly, does the option avoid depending upon a weakness that the organisation suffers?
- Does this option offer the organisation the chance to gain a competitive advantage?
- Is this option consistent with other strategies selected?
- Does this option address a mission-related opportunity presented by the evolving market?
- Is this option's level of risk acceptable?
- Is this option consistent with policy guidelines?

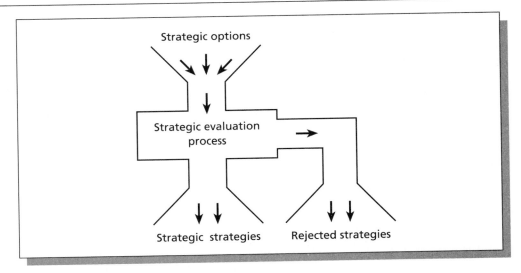

**Fig 2.29 ◆ Strategic evaluation process**

The evaluation process seeks to judge the appropriateness of the options as a screening mechanism to ensure that only those options that have a strategic fit with the organisation's environment, culture, and capabilities are considered further for testing of feasibility and desirability. An understanding of the organisation's environment, culture and capabilities was discussed in Section 2.2 purely as a strategic analysis activity. However, the results of that analysis build the understanding needed here to judge feasibility and desirability. This is presented here in the text as a linear and conscious sequence, in many instances the whole process of analysis/choice is either unconscious or simultaneous. We still do things in the light of our preferences and therefore understanding of these preferences is useful. Since more than one option will normally be being tested against each of these three, any risk analysis approach (for example criteria ranking as discussed at a much lower level of detail in Chapter 12, scenario analysis as discussed in Chapter 1, or decision tree techniques which lie outside the scope of this text) can be used to select the 'best' fit, the 'most' feasible or the 'most' desirable option. What is meant by these terms is discussed below. Some possibilities can almost immediately be excluded because they violate non-negotiable conditions, for instance through their cost implications or from cultural objections.

### Strategic fit – appropriateness

The strategic fit is the degree to which the options being reviewed fit the situation identified during the strategic analysis. A 'good' fit is logical, *maximises* available strengths and opportunities and *minimises* weaknesses and threats. In other words, it suits the nature of the organisation including its behavioural nature. Because this assessing of appropriateness relates to the situation considered during the strategic analysis process the tools that could help here are those that helped then:

- SWOT analysis
- Product portfolio analysis

- Life cycle analysis
- Cultural web analysis.

All these approaches allow the options to be *matched* against the organisation's *relative* competitive position. The approaches differ in the critical variables they use but in each case the present position is used to guide selections for the future. Once only 'suitable' options are being considered they can go forward for feasibility and desirability testing.

### Strategic feasibility

This is the assessment of the extent to which the option will work in practice. This feasibility can be judged in terms of both the returns that can be anticipated and the demands it will make. These may use detailed financial feasibility measures of predicted profitability and/or detailed cost-benefit appraisals both of which are outside the scope of this book though the concept of the economic feasibility of strategy is considered in IS specific terms in Chapter 7. Qualitative judgements of the implementation demands (discussed in Section 2.4) are also useful.

### Strategic desirability

This desirability is the extent to which the option is *acceptable* to the stakeholders of the organisation. A number of issues are associated with the strategic desirability of options. An option's desirability will depend upon the goals and objectives of the organisation and hence the way to measure the degree of the desirability must also vary. The option may be assessed in terms of:

- Profitability
- Risk profile
- Social cost/benefit appraisal
- Shareholder expectations.

All other things being equal, the higher the expected profitability the higher the strategic option will 'score'. Other aspects of desirability relate to those issues uncovered as part of the strategic analysis.

Any organisation will need to think in terms of the risk inherent in any potential strategy. The selection of a strategy will require a trade-off to be made that balances risks with returns. One very simple approach to judging this is to ask two basic questions:

- What is the pay-off of the proposed strategy, quantitatively, qualitatively or via a reasonably realistic estimate of the benefit return?
- How far off are the goal posts in terms of the current capabilities, the business or technical difficulties to be overcome or the organisational barriers?

These key variables can be modelled on a two by two matrix shown in Figure 2.30.

The early success initiatives are needed to build confidence and provide returns to finance the *glittering prizes* that are of significant competitive value but more organisationally draining. To balance the strain *sweetmeats* are needed to reap the limited but easily achieved rewards, whereas the *backburners* are to be postponed

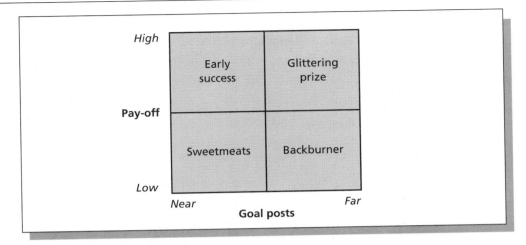

**Fig 2.30 ◆ Risks and returns portfolio matrix**

until either the difficulty factor reduces or the pay-off factor increases. At which time, of course, the option would become a sweetmeat or a glittering prize, so backburner options are never selected.

This, in many ways, models what should be common-sense prioritising but it is often helpful to be reminded of the common sense in the strategic arena! Obviously high return for little effort (or distance to go in this analogy) should be sought more vigorously than the long haul for not much reward. Nicholls (1995) discusses more fully the risks to be managed in decisions close to or far away from, not the current position as such, but the aims and capabilities of the organisation. The MCC matrix takes these three holistically: feasibility through direct relationship to core competencies as a measure of feasibility, appropriateness and desirability indirectly through relationship to the mission and vision which captures what is appropriate and desirable for the organisation to do (core competencies are one indirect measure of what the firm can do).

## 2.4 ◆ STRATEGIC IMPLEMENTATION

The final aspect of Johnson and Scholes' model of strategic management is strategic implementation. Techniques that support the formal aspects of this are considered under categories taken from that model, introduced in Figure 1.1 and repeated in Figure 2.31. This section will therefore look at aspects of resource planning, organisation structure and people and systems. Implementation of a chosen strategy is by making any necessary adaptations to structure, the systems and people of the organisation and managing the required acquisition and deployment of resources. Of course, the notion of implementation as *distinct* belongs to one view of strategic management. Others would have implementation and formulation as inextricable (*see* Chapter 1 for a discussion on various planning process views). However this view gives a convenient structural device recognising that the linear presentation of ideas may mask that they inter-relate and need to be integrated (perhaps incrementally).

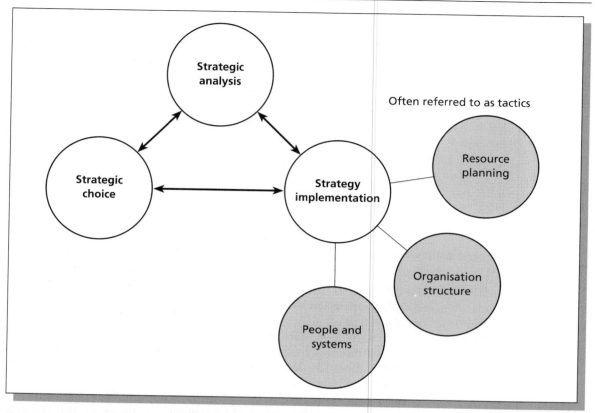

**Fig 2.31 ◆ Three elements of strategy implementation**
(adapted from Johnson and Scholes, *Exploring Corporate Strategy: Texts and Cases* (1993) by permission of Prentice Hall)

Feurer, Chaharbaghi and Distel (1995) pick up the argument for the simultaneous (and continuous) nature of strategy formulation/implementation relationship as the grounding for arguing that, if this is so, the strategy as a consistent pattern of resource decisions needs to belong to everyone. This link puts strategy implementation (and of course formulation) squarely related to the issues of the learning organisation discussed in Chapter 8 through the 'planning is learning' notion. When an organisation implements a trial decision it learns about the feasibility, appropriateness and desirability of that decision, and not as a separate issue as implied by many of the techniques discussed in Section 2.3.

When the process of strategic management has identified possible alternatives and weighed (in some way) those alternatives then the final stage is to implement the resultant choice. This element of the strategic management process aims to turn the selected strategy into action. Successful strategic implementation is just as critical to organisational success as strategic choice, and just as difficult. Such strategic implementation requires that the organisation deal with the:

- Resources required
- Organisational structure changes required
- Systems and work force necessities

Resource planning identifies the major tasks to be done and assesses how, and by whom, these tasks can be resourced. Organisation structure will commonly require amendment as part of the process of strategic implementation, and the organisation must judge how best to organise the business in order to carry through the strategy. The systems and work force must be geared up appropriately. The business procedures and information systems may need adjusting and the skill mix may also require tweaking.

## 2.4.1 ◆ Resource planning

The relationship between strategy and resources appears here as if the formulation of strategy comes before its implementation *through* resource planning. In fact, resource capabilities are, of course, a fundamental issue in strategy formulation (though one meaning of strategy is a consistent pattern of resource allocation) and may involve a change in the allocation of human and material resources. This needs to be planned at corporate and business unit level. Typically, the larger the organisation the more levels there will be (*see* the discussion of the system of strategies in Chapter 4). The corporate allocation of resources should reflect the business strategy being followed, as indicated in Figure 2.32. Functional level resource allocation normally takes place through budgeting techniques and project planning and control mechanisms. The nature of the resource allocation process will be shaped by two key variables:

- *The degree of change*. The extent of the change in resource demands is a key variable, since in unstable, fast-changing times more judgement processes are required than under more static conditions when incremental changes can be made based on historically determined formulae.
- *The extent of central direction*. This is also a key variable since the central authority may expect to adjudicate on claims or it may leave units in an autonomous position and the resource allocation process would clearly differ.

| | | **Degree of change** | |
|---|---|---|---|
| | | *Low* | *High* |
| **Extent of central direction** | *High* | 'Formula' | Imposed priorities |
| | *Medium* | Constrained bargaining | Constrained bidding |
| | *Low* | Free bargaining | Open competition |

**Fig 2.32 ◆ Corporate level resource allocation process**
(after Johnson and Scholes)

The work of Feurer and Chaharbaghi (1995) challenges the idea of central direction and the degree of change as being independent variables since they point out that for many (perhaps most) organisations the degree of change is inevitably high and they argue that *therefore* the extent of central direction should be kept relatively low and should focus upon determining boundaries and visions (the whats) rather than making strategic choices as such (the hows).

## 2.4.2 ◆ Strategy and structure

The structure of an organisation is the way it is arranged (in both the formal and the informal sense), who holds what authority and responsibility and what communication links there are. The organisational structure may be defined on the organisation chart, but it is likely that the chart captures only one facet of the structure – *the formal structure*. Understanding the culture of the organisation builds some insight into its informal structure. Mintzberg (1983) suggests that there are six basic elements to any organisation (strategic apex, middle line, operating core, support staff, technostructure and ideology) but they can be combined in an almost infinite number of ways! The size of each element and its relationship to all other elements defines the type of structure that the organisation has. These can be classified as:

- *Entrepreneurial/simple structures*. These occur where the activities are totally centralised around the owner manager. There is no division of responsibility and so this is only suitable for small organisations in their formative stages.

- *Functional structures*. Structures of this type are grouped around the primary tasks of the business, such as marketing, production, and accounts, etc. This structure is appropriate for medium-sized organisations or those that have a relatively static environment.

- *Divisional structures*. These type of structures emerge as the organisation grows or becomes more diversified. These divisions are 'chunks' of the organisation that are responsible for a coherent market or product area. These divisions are frequently called strategic business units (SBU) since they are decentralised profit centres which may have functional structures of their own. This is an appropriate structure for organisations that have grown through acquisitions or where natural divisional splits exist. This is a very common structure for dynamic environments.

- *Federal, or holding, structures*. These structures pertain where a set of virtually autonomous operating companies has a headquarters that serves as an investment company. They are suitable for conglomerates with diverse interests or where individual businesses are frequently bought or sold.

- *Matrix structures*. These combine features to give a two-dimensional chain of command. This is an appropriate structure for groups of businesses in diverse areas who nevertheless have significant inter-relationships.

The model in Figure 2.33 illustrates how the stage of maturity of an organisation may determine the problems facing that organisation and hence the parameters surrounding the structure choice. The table in Figure 2.34 illustrates how a *strategy* can avoid the meaningless debate of centralised versus decentralised structures since the *successful* implementation of a strategy requires the integration offered by centralisation and the differentiation offered by decentralisation. Hence the selected structure must allow strategy integration at the centre and strategy differ-

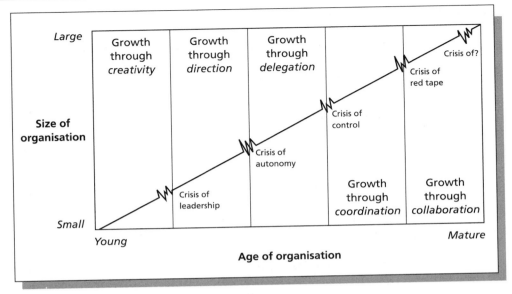

**Fig 2.33 ◆ Greiner's model of organisational growth**
(adapted and reprinted by permission of *Harvard Business Review*. An exhibit from Evolution and Revolution as Organisations Grow by Larry E.Greiner, Jul-Aug 1972. Copyright © 1972 by the President and Fellows of Harvard College, all rights reserved)

entiation at the periphery. Where there is a strong focus upon understanding the organisation's core competencies then structural decisions will be made in the light of how the structure will support those as well as the general issue of how structures add *value*.

This also shows that there is *not* a one-way relationship between strategy and structure, rather there is a two-way inter-relationship:

STRATEGY  STRUCTURE

Amburgey and Dacin (1994) explore this inter-relationship to show that the ways in which structure influences strategy are rather different (basically in terms of importance and speed of effect) to the ways in which strategy influences structure.

| Centralisation | Decentralisation |
|---|---|
| Operating efficiency | Functional |
| Competitive efficiency | Divisional |
| Innovative emphasis | Project matrix |
| Strategic consistency | Corporate matrix |
| Strategic success | Multi-structural |

**Fig 2.34 ◆ Centralisation *v* decentralisation**

## 2.4.3 ◆ Strategy and people and systems

Strategy is visible as a consistent pattern of resource decisions; that pattern happens through *people* operating within activity systems making resource decisions. In order to deal successfully with the people and systems aspects of any strategic implementation it is necessary to achieve a cultural change for the organisational acceptance of the 'new' information, control, regulatory, and political systems. Control and feedback systems allow the organisation to detect that the strategy is succeeding or failing and to take corrective actions in order to implement that strategy more successfully, or to modify the strategy itself. These control systems are often quantitative in nature but, in general, need to provide:

- Effective monitoring of performance
- Devolution of responsibilities to the appropriate level of the organisation
- Agreed performance metrics
- Highlights of both successful and unsuccessful outcomes.

Regulatory systems are those that assist in bringing about strategic change since they promote changes in individuals' behaviour. Whilst behaviour modifying systems are often associated with ethical concerns, they encompass issues of:

- The incentive and reward system of:

  Monetary rewards, such as bonuses
  Non-monetary rewards, such as status enhancements.
- Training schemes to ensure that the organisation is able to implement the chosen strategy

The management style determines how these regulatory systems can be put into effect, just as it determines many other aspects of strategic management. Management style can be classified as:

- Entrepreneurial      or      Conservative
- Autocratic      or      Democratic
- Mechanistic      or      Organic

The successful implementation of strategy is going to depend fundamentally upon the successful gaining of acceptance of the required behaviour changes. In other words the successful management of change. The commonest model of this process is the three stages of:

- Unfreeze      Create a climate ready for change
- Change
- Re-freeze      Institutionalise the new state

Change may be achieved *directly*, by altering the attitudes, beliefs and values of individuals, or *indirectly*, by changing the structure, goals or technology of the organisation. There are at least three different ways of making that three-stage process happen:

- Power – coercive change rewards or punishes different behaviours
- Rational – legal change appeals to logic and rules
- Normative – re-educative change which alters values and norms.

In Section 2.2.2 various ways of interpreting the people and systems of the organisation were presented. It is worth noting that the relationship between people and systems and strategy differs between various models of management thought as such models hold different views of what an organisation is about. Guillén (1994) usefully classifies the characteristics of the three predominant schools of thought (scientific management, the human relations school and structural analysis) including by looking at their different approaches to people and systems. A sub-set of these features is given in Figure 2.35. One of Guillén's fundamental points is that an appreciation of the general and methodological features and the particular techniques associated with each paradigm remains extremely useful since he argues that contemporary views on management (such as the learning organisation notion discussed in Chapter 8) are *always* combinations, albeit eclectic ones, of features and techniques drawn from these three.

## 2.5 ◆ SUMMARY AND CONCLUSIONS

This chapter has presented a range of tools and techniques that have been developed to assist in the process of formulating strategy. Gupta and Govindarajan (1984) believe that 'strategy plays a role in mediating an organisation's interaction with its environment'. The definition of strategy used throughout this text would believe that strategy is the organisation's interaction with its environment. Either way, the models discussed in this chapter have all been developed to help improve that interaction.

The chapter adopted as an ordering device the three element headings of strategic analysis, strategic choice, and strategic implementation. It must be stressed that this was a structuring device and the fact that the models are described in this linear fashion should not be interpreted as indicating that any process of application would be linear. Of course, an organisation's understanding of its situation is shaped by who it is (the organisational culture, the capabilities, etc) and who it is shapes how it decides to accept or alter its situation. This may be viewed as a rational logical process of creating the future but it is also a cultural, filtered cognitive approach to reacting to 'self-evident' situations. Even within the logical process view complex inter-relationships of who we are shapes what we think strategic management is, what we treat strategic management as shapes what we become. For instance, the assumption that it is valid to perform a cultural web analysis is linked to particular cultures; capabilities are put in place based upon assumptions made about what is needed to implement the chosen strategy; strategy is formulated (incrementally or as a long-term planned blueprint) based upon assumptions of capabilities; all assumptions result from the cultural web; and so on in an ever tangled scheme.

| | Scientific management | Human relations | Structural analysis |
|---|---|---|---|
| Predominant social relationships | Authority (formal) | Leadership and participation (informal) | Both formal and informal |
| Rationality assumptions | All actors can behave rationally | All actors are emotionally dependent but managers have superior skills | All actors are rationally bounded |
| View of workers | Blindly driven by self-interest | Driven by psychosocial norms, needs, emotions | Adaptable, behave according to their structural situation |
| Social and intellectual agenda | Modernism, human mastering of nature | Nostalgia, romanticism, social harmony | Disciplinary, defence of the free enterprise system |
| Distribution of tasks | Task conception and execution separatred, division of labour among individual workers, specialisation | Job enlargement, enrichment, rotation | Differentiation and integration of functions |
| Authority structures | Simple managerial hierarchy | Downplays hierarchy, emphasis leadership and communication | Complex hierarchy, line-and-staff structures, ambiguity of hierarchy |
| Organisation of the work process | Work simplification, mechanisation, assembly-line work | Small-group activities, teamwork | Departmentalisation, divisionalisation, matrix structures, profit centres |
| Preferred rewards | Wages, bonuses | Stability, security, work satisfaction, recognition | Prestige, status, power, promotion, salary |
| Preferred economic incentives | Piecework wages | Group wage incentives | Seniority-based salaries |

**Fig 2.35 ◆ Features and techniques of the three organisational paradigms**
(adapted from The Age of Eclecticism by Guillén, *Sloan Management Review* Vol 36, No 1, 1994, pp. 78–9, by permission of publisher. Copyright 1994 by Sloan Management Review Association. All rights reserved)

Some of the models discussed focus upon one aspect of the strategy situation and consider it in some depth, for instance the product portfolio analysis tools, whilst others consider the integration of broader issues, for instance the MCC matrix. Given the differences in focus and the inevitable overlapping nature of these models the chosen headings are one interpretation only; after all describing the logic of strategic planning as involving these three elements will not constrain the operationalising of that logic into tools.

It is interesting to note that Section 2.2, which discusses those tools most directly related to strategic analysis, forms nearly half of this chapter whilst Section 2.4 which discusses strategic implementation models is the slimmest. This volume difference primarily represents a history of concentration upon analysis and hence the development of a large number of models under the analysis heading. To some extent it also represents an arbitrary placing of those models that straddle the headings (as discussed above) but it does not represent any statement of relative importance, difficulty or preference.

This structural device does, of course, follow a particular perception of the strategy formulation process in which it is valid to adopt these headings. A more interpretist approach, for example, as given in Mintzberg and McHugh (1985) could see many different models of how strategy happens that would run contrary to the analyse/choose/implement model of planning. Mintzberg and McHugh name three alternative views, where strategy happens as a result of:

- Precedent set by one individual
- Thin stream of activity eventually pervading an organisation
- Spontaneous convergence in behaviour of various actors

In other instances strategy (the pattern of resource allocations) could be forced by legislative or political change. The point is that from this perspective strategy can 'form without being formulated', there may be an absence of intention, but if fortune favours the prepared mind whether the tools are to help *think* strategically or intentionally *create* strategic plans they still are useful. What could differ would be the headings selected under which to group the discussions.

**References and further reading**

Amburgey, T.L. and Dacin, T. (1994) As the Left Foot Follows the Right? The Dynamics of Strategic and Structural Change, *Academy of Management Journal*, Vol 37 No 6 Dec pp. 1427–52.

Ansoff, H.I. (1968) *Corporate Strategy*, Penguin.

Anthony, R.N. (1965) *Planning and Control Systems: A Framework for Analysis*, Harvard Graduate School of Business.

Bazzell, R.D. and Gale, B.T. (1987) *The PIMS Principles: Linking Strategy to Performance*, Macmillan.

Brannan, T. (1992) Listen to the Future, *Marketing Business*, Oct.

Chalak, T. (1993) *The Art of Business*, Pelanduk Publications.

Collis, D.J. and Montgomery, C.A. (1995) Competing on Resources: Strategy in the 1990s, *Harvard Business Review*, July-Aug pp. 118–128.

Cyert, R.M. and March, J.G. (1992) *Behavioural Theory of the Firm*, Blackwell.

David, F.R. (1989) How Companies Define Their Mission, *Long Range Planning*, Vol 22 No 1 pp. 90–7.

Deal and Kennedy (1982) *Corporate Cultures: The Rites and Rituals of Corporate Life*, Addison-Wesley.

Dess, G.G. and Miller, A. (1993) *Strategic Management*, McGraw-Hill.

Drucker, P.F. (1995) The Information Executives Truly Need, *Harvard Business Review*, Jan-Feb pp. 54–62.

Drury, C. (1988) *Management and Cost Accounting* (2nd edn), VNR International.

Dyson, R.G. (1990) *Strategic Planning: Models and Analytical Techniques*, Wiley.

Eden, C. (1992) Strategy Development as a Social Process, *Journal of Management Studies*, Vol 29 No 6 pp. 799–811.

Eden, C. and Ackermann, F. (1992) Strategy Development and Implementation – The Role of a Group Decision Support System, in Bostrom, R.T. and Kinney, R.T. *Computer Augmented Teamwork: A Guided Tour*, Van Nostrand Reinhold.

Fahey, L. and Narayanan, V.K. (1986) *Macroenviromental Analyses for Strategic Management*, West Publishing.

Fredericks, P. and Ventkatraman, N. (1988) The Rise of Strategy Support Systems, *Sloan Management Review* Vol 29 No 3 pp. 47–54.

Feurer, F., Chaharbaghi, K. and Distel, M. (1995) Dynamic Strategy Ownership, *Management Decision*, Vol 33 No 4 pp. 12–21.

Gaister, K. and Thwaites, D. (1993) Managerial Perception and Organisational Strategy, *Journal of General Management*, Vol 18 No 4 pp. 15–33.

Galbraith, J.R. and Kazanzian, R.K. (1986) *Strategy Implementation: Structure, Systems and Process*, West Publishing.

Gitman, L.J. (1976) *Principles of Managerial Finance*, Harper and Row.

Goold, M. and Campbell, A. (1987) Many Best Ways to Make Strategy, *Harvard Business Review*, Nov-Dec pp. 70–6.

Gordon, J.A. (1983) *A Diagnostic Approach to Organisational Behaviour* (2nd edn), Allyn and Bacon.

Grant, R.M. (1991) Porter's Competitive Advantage of Nations: An Assessment, *Strategic Management Journal*, Vol 12 pp. 535–48.

Greiner, L. (1972) Evolution and Revolution as Organisations Grow, *Harvard Business Review*, July-Aug.

Guillén, M.F. (1994) The Age of Eclecticism: Current Organisational Trends and the Evolution of Managerial Models, *Sloan Management Review*, Vol 36 No 1 pp. 75–86.

Gupta, A.K. and Govindarajan, V. (1984) Business Unit Strategy, Managerial Characteristics and Business Unit Effectiveness at Strategy Implementation, *Academy of Management Journal*, Vol 27 No 1 pp. 25–41.

Handy, C. (1991) *The Age of Unreason*, Century Business.

Hendry, J. (1990) The Problem with Porter's Generic Strategies, *European Management Journal*, Vol 8 No 4 Dec pp. 443–50.

Hibberty, E. (1992) The Growth of International Coalitions in Global Product and Market Strategy, *Journal of European Business Education*, Vol 1 No 2 pp. 63–95.

Hickson, D.J., Hinings, C.R., Pennings, J.M. and Schenk, R.E. (1974) Structural Conditions of IntraOrganisational Power, *Administrative Science Quarterly*, Vol 19 No 1 Mar pp. 22–4.

Hofer, C.W. and Schendel, D. (1978) *Strategy Formulation: Analytical Concepts*, West Publishing.

Hussey, D. (1978) Portfolio Analysis: Practical Experience with the DPM, *Long Range Planning*, Vol 11 No 4.

Johnson, G. and Scholes, K. (1993) *Exploring Corporate Strategy* (3rd edn), Prentice-Hall.

Kanter, M. (1985) *The Change Masters*, Unwin.

King, W.R. and Cleland, D.I. (1986) *Strategic Planning and Management Handbook*, Van Nostrand Reinhold.

McGregor, D. (1960) *The Human Side of Enterprise*, McGraw-Hill.

Mercer, D. (1995) Simpler Scenarios, *Management Decision*, Vol 33 No 4 pp. 32–40.

Miles, R. and Snow, C. (1978) *Organisational Strategy, Structure and Process*, McGraw-Hill.

Mintzberg, H. (1983) *Structure in Fives: Designing Effective Organisations*, Prentice-Hall.

Mintzberg, H. and McHugh, A. (1985) Strategy Formulation in an Adhocracy, *Administrative Science Quarterly*, Vol 30 June pp. 160–97.

Molloy, S. and Schwenk, C.R. (1995) The Effects of Information Technology on Strategic Decision Making, *Journal of Management Studies*, Vol 32 No 3 pp. 283–311.

Nicholls, J. (1995) The MCC Decision Matrix: A Tool for Applying Strategic Logic to Everyday Activities, *Management Decision*, Vol 33 No 6 pp. 4–10.

Peters, T. and Austin, N. (1984) *A Passion for Excellence*, Collins.

Porter, M.E. (1979) How Competitive Forces Shape Strategy, *Harvard Business Review*, March-Apr pp. 137–45.

Porter, M.E. (1980) *Competitive Strategy: Techniques for Analysing Industries and Competitors*, Free Press.

Porter, M.E. (1985) *Competitive Advantage: Creating and Sustaining Superior Performance*, Free Press.

Prahalad, C.K. and Hamel, G. (1990) The core competence of the corporation, *Harvard Business Review*, May-June.

Rackoff, N., Wiseman, C. and Ulrich, W.A. (1985) Information Systems for Competitive Advantage: Implementations of a Planning Process, MIS Quarterly, Dec pp. 285–95.

Rowe, A.J., Mason, R.O., Dickel, K.E., Mann, R.B. and Mockler, R.J. (1994) *Strategic Management: A Methodological Approach*, Addison-Wesley.

Schoemaker, P. (1995) Scenario Planning: A Tool for Strategic Thinking, *Sloan Management Review*, Winter pp. 25–40.

Smith, N.I. (1994) *Down-to-Earth Strategic Planning*, Prentice-Hall.

Thompson, J.L. (1995) *Strategy in Action*, Chapman and Hall.

Weihrich, H. (1982) The TOWS Matrix: A Tool for Situational Analysis, *Long Range Planning*, Vol 15 No 2 pp. 54–66.

Wheelan, T.L. and Hunger, J.D. (1987) Using the Strategic Audit, *Advanced Management Journal*, Vol 52 No 1.

Wild, R. (1984) *Production and Operations Management* (3rd edn), Holt, Rineholt and Winston.

# PART 2

# Information systems strategy formulation

The process of formulating and implementing a business strategy is the fundamental foundation upon which rests all functional strategies, IS included. In this section some aspects of formulating an IS strategy that is consistent with the business strategy are discussed. The business strategy of section 1 defines the goals of the business, and IS strategies must of course be connected with those. As we shall see in this section they may relate to them by *aligning* with the goals of the business by translating them into IS goals, they may *impact* upon the business goals by competitively enhancing them, or they may *redesign* the business processes used to achieve these goals. There is, therefore, a close, sometimes one-way, sometimes circular relationship between IS goals and business. The business goals give the 'peg in the ground' for the process of formulating and implementing IS goals. The process by which the business goals were established in one sense is now irrelevant except that it will inevitably now affect, constrain or inform the process of establishing the IS goals. Because of the IS focus of this book the *implementation* of the IS goals is discussed in Part 3.

This section considers Strategic Management with Management Information Systems and explores the way in which Information Strategies and their formulation have evolved over time; how these strategies should be, but often are not, linked to the business strategies and the benefits available when they are. The chapters again follow a 'toolbox' approach, introducing important techniques associated with this area along with assessment of their suitability in application.

# CHAPTER 3

# What *are* management information systems?

This chapter does NOT intend to explore in detail the concepts and components of management information systems – there are many excellent books that address these topics and the varied methods for actually developing systems, see the further reading section at end of this chapter. However, since the available texts do not present consistent definitions even for the notion of 'MIS' many find it difficult to articulate what various terms represent just from literature surveys. Example definitions of MIS from literature include:

> *MIS is an integrated, computer based, user-machine system that provides information for supporting operations and decision making functions.*
>
> **Awad** (1988) *Management Information Systems: Concepts, Structures, & Applications.*

> *MIS is the development and use of effective information systems in organisations.*
>
> **Kroenke** (1989) *Management Information Systems.*

> *It is a system using formalised procedures to provide management at all levels in all functions with appropriate information, based on data from both internal and external sources, to enable them to make timely and effective decisions for planning, directing and controlling the activities for which they are responsible.*
>
> **Lucey** (1991) *Management Information Systems.*

> *MIS ... is now defined to include everything which deals with the computer-assisted flow and presentation of information ...*
>
> **Wolstenholme, Henderson** and **Gavine** (1993) *The Evaluation of Management Information Systems: A Dynamics and Holistic Approach.*

Because of that difficulty this chapter defines and distinguishes between IT, MIS, DSS, SMIS and the IS function. This book uses these definitions consistently throughout. Such distinctions are vital. Whilst not intending to enter the widespread debate about precise definitions, we need some clarification of implied meaning otherwise the resultant confusion means that concepts are difficult to express. This confusion makes it impossible to effectively grasp the differing concerns associated with the distinct, but overlapping, areas of technology, systems and their management.

The chapter continues with a very brief discussion of MIS topics, to serve as an introduction for Business Studies students or as a recap for Information Systems students. These topics are:

- The instrumentation view of MIS
- General model of the levels of MIS
- The nature of decision making
- The desired attributes of systems and information
- The strategy role of different categories of systems players

## 3.1 ◆ DEFINITIONS

### 3.1.1 ◆ Information technology (IT)

This phrase covers all the machinery and software that at one time was seen as belonging to individual technology disciplines. Where once computing (or Data Processing), communication technologies, office automation and production automation were disparate they now converge so that IT describes any 'kit' concerned with the capture, storage, transmittal or presentation of *information*.

This technology convergence has brought the separate disciplines into one management arena. This has paved the way for an integrated view that permits an organisational focus upon the purpose of the whole rather than upon the technical differences of the parts. The convergence demands coherent management responsibility for all aspects of information handling. Hence, whilst still requiring technical expertise that must be specific, the nature of IS management must change. Chapter 10 considers the nature of this change in some detail.

### 3.1.2 ◆ Management information systems (MIS)

As indicated before, there are many definitions of MIS. Some choose to emphasise the word management and hence make the distinction between management and transaction activities; others emphasise the word system and point to a wider framework beyond computer-based activities. I do not denigrate these varied views and in the appropriate texts with their differing perspectives these distinctions are important. In this book however, the term MIS will represent the entire portfolio of computer-based systems and their complementary manual procedures. Together these systems strengthen the operation of a business and include everything from routine DP, transaction processing activities, through to decision oriented support.

### 3.1.3 ◆ Decision support systems (DSS) and executive information systems (EIS)

This sub-set of MIS contains those systems designed and implemented specifically to address the need to provide automated support during the decision making process, including the problem awareness and definition stages.

Sometimes these systems need regarding as distinct from other examples of MIS, particularly to consider the organisational sensitivity of EIS and the notion of assessing intangible benefits so typically associated with these systems.

### 3.1.4 ◆ Strategic management information systems (SMIS)

This term again represents only a sub-set of the total MIS portfolio. In this instance it is the set that contains systems considered critical to the current or future business competitiveness, and hence survival, of a particular organisation. By definition therefore, this is a relative rather than an absolute term; one must assess the competitive circumstances of a given organisation before attaching the title 'SMIS' to a particular system.

Much of this section is going to be addressing how to:

- judge the degree of business importance of a system;
- appropriately plan for and manage these systems; and
- distinguish potential or actual IS capabilities from strategic applications

Whilst assessing the business importance of all systems is important, identifying the strategic MIS is vital to managing successfully *with* MIS and the effective management *of* information systems.

### 3.1.5 ◆ Information systems (IS)

In discussions of the management of systems we need a name to describe the organisational aspects or function that contains IT, MIS, DSS and SMIS. This does not automatically equate to the 'DP Department', 'Computer Section' or whatever a particular organisation names its main service providers since threaded throughout business functions are many managers who take responsibility for IT, MIS, DSS or SMIS.

IS is my chosen adjective for that part of the whole organisation and/or that part of an individual manager's activity related to IT, MIS, DSS, or SMIS. An alternative term that this text could have adopted would be Information Management, at least in the way that this phrase is used by both Strassman (1995) and O'Brien (1995). However, this is a much mis-used phrase and is frequently used to refer narrowly to specific elements of the data manipulation process, especially that of database administration rather than to the managerial and organisational concerns that the term Information Systems is here taken to represent.

## 3.2 ◆ MANAGEMENT INFORMATION SYSTEMS

### 3.2.1 ◆ The instrumentation view

Management Information Systems are the instrumentation of an organisation. Their interfaces to the human controllers of business serve as the 'dials and gauges' that allow these controllers to 'read off' the current state of their organisation. They may record and model all or part of the organisation's activities and provide indicators of any actual or predicted change in state. Of most value, they record or predict the rate, direction and timing of such changes.

When a business event occurs, whether it is the issuing of an invoice, the ticking over into a new financial quarter or staff attendance at a training course the event provides the raw material for the MIS. The event may be recorded, appropriately stored, transmitted, combined with other raw materials and ultimately presented in some appropriate way. The technologies and techniques for doing all this may be complex and naturally develop and change over time but the model in Figure 3.1 represents the elements of an MIS irrespective of any particular technologies.

Over time the physical MIS represented by this conceptual model has naturally altered in nature and focus. For example, looking at just the computer-based elements, the input part of the model once used punched cards or paper tape, moved though key-to-disk equipment and dumb terminals to computer sensed inputs and may now be a PC or any one of a host of 'human friendly' input devices gathering speech or visual signals. The output section may have moved from printed reports or turnaround documents to interactive soft copy graphics. Similarly, the data storage element once representing values inextricably linked to a specific application may be now an object oriented database containing multi-media objects distributed across a number of platforms. The process box may represent anything from simple data manipulation to sophisticated mathematical modelling.

Each box on this conceptual model (and the way of transmitting data from one to another) roughly represents one field of MIS endeavour, for example, Interface Design, Data Storage Analysis and Design, Data Communications, Simulation and Modelling, etc. Detailed consideration of these fields is outside the scope of the book. However, the end of this chapter suggests some further reading for anyone wanting to go further into MIS concepts, components or development.

The relative importance attached to parts of the whole has altered over time just as the physical implementation of the elements has changed. Early management information systems emphasised the data input module; currently the presentation of output seems of more significance. Additionally, the instrumentation has moved from being made up of independent, activity-specific units to an interdependent,

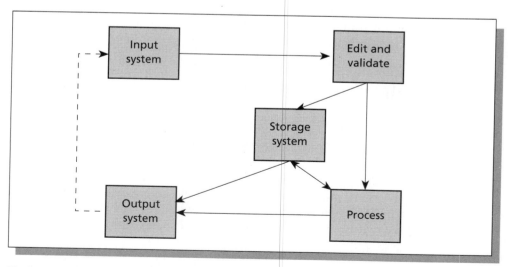

**Fig 3.1 ◆ General model of MIS**

integrated whole. However, we shall see that the most critical evolution has been from the majority effort concentrating upon the technical vehicle to focusing upon understanding the purpose and value of the resultant product and process.

The instrumentation view of MIS provides a simple and yet powerful perspective from which to approach management of, and with, these systems. Implied in this view is the need for human value judgements to support effective actions being taken; judgements are needed on:

- Which activities to record
- Which of the enterprise's variables require monitoring
- What extent to monitor them
- What format to have the dials and gauges display their message

Instrumentation must always exist for a *purpose*, and many current approaches to creating MIS concentrate on uncovering just what that purpose can be agreed to be. There are many different ways to approach the construction and installation of such instruments, with the advocates of each method often imbuing their own path with almost religious significance. However, lack of a clear sense of the instrumentation's purpose wastes expensively skilled effort. The efficiency, accuracy, and usability of the MIS depends upon the skill of those building each component of it. However, the effectiveness, and hence value, of the MIS depends upon the skill of those developing, communicating, or understanding its sense of purpose. This book's purpose is to support the development of this effectiveness skill and address a strongly identified skills gap (discussed in the preface to Part 3).

## 3.2.2 ◆ Levels of MIS

Conventionally, we view MIS as being constructed to serve various levels and aspects of management activities such that each level of the MIS has a different emphasis. The best known model of this is the one defined by R. N. Anthony in 1965, shown in Figure 3.2 relative to the planning horizon continuum.

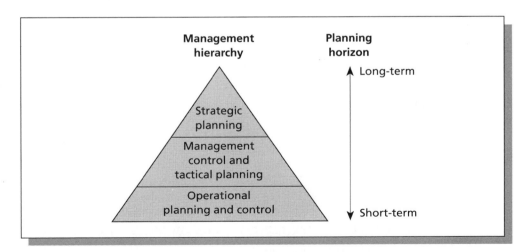

**Fig 3.2 ◆ Levels and planning horizons of management activities**

The effectiveness of MIS support to each level is cumulative; ie informed decisions making at each level depends upon the MIS constructed for that level *plus* those of the lower tiers. For example:

| LEVEL | PURPOSE |
|---|---|
| Sub-operational (transactional) | Producing an invoice |
| Operational | Reporting daily sales ledger figures |
| Tactical | Developing budgetary forecasts |
| Strategic | Making business sector comparison |

In the study of MIS this perception of serving different levels of management activity is important since it encapsulates statements of the nature of the decision making process such as the degree of structured/unstructured decisions and the significance of internal/external sources of raw material to the MIS. This hierarchical view is also relevant in Section 3.3.4 when considering information attributes.

### 3.2.3 ◆ Nature of decision making

Human decision making and decision makers are the subject of much detailed study in a number of disciplines all of which contribute to our ability to construct effective business instrumentation. Probably the most 'standard' view of all decision making is the three-stage model defined by Simon 1960 and Newell and Simon. This model is shown in Figure 3.3 and illustrates the different role played by MIS instrumentation at each stage.

As well as defining this popular view of the decision making process Simon made the distinction between what he called programmed and non-programmed decisions. This distinction is now more normally represented as a continuum between structured and unstructured decision types (*see* Figure 3.4).

Both of these models contribute to an appreciation of the required nature of MIS if it is to support *human* decision making; that is, an appreciation of how humans may respond to the data displayed on the dials and gauges.

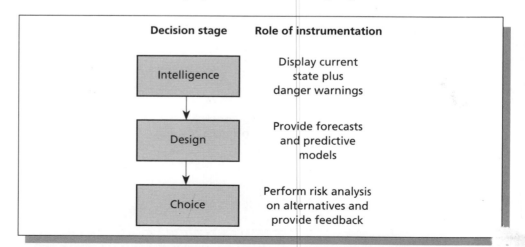

**Fig 3.3 ◆ Model of decision making**
(*Human Problem Solving* by Newell/Simon, © 1972. Adapted by permission of Prentice-Hall, Inc., Upper Saddle River, NJ)

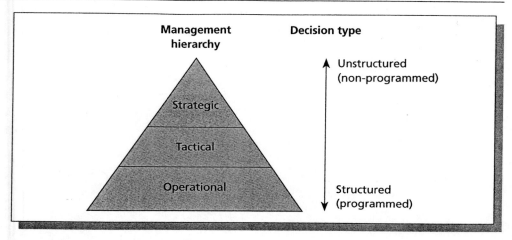

**Fig 3.4 ◆ Decision type continuum**

## .2.4 ◆ Desired attributes of MIS and information

For management information systems to provide effective instrumentation they, and their outputs, should possess a number of attributes. Figure 3.5 gives a simple summary of the required information attributes, particularly important to remember with the current emphasis upon output.

| | |
|---|---|
| Surprise value | It should startle the recipient and not be obtainable elsewhere; there is however a value in a comfort attribute |
| Relevance | To the decision maker, and the decision's scope and timing |
| Complete/concise | These two attributes are both necessary but can often be contradictory |

The Gorry and Scott-Morton model (shown in Figure 3.5) presents a more detailed picture of information attributes and illustrates how they will vary by level of the management hierarchy.

| Characteristics of information | Operational | Tactical | Strategic |
|---|---|---|---|
| Source | Largely internal | ---------------------------------------------- | External |
| Scope | Well-defined, narrow | -------------------------------------- | Very wide |
| Level of aggregation | Detailed | ------------------------------------------------ | Aggregate |
| Time horizon | Historical | ---------------------------------------------- | Future |
| Currency | Highly current | ------------------------------------------ | Quite old |
| Required accuracy | High | -------------------------------------------------------- | Quite low |
| Frequency of use | Very frequent | ---------------------------------------- | Infrequent |

**Fig 3.5 ◆ Model of information requirements by level of management activity**
(adapted from A Framework of Management Information Systems by Gorry and Scott-Morton, *Sloan Management Review*, Vol 13. No 1, 1971, by permission of publisher. Copyright 1971 by Sloan Management Review Association. All rights reserved)

Chapter 7 explores these attributes since they, and the weighting attached to each, are what determine 'information value' and form a basis for the notion of information as an economic entity. The *value* of information is relative to the needs of the organisation and the specific manager and hence is difficult to define. Chapter 7 explores the notion that IS is a value-adding process and the quantification of that adding of value will be one way of representing the value of information.

Whilst there is justifiable current concern with the problem of identifying and quantifying the value that results from information attributes, the vehicle itself must also possess a number of attributes for it to provide the business with the instrumentation it needs. The following table summarises the desired system attributes.

| | |
|---|---|
| Decision oriented | Whilst it is a legitimate decision to do nothing the system must be producing material in an appropriate way to enable informed decision making. |
| Data processing | Despite the shift in focus, MIS must still maintain DP checks, controls, timeliness, and efficient resource use. |
| Data management | The vehicle should maintain the three I's of data storage: *integrity – independence – integration* |
| Flexibility | To avoid being stuck with outdated and inappropriate technology and solutions any MIS should be sufficiently adaptable to people's varied and changing needs and behaviour. |
| HCI | The systems should capitalise upon the best of humans and of machines to obtain the optimum mix of people intuition and machine reliability and speed. |

The commonest complaints levelled at MIS are the lack of decision orientation and the lack of flexibility. The unsatisfactory systems are generally those that do not allow humans to take decisions in the *way* that they wish to.

## 3.2.5 ◆ The effects of management information systems

Extending the use of MIS in an organisation will, of course, have an impact upon the nature of that organisation and the collective impact that IS has had upon the nature of organisations is explored in Chapter 7. It is outside the scope of this text to consider the industrial sociology of MIS. However we should note that extending the automating of decision making, which is generally the action of an MIS, will frequently alter the organisation's structure. Organisations do consciously and intentionally use an MIS to revise their structure (for instance, see the discussion of Business Process Re-engineering in Chapter 7) or such changes may be the unexpected by-product of some other objective. There may be a change in the job content of many managers, particularly in the middle range whose sole purpose may have been the collecting, collating and presentation of data, along with some filtering of it! This tends to cut out unpleasant routine operations but also make the supervisory role more routine. However the decision making process may develop since 'what's left' is the informal, presumably more interesting since less routine and programmed, aspects. Perhaps less frequently the inadvertent by-product may be a degree of decentralisation since the MIS supports distributed decision making or even makes routine local decisions itself and this support ability may create a push towards decentralisation, whether sought or not.

The effects of MIS may be good or bad, where 'good' may represent an increase in job satisfaction whilst 'bad' includes the sense of alienation created from the loss of personal communications. In reality organisations are now rarely starting from scratch and therefore the degree of disruption and distress experienced from the introduction of a *new* MIS is really an issue for the management of change. To capitalise successfully upon the potential impact of MIS creates challenges high up the management ladder and this challenge is to *co-ordinate* successfully the interests of the systems players.

## 3.2.6 ◆ Strategy role of categories of systems players

By definition, MIS are for people and IS as the organisational function responsible for them will also be made up of people. Because of the often extensive impact of an MIS upon an organisation, as discussed above, it is important for there to be a strategic direction that co-ordinates the role and interests of the different groups of players in MIS. These will include senior management, user management and IS management. However, recently the distinction between user and IS management has become increasingly blurred.

The MIS Triad of Brookes, Grouse, Jeffery, and Lawrence (1982), shown in Figures 3.6a,b,c, models the relationships between these different groups of people and their differing roles. The two-way arrows along each side show the necessary flow of information. Interestingly, the management of MIS in itself requires an effective MIS!

There is a danger that the different roles will become stereotypes and caricaturised so that each player in this 'eternal triangle' is seen by the others in terms of the negative qualities and impacts they may have.

The role of the IS strategy is to ensure the effective development and implementation of IS within the strategic direction and to do this each node must play the role indicated in the circle to avoid the dangers noted.

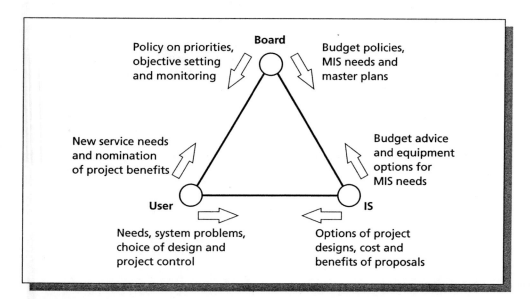

**Fig 3.6a ◆ MIS triad**

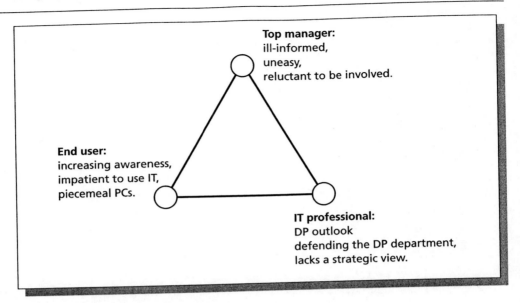

**Fig 3.6b ◆ MIS ITernal triangle caricature**

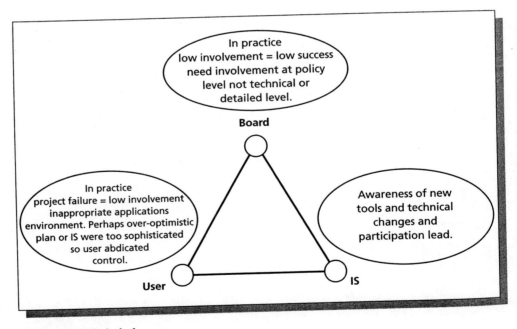

**Fig 3.6c ◆ MIS triad: dangers**

**References and further reading**

As indicated throughout this chapter, it is beyond the scope of this text to go into detail about MIS concepts, components and development approaches. However, for those interested the list below offers some follow-up reading as well as listing the works referenced.

Awad, E. (1988) *Management Information Systems: Concepts, Structures, and Applications*, Benjamin Cummings.

Curtis, G. (1989) *Business Information Systems: Analysis, Design and Practice*, Addison-Wesley.

Gorry, G.A. and Scott-Morton, M. (1971) *A Framework for Management Information Systems*, Sloan Management Review, Vol 13 No 1, Autumn.

Harry, M.J.S. (1990) *Information and Management Systems: Concepts and Applications*, Pitman Publishing.

Harry, M.J.S. (1994) *Information Systems in Business*, Pitman Publishing.

Kroenke, D. (1989) *Management Information Systems*, McGraw-Hill.

Lucey, T. (1991) *Management Information Systems* (6th edn), DP Publications.

O'Brien, B. (1995) *Information Management Decisions: Briefings and Critical Thinking*, Pitman Publishing.

Reynolds, G.W. (1995) *Information Systems for Managers* (3rd edn), West Publishing.

Rochester, J.B. (1993) *Computers: Tools for Knowledge Workers*, Irwin.

Schultheis, R.A. and Sumner, M. (1992) *Management Information Systems: The Manager's View* (2nd edn), Irwin.

Strassmann, P. (1995) *The Politics of Information Management*, Information Economics Press.

Turban, E., McLean, E. and Wetherbe, J. (1996) *Information Technology for Management: Improving Quality and Productivity*, Wiley.

Wolstenholme, E.F., Henderson, S. and Gavine, A. (1993) *The Evaluation of Management Information Systems: A Dynamics and Holistic Approach*, Wiley.

## Concepts and models

Anthony, R.N. (1965) *Planning and Control Systems: A Framework for Analysis*, Harvard University Press.

Brookes, C.H.P., Grouse, P.J., Jeffery, D.R. and Lawrence, M.J. (1982) *Information Systems Design*, Prentice-Hall.

Newell, A. and Simon, H.A. (1972) *Human Problem Solving*, Prentice-Hall.

Simon, H.A. (1960) *The New Science of Management Decisions*, Harper and Brothers.

## Components
### Data analysis and design and databases

Chen, P. (1976) The Entity-Relationship Model: Towards a unified view of data: ACM *Transactions of Database Systems*, 1,(1) pp. 9–36.

O'Neill, P. (1994) *Database: Principles, Programming, Performance*, Morgan Kaufmann.

Rock-Evans, R. (1991) *A Simple Introduction to Data and Activity Analysis*, Computer Weekly Publications.

Teorey, T.J. (1990) *Database Modelling and Design: The Fundamental Principles* (2nd edn), Morgan Kaufmann.

Veryard, R. (1984) *Pragmatic Data Analysis*, Blackwell.

### HCI

Carey, J.M. (1991) *Human Factors in Information Systems: An Organisational Perspective*, Ablex Publishing.

Dix, A., Finkley, Abowd, G. and Beale, R. (1993) *Human Computer Interaction*, Prentice-Hall.

Gerlach, J.H. and Kuo, F.-Y. (1991) Understanding Human-Computer Interaction for Information Systems Design, *MIS Quarterly*, Vol 15 No 4 Dec pp. 526–49.

Mumford, E. and Henshall, D. (1983) *Designing Participatively: A Participative Approach to Computer Systems Design*, Manchester Business School.

Preece, J. (1993) *Human Computer Interaction* (3rd edn), Addison-Wesley.

Schneiderman, B. (1992) *Designing the User Interface* (2nd edn), Addison-Wesley.

### Data communications

Gandoff, M. (1990) *Students' Guide to Data Communications*, Butterworth-Heinemann.

### Development approaches

Lantz, K.E. (1985) *The Prototyping Methodology*, Prentice-Hall.

Wood-Harper, A.T., Antill, L. and Avison, D.E. (1985) *Information Systems Definition: The Multiview Approach*, Blackwell Scientific Publications.

### Hard/structured systems

Crinnion, J. (1991) *Evolutionary Systems Development: A Practical Guide to Use of Prototyping Within a Structured Systems Methodology*, Pitman Publishing.

De Marco, T. (1980) *Structured Analysis: Systems Specifications*, Yourdon, Prentice-Hall.

Gane, C. and Sarson, T. (1979) *Structured Systems Analysis: Tools and Techniques*, Prentice-Hall.

### Soft systems

Checkland, P. (1981) *Systems Thinking, Systems Practice*, Wiley.

Naughton, J. (1977) *The Checkland Methodology: A readers guide*, Open University Press.

Patching, D. (1990) *Practical Soft Systems Analysis*, Pitman Publishing.

Stowell, F. (Ed.) (1995) *Information Systems Provision: The Contribution of Soft Systems Methodology*, McGraw-Hill.

# CHAPTER 4

# Strategy planning for information systems

This chapter develops the ideas introduced in Part 1. That section presented strategic planning as the process by which an organisation:

- Identifies its business objectives
- Selects the acceptable means to achieve them
- Initiates the necessary courses of action and allocation of resources.

Planning is an ongoing process that provides the framework that determines the implementation detail. Neither 'general' strategy planning nor IS strategy planning are simple activities but most managers would say that they perform more effectively if they plan and stick to the objectives of that plan. Indeed we show our awareness of this in day-to-day life every time we write a shopping list. One anonymous writer neatly captures the value of planning: 'if we fail to plan, we plan to fail'. And yet, whilst in an abstract way all acknowledge the value of planning, there are no commonly agreed principles for either business or IS strategy planning though both can result in hugely significant gains or losses. Most writers of the last decade agree that controlling technology development and/or acquisition is a crucial aspect of modern management; to control effectively, IS objectives must be established.

Despite a history of neglected planning, IS needs effective strategic planning as much as, and perhaps more than, other functional areas. Just as other functional areas do, IS consumes a portion of the organisation's finite resources. Without a clear view of value (the aim of planning) the allocation of resources is unlikely to match that value. Of course, it must be noted that value has many possible interpretations; the early section of this book was about exploring value at the macro level while Chapters 11 and 12 look at some issues of exploring value at the micro level. However, IS must accommodate rapid technological change, its projects are often very high cost, and increasingly competitive well-being depends upon IS delivering those systems that enable the business to function effectively, the *strategic* management information systems. Planning and implementing an appropriate IS strategy produces the organisational confidence that IS will cost-effectively deliver these strategic systems. Systems without planning will mean, for most organisations, not only financial losses but additional hidden, and often greater, costs such as lowered staff morale, missed opportunities, continuous management fire-fighting, and customer dissatisfaction. Planning helps an organisation identify its information needs and find new opportunities for using that information and it defines the activities needed to implement the chosen strategy.

Surveys throughout the 1980s consistently placed improved IS strategic planning first on any list of concerns for both user and IS management. One example was the 1986 study of chief executives and corporate level general management quoted in Brancheau and Wetherbe (1987); this study also placed using IS for competitive advantage in second place. And if, as seen in Niederman, Brancheau and Wetherbe (1991), current surveys show that strategic planning has moved from its 1980s perch into third place, it is still very important. The fall of competitive advantage into eighth place reflects an awareness that competitive advantage is actually something that *might* follow from getting the rest right. Infrastructure issues, the more technical aspects of IS management, may now dominate, but strategic planning remains in third place and has 'enjoyed' more than a decade as management's number one.

It is certainly desirable to plan ahead for the IS function and that planning should be at a strategic, organisational level. It should not be only at the level of project planning, ie where decisions have already been made about which projects to implement and planning is all over bar the shouting. Orderly planning allows IS to focus on higher levels than simply completing projects. Unforeseen or corrective work always occurs but a framework of objectives makes IS better able to handle such disturbances. Strategic planning results in a strategic plan, and like any other plan or strategy, once identified and documented it needs reviewing as part of an ongoing planning process but, until an update is produced, it is the focal point for all implementation decisions. The *purpose* of strategy planning for IS is to identify the most appropriate targets for technological support and to schedule that technology adoption. There is a strong case to put for seeking automation support for this process of identifying automation candidates. The strength of this case is argued in Copley (1989) where it is pointed out that this is particularly true for any of the planning tools or approaches that are biased towards either validating organisational models or generating repository designs. (*See* Chapter 5 for tools and Chapter 6 for approaches.) An organisation's IS strategy, and the plan that documents it, must be consistent (as shown diagrammatically in Figure 4.1) with:

- its corporate plans;
- its management's view of the role of IS in the organisation; and
- its stage of maturity of use and management of IS.

Cortada (1980) almost two decades ago was advocating that strategic planning for 'DP' (the term used at that time for the concept called IS in this book) was fundamentally the same as general business strategic planning. However, he did appear to see it as conducted separately, even if performed in the same way, and to be only possible once 'DP Management understands fully the environment in which the company operates'.

Later chapters in this section will address some aspects of how to ensure that it is consistent but before that this chapter addresses five preliminary questions relating to strategy planning for management information systems:

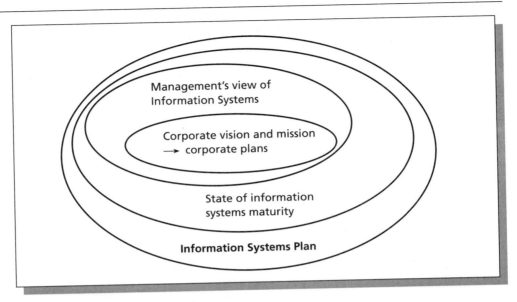

**Fig 4.1 ◆ IS strategy consistency**

- Where does an IS strategy fit within the wider set of strategies?
- What has been the history of IS strategy planning?
- What circumstances demand major re-assessment of IS strategy plans?
- Who might be employed to do the actual planning?
- What might an IS strategy plan contain?

This chapter concludes with a brief discussion of the key concerns of IS strategy planning from the perspectives of users and IS.

We must never lose sight of the fact that a strategy, by definition, is the desirable ends plus the acceptable means for achieving them and so any strategy plan documents *what* and not *how*. In the literature of MIS management two slightly different terms with slightly different meanings are encountered:

- IS strategy planning: Which is the *process* of *formulating* the IS, that is the posture to the use and management of IS; this process will define, and probably document, what IS must achieve and within what constraints of acceptability.

- IS strategic planning: Which implies that the *process* of *planning* IS activities has, as its *purpose* and time horizon, strategic levels of importance. That is, either it is performed by executives at the strategic level of the organisation; or it is concentrating primarily upon issues of significant business importance, though often these can only be judged with hindsight.

When we are talking of the process we will use the former term; only when implying business importance will we use the latter.

## 4.1 ◆ WHERE DOES AN IS STRATEGY FIT WITHIN THE WIDER SET OF STRATEGIES?

Identifying a business' goals and objectives should lead to articulating an overall business strategy and Part 1 considered this process more deeply. Taking a systems view of strategies shows why the story doesn't stop with the business strategy. The model in Figure 4.2 intends to represent where an IS strategy fits in context, and not to make any statements about the sequence of the IS planning process. In addition, since systemic relationships are an issue of perspective, the IS strategy shown here as an element of divisional strategy could equally be viewed as permeating across all divisions. The usefulness of viewing it in that way will largely depend upon the degree of autonomy within the divisions.

The single business strategy feeds down, through divisional or business unit strategies, into a number of 'functional' strategies. One of these is the IS strategy

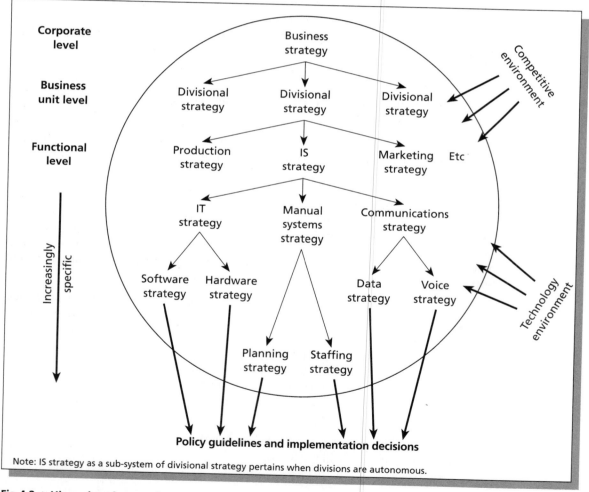

Note: IS strategy as a sub-system of divisional strategy pertains when divisions are autonomous.

**Fig 4.2 ◆ Hierarchy of strategies**
Note: the term hierarchy used here in a systemic not authoritarian sense

that, in turn, feeds into a number of sub-strategies, the IT strategy, the communications strategy, etc. These then develop ever more detailed strategy elements. This system of strategies and its hierarchy gives a context that provides much of the validation for the general approach to IS use and management discussed in Chapter 8. By considering an IS strategy as an element of a *system of strategies* we are able to draw upon the understanding generated by systems study. It is useful to understand the concepts associated with systems theory (*see* Harry 1990) and it is particularly appropriate to use this understanding when grappling with the problems of managing a business with those resulting systems.

Each level of this system of strategies contributes to the emergent property that is the higher-level strategy; this is the strategy as a pattern in the what happens sense rather than strategy in the planned but yet to happen sense. Wasted and ineffectual effort is the likely result of failing to acknowledge the required contributions. Thus the elements of the IS strategy *together* produce the emergent property that is an IS strategy. All aspects of IS endeavour exist within an overall system. Illustrated here is the system of strategies but IS projects form part of a system of projects and IS budgets form part of a system of budgets. This systems context reminds us that each level in the hierarchy contributes support to the 'owning' level. Lederer and Gardiner (1992) provide details of an entire planning methodology in such a way that *one* example of how the sub-systems might fit together can be seen.

Figure 4.2 shows the system hierarchy but it does not imply a fixed *sequence*. Indeed, many organisations make early attempts at developing an IS strategy before articulating their business strategies, despite the fact that many IS strategy development approaches depend upon the prior identification of business strategies. It is not necessarily a problem to use deduced or assumed business strategies when validated ones are not available since having to assess business issues as thoroughly as IS ones gives much of the process gains. During early experiments in IS strategy planning IS often acts as the catalyst for generating and documenting the business strategy. Because the system of strategies has, like any other system, a hierarchy it would be tempting to assume that strategy planning must be a top-down activity; this is not the case (*see* Chapter 6 for a discussion of a number of different approaches to developing the IS strategy).

This hierarchy, however, does explain some of the difficulty of IS strategic planning; as Earl (1989) said:

> We are trying to connect the exploitation of IT, which is in itself complex, rapidly changing, and often not well understood by managers, to development of business strategies where neither the principles nor the methods are yet agreed. Paradoxically in seeking to bridge these two problematic and somewhat unstructured streams the desire seems to be to find a structured methodology; management seem to want a structured approach.

In other words, developing business strategies is difficult; developing IS strategies is difficult; developing IS strategies that support business strategies is very difficult. Therefore managers are constantly seeking ways to understand better the nature of IS strategy planning and ways of appraising the planning processes they and their organisation undertake (King offers some suggestions for doing this). The study of the need for IS and business strategies to match and form a single system has resulted in some valuable awareness raising models (*see* Figure 4.3 and next chapter). However, this study has generated far less material on how to achieve confidence in

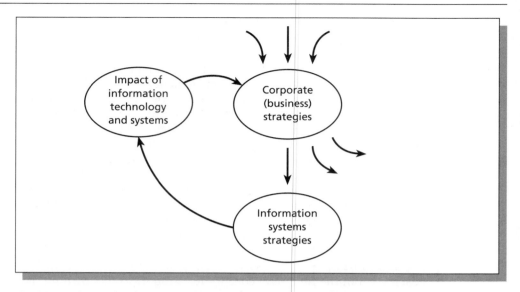

**Fig 4.3 ◆ Relationship between IT, IS and business strategies, or connections in systems terms**
(adapted from Integrating Information Systems into Business Strategies by Ward, *Long Range Planning* Vol 20 No 3, pp. 19–29, © 1987 with kind permission from Elsevier Science Ltd)

the degree of match. Section 4.6 of this chapter discusses the history of this matching, and Chapter 6 discusses some approaches aimed at increasing confidence in the degree of match. Figure 4.4 provides a more detailed outline of IT and IS strategies.

We generally discuss how to define and document an IS strategy as if it were a single item. It would be far more correct to refer to IS strategies in the plural and to see them as a collection of strategies. Corporate groupings may require a corporate

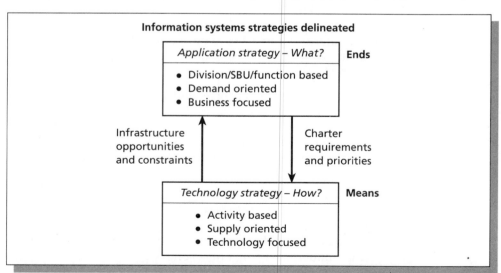

**Fig 4.4 ◆ IT and IS delineated in more detail**
(adapted from Earl, M.J., *Management Strategies for Information Technology* (1989) by permission of Prentice Hall)

| IS planning level | Breadth of computing activity | | |
|---|---|---|---|
| | *Personal computing* | *Departmental computing* | *Corporate computing* |
| *Mission defining* | Users normally take lead in spotting opportunities. IS will provide assistance when asked. | Both users and IS will seek new opportunities for departmental computing. Users may ask for systems for small groups, IS when for whole department. | IS is responsible for leading the definition of opportunities for corporate-wide systems. Users must actively participate. |
| *Strategy planning (long-term, two to four years)* | Since many personal computing products and systems have a relatively short life, strategy planning will primarily relate to the management rather than computing implications. | Department management will lead the development of strategic plans for their departmental computing. IS and Users must actively participate. | Corporate management will lead the development of corporate IS strategy. IS and business departments will define requirements, review strategic plans, and support the implementation. |
| *Tactical planning (medium-term, one to two years)* | Users will do this, assisted by IS when requested. | Department management is encouraged to lead this activity. IS will actively participate. | IS and interdepartmental management teams jointly lead this activity. Users encouraged to participate actively. |

Fig 4.5 ◆ Planning activity/responsibility

IS strategy, plus a number of business unit's IS strategy plus infrastructure strategy, etc. This equates to the levels of business strategy discussed in Chapter 1. The corporate level strategy will often establish the framework that deals with:

- Corporate level information needs, for instance the type and format of required financial reports
- Common systems architectures to get maximum benefit from internal expertise and to establish good relations with vendors
- Organisational arrangements to ensure that business units' strategies support and perhaps enhance the corporate strategy

There are also differences relating to the major roles and responsibilities associated with what is being planned for and at what level. Figure 4.5 illustrates some of these differences. The current fashion, however, is for a minimalist corporate IS, and business, strategy that gives only overall direction and leaves maximum autonomy and freedom of interpretation to the business units.

## 4.2 ◆ WHAT HAS BEEN THE HISTORY OF IS STRATEGIC PLANNING?

Whatever the perception of the general value of planning, IS strategy planning is a relatively recent phenomenon and it is still often not done or done badly. Management Information Systems are of major importance to modern business; they are either:

- Valuable tools when correctly aligned with business needs

  or

- A heavy cost burden when inappropriate or managed incorrectly.

Traditionally, business management has focused on business planning, with little understanding of, or interest in, how IS could support, and influence, its objectives. IS management has concentrated on technical issues with little understanding of, or interest in, business objectives. Naturally systems planning of sorts has always taken place but usually in the form of project planning with a concentration on getting the system done right rather than getting the right system, and, in any case, being performed in isolation from mainstream business planning. 'Traditional' IS planning has, in fact, been a specific system's plan. It has been about producing a project plan, not choosing the project or, even better, providing the framework in order to choose. Such traditional planning was entirely reactive in nature. This type of planning is practical at the systems level but leads to lost business opportunities and incompatible systems, data stores and architectures, for no good reason, and often unacceptable implementation lags. Greater integration across functional boundaries highlights the problems in the purely needs-based reactive planning and 'pushes up' concern with strategic planning. Raghunathan and Raghunathan (1993) explore the nature of the job of IS planner and identify it as involving two distinct job elements, therefore appropriately held by two managerial types. They see these two jobs as either the active participation in management decisions on IS resource allocations (by the meanings of strategy explored in Chapter 1 this is directly *forming* the IS strategy) or as a job of process facilitation whereby planning skills are exercised to help others reach management decisions on IS strategy (clearly an indirect role). The 'pushing up' of concerns with IS strategic planning may be seen in the creation of these two roles.

Strategic management emerged as a coherent discipline for study in the 1960s and much time and money has since been spent on business strategy formulation. However, it is only since the late 1970s that it has been accepted that IS, and IS planning, has a strategic importance to business survival. This acceptance has very gradually elevated planning for IS from its traditional operational or tactical level to the strategic level and begun to merge it with more mainstream business planning (*see* Figure 4.6). In theory the IS management should now be part of senior management and hence should have been part of developing the organisation's business plans for the next half decade or so and hence will have a good idea of the way to plan for IS over the same period. By and large it is still not quite like that and IS is still frequently just reactive.

Prior to the late 1970s the main emphasis of DP planning was upon efficiency, that is the ratio of outputs to inputs. With the emergence during the 1980s of a perception of information as a resource that should be managed to the advantage of the organisation, just like capital and manpower, came an appreciation of IS effectiveness issues, that is the relationship between output and goals. Any *resource* must be managed and so there grew a perceived need for an information *strategy*. Some would say that information is not just a critical resource, but rather that it is *the* critical resource allowing the organisation to manage all others. So strategy planning for IS arrived with the primary objectives of the planning effort broadening to encompass the desire to improve communication with users, to increase the degree of top management commitment, still to allocate resources of course, but to find more opportunities for improving the IS function and spot the new, higher

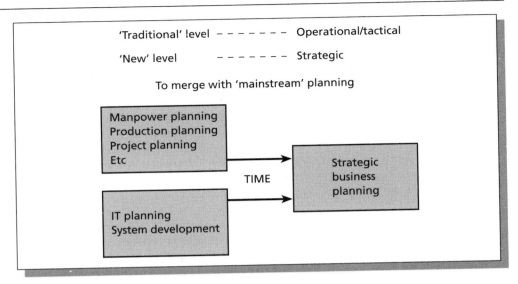

**Fig 4.6 ◆ Convergence of planning activities**

business payback MIS applications. By the late 1980s to that 'wish list' had been added the desire to describe an organisation-wide data architecture and to identify the *strategic* applications. Lederer and Sethi (1989) and Baker (1995) both give brief histories of strategy planning for IS.

For example Ford Motor Co introduced computer-controlled manufacturing, established a JIT inventory system, and constructed a network to link to suppliers. These initiatives were designed to rationalise performance and improve efficiency, which they did, and took pre-tax profits from $1.5 billion in 1979 to $5.1 billion in 1986. However, on the same *efficiency* tide was carried huge volumes of data and the unfortunate manager had to contend with masses of green-lined printouts to wade through to get to information in order to make *effective* decisions. These managers suffered a physical and intellectual information overload.

The issue of IS strategic planning may have appeared in management 'top tens' for over a decade but the planning itself has had a rockier history. It is difficult to escape the conclusion that, whilst most organisations would say that planning is a 'good thing', the reality is too often that they barely understand IS strategic planning and frequently adopt time scales and levels of detail inappropriate for it to be *strategic*.

This is illustrated by a seminal research programme into 150 major US corporations conducted by the Diebold Institute in the early 1980s. They found that 66 per cent of IS functions did go through a formal planning process and did publish formal plans. However, 63 per cent of these published plans had time horizons of less than 3 years. This means that only 25 per cent of the sampled corporations, who were amongst the largest in America, had strategic IS plans; that is, plans extending *beyond* their current application backlog. Research a year later, though into only 40 corporations, found that 62.5 per cent of the sample had no formal IS plans or had begun planning only the previous year. For many organisations there does seem to have been a turning point in the mid-1980s, with more recent studies indicating that the IS strategic planning situation is improving, with perhaps as many as 84 per cent of companies formulating IS plans in a real strategic manner (Galliers 1992).

There is, however, more to the history of IS strategy planning than just the history of whether it has occurred or not. There is also the history of its *nature*. Organisations tend to take two to five years of experimenting with their process for formulating IS strategies. During this time they 'try out' different approaches (Chapter 5 describes the techniques used in these approaches) and learn by the experience. Most notably they discover that it generally takes four to five years for the benefits of the formalised planning process and delivered plans to materialise. By learning how to plan effectively and strategically organisations find that IS and business strategies align and interact to give real business benefits. However, perhaps the most significant benefit for the majority of organisations is that the process and its resultant strategies produce a better understanding throughout the organisation of the organisation and its business.

Earl suggests that, during their five-year experimentation process, organisations will go through the five stages illustrated in Figure 4.7. Earl suggests that at the end of these five experimental stages, organisations will realise that no single approach to formulating an IS strategy will work. Hence he has developed a multiple methodology model (*see* Chapter 6 for more detail on this) that acknowledges that not only the stage during the experimentation process but also that the industry sector and the organisation's position in that sector will continually influence their choice of method. Perhaps the most important point about this model is the help it offers in judging the appropriateness of particular examples of the ever expanding collection of IS strategy related analysis tools (samples from this IS strategic analysis tool kit are discussed in Chapter 5).

| Stage | Planning context | Methodology | Objective |
|-------|------------------|-------------|-----------|
| Year 1 | Inexperience/unawareness | 'Bottom-up' DP/IT led | Management understanding |
| Year 2 | Inadequate business plans | 'Top-down' Senior management drive | Agreeing priorities |
| Year 3 | Complexity apparent | Match 'top-down' and 'bottom-up' and investigations and prototyping | Firming up the IS strategy plan |

Stage 3 is usually a 'messy stage' that involves mainly user and IS management rather than senior management. During this stage the organisation makes a few false starts before selecting a structured methodology (perhaps use of critical success factor analysis) to lead into Stage 4.

| | | | |
|-------|------------------|-------------|-----------|
| Year 4 | Impatience for resulting benefits | 'Inside-out' process Executive managers and users in control | Finding opportunities |
| Year 5 | Maturity | Multiple methods accepted Partnership of user, senior and IS management | Integrating IS and business strategies |

Fig 4.7 ◆ Planning method experimentation
(adapted from Earl, M.J. *Management Strategies for Information Technology* (1989) by permission of Prentice Hall)

## 4.3 ◆ WHAT ARE THE CIRCUMSTANCES THAT DEMAND AND MOTIVATE MAJOR RE-ASSESSMENTS OF IS STRATEGIC PLANS?

IS strategic planning, like any planning, is not a one-off activity; ideally it would be a continuous cycle synchronised with or, better yet, embedded into the cycle of general business planning. Chapter 8 discusses the nature and benefits of this synchronisation. Given that organisations may address IS strategic planning in different ways there are still potentially common circumstances that require a re-assessment of the IS strategic plan. Short-term elements of the plan will naturally require frequent revision to reflect technology changes. The re-assessment referred to in this section is to the long-term elements that provide the sense of direction; the *what* of the plan (the short-term elements providing the *how* of the plan). O'Brien (1992) provides some good coverage on supply/demand interaction, and the need for re-assessment and a not-too-rigid plan. Since any strategy is about goals it should not be necessary to adapt the detail. Three common circumstances that alter the objectives of an IS plan are:

- Major corporate changes
- External competitive opportunities or threats
- Evolutionary change in IS maturity

For each of these three categories it is worth listing some of the 'text book' symptoms expected since identification of the symptoms leads to the 'diagnosis' and this diagnosis is the first step towards a 'cure', ie understanding the likely appropriate objectives, emphasis and scope for the revised IS strategic plan. This understanding gives a nudge in the direction of the best tools to pull out of the tool bag.

### 4.3.1 ◆ Major corporate changes

When there is a major corporate change the symptoms are usually plain to see! The collective result of new owners, management, rationalisation programmes, restructuring exercises or other corporate changes is an alteration in the real or perceived role of IS in matching the *new* needs of the new business. There is now a different business that needs different things from IS. If these obvious symptoms are present then the IS strategy is likely to have as its primary objective the definition of the new role for IS. Its scope will be uncertain but the emphasis is to build upon senior management commitment to the changing role of IS within the new organisation.

### 4.3.2 ◆ External opportunities/threats

The likely symptoms of this type of change are the emergence of new markets and/or products that may be created by IS or the competitive need for major cost factor changes and improved performance. Again this need may be generated by IS itself, or the awareness of new challenges and advantages emerging, and yet again opportunities/threats may be driven by IS. This set of circumstances is likely to produce a plan whose objective is to move IS resources, in the widest sense of the term, into the new, but long-term, commitments to high benefit or threat protection. The scope of the plan created to respond to these circumstances is likely to be much more limited than the strategies produced in other situations. This plan focuses effort and resources upon those areas where the most good can be achieved. The emphasis of the plan is to exploit IS strengths and the weaknesses of competitors by being entrepreneurial and developing new attitudes, skills and uses of IS in these new commitments.

### 4.3.3 ◆ Evolutionary change

Probably the most frequent reason for re-assessing the IS strategy is that IS itself experiences an evolutionary change. The most noticeable symptoms of this are changing views on the required levels of control over IS or its budget allocations and/or the degree of dissatisfaction expressed by everyone. 'Growing' is often painful since moving from one stage to another generates fears and anxieties. Under these circumstances the plan's objectives are to get and keep senior management commitment, if not already present, and to demonstrate *managed* evolution. The scope of the plan extends the boundaries of IS but only as far ahead as can be known. The emphasis is upon setting and re-setting resourcing levels and styles and releasing or controlling IS in the *appropriate* way for the stage of growth. Chapter 6 explores the notion of stages of IS evolution since modelling the stage is a valuable analysis tool.

## 4.4 ◆ WHO MIGHT BE EMPLOYED TO DO THE ACTUAL PLANNING?

There are many approaches to establishing IS strategy planning teams. Broadly, there are three main approaches: the use of planning specialists, general IS staff or coalition teams.

Planning teams can be constructed primarily of specialist planning staff. They then will probably hold responsibility for co-ordinating, if not actually developing, many other planning efforts. This 'dedicated planners' approach can offer many advantages, with perhaps the most significant being that there is a high chance of the plan being completed. Since these teams are likely to be a 'standing army' this approach will also tend to increase the frequency of the planning activity and the chance of IS planning cycles being synchronised with the wider system of planning cycles. Additionally, since the planners are involved in many other corporate and functional plans there may be a deeper understanding of business needs. Balancing the potential advantages, however, is that their very specialism can lead to the most notable disadvantage and that is the tendency of these teams to lack an appreciation of 'reality' in IS issues. If these teams are not a standing army, then they must inevitably be externals, in which case a quite different picture emerges, with the IS strategy plan being an expensive and hence infrequent activity, and less likely to be synchronised with other planning cycles, especially if other plans are produced in house. Some difficulties associated with this 'strategy by outsiders' route can be addressed by careful attention to the issue of ensuring ownership by those ultimately taking the IS resource decisions. Adriaans (1993) discusses this issue of gaining commitment in a paper clearly aimed at just such subject specialist teams.

A second approach is to make the production of the IS strategy the responsibility of 'general' IS staff. Since teams of this type will tend, at least initially, to lack experience of strategic planning and will also tend to suffer the 'tyranny of the urgent' in calls from their everyday responsibilities this may reduce the chance of the plan being completed. However, their significant MIS awareness may produce a more implementable plan, if one is created at all. These teams are likely to be *ad hoc* in nature or at least busy in other areas, and this may reduce the frequency and increase the elapsed time needed for planning activities.

The third route is to use a coalition team drawn from a number of business functions, certainly including IS and perhaps including some specialist planning staff. This breadth of experience should increase the organisational realism within the IS strategy plan. This realism gives the organisation the best chance of an IS strategy that is aligned with business objectives. The only potential drawback is that the diversity of interests may act destructively upon team co-ordination, and that members may be 'moved on' at inappropriate, from a plan point of view, times.

These coalition teams are frequently referred to as IS steering committees, though Earl calls them joint project teams. Perhaps the most successful approach to IS strategy planning teams is to use the steering committee, which is best chaired by a senior general manager, with consideration and approval by board or equivalent. The advantage then is that it gets senior management to play a part, at an appropriate level without taking up too much of their time. It is then the responsibility of this committee to select the preferred framework (*see* Chapter 6) for the way of identifying and documenting the IS strategy. This committee defines the organisational arrangements necessary to do this and will meet when needed but, to be effective, at least quarterly. This coalition approach should provide the balancing mechanism among the three groups represented by the MIS triad and provides *visible* evidence of an integration of IS into the business. The plan produced by this type of team is *seen* to be organisational and hence should have political support. Doll and Torkzadeh (1987) discuss a steering committee approach to IS strategy planning and management in some detail and suggest that steering committees exist more frequently in organisations that have a fairly formalised approach to IS planning, defined by them to be that the organisation produces a written plan, has agreed development priorities, has separated the activities of maintenance and development, and has funding available for the planning process.

This discussion of the planning teams has focused upon the background from which the planning team may be drawn and the specific skills that the team members may bring. Since, in most cases anyway, IS strategy planning will be managed by a team all the personal level issues of team membership come into play. Therefore, in addition to specific skills already discussed team composition will also need to balance appropriately the generic team skills of the shaper, the former, the critic, the realist, the idealist, the ideas generator, the synthesiser, the motivator.

Whatever the make-up of the team is, resources must be allocated to the planning process. These resources will include staff, time and, increasingly, the provision of automated support mechanisms. Such allocations should never be seen as wasted, though it is tempting in times of recession to reduce spending on 'non-essential' activities such as planning (training also suffers from the mis-perception of being a 'luxury') but this is a false long-term economy. Without a coherent IS strategy an organisation may embark upon many expensive activities that do not significantly contribute to meeting business goals. It is *planning* that allows a favourable benefit/investment balance to be struck.

When making the choice of planning approach an organisation is in something of a chicken-and-egg situation. There must be some concept of the likely scope of the delivered plan in order to establish an appropriate planning team. Fidler and Rogerson (1996) provide a chart of planning team membership (what they refer to as 'participants in the SISP process') by intended scope (what they call strategy focus). Unfortunately, however, the planning team identifies and documents the objectives and scope. Additionally, as part of establishing the planning team the boundary of activities must be identified. It is inappropriate, but often happens, for the IS function itself to develop the strategy for its own development and use. When this situation occurs it probably results from a lack of commitment and involvement by senior management whose role it more properly is.

## 4.5 ◆ WHAT MIGHT AN IS STRATEGIC PLAN CONTAIN?

The content of a given organisation's strategic plan may vary widely depending on its particular emphasis and it should not be forgotten that the process benefits of the planning process will tend not to be captured in the plan document but are none the less real. However, once created, the plan is a conception of the future and therefore aims to achieve two things:

- Clearly identify where IS intends to go and so avoid the danger of 'getting lost', ie taking courses of action that do not contribute to the overall mission
- Provide a formalised set of benchmarks so that progress on this journey can be monitored

The emphasis between these two may differ for any given organisation, or may shift within the same organisation. An organisation comfortable with the degree of 'shared priorities' may not feel the need to emphasise the identification aspects but may emphasise the benchmark aspects.

Being *strategic*, the plan should naturally contain long-term directions which would normally be for three to five years; this will mean that most of the document will need review every year, or at most eighteen months. Given this long(ish)-term focus many plans will identify milestones perceived as critical points in achieving the view of the future. These may form natural review points. Baker (1995) in fact argues for the continual monitoring of the IS strategy plan rather than merely at such milestone points. She also offers some indications of how such *continual* reviewing could happen with the creation of feedback loops necessary to reflect upon the success of the planning process as well as the continued appropriateness of its content, that is the actual IS resource decisions.

It can be hard to persuade those involved with IS that IS must by definition exist only for a purpose. Yet too many see it as an end in its own right. One of the points of documenting the IS strategy and publishing it in the IS plan is to show, and be seen to show, that the organisation does not subscribe to this view.

Despite the possible variety of formats, it is possible to identify the necessary core elements to the IS strategy plan, they are:

1 A clear statement of the IS objectives, that give a clear sense of direction, ie where the organisation wishes to be. The following chapters introduce and discuss techniques to identify these and to determine why, and how, they should match *business* objectives.
2 An inventory and assessment of both the current organisational capabilities and problems resulting from current practices, ie where the organisation is now. Part 3 introduces many of the specific issues affecting IS capabilities and possible approaches to IS use and management.
3 A concrete implementation plan that translates the sense of direction and knowledge of the start point into a navigable route map, ie how to get from (1) to (2). The plan must identify both long-term and short-term actions and resource allocations. Additionally, the IS strategic plan must acknowledge that organisational change is an almost inevitable corollary to the planning process.

In Part 1 the nature of strategic planning was discussed. A 'good' plan must, of course, result from 'good' planning and therefore it will document the mission, goals, objectives and acceptable strategies that were defined as part of the planning process. Ward in his model of a planning process suggests that the IS strategy plan should contain three elements:

1 *Business Information Strategy*; this indicates how information will be used to support the business. Priorities that the organisation has for systems developments are defined at a general level, perhaps by suggesting a portfolio of current and required systems. It may outline information requirements via blueprints for application developments of the future.
2 *IS Functionality Strategy*; this indicates what features and performance the organisation will need from the systems. It demonstrates how the resources will be used, and provides policy guidelines for the information resource's management and perhaps policies for communication networks, hardware architectures, software infrastructures and management issues such as security, development approaches, organisation and the allocation of responsibility.
3 *IS/IT Strategy*; this defines the policies for software and hardware, for example any standards to be used and any stand on preferred suppliers. This also defines the organisation's stand on the IS organisation, for example whether it is to be centralised or distributed, what are to be the investment, vendor and human impact policies and IS accounting techniques.

The problem with Ward's model is that item (3) can hardly be considered to be *strategic* in focus. In many eyes, item (3) is not the IS strategy but the decisions taken as a result of it, ie the tactics and action of implementing it.

As with business plans, the strategic IS plan should delineate the general role that IS will play in assisting the rest of the organisation to reach its business goal. It lays out the results desired for the time period and the necessary major initiatives estimated to lead to them. This is akin to the general systems model of control where the IS strategy plan acts as second order control in that it selects the desired standard; the review of the plan then acts as first order control.

The long-term plan, although coinciding with the business plan time scale of three to five years, tends to be far more project specific than the equivalent business plan. This is the natural result of the different purpose of IS and IS plans, which is to translate business plans and IS objectives into specific major developments. So the document defines methods by which IS intends to complete projects for the business, it should also list projects that will enable IS itself to be better equipped to provide a service. The short-term IS plan is very like the short-term business plan. It defines the specific stages of projects that may run over several years. It gives specific dates, goals, and budgets for software and hardware acquisitions. Staff and other resources are allocated to projects to develop systems or make improvements to operating procedures or networks, etc. Earl (1989) integrates the strategy plan structural points of Ward and these relationship aspects and illustrates them as shown in Figure 4.8. In fact Fidler and Rogerson (1996) reproduce a template originally by Cole (1995) giving an extremely simple outline for the IT strategy elements of the overall strategy that Earl refers to as the functional plan.

Many of the strategy planning techniques require a definition of business areas in order to create an information *architecture*, where a business area is defined as a collection of closely related business processes together with the data which supports them. A business area contains processes which can be automated within one project or set of related projects. Similarly the data for an individual area suits a single database. It is very common to document the relationships between these via a matrix of processes and entities; and there will perhaps be two hundred of each for an average organisation. These relationships provide a model of the business, often called an enterprise model. Because of the complexity of creating these matrices CASE tools really have to be used. These CASE tools provide the reports docu-

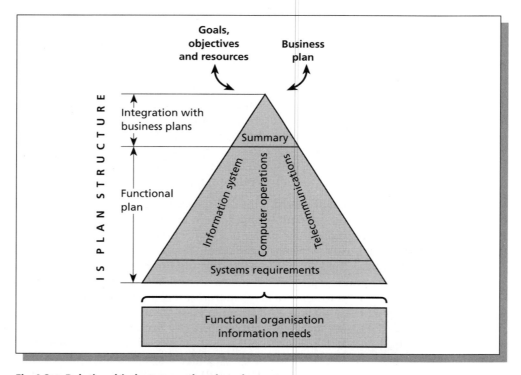

**Fig 4.8 ◆ Relationship between planning elements**
(adapted from Earl, M.J., *Management Strategies for Information Technology* (1989) by permission of Prentice Hall)

menting the relationships and so the format of the IS strategic plan may be determined, or at least significantly influenced, by the nature of the automated tools used during the planning process.

As well as the core features, any IS strategic plan may include a number of possible additional features. These may be included in response to particular planning emphases, for example executive or action summaries. A house style often exists for any published plans and this does tend to make the published IS strategy document more familiar in appearance and language and therefore more accessible to everyone. This will be particularly useful for the more detailed elements of the plan that must be read and understood by lower levels of management. However, house styles have a habit of being generated by document people rather than strategy planning people, and so the design may act as a straight-jacket to the detriment of the plan.

## 4.6 ◆ KEY CONCERNS

From the perspective of those destined to be consumers of IS services, the key concern of IS strategy planning is that they are able to interpret IS developments and services in terms of their business strategy and hence business needs. And so users are obviously concerned to establish the business demand and priorities for IS activities in order to get the best business value from IS resources and investments; by reconciling requirements to avoid inappropriately duplicated or incompatible investments. The overall objective is to regain control by the business of information, irrespective of the strategy for the technical delivery of it, and hence to be able to exploit the use of information to improve business performance. Whether this improved business performance can be said to equate to competitive advantage is discussed in Chapter 7.

From the perspective of those destined to provide and manage IS services (and this group may obviously overlap with the previous group) the overriding objective is to provide service levels and styles that are *appropriate* to the business' needs. Thus IS are concerned to reconcile and satisfy user requirements in order to identify, plan for, and so manage, the IS resources and technologies needed. They are concerned to fill the technical, probably advisory, role in identifying and exploiting opportunities to use information to improve business performance.

## 4.7 ◆ SUMMARY

This chapter has explained the historical development of the process that is called IS strategy planning. This chapter's planning emphasis places the focus upon the future; upon the process by which IS strategy is conceived to determine the future decisions of IS resource allocations. The consideration of the conscious directing of future IS resource allocations within this chapter has been through a discussion of the context of that conscious planning process, the possible players within it and its significant deliverable, the IS strategy plan.

Of course, strategy planning is not the only aspect of strategy formulation. There are also the multitude of processes, conscious and unconscious, by which the *actual* pattern of IS resource allocations will unfold. That is, those processes through which IS decisions will be interpreted and responded to. However the planned and directed outline of intent for future decisions that is the IS strategy plan remains of primary significance and therefore tools specifically to facilitate that future-oriented process are discussed in Chapter 5. The *approaches* to IS strategy formulation within which those tools may be used will be discussed in Chapter 6.

It is possible to conduct a strategy planning exercise as a 'kick start', one-off project in order to raise the awareness of the potential business impact of IS and to, hopefully, get senior management commitment to implementing the results of the strategy planning exercise. The aim throughout is to demonstrate that progress will be *revolutionary*: making a move from doing things right to doing the right things. A 'good' strategy will always pull out the application areas that are really critical to the organisation and these can only be identified by an IS strategy exercise since a purely service-oriented IS function can never uncover the really key areas. The one-off strategy planning exercise is ideal for raising the perception of the pivotal role IS has for organisations but after that IS strategy planning *must* be embedded into business strategic planning to ensure that it is regularly and routinely part of business.

To a large extent the strategy planning process must establish appropriate levels of shared commitments since such a plan is intended to shape decisions on *future* IS issues not yet apparent. The process is not just to decide now on issues visible now; such a focus would more conventionally be called an operating plan.

**References and further reading**

Adriaans, W. (1993) Winning Support for Your Information Strategy, *Long Range Planning*, Vol 26 No 1 pp. 45–53.

Baker, B. (1995) The Role of Feedback in Assessing Information Systems Planning Effectiveness, *Journal of Strategic Information Systems*, Vol 4 No 1 pp. 61–80.

Brancheau, J.C. and Wetherbe, J.C. (1987) Key Issues in IS Management, *MIS Quarterly* Vol 11 No 1 March pp. 23–44.

Cashmore, C. and Lyall, R. (1991) *Business Information: Systems and Strategies*, Prentice-Hall.

Cole, P. How to Write an IT Strategy in Six Pages, *Computer Weekly*, 18 May, in Fidler, C. and Rogerson, S. (1996) *Strategic Management Support Systems*, Pitman Publishing.

Copley, J.D. (1989) Information Planning, *Software Management Magazine*, Mar pp. 14–16.

Cortada, J.W. (1980) *EDP Costs and Charges: Finance, Budgets and Cost Control in Data Processing*, Prentice-Hall.

Davis, G.B.and Olson M.H. (1985) *Management Information Systems: Conceptual Foundations, Structure and Development* (2nd edn), McGraw-Hill.

Doll, W.J. and Torkzadeh, G. (1987) The Relationship of MIS Steering Committees to Size of Firm and Formalization of MIS Planning, *Communications of the ACM*, Vol 30 No 11 Nov pp. 972–8.

Earl, M.J. (1989) *Management Strategies for Information Technology*, Prentice-Hall.

Fidler, C. and Rogerson, S. (1996) *Strategic Management Support Systems*, Pitman Publishing.

Fink, D. (1994) Information Systems Planning in a Volatile Environment, *Long Range Planning*, Vol 27 No 6 pp. 108–14.

Flynn, D.J. (1992) *Information Systems Requirements: Determination and Analysis*, McGraw-Hill.

Frenzell, C.W. (1992) *Management of Information Technology*, Boyd and Fraser.

Galliers, B. (1992) Implementing Strategic Information Systems Plans: Barriers and Opportunities, *University of Wales Review of Business and Economics*, Vol 8 pp. 7–14.

Harry, M. (1990) *Information and Management Systems*, Pitman Publishing.

King, W.R. (1988) How Effective is Your Information Systems Planning?, *Long Range Planning*, Vol 21 No 5 pp. 103–12.

Lederer, A.L. and Gardiner, V. (1992) The Process of Strategic Information Planning, *Journal of Strategic Information Systems*, Vol 1 No 2 Mar pp. 76–83.

Lederer, A.L. and Sethi, V. (1988) The Implementation of Strategic Information Systems Planning Methodologies, *MIS Quarterly*, Sept pp. 445–61.

Lederer, A.L. and Sethi, V. (1989) Pitfalls in Planning, *Datamation*, June p. 59.

McFarlan, E.W., McKenney, J.L. and Pyburn, P. (1983) The Information Archipelago – Plotting a Course, *Harvard Business Review*, Jan-Feb pp. 145–56.

Martin, E.W., Dehayes, D. ., Hoffer, J.A. and Perkins, W.C. (1991) *Managing Information Technology: What managers need to know*, Macmillan.

Mensching, J.R. and Adams, D.A. (1991) *Managing an Information System*, Prentice-Hall.

Niederman, F., Brancheau, J.C. and Wetherbe, J.C. (1991) Information Systems Management Issues for the 1990s, *MIS Quarterly*, Dec pp. 475–500.

O'Brien, B. (1992) *Demands and Decisions: Briefing on Issues in Information Technology Strategy*, Prentice-Hall.

Raghunathan, B. and Raghunathan, B.S. (1993) Does the Reporting Level of the Information Systems Executive Make a Difference?, *Journal of Strategic Information Systems*, Vol 2 No 1 Mar pp. 27–38.

Reynolds, G.W. (1995) *Information Systems for Managers* (3rd edn), West Publishing.

Silk, D.J. (1991) *Planning It: Creating an Information Management Strategy*, Butterworth-Heinemann.

Sinclair, S.W. (1986) The Three Domains of Information Systems Planning, *Journal of Information Systems Planning*, Spring Vol 3 pp. 8–16.

Smith, A. and Medley, D. (1987) *Information Resource Management*, South-Western.

Wysocki, R. and Young, J. (1990) *Information Systems: Management Principles in Action*, Wiley.

Ward, J. (1987) Integrating Information Systems into Business Strategies, *Long Range Planning*, Vol 20 No 3 pp. 19–29.

Ward, J., Griffiths, P. and Whitmore, P. (1990) *Strategic Planning for Information Systems*, Wiley.

# CHAPTER 5

# The information systems strategic planning 'Toolkit'

This lengthy chapter introduces a range of tools that might contribute to an IS planning toolkit. The chapter title should not be taken to imply that this is the only possible toolkit or that the dozen or so models covered here represent anything other than a sample. The particular sample was chosen to represent many of the most widely known and extensively used of the tools used to facilitate the strategic *planning* aspects of IS strategy formulation, primarily therefore what was discussed as strategic analysis and strategic choice in Chapter 1. Many of the tools described in this chapter are derived from those that were discussed in Chapter 2 with no *explicit* IS focus. Indeed familiarity with particular business strategy planning tools significantly influences the selection and usefulness of any specific IS strategy planning tools.

With such a lengthy chapter in which such an eclectic set of tools is included the choice of chapter structure is particularly complex. The intent in this chapter is to provide general reference material. It is therefore unhelpful to get bogged down in an unresolvable debate over which category to place the tool, model, technique or checklist into. The chapter includes, in Section 5.8 a road map in which particular tools are catalogued and cross-referenced in a variety of ways that should facilitate their selection for various purposes.

Discussion of the *selection* of tools is the focus of Chapter 6 in which various *frameworks* (pre-collected sets of tools) for developing an IS strategy are considered. If there are no commonly agreed principles for the *process* of formulating and communicating IS strategy there certainly are lots of tools and techniques available to 'support' this process. Please treat this chapter as the provider of reference descriptions, illustrations, general comments, and critiques as appropriate for the *components* of the frameworks that will be discussed in Chapter 6.

On a related point, please note that the use of the term toolkit in the chapter title does not indicate that this is any form of cookbook chapter. The tools covered are cooking *techniques* rather than recipes. Often cooks learn by starting with simple techniques that will be useful to them independent of a recipe, never mind a full menu! To follow that analogy, here are those basic cooking techniques, Chapter 6 considers recipes, the text in its entirety is considering menus.

## 5.1 ◆ REFERENCE TO INCLUDED TOOLS

This chapter discusses many tools; some of these tools have as their emphasis the identification of the SMIS (as defined in Chapter 3) whilst others focus upon comprehensive coverage of systems to deliver information requirements. Some tools offer only placement advice, others indicate preferred alternatives. Some models raise levels of awareness when used without quantification and yet when 'pinned down' with more details will offer positioning support.

With tools that overlap in emphasis and outputs there is, of course, no one agreed way of grouping them. Any scan of the strategic planning literature will show that descriptions of tools and techniques have appeared grouped under various headings, including:

- Those that follow a model of planning or decision making stages, eg analysis, design, etc
- Those that refer to the nature of their intention, eg frameworks for awareness, opportunity and positioning
- Those that identify their origin, eg business derivatives versus IS specific
- Those that refer to their perspective, eg environmental analysis versus internal auditing
- Those that reflect current problems, eg business demand modelling versus supply modelling.

There is no doubt that the use of non-arbitrary groupings can provide a valuable aid, though only if supported by a coherently argued rationale for that grouping, which is rarely the case. I could have rationalised these tools into groups around the notion of being efficiency, effectiveness or competitiveness targeted or, conversely, whether they were aimed at business alignment or business impacting. Or again, as Earl does, around whether they form part of an awareness, opportunity or positioning framework. However to serve as general reference material this chapter needs to be as non-prescriptive as possible. The next chapter discusses 'prescriptions', or rather the issue of co-ordinating these tools into a set that achieves an identification and documentation of an appropriate IS strategy for the given organisation. Hence at this stage it is fruitless to get bogged down in an unresolvable debate over which category to place the tool, model, technique or checklist into.

In the final section of this chapter, Section 5.8, there is a set of cross-referenced classifications of the tools discussed in the chapter. The chosen classification sets are included as they may assist in the selection of a particular technique for a particular purpose. In addition, the classes represent labels that are frequently encountered in the IS strategy literature. The ability to cross-reference techniques may be helpful when studying that literature. Of course the placing of a given technique into a given category set is often based on a judgement of the *main* use of the technique. Care should be taken when using this list to recognise that many techniques 'overlap' on purpose and have different ways in which they can be used.

## 5.2 ◆ CHECKLIST ACRONYMS

There are an enormous number of checklist acronyms available. Some merely intend to give convenient headings with which to prompt discussion, or structure ideas for communication. One example would be the PLEETS (Political, Legal, Economic, Environmental, Technical, Social) acronym. Such structuring checklists typically list those areas or issues to be included in the discussion, decision or risk analysis, etc and do not tend to include *within* themselves ways of making judgements. They intend to give a framework within which to question any number of things. What business are we in? What are our strengths? How do we perform in this environment? Is the target market expanding or contracting? What alternatives/choices do we have? What is the risk level? Is the timing right for this choice? Do we have the appropriate appraisal systems (and not just financial)? Are the people attitudes right? What will be the technical demands?

Of course the chosen checklist will draw attention towards or away from certain issues so the selection of the checklist itself is not unimportant. Other acronym checklists aim to force the forming of a *judgement*, though of course the process of allocating an issue to a specific category is a judgement of sorts. The most commonly encountered technique of this type is the SWOT (Strengths, Weaknesses, Opportunities, Threats) or TOWS (Threats, Opportunities, Weaknesses, Strengths) analysis.

### 5.2.1 ◆ SWOT

**S**trengths
**W**eaknesses
**O**pportunities
**T**hreats

The SWOT analysis is ubiquitous and forms a conventional, even essential tool in any strategic planning approach. SWOT has as its strength the fact that it is so ubiquitous and so is very familiar, its purpose and categories are well known. Additionally it considers both internal and external factors and, when well used, can effectively balance them both.

An assessment of opportunities and threats (opportunities in reverse) forms part of an environment scan whilst an assessment of strengths and weaknesses is part of the capability auditing of the organisation. SWOT analysis is extremely familiar to business or case analysts. It is virtually a conventional approach to the consideration of:

- What are our weak/strong products, divisions, attitudes, etc?
- Are there gaps/opportunities we can go for?
- Are there dangers/threats we need protection from?
- Are we strong in the right way to exploit the opportunity?

The point of performing the analysis is that no business should take on a high risk strategy, ie to exploit an opportunity, if they have a significant weakness in the area. For example, assessing the SW of an organisation means questioning:

- *Approach to IS.* Whether IS is seen as a necessary evil, a scarce resource or as a transferring aid and whether the organisation seeks to lead the field, follow the flock or float with the tide.

- *Use of IS.* The number of systems which are of poor quality or not easy to use and those which are batch rather than on-line. And the proportion of systems which are administrative or 'head office' in nature rather than assisting the delivery of products or services at the 'sharp end' (see primary and support activities delineated in Porter's value chain).

- *Delivery of IS.* The proportion of resources tied up in maintenance, the extent to which the current approach towards planning new systems is technology driven rather than information-need driven, the role of users and departments, the use of fourth generation tools and the use of modern system development techniques.

- *Data management.* The degree of redundancy and dis-aggregation of data, the use of DBMS and the approach to modelling and design of data.

- *Technical skills.* The technical support available, the growth in demand and the responsibilities for voice communication, office systems and performance monitoring.

It is important to consider the impact of a possible course of action upon customers/suppliers as well as competitors since a strategy can be selected in isolation but it cannot be implemented in isolation. A SWOT analysis is a reminder of the need for balance and an attempt to judge the options available. So having become aware of the potential effect of IS we can use SWOT techniques to weigh up the risks involved. Figure 5.1 illustrates the four types of risk exposure created by the combinations of external and internal factors and indicates the type of response that might be most appropriate to deal with each type of risk. We would expect the IS priorities to lie along a diagonal top-left to bottom-right since that line represents the best chances and the greatest dangers.

When both opportunities and strengths are present then the organisation is in a position to *attack* its competitors through the use of IS with a good prospect of success. Conversely when threats are faced where there are weak capabilities then the organisation must take steps to *protect* itself from its vulnerability to attacks from its competitors. When there are value adding opportunities for IS but the organisation

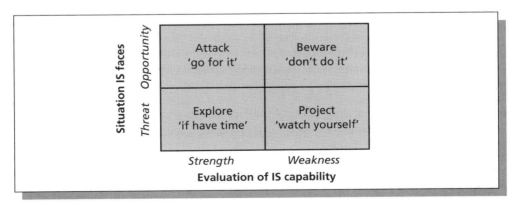

**Fig 5.1 ◆ Possible responses on basis of SWOT analysis**
(adapted from McLaughlin *et al.*)

finds itself with weak IS capabilities then they should *beware* of following these up since they are less assured of success than others in their sector with more adequate IS. Should the organisation find itself having strong IS resources alongside threatening situations then it should *explore* avenues to both maintain that quality against the opening up of opportunities and to identify overlooked potential.

These techniques are intended to focus attention upon issues and give little guidance on actions. There is a tendency when doing a SWOT analysis to be less than honest in the appraisals and to feel the need to cover up feared weaknesses by proclaiming perceived strengths. SWOT may offer rather better service at warning of the need for avoidance of some action and so the results may tend to the negative prediction in bias.

### 5.2.2 ◆ Sector analysis

This is essentially the checklist style approach but without snappy acronyms! The aim is, as with SWOT analysis, to make judgements in a structured way.

| | |
|---|---|
| Size ↓ | The current situation, in terms of a SWOT and competitive forces analysis. |
| Pressures ↓ | The external pressures on the industry in which the organisation operates. This could come from a change in the competitive forces (for example a new entrant) or from a change in the attitude of customers or society at large. |
| Trends ↓ | Identifying the trends is the element of creative business thinking since the organisation must predict what changes the pressures will induce in the business. For example, lower profit margins, more direct competition, lower demand for a traditional product, rejection of certain materials, etc. |
| IS Needs ↓ | What needs and opportunities for IS will arise in the new situation? Can IS respond, by differentiating the product, or by making the process more efficient? |
| IS Markets | Do the changes give the organisation a chance to sell information of special IS? |

In a sector analysis the organisation is asking:

- Where are we now?
- How is the world changing and what will be the new rules of the game?
- What is the way to win and where do we want to be?
- How can IS help our people?
- How can our IS help other people?

## 5.3 ◆ BUSINESS OPPORTUNITY

From the mid-1980s onwards any article or book on managing IS has been sprinkled with examples of the opportunities that result from the impact of IS on industries and businesses. As early as 1985 *Business Week* was drawing attention to the business or competitive impact of IS with their cute drawings of pushchair terminals and so on! Commonly quoted ones are:

- American Airlines and their Sabre Reservation System that was the first effective electronic reservation system in the US (the outcome of a vision of one data set per customer). SABRE gave them a market lead that they have never since lost. By 1988 American Airlines were making more money from SABRE than they were from flying aeroplanes. In 1990 their vice-president said that they got competitive edge from the creative use of information that the systems handle rather than the systems themselves (although the systems sold on to smaller operators to generate useful revenue).

- Thomson's Holidays' TOPS on-line viewdata-based booking system, where travel agents' use of this system generated major market share through technology supremacy, but at the same time, backed them – and the whole industry – into a technology cul-de-sac.

- Merrill Lynch's integrated banking service system, where its cash management account combined normally separate banking services into a single statement, and automatically moved spare funds to a high interest account. This was a totally new service that ignored the traditional view of banking being discrete from securities. It allowed Merrill Lynch to obtain $1 billion of assets in the first year alone and still provides them with more than half of the market.

- American Hospital Supply and their order entry distribution system that started when a manager gave one customer the hardware that allowed him to place last minute orders directly onto AHS's computer system. The system grew to link most customers; these customers do the order entry to the cost advantage of AHS but the customers gain greater control over their stock holdings to their advantage.

- General Tire and their telemarketing system initially conceived to provide sales support in order to free sales specialists from dealing with problems such as bill or delivery queries but then extended to include the management of marginally profitable accounts. This significantly lowered the cost of making a sale (the system's objective) but also unexpectedly increased sales.

There are far fewer quoted examples of failures, and without knowing the process that led to these often quoted successes it is hard to judge the *value* of the examples. However, anecdotes about such opportunities form the folklore of successful IS strategic planning by showing by example the business opportunities created by IS. But note that, for example, General Tire did it all to avoid unprofitable accounts and didn't expect it to increase sales so the awareness being raised is often only partial.

This folklore of examples forms the basis for a number of techniques for recognising past and future potential impacts in order to somehow respond to them. These techniques identify and classify strategic opportunities that IS presents, none of the techniques provides instruction on how to pursue the opportunity.

Those familiar examples have been joined more recently by examples of the business opportunity afforded by using the power of IS to rethink *radically* the nature of the organisation itself (see Chapter 8 for a discussion of Business Process Re-engineering and Chapter 9 for a discussion of the IS implications for the nature of work).

### 5.3.1 ◆ Opportunity categorising

There are several versions of essentially the same analysis technique. All aim to generalise classes that capture the essence of the actual or potential effect of IS. Using these categories supports the effective scanning for opportunities to use IS strategically since the categories can give the focus for the questioning done in the scan. This analysis serves, as suggested by Earl, as an awareness raising activity by making management far more conscious of past and currently exploited opportunities and also as part of establishing the organisation's position with respect to the business importance of IS.

Ward is one of the many writers who has taken examples of the *past* opportunities that IS has provided and from them generated a classification set for what he refers to as 'opportunity areas'. This set, in descending order of commonness of occurrence, is, he suggests:

(a) *Where the opportunity is to use technology-based systems to link the organisation to its customer/consumers and/or suppliers*

The most obvious example of this was AHS who provided customers with the hardware to enable them to place direct orders. Not all such opportunities, however, are in the area of order placing. For example the link could be through the ability to share information about product designs: JAL and other major airlines work with Boeing on the design of the new 777. These opportunities are by definition not solely under the organisation's own control.

(b) *Where the opportunity is to use technology-based systems to make more effective the integrative use of information in the organisation's value adding process*

General Tire's use of technology to reduce the cost of sales support is Ward's example since it highlights how all relevant information must be available to permit effective business dealings. It would be pointless, he suggests, for telemarketing to be used to sell to poor payers. In fact a better example might be to cite the many instances when IS/IT is used to relocate the information access point to the business dealing point, eg portable customer profile systems used by mobile sales staff. To actually exploit this opportunity is usually an organisational structural concern rather than a technological one since almost inevitable will be the need to restructure business groupings and redefine and reuse available skills (*see* Chapter 8 for a further exploration of IS used for business re-engineering).

(c) *Where the opportunity is for an organisation to develop, produce, market and deliver new or enhanced products or services based on information*

Here it is IS/IT that creates a product or market that could not have existed before. Merrill Lynch provides a rare example that actually resulted from a conscious strategic planning process. The opportunity to create a new market for an integrated consumer service was spotted and successfully pursued. Other examples include those companies that use extensive customer databases as the vehicle for providing customer profiling services. This opportunity area requires a good knowledge of current product provision (including that of competitors) coupled with sufficient appreciation of potential use to identify 'holes'.

(d) *Where the opportunity is to provide executive management with information to support the development and implementation of strategies*

This is the opportunity to provide systems appropriate to senior management, ie interactive access to consolidated internal and external business indicators, which is strategically important since it means that the process of developing and implementing business strategies can be more certain of success.

## 5.3.2 ◆ Impact categorising

There are rather more specific forms of awareness raising techniques which focus on the *impact* that IS can have upon business. One clear example of this is offered by Benjamin, Rockart, Scott Morton and Wyman (1983) as a system of categorising the impact IS has had or can have. They use the store of empirical evidence discussed earlier to derive a model which suggests that IS might impact in one of four ways as illustrated in Figure 5.2.

The approach to the competitive market place (external) and the approach to operations (internal) can both offer two types of strategic opportunity, either by significantly improving the traditional ways of operating or by making significant changes to the way of doing business. IT can be used for strategic purposes either in the competitive market place or in the internal operations. Uses of IS can focus upon improving traditional ways or upon creating new ways. Many examples make contributions to more than one category. Benjamin, Rockart, Scott Morton and Wyman suggest that this matrix can be used by an organisation to uncover the strategic opportunities presented by IS by asking itself two questions:

- Can IS be used to make a significant change in the way it does business and so gain a competitive advantage?
- Should it concentrate on using IS to improve its approach to the market place, or should it centre its efforts around internal improvements?

This grid is widely applicable and certainly does provide a vehicle for widening and yet sharpening the focus of management attention. Since there is both an internal and an external dimension this technique makes the assumption that the

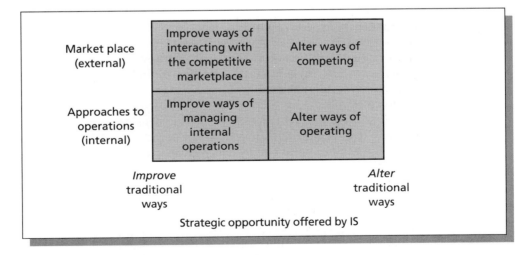

**Fig 5.2 ◆ Four potential business impacts of IS**
(adapted from Information Technology: A Strategic Opportunity by Benjamin *et al*, *Sloan Management Review*, 1984, by permission of publisher. Copyright 1984 by Sloan Management Review Association. All rights reserved)

uses of IS need not be directly related to customers to be strategic. Japanese industry has shown the West that good operating conditions can be strategically important. This is one of the few early models that explicitly suggests that internal operations can be a source of strategic gains, though it should be noted that the adoption of IS to make significant modification to current business practices may be painful and difficult (again, *see* Chapter 8 for more discussion of the difficulties of this business re-engineering).

A slightly different approach is to use the basic principle that management directs resources to achieve *results* to classify the observed examples by their generic impact; in Silk (1991) impact is referred to as benefit. The classes Silk uses are efficiency, effectiveness and competitive advantage. An efficiency impact is felt where IS has made savings on other resources. The organisation is doing the same job as it did before but IS allows it to be done in a less expensive way. This impact reduces costs. An effectiveness impact would occur when IS makes other resources more effective. IS allows the organisation to do a better job than the one it was doing before. This type of impact improves the Return on Assets (RoA) for those other resources. A strategic advantage (or edge) impact can be detected where IS has changed some aspect of what the business does, bettering the business. This results in growth, defined as an increase in revenue or throughput or profit or whatever is the relevant indicator for the given organisation. These generic impacts are illustrated in Figure 5.3.

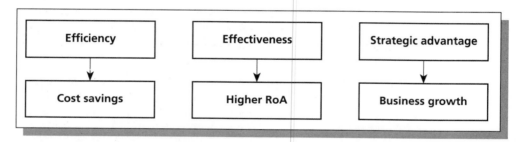

Fig 5.3 ◆ Generic impacts of IS/IT

This categorising system is similar in nature to Sinclair's (1986) 'three domains' and will obviously mean that the selection of tools should follow from the focus of the domain. A full, reasonably up-to-date, and clearly described set of example is also given by Silk.

Whether these different classification systems significantly differ from each other is largely irrelevant, their purpose is the same. The application of IT has led to a shift in the balance point between any given organisation and:

- Other direct competitors
- Non-direct competitors with potential substitute products
- Suppliers and/or customers.

This shift results from two distinct, but not mutually exclusive, categories of IS:

- Those systems that permanently change the way a particular industry operate; because of the IT impact/involvement in the product or service they redefine that business, not just relationships within it

- Those systems that affect, for a particular organisation, the relative power or ability to operate; they alter the competitive environment.

Through these techniques runs the wish to identify those instances where IS affects the very ability to compete with other players in the existing industry and where the opportunity is to change the very nature of that industry. The specific systems that have that potential are the strategic management information systems defined in Chapter 3 and, by definition, worthy of 'special' treatment

To be aware of past and current impacts of IS/IT is interesting, to analyse the categories they fall into can give a useful tool for clarifying chaos but the models are non-prescriptive. The problem is that whilst any generalised model based on the past strategic impacts of IS (such as Benjamin *et al's*) sounds useful it is difficult to make the step from the past stories into future plans. The opportunities described in those past stories are no longer strategic even if they ever were consciously chosen as such. They effectively evidence the importance of IS but is anybody doubtful of that, at least in these instances? What is needed is a greater certainty of the business potential for a given business. These models must be linked with additional tools to achieve that.

### 5.3.3 ◆ Strategic importance analysis

Derived from the BCG Matrix discussed in Chapter 2, and shown in Figure 2.16, is the Strategic Importance Matrix from McFarlan and McKenney (1983). That BCG Matrix classifies businesses, divisions or products according to presently held market share and the future growth potential of that market. Since outline strategies are recommended for each of the four possible positions the act of positioning is also the act of identifying the prescribed actions.

The IS-specific matrix offered by McFarlan and McKenney is illustrated in Figure 5.4 and separates businesses by virtue of the different degree to which the firm is functionally dependent upon IS/IT today or the degree to which IS/IT developments will create competitive edge. Similarly systems can also be positioned with

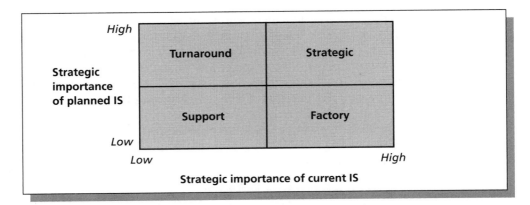

**Fig 5.4 ◆ Strategic importance matrix**
(adapted and reprinted by permission of *Harvard Business Review*. An exhibit from The Information Archipelago–Plotting a Course by McFarlan, McKenney and Pyburn, Jan–Feb 1982. Copyright © 1982 by the President and Fellows of Harvard College, all rights reserved)

respect to the importance they hold to the business under review. To what extent are the *existing* systems critical? To what extent will they be in the *future?*

Businesses in the *strategic* segment currently depend upon IS for their competitive position and expect to continue to do so. Businesses in the *turnaround,* or High Potential, segment predict that their competitive well being will depend upon IS in the future though that is not currently the case. Businesses in the *factory* segment will currently competitively depend upon IS but will not expect that importance to remain in the future. For businesses in the *support* segment, current IS is not competitively important, though IS may ease their operation, and they do not expect that to change in the future.

The strategic importance matrix can be used as described above to name the *type* of importance that IS collectively has for this business. By identifying the type of importance, advice on the style of management treatment of IS is given.

| *BCG segment* | *Strat. imp. segment* | *Outline advice* |
| --- | --- | --- |
| Star | Strategic | Invest in |
| Wildcat | Turnaround | Examine |
| Dog | Support | Divest |
| Cash Cow | Factory | Milk |

The outline advice, of course, needs to be fleshed out into specifics. For example, Support organisations are being advised to 'divest' which in IS terms probably becomes real as cost-driven outsourcing contracts (discussed in Chapter 12), as standardised systems services and components (also discussed in Chapter 12) and other mechanisms that reduce the organisational resources, energy, time, attention, emotion, creativity and so on as well as financial expenditure on IS.

In addition to being used to position and classify the organisation this matrix can be used to distinguish specific aspects of the IS portfolio of activities. For particular areas of activity their current strategic importance can be judged as can the potential strategic importance in the future.

In other words it can be said that strategically important *systems* are those upon which the organisation depends now and will do in the future. Likewise turnaround systems are those of low current business importance but predicted to be critical in the future. Factory systems are those of high current value but low predicted value. And finally, support systems are of low business importance now and are expected to remain so. In all cases the type of importance is measured and described in business terms and not in terms of technological complexity or 'newness'. This makes it explicit that it is business *value* and not any technical issue which must determine IS resource allocations and gives this model its greatest strength.

Just as the BCG matrix had movement implicit in it so does this matrix. For example, it is possible that a particular class of systems will emerge with much uncertainty as turnaround ones (or high potential), will develop into strategic systems, decline into factory systems and finally end as support ones. The history of payroll systems gives an example of this. Almost no businesses would regard their payroll system as having any great business importance and yet once they were so innovative that they gave significant advantage to those organisations that used them.

It is worth noting that the application of this particular technique has evolved to include two different forms of use with the concept of *changes* over time being a little different for each. One use, that closest to that proposed by McFarlan and McKenney (1983), is that it is a device to place an organisation (or coherent business unit). The segment names label the type of importance that IS holds for that business. The concept of time here is that it is unlikely that IS will continue to hold the same type of importance to the same organisation. Therefore, over time, organisations move into *different* segments. In this form of application there is no particular sense of the probable direction or trend of that movement.

A second type of use considers the portfolio of IS activities and names the type of importance of each area of this activity. Ward and Griffiths (1996) illustrate one instance of this type of use and refer to such IS activities as IS *applications*. Again the segment names label the type of importance, in this instance the importance that a particular area of IS has for the business. The concept of time with this type of application is again that it is unlikely that a given area of activity will always have the same type of importance. However what is very different with this form of use of the technique is that by drawing on the product portfolio work of the BCG Matrix some judgements of probable movement can be made. It is likely that the direction will be Strategic → Factory → Support with movement from Turnaround to any other segment possible. This movement is not inevitable and actions can potentially be taken to move an area of IS activity into a particular segment and the likelihood and potential for doing just that will be one issue to be explored by use of this matrix.

This model provides a valuable tool in ensuring that IS strategies reflect *real* business value. Knowing where an organisation or system sits on this matrix gives an indicator of an appropriate IS strategy. For convenience this 'appropriate strategy' is conventionally defined in the language of Parsons' generic IS Strategies, which are defined and discussed in Section 5.5.3. Figure 5.5 shows the probable relationship between the importance segment and the generic strategy. The numbers used represent 'best fit', 'second best', etc.

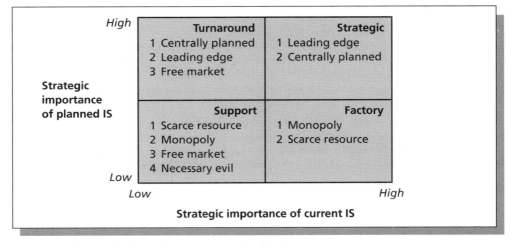

**Fig 5.5 ◆ Relationship between strategic importance grid and generic IS strategies**
(adapted from Integrating Information Systems into Business Strategies by Ward, *Long Range Planning*, Vol 20 No 3, pp. 19–29, © 1987, with kind permission from Elsevier Science Ltd)

*Strategic*      Here we would predict that a leading edge or centrally planned strategy would give the best match due to the high correlation between the success of the business and success at *exploiting* IS.

*Factory*      A monopolistic approach would probably be the best fit since it will make IS reliable and readily available. To treat IS as a scarce resource could be used to avoid building up any excess capacity but it would need to be used with caution to avoid stagnating the business' use of IS. There is no return on the expense and effort of a leading edge or centrally planned strategy since IS will not create any competitive advantage. The free market strategy is not appropriate in this instance since users would not wish to bear that amount of responsibility.

*Support*      Whilst most of the six generic strategies could work in this segment, with the exception of the organisationally 'expensive' leading edge and centrally planned strategies, the chosen one should concentrate upon obtaining a high return on investment made and upon short-term projects, both features typically associated with a scarce resource strategy. The monopoly approach can lead to excess capacity and the resultant improved performance cannot be business justified. Similarly the free market approach may demand more user involvement and effort than the business benefits justify, with the additional disadvantage that it may lead to a duplication of effort and the loss of potential economies of scale. If the free market strategy is selected then it will need to be used with caution and with extra central controls in place.

*Turnaround*      Since this segment is characterised by unpredictability, the indicated strategies are centrally planned, leading edge or free market. Circumstances will favour a centrally planned strategy if the resources required for a leading edge strategy are not available, or it is not *wanted* to make them available. A free market strategy may be an appropriate direction if the user community is sophisticated and equipped to take this degree of responsibility. If not, then again a centrally planned approach is indicated but an opportunity to devolve the ability to manage IS strategically will be lost.

Again, this matrix (illustrated in Figure 5.5) can be used as a normative model, that is it suggests what is expected to be the case, and implies the need to consider if any reasons exist for deviance from the expected norm. There are aspects of other tools in this one: there are remnants of life cycle ideas (*see* Section 5.6.3) in that there is some implication of a natural progression, and, whilst using different terms, the spirit of the BCG (*see* Section 2.2.3) is captured. The least successful mapping is within the support/dog segment; the IS intention is not, as it would be in strategic management terms, to divest the product, division or whatever, but to keep the resource and attention mix very lean. In use, this model links effectively to a model such as the illustrated generic IS strategies but would also need to be linked to some method of actually judging the degree of IS/business importance, for instance using impact analysis techniques.

This grid was originally proposed in order to determine the required level of senior management attention in managing corporate IS, but has been successfully used to identify strategic IS *applications*. The biggest problem with this model is that it leaves the strategic value of IS as something to be assessed after the fact. Additionally, it cannot model the situation when the organisation is aware of the strategic business importance but has no current or planned applications in that segment. One way of overcoming this weakness is to use a technique such as CSF analysis (*see* Section 5.7.1) to determine just what areas of IS activity are *needed* even if they are not actually in existence or even planned. This allows the matrix to be used to identify development resource allocations on the basis of business importance. This matrix is however very good at giving a snapshot of the status and role of IS now and in the near future and makes this role explicit, clearly a vital part of strategy planning. Ward and Griffiths (1996) give an extended discussion of the use of this matrix to plan application management specifics.

### 5.3.4 ◆ Benefit level matrix

There is a similar but far more detailed version of the strategic importance grid, known as the benefit level matrix. This is a nine rather than four segment matrix which charts *who* the effect is on as well as the nature of the importance. This matrix, like the previous one, captures the dynamic nature of IS and the essentially ephemeral nature of competitive advantage. This model uses the same concepts as the competitive impacts analysis in that it differentiates between efficiency, effectiveness, and competitive edge effects. Figure 5.6 shows the matrix and builds upon the same type of benefits first illustrated in Figure 5.3. This model plots the *evolution* of systems by differing business benefits and organisational impacts. To illustrate it with an example adapted from Silk (1991):

An order entry transaction processing system (TPS) is created in a mainframe environment to reduce staff demands. The effect is to reduce costs so the benefit is one of efficiency and the impact is felt at the operational level. After some time an add-on to this system is created that uses the stored data to produce sales summaries for management and creates exception reports. For the purposes of this example this management information system (MIS) is considered as a separate

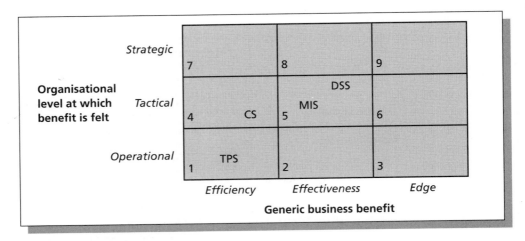

**Fig 5.6 ◆ Simple benefit level matrix**
(reproduced with the permission of Butterworth-Heinemann from *Planning IT: Creating an Information Management Strategy* (1991) by D.J. Silk)

entity but, of course, a real instance would nowadays integrate such functions. This supports better decision making to maximise the use of assets and so the benefit is one of effectiveness and since middle management are concerned with these summaries the impact is felt at the tactical level.

This system is further enhanced to include a decision support system (DSS) which can model several possible sales scenarios and is linked to production planning and inventory management to support yet more effective management. Effectiveness benefit felt at the tactical level as before, but more of it! When the system is still further enhanced and is optimised to understand the way that the sales scenarios influence production planning and inventory management then routine decisions are actually taken by the system and communicated to those who can initiate the raising or lowering of production/inventory levels. This new version is called, for want of a better term, a control system (CS). The effect of this system has fallen back to one of efficiency since there is now a lowered requirement for human management intervention and hence costs are saved. Who (or what) ever takes the decision that production/inventory levels should rise or fall, the impact is felt at the tactical level.

The final stage of this system's life is that it is fully integrated with the other business systems. This mega-system now actually triggers the alteration to production/inventory levels. In other words it efficiently and completely processes the transaction. The benefit felt is still one of efficiency since further cost savings are made but the business activity has become a predictable, routine one that means that the benefit is felt at the operational level. Another twist to the meaning of a system life cycle!

The more fully completed benefit level matrix shown in Figure 5.7 illustrates how office automation (OA), in most organisations, typically shifts in importance and focus. In a similar way, a decision support system (DSS) makes the transition into a strategic management information system (SMIS), or occasionally into expert systems, intelligent knowledge based systems (IKBS). And finally, the initial business impact of electronic data interchanges (EDI), which frequently occur as a spin-off from improvements in communication technologies, is followed by the 'routinisation' of that impact.

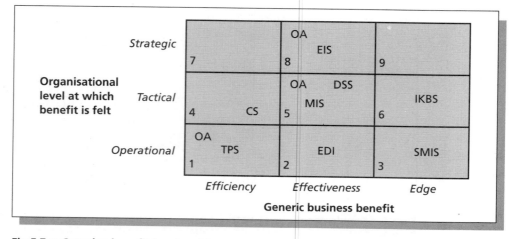

Fig 5.7 ◆ Complex benefit level matrix

The charted systems also illustrate the lack of impacts at a strategic level. Office Automation (OA) and executive information systems (EIS) have had some impact but it is likely that the next era will deliver systems that deliver efficiency and competitive edge benefits at a strategic level.

## 5.4 ◆ COMPETITIVE POSITION

A number of techniques exist that support the analysis and assessment of the organisation's competitive position from an IS perspective. This set of tools is dominated by the work of Michael Porter on the nature, structure, and responses to, competition (*see* Chapter 2).

### 5.4.1 ◆ Industry analysis

This is the analysis of the list of industry impacts, as described in Section 5.3, but used with an altered emphasis. Instead of asking 'how *has* IS/IT affected . . .?', the organisation now poses the question 'how *can* IS/IT affect?' This technique is about analysing the *future* IS opportunities rather than the *past* effect, or *current* situation (*see* Chapter 2 for fuller coverage of general business competitive strategy analysis and Chapter 8 for some discussion of the altered nature of organisations).

Gregory Parsons (1983) was one of the first writers to suggest that the strategic importance of IS could be assessed within the frameworks defined by Porter's work on the nature of competition. Parsons felt that importance analysis could be done by looking at how IS/IT could contribute to the competitive opportunities surrounding:

- *Products and services*: Their nature, production life cycle and speed of distribution
- *Markets*: Their overall demand, degree of segmentation, and geographic distribution possibilities
- *Economies of production*: The relevant range of economics of scale, the necessary flexibility versus standardisation trade-offs and the value adding stream.

To some extent this technique is another checklist one, however it draws upon a stronger conceptual basis for both the categories and how to judge the situation under each heading. This conceptual foundation was explained in Chapter 2 and is expanded into the IS context in the following two sections.

### 5.4.2 ◆ Five forces model

This model, developed by Porter and Millar (1985), operates at the level of an individual organisation rather than at the industry level, as in Section 5.4.1. Porter's competitive forces model, introduced in Chapter 2, can be used to assess whether IS can influence the relative power of the five forces, those forces that affect an organisation's overall profitability. This model is applied in a two-stage process: first to assess the most significant of the five forces and secondly to question what IS opportunities relate to those significant forces, including what opportunities exist to alter the *relative* power of the forces. A 'good' business, or IS, strategy would enable the organisation to erect barriers against potential new entrants, change the balance of power in supplier relationships in favour of the firm, increase switching costs for customers and change the basis of competition among rivals in favour of the organisation.

This model is similar to the strategic opportunities tools of Section 5.3, and it could have been included there since, if IS/IT affects the most significant force, the strategic one, then that example of IS is a strategic one. Similarly if IS affects the relative power then that change, and hence the relevant IS, is *strategic*.

The classic five-forces model of industry competitiveness provides a multipurpose model which can be used to assess, for any given industry or organisation, three things:

- The current situation
- The opportunities
- The threats

Since these forces determine profitability, by defining the elements that create the degree of return on investment, they provide a way of structuring general questions that can be asked about the role IS does/can play, for example as shown in Figure 5.8.

To a wholesale clothing manufacturer, overseas competitors and their powerful single customer will be the major external factors. The potential threats from cloth suppliers, possible new entrants onto the UK scene and from substitutes, if any, will be of lesser significance. For a retail bank the major external factors will be the threat of new entrants, other financial institutions, made possible by de-regulation and the bargaining power of customers. Depending upon the bank's market position direct competitors may be a significant force. For the police force there will be no industry competitors as such but there is now a significant threat from new

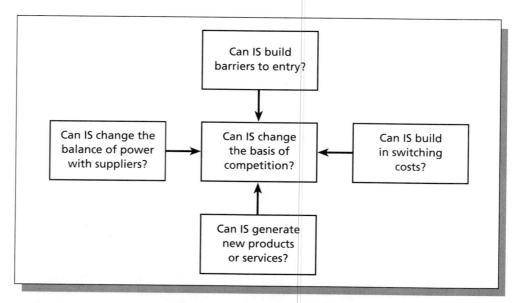

**Fig 5.8 ◆ Porter's Five Forces Model and IS opportunities**
(adapted with the permission of The Free Press, a division of Simon & Schuster from *Competitive Strategy: Techniques for Analysing Industries and Competitors* by Michael E. Porter. Copyright © 1980 by The Free Press)

entrants and substitute products in the security services field and deep concern about suppliers of resources and customers.

Once the relative power of these five forces has been assessed, or in order to change that relative power, it is possible to analyse the opportunities to use IS.

*Buyers*　　IS can be used to reduce the bargaining power of buyers by increasing the switching costs by making it more expensive for a buyer to go to another supplier. Additionally, IS can be used to categorise and differentiate buyer groups so that it is possible to reduce, or increase, costs of supply to certain groups.

*Suppliers*　　IS automation can reduce the power of suppliers, perhaps CAD/robotics could reduce the need for human labour. Alternatively, IS can identify potentially new products, etc.

*New entrants*　　Naturally when an industry is attractive, others seek to move in. IS can be used to defend a market position or to penetrate the barriers others have erected around an attractive industry.

*Substitutes*　　The determinants of the substitution threat are relative price performance, switching costs, and the inclination of buyers to use substitutes. When suppliers have alienated their customers they increase the readiness of those customers to use an alternative product whenever it becomes available. If the price performance balance of products shifts dramatically then that will increase the threat of a substitute being used, a perfect example being when word processors all but eradicated the market for typewriters.

*Rivalry*　　The intensity of rivalry between competitors is usually greater in mature or declining industries. IS determinants are industry growth, fixed assets/value-added, intermittent over-capacity, etc. It is possible to use IS to support *collaborative* efforts to lower costs.

So, at the level of a *business*, the strategic potential for IS can be classified by the five forces:

| | |
|---|---|
| *Buyers* | Switching costs |
| | Buyer selection |
| *Suppliers* | Avoid switching costs |
| | Backward integration |
| *New entrants* | Entry barriers |
| | Entry deterrents |
| *Substitution* | Relative price-performance |
| | Product features |
| *Rivalry* | New basis of competition |
| | Shared IT |

We should note that these things are, of course, what any business is about. We are using this model to assess whether and where IS can contribute.

### 5.4.3 ◆ Generic business strategies

Based upon the five forces model is Porter's classification of the three generic business strategies possible to respond to these forces. An understanding of the business strategy gives pointers to the strategic opportunities for using IS in support of that strategy. The organisation can question how IS can help to advance the chosen strategy, ie to permit lower costs or to differentiate products and services or, very rarely, both. This section has many similarities with Wiseman's work on strategic thrusts covered in Section 5.4.4.

These three corporate responses were discussed in Chapter 2 but they are mentioned again here since they are relevant as a way of focusing attention on what *matters* to a given organisation. Strategies give a sense of direction, and *generic* strategies encapsulate those directions and Porter's generic strategies give a convenient and extremely well known way of defining those directions. Expensive PR tracking systems are of little business importance to overall cost leadership organisations. This list may give the most useful and straightforward way of assessing business importance of current systems in order to place the organisation onto the Strategic Importance Grid shown in Figure 5.4. In this model Porter concentrates upon how the competitive environment affects the organisation and how the competitive strategies are the means by which that organisation alters the relative power of the forces, in its favour, or in its defence. Use of the model will show where chance can give good returns on effort and investment and highlight trends which pose significant opportunities or threats. At the strategy level, there are the following opportunity areas:

*Overall cost leadership*    Where the objective is to become the low-cost producer in all market segments, and therefore where IS seeks to:

- Reduce the overall costs directly
- Enhance the ability to reduce costs through other functions

*Overall differentiation*    Where the objective is to distinguish the organisation's products and services from others in all market segments, and therefore where IS seeks to:

- Add unique features to product/services directly
- Enhance the ability to differentiate the product/services through other functions

*Focus/niche*    Where the objective is to concentrate upon a particular market segment and then either differentiate or have cost leadership in that segment, and therefore where IS seeks to:

- Identify and create market niches directly
- Enhance the ability to create market niches through other functions.

Examples of IS support to a business strategy might include (and more are presented in Figures 5.9a and 5.9b):

- A tractor producer has used IS to help achieve the position of low-cost producer. They have developed a spare parts stock management system that allows similar parts to be identified rather than made or purchased, which has allowed them to save £9 million in two years.

- On a smaller scale is the independent costing quantity surveyor who uses project management software to provide 'standard' costing shells in order to cost building work more quickly and accurately. This low cost to produce costs is strategically necessary since if the building contractor does not get the contract the quantity surveyor receives no fee.

- Owens-Corning have used IS to support their attempts to differentiate themselves; they compute energy ratings for potential house designs as a free service for builders when they take Owen-Corning insulation products. ICI does something similar with specialist chemicals. Plumb Centre and many other DIY materials providers offer free kitchen design services that also generate automatic cost and availability schedules.

- Sears, Roebuck & Co, along with many other retailers, use IS to identify niche markets. For instance, they record purchase dates in order to send out regular maintenance reminders to past customers.

Chapter 8 provides a discussion of the benefits of using a business strategy aligned with IS strategy.

The highest level at which the concept of a generic business strategy can be meaningfully applied is at what is defined as 'the business'. It is by no means always clear nowadays what is meant by this. In an era of shifting corporate groups and increasing business autonomy many elements of the corporate whole may be following different business strategies. And so, at the point at which the organisation can say 'all of this follows the *same* strategy', they have defined one sub-group of the business; sorting out that definition can in itself be very worthwhile since it indicates much about what should be treated as a coherent and possibly autonomous grouping.

| Low-cost strategy IS application | Business area | Differentiation strategy IS application |
|---|---|---|
| Process control systems | Manufacturing | Total Quality Management systems |
| Stock planning and control systems | | Progress tracking systems |
| Project control systems | R&D | Public research data access systems |
| CAD systems | | Dispersed research communication systems and E-mail |
| Sales call prioritising systems | Sales | Easy order-entry and order-query systems |
| Advertising and promotions tracking systems | | Total customer care systems Pricing systems |
| Planning and budgeting systems | Finance | Business integration office automation systems |
| Cost control systems | | |

**Fig 5.9a ◆ IS support to low-cost or differentiation strategies**

| Areas of strategic IS potential to support a low-cost strategy would include: | The potential for a differentiation strategy might be established by asking how can IS help: | The strategic potential of IS to a niche/focus strategy may perhaps come from: |
|---|---|---|
| • Order handling and sales accounting<br>• Labour recording, incentive payments and control<br>• Cost recording, analysis and allocation | • Find out more about customer requirements<br>• Monitor customer perception of service<br>• Provide faster delivery on orders<br>• Enable market intelligence to be available to R&D staff<br>• Get customers through to the best source to answer a query<br>• Improve quality control on key components<br>• Integrate the management decision making and planning process<br>• Provide individuals with pertinent information from which ideas can be developed | • Identifying the target market<br>• Developing a unique base of information about the selected market and its needs<br>• Establishing a specialist process via systems to produce a clear cost advantage vis-à-vis general market servers<br>• Linking the organisation via systems into the business of the customers to increase potential switching costs and establish potential barriers to re-entry from general market sources<br>• Additionally, IS can enhance the secondary strategy used within the selected market segment |

**Fig 5.9b ◆ Possible IS support to business strategies**

Porter's notion of a generic business strategy is perhaps the most widely used planning technique and the popularity of it makes it an extremely convenient and useful tool since familiarity breeds skill in the appliers and comfort in the appliees! Porter's model of competitive responses to the five competitive forces is compared in Bergeron *et al*'s work with Wiseman's strategic thrusts, with the conclusion being that Wiseman's work is more outwardly oriented. Both models are impact planning techniques, that is they have a competitive position perspective and intend to *affect* the business rather than merely *reflect* it. So the goals for IS are not merely to translate business goals into an IS context, as they would be for the aligning techniques, but to alter them. Alignment planning techniques such as Business Systems Planing (BSP) and Information Engineering (IE) may lead only to a moderate amount of satisfaction since they are, by definition, reactive, reflective and delayed.

## 5.4.4 ◆ Strategic thrusts

As discussed in Chapter 2 Rackoff, Wiseman and Ullrich (1985) expanded on Porter's work on competitive strategies to offer a more comprehensive model of industry competition. That fuller model (the Strategic Option Generator) identifies five things that an organisation can do and three targets that those things can be applied to. The resultant grid, discussed in Chapter 2 and repeated in Figure 5.10, can be filled in from an IS perspective.

| Strategic thrust | Strategic target | | |
|---|---|---|---|
| | Supplier | Customer | Competitor |
| Differentiation | | ✓ | |
| Low cost | | | |
| Innovation | | ✓ | |
| Growth | | | |
| Alliance | | | |

**Fig 5.10 ◆ Strategic option generator**

This option grid can be 'filled in' by asking a number of questions, these include:

- What is our strategic target?
  Suppliers  Customers  Competitors
- What strategic thrust can be used against the target?
  Differentiation  Cost  Innovation  Growth  Alliance
- What strategic mode can be used?
  Offensive  Defensive
- What direction of thrust can be used?
  Usage  Provision
- What IS skills can we use?
  Processing  Storage  Transmission

The grid facilitates the process of making strategic choices (*see* Chapter 1) and this can serve two purposes in the IS strategy arena. Firstly the role that IS can take in *supporting* the chosen strategic thrusts can be identified. Those areas of IS activity that are acting in such a strategic support role are clearly of competitive importance. Secondly the opportunity that IS offers to *shape* the organisation's strategy by shaping the strategic thrusts can be identified. Again areas of IS activity that play a shaping role can therefore be classed as having high competitive importance and treated accordingly. In this second instance it may be that it is IS capability in aggregate that enables the shaping and not any specific area of IS activity.

Therefore the strategic option generator can act as both an aligning technique, 'what is our approach, how can IS help it?' and an impacting technique, 'what can/should be our approach, how can IS change it?' These two alternatives are not mutually exclusive.

### 5.4.5 ◆ Strategy set transformation

King (1978) suggests that if the business strategy is viewed as an information set of managerial variables, such as a mission, objectives, strategies, willingness to accept change, important constraints, etc, then strategic IS planning is the process of turning this business organisational set into the IS strategy set comprising the IS objectives, constraints and strategies. Obviously this technique must start by sorting out the business strategy set. This may or may not already be documented by the organisation; increasingly it is, but, if not, then the first strategy of this technique is to create it. King suggests the organisation go about this by identifying major stakeholders, claimant groups, identifying goals for each group and then identifying purposes and strategy for each group. The strategy set must be validated by getting comments and eventual approval from senior management. This then is the business strategy set that can now be 'transformed'. To do this each element of the strategy set is taken and an IS equivalent identified. These are then collected as the IS strategy set. This shapes the overall infrastructure architecture and the business strategy and, for each, produces an equivalent IS strategy; for example, a margin analysis tool is an MIS resulting from the corporate objective of improved profits via more high margin products.

King's article gives a table which illustrates how the organisational and IS strategy sets relate; this shows clearly the translating rather than improving emphasis of the technique and is shown in Figure 5.11.

*System objectives*    These define the purpose that IS is to serve, for example: in activity terms, 'to permit the payment of 98 per cent of invoices by the due date'; in information and communication terms, 'to collect and process all routing and cost information and provide it in a timely fashion to the dispatcher'; or in decision oriented terms, 'to permit the determination of the best routing no more than one hour after the tentative routing choice has been implemented'.

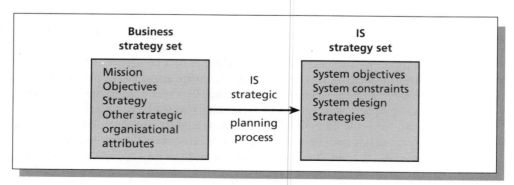

**Fig 5.11 ◆ Strategy set transformation**

| | |
|---|---|
| *System constraints* | These are external as well as internal, for example they could be the reporting requirements of government and industry bodies, the need to interface to other systems, the obvious budget constraints or the more subtle one of skill shortages. |
| *System design strategies* | These can vary, for example the parsimonious 'the systems should be designed so that the user is provided with the minimum amount of relevant information which is necessary to achieve his managerial objective'; or relate to the intended nature of the system, 'the system should operate primarily in an exception reporting mode in accomplishing its credit monitoring objective'. |

Strategy set transformation can only be as good as the accuracy of the corporate strategy set and is really only about defining an IS framework. It has long-range strategic horizons and is well aligned to business, obviously since it purports to be a *translation* of it. However, translations are often flawed (read the manual attached to any electronic gadget for a direct translation from the Taiwanese) and always subjective. To obtain a successful IS strategy by using this technique it is necessary to avoid literal translations in favour of capturing the 'spirit' of the strategic set. This capturing of the essence can be very difficult to do and therefore strategy set transformation requires a great deal of skill in use.

However, strategy set transformation is an important technique since it concentrates on those opportunities that exactly *deliver* a business objective, and hence can lead to IS strategies that are more certain of value. Unfortunately this narrowness also means that it does not exploit the potential for IS to *change* what is desired by the business, hence it is explicitly an aligning technique, indeed the archetypal one, and not an impacting or re-engineering technique. It also forms the base work for IBM's Business Systems Planning and enterprise-wide information management techniques. Both King's work and BSP assume that IS will fulfil its appropriate role if business strategies are used as the start point and continuing foundation for developing the IS strategy.

### 5.4.6 ◆ Business modelling

The issue of *business* scenario modelling was discussed in Chapter 2 as a technique of business analysis. That discussion noted that the perceived technical complexity associated with it meant that scenario modelling was not a widely used strategy tool. However, it has been realised that models do not have to be technically complicated to be *useful* and software has become more widely available to support the process of their development. Those facts plus a recent drive to enable flexibility in strategy planning and to move away from inappropriately rigid and overly detailed forecasting have accounted for the return to popularity of business modelling. Reflecting the need to produce adaptive strategies is the recognition that the use of single or multiple business models facilitate a fast response to unpredictable but *not* unimaginable changes. In the IS strategy development sense such business models may be used in one or both of two overlapping and inter-related ways:

- maintenance of a single model of the business area of concern and its processes as a more or less direct driver of IS activities

- development of scenario models that identify key issues in multiple possible futures so that the IS role, impact or opportunities in each future can be considered

The first of these two draws upon the increasing availability of simple, fast and graphical process modelling tools. These tools allow, and indeed force, business *needs* to be the driver of IS activities, either by being a communication device to provide a chain of argument or, even more directly, through a chain of automated tools to the applications themselves. Scott (1996) discusses examples of such uses of business modelling whilst Hugo (1996) describes instances of software that can be used in just such a manner. Adriaans (1993) indicates that production of a business model is a fundamental step in the process of gaining support for the IS strategy. The demonstrable connection between the model of the business process and the IS activities gives the business argument. Clearly, when used in this way, modelling is an explicitly aligning technique and is frequently associated with ensuring that IS follows any business process alteration initiatives. Of course, such initiatives almost *inevitably* produce a business model which embodies the various value choices that have been made; it is sensible to then use that model to ensure that those value judgements are reflected into IS choices.

The second use of business modelling as an IS strategy tool is in a *scenario* modelling sense that mirrors the typical uses of scenarios as discussed in Chapter 2. In other words, by using models of alternative futures within the process of formulating an IS strategy will force the inclusion of adaptability to various possibilities. The IS resource allocation decisions (the IS strategy) will encompass the 'breakpoints' and branches identified from the scenarios. To be useful in such a way, the scenarios modelled will need to include aspects of possible technological futures in addition to aspects of possible social, political, competitive, legal, cultural, organisational, etc, etc changes. By *building* in an awareness that many different futures are possible it is hoped that the pattern of IS resource decisions will be such that the *actual* future is one which the organisation's IS is equipped for.

## 5.5 ◆ INTERNAL POSITION

There are a number of IS strategy planning techniques that model or assess aspects of the internal operations of the organisation, including its IS management process. Of course, many other techniques from other sections could have been placed under this heading, for instance the Stages of Growth model discussed in Section 5.6.1 or the Strategic Importance Matrix discussed in Section 5.3.3. Please see Section 5.8 for a cross-reference of possible categorising of the IS strategy tools this chapter discusses.

### 5.5.1 ◆ Generic IS strategies

Just as Porter's analysis leads to the identification of four possible business competitive postures so Gregory Parsons (1983) suggested that all possible IS strategies, or IS postures, can be summarised on a six member classification list. Like business strategies, these IS strategies may be deliberate or emergent and so this classification system can be used to name a chosen strategy or to conveniently classify the set of *observed* activities. The essence of each of the six postures is described below. Naturally the *precise* nature of each for a particular organisation will differ (just as is the case with Porter's work on Generic Business Strategies).

The essential decision making logic of this tool (and many others included in this chapter) is explored and discussed in O'Brien (1995) who points out that each of the six instances focuses upon only one or two dimensions of the IS strategy. He does point out that even untangling the specific issues is of some value, perhaps another way of pointing out that the process of fleshing out for the particular circumstance is the vital activity. However describing or prescribing as central to the future IS strategy even one or two IS dimensions is of real value.

## Centrally planned

If this strategy is adopted, it is most unlikely to be an *emergent* strategy, because management believe that it facilitates uncovering the whole picture and that this larger, overall, view makes for better decisions. In order to make these 'better' decisions, it requires a significant degree of involvement and knowledge on the part of senior management. It is not possible to follow this strategy unless the strategic significance of IS is well understood and fully acknowledged. Because of this it also requires that the planning cycles of business and IS are closely integrated, indeed IS strategy planning should be embedded within business strategy planning. Further, this management treatment of IS places its primary emphasis upon the strategy planning processes, using them as the path towards business value from IS.

The resultant role of the IS function is one of service provider, closely linked to the user community in order to deliver the business demands. The complementary user role is of an opportunity spotter to identify the appropriate demand to make upon the IS function to ensure the full exploration of IS potential throughout the business.

NOTE: Centrally planned does *not* equal centrally controlled. It is a very common misunderstanding to label centralised IS as being centrally planned. The logic of this approach is of strategic direction understanding and co-ordination rather than on control. Where control *is* the primary emphasis then it is likely to be a monopoly posture that is being described.

## Leading edge

This strategy is adopted because of a belief that innovative technology use can create business gains and therefore the highly risky investment can generate huge payback. In order to be able to take these risks the organisation must have the ability and willingness to commit large amounts of money and other resources and to have very innovative IS management who can draw upon strong, varied and flexible technical skills.

The resultant role of the IS function is one of an experimenter and promoter to push forward the boundaries of technical capabilities throughout the organisation. Much technology environment scanning must go on along with a willingness to support major in-house development initiatives. The complementary user role is of a willing user of new advances in order to assess their current and future business potential.

There is a tendency for this technology-led strategy to result from distorted internal power relationships rather than business motivated choices or for it to result from a 'crisis cult' of the type discussed in Chapter 7. Organisations that focus upon the physical, so usually technological, aspects of the famous examples of competitive gain through IS may believe they must be innovative only in their technology and adopt this strategy as a result of that belief. A more successful instance of this strategy will place as much emphasis upon the organisational issues of education and innovation as on the more directly technological issues of IS.

## Free market

This strategy is adopted out of a belief that the 'market' makes the best decisions and since users are responsible for business results they are the most equipped to make these best decisions. Hence there can be no strongly held need for integration. In order to take up this responsibility this strategy requires knowledgeable users who are able to assess the relative merit of wide-ranging options. To be able to do so there must be an organisational willingness to accept a degree of duplication of effort in return for devolved responsibility. This IS function must be financially accountable in order to 'compete' and the organisation cannot exert tight financial controls over total IS budgets.

The resultant role of the IS function is of a competitive business unit, quite probably a profit centre. It must be prepared to achieve a return on its resources and use its understanding of the organisation to leverage against 'outside' competition. The complementary user role is one of service negotiation since they must identify and acquire IS services and manage that choice, acquisition and contract process.

This has been an enormously popular strategy, particularly explicit within government bodies. The removal of technical barriers to integration pushed it forward in favour along with the 'fashion' for greater autonomy in flatter organisations. However, recessionary times need tighter cost controls and a greater intolerance of duplication (seen as equating to waste) emerges. The 'softer' aspects of integration, for example perceptions regarding data models of the business, have proved harder to deal with than file/operating system format incompatibilities. The limited success of open systems in addressing these organisational integration issues limits the applicability of this IS strategy.

## Monopoly

This strategy, the opposite to free market, is adopted because of a belief that information is a corporate asset produced across functional boundaries and hence can only be cross-functionally available if controlled by a single service source. In order for such single sourcing to prevail there must be a user acceptance of the philosophy backed up by policing policies to force it through. To maintain user acceptance the single source provision should be based upon good forecasting of service demands and a strong focus on customer satisfaction.

The resultant role for the IS function is a reactive one of satisfying articulated requirements as soon as they arise rather than directing future developments. The complementary user role is one of articulation of needs and negotiating for provision of them from the single source. Since there is a single source provider, much of this negotiation is one of bidding for a *share* of resources rather than for a service contract.

This is an appealing strategy in times of tight financial constraints because of its potential for economies of scale. However, unless IS is responsive to the need to be 'cost efficient' by exploring new approaches to IS productivity the organisational expectation of lowered overall costs can be misplaced. Almost by definition this IS strategy can flounder in bureaucratic structures. In more successful instances the strong emphasis upon standardised solutions facilitates integration and *corporate* exploitation of resources.

### Scarce resource

This strategy is adopted, though it very often simply emerges, because of a belief that information is a finite and hence limited resource whose development requires a clear justification. In order for these justifications to exist there must be very tight budgetary controls in place over all aspects of IS expenses and there must be policies which ensure that both IS and users adhere to these budgetary controls.

The resultant role for the IS function is to make the best use of their limited resource by effective cost control of projects and the adoption of all cost saving measures. The complementary role of users is to bid for a slice of the cake via project justifications in terms of bottom line cost/benefit presentations. This strategy is unlikely to accommodate sophisticated selection processes based upon 'softer' values (*see* Chapter 7).

This strategy will clearly have a negative influence upon information exploitation and will tend to generate a passive user community, or one adept at accurately quantifying benefits. Similarly, this strategy may tend to produce a 'penny pinching' IS function or one that is adept at low cost productivity. It tends to force players to follow the 80:20 rule of getting 80 per cent of the benefits for 20 per cent of the costs!

### Necessary evil

This strategy is adopted, very infrequently now, in those organisations that believe that information is not important to their business. Indeed in Ward and Griffiths' (1996) description of this set of strategies the necessary evil strategy has been dropped from the list. Perhaps the only remaining instance where it can be seen is in the small organisation.

There is a very tightly controlled grudging allocation of IT only to meet basic needs. The resultant IT role is to provide a minimum level of resource and skills and to encompass only those projects that have been identified to have a good return on investment. The complementary user role is very passive since they take no part in the development or management of IS.

Increasingly this strategy is challenged by the constant stream of evidence available of the importance of IS/IT. It therefore is likely that this strategy is an ill-advised one except in very rare instances. The skill is in identifying what are basic needs. However it does remain in some instances and gives a convenient name to the IS strategy adopted in a number of smaller organisations.

This classification set is primarily used to name (having a single phrase or word to represent a mass of detail allows the name, which is a shorthand form for much else, to simplify complexity) the identified planned strategy but it is very much part of the process of developing that strategy plan to be aware of what the currently followed strategy is. The relationship between the generic IS strategy and an organisation's position on various other models forms the basis of some of the frameworks for toolsets explored in the next chapter. See, for example, generic strategies related to business importance in Section 5.2.3 and in Chapter 6 where Ward's entire planning approach builds upon such relationships.

As mentioned earlier, the intention in using this model is two-fold, one to have a way of understanding complexity, and two to have a *shared* understanding of it. The IS strategy forms the 'peg in the ground' for the tactical decisions taken by the IS function and so there must be a way of effectively and efficiently communicating it. Many frameworks for strategy development, as discussed in Chapter 6, draw upon this classification set to conceptually demonstrate the relationships between business and IS strategies.

## 5.5.2 ◆ Value chain and value system analysis

Porter (1985a) suggests that all organisations have an internal value chain and in turn belong to an overall industry value system (*see* Chapter 2). The value chain models the internal processes that are *how* an organisation achieves the generic strategies he defines as responses to the competitive situation he describes in his five-forces model of industry structure. The value chain model provides the basic structure through which to assess the information intensity of the organisation's activities as discussed in the next section. With the value chain and value system models IS opportunities can be identified by analysis of value chain activities and linkages. As part of an opportunity framework this technique is now used to iden-tify the opportunities to enhance the internal value chain or access a greater share of the total profits available in the industry value system.

Porter distinguishes between those internal activities that are primary, ie value adding activities, and those that support them. Looking at what IS can contribute in the way of support activities increases the efficiency of the organisation. Those opportunities for IS to impact upon the primary activities are opportunities to increase the competitive effectiveness of the organisation. Since value added – cost = margin, the organisation can usefully assess whether IS can increase value adding as well as reduce costs. To reduce costs by contributing to support activities has been the traditional focus of IS. Of course it can be argued that using IS to enhance the support activity gives opportunities to add value across a large number of processes. Analysis of the nature of the value chain for an organisation and consideration of the current impact of IS can give a picture of the business importance of IS and of potentially strategic opportunities for the future.

The value chain (Figure 5.12a) diagrammatically represents the production process in a way that distinguishes between primary activities which directly relate to the production of the goods or services and secondary activities which have an indirect, or infrastructure, relationship to that production. Total cost of all activities is, of course, the total cost of the production process, the value chain. Whilst Porter and Millar gave as their example a manufacturing operation the concept of the value chain can be applied to service sector or non-profit making organisations, indeed all organisations can model their value chain. It is interesting to note that, at a more specific level, we talk about the IS infrastructure and we usually mean precisely this distinction, ie not those systems or applications that directly provide the service but those that indirectly support that happening. Therefore the value chain model could usefully be used to illustrate IS to show those distinctions more forcefully.

The concept of the value chain was developed in the two 1985 Porter texts with the main aim being to discover how IS can impact upon the performance of a firm by altering the entire process of product or service creation, development and sale

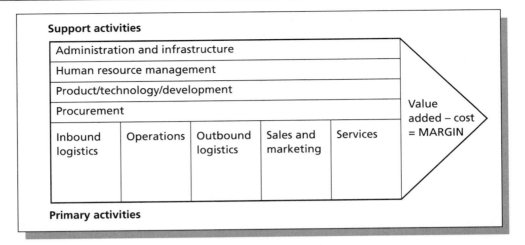

**Fig 5.12a ◆ Porter's Value Chain Model**
(adapted with the permission of The Free Press, a division of Simon & Schuster from *Competitive Advantage: Creating and Sustaining Superior Performance* by Michael E. Porter. Copyright © 1980 by The Free Press)

to clients. Value chains target competitive advantage. They are a way of modelling the organisation in order to answer questions activity by activity. Once an organisation has modelled its value chain it can ask:

- Can we enhance the value added by that activity?
- Is there an opportunity to reduce the cost of that activity?
- Or eliminate that activity?
- Can we use that activity to differentiate the organisation?

In order to answer these questions the organisation must study the primary activities that get the product to the customer and the support activities that facilitate that. In addition there are linkages between these activity processes. Increasingly it is with improvements to the linkages that IS can offer most support.

The value chain model was developed rather later than the five forces and competitive strategy work although competitive advantage in either cost leadership or differentiation is a function of the chain of activities. Vitale's 1986 survey found that the notion of a value chain was the most widely used planning technique. This despite the criticisms of its difficulty in use for service organisations and the difficulty of reconciling the fact that the use of this model potentially increases the local optimising of activities at the expense of overall effectiveness.

The value system concept, also proposed by Porter, takes this idea still further (Figure 5.12b). Porter suggests that all businesses form one part of an industry's value system. By modelling the value *system* for the entire industry an organisation is able to assess how significant IS is to the linkages in this system, back to industry impacts. In addition, reducing costs in the *whole* system frees up additional margins from which the initiating organisation can take a greater share. Here the organisation seeks to identify the potential role IS can play in the link between organisations. By viewing themselves as one activity in a larger system that

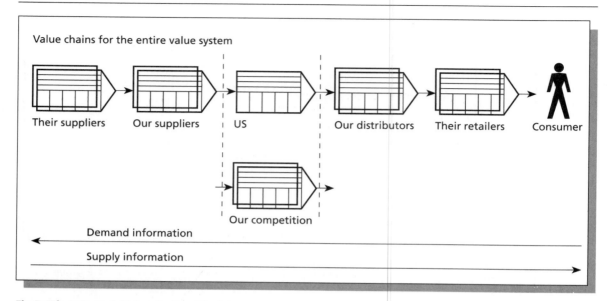

**Fig 5.12b ◆ Porter's Value System Model**
(adapted with the permission of The Free Press, a division of Simon & Schuster from *Competitive Advantage: Creating and Sustaining Superior Performance* by Michael E. Porter. Copyright © 1980 by The Free Press)

includes their suppliers, customers, and perhaps competitors, they can assess where costs can be decreased or the value added increased. The appendix on IS in the context of the value chain in Andreu *et al.* (1992) provides a more detailed discussion of this process.

With an increasing concern to *configure* rather than simply support the arrangement of business activity the value chain model becomes more useful. As one of the early process based views of an organisation its ideas are clearly related to that of those generated methods and models to support Business Process Re-engineering (BPR). Porter's concern that organisations should configure both processes and their linkages is an instance of advocating at least business process design. *See* Chapter 8 for a more detailed discussion of BPR.

The various models that are used to support BPR initiatives also could have been included here; however, BPR is a significant category of activity in its own right. For that reason it has its own section within Chapter 8.

### 5.5.3 ◆ Information intensity matrix

For any organisation it is possible to assess the information content, that is the information *intensity*, of the value chain activities and linkages as discussed in the previous section (*see* Chapter 2 for more detailed coverage of Porter's value chain model), and the organisation's products and services. Porter and Millar's information intensity matrix provides a tool for doing this. This matrix has as its X-axis a measure of the information content of the product/service. This is very low in a product such as cement, but is very high in a product such as a newspaper. The Y-axis measures the quantity and cost of information exchanges which must happen in order to complete a transaction. The two by two matrix is illustrated in Figure 5.13.

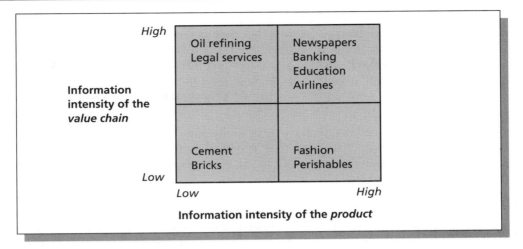

**Fig 5.13 ◆ Information intensity matrix**

Porter and Millar suggest that information intensity, which presupposes the use of Porter's value chain model to categorise it, determines the business importance of IS since every activity in the value chain has an information processing component as well as a physical component. IS is strategically important in the high/high matrix segment.

By positioning an organisation in a given segment, advice can be 'read off' as to *where* IS is going to be critical to business activities. This model can be used to provide measures of the business importance of IS but, more usefully, it can refine the crude view into a more detailed picture of where and how it holds that business importance. For example, consider the two extreme segments:

**(a)** *Low product information content/Low value chain information content*
This segment contains traditional process manufactured, widely available, commodity products with several potential producers, such as cement and bricks. The fact that information content is low does not, however, mean that there is no scope for exploiting IS to business advantage. Most organisations in this segment are going to be low-cost producers and hence IS can contribute to that overall cost leadership. There may, however, be a niche market for specialist cements where expertise is in short supply, so offering information about its use can provide some added value. This happened in fertiliser production when farming advisory services were offered to farmers as part of an integrated service. IS can allow the producer to build an all-round service to customers and hence leverage some switching costs. There may be little scope for IS in the production process but since the process is well known and closely controlled IS could be used to better inform that process and hence run far closer to the optimal safe operation. For example airline pilots are encouraged to rely on instrument flying and not fly planes themselves since fuel consumption may rise by as much as 30 per cent during manual flight.

**(b)** *High information product content/High value chain information content*
This segment is typically represented by banking and financial services. For example ATMs, credit/debit cards, and customer databases have all been inte-

grated to give a much more personalised service whilst lowering service costs. This has gone so far now that there are banks in the UK (eg First Direct) that have no branches at all and retail solely through ATMs and 24-hour phone links. In wholesale banking, corporate customers are offered direct terminal access and DSS to offer help in optimising investment opportunities. So this is a wholly information-bound product and the process relies more and more heavily on IS to get that product to the customer.

The matrix offers a way of analysing the industry sector according to the information intensity of that specific industry and can be used to assess *where* information is important in the given business and hence where IS is, potentially at least, strategically important. It provides a focus for the question 'where is information an important ingredient?' The answer to this might be that it is in the product/service that is sold, whether it is a traditional physical product or a less tangible service. Additionally the answer could be that it is in the process that allows the organisation to make or sell or deliver that product/service.

# 5.6 ◆ EVOLUTIONARY MODELS

There are now a large number of intuitively appealing evolutionary models. Many of them offer models of stages an organisation will progress through. An awareness of these stages is frequently of relevance during the strategy implementation process. A few models, however, are directly related to defining and documenting the IS strategy. Three of these are included here. All of the evolutionary models of course make assumptions about the nature of organisational learning about IS and about the predictability of progression. Other aspects of organisational learning and change were discussed in Chapter 2, and will be further discussed in Chapter 8.

## 5.6.1 ◆ Stages of growth model

In 1974 Richard Nolan and Cyrus Gibson presented a way of understanding the developing sophistication of IS use and management and have subsequently presented enhancements upon the basic model via a number of new versions. These have been taken up and further enhanced by other writers. In the Stages of Growth Models the basic premise is that any organisation will move through stages of maturity with respect to the use and management of IS. This model of stages offers an attempt to help managers interpret the position, and the meaning of that position, of their organisation with respect to IS. The initial intention was to map expenditure from empirical research since typically DP spending grew very quickly from a low base (the contagion stage); when planning and control caught up, spending levelled off. The shape of the expenditure curve corresponded to major changes in the use and management of IS.

Stage 1: The technology is placed in the organisation
Stage 2: This is a period of rapid and uncontrolled growth in the number and variety of applications of the particular technology
Stage 3: Management now gains control over the technology's resources by implementing formal control processes and standards that stifle almost all new projects

Stage 4: The use of the new technology increases rapidly, providing new benefits and supporting the overall business strategy

Stage 5: The data handled by the new technology are recognised as an important resource and so efforts are made to *manage* that data

Stage 6: Maturity – perfection?

It was found that many other aspects of IS use and management also changed over time and so more stages were added and they were described in ever more complex ways to include:

- The role of users
- The spread of automation across applications
- The organisation of the DP's management
- The type of planning controls used

Versions of the Stages of Growth Model (the model is also known as the MIS Maturity Continuum) were developed with subsequent enhancements made to adapt the model to modern IS life. The diagrams in Figures 5.14a–d show the typical characteristics of each stage for the four, six or repeating stage model. The enhancements allowed the model to provide a universal view of IS problems to give reassurance and some clues for the future. They explicitly define the extent to which IS pervades the organisation and how it affects all sorts of things such as financing the purchase of MIS to planning for their control to different styles of user involvement.

The Stages of Growth Model gives a better understanding of the factors influencing the strategy and so management are able to do a more successful job of planning. The management principles will differ from one stage to another and different technologies and perhaps different areas of the organisation are in differing stages at any one time. Therefore this model also makes explicit the need for a *portfolio* of strategies to cater for these differences.

Each strategy needs to be consistent with the organisation's stage, with respect to that technology. So, for example if the organisation's stage of maturity is Control stage then it will be difficult to adopt any projects without strong economic justifications. In this stage any/all proposals must clearly define the expected cost savings or the expected increases in revenue if they are to have any chance of approval. The only projects treated 'kindly' should be those that *help* management gain control over that particular technology's use and costs; user chargeback systems as discussed in Chapter 12 are a perfect example of this.

|  | Stage 1 Initiation | Stage 2 Expansion | Stage 3 Formalisation | Stage 4 Maturity |
|---|---|---|---|---|
| *Justification* | Short-term cost saving | Any/none | Long-term cost saving | Effective |
| *Controls* | Very short-term | None | Financial | Balanced |
| *Expenditure level* | Steady from zero base | Steep rise | Steady rise | Appropriate |

**Fig 5.14a ◆ Stages of growth model – four stages**

At each stage organisational changes occur. This process involves a growth in computer applications, specialist personnel and specifically IS management techniques. The stage names in this version of the model are:

1 *Initiation*. The first introduction of computers in order to make cost savings. The long-term implications for the organisation are rarely considered and hence the computer itself usually 'belongs' to accounting so that costs can be monitored. This may become a barrier to future developments. Complete lack of management interest.

2 *Expansion*. This is the stage of the sudden blossoming into new areas, a stage of contagious, unplanned and therefore unmanaged growth. During this stage senior management may abdicate all responsibility, leaving it in the hands of the technocrats. This stage may easily be chaotic and failures begin to be more common than successes. Over-ambition for projects justified on basis other than cost can exacerbate resentments. Typically computer staff feel free to concentrate on the technically exciting rather than the business worthy. Budgets grow.

3 *Formalisation*. Senior management become concerned about the budget growth and can slim down staff members and centralise for both tighter control and lower costs. All informal aspects of design, planning and budgeting become formalised, though this often swings rather further than necessary. Concentration is upon systems to save money, very little upon systems to make money. The different roles of different groups become more crystallised. The stage of formal plans, methodologies, and hence extensive backlogs.

4 *Maturity*. Senior management now includes senior IS staff. A stage of balance; between stability and innovation; between control and chaos; between autonomy and cohesion. The MIS Triad co-operates fully.

The later model of the stages of growth suggests, as illustrated in Figure 5.14b, that 'maturity' can be sub-divided into three, more specific, stages. This is an enhancement and not a replacement for the earlier model. There has also been some name changing:

| 6-stage | 4-stage | Leadership |
|---|---|---|
| 1 Initiation | Initiation | Technical |
| 2 Contagion | Expansion | |
| 3 Control | Formalization | Managerial |
| 4 Integration | ⎫ | |
| 5 Data administration | ⎬ Maturity | |
| 6 Maturity | ⎭ | Executive |

The first three stages, those concerned with computer management, remain the same (obviously, if it is a realistic model only the terminology and sophistication of the perception should alter) but after the critical transition point into stage 4 Nolan found that lumping *all* experience as one amorphous stage was inadequate and so:

4 *Integration*. Lowers the control levels of stage 3 in order to encourage innovation. The IS function will be reorganised to allow the IS staff to become more involved with the working of the organisation as a whole. Some considerable expenditure

| | Stage 1<br>Initiation | Stage 2<br>Contagion | Stage 3<br>Control | Stage 4<br>Integration | Stage 5<br>Data<br>administration | Stage 6<br>Maturity |
|---|---|---|---|---|---|---|
| *Planning and control* | Lax | More lax | Formalised planning and control | Tailored plans and control systems | Shared data and common systems | Strategic planning |
| *IS organisation* | Specialised for technology learning | User oriented programmes | Middle management | User/IS account teams | Data administration | Data resource management |
| *User awareness* | 'Hands off' | Superficially enthusiastic | Arbitrarily held accountable | Accountability learning | Effectively accountable | Acceptance of joint user and IS accountability |
| *Expenditure level* | Steady from zero base | Steep rise | Steady rise | Steep rise | Steady rise | Appropriate |

Fig 5.14b ◆ Stages of growth model – six stages

may be incurred on integration architecture 'backbone' developments for data and communications. The first stage recognising user accountability and IS as *service* function.

5  *Data administration*. The organisation's requirements for information drive developments during this stage. Great recognition of the business value of cross-functional data access. The stage of the corporate database.

6  *Maturity*. As before, the nirvana stage. Planning and development of IS in the organisation is embedded into the business' development.

Despite the more detailed breakdown provided by the 1979 six-stage model there has been an awareness that still the whole picture was not being represented. As organisations embark upon ventures with *new* technologies, perhaps minis or micros after a history of mainframes, or networks after a history of stand-alone machines, they will experience a repeat of the characteristic S-curve and of the stages of growth. The start point is not zero, but nor is it a smooth continuous progression. Not surprisingly, new technologies significant enough to be *strategic* bring about discontinuities. The nature of this discontinuity is illustrated in Figure 5.14c.

There is some evidence that organisational approaches to IS, as well as the technology associated with it, show the same repeating stages. The organisation needs new 'learning' when it moves from centralised IS to devolved computing or from in-house provision to the management of a web of outsourced services. Most noticeably the emergence of personal systems as associated with End-User Computing (*see* Chapter 10 for a more detailed discussion of E-UC) generated one such repeating curve. An organisation's stage with respect to corporate systems managed and controlled by IS 'professionals' (*see* Chapter 11 for a discussion of the evolving nature of the IS profession) will be very different, and probably far more mature than with respect to the management of those personal systems. Similarly a more recent phenomena, that of mobile and global IS, also generates a 'new' maturity learning continuum.

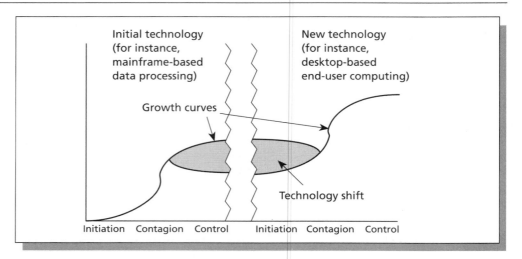

**Fig 5.14c ◆ Stages of growth model – repeating stages**

This 'learning' notion is one of the key assumptions behind the stages of growth model. These key assumptions must be accepted if this model is to be used. These assumptions are:

- Organisational learning permits the movement through the stages. It is the experimentation of Stage 1 that *leads* to the expansion of Stage 2. It is this expansion that 'teaches' the need for control in Stage 3.

- Stages cannot be 'skipped' since *every* experience is necessary to be equipped for the next stage. So no experimentation, no promoters for the contagion stage.

- Although there is a 'natural' progression, the transitions can be planned, co-ordinated, and managed to permit painless movement. Recognition of the stages is recognition of a sequence for planned and managed change.

This contingency theory supports the exploitation of strategic IS opportunities. Knowledge of the current maturity position provides a base from which to develop appropriate strategies, management styles, control approaches and investment levels. The approaches that build upon this are discussed in Chapter 6.

Since an evolutionary move is so often the reason for devising or revising an IS strategy the ability to model this development is plainly valuable. The stages of growth model has predictive value. Being a contingency model, if the 'textbook' symptoms can be spotted then it is likely that an organisation is at a particular stage of evolution, frequently as a change point. Of more value, if the stage is known, much can be surmised of the appropriate management techniques. For example, setting aside the change management *process*, the identification of an organisation as being at the boundary between Stage 2 (contagion) and Stage 3 (control) indicates that the chosen IS strategy will concentrate upon formalising the procedures by which IS decisions are made. This moves the responsibility for those decisions from the technologists to the middle level, budget setting management and charges the user community with the need explicitly to produce an argument for the particular IS activity (the structure of such an argument being defined by the nature of the approvals process now formalised). This would be true whether we believe that the model represents a learning curve or simply sequential development.

In the model the turning points on the curve represent crisis points where major management shifts have to happen. Nolan always foresaw that his four-stage model would require additional stages. And he makes the careful point that an organisation would not take any one of the symptoms in isolation when trying to diagnose the stage – organisations are rarely 'textbook' cases. He suggests two levels to the analysis of benchmark indicators and feels that a division will always have a single coherent stage for a given technology. There are a number of problems in applying Nolan's model itself since it was created in the days of the mainframe and the symptoms are described in the context of that environment. It takes a fair bit of contorting to make the model work in detail. It does however still make valuable general points. Even more usefully it has formed the basis of several tool combinations that will be described in the next chapter.

The most significant advantages to this model are:

- It is simple
- It is easy to understand, use, and see that some natural development is to be expected
- It is relevant to acknowledge the past in the present
- It acknowledges that sections of the business can be in different developmental stages and hence need different management treatment.

The last point is particularly important. There is no implication of trying to 'get all sections up to the same stage', but rather of legitimising the difference in IS strategies. Initially the model was considered to be developed from a poor empirical base but it has now left that consideration behind because of the usefulness of the questions it forces to be asked. Perhaps the actual benchmarks may evolve but the concept still holds true. This model gives a better understanding of the factors influencing the strategy and so management do better at planning. Management principles differ from one stage to another and different technologies are in differing stages at any one time so it makes explicit the need for different *strategies* in each stage of each technology. One additional useful feature of this model is its focus upon the issue of change. The model as presented gives an outline only of the *results* of the changes experienced. Others have given more attention to the nature, processes and barriers to those changes. The managerial behaviour aspects to this change process are explored in Lu (1995).

Galliers (1991) presents and discusses the amended version of the stages of growth model, developed in Galliers and Sutherland (1991), as part of a discussion of the failures of strategic planning for IS. He notes that many tools associated with such planning address ways of determining an organisation's desired end state, the destination they wish to get to. Strategic planning, however, needs not only these 'visions of the future' but an awareness of the start point and alternative, acceptable ways of moving from here to there at least implicitly adopting this text's definition of strategy as ends plus means (*see* Chapter 1). These, of course, are the IS strategies. The stages of growth model gives a powerful tool in assessing where 'here' is. A number of other writers have presented versions of the stages of maturity concept, for example McFarlan and McKenney (1983) presented one in which they called the four stages:

- Identification and initial investment
- Experimentation and learning

- Management control
- Widespread technology transfer.

Their version is most notable for its different perception of the second stage. There is not the negative connotations of the Nolan terminology. They present that stage in the positive light but making explicit the point that too much control too early 'kills off' the use of a new technology. This perception of 'appropriate' levels of control will form a fundamental concept behind the assessment of IS strategy implementation discussed in Part 3. In a generalised view of stages of maturity of the use and management of any new technology we see:

- *Stage 1: Early success.* The beginning of a use of any new technology will be a time of some errors but many early successes that create an increased interest and experimental air.
- *Stage 2: Proliferation.* Based upon the early successes, interest in the new technology grows rapidly as new products or services based upon this new technology arrive in the market place. The new technology is tried out in a variety of application systems.
- *Stage 3: Control of proliferation.* Eventually it becomes apparent that the proliferation must be controlled. Management begins to feel that the costs of using the new technology are too high and the variety of ways it is used generates waste. The integration of applications is attempted but proves difficult.
- *Stage 4: Mature use.* At this stage the use of the particular new technology is considered mature. The stage has been set for introducing still other new technologies, and the pattern is repeated. So the organisation is in several stages simultaneously for different technologies.

Unfortunately however, the available stages models omit to encompass the human dimensions as well as the technological ones. Galliers and Sutherland (1991) therefore offer a version of the six-stage model that includes acknowledgement of the organisation's goals, culture, skills and structure. This is illustrated in Figure 5.14d.

Galliers and Sutherland find the available stage models overly narrow in focus, though they do *not* challenge the concept of organisational learning with respect to IS management or the notion of a stage model. This enhanced model, they argue, is not only an effective descriptor but also an effective prescriptive device. Interestingly they assert that it is *not* necessary to work through all elements of all stages if there is a strong top-down planning drive performed by sufficiently well-experienced senior management. Their version of the stage model implies that it is possible to *select* which aspects of the IS management to move forward on deliberately. This is conceptually rather different to the Nolan technique.

So to summarise, there have been many challenges to the basic concepts of the MIS maturity stage model and therefore it has been much criticised. Drury (1983) considered the model as an important idea that offered practical and conceptual appeal. Whilst appearing to structure the process of planning, the difficulty when applying this technique means that it actually acts as a framework within which interpretation occurs. He also was already questioning whether the turbulence surrounding the 'new technologies' made it no longer applicable without adaptation.

| Element | I | II | III | IV | V | VI |
|---|---|---|---|---|---|---|
| Strategy | Acquisition of hardware software, etc | IT audit Find out and meet users needs | Top-down IS planning | Integration, co-ordination and control | Environmental scanning and opportunity seeking | Maintain comparative strategic advantage<br><br>Monitor futures<br><br>Interactive planning |
| Structure | None | Label of IS<br><br>Often subordinate to accounting or finance | DP department<br><br>Centralised DP shop<br><br>End users running free at Stage 1 | Information centres<br><br>Library records, QA, etc in same unit Information services | SBU coalition(s) (many but separate) | Centrally co-ordinated coalitions (corporate and SBU views concurrently) |
| Systems | *Ad hoc* unconnected<br><br>Operational<br><br>Multiple manual and IS<br><br>Unco-ordinated<br><br>Concentration on financial system<br><br>Little maintenance | Many applications<br><br>Many gaps<br><br>Overlapping systems<br><br>Centralised<br><br>Operational<br><br>Mainly functional systems<br><br>Many areas unsatisfied<br><br>Large backlog<br><br>Heavy maintenance load | Still mostly centralised<br><br>Uncontrolled end user computing<br><br>Most major business activities covered | Decentralised approach with some controls, but mostly lack of co-ordination<br><br>Some DSS (*ad hoc*)<br><br>Integrated office technology systems | Decentralised systems but central control and co-ordination<br><br>Added value systems (more marketing oriented)<br><br>More DSS (internal less *ad hoc*)<br><br>Some strategic systems (using external data)<br><br>Lack of external and internal data integration<br><br>Integration of communication technologies with computing | Inter-organisational systems (supplier, customer, government links)<br><br>New IS based products<br><br>External/internal data integration |
| Staff | Programmers/ contractors | Systems analysts DP manager | IS planners<br><br>IS manager | Business analysts<br><br>Information resource manager (chief information officer) | Corporate/business/ IS planners (one role) | IS director – members of board of directors |
| Style | Unaware | Don't bother me (I'm too busy) | Abrogation<br><br>Delegation | Democratic<br><br>Dialectic | Individualistic (project champion) | Business team |
| Skills | Technical (very low level) (individual expertise) | Systems development methodology | IS believes it knows what the business needs<br><br>Project management | Organisational delegation<br><br>IS knows how the business works<br><br>Users know how IS works (for their area)<br><br>Business management (for IS staff) | IS manager- member of senior executive team<br><br>Knowledgeable users in some IS areas<br><br>Entrepreneurial/ marketing skills | All senior management understand IS and its potentialities |
| Superordinate goals | Obfuscation | Confusion | Senior management concern | Co-operation | Opportunistic<br><br>Entrepreneurial<br><br>Intrapreneurial | Interactive planning |

**Fig 5.14d ◆ Stages of growth model – socio-technical version**
(reproduced by permission of the publisher from Information Systems Management and Strategy Formulation by Galliers and Sutherland, *Journal of Information Systems*, Vol 1 No 2 (1991) p.111)

Benbasat *et al.* (1984) similarly attempted to explore the empirical foundations of this model and found little to support the basic logic that the key benchmarks would all move in the same direction and in a similar manner. Their overall findings say little in support of the fundamental notion of an MIS management maturity continuum and explicitly doubt the utility of the benchmark measures included in Nolan's work.

In contrast to these two negative comments on stage models Raho *et al.* (1987) focus upon McFarlan and McKenney's more general continuum and argue that empirical evidence does support its validity as a description of the process of managing technology assimilation. However their evidence does not support the specific stages identified by McFarlan and McKenney and Raho *et al.* speculate that there may actually be six stages, although they do not define them and appear to adopt the notion of six simply to be symmetrical with other models (including stage models as used specifically to describe the organisational assimilation of end-user computing as discussed in Chapter 10).

Most challengingly, O'Brien (1995) explores the difficulties associated with the very notion of stage theories and with the specifics of Nolan's and other more specific instances. Whilst rejecting the utility of the basic logic that says 'if here, then do this' associated with many of the models, he follows Galliers and Sutherland in seeing some utility in the issue-raising potential 'as a quarry for extracting aspects, distinctions and gradations of possibilities . . .'.

### 5.6.2 ◆ Era models

In contrast to the stages of growth models discussed in the previous section, in which particular benchmarks are offered with which to diagnose *specific* positions and therefore (perhaps) prescribe specific IS management actions, are a number of 'Era' models. These models focus on the significant, even revolutionary, shifts from one era to another. In one sense they are stage models without the detail; indeed Ward and Griffiths (1996) refer to the fact that when looking at Nolan's model from 'a more distant perspective' it is an era model. Nolan referred to there being two eras with a critical transition between the computer management concerns of stages 1, 2, and 3 and the information management concerns of stages 4, 5 and 6.

A number of models highlight the key transitions, such models include those by Silk (1991) and Ward *et al.* (1990). Ward *et al.* argue that there are significant changes; the ideas of their eras are shown in Figure 5.15 (note: Ward's use of the term SIS is the same as that defined as SMIS in Chapter 3).

Another model focusing on this issue of important changes in IS is the notion of a paradigm shift explored in Tapscott and Caston (1993). This issue of fundamental and revolutionary change is often operationalised as a BPR initiative. It also echoes the basic principles of chaos theory and its relationship to strategy planning as discussed in Chapter 1. Models that focus upon recognising when periods of relative stability are ending offer more utility than models that imply steady progressions. The primary difficulty with this notion is that although all available era models alert 'trailing' organisations to the arrival of a 'new era', they offer little explicit IS resource decision making assistance to them and none at all to those ground breaking organisations *creating* that new era.

| 1960s<br>DP Era | 1970s<br>MIS Era | from 1980s<br>SIS Era |
|---|---|---|
| Increased efficiency<br>IS automated functional<br>activities of organisation,<br>transaction handling and a few<br>exception reports<br><br>Bottom-up | Increased effectiveness<br>User initiated enquiry systems all<br>to assist management activities.<br>Built on the common base of<br>systems produced during DP Era<br><br>Top-down | Improved competitiveness<br>Encompasses more intelligence<br>so DSS and expert systems.<br>Wider variety of data types –<br>voice, data, graphic images, etc.<br><br>Outside-in |

**Fig 5.15 ◆ Three-Era Model**
(reprinted by permission of John Wiley and Sons Ltd. from *Strategic Planning for Information Systems* (1990) by J. Ward, P. Griffiths and P. Whitmore)

## 5.6.3 ◆ Industry life cycle

One such placement technique is J. M. Higgins' (1985) model of industry and product life cycles. This focuses on the demand/supply relationship for products or industries and hence this can be used to model and subsequently analyse either.

This model combines three components; in this instance any product or industry is defined as progressing through four stages (Figure 5.16). The relationship between supply and demand differs for each stage. The important point about this model (and indeed any model used as an analysis tool) is that if you can identify the position of a given organisation on the model then you have access to a pre-defined framework that suggests the greatest value for IS – in this instance the business emphasis and hence where IS is best serving the business.

A product or industry can be positioned on this model by assessing the relationship between supply and demand. That assessment lets the analyst 'read off' the current stage in the cycle and hence 'look up' the normative best use of IS. Remember that normative merely says 'normally will be this'; any potential cause for deviation from this should be considered.

All this implies that for each stage the emphasis for the effective use of IS will be different because the business environment or the product viability is different for each. In other words, in industry terms, the systems critical to survival in that industry vary by stage. In the development stage of this cycle those systems critical to survival will be those that most directly assist in the definition of the product and the prediction of the industry growth. Conversely, in a mature industry those systems most crucial to survival will be those that act to reduce unit costs. The identification of what holds the greatest *importance* should, of course, then be matched to a set of IS activities that reflects that importance (or lack of it).

| *Stage* | *Normative best use* |
|---|---|
| Emerging | To define the product and predict the industry. |
| Growth | To enhance the product and develop the industry. |
| Mature | To reduce product unit costs and focus the industry. |
| Declining | To divest the product and withdraw from the industry. |

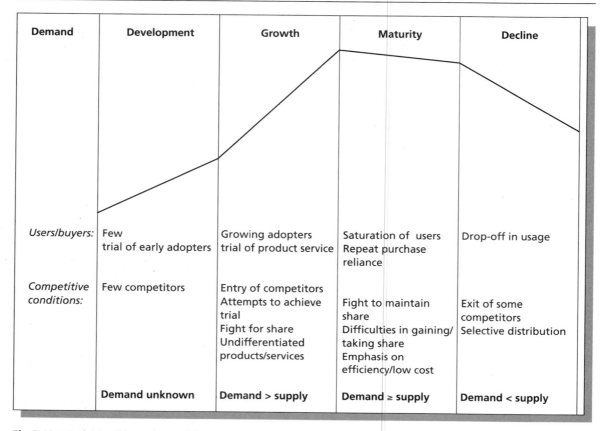

| Demand | Development | Growth | Maturity | Decline |
|---|---|---|---|---|
| *Users/buyers:* | Few<br>trial of early adopters | Growing adopters<br>trial of product service | Saturation of users<br>Repeat purchase<br>reliance | Drop-off in usage |
| *Competitive conditions:* | Few competitors | Entry of competitors<br>Attempts to achieve trial<br>Fight for share<br>Undifferentiated products/services | Fight to maintain share<br>Difficulties in gaining/ taking share<br>Emphasis on efficiency/low cost | Exit of some competitors<br>Selective distribution |
| | Demand unknown | Demand > supply | Demand ≥ supply | Demand < supply |

Fig 5.16 ◆ Industry life cycle model

## 5.7 ◆ INFORMATION REQUIREMENTS ANALYSIS

A number of techniques exist that aim to develop a picture of an organisation's strategic information requirements, the MIS output. This is not at the level of detail that would form part of a systems development project but identifying the information that is needed in order to operate and manage an organisation so that the organisation can identify *what* IS should deliver. Three are included here with examples, some examination of their strengths and weaknesses and a comparison of their likely outcomes. Additionally a model for matching method to environment is offered.

### 5.7.1 ◆ Critical success factor analysis

This non-proprietary, business-aligning rather than business-impacting, technique suggests that strategic information requirements can be uncovered by a three-stage process: firstly the identifying of a number of critical success factors, secondly the critical decisions to be made, and hence finally the information required to support those decisions. Critical Success Factors are those handful of things that within someone's job must go right for the organisation to flourish. They are the factors that the manager wishes to keep a constant eye upon. The conceptual structure of a CSF analysis is shown in Figure 5.17a which shows the concept of Key Decisions serving as a bridge into information requirements identification. Alternatives for this linking role are discussed later in this section.

Although CSFs are specific, they differ from industry to industry, between organisations within the same industry and from one time period to another even in the same organisation. There are therefore five influential factors to consider when eliciting a manager's handful of CSFs:

- *The industry*: all organisations within one industry will share these
- *The competitive strategy/industry position*: large players may determine these for the smaller players
- *Environmental factors*: the economy, country or politics, etc.
- *Temporal factors*: those not 'normally' of concern but are so 'for a time'
- *Managerial position*: the CSFs will vary with the level in the hierarchy, the higher up the management triangle the more likely it is that CSFs will be of the 'building' variety – tracking the progress of changes. Lower levels of management have CSFs relating to 'monitoring' of current operations.

Critical Success Factor analysis was first proposed by Rockart (1979) as a way of allowing IS management to deal with the problems of the then available techniques. These problems were:

- *Null approach*: CEOs are complex, mysterious and changeable creatures and so we can do nothing. So we do nothing.
- *By-product*: information results as a by-product of processing transactions.
- *Total study*: information needs can only be known after an exhaustive, and an exhausting, study, for example BSP.
- *Key indicator*: systems can generate exception reports if told of the key performance indicators.

The process of a CSF analysis allows managers, initially senior ones, to articulate their needs in terms of the information that is absolutely critical to them. These areas Rockart defined as 'the limited number of areas in which results, if they are satisfactory, will enable successful competitive performance . . .' Rockart (1979); the process of application is illustrated in Figure 5.17b. These CSFs can come from the

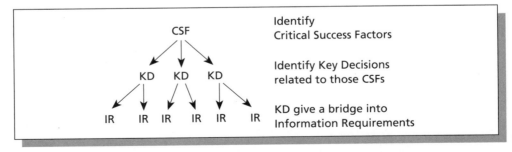

**Fig 5.17a ◆ Relationship between critical success factors, key decisions and information requirements**

industry structure, competitive strategy, industry position, business environment, etc. CSFs are not information needs for strategic planning, which would probably be far too unpredictable, but the information needs for management control, so the data needed to monitor and thus improve business areas – this can be defined. Ward and Griffiths (1996) argue that there will be a structured relationship such that the industry CSFs will influence organisational CSFs which in turn shape the CSFs of the particular area of the business which, of course, form the CSFs of a particular manager. They also comment on the necessity to be clear about objectives *before* embarking upon a CSF analysis.

Prior to the use of CSFs there was a chasm between the consumers of information, ie user management, and the providers of information services, ie IS. So CSFs can give some guidance on needs in such a way that the effect of this chasm is minimised. CSFs are needs and not development plans, or requests for specific systems. CSFs must be:

- Intelligible to senior managers
- Intelligible to IS/DP managers
- Possible to act on

Leidecker and Bruno (1984) describe eight possible ways to identify *what* the CSFs of a particular areas of concern are.

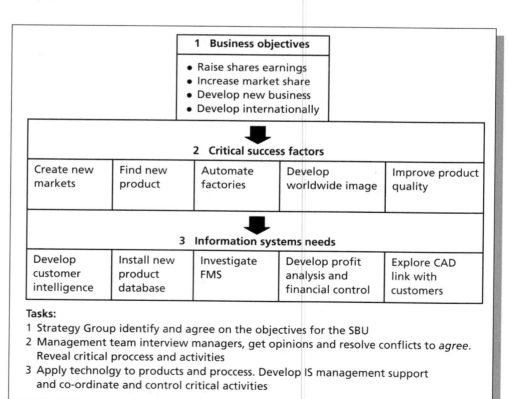

Fig 5.17b ◆ Applying a CSF analysis

**Example 1:** The national parts department within a large organisation with a basic business strategy of providing superior product support while maintaining an efficient operation that achieves a high return on investment might be:

CSF        Minimise length of time a part is kept in stock
KD         Decide what quantities must be ordered
IR          Order demand

Meeting the CSF ensures that the investment in stock is kept low and that parts reach dealers quickly. IS provides support to this, for example a key report would compare part purchasing to part demand patterns to enable managers to anticipate order demand without overstocking and at the same time help avoid shortages.

**Example 2:** The field engineering department of a world-wide oil company with refineries:

CSF        Minimising oil well uncertainty
KD         Estimating profitability of drilling sites
IR          Geological and engineering calculations

They can be applied lower down the management structure but it gets more and more difficult to articulate only a few things that must go right the lower down one goes. This becomes particularly difficult for those many management layers that focus on gathering and filtering data for other parts of the organisation. This could be a pointer to the fact that they have no CSFs, nothing they do is critical, and obsolescence and removal is the logical conclusion! It is possible, however, to generalise by Anthony's levels of management. To illustrate this Figures 5.18a, 5.18b and 5.18c show the possible relationship for the three 'standard' levels of management within a manufacturing organisation.

Note that the version of a critical success factor analysis described here uses the notion of there being key decisions that must be taken in order to *manage* the

| Decision making | | | Information requirements | |
|---|---|---|---|---|
| **Characteristics** | **CSF example** | **Key decision** | **Type of IS** | **Examples** |
| Top management | Attain profits | What to make | Simulation models (corporate plans) | Profit forecasts |
| Long term (> 1 year) planning | Market share | How to sell | | Economic trends |
| | Right products | Sales targets | Private viewdata | Industry trends |
| Unstructured | Customer services | R&D investment | Public viewdata | Sales analyses |
| Open loop | Quality control | Location of new factory | Graphical EIS | Cost centre analysis |
| Difficult to measure | Cost control | Physical requirements | Information retrieval | SBU performance |
| High risk | | Investment needs | Operational summaries and trends | Market research |
| Major impact | | Profit targets | | Demographic survey |

NOTE: This level uses extremely summarised data with extensive drawing upon external sources

**Fig 5.18a ◆ CSF analysis: strategic level of a generalised manufacturing organisation**

particular CSF adequately. These key decisions require information in order to be taken. Alternatively a CSF analysis may be described as using 'key performance indicators', as in Fidler and Rogerson (1996), or 'measures', as in Ward and Griffiths (1996), as the bridge between what is important (the CSF) and the IS activity necessary to support it (the information requirement). The point is to structure and highlight the link between what must be done and why it is needed, either to support a key decision or because it forms a key performance indicator or because it would be a measure of situation control or situation effectiveness. The choice of a specific form of the analysis structure should draw upon language and style preferences of the particular area of concern.

| Decision making | | | Information requirements | |
|---|---|---|---|---|
| Characteristics | CSF example | Key decision | Type of IS | Examples |
| SBU head | Effective | What standards | Budgeting | Sales analysis |
| Focus on control | management | Monitor and action | Performance reporting | Variance reports |
| Short-term | Control of: | on variances | Modelling | Summary totals |
| (budget year) | • people | Determine order | Exception reporting | Cash flow forecast |
| Probabilistic | • money | levels and quantities | Quantitative techniques | Personnel records |
| Performance | • stock | Select best option | Office automation | Management |
| monitoring | • machines | for identified need | Report generators | reports (for |
| Setting rules | • resources | Introduce overtime | | editing) |
| Motivating | | Specify training | | |
| Medium risk | | | | |
| (commitment) | | | | |

NOTE: This level uses summarised data from operational level and produces summaries for strategic level. Information required fast to enhance chance of successful problem solving

Fig 5.18b ◆ CSF analysis: tactical level of a generalised manufacturing organisation

| Decision making | | | Information requirements | |
|---|---|---|---|---|
| Characteristics | CSF example | Key decision | Type of IS | Examples |
| Supervisors and | Attain targets | Re-order stock | Transaction processing | Stock list |
| clerks | Follow procedures | Price an order | Build database | Picking note |
| Day-to-day control | Meet standards | Allow credit | Support enquiries, eg | Invoices |
| Highly structured | | Priority change | • production control | Outstanding debts |
| Closed loop | | Schedule production | • sales ledger | Production order |
| Deterministic | | Requisition materials | • purchase ledger | Completion dates |
| Stable | | Buy stock | • order processing | |
| Low risk | | | | |
| (commitment) | | | | |
| Routine | | | | |

Note: This is all standard stuff, the ways and means might vary but the basic techniques are all 'packageable'

Fig 5.18c ◆ CSF analysis: operational level of a generalised manufacturing organisation

Jenster's article (1987) gives a detailed explanation of how to apply an overall planning approach based upon CSFs. Shank and Boynton's article (1985) gives a case study of the use and effects of CSFs and also gives some useful general guidelines:

- CSFs are very flexible which can entice some organisations to be too casual about their use. Casual application can provide false results. CSFs should be used with the same precision as formal methods.

- The person managing the CSF study should have a thorough understanding of the organisation's business. As with many other techniques the real discriminator for success is going to be the skill of the team and the degree of high-level commitment. IS and senior management cannot speak the same language unless they both understand their common business goals.

- It is helpful to have a senior management champion, again, as always. This can motivate others to be more receptive in the early stages.

- Education of staff members in the CSF method before the actual interview is useful. A basic understanding of the concept and time to think before the first interview will make it more productive.

- Do not link to concrete things such as information needs, computer applications, etc during the first round of interviews. Staff can be more productive and creative in identifying CSFs if their attention is directed away from current IS realities (*see* Chapter 7).

- Try to use several management levels in order to validate the CSFs and to get a broader picture and higher quality organisational CSFs.

CSFs have been widely used. Their purpose is to identify the most important ingredients for the IS strategy since they define the most important ingredients of the business' success. As O'Brien (1995) points out as a 'realistic view' of CSF analysis, it is the act of deciding what is important that give this tool its utility. CSF analysis keeps a firm focus upon strategic issues, but obviously its weakness is that it needs very skilled and very perceptive interviewers to do the abstracting of CSFs from senior managers. The main strengths of CSF analysis are that it provides effective support to planning since the consideration of *critical* activities develops management insights and CSF analysis serves as the effective top level for a subsequent structured analysis. CSFs receive an enthusiastic welcome from senior management. By contrast, another major weakness of the approach is that the more removed from the management apex a specific manager is the harder it is to apply CSF analysis; many managers who are not already involved in strategy planning activities find CSF analysis too conceptual and it is particularly difficult for those managers who experience the greatest turbulence. Additionally, it is usually impossible to build a *true* picture of the organisation's information requirements using *only* CSFs. A further difficulty associated with CSF analysis is that the resultant decisions may ignore any resource constraints surrounding their management. Boynton and Zmud (1984) provide an extended discussion of the strengths and weaknesses of CSFs.

Like strategy set transformation, this is a technique that intends to *translate*. Here the translation is the information requirements of senior managers into an identification of the critical areas for IS effort and expenditure. There are lots of derivatives of the basic approach and they are all top-down in nature. For example, discussed below is one where critical success factor analysis is extended into critical *information* set analysis.

## 5.7.2 ◆ Critical set analysis

Henderson's work on critical sets is a variant of CSF analysis but which includes analysis of the critical assumptions made as well as the critical success factors and the key decisions. Basically the model suggests that a three-stage process can identify the IS strategy. These steps are:

1 Understanding the business using:

- Five forces model
- Value chains

2 Identifying information needs using:

- Critical sets
- High-level data model

3 Ranking the IS/IT opportunities.

The use of the term 'ranking' here is rather misleading since the approach actually requires placement onto a two by two segment matrix. This is done by analysing the critical/key assumptions by their degree of stability and their importance to the business strategy and then analysing the critical/key decisions by their importance to the business strategy, and the scope there is for IS/IT to enhance the decision making process. The resultant matrices are illustrated in Figures 5.19a, 5.19b and 5.19c.

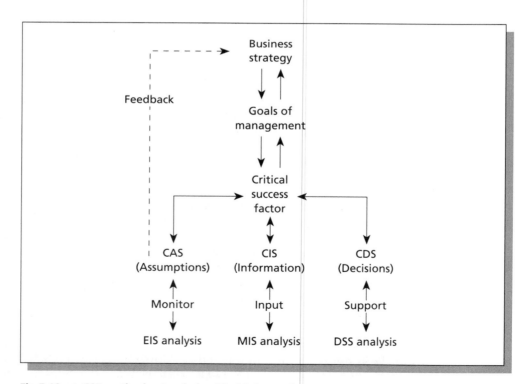

**Fig 5.19a ◆ CSF method extended: critical information set**

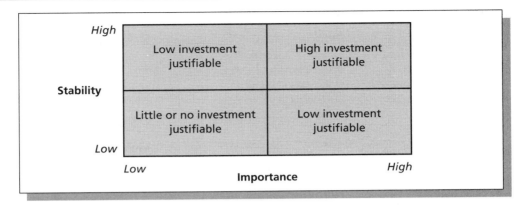

**Fig 5.19b ◆ Critical assumptions 'ranked'**

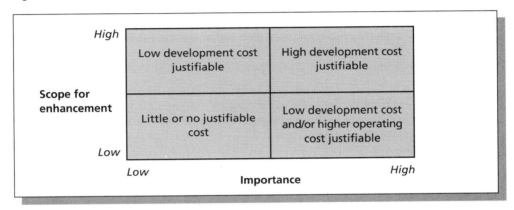

**Fig 5.19c ◆ Critical decisions 'ranked'**

This approach is very much about business *alignment* and it is not going to be used as a tool of *impacting* or business re-engineering. This is an approach for ensuring that IS vision aligns with senior management vision and any such revolutionary steps as process redesign are not likely to be adopted.

## 5.7.3 ◆ Ends-means analysis

Drawn from the general systems theory model of first and second order control systems, this technique requires that managers define not only their information requirements, the outputs, but also measures of efficiency (first order feedback) and effectiveness (second order feedback). The structure of the technique is illustrated in Figure 5.20.

This technique, therefore, aims to identify information requirements. The organisation must look first at outputs, the *ends* in the terminology of this technique, of a business area, and then, for that business area, define the inputs and processes, the *means* in this terminology, used to get there. The outputs of one business process form the inputs of another, making *explicit* the internal customer relationship modelled by Porter's value system, and the organisation has to define *effectiveness*, how good the outputs are at being the next inputs, as well as *efficiency*, that is the minimum use of resources to perform the move.

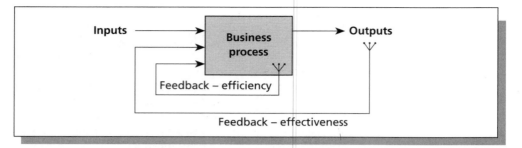

**Fig 5.20 ◆ Ends-means analysis**

The stages in an Ends-Means Analysis are:

1 Specify ends
2 Specify means
3 Specify efficiency measures (what information is needed to know that the organisation is efficient)
4 Specify effectiveness measures (what information is needed to know that it is effective)

As an example, for a stock control manager, the ends or outputs should be a stock level that is as low as possible whilst still maintaining an acceptable degree of availability. The means might include keeping forecasts of future needs, the amount of stock on hand and on order, the unsalable/unusable stock, the demand variations, the cost of ordering and the cost of not filling orders. The measures of efficiency might include the number of orders placed, the cost of holding stock, any loss on disposal of unsalable/unusable stock, whilst the measures of effectiveness might include the level of stockholdings and the frequency and seriousness of any running out of stocks.

This is not a particularly widely used tool but is included for completeness and because of its potential appeal to anyone familiar with systems theory, and particularly control systems. Since ends-means analysis makes *explicit* a concern with effectiveness it is a good method for focusing management attention upon it. Also, since there is a current concern with the issue of business re-engineering, redesign is needed to respond to the different climate created by IS/IT. This technique has inherent in it the ability to *redefine* the nature of the business processes studied and their outputs and inputs. Versions of this tool are therefore likely to come to prominence in the wake of this concern with business redesign. This is particularly since the received wisdom is that to re-engineer a business needs fast responses (the new environment is about speed of change) rather than tortuous planning processes and E-M analysis can be speedily performed. This technique can equally readily be applied by individuals as by much larger planning teams, at all levels of aggregation of the process, and increasingly managers are familiar with the notion, value and concepts of control systems theory and therefore are *inherently* equipped to use this planning tool.

## 5.7.4 ◆ Business systems planning (BSP)

An IBM proprietary technique (also known as enterprise modelling or information resource management) developed for use in both public and private sector organisations, it was devised initially for IBM internal use and then sold as a service to their customers in the mid-1970s. It is a fairly lengthy process that offers a structured approach to planning via a number of fairly rigorously defined stages that lead from the identification of business processes to a definition of required data structures. The steps needed to conduct a BSP study are summarised in Figure 5.21. Data is tracked as it flows throughout the organisation by the business activity it supports or results from. Outputs then go on to become inputs so data use and creation can be mapped for the whole organisation. It provides a bottom-up view of information for the organisation that takes as its base premise the notion that data is a corporate resource and so it should be managed from an overall organisational viewpoint.

The approach concentrates upon conceptually designing an overall corporate database, the 'enterprise data'. The systems that result are supposed to be lasting since they deliver the long-term needs, they reflect the business strategy and they take advantage of database technologies. However, whilst this structured approach works well in structured organisations, the increasing tendency towards decentralisation and devolution calls into question the value of it. It assumes the politics of the organisation encourage or at least permit data to be a single corporate asset and hence make business elements far more transparent to other business elements. BSP's main features are:

- Assumption that a central data repository exists
- Requires the definition of business processes
- For each process it must define the:
  1 Key success factors
  2 Key decisions
  3 Key problems
- Primarily aims to produce models of the data structures
- Since it has no built-in recognition of the organisation's position it tends to be rather unrealistic
- Can be very difficult to complete the study

BSP is well supported by IBM and it works well in organisations where the environment is organisationally or physically centralised. It is better suited to 'command and control' organisations rather than 'motivate and lead' ones. It forces the team to look at the workings of the organisation in great detail. It is a widely known planning approach since it is rather more than just a technique or tool.

BSP is an enhancement of King's strategy set transformation and was developed to create senior management commitment and also to improve the performance of the IS function. It presupposed an intention to create a corporate or integrated database. BSP involves top-down *planning* followed by bottom-up *implementation*. Senior management involvement is critical because of the scale and cost of the exercise and, while IS analysts may act as advisors, the study *must* involve

| | | |
|---|---|---|
| 1. | *Gaining executive commitment* | Needs a top sponsor and a team leader, might be the same person, to head the study team of 4–7 managers. |
| 2. | *Preparing for the study* | Team trained in BSP. They compile data of organisation's business functions and current IS support, produce a work plan, interview and review schedule and final report outline. |
| 3. | *Starting the study* | Sponsors review study's purpose with the team. Team leader reviews the compiled business data and IS explains recent IS activities and problems to the team. |
| 4. | *Defining business processes* | Team identifies the business processes which form the basis for management interviews, the definition of the future information architecture and other study activities. |
| 5. | *Defining data classes* | Data are grouped into classes based upon their relationships to the business processes. Charts are built. |
| 6. | *Analysing current systems support* | Team identifies how IS currently supports the organisation. Charts to show organisational processes and the responsible departments. |
| 7. | *Determining the executive perspective* | Executive interviews gain commitment and help team to understand the problems whose solutions will be the future systems (modern versions of BSP use CSFs). |
| 8. | *Defining findings and conclusions* | Team develops categories of findings and conclusions and then classifies previously identified problems into the categories. |
| 9. | *Defining the information architecture* | Team uses the business processes and data classes to design databases. Charts relating processes to classes and systems to sub-systems. |
| 10. | *Determining architectural priorities* | Team sets system development priorities based on potential financial and non-financial benefits, likelihood of success and organisation's demand for each system. |
| 11. | *Reviewing information resource management* | Team evaluates current IS organisation's strengths and weaknesses. Steering Committee set up to set policy and control the function. Stages 9 and 10 can run in parallel with this stage. |
| 12. | *Developing recommendations and action plan* | Team prepares an action plan with recommendations about software, adjustments to current systems and ways of strengthening IS management. |
| 13. | *Reporting results* | Team gives a talk and a brief summary and a more detailed (very thick) report covering the study's purpose, methodology, conclusions, recommendations and prescribed actions. |

Fig 5.21 ◆ BSP study steps

managers. A BSP study generates huge volumes of information and so IBM market an automated version. Whilst the definition of business processes gives it the potential to be a business impacting tool, the overall 'wrapping' of the technique ensures that it is inherently conservative and therefore it is most unlikely to do anything beyond produce data models of existing practices.

### 5.7.5 ◆ Comparison of CSF, E-M and BSP

Three of the previous techniques (Sections 5.7.1, 5.7.3, 5.7.4) seek to build a high-level picture of the information needs of the organisation. These information needs form part of the *demand* pressures upon IS. Each technique aims to model critical, or strategically important, information needs. CSF and BSP are both very widely used and all three aim to cut through the clutter of what *is* done to the value of judging what *should* be done. In practice the actual information requirements identified may vary and this variety reflects the different assumptions and objectives underlying each tool. This variety is also probably an argument for mixed is best! Wetherbe (1991) gives a comparison of these three, as shown in Figure 5.22.

The difference between these three can best be highlighted by examples of the different types of questions associated with each.

CSF: What are the CSFs of this business area (most managers have between four and eight)? And what information is required to ensure the CSF is well managed?

E-M: What makes goods/services provided by this business area effective to users? And what information is required to ensure effectiveness in providing the goods/services?
How do the business areas define efficiency in the provision of goods/services? And what information is needed to evaluate the area's efficiency in providing goods/services?

BSP: What are the major problems in accomplishing the purposes of this business area? And what are 'good' solutions to those problems? And what role does information play in those solutions?
What are the major decisions in managing this business area? And what information is needed to improve those decisions?

Any or all of these questions can be self-asked or used as the focus of brainstorming sessions or be the structure of a consultancy intervention via interviews or questionnaires. Wetherbe (1991) provides a number of tables in which the same organisational process (the order processing system) is analysed by each technique. In these tables it is clear that the overall 'feel' of the results from each technique is very similar, but that the *detail* may vary. For instance, Wetherbe indicates that CSF analysis may not identify the need for *specific* data sets such as shipping schedules that a BSP process would uncover, nor would an Ends-Means analysis. In fact this simply reflects the concentration within BSP to uncover *data* necessities whereas both CSF and E-M analyses focus upon the contextualised issue of *information* necessities. Whilst O'Brien (1995) feels that the different questions posed by BSP and CSF analyses are 'distinctions without a difference' the difference is the important one of levels of *detail*. That

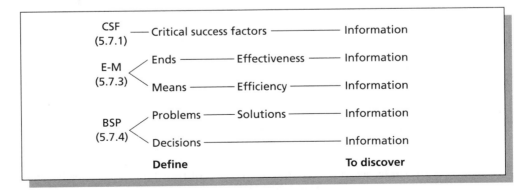

**Fig 5.22 ◆ Framework for information requirements**
(adapted from Wetherbe (1991) by special permission of *MIS Quarterly*)

is not an insignificant difference when related to a choice between these techniques. Where data detail is wanted then BSP may score over CSF analysis. Where business direction focus is wanted CSF will score most highly. Ends-Means analysis may score most highly when the objective is not only to improve current processes but to provide for continual monitoring of whether the process of concern is itself a necessity (*see* Chapter 8 for a discussion of other process improvement issues).

## 5.8 ◆ SUMMARY AND COMPARISONS

This chapter has included an almost indigestible number of strategic planning tools and there are an equal number of strategic planning techniques which have been omitted! For this reason no organisation would dream of using other than a small sub-set of the available tools. Some approaches to *choosing* the sub-set of tools that an organisation might use are covered in Chapter 6.

A number of writers have produced surveys of the available techniques. These include Andreu *et al.* (1992) who place Impact Categorisation, Information Intensity, Life Cycle Analysis, Five Forces Analysis, Strategic Importance Matrix, and a number of others within Earl's (1989) classes of Alert, Opportunity and Positioning. However few authors have actually compared the techniques. One exception is Bergeron, Buteau and Raymond (1991) who go into some depth in comparing the use of the notion of a value chain analysis and of strategic thrusts to identify strategic opportunities. They found both to be effective at identifying opportunities but the strategic thrusts framework, with its more external orientation, to be particularly useful for organisations in unstable environments. O'Brien (1995), while not *comparing* techniques as such, does assess the strengths of a number of them in terms of their ability to assist in making *real* IS strategy decisions.

The lack of empirically or conceptually based comparisons of the available techniques is therefore a remaining and fundamental difficulty when attempting to select IS strategy tools. To some extent the adoption of a particular *framework* (*see* Chapter 6 for a discussion of these) side-steps this issue by prescribing the techniques to employ. Galliers (1992) describes a coherent way of reaching judgements about which technique to use. Galliers argues that there are ten issues which are critical to the process of formulating an IS strategy. He suggests using these ten issues as a framework against which to judge candidate techniques. By doing this it becomes possible to identify those areas of weakness associated with the selected technique(s). Such structured awareness of limitations enables tool *sets* to be chosen, or 'special' attention to be applied as necessary. Galliers' ten issues framework is illustrated in Figure 5.23. Note this is a subset of Gallier's original table, for clarity the version given here shows only the two techniques covered within this chapter. Also to improve the clarity of the table, the wording of the key considerations has been extended.

In the absence of assessments of each technique at least understanding the focus of each may assist the tool selection process. For that reason Figure 5.24 gives a cross-referenced set of ten different ways of classifying the tools discussed in this chapter. Note that not every technique appears in every 'set'. Where a technique cannot be meaningfully distinguished within a particular 'set' it has not been included at all. This should improve the clarity of the table by reducing unhelpful duplication. For example, because a SWOT analysis captures the relationship between the organisation's environment and its internal capabilities, this technique cannot be placed on any Internal Auditing/Environmental Analysis Classification system.

| Key considerations | Porter's 5-forces and value chain | Rockart's CSF analysis |
|---|---|---|
| Ensuring management involvement | XXX | XXX |
| Ensuring management commitment | XX | XX |
| Ensuring debate | X | X |
| Surfacing alternative views | X | X |
| Considering company goals | XXX | XXX |
| Considering business environment | XXX | X |
| Considering IS capabilities | X | X |
| On-going reviews of benefits | X | XX |
| Integration with business strategy | XXX | XX |
| Incorporating change management | X | X |

Coverage of key considerations is indicated as follows:
XXX = good  XX = reasonable  X = weak

**Fig 5.23 ◆ Assessment of two IS strategy tools**
(adapted from Galliers (1992), published by the *University of Wales Business and Economics Review*)

**(a)** Categorised by the side of the demand ◄── ──►supply relationship they focus upon.

| Demand assessment | Supply assessment |
|---|---|
| • Opportunity categorising | • Generic IS strategies |
| • Impact categorising | • Stages of growth model |
| • Benefit level matrix | • Era models |
| • Industry analysis | • Ends-means analysis |
| • 5-Forces model | • Business systems planning |
| • Generic business strategies | |
| • Strategic thrusts | |
| • Strategy set transformation | |
| • Business modelling | |
| • Value chain and system | |
| • Information intensity matrix | |
| • Industry life cycle | |
| • Critical success factors | |
| • Critical set analysis | |

**Fig 5.24 ◆ Various classifications of the IS strategy tools discussed in Chapter 5**

**(b)** Categorised by whether their primary concern is with issues or with actions.

| Issue focus | Action focus |
|---|---|
| • SWOT | • Strategic importance matrix |
| • Sector analysis | • Benefit level matrix |
| • Opportunity categorising | • Generic business strategies |
| • Impact categorising | • Strategic thrusts |
| • Industry analysis | • Strategy set transformation |
| • Value chain and system | • Business modelling |
| • Information intensity matrix | • Industry life cycle |
| • Era models | • Critical success factors |
| | • Critical set analysis |
| | • Ends-means analysis |
| | • Business systems planning |

**(c)** Categorised by the element of the model of the strategic planning process.

| Strategic analysis | Strategic choice |
|---|---|
| • SWOT | • SWOT extended |
| • Opportunity categorising | • Impact categorising |
| • Strategic importance matrix | • Strategic importance extended |
| • Benefit level matrix | • Strategy set transformation |
| • 5-Forces model | • Business modelling |
| • Generic business strategies | • Generic IS strategies |
| • Information intensity matrix | • Industry life cycle |
| • Stages of growth | • Critical success factors |
| • Era models | • Critical set analysis |
| | • Ends-means analysis |
| | • Business systems planning |

**(d)** Categorised by whether they work from aims or from situations.

| Top-down | Bottom-up |
|---|---|
| • Opportunity categorising | • Business modelling |
| • Impact categorising | • Value chain and system |
| • Strategic importance matrix | • Information intensity matrix |
| • Benefit level matrix | • Stages of growth |
| • Industry analysis | • Ends-means analysis |
| • 5-Forces model | • Business systems planning |
| • Strategy set transformation | |
| • Business modelling (scenario) | |
| • Industry life cycle | |
| • Critical success factors | |
| • Critical set analysis | |

**Fig 5.24 ◆ Continued**

**(e)** Categorised by the objective they focus upon.

| Efficiency focused | Effectiveness focused | Competitiveness focused |
|---|---|---|
| • Business systems planning | • Strategic importance matrix | • Opportunity categorising |
| | • SWOT | • Impact categorising |
| | • Business modelling | • Industry analysis |
| | • Stages of growth | • 5-Forces model |
| | • Industry life cycle | • Generic business strategies |
| | • Critical success factors | • Strategic thrusts |
| | • Critical set analysis | • Strategy set transformation |
| | • Ends-means analysis | |

**(f)** Categorised by the place they take in overall decision making.

| Alerting | Opportunity | Positioning |
|---|---|---|
| • SWOT | • 5-Forces model | • Strategic importance matrix |
| • Sector analysis | • Strategic thrusts | • Benefit level matrix |
| • Opportunity categorising | • Generic business strategies | • Information intensity matrix |
| • Impact categorising | • Value chain and system | • Stages of growth |
| • Era models | • Industry life cycle | • Critical success factors |
| | • Ends-means analysis | • Critical set analysis |
| | | • Business systems planning |

**(g)** Categorised by the assumed relationship to the business strategy.

| Impact | Aligning |
|---|---|
| • SWOT | • Strategic importance matrix |
| • Sector analysis | • Generic business strategies |
| • Opportunity categorising | • Strategic thrusts |
| • Benefit level matrix | • Strategy set transformation |
| • 5-Forces model | • Business modelling |
| • Value chain and system | • Critical success factors |
| • Information intensity matrix | • Critical set analysis |
| • Ends-means analysis | • Business systems planning |

**(h)** Categorised by their orientation.

| Environmental scanning | Capability auditing |
|---|---|
| • Opportunity categorising | • Benefit level matrix |
| • Impact categorising | • Generic IS strategies |
| • Strategic importance matrix | • Value chain and system |
| • Industry analysis | • Information intensity matrix |
| • 5-Forces model | • Stages of growth |
| • Strategic thrusts | • Critical success factors |
| • Era models | • Ends-means analysis |
| | • Business systems planning |

**Fig 5.24 ◆ Continued**

---

**(i)** Categorised by their modelling intent.

| Descriptive | Prescriptive |
|---|---|
| • Opportunity categorising | • Strategic importance matrix |
| • Impact categorising | • Strategic thrusts |
| • Benefit level matrix | • Strategy set transformation |
| • 5-Forces model | • Stages of growth |
| • Value chain and system | • Critical success factors |
| • Information intensity matrix | • Ends-means analysis |
| • Industry life cycle | • Business systems planning |

And on a final note it may be worth noting that the following techniques are all fairly direct derivatives of techniques common in the 'general' strategy formulation arena.

**(j)** Those derived from general business techniques.

- SWOT
- Sector analysis
- Strategic importance matrix
- 5-Forces model
- Generic business strategies
- Strategic thrusts
- Scenario modelling
- Value chain and system

**Fig 5.24 ◆ Continued**

---

**References and further reading**

Adriaans, W. (1993) Winning Support for your Information Strategy, *Long Range Planning*, Vol 26 No 1 pp. 45–53.

Andreu, R., Ricart, J.E. and Valor, J. (1992) *Information Systems Strategic Planning – A Source of Competitive Advantage*, NCC Blackwell.

Benbasat, I., Dexter, A., Drury, D. and Goldstein, R. (1984) A Critique of the Stage Hypothesis: Theory and Empirical Evidence, *Communications of the ACM*, Vol 27 No 5 May pp. 476–85.

Benjamin, R.I., Rockart, J.F., Scott Morton, M.S. and Wyman, J. (1983) Information Technology: a strategic opportunity, *Sloan Management Review*, Spring 1984.

Bergeron, F., Buteau, C. and Raymond, L. (1991) Identification of Strategic Information Systems Opportunities: Applying and comparing two methodologies, *MIS Quarterly*, Mar.

Boynton, A. and Zmud, R. (1984) An Assessment of Critical Success Factors, *Sloan Management Review*, Summer Vol 25.

Cashmore, C. and Lyall, R. (1991) *Business Information: Systems and Strategies*, Prentice-Hall.

Copley, J.D. (1989) Information Planning, *Software Management Magazine*, Mar pp. 14–16.

Davis, G.B. and Olson, M.H. (1985) *Management Information Systems: Conceptual Foundations, Structure and Development* (2nd edn), McGraw-Hill.

Drury, D. (1983) An Empirical Assessment of the Stages of Data Processing Growth, *MIS Quarterly*, Vol 7 No 2 June pp. 59–70.

Earl, M.J. (1989) *Management Strategies for Information Technology*, Prentice-Hall.

Fiddler, C. and Rogerson, S. (1996) *Strategic Management Support Systems*, Pitman Publishing.

Flynn, D.J. (1992) *Information Systems Requirements: Determination and Analysis*, McGraw-Hill.

Frenzell, C.W. (1992) *Management of Information Technology*, Boyd and Fraser.

Galliers, R.D. (1991) Strategic Information Systems Planning: Myths, Reality and Guidelines for Successful Implementation, *European Journal of Information Systems*, Vol 1 No 1 pp. 55–64.

Galliers, R. (1992) Implementing Strategic Information Systems Plans: Barriers and Opportunities, *University of Wales Business and Economics Review*, Vol 8 pp. 7–14.

Galliers, R. and Sutherland, A. (1991) Information Systems Management and Strategy Formulation: The 'Stages of Growth' Model Revisited, *Journal of Information Systems*, Vol 1 No 2 pp. 89–114.

Higgins, J.M. (1985) *Strategy – Formulation, Implementation and Control*, Dryden Press.

Hugo, I. (1996) Business Developers do IT with Models, *PC Week*, 4 June pp. 8–9.

Ives, B. and Learmonth, G. (1984) The Information System as a Competitive Weapon, *Communications of the ACM*, Vol 27 No 12 pp. 1193–201.

Jenster, P.V. (1987) Using Critical Success Factors in Planning, *Long Range Planning*, Vol 20 Aug pp. 102–9.

King, W.R. (1978) Strategic Planning for Management Information Systems, *MIS Quarterly*, Vol 2 No 1 Mar pp. 27–37.

Lederer, A.L. and Gardiner, V. (1992) The Process of Strategic Information Planning, *Journal of Strategic Information Systems*, Vol 1 No 2 Mar pp. 76–83.

Lederer, A.L. and Sethi, V. (1988) The Implementation of Strategic Information Systems Planning Methodologies, *MIS Quarterly*, Sept pp. 445–61.

Lederer, A.L. and Sethi, V. (1989) Pitfalls in Planning, *Datamation*, June pp. 59.

Leidecker, J. and Bruno, A. (1984) Identifying and Using Critical Success Factors, *Long Range Planning*, Vol 17 No 1 pp. 23–32.

Lu, H.-P. (1995) Managerial Behaviour Over MIS Growth Stages, *Management Decision*, Vol 33 No 7 pp. 40–6.

McFarlan, F.W. and McKenney, J. L. (1983) *Corporate Information Systems Management*, Irwin.

McFarlan, F.W., McKenney, J.L. and Pyburn, P. (1983) The Information Archipelago – plotting a course, *Harvard Business Review*, Jan-Feb pp. 145–56.

McLaughlin, M., Howe, R. and Cash, J. (1983) *Changing Competitive Ground Rules – the impact of computers and communications in the 1980s*, unpublished.

McNurlin, B. and Sprague, R. (1989) *Information Systems Management in Practice* (2nd edn), Prentice-Hall.

Martin, E.W. Dehayes, D.W., Hoffer, J.A. and Perkins, W.C. (1991) *Managing Information Technology: What managers need to know*, Macmillan.

Mensching, J.R. and Adams, D.A. (1991) *Managing an Information System*, Prentice-Hall.

Nolan, R.L. (1979) Managing the Crisis in Data Processing, *Harvard Business Review*, Mar-Apr pp. 115–26.

O'Brien, B. (1995) *Information Management Decisions: Briefings and Critical Thinking*, Pitman Publishing.

Palmer, C. (1992) An IT World in Turmoil, *IT Matters*, Summer pp. 5–8.

Parsons, G. (1983) Fitting Information Systems Technology to the Corporate Needs: The Linking Strategy, *Harvard Business School Teaching Notes* (9-183-176) June.

Porter, M.E. (1985a) *Competitive Advantage: Creating and Sustaining Superior Performance*, Free Press.

Porter, M.E. (1985b) Technology & Competitive Advantage, *Journal of Business Strategy*, 5, 3 Winter pp. 60–78.

Porter, M.E. and Millar, V.E. (1985) How information gives you competitive advantage, *Harvard Business Review*, Vol 63 No 4 July-Aug pp. 149–60.

Rackoff, N., Wiseman, C. and Ullrich, W.A. (1985) Information Systems for Competitive Advantage: Implementation of a planning process, *MIS Quarterly*, 9,4 Dec pp. 185–294.

Raho, L., Belohlav, J. and Fielder, K. (1987) Assimilating New Technology into an Organization: An Assessment of McFarlan and McKenney's Model, *MIS Quarterly*, Vol 11 No 1 Mar pp. 46–57.

Reynolds, G.W. (1992) *Information Systems for Managers* (2nd edn), West Publishing.

Rockart, J. (1979) Chief Executives Define Their Own Information Needs, *Harvard Business Review*, Mar-Apr.

Scott, B. (1996) Try the Future Now, *OR/MS Today*, Vol 22 No 3 June pp. 58–63.

Shank, M.E. and Boynton, A.C. (1985) Critical Success Factor Analysis as a Methodology for MIS Planning, *MIS Quarterly*, June pp. 121–9.

Silk, D.J. (1991) *Planning It: Creating an Information Management Strategy*, Butterworth-Heinemann.

Sinclair, S.W. (1986) The Three Domains of Information Systems Planning, *Journal of Information Systems Management*, Spring, pp. 8–16.

Smith, A. and Medley, D. (1987) *Information Resource Management*, South-Western.

Tapscott, D. and Caston, A. (1993) *Paradign Shift: The New Promise of Information Technology*, McGraw-Hill.

Vitale, M. (1986) The Growing Risks of Information Systems Success, *MIS Quarterly*, Dec pp. 327–34.

Ward, J. (1987) Integrating Information Systems and Business Strategies, *Long Range Planning*, June.

Ward, J. and Griffiths, P. (1996) *Strategic Planning for Information Systems* (2nd edn), Wiley.

Ward, J., Griffiths, P. and Whitmore, P. (1990) *Strategic Planning for Information Systems*, Wiley.

Wetherbe, J.(1991) Executive Information Requirements: Getting It Right, *MIS Quarterly*, Vol 15 No 1 Mar.

Wetherbe, J.C. and Davis, G.B. (1982) *Strategic Planning Through Ends/Means Analysis*, University of Minnesota, MIS Research Centre Working Paper.

Wiseman, C. (1985) *Strategy and Computers: Information Systems as Competitive Weapons*, Dow Jones-Irwin.

Wysocki, R. and Young, J. (1990) *Information Systems: Management Principles in Action*, Wiley.

# CHAPTER 6

# Frameworks for integrating IS strategies with business strategies

The basic premise of this book is that strategies for IS must be related to business strategies, and will, in turn, influence them. We saw in Chapter 4 that conceptually IS strategies form a subsystem within a system of strategies and hence, from general systems theory, will have both connections and interactions, and the set of subsystems may exhibit sub-optimisation unless the organisation acknowledges this system's hierarchy. This conceptual-based reasoning is supported by much empirical evidence that, even if it is still mainly anecdotal, shows that when any one subsystem of a business ignores its impact upon others the entire business suffers. Also Chapter 4 showed that, to be connected to the business strategy, the IS strategy must be consistent with a number of things, the business vision of course being one of them. It should not be forgotten, however, that whilst a 'good' IS strategy is vital, it is not the entire story. The plan that documents the IS strategy must be implemented; Part 3 of this text considers some of the implementation issues.

When an IS strategy has been 'crafted' and implemented, empirical research indicates that the matrix given in Figure 6.1 represents an organisation's chances of success from IS. This chapter explores the different definitions of *consistent* and some of the different approaches employed to achieve this consistency. Chapter 8 will explore some possible meanings of *success* and what it may represent for the business.

This matrix simply sums up the advantages of having consistency between IS and business strategies and indicates the absence of total *certainty* even when this is the case. Given the fact that success probability is increased if consistency is achieved it is not surprising that a great deal of attention has been given to achieving some certainty of this consistency. This, of course, serves as a form of risk management since certainty of consistency *in advance* lowers the risks associated with any given IS strategy.

We saw in Chapter 4 that there are no standards for *what* an IS strategy plan should contain nor for *who* should do the strategy planning and, not surprisingly, there is no agreement as to *how* to produce it. This lack of consensus is to be expected since precisely the same dilemmas exist in the arena of 'general' business planning. However, some general principles are beginning to emerge. These principles seem to revolve around three different perceptions of the process for achieving consistent IS strategies, and Section 6.4 discusses these different perceptions.

| | IS strategy/ business strategy ARE consistent | IS strategy/ business strategy ARE NOT consistent |
|---|---|---|
| Execution of the plan is GOOD | Success is LIKELY | Success is POSSIBLE |
| Execution of the plan is POOR | Problems are LIKELY | Failure is EXPECTED |

Fig 6.1 ◆ Success probability matrix

# 6.1 ◆ REASONS FOR A PLANNING FRAMEWORK

Many organisations realise the value of having an IS strategy; the sense of direction it provides allows them to prioritise a set of opportunities to pursue. They may even have decided who should go about creating it, but how? When an organisation begins to collect together a set of tools into an overall planning approach they begin to construct the first significant determinants of their success. At this stage, what is required is a framework that allows the organisation to achieve its objectives. This framework should not straight-jacket innovation. The framework should provide a flexible and adaptable way to relate planning objectives to the choice of planning tools. By doing this, the organisation can develop the necessary deliverable, that is the consistent IS strategies.

The IS strategy is the *outcome* of the IS strategy planning process and having a framework for that process helps the organisation avoid getting bogged down in inappropriate detail. What are not required are detailed data models, system specifications, subsystem dependencies, etc, and so tools for creating these things should not form part of an IS strategy planning toolkit (though, obviously they may make complementary partners for effective implementation).

## 6.1.1 ◆ A framework or a methodology?

There are many different approaches to collecting the individual strategic analysis tools and techniques into a set that creates the IS strategic planning *process*. The advocates of certain collections call their planning approach a planning *methodology*. In this instance, methodology means a collection of postulates, rules, and guidelines that provide a standard proven process to follow. The nature of methodology is shown in Figure 6.2.

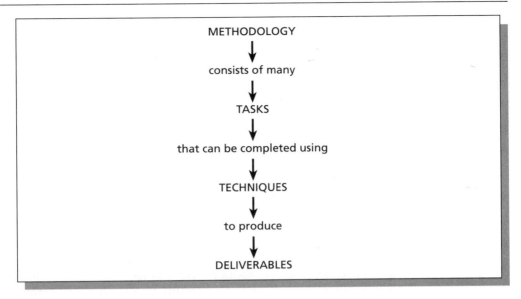

**Fig 6.2 ◆ Nature of a methodology**

A methodology should use a *standard* set of techniques and supporting tools. A methodology provides management with the facilities to help them plan, review and control the IS strategic planning project. Peter Drucker (1964), suggests that the importance of using a methodology is that 'knowledge organised in a discipline does a good deal for the merely competent; it endows him with some effectiveness. It does infinitely more for the truly able; it endows him with excellence.' And yet, at the same time, he cautions 'no book will ever make a wise man out of a donkey or a genius out of an incompetent.' Any methodology will contain the following four elements:

- A structure that gives guidance on what to do, and when to do it
- A definition of techniques to do what needs to be done
- Advice on how to manage the quality of the results
- Tools to automate the process

A methodology can, therefore, always use alternative techniques to achieve the overall aim, and, of course, alternative tools to support those techniques. Many of the planning approaches advocated in countless papers and books will provide the first two of the above list, they more often omit the latter two!

Lederer and Gardiner (1992) provide a detailed explanation of the application of one methodology 'Method/1' from start to finish showing how all the bits fit together.

Whilst some *standardising* of the IS strategic planning approach is useful, an organisation must realise that no 'cookbook' can provide all the answers. The approach must also allow the strategist to be flexible and pragmatic when applying it. Mainelli (1988) suggests that the primary success factors when developing and using a methodology are:

- Applying the correct procedures
- Knowing when to stop

Using the wrong tools will waste significant amounts of valuable time and may result in total confusion, and failing to stop at the *right* time will be waste of effort and may prejudice the conclusions of any strategic study. Many inexperienced strategic planners will go into far too much detail and only practice can effectively overcome this particular problem. As noted in earlier chapters, particularly in Chapter 1, with the increasing pace of change and growing turbulence in the environment there is a need to develop speed and flexibility of response. Just as in the general business sense, IS strategy planning frameworks enable fast development of the IS strategy, and facilitate maximum commitment to the resultant IS strategy. It should focus upon developing the sense of overall direction rather than providing detailed and prescriptive responses to every predicted future situation. The future *cannot* be predicted, IS strategy planning should not waste effort assuming it can be.

Rather than enter a debate about the strict differences between the terms technique and methodology, I will use the, hopefully non-contentious term, *framework*, and rather than define a new approach will rest content to provide some commentary on the different *frameworks* that are currently promoted.

## 6.2 ◆ ALTERNATIVE CLASSIFICATIONS OF PLANNING FRAMEWORKS

Rather than debate whether *grouping* the techniques covered in Chapter 5 into a set gives a methodology or not, the *actual* sets that organisations have used are considered. There are a variety of ways to classify an IS strategic planning approach. Three different ways of viewing the planning approach are given below. These are different *perceptions*; the actual approaches will, of course, use *overlapping* sets of techniques.

### 6.2.1 ◆ Classified by the intention/effect of the framework

By focusing upon the intention, or emergent effect, of the planning outcomes, that is the IS strategy itself, an organisation can perceive planning frameworks as being either:

- Business impacting
- Business aligning

### Business impacting

Impact planning techniques might include, as suggested by Bergeron, Buteau and Raymond (1991):

- Competitive forces:      Porter (1979)
                                      McFarlan (1984)
- Competitive strategies:      Porter (1980)
- Value chain:      Porter (1985)
                                      Rackoff (1985)

- Consumer resource life:  Ives and Learmonth (1984)
- Impact of IS/IT:  Parsons (1983)
- Strategic opportunities:  Benjamin (1984)

All of these techniques aim to determine which IS strategy to adopt in order to impact, presumably favourably, upon the business. This must mean that, as a consequence, the business strategy evolves. For instance, Rackoff *et al.* (1985) talk through what they refer to as a 'process for generating competitive advantage' based upon Wiseman's strategic thrusts; this process is basically a method of brainstorming ideas and this method is wrapped in some evaluation techniques to turn it into an entire process but it is clearly targeted at impacting upon the business. Ends-means analysis has the potential to be a business impacting tool. There has not yet been enough data gathered to verify the usefulness of these impacting tools at generating new and innovative strategic opportunities, in other words there is little evidence yet as to how good they are at impacting on the business. Obviously, all the techniques of the business re-engineering or business process redesign schools are explicitly aiming at business impact.

### Business aligning

The business aligning techniques assume that IS will fulfil its most appropriate role if the organisation's business strategy is used as the *basis* for developing the IS strategy. Probably strategy set transformation is the quintessential business aligning tool. The following list shows some of the aligning techniques:

- Critical success factor analysis
- Business systems planning
- Strategy set transformation

One technique that *explicitly* translates business strategies into IS terms is strategy set transformation. Any business can be said to have a set of business strategies, whether they are *formally* articulated or not. The technique proposed by King (1978) involves a number of stages that, when completed, will have translated those business strategy(ies) into IS terms. This translation will have ensured that strategic IS plans directly support business plans. Chapter 5 explained this technique.

Similarly Henderson's work on critical sets, a variant of CSF analysis that was covered in Chapter 5, intends to align IS to business demands. This particular approach attempts to be both business *aligning* and business *impacting* in its effect, but it is obviously going to be mainly about aligning. This approach makes extensive use of ranking to sharpen the focus of what is planned. The use of ranking requires a process of agreeing on what to regard and treat as the most important issues. This makes it explicit that Critical Sets and CSFs are not an objective 'truth' but the result of a process of interpretation and judgement.

Finkelstein (1989) writes of the information engineering (IE) approach. The aim of IE is to align hardware and software resources to the corporate plan. A major point of IE is that it must be a *continuous* process, unlike Ward's approach that can be an intermittent, triggered process. IE also includes an assessment of the informal as well as of the formal. The outputs of IE are known as 'strategic statements'. IE starts from the fact that, even if it is not formally documented, the business always has a business strategy. The IE approach, therefore, must start with judging what is that actual business strategy. This process of deduction may use the strategy intent shown in any formal documents but it must also consider the actual strategy demonstrated in business resource allocation decisions. It is this composite, and hopefully more realistic, view of the business strategy that is used as the reference of what to align to.

Finkelstein suggests the use of a life cycle model for analysing the organisation's products or services with regard to the environmental factors such as the market and competitors. Dickson and Wetherbe (1985) also describe a business aligning technique. Any aligning technique will be a formal attempt to match the investment in IS with an identifiable business need, to create *certainty* that spending derives gains. One example that places a strong focus on this financial chain of reasoning is that by Kovacevic and Majluf (1993) in which they describe fifteen activities grouped into six stages. They argue that the approach, although potentially overwhelming, is actually straightforward for seasoned managers. However, since the method requires 'managers to have a lot of specialised and deep knowledge of both the firm's different businesses and the intricate aspects of the technology' it will be an impractical framework in many, even most, IS situations.

All aligning techniques work by identifying business goals and plans, and deduce IS requirements via a formal method for translating them. Unfortunately, these techniques are often forced to articulate business goals first in suitable language to do this.

## 6.2.2 ◆ Classified by the nature of the planning environment

By focusing upon the nature of the planning *environment* within which the planning takes place an organisation can perceive the planning frameworks to be either:

- socio-technical, or
- developmental

The *holistic* approach of the socio-technical school requires that the *process* of getting the organisation from its current state to some desired state must be *managed*. Because of this focus upon the process of change there is a shift in the focus of strategic management, from the major interests being strategic analysis and strategic choice to a growing concern with strategic implementation. Earl (1989) made a clear distinction between *IT* strategies and *IS* strategies, the first being concerned with understanding and defining the *how* while the latter is primarily concerned with understanding and defining the *what*. Earl's multiple approach discussed later in this chapter, with its recognition of the different strategy *elements* and the different *approaches* needed to get to them, falls very much within this socio-technical perspective.

The more 'technical', developmental schools take a focus that is, at best, upon the interface between the 'box' that is the IS strategy and its environment; this box is illustrated in Figure 6.3. This focus upon the interface means that the IS strategy and the business strategy are seen as two, distinctly separate entities. By treating each as a 'black box' whose internal workings are not known (and whose workings it is not necessary to know) there will tend to be little richness in the resultant IS strategy. The interaction between these two entities is single dimensional. Interaction is only through the technical process of using the complete business

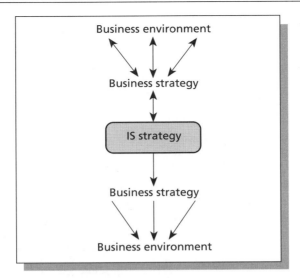

**Fig 6.3 ◆ Nature of the planning environment**

strategy as a baseline from which to construct the IS strategy (in the case of aligning methods such as that described by Kovacevic and Majluf (1993)) or through the technical process of using the complete IS strategy to shape the business strategy (in the case of impacting methods such as the value chain based techniques). Technical approaches aim either to *align* IS with the business, in which case the lower element of the diagram is missing, or to use IS to impact upon the business, in which case the two-way links *are* present.

The socio-technical planning environment 'explodes' the IS strategy box and considers all the interacting elements that connect to create the IS strategy; this takes a systems view that an IS strategy is an emergent property. The expanded box is shown in Figure 6.4.

Galliers (1991) speculates that much of the continual senior management disinterest in the *process* of IS strategy planning results from the refusal of many organisations to concentrate upon the core line of business-related strategies. The technological issues, addressed by the IT strategy, and the infrastructure issues, addressed by the IM strategy, are secondary to the core business strategies. When this multiple nature is recognised it does, of course, demand a variety of planning approaches. Single dimension planning perspectives all work by identifying the desired state, though obviously there are various views of how to identify this. Many of these single dimension approaches acknowledge the current position, either as part of strategic selection or as a variable for strategic analysis, and then they itemise the necessary moves to get the organisation from 'here to there'. The socio-technical perspective generates planning approaches that go further and analyse, choose and implement the how to make that transition. In other words change management becomes a significant part of strategic management.

Sullivan (1985) reports on research into 37 major US corporations that has indicated a relationship between the technology impact and the probable use of a particular planning tool; this relationship is portrayed in Figure 6.5. The technology measures form the axes (Figure 6.5) and the matrix cells are identified by name

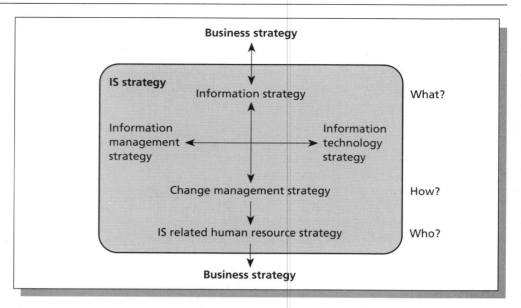

**Fig 6.4 ◆ Socio-technical perspective of the planning environment**

and by the likeliest IS strategic planning technique. The use of this model requires some prior tool be used in order to establish the degree of importance of IS to the organisation; the high infusion segments relate to systems that are *strategically* important and tools must be used that support making that judgement. Whilst systems diffusion may be a term that is harder to define, in practice it may be much easier to measure. Crudely, systems diffusion is a composite measure of the degree of decentralisation of three facets of IS use and management. These three facets are the decentralisation of IS:

- organisational
- physical
- responsibility/authority

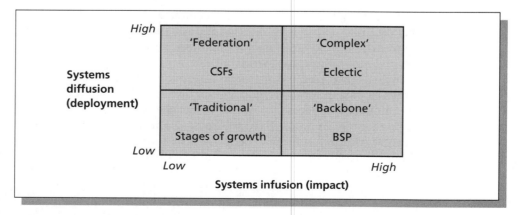

**Fig 6.5 ◆ Technology/technique match**

Hence the low diffusion segments equate to 'old style' centralised DP whilst the high diffusion segments represent a devolution to end user computing. If we look at each segment in turn we can see how the quite different parameters to the IS strategy planning process affect the degree of match to a planning tool.

- *Traditional*. This segment of low infusion and low diffusion represents the world of the old style, conventional DP shop, normally with a heavy efficiency bias. In this environment, with its centralised single provider of new technologies and no user autonomy, the stages of growth model for any particular technology provides a very appropriate planning tool.

- *Backbone*. In this high infusion, low diffusion segment systems have a strategic importance to the organisation but they are centralised under the control of one service provider. In this segment there will tend to be a 'factory' focus upon implementing and supporting a single central database as is the case in CAM/CIM, and since that is precisely what an IBM repository is, and this is exactly the environment that BSP presupposes exists, it is no surprise to find that BSP will be the technique matching well in this segment.

- *Federation*. In this low infusion, high diffusion segment the organisation has very decentralised and devolved systems that are not critically important to the business. The organisation itself is likely to be a loosely related set of entities where only some co-operation is needed. The managerial independence means that critical success factor analysis works very well in this segment and the central issue for IS may be to identify what to share and how to support the remote access to systems.

- *Complex*. In this segment IS is strategically important to the organisation and yet it is extensively devolved rather than centralised. In this complex 'stew' no one technique is likely to be appropriate since no one technique adequately covers all of the complex web of concerns. Organisations in this segment, therefore, are going to need to use a mixture of techniques in order to avoid 'black holes'. Often some subdivision of the complexity will be attempted with techniques matched to the characteristics of component elements. See Section 6.6 for one such approach.

### 6.2.3 ◆ Classified by the nature of the planning process

By focusing upon the nature of the *process* that will produce the IS strategy an organisation can perceive planning frameworks to be either:

- Top-down
- Bottom-up
- Innovative
- Eclectic (also referred to by Earl as multiple)

Top-down planning is proactive whereas bottom-up planning is reactive but both are intermittent 'planning project' based. Innovative planning is intuitive, interactive, instant and yet continuous in nature. There is an explicitly top-down approach defined in Emberton and Mann (1988) which has a heavy emphasis upon the production of data models. Many of the 'traditional' techniques for identifying information requirements, such as IBM's BSP, are *project*-based, that is they have a definite start and stop point. They also tend to be bottom-up in so far as it is the current nature of the organisation that generates the strategies. A general model for top-down matching of IS strategies to business strategies might be as shown in Figure 6.6.

This general model can be used to select appropriate planning techniques for the stage in the process. A number of techniques might support each stage and, therefore, issues such as familiarity with the technique, the nature of the planning environment, stage of planning 'learning', etc, can be the driver of the selection process provided the objective of that stage is met. All the analytical top-down methods are formalised and they all aim to appeal to the business manager. In addition, they can be re-done as business needs change, and they give IS direction setting and not detailed plans (given the growing recognition that detail hinders by reducing flexibility rather than helps this is a strength of these approaches). Examples include Ward's strategic information systems planning approach, King's strategy set transformation and CSF analysis (which are particularly useful if no prior business strategy has been articulated).

Many 'umbrella' planning approaches aim to give a degree of direction to the technique selection process and two of these are considered in Sections 6.3 and 6.4. The first planning approach discussed (in Section 6.3) is a rational analytical one suggested by Ward (1996) and the second one (in Section 6.4) is the more complex, less prescriptive, more flexible, one suggested by Earl (1989).

Silk (1991) also presents a view of stages of planning experience that is very similar to Ward's three-eras model (*see* Chapter 5). Silk suggests that at each stage linkage is obtained in a different way since the planning *objectives* of each stage are quite different (Figure 6.7).

Every organisation wants confidence in its strategies since they define its sense of direction. However, just as there are a number of business benefits that can be obtained from IS there are a number of ways of going about the process of deciding and documenting an IS strategy. They can be classed, as they have been by Earl, as being:

- Infrastructure led – where the emphasis is bottom-up
- Business led – where the emphasis is top-down
- Mixed – where the emphasis is inside-out.

| 1 | Business objectives: | What *want* to achieve |
|---|---|---|
| 2 | SMIS requirements: | What *need* to do and be |
| 3 | Current position: | Where *start* from |
| 4 | Goals/position comparison: | Map of *gaps* |
| 5 | IS policies: | Strategic *decisions* |
| 6 | Plans for IS/IT: | *Project* selection |
| 7 | Implementation: | Procurement and project management in *widest* sense |
| 8 | Review: | What *changed* and what *learnt* |

**Fig 6.6 ◆ General model of top-down alignment planning process**

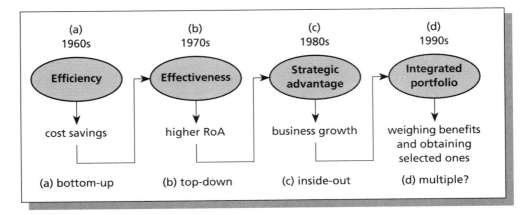

**Fig 6.7 ◆ Evolution of the planning process**
(adapted with the permission of Butterworth-Heinemann from *Planning IT: Creating an Information Management Strategy* (1991) by D. J. Silk)

The likelihood of one approach being prominent can be charted by the *nature* of the organisation and the business importance of IS to it at the given time. This business importance can take three forms, so IS can be important:

- As a means of delivery of products or services
- Since business strategies depend upon IT for implementation
- Since IT provides new strategic opportunities

There is an increasing focus upon the idea that the planning process must be different at different stages; this is captured in Figure 6.8 in which Galliers (1987) indicates a 'learning' path by which organisations move through different single-focus IS strategy planning approaches. The 'mature' situation is the recognition of

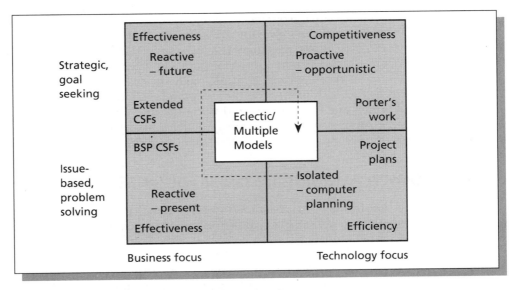

**Fig 6.8 ◆ Development path for strategic IS planning process**
(after Galliers (1987))

the need to deal *simultaneously* with business and technology issues and goals (similar to Earl's (1989) multiple methods as illustrated in Figure 6.13 p.193). The experiences gained by moving along this path also give the skill to deal with multiple models.

Just as many analysis tools draw upon the idea of eras or stages of growth so too have there been ways of perceiving the role of IS planning and hence ways of deciding if the IS plan suited the business or not. This is modelled in Figure 6.8. The segment referred to as *isolated* is where planning is an internal matter for the IS function. Planning here is about improving computing efficiency. There are two reactive segments where planning seeks to address effectiveness. The first of these is where the planning effort becomes aware of the need to create systems to deal with the business' problems and so reacts to the *current* set of issues and opportunities. There is some planning success in this segment but no forward perspective. Hence the development of the second reactive segment where the *future* dimension is added. In this segment, planning is still reacting to business goals but these include future as well as current ones. The *proactive* planning segment is where the planning process seeks to find the IS opportunities by focusing upon the business environment. Even this middle-out or inside-out planning process leaves some issues unresolved and hence the centre planning segment is where an *eclectic* mixture of planning process models are used in order to capitalise upon the strengths of each since IS strategic planning is itself a complex and eclectic set of issues.

There is an observable tendency for large firms to 'try out' different approaches to planning. They experiment with different processes for IS strategy formulation. Earl (1989) suggests that this experimentation is likely to go on for the four to five years it typically takes before 'hard' business benefits can be reaped. During the early stages of this learning process the benefits are from learning about IS strategic planning and themselves. It is only when the use of multiple models is adopted that these 'soft' process gains are joined by 'hard' product gains. It is only when the organisation recognises and accommodates multiple planning models that the organisation produces 'better', ie more business consistent, IS strategies. Of course, throughout this development path the organisation is learning how to plan effectively.

The five-year time-frame for this suggested by Earl was illustrated in Chapter 4. At each of the five stages there is a different objective for the planning process and so obviously a different approach should be selected. The organisation will 'settle' down to an acceptance of multiple methods each moving into sharper or dimmer focus as the current environment demands. There is likely to be a dominant leg, and which one it is will depend upon the industry the organisation is in. So the eclectic centre segment of Galliers' model contains a number of planning processes each of which is given more or less attention as business issues dictate.

## 6.3 ◆ TOP-DOWN ALIGNING OF IS AND BUSINESS STRATEGIES

The first framework considered in some detail is that from Ward (1987). This is a rational, clearly explained, compendium approach that suggests *how* a collection of conceptual models are to be combined. Ward's approach uses the set of models to provide logical pointers to strategies for IS resourcing, structure and management that are *demonstrably* linked to business objectives. More detailed coverage of the tactics of IS resourcing, structure and management is provided in the discussions of strategy implementation included in Part 3.

Ward's method takes, as its start point, the definition of the organisation's competitive posture, in other words the generic business strategy is defined using Porter's terminology as discussed in Chapter 2. We can already see that Ward's approach will only be appropriate at a SBU level, where a coherent, single, competitive stance is definable.

Ward suggests that for any given generic business strategy there is a default relationship to Parsons' generic IS strategies, that is given a particular business approach, certain IS approaches would be expected to emerge where there is perhaps no conscious *direction* of the pattern of IS resource allocations. This default relationship Ward suggests is:

- Low cost tends to:       Scarce resource
                                Free market
                                (less likely to necessary evil)

- Differentiation tends to:   Monopoly
                                Leading edge
                                (less likely to centrally planned)

- Focus/niche tends to:     a secondary business strategy

Ward is very careful to point out that this is the *default* relationship and the default, or emergent, strategy may be entirely inappropriate, particularly for organisations for which IS is very important. Ward argues that the *appropriate* IS strategy is one that is business consistent. He suggests a process for gaining this consistency. This suggested process builds consistency with the IS management maturity of the organisation and with the strategic importance IS has for it. By building on these two particular analysis tools an IS strategy that is both feasible (matches the IS maturity stage) and desirable (matches the strategic importance segment) will be adopted.

The first step in this process therefore is to use the notion of match between IS strategy and stage of maturity. The nature of this match is illustrated in Figure 6.9. The application logic is that, having established at what stage position an organisation (or SBU) is with respect to a specific form of IS, then the suggested IS strategy can be 'read off'. So different IS strategies are going to be *consistent* with different stages of maturity of use and management of IS. The IS strategy indicated by this model may not be the one emerging as a result of the nature of the business' competitive stance. In addition, the 'complete' stages of growth model indicates that repeating cycles of stages 1–3 are to be expected but associated with different, new, technologies. So we have some clear pointers that a set of IS strategies will be needed and that these should be chosen upon the basis of the organisation's experience level with a given technology. It would be inappropriate to adopt the same strategies for managing the newly emerging workgroup technologies as for the well-understood mainframe multi-processing technologies because the IS management maturity, of the *experience* of managing it, will be very different for each. The same need for a variety of strategic stances was very noticeable when personal computers grew to corporate prominence during the 1980s.

Next, the strategic importance grid is used. This can define two things, firstly the aggregated strategic importance of IS to the business, and secondly, and more importantly, the disaggregated business value weightings of *different* elements of the IS portfolio. So the current and planned systems portfolio represents a basket of IS activities, each of which holds a different *value* to the business and so should be

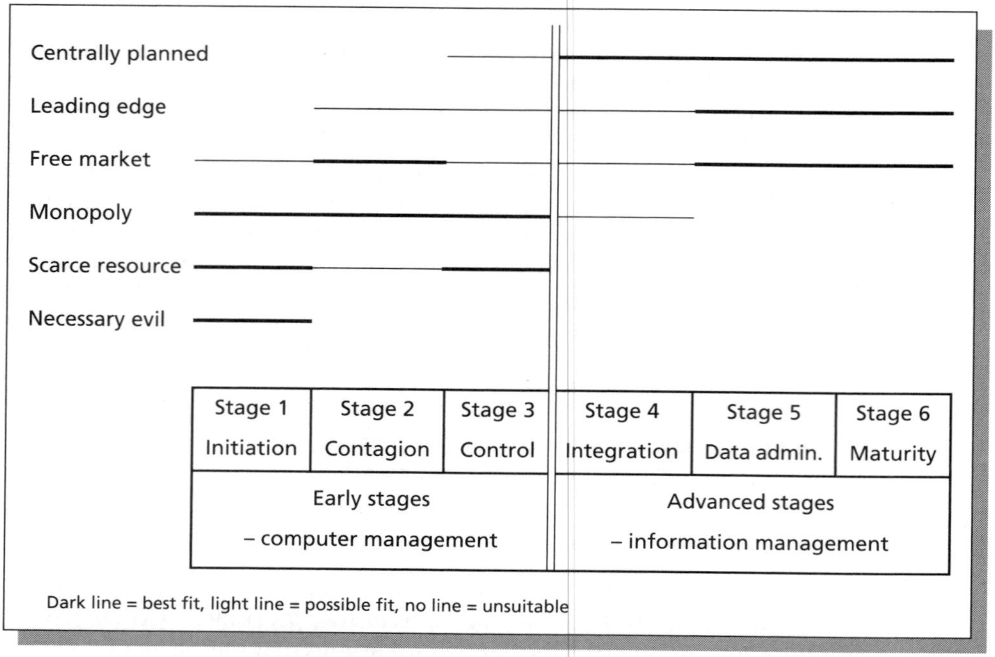


**Fig 6.9 ◆ Relationships between IS strategies and IS maturity**
(adapted from Integrating Information Systems into Business Strategies by Ward, *Long Range Planning*, Vol 20 No 3, pp. 19–29, © 1987, with kind permission from Elsevier Science Ltd)

treated differently. The generic IS strategies have a relationship to the four segments of the strategic importance grid. Each segment has a 'best fit' IS strategy shown in Figure 6.10. Ward's approach is building up an ever more varied portfolio of IS strategies!

This growing portfolio is further expanded because of the life cycle implications inherent in the strategic importance grid. Obviously, organisations would not necessarily be placed in the same segment today as they would have been placed in

| **STRATEGIC** | **TURNAROUND** |
|---|---|
| CENTRALLY PLANNED<br>Leading edge | LEADING EDGE<br>Free market<br>Centrally planned |
| **FACTORY** | **SUPPORT** |
| MONOPOLY<br>Scarce resource | SCARCE RESOURCE<br>Free market<br>Necessary evil |

**Fig 6.10 ◆ Strategic importance grid and 'best-fit' IS strategies**
(adapted from Integrating Information Systems into Business Strategies by Ward, *Long Range Planning*, Vol 20 No 3, pp. 19–29, © 1987, with kind permission from Elsevier Science Ltd)

1990 or 1985. Even more obviously, a *type* of system would definitely not be placed in the same segment today as in 1990 or 1985. This is a very useful reminder that these 'snapshots' of *dynamic* models must be treated with caution, and also makes explicit the need to *evolve* the IS strategy to keep it consistent with business value.

Ward uses Porter's work to illustrate how the business value of the applications portfolio will evolve. Since the strategic importance grid is so closely related to the BCG's benefit generation/resource use matrix (*see* Chapter 2) the product portfolio management implications can be 'lifted' into the IS strategy world. Hence, not only can the organisation match the segment to an IS strategy whilst being conscious of the evolutionary path that they can hope to manage applications portfolio elements along, but they find that appropriate management styles and resource levels are prescribed once the business importance has been diagnosed. Resource levels should not be 'even' but should rise and fall with a given application's strategic value. Organisations will never find that *all* of their applications are strategically important and so a scarce resourcing strategy will be appropriate for some parts of the portfolio. Similarly no organisation will find that *all* of their applications are valueless and so perhaps a centrally planned strategy will be appropriate for some parts of the portfolio.

The fuller implications of the product portfolio analysis aspects of the strategic importance matrix are illustrated in Figure 6.11. This diagram notes the BCG matrix segment name 'matched' onto the segment name used here. This diagram also illustrates the prescriptive influences that can be drawn as a result of this model's derivation from that BCG matrix. In terms of the specifics of IS strategy use of this one model provides statements about the viable IS strategy; the dominant structural pressure; the strongest influencing factor; the level of justified resource use; behavioural focus of the responsible manager or group. The IS strategy design resulting from the application of Ward's method can therefore include explicit coverage of these issues.

The IS strategy planning process can 'learn' from the experience of product portfolio management. IS needs to be sensitive to the fact that different management styles are needed to reflect the different segments:

- Strategic is the segment that needs flexible and sensitive handling to exploit opportunities to the full. This needs the management skill of a developer to head an adept team.

- Support segment applications should be starved of unnecessary resources and so need the managerial skills of a caretaker who is prepared for the unglamorous role of resourcing only to reduce net costs.

- Factory segment applications are those that need the care of a controller to milk them for all their possible benefits by well judged enhancements. Applications in this segment should be resourced in ways that will increase their quality but not cause any business disruption.

- Turnaround segment applications are associated with uncertainty and so the risk-handling skills of an entrepreneur are needed to push for advances when needed and yet be willing to accept the need to drop unsuitable developments.

The managerial style and resource level are, of course, very much part and parcel of an IS strategy but Ward's approach makes explicit the need to cater for variety – and a changing variety at that.

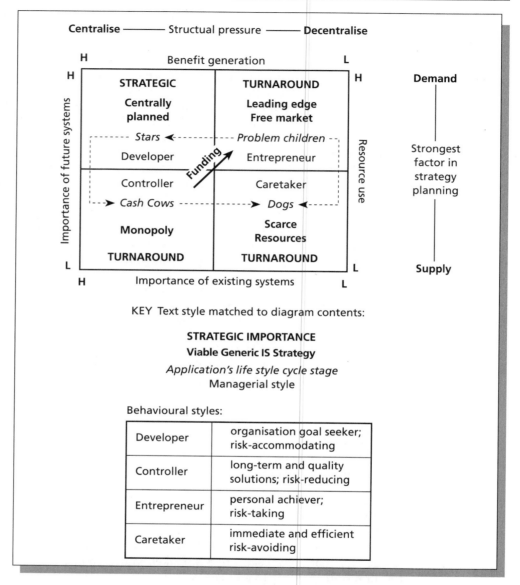

**Fig 6.11 ◆ Portfolio matrix comparisons, managerial styles and resource levels**

The net result of using models of maturity and models of business importance is the tentative identification of two sets of potentially viable IS strategies. These lists need to be cross-considered to select actually viable alternatives. The real business value of a system should be reflected in how it is treated. There is no doubt that IS has a distressing tendency to manage the systems portfolio to reflect its technical complexities and not to reflect its business importance.

So Ward's explicitly business aligning approach is fundamentally a top-down one, though it is tempered (rather than driven) by an awareness of infrastructure issues; this awareness is reflected in the assessment of IS maturity (Figure 6.12).

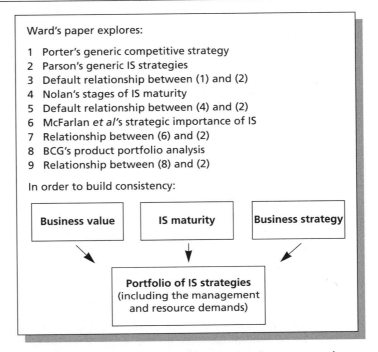

**Fig 6.12 ◆ Aims and overview of Ward's top-down approach**

Ward outlines the overall approach as:

1 Analyse the strategic business importance of IS using:

- Industry and competitive impact analysis
- Competitive five forces analysis
- Operational dependency analysis
  to chart existing and planned applications on Strategic Importance Grid

2 Analyse the IS strategy options using:

- Strategic importance charting from (1)
- BCG portfolio management model
- Stages of growth model
  to define the set of IS strategies required

3 Manage the *evolving* portfolio in direct proportion to business value and not technical peculiarities using:

- IS strategy from (2)
- Resource and management portfolio analysis
- Current approach analysis
  to define the demands for the effective management of known and predicted developments.

Ward's powerful compendium of analytical and top-down approaches develops into a conceptually satisfying planning framework that is particularly appealing because the approach hinges upon the *relationships* between a number of well-known tools. Many organisations are familiar with these tools since they form almost 'standards' of IS strategic analysis. The clear pattern of:

- document symptoms
- make a diagnosis
- read off a cure

implies that IS strategy defining is a simple, almost a trivial, activity and therein lies the strength and weakness of this approach. If it is as simple as that, why isn't everyone getting it right? There is, of course, no real answer to this question. Ward's method is a strong example of the formal-rational approach to IS strategy formulation. The IS strategy will be *designed* on the basis of the systematic steps of the analysis. However the process of operationalising the method actually requires a great deal more skill of synthesis and creativity than a description of the steps of the method implies. At the most obvious level, the process of selecting the IS strategy from the advised set and the process of turning this *generic* selection into a real flesh and blood organisationally grounded pattern of IS resource allocations are both processes of choice bound up in interpretation and values. At a less obvious level, the process of identifying the stage of maturity and the process of deciding upon the strategic importance of areas of IS activity are also value judging selection processes. The IS strategy design resulting from the application of this method will be only as useful as the degree to which the *actual* organisation's situation and values are captured.

## 6.4 ◆ ECLECTIC, ALIGNING AND IMPACTING PLANNING PROCESS

The complexity of live situations is often too great for a single technique to be universally successful and hence several approaches advocate *combining* techniques. Earl's (1989) model of the need for multiple methods for developing IS strategies is chosen for its sophistication. This approach suggests that it can be used to judge the *appropriateness* of models and techniques and so judge which ones an organisation should concentrate upon.

Earl suggests that the ideas developed when assessing the impact of IS upon an organisation and its industry can be used to identify the three ways in which IS may be *strategic* for them:

- As a means of delivering products or services
- Business strategies depend upon IT for implementation
- IS provides new strategic opportunities

These three classes of strategic *importance* each have a close relationship to particular approaches to the IS strategic planning process. Earl suggests that these three *approaches* are:

- Top-down which links the IS strategy inextricably to what the business *must* do
- Bottom-up which links the IS strategy to supporting what the business *does* do
- Inside-out which links the IS strategy to what the business *could* do

The likelihood of any one approach being prominent can be charted by the *nature* of the business importance of IS to the given organisation at the given time. The *multiple* methods implication is that, while one approach may appropriately be prominent, all should be accommodated for effective IS strategy planning.

### 6.4.1 ◆ Strategic importance of IS and infrastructure-led bottom-up planning process

For this class of organisation IS is the means of delivering the goods and services of the sector. Banks and Financial Services are the classic example of this. The computer-based transaction systems underpin the business operations and the organisation depends upon IS. Any failed systems would stop their operations, an *inefficient* one would drive up their costs and an *inflexible* one would stop product development. Organisations in this class have to be driven by their infrastructure decisions and so must be *guided* by their technologists on what to do. Often the organisations must make choices in ignorance of future business needs and so this class is one of inherently high risk and uncertainty.

Giving prominence to the bottom-up approach will be appropriate for any organisation where the impact of IS is felt in this way. The organisations will need to understand their current position and to be able to evaluate it in a meaningful way. They may need to demonstrate the quality and coverage of existing IS to get or regain credibility. No organisation is without a history and the more that has been achieved in the past the more those achievements influence the future. Recognising the strengths and weaknesses of the current portfolio and infrastructure is necessary for *controlled* developments. This evaluation may identify potential for better exploitation or value adding building. Earl refers to this approach as the bottom-up leg and this leg of the multiple method needs evaluative tools, for instance auditing the current position by examining business value (preferably by users), or examining technical quality (preferably by specialists) of major systems and considering existing performance and potential. The bottom-up planning process must appraise the skills, attitudes, user awareness, technical ability, etc of the organisation, and could for instance use Nolan's IS maturity model to do this. This is not identical to the re-active project planning that has always been associated with DP activities. Infrastructure-led IS planning can still be strategic in focus rather than specific and isolated needs driven, whether the project plans are drawn up irrespective of the *relative* priority or whether they mesh into an overall direction.

### 6.4.2 ◆ Strategic importance of IS and business-led top-down planning process

For this class of organisation the business strategies increasingly depend upon IS for their implementation. The business and functional strategies require a major automation, information, and communications capability and are only made possible by these technologies. The classic example of this class is the automotive industry where business plans for survival and regeneration define the investments in IS for manufacturing, distribution and marketing. The IS plans are important to, but derivatives of, the business plans.

Any organisation that can analyse to be certain of, and hence manage, the need for IS in its business direction is likely to find that a business-led planning process is most appropriate because of the reduction in risk. Therefore a top-down analytical approach should be selected, all of which rely upon the ability to apply models, such as portfolio analysis and information analysis, by decomposing the organisation and its objectives to the level of business process and resultant information needs. Ward's top-down approach of Section 6.3 was a clear example of this.

### 6.4.3 ◆ Strategic importance of IS and mixed, eclectic planning processes

For this class of organisation, IS has the potential to provide *new* strategic opportunities. For this class the specific applications of technology are exploitable to develop the business and change the processes of managing it. Where there is potential in specific areas for the exploitation of IS the organisation needs a mixed approach to the planning process. The IS infrastructure will be the *enabler* that delivers the new idea but not the generator of that innovation. If organisations do not use a mixed approach that 'anchors' and connects such exploitation into the business goals and the organisational capabilities then exploitations will not *alter* the business.

These organisations must include an inside-out, opportunity-led planning process. The innovative use of IS does not result solely from *analysing* needs or *building* upon capabilities. The formal, structured, approaches are not the best ways to identify or pursue innovations, including those in IS. Technological innovation can come about from entrepreneurial managers outside the formal planning process or in very focused, one-off targeted plans. Strategic opportunities in this way are about 'bright sparks' and 'champions' and working around any formal procedures. In turbulent environments an organisation needs alert and aggressive managers at the IS/Business interface and it needs champions in a position of power to muster any resources necessary. Inside-out planning is a creative approach, relying on generating ideas for business opportunities that can be pursued by using IS. This is akin to the ideas of business re-engineering discussed in Chapter 8. Inside-out 'planning' needs a creative innovative environment that allows off-beat approaches that by-pass normal rules. The organisation is going to need to prepare an environment that is ready for this (*see* Chapter 8) and people able to innovate within it (*see* Chapter 11). It is not analytical or evaluative but innovative and the processes of innovation in IS strategy formulation have not attracted as much attention as have the processes of analysis and evaluation. Zhuang (1995) documents a study that attempts to address this lack but the study has yet to form any conclusions.

Earl suggests a method for the development of IS strategies that has three 'legs' (Figure 6.13). These are top-down, to translate business objectives; bottom-up, to develop incrementally from the current position; and an 'inside-out', less structured, leg to support innovation. An organisation's classification will determine which of the legs will be dominant at any one time but *all* may/should be employed, since the three IS strategy planning approaches are *not* mutually exclu-

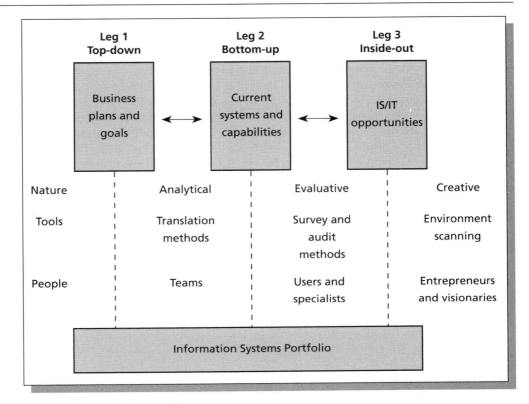

**Fig 6.13 ◆ Earl's multiple methods**
(adapted from Earl, M.J., *Management Strategies for Information Technology* (1989) by permission of Prentice Hall)

sive. They are all simultaneously required if IS plans are to capture the true business situations, although each will enjoy stages of greater or lesser emphasis. This mixed approach, Earl suggests, allows the organisation to deal with the three *simultaneously* vital questions:

- What are our business needs?                Business-led
- What are the technological opportunities?   Inside-out
- What is our current position and capability?  Infrastructure-led

In different eras of the organisation's IS strategy learning path and in different businesses the *emphasis* will, and should, shift. It is a three-dimensional model that Earl proposes since the foreground and background can alter. Therefore the organisation in the infrastructure-led class cannot *ignore* business plans, but acknowledges that getting the infrastructure right is the first priority and will generate those business plans. Organisations in the business-led class should not be deaf to the indicators arising from Earl's 'leg 2' and the ideas arising from 'leg 3'. Organisations in the mixed class need a minimalist set of corporate IS policies; this is very much the current fashion, giving freedom and autonomy to follow up ideas. This class must concentrate upon getting the 'soft' infrastructure (people and support, etc.) in place but will need the 'hard' infrastructure as well. The ideas arising from 'leg 3' may need tempering by needs arising from 'leg 1' and indicators arising from 'leg 2' if chaos is to be avoided.

All this takes time. As Nolan found, organisations learn slowly and they must learn about IS strategic planning just as about IS use and management. The soft outputs are process gains in which the 'good' that results from the planning process is learning about planning in the organisation rather than the IS strategy, a view supported by Earl's research. IS/Business integration does not mean *translation*, and this integration of business and IS takes time. The process achievements must gain business and IS commitment. To do this the organisation must create a 'peg in the ground' that records where the current position is. Hence the evaluative, bottom-up leg takes the foreground for the first two years. As confidence and competence grow, legs 1 and 3 begin to emerge as the organisation learns that strategic directions *and* innovation are important.

Four to five years after formally recognising the need for IS strategic plans the organisation can expect to have plans that are integrated with the business. During this learning time the organisation can get over-ambitious and unrealistically expect *guaranteed* competitive advantage from IS. It is important to recognise that all three legs must continue to exist since innovation always needs a supporting infrastructure, yet all infrastructure with no direction achieves nothing and direction without creativity is sterile. Earl's is a dynamic model that aims to help organisations *recognise* that IS strategies are competitively important but creating *realistic* ones takes time, effort, and resources. Earl's model does not prescribe in detail what techniques to use, rather it identifies a framework for that selection. In fact Earl offers a strategy for IS strategy planning!

## 6.5 ◆ SUMMARY

Sinclair's (1986) work argues that organisations should give less effort to grasping for a methodology for planning and more consideration of what he calls 'the three domains of planning objectives'. These are very similar to Silk's (1991) IS objectives. In Sinclair's article he points out that the organisation must conduct a preliminary project to identify which of the three domains is of most concern to the organisation. His three domains are:

- efficiency
- effectiveness
- competitiveness

These are much in line with several views of the need for differing emphases during IS strategy planning. The organisation must establish which of these is their *primary* goal since the choice of planning method and/or techniques will vary with the domain. Not all approaches will address the correct domain and none address all three. For example, Business Systems Planning with its bottom-up data design oriented approach will be good at efficiency and will provide some coverage of effectiveness. BSP charts what *is* and not what *could/should be* and is not only internal to the organisation, but practically internal to the IS function. Therefore BSP provides no means of addressing the third domain, that of competitiveness, and so will require some 'back-up' by way of more holistic questions in order to judge where to take IS beyond a data plan.

In contrast portfolio approaches such as that of the BCG Matrix allow the *role* of IS to be identified. From this the possible contribution of IS to a number of variables can be evaluated. The portfolio approaches re-enforce an acceptance of change since they make explicit that they are only a snapshot view. Unfortunately, their use is so very subjective that it can be very difficult for the organisation to reach a consensus. Critical success factor analysis is, quite obviously, very competitively focused, but here the analysis demands very skilful interviewers in order to actually establish the critical success factors. So, Sinclair concludes, it is vital that the pre-planning effort identifies which domain(s) is to be targeted in order to choose the tools wisely. This preliminary work needs to ensure that:

• The objectives of IS within the organisation are clarified
• The planning tools for managing the IS function are discussed and agreed upon.

Both empirically and conceptually there seems to be much evidence of 'horses for courses' in planning frameworks. Tools and models are constantly being developed, though evidence of their usefulness is usually only anecdotal, and more stories are told of the great good that can be done *if* IS is linked into the business than of how to achieve this. Simultaneously, evaluations have been done to try to find the one *best* approach to IS strategy planning. For instance, a number of comparative studies have been done of planning approaches such as CSFs and BSP, etc. By the late 1980s many organisations felt that what offers the 'best' chance of planning success is contingent upon a number of things, including obviously the organisational commitment to the chosen approach and the skills available to apply it, but the choice of approach and its subsequent chance of success also depends upon the planning environment. (This planning environment includes the business *environment*, the management style, the technological context and the organisational structure.) Sullivan (1985) also showed that different methods suit different contexts, and argued that the determining factors are how diffuse is the technology throughout the organisation and how infused, that is how well developed and important to the business, are the applications. Of course, one important aspect of the planning environment is the planning objective. Ward *et al.* (1990) presents a three-eras model (*see* Chapter 5 for more discussion of Era Models) that suggests that bottom-up planning is appropriate for Era 1 (DP), but Eras 2 and 3 need a planning approach that is implicitly and explicitly top-down.

Currently perhaps as many as 60–70 per cent of UK companies feel that they have an IS strategy that closely relates to their business strategy or is part of it. They may always document their IS strategy in a top-down manner but it is very likely that the ideas have emerged bottom-up, only to be validated in a top-down way. There are many different approaches to defining the IS strategy but despite the different interpretations the organisation seeks certainty of 'correctness'. This certainty of suitability is sought because of the enormous cost of getting it wrong and selecting (or allowing to emerge) IS management styles or systems that are not appropriate. The Pareto 80/20 rule applies in IS strategy as it does everywhere else; so the organisation can *hope* to expend 20 per cent effort for 80 per cent of the possible business gain; however the real danger is that they will expend 80 per cent effort for 20 per cent of the potential gain. A similar version of this has been suggested as a 9-7-5 rule, that is any plan can knock off 10 per cent of the non-strategic frills and get 90 per cent of the system for 70 per cent of the estimated effort and cost in 50 per cent of the elapsed time.

At all stages of the strategic planning process decisions already taken may form the constraints, for instance where lots of expensive systems already exist it is likely that future ones will have to *interface* rather than replace at least for the economic life of the existing ones. An organisation that has found choices barred off because of being 'too locked in' is likely to constrain all future strategies to be open and not proprietary.

Countless journal articles trumpet a given organisation's discovery of the 'perfect' planning technique: presumably as they move through the strategic planning stages they trumpet a different one! It is unlikely that they have hit upon a universally appropriate IS planning method since much evidence points to the need for *each* organisation to put together its own mixture. As Earl (1989) suggests, three different approaches are *simultaneously* required, and which is *prominent* is contingent upon the organisation's stage of learning about IS strategy, its industry, and other such ideas once used to select the one approach to planning. So whilst prominence can be established somewhat generically, the exact nature of the *mix* will be organisationally specific and specific to a particular instance for that organisation. Earl's work on multiple methods is extended in Earl (1993) in which he describes five types of planning approaches and concludes that it is the eclectic and continuous organisational approach that appeared the most effective. Earl describes the five approaches as being:

- Business-led approach: which takes business plans as the reference point from which to analyse what IS plans must be. Business *drives* IS in a common sense way. However, business strategies are rarely this clear and in any case it becomes difficult to argue for IS *enabled* change.

- Method-driven approach: which uses a structured IS planning method (often with consultants taking a significant role) believing that formality and rigor is necessary for quality. The plans tend not to be 'owned' by those who will take IS resource decisions and remain 'unreal'.

- Administrative approach: which emphasises the process of resource allocations and the approvals procedures. This may fit the organisational control style and because financial criteria can be manipulated as symbols of non-financial values IS choices may closely reflect organisational values. However, radical change is unlikely to overturn the 'business as usual' dominance.

- Technological approach: which produces a model (or set of models) of the business in order to derive blueprints for IS activities. The technical complexity, the difficulty of comprehending the models generate a lack of organisational commitment. Only small-scale instances are likely to be effective.

- Organisational approach; which takes IS strategy planning to be a messy activity inextricably bound into all other organisational activities. Methods are tools adopted to facilitate particular purposes as the confirmed process unfolds. Teamwork is emphasised; IS resource allocation decisions are constantly taken. The approach may be vulnerable to management changes and may be weak at creating IS infrastructures.

Earl concluded that the last of these approaches was the most effective. This approach includes mixtures of planning tools, as already discussed, but it also explicitly sees IS strategy planning as a *continual* unfolding process. This is in contrast to the structured planning methods (for instance, that of Ward as discussed in Section 6.3) that assume IS strategy planning to be a discrete activity, triggered off (*see* Chapter 4 for examples of the types of circumstance that might act as such triggers). By this assumption IS strategy planning is a project in its own right and so needs a project team who will choose the models to use and allocate the resources to do the planning. This team may be headed by a senior manager but must also include specialist staff who are skilled in using the collected techniques. In contrast to this project view of IS strategy planning, the organisational approach has a continual process by which the pattern of IS resource allocations emerge, this being broadly similar to the issues of strategy emergence and incrementalisation discussed in Chapter 1.

The approach which Earl refers to as 'organisational' is an approach to planning that focuses upon behavioural aspects of the process by which decisions unfold rather than considering only the technical, formal and rational elements. Effective IS strategy formulation, ie forming the pattern of IS resource allocations that is deemed to be successful, may require a hybrid of analysis and emergence. Emergence alone may not accommodate those elements of IS activity that form its infrastructure (cabling, data structures and so on) since these cannot readily accommodate incremental decision making. Rationality alone may not reflect the 'humanity' of organisational situations (power, politics, multiple objectives, values and so on). Earl comments on some attempts to shape such a hybrid approach to IS strategy planning and Venkatraman *et al.* (1993) describe a fairly formal instance of the same notion.

Note that the need for IS planning tools is re-affirmed by these findings. It is the tools and techniques of Chapter 5 and of Chapter 7 that will be used as need demands either to form an approach to planning or to serve particular purposes within and emergent approach to planning.

**References and further reading**

Alter, A. (1992) *Information Systems: a Management Perspective*, Addison-Wesley.

Benjamin, R.I., Rockart, J.F., Scott Morton, M.S. and Wyman, J. (1983) Information Technology: a strategic opportunity, *Sloan Management Review*, Spring 1984.

Bergeron, F., Buteau, C. and Raymond, L. (1991) Identification of Strategic Information Systems Opportunities: Applying and comparing two methodologies, *MIS Quarterly*, Mar.

Cashmore, C. and Lyall, R. (1991) *Business Information: Systems and Strategies*, Prentice-Hall.

Copley, J.D. (1989) Information Planning, *Software Management Magazine*, Mar pp. 14–16.

Davis, G.B. and Olson, M.H. (1985) *Management Information Systems: Conceptual Foundations, Structure and Development* (2nd edn), McGraw-Hill.

Dickson, G.W. and Wetherbe, J. C. (1985) *The Management of Information Systems*, McGraw-Hill.

Drucker, P. (1964) *Managing for Results*, Harper & Row.

Earl, M.J. (1989) *Management Strategies for Information Technology*, Prentice-Hall.

Earl, M. (1993) Experiences in Strategic Information Systems Planning, *MIS Quarterly*, Mar pp. 1–24.

Emberton, J. and Mann, R. (1988) Methodology for Effective Information Systems Planning, *Information and Software Technology*, Vol 30 No 4.

Finkelstein, C. (1989) *An Introduction to Information Engineering*, Addison-Wesley.

Flynn, D.J. (1992) *Information Systems Requirements: Determination and Analysis*, McGraw-Hill.

Frenzell, C.W. (1992) *Management of Information Technology*, Boyd & Fraser.

Galliers, R.D. (1987) Information Systems Planning in the UK and Australia – a comparison of current practice, *Oxford Surveys in Information Technology*, Vol 4 pp. 223–55.

Galliers, R.D. (1991) Strategic Information Systems Planning: Myths, Reality and Guidelines for Successful Implementation, *European Journal of Information Systems*, Vol 1 No 1 pp. 55–64.

Galliers, F.R. and Sutherland, A.R. (1991) *Information Systems Management and Strategy Formulation*, Addison-Wesley.

Ives, B. and Learmonth, G. (1984) The Information System as a Competitive Weapon, *Communications of the ACM*, Vol 27 No 12 pp. 1193–201.

Kaye, D. (1992) Formulating Business Strategy to Exploit the New IT, *Unicom Seminar Proceedings: Creating a Strategic Business Based IT Policy*.

Keen, P.G.W. (1991) *Shaping the Future: Business Design through Information Technology*, Harvard Business Press.

King, W.R. (1978) How Effective is Your Information Systems Planning?, *Long Range Planning*, Vol 21 No 5 pp. 103–12.

Kovacevic, A. and Majluf, N. (1993) Six Stages of IT Strategic Management, *Sloan Management Review*, Summer pp. 77–87.

Lederer, A.L. and Gardiner, V. (1992) The Process of Strategic Information Planning, *Journal of Strategic Information Systems,* Vol 1 No 2 Mar pp. 76–83.

Lederer, A.L. and Sethi, V. (1988) The Implementation of Strategic Information Systems Planning Methodologies, *MIS Quarterly*, Sept pp. 445–61.

Lederer, A.L. and Sethi, V. (1989) Pitfalls in Planning, *Datamation*, June pp. 59.

McFarlan, E.W., McKenney, J.L. and Pyburn, P. (1983) The Information Archipelago – plotting a course, *Harvard Business Review*, Jan-Feb pp. 145–56.

Mainelli, M.R. and Miller, D.R. (1988) Strategic Planning for Information Systems at British Rail, *Long Range Planning,* Vol 21 Aug pp. 65–75.

Martin, E.W., Dehayes, D.W., Hoffer, J.A. and Perkins, W.C. (1991) *Managing Information Technology: What managers need to know*, Macmillan.

Mensching, J.R. and Adams, D.A. (1991) *Managing an Information System*, Prentice-Hall.

O'Brien, B. (1992) *Demands and Decisions: Briefings on issues in Information Technology Strategy*, Prentice-Hall.

Parsons, G. (1983) Fitting Information Systems Technology to the Corporate Needs: The Linking Strategy, *Harvard Business School Teaching Notes* (9–183–176) June.

Porter, M.E. (1979) How Competitive Forces Shape Strategy, *Harvard Business Review*, Mar-Apr, pp. 137–45.

Porter, M.E. (1980) *Competitive Strategy: Techniques for Analysing Industries and Competitors*, Free Press.

Porter, M.E. (1985a) *Competitive Advantage: Creating and Sustaining Superior Performance.* Free Press.

Porter, M.E. (1985b) Technology & Competitive Advantage, *The Journal of Business Strategy*, 5, 3 Winter pp. 60–78.

Porter, M.E. and Millar, V.E. (1985) How information gives you competitive advantage, *Harvard Business Review*, Vol 63 No 4 July-Aug pp. 149–60.

Rackoff, N., Wiseman, C. and Ullrich, W.A. (1985) Information Systems for Competitive Advantage: Implementation of a planning process, *MIS Quarterly*, 9 4 Dec pp. 185–294.

Reynolds, G.W. (1992) *Information Systems for Managers* (2nd edn), West Publishing.

Silk, D.J. (1991) *Planning It: Creating an Information Management Strategy*, Butterworth-Heinemann.

Sinclair, S. (1986) The Three Domains of Information Systems Planning, *Journal of Information Systems Management*, Vol 3 Spring pp. 8–16.

Smith, A. and Medley, D. (1987) *Information Resource Management*, South-Western.

Sullivan, C. (1985) Business Planning in the Information Age, *Sloan Management Review*, Winter pp. 3–12.

Tapscott, D. and Caston, A. (1993) *Paradigm Shift: The New Promise of Information Technology*, McGraw-Hill.

Venkatraman, N., Henderson, J. and Oldach, S. (1993) Continuous Strategic Alignment, Exploiting Information Technology Capabilities for Competitive Success, *European Management Journal*, Vol 11 No 2 pp. 139–49.

Ward, J. (1987) Integrating Information Systems into Business Strategies, *Long Range Planning*, Vol 20 No 3 pp. 19–29.

Ward, J. and Griffiths, P. (1996) *Strategic Planning for Information Systems* (2nd edn), Wiley.

Wysocki, R. and Young, J. (1990) *Information Systems: Management Principles in Action*. Wiley

Zhuang, L. (1995) Bridging the Gap between Technology and Business Strategy: A Pilot Study on the Innovation Process, *Management Decision*, Vol 33 No 8 pp. 13–21.

# CHAPTER 7

# Information value and IS investment

As has been indicated a number of times throughout this text, the formulation of an IS strategy involves the planning or emergence of a pattern of IS resource allocation. This pattern of decisions encompasses an inextricable mix of the ends those taking the decisions are seeking plus their judgement of what are acceptable and unacceptable means of achieving them. The point at which planning becomes action, the point at which emergence unfolds, is the actual IS resource allocation process. This chapter therefore discusses the issues surrounding this resource allocation process. This notion of desirable ends plus judgement of acceptable means would also serve as a definition of a cost-benefit appraisal, though not simply in the narrow financial sense. The complex interaction of many factors leads to a potential IS activity being desirable or undesirable, to being acceptable or unacceptable, and financial factors are one, but only one, part of this interaction.

Making IS strategy real through IS resource allocations therefore requires the management of three inter-related sets of issues:

- Issues related to IS costs
- Issues related to IS benefits
- Issues related to the balance between the IS costs and the IS benefits

It must be stressed again that the use of the two terms 'costs' and 'benefits' in no way indicates an exclusively financial meaning. The meaning of cost here is of the giving up of some resource or attribute that is deemed important. Such resources will include capital but will also include energy, time, emotion, power, commitment and many others. In the case of most potential IS activities one attribute that will be 'given up' is certainty, it will *not* be known what the actual outcome of the candidate activity will be. Similarly the meaning of benefits here is the gaining of some resource or attribute that is deemed useful. Again such resources will include capital but will usually also include power, status, conformance, certainty and so on. Note the certainty referred to here as a potential benefit is from improved information availability for decision making and not that the effects of the activity are known.

This chapter will not contain a *separate* section in which risk is discussed as a discrete and distinct issue. It can be seen by the nature of the attributes potentially gained or given up that issues of risk suffuse all aspects of IS resource allocations. One *cost* may be that a particular IS activity moves the organisation from the familiar to the unknown. This increases risk by decreasing certainty and many *innovative* uses of IS would, by definition, fall in to this category. Long-term infrastructure building IS activities would also fall into this category by virtue of the fact that their time horizons extend well beyond current technological knowledge. One *benefit* may be that a particular potential IS activity moves the organisation from the known to the more known. This decreases risk by increasing certainty and many instrumentation examples of MIS would fall into this category as would IS activities to automate itself and therefore *shorten* those time horizons generating risk.

Overarching both cost and benefit notions is the fact that it is the balancing of *risks* that is being achieved through the process of managing cost/benefit judgements. Risk is not a separate issue here, risk *is* the issue in IS resource allocations.

A major concern for the management of most organisations is to assess and set the *extent* of their investment in *is*; how much to spend is always critical. When struggling with this concern a range of often despairingly voiced questions are posed, these include:

- Do we know how much is currently spent on IS?
- What value results from this spending?
- How should IS alternatives be justified/prioritised/financed?
- Why do IS budgets continue to rise if IT unit costs fall?
- How can we regain our belief in IS returns?

Whether these questions are asked in anger or in despair some of them can never be fully answered, some indeed are not questions but rather the voicing of the management concerns associated with information value and IS investment. This chapter will concentrate upon addressing issues associated with IS investment, information value and IS performance appraisal. It is with IS investments that the vision that is the IS strategy gets turned into reality through the allocation of resources. Many works on IS management talk of the need for senior management commitment, a commitment that can only be gained through appropriate cost and benefit information. This means thoroughly and accurately *understanding* those things that form IS costs and benefits for the organisation and may or may not involve measuring them. Chapter 12 will include some discussion of the financing alternatives for acquisitions and the notion of corporate recovery of IS investments, known as internal charging or IS chargeback.

So what is involved in understanding an organisation's IS costs and IS benefits and the balance between these for *that* organisation? Both costs and benefits are made up of a complex web of tangible and intangible issues of varying degrees of predictability. Costs may be significantly higher than most organisations realise whilst benefits may be lower – or perhaps just different. Balancing the two involves understanding strategic directions and risk profiles and identifying techniques suitable to judge performance appraisals of both business and IS over appropriate time scales. At the simplest level, it can be said that an organisation must match its spending to its strategy demands but life is never that simple. It is important to judge any business decision in the context of the benefits it brings for the costs it will incur. After all, factory expansion, advertising campaigns or staff training programmes, for instance, are all *chosen* and any project is undertaken at the expense of others that are not. For one set to be chosen in preference to another there must be some picture drawn of costs and benefits and some opinion formed of the balance between them.

An appropriate way to allow everyone within the organisation to form the picture of costs, benefits and the balance between them is needed. Zmud *et al.* (1986) called this picture the investment architecture that forms part of a healthy information economy within an organisation. The sense of direction that is provided by the business and IS strategies become actions through the set of mechanisms for defining costs, benefits and hence the relationship between them for candidate business activities, including IS ones. Section 7.3 will discuss these mechanisms but first Sections 7.1 and 7.2 will discuss some of the issues surrounding IS costs and IS benefits respectively.

## 7.1 ◆ IS COSTS

Like the IS benefits that the organisation hopes to achieve, the IS costs it incurs are made up of two elements, the tangible plus the intangible. However, when discussing costs these two are often referred to as visible or hidden. Also like the IS benefits, IS costs need to be predicted, and then reduced where appropriate, though not at the expense of the net benefit level, and, in short, managed. IS cost predicting or estimating, even for the 'visible' projects, that is those under IS section's control, has been notoriously bad. An error factor of ten or even higher is not uncommon. Keen (1991), who has done much to quantify aspects of IS investments, suggests that the percentage error does depend upon the nature of the IS project. In-house work, drawing as it does upon more accessible expertise, is likely to be more accurate than bought-in solutions. Figure 7.1 illustrates the possible ratio of expected to unforeseen costs for medium-sized projects (Keen suggests those with budgets of $1 million to $15 million). The inaccurate forecasts lead to a number of problems, which include:

- Perhaps most obviously, a lack of confidence in IS
- The fact that projects are chosen that should not be
- But even more seriously, that worthwhile projects are not undertaken because the organisation's finite resources dry up

The main difficulty in IS cost estimating is that most forecasting techniques need two things that candidate IS projects do not offer. Firstly forecasts usually require a detailed knowledge of the intended project in *advance*; this is usually not obtained or not obtainable, and the costs of IS projects are estimated with the same degree of precision as if the cost of building a new skyscraper was estimated by walking down the empty street. Such detailed knowledge must obviously be based upon a large number of specific parameters, whereas the defining of many of them forms the project itself. Secondly accurate cost forecasts usually need some historical basis from which to generate the estimate. Such historical data is simply not available when so many IS projects are the first of their type. It is not only these objective difficulties that bedevil the IS cost estimating process. Many behavioural factors also distort the validity of the estimating procedures. Lederer, Mirani, Neo, Pollard, Prasad and Ramamurthy (1990) give a very useful explanation of both a

| | In-house software development project | | Purchased software package | | |
|---|---|---|---|---|---|
| | Expected % | Hidden % | | Expected % | Hidden % |
| Planning and design | 40 | | Planning and design | | 40 |
| Programming | 10 | | Analysis/evaluation | 25 | |
| Testing | 10 | 20 | Testing | 5 | 10 |
| Installation | 10 | 10 | Installation | | 20 |
| Total (% of actual costs) | 70 | 30 | Total (% of actual costs) | 30 | 70 |

**Fig 7.1 ◆ Visible and hidden IS costs**
(adapted and reprinted by permission of Harvard Business School Press. From *Shaping the Future* by P. Keen, Boston, MA, 1991, p. 157, © 1991 by the President and Fellows of Harvard College, all rights reserved)

rational and a political model of the cost estimating process that does much to show why, under either model, costs are frequently hugely wrong.

It is not only the *potential* costs of IS projects that are mysterious. Many organisations simply have no idea what their *current* level of IS investment is, nor what costs account for what percentage of that investment. What is currently spent on IS is surprisingly hard to quantify.

Recent growth in interest in the issue of IS asset management has led to growth in tools that can assist by automating some parts of the IS asset auditing process. The focus of these tools has been upon auditing the hardware and software *throughout* the organisation. Most of these tools focus on the ability to log *continually* the nature of the hardware and software of computers connected in networks. The interest in such auditing is of course fuelled by a number of forces other than the wish for more effective asset management. The need to be seen to take action to avoid having any pirated software, to be alert to computer component thefts and the need to integrate complex combinations of software and hardware all play a significant part in the popularity of automated asset management systems.

A key limitation of all automated asset management systems advocated by a number of authors, such as Smith (1996), Salamone (1995), Mansell-Lewis (1994) and Fawcett (1994), is that these are tools to audit the physical even if hidden elements of costs. A true asset management approach must also consider the value held in data stores, in staff skills and capabilities and in business models captured in software systems. Clearly auditing physical assets is necessary but it is not sufficient and organisations must also evaluate and judge the *value* of those non-physical assets. The possible sources of the value of these IS assets is discussed in Section 7.2 whilst issues associated with evaluating and judging that value are discussed in Section 7.3.

## 7.1.1 ◆ Checklist for IS costs

Hochstrasser and Griffiths (1990) provide a useful appendix to their work on managing the economics of IS. In this they offer a checklist that assists organisations to identify, quantify and evaluate IS costs. The checklist covers:

- *Hardware costs*: not just the processing hardware but all machinery such as printers, storage and accessories, etc. Although they are inherently visible, the increasing dispersal of these items means that even this very tangible element can be difficult to locate and audit.

- *Software costs*: the cheapest solutions will be off-the-shelf packages though even this route involves significant specification and evaluation costs if the selected software is to be of effective use. In-house developments can account for huge, and unknown, sums. The middle ground of in-house use of application generators still incurs costs, particularly start-up ones whilst learning the capabilities of the tool.

- *Installation costs*: system installations vary in complexity and so in cost. Some may require external expertise the cost of which must be included, as must the data entry cost when converting from manual systems or the data conversion costs when changing from already computer-based systems.

- *Environmental costs*: by which Hochstrasser and Griffiths mean the physical environment of IS, wiring, furniture, air-conditioning, etc. Human environmental costs such as safety, health and legal costs must also be included.

- *Running costs:* electrical power, data communication costs for remote work (telephone lines) and subscription fees for any external data services such as on-line databases, Prestel, or bulletin boards all contribute to IS costs.

- *Maintenance costs*: these must be established whether they are to be incurred in a planned and predictable way through service and maintenance contracts or in the less certain way of in-house staffing. Software breaks just as hardware does.

- *Security costs*: measures taken to reduce the danger from deliberate or accidental damage to physical or logical elements of IS must be allowed for, as must the cost of the unavoided risk and the disaster recovery planning and plans.

- *Networking costs*: network hardware, software and management all incur costs over and above any application using the network. Such costs are now so significant, and IS infrastructure costs so high on any list of management concerns that, whilst often underestimated, they are rarely overlooked. Perhaps data management costs should be substituted here since enterprise data modelling, repository planning, data warehouse management, and data infrastructure management, incur heavy costs that are not exactly overlooked but, rather, undocumented.

- *Training costs*: these are almost invariably underestimated and it is almost 'accepted' that the real extent of training costs, background education, specific training, and on-going support and updates will be undocumented.

- *Wider organisational costs*: under this catch-all heading Hochstrasser and Griffiths placed incompatibility costs, new salary structures, transitional costs, and management costs. They could also have focused upon these as organisational change management costs (software-change management costs will also form part of software costs).

The use of such checklists is intended to alert organisations to think about the *real* cost of a particular potential IS activity. The lack of tracking of past costs incurred (as discussed in Section 7.1.4) is one difficulty in identifying costs as is the impossibility of knowing future costs if the activity is truly leading edge. Equally much difficulty results from simply not recognising the *extent* of the costs implications. Both Mangoletsi (1994) and Doyle (1996) are attempting to address this blindness by cataloguing the *full* costs, of PC based systems and of printing technologies respectively.

## 7.1.2 ◆ IS cost dynamics or cost compounding

One important, and frequently overlooked, point about IS investments is that they are not a one shot action. IS projects are generally initiated to extend the organisation's IS capability. The 'project' may end but the system continues to be used. Keen (1991) suggests that a $1 million software development project is, in fact, committing the organisation to a $4 million investment over the first five years since for every development $1 an additional $0.20 must be added for operations and $0.40 for maintenance. These follow-on costs are automatically generated and hence are non-discretionary. Unfortunately they are also usually overlooked in the identification of IS costs. Until very recently most organisations saw the costs associated with IS projects as being finite and time boundaried. The reality is that the initiation of most IS projects is also the initiation of a permanent commitment to resource demands that can 'clog-up' the IS expenditures such that little disposable IS income remains. Keen graphically illustrates the implications of this reality when he shows the budget volumes over five years for four different approaches to IS investments.

Figure 7.2 shows Keen's somewhat simplified view of the compounding costs of IS and the 'natural' rate of growth in IS costs. During some IS initiatives the level may be even higher, though such levels cannot be sustained unless benefit levels are also very high. Only software development and, more significantly, maintenance automation will ever alter this situation. Since these consequent costs are frequently overlooked they are the epitome of hidden costs!

An organisation's large, and long-term, commitment to IS must be perceived to generate commensurate gains. When it did not seem to, the first response by many organisations was to see the 'business' as at fault and institute manager education and awareness programmes and appoint IS Directors to oversee business' exploitation of IS. When neither response seemed to significantly improve IS benefit realisation perceptions the emphasis shifted. The current response to poorly managed benefit realisation is to require IS to *demonstrate* that it delivers value for money. In addition, in the rush to 'blame' IS, many IS Directors or their equivalent have been removed or demoted (at the turn of the 1990s as many as 50 per cent of US IS Directors were removed) and IS activities have been outsourced so that contracts can act as the cost management tool.

## 7.1.3 ◆ Levels of IS investments

IS investment levels are frequently quoted as revenue ratios. The *explicit* statement by many IS pundits that IS investments should be in the 1 per cent to 5 per cent range is usually making the *implicit* statement that 'unsuccessful' organisations will be at the 1 per cent end of that range whilst more 'successful' ones (some possible definitions of 'success' are explored in Chapter 8) will be at the 5 per cent end. This implicit statement is based upon the assumption that the low ratio results from a 'spend as little as we can' attitude that will always be competitively dangerous, in IS as in everything else. Figure 7.3 shows total UK levels of IS investment for the years 1990–92.

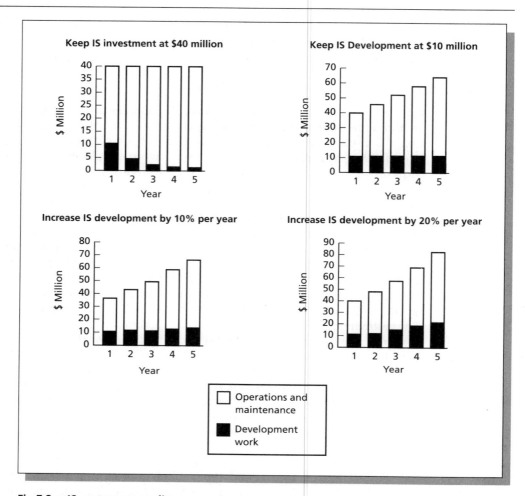

**Fig 7.2 ◆ IS cost compounding**
(adapted and reprinted by permission of Harvard Business School Press. From *Shaping the Future* by P. Keen, Boston, MA, 1991, pp. 150–1, © 1991, by the President and Fellows of Harvard College, all rights reserved)

Managing IS costs is firstly about identifying all costs, the hidden as well as the apparent; secondly it is about understanding the contribution that each element makes to the total picture; and thirdly, establishing appropriate levels for these costs. In other words, once what is spent is guessed then what should be spent on what can be decided. The ratios that are available offer one tool in judging the possible level of IS costs; however an organisation is seeking to match the IS cost level to the strategy imperative – to spend what it *has* to spend, bearing in mind that financial feasibility forms part of the strategy development process. This then is a key factor in that critical distinction between computer management and information management. Computer management sees IS costs as an operating expense and so management attention should be primarily on reducing costs for efficiency sake. Information management, since it views information as a corporate resource,

|  |  | 1990 | 1991 | 1992 |
|---|---|---|---|---|
| Total spending | £ (Billion) | 25.7 | 27.1 | 28.1 |
| Number of sites | 000s | 52 | 53 | 54 |
| Average spending | £(000s) | 49.5 | 51.0 | 52.8 |

**Fig 7.3 ◆ Total UK IS investment levels**
(sources: Computer User's Year Book and OTR-Pedder)

sees it as a capital investment for which most management attention should be upon a benefit maximisation (*see* Figure 7.4).

When it is an IS strategy that provides the framework for what is spent then that spending can be defined as an investment. However, when there is no sense of direction then IS spending must simply represent an ongoing expense. This distinction is akin to the distinction between viewing staff costs as purely a wages bill or as a skills investment. This perception shift such that information becomes seen as a corporate resource and hence IS as an asset needing asset management not blind cost reduction is what Nolan (1979) refers to as the critical transition from computer management to information management and Tapscott and Caston (1993) refer to as a paradigm shift. This basic perception shift is such that the 'percentage of sales revenue' ratio approach to IS investment that was always an over-simplification becomes less and less relevant except as a review or talking point. The concerns change from IS budgeting as a 'separate' issue to business investment as an integrated whole, to meet business goals with business profitable projects. This perception shift moves the IS economic debate from one of cost cutting to one of benefit maximisation and management and so adds business *value* appraisal to the equation (*see* Figure 7.5).

Ratios and comparisons can be dangerous. As Keen (1991) asks, if the industry average is 2.4 per cent of sales revenue is the organisation that is spending 8 per cent of its revenue on IS a visionary or a fool, catching up or trail blazing? The simplistic view of IS costs as a percentage of sales or turnover is an inadequate one and of far more significance are three factors that are looked at in the following sections.

The *reason* for a particular ratio is of more interest than the ratio itself, and a *change* in that ratio most interesting of all. For example it says more about the role of IS to Birds Eye Walls that during 1995 they increased spending on IS by £1m on a particular major project than it went from 0.8 per cent of turnover to 0.9 per cent or that its parent organisation, Unilever, typically spends more with 1.2 per cent of

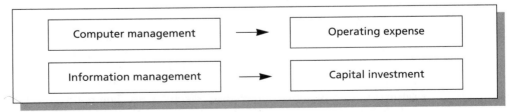

**Fig 7.4 ◆ Views of IS costs**

| IS Spending seen as expense | | IS Spending seen as investment |
|---|---|---|
| Small sums of money | ➤ | Large sums of money |
| Operational/tactical view of benefits | ➤ | Strategic view of benefits |
| Must we spend this? | ➤ | We must spend this! |
| Discontinuous and discrete spending | ➤ | Continuous investing |
| Cost analysis | ➤ | Investment appraisal |
| Self-financing by cost saving on other areas | ➤ | Capital planning |
| Manage the costs focus | ➤ | Manage the benefits focus |
| Expense accounting techniques | ➤ | Asset accounting techniques |

**Fig 7.5 ◆ Different perceptions of IS cost**

turnover going on IS. It may be interesting to know that, according to Kelly (1996), Shell is the largest spender on IS in the UK, spending £1.1bn in 1995. But what does this say about them as a successful exploiter of IS when Burmah Castrol has the lowest percentage of turnover spent on IS at just 0.2 per cent? The answer is that the two figures really tell us nothing until we investigate further.

### IS investment level over time

The level of an organisation's expenditure on IS will constantly rise but, given the concept of IS maturity modelled by works such as Nolan's (see Chapter 5), the *gradient* of that upward trend should rise and fall with the stage of maturity. Nolan's work showed that over time for a given organisation it is inevitable and desirable that relative investment levels will vary by the degree of maturity in the use and management of IS. Analysis of the current maturity position will indicate whether the rate of increase in the IS investment should be increasing or decreasing. In particular the expansion and integration stages are associated with very steep rises. A steady gradient may provide a danger sign for any organisation. Figure 7.6 illustrates some possible charts of IS expenditure over time for a range of industries compared with Nolan's generalised model of IS expenditure.

The ratio of IS spending to sales goes up over time and for the industry leader it might go up more and faster. It is not, however, a safe assumption to make that spending more on IS makes an organisation the industry leader. It is equally likely that an organisation strong and well managed enough to be the industry leader is also able, confident, and skilled enough to be able to identify and pursue the IS opportunities that increase the sales ratio spent on IS. Indeed a flurry of surveys at the turn of the 1990s seem to show conclusively that the *amount* spent on IS investments offers no predictor of success or failure and high spenders could be either. Levels of spending have no significance and it is the *use* made of the information that is the determinant of success. Whilst many writers and practitioners are seeking the *optimum* level of investment that will generate the best pay-off others question whether overspending is not simply subject to the law of diminishing returns and may actually decrease effectiveness. The reality has been that IS budgets have constantly increased for three decades at annual levels that far outstrip

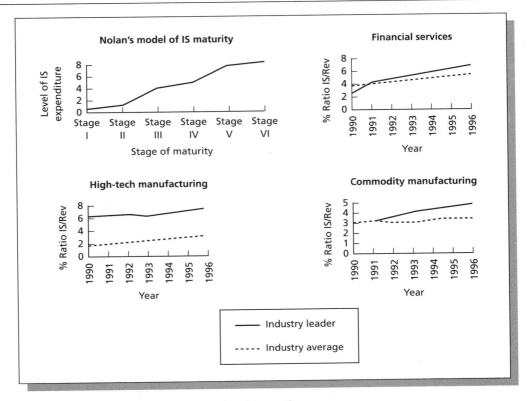

**Fig 7.6 ◆ Hypothetical IS investment levels over time**

the business growth of most organisations. Irrespective of Nolan's work, such constant increases cannot economically continue. The management dilemma is that competitively an organisation can never afford a reduction in IS investments! The recessionary pressures of the early 1990s did cause a slow down and some few instances of decline (notably in construction companies) but by 1994 IS expenditure was increasing again (Riley 1994).

## IS investment level by industry sector

It is in the nature of certain industries to demand or suit a greater or lesser investment in IS and hence an industry sector comparison of costs is sometimes helpful. An industry analysis is worthwhile since IS investment levels will normally vary with the relative information intensity of that industry's products and services. This should not be taken to the extreme of allowing the 'others are doing it' argument to form the sole justification of IS costs. The 'typical' differences between industries are very large and so industry analysis and comparison forms only one tool in assessing IS costs. Figure 7.7 shows one hypothetical industry comparison.

Service industries with their high product and process information intensity will spend more on IS than will traditional process industries with their low product and value chain information intensity. The average business importance of IS to the industry is represented by these figures. However, since it is only an *average* that

| Industry sector | % Ratio IS/turnover 1991/92 | % Ratio IS/turnover 1992/93 | Spending as % of turnover 1993/94 | Spending as % of turnover 1993/94 |
| --- | --- | --- | --- | --- |
| Manufacturing | 2.25 | -3.75 | 1.3 | 1.4 |
| Process industries | 5 | 2.25 | 1.6 | 2.2 |
| Retail/distribution | 4.5 | -3.75 | 1.0 | 0.8 |
| Finance and business services | 8 | 1.25 | 2.5 | 2.8 |
| National and local government | 3.25 | 2 | 2.9 | 2.5 |
| Education | 1.5 | 3 | 4.2 | 7.5 |
| Average | 5.25 | 1.5 | 2.25 | 2.87 |

Fig 7.7 ◆ IS investment by industry-sector
(sources NCC figures for 1992 and 1995)

they show, an individual organisation's specific competitive position and strategy and stage of maturity must also be considered. Given that this average changes over time, and for some industries quite rapidly, the primary difficulty for any organisation hoping to make an industry comparison is to obtain up-to-date figures of competitors' IS investments (remember many organisations do not know what they themselves are spending). Industry updates are reported by a number of major IS consultancy and survey companies such as Price Waterhouse and Romtech though there will always be a time lag in such reporting systems.

### Allocation of the IS investment

So far this chapter has talked about IS investments as if they were investments into a single thing. However the investment breakdown will change over time and so it is inadequate to behave as if the total cost represented a homogenous lump. The percentage split between costs attributable to the IS 'supplier' and those allocated to the IS 'user' will alter. The steady and significant trend has been away from 'traditional' IS costs towards the majority of the total being from devolved IS. This shift is closely associated with the critical evolution from computer management to information management, to the point that, for many companies, the 1990s brought a situation where devolved IS accounted for half the total organisation's IS costs at twice the cost of what might be seen as central IS.

In Figure 7.8 the dates 1990 and 1980 are not arbitrarily chosen dates. For many writers 1980 was considered the end of the DP era of computing and the start of the information era. The total cost of IS has doubled in that time but central IS has lost relative significance, though not absolute costs, hence the current preoccupation with reducing this absolute level. Given the organisational specific nature of end-user computing it is in the domain of functionally specialist IT and traditional DP that outsourcing would appear. Organisations face major difficulties in identifying and then managing the costs associated with devolved IS. Strassmann (1985) gives some clear, worked examples of both the actual costs of some IS projects and the split between technological and organisational cost elements.

It is not only the element of IS that is responsible for the cost that has changed over time. The nature of the cost itself has also altered. The split between people, permanent infrastructure, past development maintenance and discretionary devel-

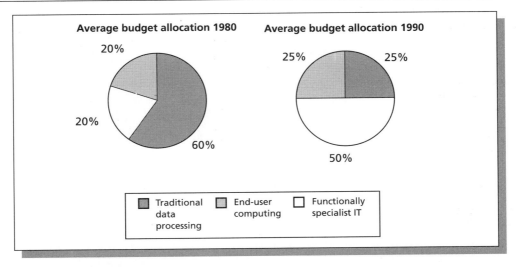

**Fig 7.8 ◆ IS investment by budget centre**

opment costs components changes with time, certain strategies and maturity stages. This is illustrated in Figure 7.9 and during 1994 according to Green-Armytage (1994) staff costs accounted for 36 per cent, hardware costs for 24 per cent, software costs for just 15 per cent, communications-related costs for 10 per cent with the remaining 15 per cent going to cover everything else.

Certain IS strategies demand more or less investments in particular components. For example, the integration stage is likely to generate the need for high-cost networking technologies whereas the contagion stage's strategies suggest low-cost demand-generating activities of a low tech mass market nature. Not only is the ratio of IS spending to turnover going to vary over time and by industry sector, it will also vary by both organisation size and IS resource element.

IS costs cover those for two types of resources; these are the technology itself and the personnel associated with managing and operating it. Figure 7.10 illustrates how much of the IS investment these two elements have accounted for. Whether the 60/40, but reversible, allocation to organisational and technology resources will continue is, of course, uncertain. The high allocation to the visible elements in the

|  | 1990 | | 1991 | | 1992 | |
|---|---|---|---|---|---|---|
|  | £ (Billions) | % | £ (Billions) | % | £ (Billions) | % |
| *Hardware* | 5.55 | 21.60 | 5.45 | 20.20 | 5.86 | 20.50 |
| *Software and services* | 4.68 | 18.20 | 5.13 | 19.00 | 5.57 | 19.50 |
| *Supplies* | 0.67 | 2.60 | 0.75 | 2.80 | 0.79 | 2.80 |
| *Telecoms services* | 0.56 | 2.20 | 0.61 | 2.20 | 0.73 | 2.60 |
| *IT specialist staff* | 7.15 | 27.80 | 7.38 | 27.30 | 7.60 | 26.60 |
| *Other expenditure* | 7.12 | 27.70 | 7.73 | 28.60 | 7.99 | 28.00 |

**Fig 7.9 ◆ UK IS investment by IS resource element**
(sources: *Computer User's Year Book* and OTR-Pedder)

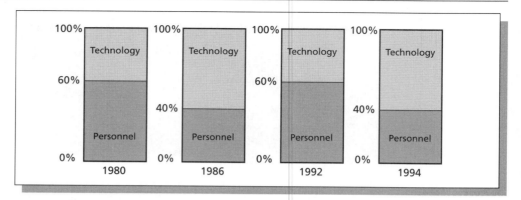

Fig 7.10 ◆ IS investment by IS resource element

mid-1980s is because of the emphasis then on putting in the technology of the infrastructure, for instance major network backbones. The people 'catching-up' seemed to be complete by the mid-1990s.

The recessionary slow-down in IS budgets during the early 1990s caused a number of projects to be halted because of budget cuts (*see* Figure 7.11). However the situation seems to have changed. The focus is now upon gaining benefit rather than cutting costs; on getting value for money, not on spending less money absolutely. In 1993 just over half of organisations were predicting static or declining spending on IS for the medium-term future. By 1994, however, only about a quarter of organisations were predicting this for their futures.

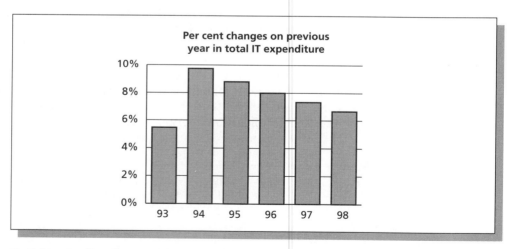

Fig 7.11 ◆ Predicted IT spending to 1998
(Source: *Computer Weekly*, 16 Feb 1995)

### 7.1.4 ◆ Auditing IS costs

What can loosely be referred to as auditing the IS investment involves identifying all costs and valuing the past IS investments. It is not enough to be aware of what

IS elements incur costs, to appreciate the need to estimate the visible and hidden costs of any potential project and to be aware of how IS investment levels vary. It is also necessary to know how much the organisation's past investment in IS is currently worth. Keen (1991) suggests that this process can be helped by creating an IS asset balance sheet even though the most valuable elements of IS, the data and software, cannot be counted as assets for tax purposes; they still add to the value of the organisation. He gives an example IS asset sheet for a large (US) bank with an annual IS investment of $200 million. This is illustrated in Figure 7.12. The IS asset sheet therefore records the *value* to the organisation of the situation that results from incurred IS costs. This notion of an IS asset sheet is related to the notion described in Vowler (1994) as a benefits register that would provide:

- a definition of the benefit proposed and the rationale it is based on
- a statement of the full value of the promised benefit, and the pay-back time in which it has to be delivered
- the identification of the manager responsible for delivering that benefit

The crucial difference between these two concepts is that the IS asset sheet is a record of the *actual* value of IS whereas the IS benefits register is a record of the value *intent*.

Looking at IS in this asset appraisal way is part of the critical transition from computer management to information management discussed in Chapter 5. If the perception is that it is just a computer that is being managed then everything other than hardware becomes viewed as its operating costs, or expenditure, and this perception causes the business value of data and software to be hidden. When costs are hidden then they can so easily be ignored and hence escalate. The value of IS assets needs to be acknowledged in order to identify the appropriate level of management attention that the value deserves. Many organisations that do not currently devote much management energy to IS concerns would perhaps do so if they appreciated the value of the area they are neglecting. As noted in Mansell-Lewis (1994), Smith (1996) and others, when the *scale* of the costs is fully recognised then management 'sit up and take notice'. IS itself would find it hard to quantify these assets unless an IS asset balance sheet is produced.

It can be very difficult to quantify the IS asset set in an environment of distributed hardware and devolved data and software responsibility. Keen suggests using the distinctions between IS supplier costs and IS user costs; this is the very distinction that UK local authorities have had forced upon them. An element of IS supplier costs would be the management of network backbones, another of maintenance of development methodology skills. Examples of IS user costs could include printing costs, time spent in service negotiation or actual software operation. This distinction is also the one made by organisations wishing to de-couple IS functions in order to judge whether IS supply should remain within the organisation or go to an outside agency (outsourced). Obviously IS costs come from both the supplier and the user side and collectively these create the IS asset set.

IS supplier costs are those incurred in running the corporate IS function, the data or super-centre of Chapter 9. The costs of running this utility are largely accounted for by maintenance and service work. The new developments are the only variable cost in its equation although data centre operation automation, off-the-shelf

| Total IS assets | | Asset worth ($ Millions) 2 240 | The figures and comments below are intended to give some guidance as to how this figure is arrived at |
|---|---|---|---|
| Total hardware | | **368** | |
| | Centrally managed computers | 120 | Keen feels that this is the most visible element of IS investment. Certainly it is the one that accountants track but it represents only 5% of the real IS assets for the example that Keen gives. |
| | Distributed computers | 84 | These will usually be PCs. For many organisations this overlooked asset actually accounts for more spending than centrally controlled equipment does. |
| | Network equipment | 105 | Even the centrally controlled network services are hard to track since they usually appear across a number of different budgets. |
| | Distributed telecoms | 59 | The value of the local area networks. |
| Total software | | **488** | |
| | Application development | 420 | Both software figures are little more than guesses since the bank quoted by Keen, like many other organisations, does little to track the value of developments. |
| | Other, including PC software | 68 | In this instance the replacement cost was estimated as $1.2 billion or three times the original cost. |
| Data resources | | 1 200 | This is the estimated capital cost of salaries, processing, storage media, etc to create the on-line data resources that form the basis of the bank's products and services. Obviously banking is an industry with a very high information intensity. These assets do not wear out with increased use. |

**Fig 7.12 ◆ An IS asset balance sheet**
(adapted and reprinted by permission of Harvard Business School Press. From *Shaping the Future* by P. Keen, Boston, MA, 1991, p. 144, © 1991 by the President and Fellows of Harvard College, all rights reserved)

software development and productivity tools can all help to reduce overall costs. As the IS supplier element represents an ever smaller percentage of the total IS value it can look very attractive to remove the management effort it causes the organisation by establishing outsourcing arrangements – or at least consolidating and commercialising the in-house data centre(s).

IS supply costs are not sharply divided from IS user costs and the two become extremely fuzzy-edged when items such as support and technical services are considered. For example, the true cost of a £1 000 PC may become £4 000 a year when support, service and maintenance are included. Some IS supply costs are borne as overheads, others may be charged back to become part of IS user costs (*see* Chapter 12 for more detail of IS charging). IS user costs are, however, greater than just the charged-back costs from IS supply. Direct acquisitions if and where these are permitted, plus all the user related costs, must be included. Compounded costs are probably the biggest IS use issue; there is an enormous difference between dealing with ten separate £1 000 PCs and dealing with ten linked PCs that wish to share data and messaging and so require communication links and on-going support. The apparently attractive cost equations of downsizing are often seriously misleading when the true costs for both IS supply and IS use are considered. Real and yet hidden organisational costs make the visible costs look like peanuts.

Any portfolio of IS projects must, of course, encompass maintenance activities and most of these are non-discretionary, although a surprising number of bug-fixes need never be tackled. Without an investment strategy that explicitly manages enhancements the expenditure on such changes can quickly grow uncontrollably. Of more importance, however, is the fact that the value to be gained from these 'enhancements' is rarely appraised. Many organisations could spend every 'IS £' in this way without ever clearing the backlog of enhancement requests, a fact that is one of the drivers of end-user computing.

IS investment discretion enters the equation when selecting between infrastructure projects, new application projects and research projects. Each of these carry different demands and offer different gains, and a mixed portfolio is desirable. User support must form part of the investment to actually realise the intended benefits, from past as well as current and future investments. Investment comparisons across time, industry and spending elements help in the process of investment management, but the understanding of what gives value to information (*see* Section 7.2) and the understanding of what techniques to employ to choose between investment candidates (*see* Section 7.3) is essential.

## 7.2 ◆ IS BENEFITS – INFORMATION VALUE

The evolution from computer management, with its focus upon input and technical vehicle control, to information management, with its focus upon business useful outputs, has caused a corresponding shift of emphasis from cost justification to benefit realisation. Effective IS management we have seen is very much about the shift from controlling the technical process, of cost control, to the management of benefit realisation. With this conceptual shift the issue of information *value* becomes a cornerstone of benefit judging. Computer management, quite properly, concentrates upon cost reduction since, with its expenditure perception, IS activities form a constant outgoing drain. The asset management perception of information management implies the need to judge the value gained as well as the costs incurred.

An organisation will have to make some judgement of information value in order to judge 'appropriate' investment levels. After such a balancing act management must feel that it has achieved value for money and it is not at all certain that all organisations feel that they have. Price Waterhouse suggest that the common perception of IS is one of not providing value for money and quote the senior manager who feels that IS investments are the result of:

> *Being blackmailed by the computer suppliers and by our own staff, who are forever quoting the IS spend of competitors.*

Doubts about a lack of value for money may not be just a perception since a 1992 City University Business School survey showed that 82 per cent of IS projects returned very few real *business* benefits and a 1993 KPMG Peat Marwick survey of Building Societies found that, although they were all investing in new IS ventures, only 40 per cent felt that they were getting value for money. A 1995 survey, also by KPMG, concluded that the situation had not improved. Bicknell (1996) reports on a survey that indicates that 33 per cent of City of London firms do not even monitor to discover just what benefits do result from IS activities. If they do know the benefits situation significantly less than half will feel that they have gained the required benefits. Figure 7.13 shows some 1992 Price Waterhouse estimates of some of the results of the large IS investments; however, if other figures are to be believed many organisations will not know whether *effects* are benefits of not.

So just what are the benefits that result from IS activities? They are the ways in which an organisation is able to improve its situation as a result of the manner in which information is managed. Benefits come as a result of what it becomes possible for the organisation to do. What makes information valuable is the cornerstone notion that is supporting the issues of organisational change discussed in Chapter 8. Value potentially comes from a number of facets of information, and the list provided by Angell and Smithson (1991) is as extensive as most. They identify the points where value accrue as:

| | | | |
|---|---|---|---|
| Accuracy | User satisfaction | Relevance | Profitability |
| Quality | Functionality | Productivity | Speed |
| Usability | Reliability | Security | Volume |
| Flexibility | Utilisation | | |

Such lists of information attributes *define* those things that potentially give value to information. It is the nature of these attributes that is *altered* by IS activities and it is that change that brings benefit. This issue of altering the attributes of information to bring about benefit relates to concepts of information and decision making discussed in Chapter 3. The relationship of valuable information attributes to management decisions is illustrated in Figure 7.14.

| | 1983 Million | 1990 Million | Increase % |
|---|---|---|---|
| Number of PCs in 'Fortune 500' companies | 2.5 | 18.4 | 740% |
| % of white collar staff using PCs | 7% | 56% | 800% |
| Spending on PCs | <1 | 12+ | 1200%+ |
| Number of paper pages generated by 'Fortune 500' companies | 120 | 1500 | 1200%+ |
| **Increase in white collar productivity** | | | **1%** |

**Fig 7.13 ◆ Results of IS investment**
(source: Price Waterhouse)

| Attribute feature | By management level | | |
|---|---|---|---|
| | Operational | | Strategic |
| Timelines | | | |
| ● Currency | Up-to-date | ◄——► | Relatively old |
| ● Response time | Instant | ◄——► | Slow |
| ● Frequency | Constant | ◄——► | Varies |
| Content | | | |
| ● Accuracy | High | ◄——► | Relatively low |
| ● Relevance | | No difference | |
| ● Completeness | | No difference | |
| ● Conciseness | | No difference | |
| ● Aggregation level | Very detailed | ◄——► | Very aggregated |
| Format | | | |
| ● Medium | Mostly on-line | ◄——► | Mixed formats |
| ● Structure | Fixed | ◄——► | Flexible |
| ● Image | Fixed | ◄——► | Flexible |
| Cost | | | |
| ● Cost | Easily assessed | ◄——► | Hard to assess |
| ● Benefit | Tangible | ◄——► | Intangible |

**Fig 7.14 ◆ A model of information attributes**

Efficiency can be considered as a facet of information value and quality in this context generally means meeting the target or conforming to the standard. This relates primarily to those tasks that *must* be done, since if this is the case they should be done *right*. Effectiveness chooses *what* to do and hence involves the subjective issue of judging value. Many of the techniques discussed in Section 7.3 fall into these two camps with management effort swinging between the two.

Throughout the 1980s IS 'fashion' dictated what was almost a disdain for efficiency measures in favour of chasing effectiveness. However, the harsher competitive times have forced a reawakening interest in good efficient activities, and of course the reality is that once selected a project must be efficiently managed.

The distinction between efficiency, doing something right, and effectiveness, doing the right thing, is here revisited from an economic perspective. Economic *effectiveness* in this context depends upon the complex issue of balancing the benefits gained for the costs incurred and hence is a management rather than a technical issue. From the definitions of efficiency and effectiveness we can see that efficiency in the IS resource is obtained by producing a defined system, service, accuracy or whatever, as cheaply as possible, where quality can be defined as the ability to do something, the capability. Figure 7.15 illustrates the single variable dependency of efficiency and shows how any two IS activities can be compared for efficiency in producing a like capability. The line, referred to as the efficiency frontier, represents the lowest level of costs *currently* to be incurred to achieve a given capability.

If A and B in Figure 7.15 are actual systems then there is a *measurable* amount of inefficiency in system A that is the amount of additional cost incurred for the *same* capability or, conversely, a measurable efficiency improvement in system B. They both deliver the same quality but system A incurs more costs to do so. If the IS resource can, perhaps by using automated productivity tools or improved manage-

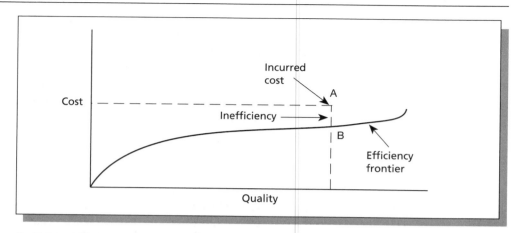

**Fig 7.15 ◆ Efficiency depends only upon cost of vehicle**

ment methods, produce a system C, with even lower costs for the same defined quality then both System A and System B become 'inefficient', again by an amount that can be measured. Such a possibility means that there is no *optimum* point (except perhaps at zero costs) of efficiency, merely the currently attained frontier, which like any other frontier will be constantly pushed forward by new developments. Any given system exists at a point relative to the current frontier and it is the *obligation* of IS, particularly within the data centre elements discussed in Chapter 9, to keep moving this efficiency frontier to the advantage of the organisation.

From our earlier definitions effectiveness, with its issue of 'doing the right thing', adds the dimensions of value (potential benefit) to our equation and so is a more complex issue than efficiency. Figure 7.16 illustrates how IS benefit is the result of a balancing act between the costs incurred for the value gained.

Figure 7.16 shows that there is *usually* a rise in costs as quality is improved; this produces the cost curve for a given system or project in the same way as in Figure 7.15. The *value* curve, representing the benefit to the organisation, however follows quite a different line. Capability does *not* equal value; for instance, in the early days

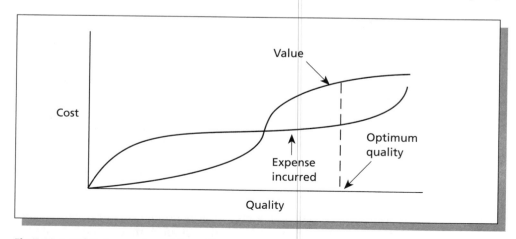

**Fig 7.16 ◆ Balancing costs and benefits**

of interactive software, making an investment to improve response times by a factor of ten from 20 seconds to 2 seconds certainly increased the capability of the system and probably increased the value of the system because of the increased human usability. A further, and probably larger, investment to improve response times by another factor of ten from 2 seconds to 0.2 seconds will certainly increase the capability of the system but will probably *not* increase the *value* of the system since humans rarely operate at such a pace! On this diagram there is an optimum point where the positive difference between value gained and cost incurred is greatest, where the best balance is obtained. This diagram should be used as a constant cautionary reminder of the fact that if the value never exceeds costs incurred then do not do it!

This distinction between efficiency and effectiveness is obviously a critical one. With an IT investment level of around 1 per cent of sales revenue then IS *efficiency* savings will have a fairly small net effect upon the overall organisation, though they may be of significance to the IS function. Effectiveness, however, produces benefit that can apply to the entire organisation. Information efficiency is the province of lowering the cost as far as possible by using productivity and project control tools. Information effectiveness can only be judged by establishing the value curve. To do this requires an understanding of the value-generating attributes associated with information.

It is not only information attributes that can be considered by organisational level, the benefit that results from the use of information can also be felt at every level. Silk (1991) gives a clear and concise explanation of the differences and the relationship between the generic business benefit and the organisational level that experiences this benefit. The illustrative example given in Figure 7.17 is of a decision support system (DSS) project where the value is of effectiveness and where this value translates into a business benefit felt primarily by the tactical level of the organisation's management. In other words, strategic systems can be for operational management.

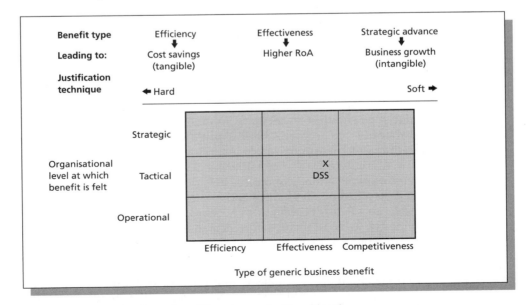

**Fig 7.17 ◆ Generic business benefit and organisational level**

IS benefits felt by particular management levels within the organisation can easily be confused with IS investments intended to have differing impacts upon the business. The latter are:

- *Operational Value Investment.* These productivity-improving projects are investments in transaction processing projects with short-term gain horizons, usually to reduce costs in business processes. These may be one form of IS investment for which traditional financial justifications are appropriate, though they must not be confused with a strategic investment whose impact happens to be upon business operations.

- *Strategic Value Investment.* When a business-enhancing or risk-minimising project intends to improve the revenue-generating potential of the organisation then the gain horizon (the time scale anticipated to reap a particular benefit) will probably be long-term; the value of this project will be direct but extremely hard to quantify though revenue growth rates may offer some approximation. Frequently investments that were conceived under one of the other three headings is claimed in retrospect as a strategic investment. Indeed, as Cunningham (1985) points out, the market is frequently the only definer of strategic value, and it quickly tells the competition:

    *You only know that you have a strategic system when the competitors start spending money they didn't know they had available to spend.*

However, business benefits do not only come in operational versus the strategic variants and there are at least two other types of value generating IS investments, these are:

- *Threshold Investment.* These are the investments in IS projects that an organisation must make to operate within the industry. Whilst 'returns' are not easy to identify the investment is effectively mandatory. These projects may actually have a *negative* RoI but the investment must still be made for competitive survival.

- *Infrastructure Investment.* These investments typically have medium-term gain horizons and cannot normally generate any direct benefits, such as staff cost savings, but provide the enabler for many other value generators, such as improved management communication. These projects intend to create a backbone for the organisation and hence can be viewed and assessed as *assets*.

Each style of IS investment is associated with a different type of value and each value type should be articulated and assessed, though not necessarily quantified. Furthermore, as Section 7.3 will show, the different objectives and benefit types will require different approaches to justifying the investment.

An alternative way of considering classes of information value comes from the ideas of Information Economics (IE is primarily intended to provide a set of investment justification techniques and as such will be further discussed in Section 7.3). Parker and Benson (1988), in their work on Information Economics, define six categories of value in the use of information. These may, of course, form the basis for investment justifications. The six classes of value are:

1 *Return on investment*: perhaps the most traditional type of value where financial cost/benefit analyses show up a positive difference between the development and operating cost stream and the business cost reduction and revenue increasing stream to give a net value over time.

2 *Strategic match*: this is the direct support of a stated business strategy by a particular project.

3 *Competitive advantage*: a value created from a new business or product, or increased market share.

4 *Management information support*: providing information about critical aspects of the business. Those aspects that must be done well for the business to succeed – these are the CSFs or Nolan Norton's 'do wells'.

5 *Competitive response:* IT activities aimed at catching-up with competitor's position or even leap-frog them in ways that will be difficult to duplicate or overcome.

6 *Strategic IS architecture*: a basic and necessary investment that enables subsequent strategic applications to occur.

One of the greatest problems in judging information value is to recognise the distinction between tangible and intangible benefits and having some method of estimating the worth of intangible benefits since, as a 1991 survey by Clarke McKee Management Consultants on behalf of the Prudential Corporation found, the vast majority of organisations (over 80 per cent) will find that intangible benefits account for at least 30 per cent of the value resulting from their IS investments. This same survey investigated which intangible benefits were rated as most important, and therefore presumably as having the greatest value. These results are shown in Figure 7.18.

How these intangible benefits were rated for their degree of difficulty to measure will be looked at in Section 7.3, indeed much of the difficulty in finding techniques suitable for IS investment justifications comes from the difficulty in quantifying intangible benefits. The value to a bank of an integrated network comes from the ability to alter what staff do rather than from the ability to reduce the number of staff, as happened with early banking systems. This value is both intangible and inextricably involved with the many other changes that are happening in banking, so a casual relationship is hard to defend. Value attaches to the way information is

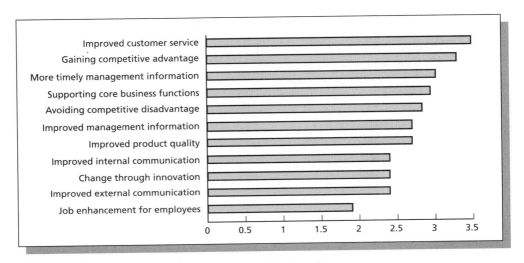

**Fig 7.18 ◆ Relative importance of some intangible benefits**

used and not to the information systems themselves (except in the sense that they provide an asset capable of generating valuable information). Given that it is information that has value this value results from maintenance activities and from small IS projects as well as from major IS investments. In fact there seems to be no correlation between the scale of the IS investment and the value ascribed to the resultant information.

If *direct* but intangible benefits from IS investments are hard enough to quantify then judging the *indirect* intangible benefits resulting from investments in core business backbone systems is even more difficult. Intangible benefits accruing from investments in IS backbone services are impossible! The value of an IS investment may be harvested here and now from this specific IS project, or not until far in the future from other projects that only become possible because this one was undertaken. To make value even more complex to assess, the value may derive from future business dangers that are avoided. Business infrastructures have a direct relationship only to costs and their benefits are indirectly felt through the line of business activities that they enable or improve. IS infrastructures also have a direct relationship to costs but their relationship to benefits is further removed than that of business infrastructures. IS infrastructures enable IS activities to happen, IS activities enable business activity improvements. Costs incurred for IS infrastructures have a lot of links to go through before they can be balanced by benefits.

Changes in these two infrastructure elements are compounding the problems of each. Increasing IS devolution makes more managers responsible for IS costs and yet they are ill-equipped to understand the growing need to spend on maintenance and upon infrastructure assets such as communication networks, system software skills and corporate data services. Some aspects of value can be readily assessed, even if not fully quantified. This value, however, never comes from the technology itself, it comes from the improved ability to compete, that is to have a better management process.

In a general economic sense the expected value of information is always defined by the simple relationship illustrated in Figure 7.19. The *calculating* of this equation however is anything but simple. Just as IS investments involve tangible and intangible costs, so too do they involve tangible and intangible benefits. Most would agree that it is important to attempt to evaluate the gains represented in this equation, though such estimates may need to take a qualitative rather than a quantitative form and so will vary from unsupported guesses to pseudo-scientific calculations. Any degree of accuracy about benefits is impossible to maintain but then many forecasts of *costs* suffer in just the same way and yet most organisations put a larger amount of management attention into estimating and then controlling costs than they are prepared to put into estimating and controlling the *benefits*.

The equation shown in Figure 7.19 defines the *boundaries* of information value. Whilst it is generally impossible to define the exact value of any given information

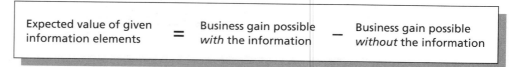

| Expected value of given information elements | = | Business gain possible *with* the information | − | Business gain possible *without* the information |

Fig 7.19 ◆ The theoretical calculation of expected information value

element it is possible to establish the upper boundary, the value of perfect information, that is a removal of all risk associated with future actions. An example situation illustrates this and is given in Figure 7.20.

To re-state the obvious, information value results from the business gain made *with* the given information *minus* the business gain made without it. It is this second stage in judging value that is often forgotten. Because computing this difference is an often forgotten stage new products frequently 'steal' from old ones. The *with* situation rarely emerges in a green field site; information is already obtained, from manual or old automated systems, from guess-work or very slowly, but it is still acquired. However the *without* circumstances are not the status quo either; 'old' products will decline in effectiveness anyway and such a decline must be off-set against costs. The resulting gain may simply be from some 'not worse' situation. Similarly business gain may result from soft gossip style information if that information acts to generate an awareness of a *need* to act.

It is worth noting that such a representation makes certain assumptions about the role information plays in making decisions. It assumes that information directs decisions in a straightforward way; information is 'perfect' if it is relevant to the decision to be made and if it is precise and reliable. Feldman and Marsh (1981) however, note that the way organisations use information may not conform to that

---

A cosmetics manufacturer can create ten new products a year. A product launch costs £1 million and has no residual value. Each launch is an independent event. Ten per cent of such product launches succeed. The net return from a successful launch is £12 million and all launch costs are lost with an unsuccessful one.

**Scenario 1**

| Expected gain from launch | = | (Probability of success | × | Value of gain) | + | (Probability of failure | × | Value of failure) |
|---|---|---|---|---|---|---|---|---|

$$\text{Expected gain from launch} = (0.1 \times £12\text{ million}) + (0.9 \times -£1\text{ million})$$
$$= £0.3\text{ million}$$

Such potential value can now be compared with alternative uses of the £1 million launch funds.

**Scenario 2**

If a new and infallible market research system was able to supply perfect information (though it will do nothing to alter the probability of product success) then the situation is changed.

$$\text{Expected gain from launch} = (0.1 \times £12\text{ million}) + (0.9 \times \text{zero})$$
$$= £1.2\text{ million}$$

Expected = Business gain possible *with* the information − Business gain possible *without* the information
= £1.2 million − £0.3 million
= £0.9 million

Under these circumstances the *maximum* value that can accrue to perfect information is £0.9 million. Whilst reality obviously never offers such perfect removal of all risk nevertheless the idea of the boundaried value to information is a useful one.

**Fig 7.20 ◆ An example illustrating expected information value**

simple relationship. They speculate that, based on a volume of research literature, the following observations are more realistic about information use than the simple assumption that it directs choices:

- Much of the information that is gathered and communicated by individuals and organisations has little decision relevance.
- Much of the information that is used to justify a decision is collected and interpreted after the decision has been made, or substantially made.
- Much of the information gathered in response to requests for information is not considered in the making of decisions for which it was requested.
- Regardless of the information available at the time a decision is first considered, more information is requested.
- Complaints are often made that an organisation does not have enough information to make a decision while available information is ignored.
- The relevance of the information provided in the decision-making process to the decision being made is less conspicuous than is the insistence on the information.

Feldman and Marsh go on to argue that these observations indicate a weakness in assumptions about the role of information and standard perceptions of decision making. The *value* of information lies in more complex issues related to the symbolic significance it holds with respect to legitimating decisions, in giving an affirmation of rationality, to incentives to be *seen* to gather information, and to fears of 'missing out' and not 'knowing what's going on'. In short the value of information is a social and cultural value laden issue. This can be interpreted as a recognition, linking back to the earlier points made, that although the losses and gains represented in a cost-benefit judgement *may* be couched in terms of financial value, the *actual* issues of value will include power, emotion, commitment and so on as noted in this chapter's opening paragraphs. Indeed some consideration of specific issues other than finance are required, law and ethics for instance, or morality for Islamic organisations as discussed by Gambling and Karim (1991), perhaps environmental impact or any number of other attributes deemed of key importance.

Gain is always a *net* term made up of the relationship between cost and benefits, and the objectives of managing the economics of making choices about IS activities must always include:

- 'Knowing' all costs – tangible and intangible
  here the emphasis is on trying to decrease them
- 'Knowing' all benefits – tangible and intangible
  here the emphasis is on trying to increase them (or at least ensure that they are successfully harvested)

Since gain is a net term it can only be established by some sort of benefit for cost judgement where the IS resource allocation decision maker (who that will be varies by IS structure, location and management responsibility) is seeking to make *informed* decisions based upon the IS investment risk balancing act. Whilst IS and user teams involved in IS projects before the investment is made remain unsure of the potential business value they will find it hard to sell these to a sceptical management. Remaining unsure of the business benefits *after* the investment has been made makes it doubly hard to justify the next generation of IS projects.

This section has looked at where information value may lie but these benefits do not *automatically* result and they must be carefully harvested. To harvest the potential business benefits made possible by information value requires the use of techniques to identify the most fruitful IS projects. A consideration of such techniques is found in Section 7.3. The management of benefit realisation will also require a constant review of the validity and accuracy of the chosen techniques by considering the distance between predicted value and obtained benefits.

## 7.3 ◆ MAKING THE INVESTMENT DECISION

Assessing the value of information in a generalised sense is still done by asking the same old questions:

- What triggers are received and how often? In other words what surprises will be generated by the information and how often?
- What changes are provoked and how often? In other words what decisions can and will be changed for the better if such a surprise is received, and how often?
- What is the business payoff from the improved actions?

To actually answer these questions involves some complex techniques. In Section 7.2 we were concerned with looking at where information value lies in order to assess the business value of IS investments. Here the focus is rather sharper, namely how to compare candidate IS projects to select an IS investment. Figure 7.16 on p. 218 showed that the value curve for any project must be established in order to judge value for money. In this section we consider some techniques for generating this curve.

The most fundamental reason for developing an IS strategy is that it defines what are the necessary IS investments. Indeed one definition of an emergent strategy is that it is shown by the process of resource allocations, that is investments decisions. The process of selecting IS investments should be guided by the IS strategy but many organisations face conflicting investment pressures. On the one hand they need immediate hard benefits such as lowered costs or improved cash flow and yet also need the long-term soft benefits such as improved customer service levels or improved staff productivity. Having looked at some of the issues associated with the cost side of an investment decision, and at some of the issues associated with the value side of the decisions, now we must look at how organisations can evaluate and decide about a given IS opportunity.

By the evaluation process an organisation is revealing a judgement of its preferred alternatives and establishing its priorities. Such preferences must be acknowledged since any organisation will have a finite set of resources and yet may have an infinite number of potential projects from which to choose. Any selection is at the expense of other things that could have been done with the allocated set of resources and therefore has an opportunity cost. Many of the beneficial business effects of IS are not adequately captured by any accounting system. Since information value is not readily captured by financial reporting techniques an organisation should not assume that IS has no value, even the most basic common sense shows that it has a huge significance. Remenyi *et al.* (1991) in their detailed treatment of information as an economic entity report on some perceptions of IS importance:

- IS helps us to gain a competitive advantage      30 per cent
- Our business would not be possible without IS  21 per cent

It is no longer possible to evaluate business performance solely on the basis of *traditional* accountancy frameworks, which is not to say that the techniques intending accurately to measure bottom line implications are obsolete but they are insufficient alone. There are many problems with purely accountancy evaluation techniques, not least that, just as they do not allow all costs to become visible, they do not allow all gains to become visible. They are short-term evaluations on a quantitative basis that favour risk aversion and cost-lowering activities with the financial year as their natural horizon and so are inevitably inappropriate for the high-risk long-term projects that hope to make qualitative gains that are often of an indirect nature. As Hochstrasser (1992) suggests, organisations need a way of dealing with the mismatch resulting when traditional selection frameworks (designed to measure bottom-line financial benefits that have actually been achieved or are accurately forecast to be achievable) are used to evaluate IS activities against IS projects aimed at supporting and improving the organisation's long-term performance. IS benefits are always uncertain and realising them takes a long time (Figure 7.21); Nolan Norton suggest that any IS project requires two to three years before its benefits are stable enough to be measured. Financial measures are weighted towards short-term returns and not the meeting of long-term goals and the concentration upon costs can conflict with efforts to gain benefits.

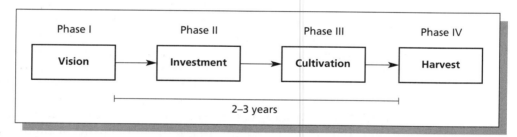

**Fig 7.21 ◆ Realising IS benefits is a long-term process**

The net result of the situation is, as reported by Green-Armytage (1994), that chief executives are increasingly dissatisfied with IS, with less than half (44 per cent) convinced that IS contributes to profitability. Interestingly, in the same report the vast majority of IS professionals (76 per cent) were convinced that it *did* contribute to profit. There may be many factors contributing to this level of dissatisfaction but it plausibly indicates poor quality evaluation practice since ineffective (in business value terms) IS activities are being chosen. Of course it should be noted that this dissatisfaction with IS is of IS in *overall* terms and the quality of specific choices may be high. Mukhopadhyay *et al.* (1995) demonstrate the significant contribution to profitability a *specific* IS activity (an instance of EDI by the Chrysler Corporation) undertaken for a *specific* purpose can make and therefore caution against treating IS as a single factor. The fact remains that IS investment decisions have been taken but the resulting situation is not perceived to be successful.

In many respects the IS investment decision is treated differently to the financing decisions of other business functional areas. Remenyi *et al.* (1991) suggest that any functional area's treatment of expenditure is determined by:

- The size of the expenditure required
- Whether performance or value in return for expenditure is taken for granted
- Whether expenditure is seen as unavoidable ongoing expenses or discretionary capital investments

Figure 7.22 illustrates the position of a number of functional areas with respect to the investment decision making process and shows some of the key differences between functional areas. Marketing, for example, spends large amounts of money but the sum is generally perceived as a necessary operating expense whilst the large sums spent by IS are treated as capital investments. Remenyi *et al.* (1991) suggest that the combination of IS factors demands the existence of a manager whose sole responsibility it is to ensure the realisation of IS benefits (they refer to an IT Benefits Manager) who will co-ordinate the complex investment decision making process, be charged with measuring and evaluating the predicted and actual benefits, and eventually evaluating the degree of 'success'. This is broadly the same as the concept of the IS benefits register discussed earlier.

Much of this chapter has considered the different types of benefits that IS can bring to a business. Many writers, including Silk (1991) and Tapscott and Caston (1993), make the distinction between the three eras of information, what Remenyi *et al.* are amused to see referred to as E³. With three distinct eras there are also, obviously, distinct benefits, and not surprisingly there is a need for different approaches to evaluating IS projects in order to make the IS investment decision. The attributes of the three information eras are shown in Figure 7.23.

Figure 7.23 illustrates why *complementary* assessment techniques are needed. These are likely to lie along a scale of 'hardness' with the traditional accountancy evaluation techniques such as net present value and discounted cash flow analysis at one extreme. This extreme is the 'we must measure it to manage it' school. The middle ground is held by the 'if it supports our strategic direction we must do it' school that completely de-emphasises financial figures and ratios and replaces them by statements of faith. Although this area concentrates upon defining the reason for the benefit it may monitor the direction and size of the change and particularly focuses upon marginal changes when going through the process of

| Function | Finance (same for personnel ) | Manufacturing | Marketing | R&D | IS |
|---|---|---|---|---|---|
| *Size of spending* | Small | Large | Large | Large | Large |
| *Agreed value* | Yes | Yes | Yes | Yes | Undecided |
| *Expense or capital* | E | C | E | E | C |
| *Degree of risk* | Low | Medium | Medium | High | Very high |
| *Concern to measure* | Low | High | Low | Medium | Undecided |

**Fig 7.22 ◆ Business investment decisions**
(after Remenyi *et al.*)

| Era | $E^1$ | $E^2$ | $E^3$ |
|---|---|---|---|
| Goal | Automate | Informate | Transformate |
| Generic benefit | Efficiency | Effectiveness | Exploitation |
| Nature of benefit | Hard | | Soft |
| Scale of benefit | $B_1$ | $B_2 = B_1 \times 10$ | $B_3 = B_2 \times 10$ <br> $B_3 = B_1 \times 100$ |
| Metrics | Requires metrics that focus on cost displacement and/or cost avoidance analysis, any intangible benefits are extra gains best measured by surveys. | Requires metrics that include some element of automate era and so measured as for $E^1$. | Requires full capital investment appraisal techniques needing long-term horizons, not likely to include many measures from $E^2$ but will include some from $E^3$. |

Fig 7.23 ◆ Information eras and IS investment

selecting candidate projects. The other extreme is the 'how do we run the business' school of business activity assessment approaches that does not separate out IS at all. The dictated changes, the must do projects, do not really come under the heading of an investment *decision* at all since, by definition, the investment must be made! (*See* Figure 7.24.)

All these approaches are attempting to assess the worth to the organisation of value generating information attributes. Before we move into looking at some of the specific tools for doing this we need to make one important distinction. That is between tangible, and therefore empirically measurable, benefits and intangible, and therefore assessable but not empirically measurable, benefits.

| Assess *financial* impact of change | Assess *value* of change | *Causal* logic for change | Act of *faith* change | Must Do/ *Dictated* change |
|---|---|---|---|---|
| Hard | | | Soft | |
| Tangible | | | Intangible | |
| NPV, IRR, etc to document quantifiable net savings | RoM or similar to document net value | IE or other weighting method to select 'best' | CSF or similar for strategic contribution | N/A <br><br> Not really a 'decision' |

Fig 7.24 ◆ Continuum of approaches to investment decisions

## Tangible benefits measurement

One of the best known intangible benefit appraisal techniques is Information Economics (*see* Section 7.3.4). Although Information Economics concentrates upon extending traditional measurement techniques to encompass intangible benefits,

Parker and Benson (1988) are careful to ensure that the tangible benefits are quantified as the first stage of the IS investment decision making process. They suggest the following seven stages to calculating the value of the tangible benefits:

1 Break down the effort on the basis of the work functions affected by implementation.
2 For each area from (1) identify alterations, additions or eliminations associated with the specific job processes.
3 Determine the cost of performing the job process affected. Cost categories might include labour, equipment, facilities, materials, etc. Cost sources might include organisation and function budgets or projections of the basis of time, volume and labour rates.
4 Determine the effects of the change on indirect costs such as taxes or stock holdings.
5 Determine the cost of performing the process *after* modification.
6 Determine where additional costs will occur in the future if no change occurs in the job process. Categories include additional volume needing more labour, equipment, materials, new or modified facilities, and additional indirect costs.
7 Calculate the difference between performing the process the old way and the new way. The result of this calculation will be the expected tangible benefit or an added cost of doing business.

Obviously this seven-stage process forms a major part of the investment decision process on the left side of the scale in Figure 7.24 and only a minor part to the right of the scale.

As we saw in Section 7.2, one of the greatest problems in judging information value is to have some way of estimating the *worth* of intangible benefits. The continuums shown in Figures 7.23 and 7.24 show that as we move along the scale such intangible benefits account for a larger and larger part of the value of the project. The 1991 Clarke McKee Management Consultants survey on behalf of the Prudential Corporation showed that over 80 per cent of organisations find that intangible benefits account for at least 30 per cent of the value resulting from their IS investments. Figure 7.25 shows how these intangible benefits rate by the degree of difficulty to measure them. All intangible benefits relate to risk in attainment and therefore are *inherently* difficult to measure.

Simply to *quantify* the benefits, be they tangible or intangible, is not enough for an effective investment decision making process. To select specific IS activities there is the fundamental need to define the relationship between benefits and costs to consider just *what* resources are those that most effectively express the necessary value judgements and the rest of this chapter will concentrate upon approaches to assessing this relationship.

## 7.3.1 ◆ Hard financial justifications

There are a number of traditional cost-benefit analysis techniques that are used to provide a financial justification for a given IS project. Each seeks to quantify everything that can be considered instruments that generate cash flow:

↑ Amount of increased revenue    ↓ Amount of decreased expenses
→ Amount of increased expenses avoided

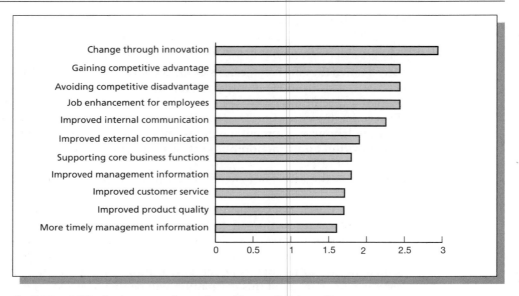

**Fig 7.25 ◆ Difficulty in measuring value of intangible benefits**

The financial nature of capital investment appraisal is intended to make the decision fully 'rational', and can do so fairly effectively for efficiency era systems that return primarily tangible, cost reduction or avoidance, benefits that result from well-understood processes. Such traditional financial methods of defining the relationship between benefits and costs are still required for two reasons:

1 Such systems are still being implemented
2 Many value judging methods extend rather than replace the traditional methods

A number of possible methods for calculating the amount by which a project's return exceeds its investment are included here but many others are used by organisations to meet their particular needs. The use of strictly financial judgement of the cost/benefit balance has been much criticised, mostly on the grounds that it is a much too simplistic approach to adequately capture the risks and gains associated with IS. However the familiarity to management of this form of expression of value means that they remain a popular component of the business case for or against particular IS activities. A comprehensive treatment of investment decision making is outside the scope of this text.

### Return on investment (RoI)

This is sometimes referred to as the *simple* return on investment and is the ratio of average annual net income of the project divided by the internal investment in the project. This is calculated by considering the annual benefit divided by the investment amount. Sometimes an average rate of return is calculated by averaging the annual benefits, otherwise it is done on a year by year basis using individual benefit amounts.

$$\text{Return on Investment} = \frac{\text{Annual Benefit}}{\text{Investment Amount}}$$

### Discounted cash flow (DCF)

A key issue when attempting to evaluate the worth of a potential IS activity quantitatively is to consider the time-dependant nature of value. Money held *now* is worth more than the same volume of money held *later*, the opportunity cost of what that money could achieve in compounded interest from investment. With any given activity costs are normally incurred sooner rather than later whilst benefits are usually gained later rather than sooner, but the distribution of these two differs for each particular IS activity. A potential activity can be described in terms of its time-dependent value. There are two popular methods of doing this: by calculating the net present value (NPV) of the activity or its internal rate of return (IRR). Both of these techniques use a discount rate that expresses future value in terms of its worth to the organisation *now*.

### Net present value (NPV)

This can be defined as the difference between the sum of values of the cash inflows, discounted at an appropriate cost of capital, and the present value of the original investment. If the NPV is greater than or equal to zero then the investment will earn the required rate of return; the project with the largest positive net present value is the most profitable.

$$\text{PV of Benefit} = \frac{\text{Benefit}}{(1 + i)^n} \qquad \begin{array}{l} i = \text{rate of interest} \\ n = \text{number of years} \end{array}$$

NPV =    Present Value of Benefit – Present Value of Investment
If NPV >= 0    Invest
If NPV < 0    Do not invest

This method uses a discount rate determined by the organisation's cost of capital to establish the present value of a project and so provides some estimate of the value of money to the given organisation. This discount rate is used to determine the present value of cash receipts and cash expenditures and can be set to include risk elements. All cash flows affecting taxable income must be credited to the project on an after-tax basis. Depreciation is an exception to this rule since it does not involve an actual disbursement. The amount of tax relief from depreciation must be included into the cash flows. Figure 7.26 gives an example NPV calculation where the organisation's tax rate is 34 per cent and their cost of capital is 20 per cent. The cost of capital is the average cost to the organisation of the funds used to finance its operations. Since this is what it will cost the organisation to have capital 'tied up' this is the minimum rate of return that would be desired. The notion that it forms a critical hurdle is why it is also often known as the hurdle rate or cut-off rate. (Note that these methods are frequently criticised for using an unrealistically *high* cost of capital in an attempt to build into the method some recognition of risk elements.) This measure, like all profitability measuring techniques, is only as good as the accuracy and reliability of the estimates used within it. The more realistic the estimates of cash flows and discount rates are the more useful is this measure. The organisation can consider the NPV as either:

- A measure of the surplus which the investment makes over its required return

  or
- A margin of error in the size of the approvable investment amount

| Item | Year | | | |
|---|---|---|---|---|
| £000s | 1 | 2 | 3 | 4 |
| 1  Cash inflow | 25 | 105 | 125 | 200 |
| 2  Cash outflow | −135 | −25 | −30 | −35 |
| 3  Pre-tax cash flow | | | | |
| (Row 1 + Row 2) | −110 | 80 | 95 | 165 |
| 4  After-tax cash flow | | | | |
| (1 − tax rate) × Row 3 | | | | |
| [assume 34% tax rate] | −70 | 53 | 63 | 109 |
| 5  Depreciation | 60 | 50 | 40 | 30 |
| 6  Tax relief from depreciation | | | | |
| (tax rate × Row 5) | 20 | 17 | 14 | 10 |
| 7  Net after-tax cash flow | | | | |
| (Row 4 + Row 6) | −50 | 70 | 77 | 119 |
| 8  Discounted cash flow | | | | |
| [assume 20% cost of capital] | −50 | 58 | 53 | 69 |
| Net present value | | | | |
| (sum of amounts in Row 8) | 130 | | | |

**Fig 7.26 ◆ Example NPV calculation**

### Internal rate of return (IRR)

The internal rate of return is based upon the net present value but calculated using an interest rate that will cause the NPV to equal zero. This is the discount rate at which the present value of cash receipts equals the present value of cash expenditures. The IRR intends to make projects more directly comparable by showing what interest would have to be received on the sum of the investment to get the same return offered. This is also called the yield of the investment and is often used to define a hurdle rate, for example no investment is approved unless its IRR is greater than 12 per cent.

$$0 = \frac{\text{Benefit}}{(1 + i)^n}$$

$i$ = rate of interest
$n$ = number of years

Solve for $i$ rather than for NPV:
  If $i >= 12\%$    Invest
  If $i < 12\%$    Do not invest

### Payback period

This technique determines the amount of time, usually in years and months, required for the cumulative cash inflows to equal the initial investment. The most popular form uses the exhaust method where each year's cash inflow is identified until zero is reached. In contrast to the exhaust method is the average payback calculation that gives only an approximation of the payback period. This average method is only useful if the annual benefits all lie *close* to the average.

**Exhaust method**
Payback (in time) = Investment – Cumulative benefit

**Average method**
$$\text{Payback (in time)} = \frac{\text{Investment}}{\text{Average annual benefit}}$$

Figure 7.27 shows the time curves of costs and benefits. The payback period is the period until the net benefit becomes positive. A shorter payback period reduces the risk of the project going astray and hence many organisations will select projects on the basis of short payback periods even at the cost of ultimately lower net benefit levels. This response is particularly associated with times of financial or IS confidence crises.

These general forms of the payback period calculations are straightforward and hence popular; however they suffer from the fact that they take no account of the opportunity cost of capital use but they can be enhanced as discounted payback period to produce a time value based payback measure that reflects the cost of capital. Discounted payback always shows a longer time period than nominal, or non-discounted, payback does.

Payback period analysis, along with NPV and IRR analyses, can form part of an organisation's control over resource allocation as well as part of its investment justification method.

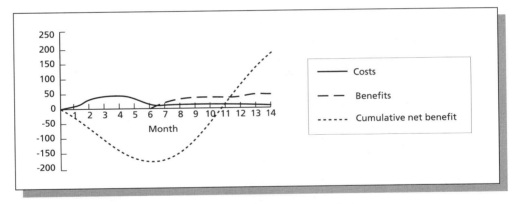

**Fig 7.27 ◆ Cost, benefit, cumulative benefit and payback period**

## 7.3.2 ◆ Risk recognising techniques

IS activities are increasingly associated with high risks because they can be, as Moad (1995) points out, 'unleashing potential for huge change'. For this reason they are associated with great uncertainty about just what the *real* effects of them may be; what the real costs and real benefits will be. For that reason it is not surprising that there are a number of evaluation techniques which attempt to describe potential IS activities in terms of their associated risk. A full discussion of the full range of the techniques available to support the handling of risk and decision making under uncertainty is outside the scope of this text; however, one of the simplest risk recognising techniques is included here as an illustration.

## Probability of attainment/Bayesian analysis

This is the only one of the financial justifications included here that *explicitly* considers the risk aspect of the investment decision. Probability of attainment analysis is an expansion of the simple RoI based upon Bayesian economics that describes the varying levels of confidence in the expected benefits. Conventionally these are given for three levels, perhaps:

- Certainly    (80 per cent confidence and above)
- Probably    (50 per cent and above)
- Hopefully    (only obtained if all goes well)

The underlying assumption is that someone within the organisation, by virtue of past experience or knowledge, can quantify the relative likelihood, or probability, of benefits being achieved. If there is no past data available then the best source of these estimates would be the intended information user. The expert or user is questioned as to the likely results of having the system in order to quantify the value of the benefits but also to give these for three different levels of certainty of outcomes. Figure 7.28 gives an illustration for an example system, one that analyses potential competition (such competition analysis systems will appear as examples of systems that may be justified under strategic contribution to a differentiation generic strategy). Obviously the benefits from such a system are subject to a risk factor in their attainment.

These 'hard' evaluation techniques draw upon the traditional skills of the financial analyst and tend to be familiar territory for all senior managers and therefore have an intuitive appeal particularly when cost savings seem essential. As number-based approaches they offer a reasonable way of choosing between mutually exclusive alternatives, but are generally only totally satisfactory for projects of relatively low business importance. IS activities that are of high business importance will probably be ones that will alter the ways of doing business, alter the factors of competition or perhaps alter the very nature of the organisation. Such projects will be high in risk with benefits that are not amenable to accurate prediction and quantification. Such projects are usually going to lie within one business area and primarily be about cost savings. It is interesting that such techniques define benefits in terms of costs, even if it is cost *saving*. Net present value, for instance, looks

| System *could* give increase in sales of (%) | Probability that it will | Sales value £000s | Return £000s |
|---|---|---|---|
| 1% | 0.80 | 750 | 600.00 |
| 3% | 0.15 | 2250 | 337.50 |
| 5% | 0.05 | 3750 | 187.50 |
| Return combining all probabilities | | | 1125.00 |
| With 15% before-tax profit on sales | | | |
| Profitability | | | 168.75 |

Fig 7.28 ◆ Probability of attainment analysis

at the 'real' increased income and/or the 'soft' decreased outgoings that are potential costs avoided. Whatever features are looked at they have to be given numeric values. Since such hard line approaches quantify everything, they work well for visible and tangible costs and benefits. Financial justification is appropriate at certain stages of IS use and management maturity, for example the control stage on Nolan's stage of growth model; or for particular aspects of the applications portfolio, particularly the support system segment of the business importance grid; or for certain styles of IS direction, for instance the scarce resource generic IS strategy. Equally, it is inappropriate for certain others.

The major weakness of these techniques is that they simply do not work for instances where the strategic impact of the project is extensive. Such impacts will generally be through indirect and intangible benefits (if they are *benefits* at all) that cannot be defined in terms of costs, incurred or saved. These techniques capture the epitome of a 'with or without' perception of IS projects, that is that they make the base assumption that IS activities *can* be vetoed or that a *before* can be envisaged. Such simple, causal relationships rarely exist in IS. These approaches do not adequately forecast or record the effect of mission critical activities or indirect but extensive infrastructure investments.

So to sum up, the main strength of these traditional numbers-based methods is that they permit the comparison of alternatives and they express value in the language of capital in a way that is familiar to many managers, but their greatest weakness is that many worthy candidate IS activities cannot adequately be described in terms that really capture their business effect.

### 7.3.3 ◆ Return on management

As more IS activities move towards the second and third eras of effectiveness and exploitation, as charted by the Era Models discussed in Chapter 5, the traditional assessment techniques prove inadequate. It was Strassmann (1985) who confirmed the fears of many organisations when he found, after extensive investigation:

> no correlation between the level of investment in IT and performance.

If anything, industries that invested most in IT have shown relatively poor productivity growth. Strassmann concluded that this was because it is *management* and not *capital* that is the decisive input to modern business and so any surplus value is because of management and not capital. He argues that a 'new' economics is needed if management and not labour or capital is the scarce resource. It is management capabilities that need to be 'shared out' and prioritised by the evaluation techniques. Traditional measures make the base assumption that it is capital that carries the inherent value. Since the real business benefit from IS comes from its potential for improving management productivity he suggests that his return on management (RoM) is a more valid measure for assessing potential IS investment than RoI is. RoM is a technique that seeks to quantify the management added value and divide it by the management cost to give an index of returns. Strassmann feels that the impact on management is the key result of IS and hence the key variable to measure to determine value.

$$\text{RoM} = \frac{\text{Management value added}}{\text{Management cost}}$$

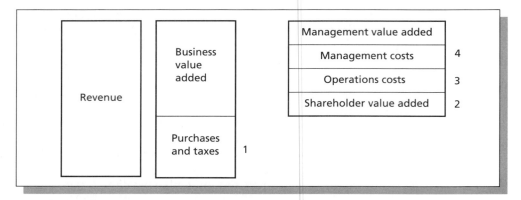

**Fig 7.29 ◆ Strassmann's return on management (RoM)**
(reprinted by permission of The Information Economics Press from *The Business Value of Computers* by
P. Strassman, 1990)

where management value added is the residue after every contribution to a firm's inputs is paid. If this residue exceeds the management cost then management is 'productive'. The nature of management value added is shown in Figure 7.29.

Revenue is composed of purchases and taxes and business value added. The calculation of RoM requires the calculation of the management added figure. This is done by deducting the elements at (1) to leave the figure for the business value added. It is then possible to isolate the required figure by subtracting the dividend that is the shareholder value added (2) followed by the direct and overhead costs that are the operations costs (3); finally, removing the management costs (4) leaves only the management value added sum. For an organisation to be deemed 'successful' the RoM should be greater than 1.

Strassmann worked with the results of many IS initiatives to try to predict what types of project typically gave a high RoM. His important finding was that it was actually possessing a high RoM *before* the IS initiative started that was the best discriminator for a high RoM resulting *from* the projects, in other words success. The RoM measure provides an indicator of the organisation's business vitality and the higher the value added percentage compared to purchase costs the better is the return on management. Strassmann claims that the strength of his approach is that it:

- Combines financial statement and balance sheet entries
- Isolates the productivity of management
- Is self-indexing
- Is particularly suitable for service-based businesses who typically use less capital than manufacturing businesses do
- Allows diagnostic evaluations

The technique does however have some problems. Firstly there is some ambiguity in quite what should be included as 'management', for example do secretarial and supervisory staff get included? Perhaps the fine distinctions do not matter as long as consistent definition are used. More significantly this technique uses *estimates* of:

- Revenue after the change is implemented
- Changes to resource costs and contributions

Both of these are difficult to do with any degree of accuracy and RoM seems to work better as an evaluation technique than as a justification one. Evaluation is the process of assessing the value of a specific aspect of IS and may be related to some aspect for which *selection* is not relevant. Justification, however, carries with it the implication of selection, of choice between alternatives.

This technique is 'good' in that it focuses attention upon the management process but Strassmann's work has not really proved a causal relationship between this process and, what he describes as, the value added by management. This additional value may, in reality, come about for reasons other than an improved management process and a multitude of external factors could be the cause. However, since the technique draws upon data that is relatively readily available it can be applied relatively cheaply and so it can be useful for evaluations and organisational 'health checks', and in particular, the longitudinal monitoring of improvements. Most usefully it can be used to chart how effective the priority setting procedures are proving to be. If the organisation consistently uses hard financial measures to select IS activities *and* it finds that the RM index rises then those techniques are proving useful. If the RoM is low or falling then perhaps other decision making techniques should be used.

### 7.3.4 ◆ Information economics

Business performance can be enhanced, perhaps by the effect of IS rather than IS itself, but which projects have the most beneficial effect? Beneficial is not an objective, context-free word, it is dependant upon many organisational specific variables, and information economics is intended to be a framework of techniques that allows an organisation to define for itself its own relationship between the *investment in IS* and improved business performance. If Return on Management is most effective as an evaluation tool, information economics intends to be an effective investment *justification* tool. Information economics explicitly evaluates investment alternatives by identifying and then evaluating, scoring and ranking the potential positive factors (the value) and the potential negative factors (the risk or uncertainty) of each candidate.

Information Economics is described and developed in the works of Parker and Benson (1988 and 1989) and in these works they suggest that value is something that is assessed by the process of defining the relative business domain feasibility and the relative technology domain viability for candidate projects. The distinction between the two domains is shown in Figure 7.30.

Every organisation has at least one line of business (LoB), that is the value chain of activities from the buying of supplies, goods or services through to the sale of products, goods or services. Many organisations will have several LoBs and Parker and Benson illustrate this by describing a university that has undergraduate education, professional education, research, healthcare, housing, food services and retail. These seven LoBs all hold the *potential* to have value added to them by IS, and this gives improved business performance to that LoB whilst improved organisation performance is the net result of all.

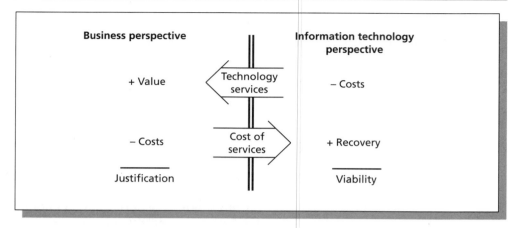

**Fig 7.30 ◆ Information economics**

Information economics suggests that the decision to make a specific investment can be made on the basis of four justifications and these possible benefits are illustrated in Figure 7.31.

Information economics extends traditional cost benefit appraisal methods to include the assessment of intangible benefits. The return on investment of a candidate project must be assessed and information economics uses an extended form of RoI:

Traditional
Cost Benefit + Value + Value + Value + Innovation
Analysis Linking Accelerating Restructuring Valuation

where linking and accelerating are attempts to assess the ripple effect of technology change. Restructuring attempts to assess changes in productivity. This extension of RoI caters for some aspects of information value but still remains unable to capture *some* aspects. The sources of value considered in Section 7.2 are the elements that must be given a score and a rank as part of the justification process.

Information Economics is not intended to replace traditional cost benefit analysis techniques but rather sets out to extend them to cater for the many value generating aspects that are excluded by such traditional analysis techniques. The factors uncaptured even by the extended RoI fall into two sets, relating to the business

| Organisational element | The Line of Business (LoBs) | Corporate backbone (infrastructure) |
|---|---|---|
| Possible justifications | Direct cost reduction | Enhancements offering added value to the LoBs |
| | Enhanced business performance | Direct cost reductions |

**Fig 7.31 ◆ IS investment justifications**

| | Business domain | IT domain |
|---|---|---|
| *Positive factors that add to the the appeal of the candidate project* | Strategic match<br>Competitive advantage<br>Management information<br>Competitive response | Strategic IS architecture |
| *Negative factors that detract from the appeal of the candidate project* | Organisational or project risk | Definitional uncertainty<br>Technical uncertainty<br>IS infrastructure risk |

Fig 7.32 ◆ Information value assessment factors for information economics

domain or to the information technology domain, and either *add* to the relative appeal of a candidate project or *detract* from its appeal. These factors are shown in Figure 7.32.

Information Economics requires that each of these project appeal increasing or decreasing factors be given a score. From the business domain they are:

- *Strategic match*: the organisation must quantify the degree of direct support this candidate project gives to business strategies. Value results from improving the efficiency of the areas where costs are most significant and so the score must reflect the money value resulting from the more efficient use of assets.

- *Competitive advantage*: with this factor the organisation must quantify the degree to which the candidate project improves the organisation's competitive position. Hence, whilst similar to strategic match, here the concern is with outward rather than inward looking features. The score is based upon the money value of value chain improvements such as increased profit margins, increased sales or lower supply costs.

- *Management information support*: here IS projects are scored on their ability to support core activities measured in terms of increased sales, lower sales costs or lower product management costs.

- *Competitive response*: to quantify this factor the projects are scored with respect to how their lack would affect the organisation's competitive position; this is particularly important when firms must 'catch up' with the strategic developments of others. IBM's SESAME (Systems Effectiveness Study and Management Endorsement which is a formal payback checking methodology that studies the cost of the system from development to maintenance stage and asks users how they would meet their current objectives without its help and how satisfied with it they are) uses a similar approach since it quantifies the costs of performing a business process without the candidate system.

- *Organisational or project risk*: this scores the degree of risk in the project in terms of how well the organisation is placed to carry it out. The bigger the gap between required skills or resources and those available the higher the risk and hence the higher the score.

And from the technology domain they are:

- *Strategic IS architecture*: this scores projects on the basis of the value that accrues from keeping IS capabilities 'up-to-scratch'. This is the cost of freedom from chaos by ensuring that the basic IS methods, standards and hardware and software building blocks are in place ready for future projects. Scoring must reflect how well aligned this project is to the overall IS strategy.

- *Definitional uncertainty*: the project must be scored for the extent to which the requirements are known in *advance*. Since any IS project will make changes to the business there is always some uncertainty. The bigger the change, the bigger the risk and so the larger the negative score for the project.

- *Technical uncertainty*: this assesses the skills, hardware and software innovations required by the project in order to attach a score to the uncertainty. The more innovative, that is the bigger the change from current technological approaches and capabilities, is the project the higher are the risks and the bigger is the negative score for the project. When organisations have no experience in a particular technological area (Open Systems, client/server architectures, object-based databases or whatever) they are especially vulnerable to problems with that technology.

- *Infrastructure risk*: candidate projects will sometimes require fundamental infrastructure changes to be made. The more changes to be made, the higher the risk and the bigger the negative score.

This all leads to the fundamental tool of information economics based selection of IS projects, and that is the information economics scorecard. Where the enhanced cost benefit analysis and the assessment of appeal and risk from both the business and technology domains are all combined to give one overall ranking for that project, that fully describes the total value to the organisation and allows candidates to be discriminated between. This scorecard is illustrated in Figure 7.33.

Assessing and scoring each project with respect to these value elements is an inexact science but, whilst the results may be imprecise, the *consultative* process does ensure that definitions of value that are organisation specific are debated. Information Economics involves four more stages once the portfolio of candidate projects has been generated and they have been assessed and scored. These stages are:

1  Establish a standard weighting for each value factor (positive or negative)
2  Multiply the score for each factor by this weight
3  Sum the score for each project
4  Rank by score and select

Whilst this list makes the method look very simple the hugely significant business of giving a measure of *relative* importance to each of these factors makes it even more complex, subjective, political and frequently contentious than the process of scoring for each factor. Not all projects score equally in each area, but the areas themselves vary in their importance to the organisation. It is the heart of information economics that it seeks to capture both dimensions of project justification.

The method builds in the distinction between business justification (value compared to cost) and technical viability (resources available compared with resources needed). Since the two domains, and their respective project factors, are explicitly recognised the method also makes explicit the need to involve *both* business and IS in the justification of *every* project. This is perhaps its greatest strength.

| Evaluator | Business domain | | | | | | Technology domain | | | | |
|---|---|---|---|---|---|---|---|---|---|---|---|
| (Factor ⇒ ) | Rol + | SM + | CA + | MI + | CR + | OR - | SA + | DU - | TU - | IT - | |
| Business domain | | | | | | | | | | | |
| Technology domain | | | | | | | | | | | Weighted score |
| Weighted value | | | | | | | | | | | |

Where: **Rol measurement**
Enhanced traditional accounting quantification score

**Business domain assessment**

SM = Strategic match
CA = Competitive advantage
MI = Management information support
CR = Competitive response
OR = Organisational or project risk

**Technology domain assessment**

SA = Stategic IS architecture
DU = Definitional uncertainty
TU = Technical uncertainty
IT  = IS infrastructure risk

**Fig 7.33 ◆ The information economics scorecard**
(adapted from *Information Economics*, Parker and Benson © 1988, by permission of Prentice-Hall, Inc., Upper Saddle River, NJ )

The strengths of the approach are summed up by Wiseman (1992) as the 7 Cs of:

- *Comprehensiveness*: that all relevant business, economic and technical issues are addressed
- *Consistency*: in the decision making process
- *Clarity*: of organisational objectives, values and attitudes
- *Communications*: vastly improved across and between functions
- *Confidence*: that projects have been rigorously and soundly analysed and justified
- *Consensus*: amongst all managers from different business units and functions
- *Culture*: closing the gap

Perhaps the greatest weaknesses of the approach also lie in this list. The process of debating and agreeing scores and weightings is always difficult, often lengthy and sometimes impossible. The approach also continues to assume that investment capital is the primary scarce resource.

### 7.3.5 ◆ Strategic contribution assessment

As we move to the right along the scale of project justification illustrated in Figure 7.24 then the degree of quantification declines. The group of approaches referred to here as strategic contribution assessment are what Silk (1991) calls 'act of faith' justification. This type of approach is concerned with the *purpose* and *impact* of the change rather than the absolute *amount* of that change. The logic is that for the radically beneficial IS initiatives the real effects can only be established *after* the initiative. The evaluation process might allow a quantification statement to be made, such as:

> *Our new integrated supply chain system has increased the number of orders processed by 30 per cent/man years, invoices are processed with 50 per cent less people, our finished goods inventory and slow movers have dropped by 25 per cent and we have reduced the number of stock-out occurrences at our distributors and retail outlets by 40 per cent.*

At the investment decision stage, however, such figures could not have been attached without such a degree of uncertainty that they were effectively spurious.

In assessing the strategic contribution candidate projects are assessed almost entirely on the basis of their intangible benefits. This assessment is often solely on the marginal differences between them rather than on their full content, so that they can be ranked. Strategic match was discussed in the previous section as a value generating area within Information Economics but the degree of strategic contribution can be taken alone as a justification technique. This is a ranking or scoring technique that requires all candidate projects to be assessed in terms of their degree of meeting the corporate strategy. Generally this business strategy will be either one of differentiation or of cost reduction. Figure 7.34 shows some examples of systems that could support either generic strategy. Illustrations of systems chosen because of their support to a low-cost strategy are given along with their score.

The intention with this type of approach is to give a degree of certainty that the IS activities are targeted at the business goals. Whilst there are few metrics available to help in the ranking process it is certain that the more clearly defined are the business and IS strategies the more successfully this assessment can be done. When the two strategies are closely aligned then each candidate project can be tested for a clear line of support to these strategies. By implication when either the business or IS strategy is not well defined then this linkage-based justification is weakened.

It can be extremely difficult to choose between projects that all appear to contribute to the strategic direction of the organisation since the essential logic of the approach is:

| If | project contributes to meeting business goals |
|------|-----------------------------------------------|
| Then | invest |
| Else | do not invest |

Often the strategic contribution assessment comes in the form of a true act of faith in that a senior management champion challenges others to demonstrate the justification for *not* investing.

There is some variety in this group of methods, some identify the strategic contribution of an IS project whilst other (even further along to the right of the justification scale) justify *business* projects. Once you view business projects as an integrated whole it makes little sense to justify the IS element in isolation. Often the business initiative cannot exist without IS support and paradoxically it can be much simpler to justify the entire business activity than its elements. This is not perhaps that surprising since IS projects other than cost displacement ones have no value in themselves and it has no relevance to value the threads separately from the cloth.

The strategic contribution investment decision approves those projects with strong linkage to the business strategy and rejects those with little or no linkage. In addition to serving as an investment justification technique the approach can also

| Function | Possible to support differentiation strategy | Possible to support low cost strategy | Low cost actual systems | Rating |
|---|---|---|---|---|
| *Product Design and Development* | R&D databases<br>Electronic mail<br>CAD | Product engineering systems<br>Project control systems<br>CAD | Project control systems | 6 |
| *Operations* | CAM for flexibility<br>Quality assurance systems<br>Quality monitoring systems for suppliers | Process engineering systems<br>Process control systems<br>Labour control systems<br>Inventory management systems<br>CAM | Process control systems<br>CAM | 3<br><br>7 |
| *Marketing* | Market databases<br>IT display and promotion<br>Competition analysis<br>Modelling | Streamlined distribution systems<br>Centralised control systems<br>Economic modelling systems<br>Telemarketing | Telemarketing | 5 |
| *Sales* | Differential pricing<br>Office-field communications<br>Sales support<br>Dealer support<br>Systems to customers | Sales control systems<br>Advertising monitor systems<br>Systems to consolidate sales function<br>Strict incentive monitoring systems | Systems to consolidate sales function | 4 |
| *Administration* | Office automation for integration of functions<br>Environmental scanning and non-quantitative planning systems | Cost control systems<br>Quantitative planning and budgeting systems<br>Office automation for staff reduction | Cost control systems<br>Office automation for staff reduction | 8<br>4 |

**Fig 7.34 ◆ Example of possible strategic match**
(after Remenyi *et al.*)

be used each year to give some indication of the strategic direction the organisation is progressing in. The strength in this type of approach is that it discards all projects that do not serve the organisation's critical success factors and hence keeps all IS effort channelled for the greatest business benefit. The approach obviously has a number of weaknesses:

- The non-quantified nature of the process makes it difficult to decide between two strategy supporting projects.
- With no need to provide numbers in order to justify the project there is little concentration on quantifying any costs or benefits, making project control culturally difficult.
- Unlike information economics that explicitly forces business and IS to work together on project justifications, this approach can divorce the costs from the benefits. The investment approval process considers the gains as defined by business whilst ignoring costs and viability.

Inevitably the act of faith has not always been rewarded and the *real* gain has not always exceeded the *real* cost.

## 7.4 ◆ SOME FINAL POINTS

As we have seen in Section 7.3, most of the IS activity prioritising techniques involve:

1 Identifying the measure of 'success'
2 Defining it in terms of units and scales
3 Doing the actual measuring

Steps (1) and (2) are obviously judgemental and so, to a lesser extent, is (3). Organisations will tend to choose measures in step (1), either on the basis of what seems likely to lead to the easiest implementations of steps (2) and (3), or as those measures that have been pre-judged as being the ones most likely to give the results *desired*.

Despite a widespread recognition of the impact of intangible benefits on the net gain or value obtained from IS, traditional quantitative measures still dominate the IS investment decision making process. There is some use of qualitative measures such as the judging of strategic fit and contribution. There is, as yet, little evidence that organisations are actually using Parker and Benson's Information Economics, Strassmann's Return on Management or IBM's SESAME. (*See* Figure 7.35.)

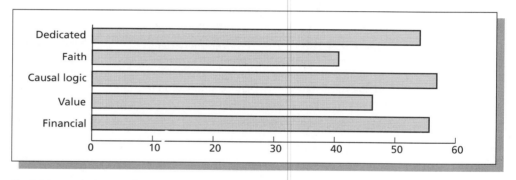

**Fig 7.35 ◆ Relative preferences in investment decision methods**
(adapted with the permission of Butterworth-Heinemann from *Planning IT: Creating an Information Management Strategy* (1991) by D.J. Silk)

It can be hard to uncover accurate evidence of what methods organisations actually use since they tend to over-emphasise the formal aspects of their investment appraisal process in a genuine ignorance of the informal aspects. It is worth noting that the symbolic role that financial cost benefit appraisal takes is part of the formal language with which organisations can *legitimately* describe their actions, even when these actions may happen for less clear-cut reasons. A *Computer Weekly* (1990) survey reported the surprising result that few managers responsible for IS activities wanted more resources absolutely, though 18 per cent wanted to improve the investment selection process. The same survey reported the degree of success at measuring the contribution to business performance as:

Very successful          3 per cent
Fairly successful        40 per cent
Very unsuccessful        16 per cent

and yet Strassmann (1985) claims that IS investments are not just of uncertain benefits but that they are actually the cause of poor productivity. Of the same respondents:

| | |
|---|---|
| Using formal quantitative methods | 56+ per cent |
| Using qualitative methods | 16+ per cent |

Of those reporting that they use formal quantitative methods, 33 per cent used RoI. This preponderance of formal methods may reflect the likelihood that it will be financial groups that make the ultimate resourcing decisions. The degree of dissatisfaction with the results of these decisions may be connected to the ignorance such groups may have of IS and its potential. IS activities draw upon technological innovations that finance groups will be unaware of. *Computer Weekly* reported in a 1996 survey that a third of Finance Directors had never heard of client/server whilst over 98 per cent had never heard of OLAP. The Remenyi *et al.* (1991) survey of impact perceptions was described earlier, it also investigated the techniques organisations used to justify IS projects and reported:

| | |
|---|---|
| We rely on individual departments to justify IS | 18 per cent |
| We use rigorous methods to calculate the benefits | 16 per cent |
| We aim to match investment levels of the industry | 15 per cent |

Clearly practitioners are still using traditional investment appraisal methods despite the amount of criticism that such methods have received for so long. We can see arguments that the accounting bias of traditional cost benefit and return on investment analyses have three problems:

- Traditional CBA and RoI approaches are microeconomics and encourage low risk investments with small returns
- They result from manufacturing economy where labour is treated as an expense
- The analysis is static and short-term

O'Brien (1992) argues that the problem is not really one of finding the 'best' measurement system and points out that the process of making investment decisions does not always require the quantification of all features of all rival projects. He suggests that there are particular motivations for IS projects that make full quantification an unnecessary burden. Under this category he includes:

- *Experimentation project.* Although this is perhaps another name for Information Economics' IS infrastructure, there is no real need to exactly justify projects whose value is the learning experience.
- *Inseparable from business project.* These were mentioned earlier and O'Brien suggests that there is no need to quantify IS separately if a business venture is only possible with the IS element included; rather quantify the business venture.

Even with projects that do not fall into one of these two categories it may not be necessary to quantify all aspects of their value generating potential. The choosing between alternative can be done by assessing the *marginal benefits* of one over another. O'Brien gives three justification techniques that he feels offer a more successful way of dealing with the intractability of IS investment decisions than just generating spurious numbers. These are:

- Use stepped decision logic to quantify only the differences between the candidate options since this narrows down the options for debate.
- Use justification by portfolio since this allows rational decisions to be made on the basis of having the entire portfolio rather than any one specific project.
- Use the inseparability of factors justification that is an extension of the justification by portfolio method. Since IS so often forms a fundamental part of an overall business venture do not separate the justifications.

Most writers on the subject of IS investments imply that it is essentially about a search for the perfect set of techniques in order to make the best *rational* decision. Some however, notably Hirscheim and Smithson writing in Galliers (1987), suggest that all assessment and evaluation is an intrinsically subjective and political activity. If this notion is accepted, then searching for the best and most appropriate *measurement* method is an irrelevancy and seeking to interpret and understand the social forces at work forms the heart of the subject. What leads an organisation to *feel* that certain IS activities are important must be investigated.

There is a difference between justification and evaluation. After justifying selecting and implementing an IS investment decision some sort of follow-up evaluation of the results of that decision would seem necessary. Whether such evaluation be interpretative, qualitative and informal or whether it be formal, rational and analytical it forms an important stage in *learning about* the resource allocation process. Despite the importance of such reflections, as Figure 7.36 illustrates, it is most probable that any given organisation will do nothing to establish whether their IS investment decision has proved to be an effective one. It is to avoid such wasted reflection opportunities to learn that is central to the notion of the 'learning organisation' as discussed in Section 8.6.

At both the justification and, perhaps more importantly, the evaluation stage the different investment objectives require, not only different techniques, but also a different domain emphasis. This means that there will be a different business to technical ratio of judgement involved (*see* Figure 7.37).

Many books and articles on the subject of IS opportunities exhort organisations to exploit the value adding potential of information by making significant investment

|  | In finance sector | In retail sector | In manufacturing sector |
|---|---|---|---|
| *Formal evaluation of results* | Rarely (25% of times) | Very rarely (18% of times) | Possibly (30% of times) |
| *Informal evaluation of results* | Possibly (34% of times) | Probably (40% of times) | Possibly (30% of times) |
| *No evaluation of results* | Probably (41% of times) | Probably (42% of times) | Probably (40% of times) |

Fig 7.36 ◆ Will organisations do a follow-up evaluation of the success of IS resource allocations (and therefore of the decision techniques used)?

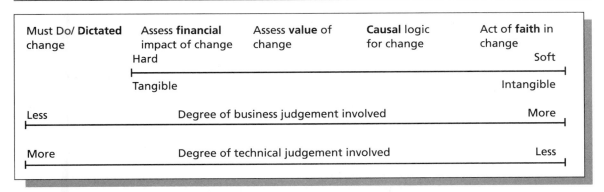

**Fig 7.37 ◆ Ratio of business/technical judgement in justification/evaluation**

in IS. Information Economics' value categories have already been looked at and many other alternative checklists exist, for example value can be listed under the following two headings:

Competitive Impact:

Competitive edge
Maintenance of leadership or share
Entry to new product/market area

Performance Improvements:

Reduction in operating locations/entities
Increased resource use efficiency
Improvements in customer services
Increased staff efficiency

The value listed in the various checklists results from the change that information can make to business processes. Whether the value resulting from the change can be *measured* or not, there has clearly been some alteration to these areas. The organisation assumes there have been some benefits but these are difficult to appraise since neither the costs nor the benefits are certain. Organisations may have to make many IS investments 'blind' or make them later when they have become the standard operating procedures within the industry with all of the costs and few of the gains (although the technology strategy of the early follower is perhaps one of the most successful). Cost effectiveness versus strategic contribution are, usually though not invariably, the opposing tensions when dealing with strategy implementation issues. Some of the resource decisions considered in Chapter 12, for instance downsizing and outsourcing projects, may all be justified and hence selected to save costs, but they can also result in leaner companies that can respond faster to competitive change so they have also a strategic role. The *same* IS initiative is both cost effective and strategically strong.

**References and further reading**

Alpar, P. and Kim, M. (1990) A Comparison of Approaches to the Measurement of IT Value, *Proceedings of the 23rd Annual Hawaii International Conference on System Sciences*, IEEE Computer Society Press.

Angell, I.O. and Smithson, S. (1991) *Information Systems Management: Opportunities and Risks*, Macmillan.

Bicknell, D. (1996) City IT Costs Out of Control, Says Survey, *Computer Weekly*, 4 Jan p. 3.

Cashmore, C. and Lyall, R. (1991) *Business Information: Systems and Strategies*, Prentice-Hall.

Chapman, P. (1991) Information Technology is Good for You – Isn't it?, *Management Decision*, Vol 29 No 2 pp. 15–17.

Clemons, E.K. and Weber, B.W. (1990) Making the Information Technology Investment Decision: A Principled Approach, *Proceedings of the 23rd Annual Hawaii International Conference on System Sciences*, IEEE Computer Society Press.

Computer Weekly (1994) Dataview: IT Budgets Growth to Slow Down, *Computer Weekly*, 16 Feb p. 1.

Computer Weekly (1996) Dataview, *Computer Weekly*. 18 Apr p. 1.

Cunningham, J. A. (1985) Information Technology Stirs GE Marketing Renaissance, *Information Systems*, Dec pp. 32–7.

Doyle, E. (1996) Counting the Cost, *PC Week*, 28 May pp. 8–9.

Ernest-Jones, T. (1989) Tracing the Intangible Fruits of Technology, *Computer Weekly*, 23 Feb p. 28.

Farbey, B. Land, F. and Targett, D. (1993) *How to Assess Your IT Investment: A Study of Methods and Practice*, Butterworth-Heinemann.

Fawcett, N. (1994) PC Monitoring, *Computer Weekly*, 10 Nov p. 49.

Feldman, M. and Marsh, J. (1981) Information in Organisations as Signal and Symbol, *Administrative Science Quarterly*, Vol 26 pp. 171–86.

Galliers, R. (Ed.) (1987) *Information Analysis: Selected Readings*, Addison-Wesley.

Gambling, T. and Karim, R. (1991) *Business and Accounting Ethics in Islam*, Mansell.

Green-Armytage, J. (Ed.) (1994) IT Budgets Set to Rise, *Computer Weekly*, 3 Mar p. 16.

Green-Armytage, J. (1994) The Business Value of IT, *Computer Weekly*, 21 July p. 16.

Henry, B. (1990) Measuring IS for Business Value, *Datamation*, 1 Apr pp. 89–91.

Hochstrasser, B. (1992) A Framework for Evaluating and Prioritising IT Investments in *Proceedings of Evaluating and Managing the IT Investment*, London, Unicorn.

Hochstrasser, B. and Griffiths, C. (1990) *Regaining Control of IT Investments: A Handbook for Senior UK Management*, Kobler Unit.

Hugo, I. (1992) Keeping Count, *Computing*, 21 May pp. 20–1.

Keen, P.G.W. (1991) *Shaping the Future: Business Design Through Information Technology*, Harvard Business School Press.

Kelly, S. (Ed.) (1996) IT Spending in UK Companies, *Computer Weekly*, 23 May p. 18.

Lederer, A.L., Mirani, R., Neo, B.S., Pollard, C., Prasad, J. and Ramamurthy, K. (1990) Information System Cost Estimating: A Management Perspective, *MIS Quarterly*, June pp. 159–76.

Mangoletsi, P. (1994) A Game of Hide and Seek, *PC Week*, 1 Feb pp. 8–9.

Mansell-Lewis, E. (1994) Totting up your Assets, *Computer Weekly*, 12 May pp. 50–1.

Miles, R. (1992) A Successful Switch, *Computing*, 9 July p. 31.

Moad, J. (1995) Time for a Fresh Approach to RoI, *Datamation*, 15 Feb pp. 57–9.

Mukhopadhyay, T., Kekre, S. and Kalathur, S. (1995) Business Value of Information Technology: A Study of Electronic Data Interchange, *MIS Quarterly*, June pp. 137–56.

Nolan, R.L. (1979) Managing the Crisis in Data Processing, *Harvard Business Review*, Mar-Apr pp. 115–26.

O'Brien (1992) *Demands and Decisions: Briefing on Issues in Information Technology Strategy*, Prentice Hall.

Parker, M.M., and Benson, R.J. (1988) *Information Economics: Linking Business Performance to Information Technology*, Prentice-Hall.

Parker, M.M. Trainor, H.E. and Benson, R.J. (1989) *Information Strategy and Economics*, Prentice-Hall.

Remenyi, D., Money, A. and Twite, A. (1991) *A Guide to Measuring and Managing IT Benefits*, NCC Blackwell.

Reynolds, G.W. (1992) *Information Systems for Managers* (2nd edn), West Publishing.

Riley, J. (1994) Growth in User Spend to Double, *Computer Weekly*, 6 Jan p. 1.

Salamone, S. (1995) Assets on the Line, *Byte*, Sept pp. 37–40.

Silk, D.J. (1991) *Planning IT: Creating an Information Management Strategy*, Butterworth-Heinemann.

Smith, S. (1996) It'll Cost You, *Computer Weekly*, 18 Jan pp. 28–9.

Strassmann, P.A. (1976) Managing the Costs of Information, *Harvard Business Review*, Sept-Oct pp. 133–42.

Strassmann, P.A. (1985) *Information Payoff: The Transformation of Work in the Electronic Age*, Macmillan.

Strassmann, P.A. (1990) *The Business Value Of Computers*, The Information Economics Press.

Sullivan-Trainor, M.L. (1989) The Push for Proof of Information Systems Payoff, *Computerworld*, 3 Apr pp. 55–61.

Tapscott, D. and Caston, A. (1993) *Paradigm Shift: The New Promise of Information Technology*, McGraw-Hill.

Turnball, P.D. (1991) Effective Investment in Information Infrastructures, *Information and Software Technology*, Vol 33 No 3 pp. 191–99.

Upton, P. (1990) Proving the Value of Strategy, *Software Management Magazine*, Apr.

Vowler, J. (1994) A Yardstick for Progress, *Computer Weekly*, 3 Nov p. 30.

Weill, P. (1990) Strategic Investment in Information Technology: An Empirical Study, *Information Age*, Vol 12 No 3 pp. 141–7.

Weill, P. and Olson, M.H. (1989) Managing Investment in Information Technology: Mini Case Examples and Implications, *MIS Quarterly*, Mar pp. 2–17.

Wiseman, D. (1992) Information Economics: The Practical Approach to Evaluating IT Investments, *Proceedings of Evaluating and Managing the IT Investment*, Unicom Seminar.

Zmud, R.W, Boyton, A.C. and Jacobs, G.C. (1986) The Information Economy: A New Perspective for Effective Information Systems Management, *Data Base*, Fall pp. 17–23.

# CHAPTER 8

# IS, business competition and organisation

The earlier chapters in this section have explored approaches and techniques associated with the formulation of an IS strategy. These have focused on the core notion of using IS activities to create and reflect business value. Overarching those specific issues are two interdependent sets of broader concerns. The first is to assess just what the *effect* of all those IS strategies has been on the nature of competition and the nature of organisations. The second is to consider the implications for IS of new organisational thinks. It should be stressed that these two areas are inextricably bound together. This chapter however takes each of these two faces sequentially for clarity. It first explores the notion that IS can be consciously used to generate 'competitive advantage' and then identifies just what has resulted from the collection of directed and undirected IS strategies. The chapter then proceeds to consider another face of contemporary organisational change by discussing the notions of radical process improvements (eg business process re-engineering) and organisational learning, these notions being considered particularly in terms of their implications for IS strategy issues of priorities, roles, structure, etc.

## 8.1 ◆ COMPETITIVE ADVANTAGE FROM IS STRATEGIES?

A number of well known examples of competitive gain from the use of management information systems exist, some were given in section 5.3. Does the adoption of the techniques and methods discussed in that section guarantee an organisation competitive advantage? Many writers argue for the possibility of an organisation consciously and deliberately exploiting MIS for competitive advantage. In summary, this view is that, given the presence of key factors, then the organisation will develop plans that are a strategic success and therefore, by definition, give competitive advantage. These key factors are:

- The application of available techniques to spot strategically significant IS

- A knowledge of the effects of the information revolution on the business environment

- An understanding of the process of IS strategic planning to generate, concrete, implementable, plans for SMIS

These three requirements are discussed along with the findings of a number of surveys into the nature and degree of perceived success.

There are contradictory views on whether the perceived 'success' in fact equates to 'competitive advantage'. Certainly the success achieved does seem to provide the benefits discussed in Chapter 6, which are, in summary:

- IS relates to the business goals
- There is an agreed set of priorities
- The management of systems is appropriate to their business value
- There is an improved business/IS communication

However, whilst desirable, these success factors are inward looking and have little to do with an organisation's competitive position. This view suggests that what is achieved is a competitive *environment* that supports innovation by following a competitive approach. This competitive *approach* does give real gains, including the possibility of serendipitous applications.

This chapter considers the characteristics of this competitive approach environment, and also of the technologies currently likely to be associated with this environment. Even Rackoff *et al.* (1985), who actually target competitive advantage, note that the use of IS may not always lead to industry domination. They acknowledge that the famous examples were found in an *ad hoc* way, but suggest that organisations now have the 'best way' to select the most *promising* prospects to yield competitive advantage. Despite this 'best way' they do not promise that competitive advantage will be certain. This chapter identifies and discusses the factors common to the businesses and applications that do seem to have generated a competitive gain.

We have looked in the preceding chapters at a series of tools, models and techniques and at some of the ways they can be collected together into an overall planning *approach* but hesitated to call it a methodology for IS strategy planning. The tools have addressed organisational, structural and technical facets of both business and IS. The previous chapters also showed that there is some, though as yet not clearly defined, value in doing this planning; that organisations can expect a greater chance of 'success' if they plan than if they do not. The chapters of this section have considered a directed approach to the development of IS strategies – an IS strategy which is developed during the strategic IS planning process and is defined and documented as the IS strategy plan.

Throughout all of this, the implicit assumption has been that an organisation *can* identify an approach or direction for the use and management of IS, the IS strategy, and articulate it via their IS strategic plan, and if the process is 'good', that is if the plan that defines the strategy is consistent with business goals, and consistent with current maturity of experience, resource constraints and the technological availability then ... WHAT?

Judging by the slant of the IS strategy literature it would seem that, since doing all of that is very difficult, then what the organisation gets, as a 'reward', is competitive advantage. Can this be true? The purpose of this chapter is to test this *implicit* assumption that understanding the key inputs and outputs of IS strategy planning and so getting an *appropriate*, that is business aligned, capability consistent plan equals competitive *advantage*. The previous chapters have concentrated upon *why* and *how* to do the IS strategy formulation, Sections 8.2 to 8.4 of this chapter seeks to

Fig 8.1 ◆ Strategy planning key inputs and key outputs

step back and consider more fully what the results of IS strategies *are*. The focus until now has been on getting IS strategy development done right, being planning efficient and avoiding 'inappropriate' IS strategies:

> *The way to get into a planning bind is to go at everything piecemeal. First the organisation chart – that's done... Then the plan – that's done... Then the budget - that's done... The IS plan – that's done... All that hard work and nothing fits.*

Now this chapter needs to test what IS strategy *effectiveness* might mean.

Figure 8.1 models what the previous four chapters have covered. The top half shows the key inputs and the bottom half the key outputs, the IS strategy is then the collection of outputs.

We may give different names to some of the boxes but the logical purpose is as shown. Note that the strategy planning techniques and tools are *both* an input and an output since new approaches come about *because* of the application of the process and are then, in turn, *used* by that process. Behind this model is the assumption that a 'good' strategy acknowledges all inputs in *producing* the outputs. The process may do this in any number of ways that use a different sequence, or weight the relative importance of each of the boxes differently (see Chapter 6), and so this diagram represents the chapters covered to date.

## 8.2 ◆ THE CLASSIC ARGUMENT FOR COMPETITIVE ADVANTAGE

The culture of any organisation includes the 'tales told' and the fact that so many stories *are* told of IS giving competitive advantage indicates that the culture of many organisations believe in this. The tales could have been presented in another way. There are many such stories, a sample is given in Figure 8.2. Many of these examples are now fairly elderly and it may be that the newer 'tales told' focus, not upon competitive advantage, but upon the radical process improvements of business re-engineering (*see* Section 8.5).

The anecdotes of cases such as American Hospital Supply, McKesson, Merrill Lynch, Thomsons Holidays, American Airlines, ICI, Otis and others are told as attention grabbers and then analysed and hence categorised in different ways in order to define the actual *effects* of the information revolution. One example set of categories is that suggested by Ward and Griffiths (1996), that the instances of IS for competitive advantage are where IS is:

1 Linking the organisation to customers or suppliers
2 Creating effective integration of the use of information in a value-adding process; value-chain primary activities
3 Enabling the organisation to develop, produce, market and deliver new products or services based upon information
4 Giving senior management information to help develop and implement strategy

| | |
|---|---|
| **American Airlines** | American Airlines' SABRE reservation system is probably the most commonly quoted instance of an organisation gaining a competitive advantage from their use of IS. This system was the first effective electronic reservation system in the US (the outcome of a vision of one data set per customer). The sophistication of this on-line reservation system was a major breakthrough, and came about as a response to the *potential* threat of travel agents developing their own booking system. United Airlines also developed a similar system (Apollo) that also offers travel agents some office automation support. These systems built upon the already extensive internal computerisation that airlines have always engaged in. The competitive value of SABRE is still being felt thirty years after its introduction. SABRE gave AA a market lead that they have never lost and by 1988 American Airlines were making more money from SABRE than they were from flying aeroplanes. In 1990 their vice-president said that they gained a competitive edge from the creative use of information that the systems handle rather than the systems themselves (although the systems sold on to smaller operators do generate useful revenue). |
| **Dow Jones** | The innovative use of satellite transmissions in the production and distribution of a newspaper (the Wall Street Journal) reduced both production costs, but more importantly, production *time*. This IS application also permits European and Asian versions to be created, significantly widening the Wall Street Journal's competitive scope. To achieve this level of IS dependency, the data that Dow Jones handles is *all* stored electronically and hence entirely new data provision services have been launched. Internal cost savings was, as is often the case in these classics, the driving motive at the start but strategic gains have been made. |
| **General Tire** | General Tire created a telemarketing system that was initially conceived to provide sales support in order to free sales specialists from dealing with problems such as bill or delivery queries but then extended to include the management of marginally profitable accounts. This significantly lowered the cost of making a sale (the system's objective) but also unexpectedly increased sales. But note that General Tire did it all to avoid unprofitable accounts and didn't expect it to increase sales. |

**Fig 8.2 ◆ The 'classic tales' of strategic advantage**

| | |
|---|---|
| **American Hospital Supply Corporation (AHSC)** | The instance of AHSC's Analytical Systems Automotive Purchasing (ASAP) system is almost as frequently quoted as SABRE. ASAP helped customers of AHSC automate the ordering part of their stock control by placing order entry terminals in their hospitals. This elimination of effort for the customer was, inevitably, popular and that popularity and the downgrading of the skill content of order placing jobs significantly increased AHSC's customer's switching costs. The system was initially developed in the 1960s as an *internal* system to deal with AHSC's order fulfilment problems with one of its most significant customers, Stanford Medical Centre. This system started when a manager gave *one* customer the hardware that allowed him to place last minute orders directly onto AHSC's computer system. The system grew to link most customers; these customers do the order entry to the cost advantage of AHSC but the customers gain greater control over their stock holdings to their advantage. Since AHSC's customers can now exploit the increased flexibility of order placing to *their* advantage they are enjoying significant value adding along with AHSC. Unlike Merrill Lynch's CMA system (*see* below), this system has been continually enhanced in order to maintain its business significance. |
| **Merrill Lynch** | In the mid-1970s Merrill Lynch felt they had to diversify their operation because of the declining attractiveness of stocks investments (it was a time of rising interest rates). The strategic option that was generated, evaluated and then selected in 1977 was that of a single integrated cash management system for customers tired of the confusion and inefficiency of different accounts in different places to get credit, make cash withdrawals, or invest in money markets. This Cash Management Account (CMA) which combined normally separate banking services into a single statement, and automatically moved spare funds to a high interest account, was technologically complex, but it was made possible because of the spare processing capacity within Merrill Lynch, plus an electronic link with Basic One for the legally required involvement of a bank for the credit card and cheque services. This innovative integration of services that ignored the traditional view of banking being discrete from securities allowed Merrill Lynch to obtain $1 billion of assets in the first year alone and gave Merrill Lynch over 90 per cent of the market for a full five years. However, whilst CMA still provides them with more than half of the market they failed to press the advantage via systems enhancements and updates and so the advantage slipped away from them. It is worth noting that Basic One, the collaborators in the CMA venture, were also involved in a wider range of strategic initiatives including providing credit card processing for other banks. |
| **Digital Equipment Corporation (DEC)** | The expert system (XCON) that DEC uses to support the process of designing and specifying systems is one of the classics of competitive advantage *and* of the use of expert systems. XCON reliably uses the best practice of DEC engineers in the system design stage and so gains increased customer satisfaction and lowers costs by reducing the potential for inappropriate systems. |
| **McGraw-Hill** | McGraw-Hill have been redefining the nature of their business for a number of years, moving from purely publishing into being an *information business*. During the 1980s, McGraw-Hill moved into on-line data and strove to computerise all operations in order to provide 'an electronic bookshelf'. Data about publications, about ordering and credit card sales themselves can all be had via public access to an American Bulletin Board. |

**Fig 8.2 ◆ Continued**

| | |
|---|---|
| **Federal Express** | Federal Express' start-up in 1973 as an overnight delivery service was closely related to IS capabilities. There was a large investment in technology and automation to control the business and reduce operating costs. The planned heavy reliance upon IS at inception makes Federal Express unique among the competitive advantage 'classics'. The low cost and high efficiency of the business is supported by systems such as the 'cradle to grave' tracking of packages. The IS dependency envisioned by Federal Express' founders has been well managed, with the world wide market share capture of Federal Express standing testimony to this. |
| **McKesson Corporation** | This healthcare distributor developed a system, Economost, that helps retail customers (American drugstores and pharmacists) calculate *what* to order, *when* to do so and *how* to do so automatically. The system will also tag the ordered products with their shelf destination and price. This system was created at least as much to reduce McKesson's costs as to lock in customers. The hand-held order-entry based system not only eases order placing but it also generates management information for the customer with its analyses of sales trends, profit margins and departmental performance, etc. So McKesson gains a reduction in manpower needs in order-entry and sales processes, an improvement in storage efficiency and a significant, six-fold, increase in sales. McKesson's customers have gained management information they could not have afforded to generate for themselves, reduced staff costs associated with all aspects of placing and receiving orders, created better discount potential and lower stock holding costs. This classic system for competitive advantage only exists because a discredited pilot project of the early 1970s was resurrected on the advice of consultants hired to assess the continuing viability of the tightly squeezed healthcare industry. |
| **Kraft Foodservice** | Kraft developed Kraftlink to provide restaurants with a complete IS/IT system. This 'hardware plus restaurant management software' system is also linked to Kraft's order-entry system. Kraft make acceptance of the service painless by installing and maintaining the system and training staff. The restaurant gains much closer control over stock costs, wastage, portion control, the ability to provide customers with a more reliable service and effective costing and pricing and management information. Kraft, obviously, gain a committed customer and lower costs associated with sales and order processing. |
| **Thomsons Holidays** | Thomsons Holidays' TOPS on-line viewdata-based booking system is the most famous UK story of IS leading to competitive advantage. The travel agents' use of this system generated a major market share for Thomsons through technology supremacy, but, at the same time, this supremacy backed them – and the whole industry – into a technology *cul de sac*. |

**Fig 8.2 ◆ Continued**

Another form of categorising is to distinguish, as Rayport and Sviokla (1995) do, between effects felt in the market *place* (a physical world) and those felt in the market *space* (a virtual world created by IS). Some examples of IS impacts have altered the nature of the physical world, such examples include bank ATM's. Other examples are of IS creating and exploiting the virtual market space and would include instances such as electronic banking and all newly created information handling industries.

These examples, whether we categorise them or not, certainly do seem to demonstrate that driven by dramatic improvements in the cost/performance ratio of technology (both the hardware and the software) and fuelled by innovative *applications* there has been a revolution caused by the use of information technologies. This revolution has permanently changed:

- *Supplier to customer relationships*: where IS can fundamentally influence competitive relationships and support the existence of partnership without ownership.
- *Distribution channels*: for example the distribution of cash is very different post ATMs, and EDI changes the 'rules' of retail distribution.
- *Production economies and product life cycles*: in, for example, publishing where it has been most noticeable, large papers get economies of scale and the new ability to include colour, whilst small circulation publication is now feasible since it can be faster and accurately targeted; for books, whole levels of the production cycle have gone. Similarly, CAD/CAM/CIM and robotics fundamentally alter the nature of more physical production industries.
- *Value-added services*: for example information wholesaling and home and business information services and brokerages related to the acquiring, storing and enhancing by re-packaging of information.

These changes have restructured whole industries and enormous changes are observable, particularly in the traditionally information-based industries such as banking and finance, publishing, estate agencies, retailing, etc. Perhaps even more radically, totally new industries have been *created*. None of this is particularly new however; *Business Week* (1985) very much captured it all with their cosy pictures of pushchair terminals, terminals in castles, terminals in rucksacks and so on to illustrate how technology was giving companies a competitive edge from new business, locking in customers, and mobility of sales respectively.

The information revolution and the tales of competitive advantage have certainly altered how managers throughout business see the role of IS. Where it was once perceived to be only part of the *operating* of a business, there is now an increasing recognition of the value of *information*. Furthermore, it is recognised that information is a depreciating asset and must be treated as an economic entity. Management recognises the contribution that information makes as a resource that the organisation could/should use in its business. This change in management perception equates to the critical transition represented by the move from Nolan's early stages 1–3 to the later stages 4–6 (*see* Chapter 5). During this critical transition IS moves from its supportive role to an integral role.

Certainly the transformation wrought by the information revolution does mean that all organisations realise that IS influences *both* sides of the general business equation, since it recognisably adds to both the revenue and the cost streams; revenue – earner: cost – spender. And from the anecdotes it would seem that some early adopters have harnessed the whirlwind to some advantage.

Porter and Millar's (1985) work was seminal in *creating* the perception that the information revolution means that IS can be used for competitive advantage. This article suggests that the effects of that revolution defined the strategic significance of IS and equated this, not only to the *potential* for gaining competitive advantage, but to the potential for *deliberately* gaining competitive advantage by following their five-step process (yet another strategic planning approach!):

1 Assess the information intensity
2 Determine the role of IS in the industry structure
3 Identify and rank the ways in which IS might create competitive advantage
4 Investigate how IS might spawn new businesses
5 Develop a plan for taking advantage of IS

It is noticeable that the paper does not debate whether the inevitable impact is *harnessable*.

Clearly, to gain a competitive *advantage*, if that is to be possible, an organisation must be able to define when IS is *strategic* to their business, that is they must be able to make distinctions between technology *hype*, technology *capability*, *useful* technology, and *strategic* technology as explored by Feeny (1989). These distinctions are represented in Figure 8.3a.

- *Technology hype*: This is the layer that is *dangerous* since unfounded belief and over-selling leads to management suspicions and disillusionment with IS. This is the area of the salesman's pitch, the area for which the term 'vapourware' was coined.
- *Technology capability*: This is the smaller sub-set that represents what current technologies can actually do today, or better still, could do yesterday so that the organisation can see them demonstrated!
- *Useful technology*: This is the layer that, out of that larger set of actual capabilities, can be called the fairly small set that any given organisation would find useful.
- *Strategic technology*: This is the hub that any organisation is seeking. The subset of IS that, if not adopted, would lead to business performance suffering.

To judge whether the organisation is looking at an instance of IS in that charmed inner circle they must be able to answer positively to the following three key points:

1 Functioning of the IS activity is critical to operations on a daily basis
2 Applications planned or under development are critical to future competitiveness
3 Information content/intensity of products and functional area is high

If they answer yes to each of these three then they know that what they are looking at *is* part of the set of strategic IS shown as the inner circle of Figure 8.3a. The strategic analysis toolkit of Chapter 5 offers some techniques to assist in considering

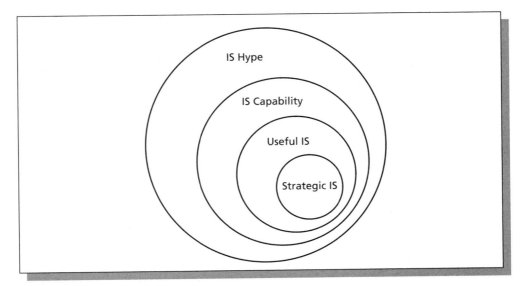

**Fig 8.3a ◆ Technology onion diagram**
(adapted from Feeny)

| Industry Impacts on: | Competitive Impacts on: |
|---|---|
| Nature of products and services | Product development cycle |
| Product life cycle | Product quality enhancement |
| Geographical scope | Sales force and selling support |
| Economies of scale in production | Order cycle automation |
| Shift in value-added locus | Office cost reduction |
| Bargaining power of suppliers | Channel and inventory management |
| New business creation | Reduction of management levels |
| | Product features enhancement and threat of substitution |

Fig 8.3b ◆ Industry and competitive impacts of IS

these points, for instance the organisation could use industry and competitive impact analyses shown in Figure 8.3b, or the information intensity matrix as discussed in Section 5.5.3.

Peter Begley, IT Planning Manager at the National and Provincial Building Society, set out some characteristics of the technologies that will be in that inner circle:

- They are *incremental* extensions of in-house work and use existing well proven technologies but build upon them in new ways.

- They have been identified and pursued irrespective of the IS services delivery section since the IS function is not the best source of innovative uses, having a technical advisor role, and the innovation will come from the business 'sharp end'.

- They are difficult to define in a traditional systems sense but are simply about supporting the way to compete. In other words, they are not about processing transactions, that is easy to define, but about communicating to the manager in a way that is the business.

- They tend to be focused on retaining customers or gaining new ones from the innovative *application* rather than the innovative *technology*. For most organisations, business benefits are gained through the customer interface *not* internal operations. The benefits are usually risk prone, opportunistic and of potentially high value though mainly expressed as intangibles.

- In general, the technologies are *futuristic* in the sense that they face forward and outwards rather than inward and backwards. So they will focus on presenting simulations and forecasts rather than reports.

Part 3 of this book will discuss the decisions that implement these strategic technologies that form part of strategic IS.

Moriarty and Swartz (1989) provide a more concrete and quantitative perception of competitive advantage than provided by many writers. They illustrate, with reference to the Sales and Marketing function, how automation – which is the application of IS – *can* generate a competitive advantage. They suggest that the use of certain technology can collectively aid productivity, such as:

- Salesperson productivity tools
- Direct mail systems
- Telemarketing
- Sales and marketing management systems

They define this *increase* in productivity as a financial advantage and hence it is, in their eyes, a competitive advantage. This gain is illustrated in Figure 8.4.

Certainly, the shaded area on the diagram represents a financial gain. However, this may simply be an efficiency gain. It can only be defined as a competitive advantage if it is sustainable and others don't have it! Moriarty and Swartz suggest that the smaller organisation will have greater flexibility and hence be more likely to be able to use IS to gain a competitive advantage; this view is by no means backed up by the weight of empirical evidence. Most of the 'classic tales' are of large organisations, already major players in the markets and often exploiting that position as much as the use of IS. It may be that only such large-scale examples are

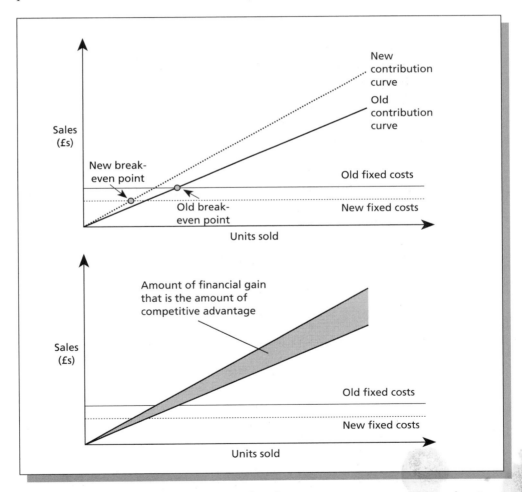

**Fig 8.4 ◆ Marketing and sales productivity (MSP) systems creates a competitive advantage**

reported. Certainly the alterations that IS makes to supplier-customer relations *can* enable the smaller organisation to compete economically with the larger ones, as discussed in a retail context by Reid (1995).

It would seem from examples of beneficial IS exploitation given so far that a key theme is that IS allows relationships *between* organisations; IS links them in ways never before possible. More detailed discussion of these links and their effects can be seen in much recent literature, see for example Brown and Pattison (1995), Nidumolu (1995) and Reid (1995). IS also impacts on internal relationships, a fact that is explored from different perspectives in many places in this text: in Sections 8.5 and 8.6 as a discussion of contemporary organisational thinking, in Chapter 10 as the diffusion of IS responsibility to IS non-professionals, in Chapter 12 as IS enabled human resource provision and Chapter 13 as the management of the dangers and risks of IS interactions.

Here however the discussion mirrors literature that focuses on the competitive impacts that IS-enabled organisational connections bring. The volume of public interest in inter-connectivity is at its highest with respect to the 1990s discovery of the 1960s phenomena, the Internet. In fact most of this interest lies with the *possibilities*, rather than realities as yet, that it seems to open in two areas, on-line commerce and speedy internal and global communications. Both of these opportunities relate to its continual development and provision of a set of low-cost and readily available tools that embody global standards. The Internet, despite the fears of anarchy, corruption and compromised security that it generates, may prove to be cheaper and more 'people friendly' than proprietary methods of internal and external communications. It is 'open' in every sense of that word. *See* Chapter 12 for a fuller discussion of inter and intra-nets.

## 8.3 ◆ PROBLEMS WITH THE CLASSIC ARGUMENTS OF IS FOR COMPETITIVE ADVANTAGE

Ward and Griffiths (1996) remind us that many examples of *competitive* advantage are actually an advantage from *information* itself and not necessarily anything to do with IS. Whilst it is difficult to quibble with the evidence of the major *impact* of the information revolution, does that impact equate to competitive advantage? Can it be voluntarily sought? In presenting a more critical case, we wish to weigh up and judge the notion of IS leading to competitive advantage; and so to judge whether the use of IS *does* lead to competitive advantage we need to consider four points:

- What does analysis of the evidence indicate?
- Can it be an advantage if it hurts?
- Are there guarantees of success?
- What are the characteristics of such success?

## 8.3.1 ◆ Analysis of the 'tales' – management not technology

The 'stories told' tend to be presented from a technological perspective, focusing upon what the systems did, and how they work, but these events did not happen in a vacuum and using something such as Porter's five-forces may more effectively show the net result of the vectors affecting the organisations concerned. Looking at any of the 'classic cases' just in relation to the technology sells them short. These cases must also be seen in the context of the market place in which the organisations operate: competitive gambles depend for their success as much on the strength of the players as upon the state of the hand. A major problem is that the technology is the *visible* aspect of the success stories (and of the stories of failures covered in Section 8.3.2). Beneath the surface are complex management, organisational and marketing factors. The reaction of other organisations to these stories may be akin to those of the crisis belief systems which emerge to respond to major culture shocks. A particularly apt example is that of the Melanesian Cargo Cults in the early 1900s in New Guinea where the natives perceived the newly arrived Europeans as essentially lazy and yet overloaded with desirable goods; the reaction was to decide that these goods must come from supernatural sources, namely the ancestors. These natives aped the *outward* appearance of processes, such as using theodolites, telegraphs, etc without any understanding of the *actual* process. There is a similar danger here for organisations *aping* IS success – the fundamental management *processes* must be understood, not just the outward technological appearances.

So the real meat to these 'tales told' is to be found in the decision making processes and strategy which led from the identification of opportunities to their realisation and when an organisation does not know the process that led to these often quoted successes it is hard to judge the *value* of the examples. However, anecdotes about such opportunities form the folklore of successful IS strategic planning. They may be folklore but they are not totally mythical and from this folklore general categories can be derived. The intention behind using these examples is generally two-fold. First to confirm the importance of IS to business and second to suggest that knowing the past impact of IS acts as a reminder to look for it again.

Neo's (1988) research paper, and his subsequent doctoral work, has done much to detail and cross-reference the quoted cases of competitive advantage. Although he contents himself with talking about *strategic* IS, that is whether the cases have found their way to the inner circle of strategically important IS, he is seeking common factors that facilitated the *process* of identifying that inner circle. His findings are summarised in Figure 8.5.

His findings indicate that the most important factor driving the use of IS is internal efficiency needs. The same systems needed for day-to-day *operating* of the company, like airlines or information service industries, are later adapted for *strategic* purposes. What appears to happen is that internal systems are improved and the opportunities for using enhancements to achieve business plans are spotted, often when new external opportunities or threats emerge. Precipitating, catalyst, events seem to have to occur. So the gains happen when management realise they *need* it, and seems to have

| | | | | | Facilitating factors | | | | | |
|---|---|---|---|---|---|---|---|---|---|---|
| | 1 | 2 | 3 | 4 | 5 | 6 | 7 | 8 | 9 | 10 |
| *Airlines* | | | | | | | | | | |
| American Airlines | | | | | ✳ | ✳ | ✳ | ✳ | | |
| United Airlines | | | | | ✳ | ✳ | ✳ | ✳ | | |
| *Distributors* | | | | | | | | | | |
| American Hospital Supply | | | | | ✳ | ✳ | | | | |
| McKesson | | | | | ✳ | ✳ | | | ✳ | ✳ |
| *Financial Services* | | | | | | | | | | |
| Banc One | | | ✳ | | | | ✳ | ✳ | ✳ | |
| Citicorp | | | ✳ | | ✳ | ✳ | | | ✳ | |
| Merrill Lynch | | | | ✳ | | | | ✳ | ✳ | ✳ |
| USAA | ✳ | | ✳ | | ✳ | | ✳ | | ✳ | |
| *Information Services* | | | | | | | | | | |
| Dow Jones | | | | | ✳ | | ✳ | ✳ | | |
| Dun and Bradstreet | | | | | ✳ | | ✳ | ✳ | | |
| Gannett | ✳ | | ✳ | | ✳ | | | | ✳ | |
| McGraw-Hill | | | | | | | | | ✳ | ✳ |
| *Others* | | | | | | | | | | |
| Digital Equipment | | | | | ✳ | ✳ | | | | |
| Federal Express | ✳ | | ✳ | ✳ | ✳ | ✳ | | | ✳ | |

| | | | |
|---|---|---|---|
| 1 | Alignment with business planning | 6 | Customer needs |
| 2 | Improved communication between IS and management | 7 | Strength in IT |
| 3 | Consideration of IS's role | 8 | Extensive computer facilities |
| 4 | Competitive pressure | 9 | Management vision and support |
| 5 | Internal needs | 10 | Consultants |

**Fig 8.5 ◆ Factors facilitating the strategic use of IS**
(after Neo)

little to do with IS but plenty to do with management having to look at all the available business tools. This suggests that incremental development is always best and internal systems can be a goldmine for strategic applications and not always needing to be new systems, as much of the literature implies.

Probably the early users of SMIS were motivated by internal pressures but then they generate the competitive pressures on the rest of the industry that others are then driven by. It certainly seems that none of the ideas came from the IS function, and only start-up organisations such as Federal Express explicitly considered the strategic role of IS in *advance*. Outside consultants seem to be generally used to generate the new ideas and are often called in response to customer complaints beginning to hurt the bottom line.

American Airlines and United Airlines were a case of 'first screen advantage' since 90 per cent of flight bookings are made from the first screen and this gave them the 'first mover' advantage since, even if competitors spent the necessary millions that reservation systems require, they cannot 'catch up' with AA and UA's ability to analyse industry behaviour and put in flights and cost deals to undermine competitor actions. McKesson's system of retail reordering terminal devices gives an advantage to McKesson by reducing their costs and making a much higher barrier to new entrants since any drug distribution organisation has to have such a system.

However, in the telling, most of these tales lose all uncertainties! Schemes to change relationships between customers and suppliers do not happen in a vacuum. Olympic Holidays was the first UK company to introduce a viewdata reservation system – they *failed* and that tells us as much about competitive advantage as Thomsons' much vaunted success story does. An organisation must get their underlying technology right but their strength in the market place, the inducements they can offer to change methods of working and industry politics, are more significant issues. Critical mass worked very much in favour of Thomsons as the market leader; Olympic's lighter weight worked against them. Another issue in Thomsons' success was their insistence upon following through the potential for further benefits. Internal re-organisation, including the centralisation of all booking activities, enabled costs to be reduced while the volume of business was increased, thereby reinforcing the competitiveness of the company. This is just what the notion of BPR (*see* Section 8.5) concerns itself with, making the re-organisation *necessary* to exploit technology opportunities.

Other success stories are proving slow to emerge to add to the original 'classics' and putting a terminal on every customer's desk is not a sure-fire winner! Perhaps cultural concern, and hence 'tales told', has shifted from competitive advantage to radical process improvements (*see* Section 8.5). Such a shift of concern matches the shift in economic climate from the expansive and entrepreneurial 1980s to the harsher realities of the demanding 1990s.

### 8.3.2 ◆ An advantage that can hurt

The IS literature does include failed IS projects, but there are far fewer quoted examples of failure of the strategy of deliberately seeking competitive advantage by using IS. One known example is when Wells Fargo lost so much that they were forced to sell off a major division and lost $14 million. The Bank of America, written up by Lansman (1984) as having total success with their IS strategy, were shown by Business Computing and Communications (1988) to have spent $80 million on the failing Masternet accounting system and had 29 of their most lucrative trust fund customers move to a competitor.

American medical insurance giant Blue Cross and Blue Shield found some of the strategic dangers of IS strategies. In the mid-1980s the organisation was pursuing an ambitious IS strategy. This strategy was defined largely by the IS function itself and was both inconsistent with the capabilities of the organisation at that time and had little real senior management commitment to it since it was not in tune with the business goals. Attempts to implement the strategy were disastrous, with projects poorly estimated for time and complexity. However, the disaster recovery process acted as a positive catalyst for far-reaching and ultimately beneficial business analysis and re-engineering. It is possible that Blue Cross and Blue Shield are now more competitively fit as a result of a misjudged seeking after competitive advantage from IS. Such fitness may result from any or all of the lessons learnt from failure, a concept further explored in Section 8.6. The integration of all business functions into a single system is an early, and failed, example of the sort of initiatives so typically associated with business re-engineering (*see* Section 8.5).

Even while IS was being championed as a strategic weapon warnings were given and questions raised about whether what can be gained *is* competitive advantage, even when the system is a *success*. Many initiatives that result from an organisation seeking competitive advantage actually give its *customers* far greater access to its internal data. This then increases *their* bargaining power and hence the profitability of the entire industry may fall. A clear example of this is that whilst American Airlines' SABRE system gave them a greater market share, the real *net* effect was that flight prices fell and so the profit margin available within the airline industry was squeezed. However it should be noted that the effect was felt far more adversely on all others in the industry, so AA gained the least worst rather than competitive advantage!

Vitale (1986) provides one of the few directed treatments of the potential competitive damage that can be done by IS. He suggests that, just as Porter's five-forces model gives a powerful tool for locating strategic IS opportunities, so it gives a good framework for looking at the potentially harmful affect of strategic IS:

- *Changing the basis of competition*: frequently IS *becomes* the basis for competition and any organisation must be prepared to make the IS investment to stay the course. Initial advantages can be quickly lost and, by having made IS the basis for competing, the initiator who fails to keep up has created their own IS-driven competitive disadvantage.

- *Entry barriers*: there are two aspects to this, IS being used to *raise* entry barriers or to *lower* them. In the first instance an organisation may attempt to 'up the ante' to protect itself from potential new competitors. In the second instance it may attempt to create a situation where it can enter an industry previously closed to it. In both cases IS may 'open up a can of worms' from which *others* may emerge the gainers. In the first instance it may be raising its own cost of competing to unprofitable levels, in the second it is creating and entering a situation of fierce competition.

- *Increasing switching costs*: applications of IS can make it very difficult for customers to move away to alternative suppliers – when this moves into the area of perceived unfair trading terms the government or trade body penalties can hurt!

- *Supplier/customer bargaining power*: it is in the area of supplier and customer links that IS has been most effectively deployed (see earlier discussion). There is a very real danger that an organisation may use IS to give customers and suppliers the ability to operate *without* them (through direct links, cutting out any middle-men) or the ability to compare them easily with competitors (through low-cost pricing information, etc). Any system that encourages customers to rely upon IS may mean that they are more willing to consider the IS-based advances of competitors (and they will be capable of comparing alternatives on the basis of IS quality). A final 'hurt factor' is that the success of IS gives greater power to those who supply the organisation with key elements of IS.

- *New product development*: while there is an obvious danger of diverting business attention from business activities to IS there is another danger where IS creates new products to the detriment of the creator! The integrated cash sweep accounts offered by banks may lower margins for no gain.

The lessons are emerging that the information revolution hurts as well as helps. A specific, though often only temporary, gain can be achieved, and so perhaps it is reasonable to claim the possibility of competitive advantage from IS, but this advantage is transitory. However, in many cases this gain is only achieved by making the overall industry a long-term victim, by making it structurally less profitable to the organisation's overall detriment. This overall effect should not, however, come as any great surprise since Porter's value system model is a generalised model of *precisely* this point. If IS can change the power of the five forces that model the structural profitability of an industry, then those changes must include the possibility of damage as well as gain.

### 8.3.3 ◆ What are the chances for competitive advantage?

The implicit case presented by the 'stories told' is not just that competitive advantage *exists* but that it can be *sought* and organisations can have a guarantee of success. They must acquire the skills necessary to use the strategic planning toolkit in an *appropriate* planning approach and then the IS plan that documents the IS strategy will be delivered by a process *infused* with the notion of aligning it with business goals and the shangri-la concept of competitive advantage. What are the chances of success? The table in Figure 8.6 shows the results of a 1989 survey conducted by Templeton College, Oxford into the degree of IS strategy satisfaction held by major UK companies. The results certainly make interesting reading. Since there is still fairly limited experience in this field, virtually all of these formal plans will have been produced with some involvement by external consultants. Internal management are broadly in agreement with about two thirds reporting that they judge their IS strategies to be successful. However over 90 per cent of those whose sole role was defining and documenting them report them a success!

The picture presented in Figure 8.6 seems fairly hopeful since so many are satisfied with their IS strategy. Whilst there is no *absolute* guarantee that the organisation will be satisfied with the IS strategy (if the process was guaranteed to give a satisfactory IS strategy then obviously the success figures would be 100 per cent) the odds are certainly favourable. By 1995, see Green-Armytage (1995), 82 per cent of firms had an articulated IS strategy and a further 14 per cent planned to create one. However 40 per cent of firms had no close co-ordination between their business and their IS activities (either they had no formal IS strategy or it was not tied to wider business goals). A number of reasons for this disconnection are given:

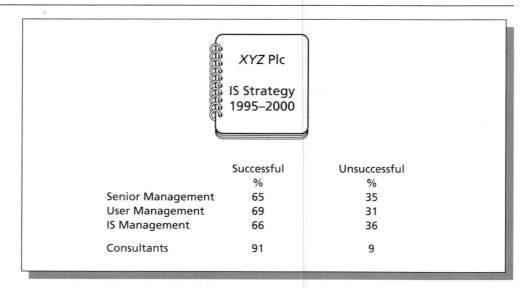

| | Successful % | Unsuccessful % |
|---|---|---|
| Senior Management | 65 | 35 |
| User Management | 69 | 31 |
| IS Management | 66 | 36 |
| Consultants | 91 | 9 |

**Fig 8.6 ◆ Chances of success**

- Absence of a business strategy | 32 per cent
- IT not involved in strategy and planning | 39 per cent
- Managements' lack of IT understanding | 38 per cent
- IT function's lack of business understanding | 14 per cent
- Legacy of mistrust and misunderstanding | 13 per cent

Many 'tales told' will be after-the-event rationalisations, for instance a large pharmaceutical company claimed competitive advantage from the early innovative equipping of their sales force with portable computers and communication software – the reality was that the portables were bought to lower order processing costs and the communications software came bundled for free with another hardware purchase and so they 'just happened' to use it.

It may be that the phrase 'IS for competitive advantage' is, in any case, only journalistic and academic hype. It may be that actual organisations do not *expect* to gain it. There is some evidence to support this in Excellence and The IT Factor, MSA Business 1990 survey into 10 large UK companies, reported in *IT Matters* (1992). In this it was noted with surprise by the surveyors, possible purveyors of such 'hype', that competitive advantage was not mentioned *explicitly* in connection with IS, though competitor awareness was. All ten companies were defined as 'excellent' in terms of:

- Steady growth in both sales and pre-tax profits
- Steady growth in terms of assets
- Good reputation
- One of the leaders in their sector.

KPMG (1992) note that many of the strategies for competitive advantage were, in any case, never implemented as the boom of the 1980s turned to recession in the 1990s. So senior management interest in IS is now one of getting maximum *value for money*, often leading to cost cutting. Perhaps all that drive to raise senior management awareness of IS has been a double-edged sword since IS now has far less mystique and is more likely to be subjected to searching questions about its value. Staying in business becomes as important as being the best. Strategy is a creative thing and so not merely the certain product of careful application of techniques by professionals – often the opposite is true and ideas from IS *amateurs* are the profitable ones since they can be far less locked into pre-conceptions.

What are the characteristics of 'satisfaction' if the organisation can achieve it? It is not enough to say that, whilst competitive advantage cannot be guaranteed, the chances of success are very good. What is this success, is it actually competitive advantage? What did those Templeton Survey respondents mean when 66 per cent of them reported satisfaction with their IS strategies? They gave four measures of their success:

1 They now had alignment of their IS and business plans; this was generally referred to as their IS plans being aligned to their business goals
2 They now had agreed priorities, that users and IS agreed
3 They now had improved control and satisfaction with the development process; all aspects of this were now more satisfactory, including the increased acquisition of packages
4 They now had improved communication between IS and the 'business'; there was a feeling that they now, at least, shared a common language.

These four are certainly very valuable gains but they are all *internal* in nature. Competitive advantage is, by definition, a relative not absolute term (*ahead* of the others) and external (ahead of the *others*) so these valuable, but internal, achievements cannot relate to competitive advantage. The satisfaction is *real* but it is *not* of itself competitive advantage. And that is even among those organisations ready and able to be successful in *seeking* competitive advantage!

## 8.4 ◆ WHAT IS THE ORGANISATIONAL GAIN?

What is the judgement? Well, an organisation cannot be sure to get competitive advantage. If choosing and implementing an IS strategy was enough to get competitive advantage then every one would be first in the race! It is not that straightforward. The information revolution can hurt, there are no guarantees of success and anyway it is the *business* that gains or loses competitive advantage *not* IS. 'If differentiation alters the customer's perception favourably and when this differentiation can be maintained competitive advantage results' (Coyne 1986). 'Competitive advantage should result in a long-term added financial return for the organisation even if benefits are hard to quantify' Cooper and Kaplan (1988). There are a number of different views about the meaning of competitive advantage:

- There is the economics of innovation view. This is that the organisation has competitive advantage if it is able to get a return on its investment that is better than 'normal' in a given industry and this is long-lived enough to be considered as altering the industry structure. Clemons and Kimbrough (1986) consider that IS for competitive advantage should reduce costs, add value, and entail substantial switching costs for customers and users, and give enough time for the innovating organisation to reap the benefits before all others imitate. By this view opportunities are very rare and imitators can out perform the innovators, Teece (1987). Banker and Kauffman (1988) found that the use of IS was beneficial, but did *not* equate to competitive advantage, even in the case of McKesson's Economost, which is one of the 'classics' of competitive advantage. Clemons and Row (1988) found that IS was a strategic *necessity* but not a *source* of competitive advantage.

● There is a far less restricted view of competitive advantage which can be taken, whereby it can be argued that innovator can conserve the advantage by continually adding valuable new capabilities to the system. Wiseman (1988) takes this view, and suggests that opportunities exist for a wide range of advantages, including those that can be measured, such as market share, number of new customers, as well as return on investment. It may be that an organisation cannot know, in advance, whether the gain will equal competitive advantage; but they can know, in advance, that the gains will be worthwhile. Strategically important systems exist and these, if they are to impact upon the competitive position of the organisation, must modify the structure of the industry, improve the competitive position of the organisation, or create new business opportunities.

When attempting to use technology for a competitive advantage there is rarely any problem thinking up ideas. The problem is generally with making them work. In attempting to use technology strategically there are a number of strategies that the organisation might employ:

● *Proprietary advantage*: the organisation develops a distinctive technology, one that sets it apart from the rest of the industry. Then it protects this lead with barriers such as patents, extraordinary investment, long lead times or rare skills base. Hence the organisation can keep the technology away from its competitors long enough to profit and gain market share. Lotus 123 is an example where the Lotus Corporation defined the nature of the spreadsheet market long enough to gain a significant advantage, though one that was eventually lost.

● *One step ahead*: this demands that the organisation continually release new and improved technology. This on-going innovation keeps it just ahead of the competition, despite rivals' abilities to duplicate particular aspects of the technology. The Pittsburgh National Bank in America is an example of this since they were the first in the market to approve car loans within 24 hours, they then speeded this up to a two-hour turnaround and then to a ten-minute one. Improvements like these have brought Pittsburgh National increased market share and kept the bank ahead of its competition.

● *Discontinuity*: here an organisation applies technology to produce a quick, decisive shift in the market it serves. An example is Citibank. Its widespread installation of ATMs reportedly almost tripled its market share. When other banks installed their owns ATMs they found it difficult to recapture the lost customers. Citibank had created a discontinuity in the market.

- *Implementation*: here the organisation applies commonly available technology uncommonly well. This strategy can offer a double pay-off, both delivering a competitive advantage in itself and improving the performance of other strategies. The advantage comes neither from the cutting edge nor from being the first to lock in customers. It comes from the detailed management know-how that makes it possible to achieve the best performance. And then adds power to every other IS strategy.

Understanding the impact of the information revolution, the process of IS strategy planning and its key inputs and outputs and implementing that strategy will lead to satisfaction but what is it?

The things that can be seen in IS 'happy' organisations and not in IS 'unhappy' organisations may be the discriminators for success, that is they can *pragmatically* be seen in organisation reporting and/or seen to be successful in their use of IS and therefore to gain *something*:

- The unit manager sees IS to be strategically important. You cannot infiltrate from below. Changes are needed in non-trivial ways. The 'unit manager' is a term used to describe the manager of whatever is the largest aggregation that makes sense as a *single* business although, in these days of corporate holdings, it may not be actually at company level. The grouping is of elements that can be seen to have a coherent set of business goals.

- The IS manager is a full member of the unit management team. Their *actual* title is unimportant but they have to be at a senior management level and therefore be present through *all* the agenda items and not just be 'techies' brought in for Item 6 – resources. It is from this real involvement that an organisation builds the two-way understanding necessary for true interaction between IS and business.

- There are business/IS bridge builders within the business unit. These are the hybrids who are comfortable with the language and concerns of both sides. They will be the mechanics who will flesh out the IS strategy and be the source of the innovation at the interface.

- Their business and IS planning are inextricably linked. Should be coincident so that the organisation can identify the vitally important application portfolio *driven* by the business.

- The maximum realistic planning horizon is two to three years. Despite all that is said about strategic planning having a long-term horizon of five years this has shortened. So the organisation is likely to be seeking as much *automated support* as possible for the process of strategy planning in all areas to cope with this squashed horizon and the need for greater flexibility and openness in the options.

- The unit will be an early *follower* rather than a pioneer in the use of new technologies. The R&D effort will be into business problems and the potential application of existing technologies in order to learn if /and where contributions are possible.

- Technology is not used for its own sake, any projects address specific business problems.

- External consultants are facilitators and not a strategic management resource. Need to be sure of the loyalties!

These factors do not include issues of ownership, technologies, machines, software, centralised or distributed location, etc since these factors are *not* found to be discriminators for success because of the ready repeatability.

What the organisation will have done by implementing the deliverable (the deliverable is an IS strategy) and by having gone through the process itself ensures a competitive *approach*. This type of approach means that they have ensured the existence of sound, relevant core systems that have been built with simplicity and flexibility in mind. They will have a high performance systems support infrastructure where IS is kept productive by exploring CASE and I-CASE, performance monitoring, quality management, staff base development, etc. IS will, of course, be subject to an appraisal cycle but will probably *not* be a profit centre. This competitive approach supports innovation at the business/IS interface since that is where it *emerges*. IS works to push technology to the environment of the customer and supports those who can assess its potential. This approach:

- Creates and encourages an organisational culture that handles soft value-based judgements effectively (*see* Section 8.6)

and, in tandem:

- Uses hard project management culture to ensure that the delivery happens efficiently

This competitive approach creates a competitive *environment* where there is an appropriate approach to systems management that has been established in line with the business value of those systems, where bridgeheads exist into both systems service division and the user divisions. This happens as much from the planning process, the project management teams, and the more varied approaches to investment, as from IS itself. Partnerships are accepted and encouraged, with agreed roles and responsibilities. These partnerships give a forum for deciding between potential advantages, an understanding of the critical differences between business processing systems and business management systems, and, most importantly, ensures that the organisation uses and manages them *appropriately*. This environment has the correct emphasis; this is generally lower than the traditional over-emphasis upon IS support systems and lowers the over-emphasis upon technical issues related to the vehicle rather than the product.

This competitive environment comes about because of, and in turn strengthens, the competitive approach. The competitive environment was referred to by Zmud *et al.* (1986) as the information economy, not to be confused with information economics. They suggest that concentrating upon this information economy is what is necessary in order to support/encourage innovation. Certainly Neo's paper found that good new ideas were never generated by the IS function so the innovations emerge from, and are managed by, the line managers.

The IS function is not the only player in this information economy although it may for historical reasons hold a market advantage. The IS function may be the holder of significant technical and managerial expertise either because they have known about information processing technologies for longer than the rest of the organisation or because of the established products and services they provide to the other business units. Increasingly though, the desirable skills are *not* held by them! So the information economy is a business within the business and its complexity can be understood by the use of tools such as the five-forces model, competitive strategy classifications, etc just like any other business. It may be that building a healthy information economy is the *appropriate* focus for IS management since without it there may be no possibility of gaining competitive advantage, especially because such advantage seems to be the emergent result of business 'best practice'.

Huff and Beattie (1985) made an extremely useful distinction between strategic and competitive information systems:

- *Strategic information systems* 'directly support the creation and implementation of an organisation's strategic plan'. So here the emphasis is on IS that supports the strategic management process.

- *Competitive information systems* 'directly support the execution of strategy by improving the value/cost relationship of the firm in its competitive environment'. So here the emphasis is on IS improving the organisation's business performance.

One thing IS *can* do is support the customer's holistic view of the company. One eternal business problem is that an organisation may be internally split into functional areas such as accounts, delivery, sales, production, etc, each with its own slice of the systems and particularly the data. However the customer deals with the *company* and does not want *internal* divisions reflected in external dealings. IS has the technical capability to increasingly support integration but politically separate development histories have a huge momentum which must be overcome. IS may allow companies to manage the total relationship associated with a sale to a customer; see Section 8.5 for a fuller discussion of the changes necessary to achieve this customer-driven process arrangement of the organisation.

So what good *does* come about? Competitive advantage, no, but improved profitability, possibly. Examples exist at all sizes of organisation from the large 'classic cases' to the individual freelancer who sells his services on the basis of fast costing and could not do so without automated support. Many valuable and real benefits are gained, though it would be naive to assume that every organisation should go 'all out' for competitive advantage since it is not likely to be the result of conscious searching. The answer may not be competitive advantage from strategic planning for IS but rather competitive disadvantage if you don't. Whether competitive advantage can actually be gained from IS and an IS strategy or strategic IS planning I leave the reader to judge for themselves:

- 'Successfully using IS for competitive advantage has become one of the greatest adventures; it involves a wealth of skills, acute business knowledge, a good measure of self-confidence and courage and that other magic ingredient, strategic insight'

- 'Make it another cutting edge, supplementing my marketing skills, make it an earner not a spender'

- 'If the IS Director thinks he is getting an increase in his next budget he must think we have suffered a collective sense of amnesia'

- 'Investing more money in IS is an unprincipled act of faith based on poor precedent'

- 'Sure all problems are opportunities, especially when the problem is 27 on-line, over-engineered databases all integrated/multi-threaded and one of them needs an urgent fix, and we don't know which one at the moment'

## 8.5 ◆ BUSINESS RE-ENGINEERING

There is a growing awareness, driven by the recession, that an organisation's IS strategy can be used to focus actions and hence *lower costs*. So management attention has moved from the debate about competitive advantage to one of competitive survival. Whether this is a sub-set of competitive advantage, a super-set of competitive advantage, or the same set as competitive advantage is largely irrelevant. Perhaps the 1990s is the era of 'IS for value for money', and not 'IS for competitive advantage'. Here again, it will be essentially a matter of business not technology. Chapter 6 discussed the possible perceptions of IS strategy development:

- To *align* with the business by *translating* business goals
- To *impact* upon the business by *defining* business goals

Now IS use and management needs to add the dimension of:

- To *improve* the business by *redesigning* its processes

The redesigning of an organisation's processes is variously called business re-engineering, business process re-engineering, business process design, business re-design and so on. Each of these terms can be used to carry distinct nuances of meaning about the type of initiative being described. For instance, whether something is being designed for the first time or not (represented by whether the re- suffix is used or not), and whether the scope is organisation wide or more limited (the term re-engineering usually figuring in the broadest definitions). For the sake of simplicity and clarity, in this text the term BPR will be used throughout and taken to subsume all variations of nomenclature. A useful working definition of BPR is given in Smith (1996) when she describes it as;

> *the fundamental rethinking and radical redesign of an entire business - its processes, jobs, organisational structure, management systems, values and beliefs,*

BPR is undertaken to achieve order-of-magnitude improvements over the 'old' form of the organisation. It is competitive *restructuring* that forms the current focus of concern as distinct from simply that of competitive *gain* as discussed in the early section of this chapter.

Efficiency ➤ Effectiveness ➤ Competitive Gain ➤ Competitive Restructuring

This shift is heavily discussed at conferences and now forms the thrust of a new school of literature. If current management concerns can be inferred from the items covered in expensive management conferences, then the issues surrounding process redesign are:

- Techniques for implementing
- Scale of opportunities
- Where to start process design
- The role of IS in and after BPR
- Resolving the questions of ownership of cross-functional processes
- The implications for management practices

- The implications for technology support of 'new' team-based processes
- The relationship between initiatives and quality

It is probable that the issue of industry-level re-engineering that is also sometimes mentioned is the same notion as that encapsulated by IS industry and competitive impact analysis (*see* Chapter 5).

### 8.5.1 ◆ The need for redesign – a paradigm shift?

At the heart of business re-engineering is the notion of *discontinuous* thinking, of recognising and breaking out-of-date rules and assumptions that underlie current business operations. Quality, innovation, and service are now more important for survival than cost, growth, and control. So processes that suited command and control organisations no longer suit service and quality driven ones and earlier assumptions of necessary roles are no longer valid.

During the post-war decades organisations needed to funnel information to the handful of people who knew what to do with that information but this funnelling is now obsolete and can lead to people substituting the narrow goals of their department or section for the overall ones of the organisation – of the process as a whole. When work passes from process to process, delays and errors are inevitable, and hence large numbers of processes exist solely to expedite delays and repair errors, accountability blurs and critical issues fall between the cracks. The situation is now fundamentally different: large parts of the organisation are educated and able and eager to contribute and to be *empowered*; IS offers a way of doing this.

Managers have tried to adapt their processes to the new circumstances, but usually in ways that just create *more* problems. If, say for example, customer service is poor, they create a mechanism to deliver service but overlay it on the *existing* organisation. If cash flow is poor, debt chasing is stepped up rather than taking steps to avoid marginal accounts. Bureaucracy thickens and so costs rise giving away market share to other, more enterprising, organisations. Dealing with this problem is the concern of re-engineering and is obviously closely akin to total quality management (TQM) where management seeks to remove the *cause* of faults rather than merely *detect* when they have occurred. Ford, for instance, threw away the old rule 'we pay when we get an invoice' which no one had articulated anyway and replaced it with the *designed* rule 'we pay when we get the goods'.

A seminal work on the changes and the new circumstances of business and IS is Tapscott and Caston (1993). The paradigm shift currently being experienced by IS (*see* Figure 8.7) demands a business re-appraisal since, as with any other paradigm change, our view of what is *real* has changed. (A paradigm is a scheme for *understanding*, for making sense of, reality.) It is not only IS that experiences such paradigm shifts, indeed Tapscott and Caston's work suggests that four key factors have *all* radically altered. The information revolution referred to earlier in this chapter may be entering its second stage. The four forces for openness that drive this are shown in Figure 8.8.

The power of these four forces is obvious. The world is opening up, leading to the consequent issue of *globalisation* of trade. Not only have many of the old political orders gone but so too have many of the old trade groupings and so the days of limited competition are over and the new business environment is far more *open* and dynamic.

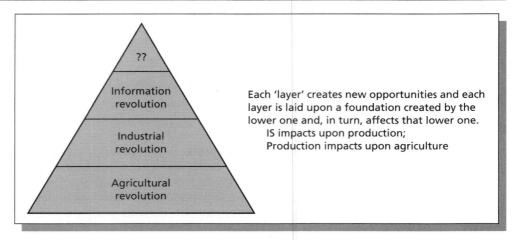

Each 'layer' creates new opportunities and each layer is laid upon a foundation created by the lower one and, in turn, affects that lower one. IS impacts upon production; Production impacts upon agriculture

**Fig 8.7 ◆ Paradigm shifts**

Since the world and its commercial activities are different a different organisation is created, the 'traditional' ones simply do not survive the new circumstances. The new organisation is flatter, simpler, team oriented, with a team commitment rather than a command and control mentality. In this situation the warrior-based metaphors associated with command and control should give way to thinking about activities in terms of co-operation; see Robson (1996) for a discussion of alternative metaphors for business.

The final force generating the paradigm shift is the technology itself. The changes in the other three forces have caused a new role for IS to be created and, in turn, the 'new' IS has driven the changes in those other three forces. IS is now made of interchangeable parts of an increasingly open whole. IS is no longer composed of discrete islands of technology, as it was during the first stage of the information revolution. The entire framework for IS decisions has changed, costs fall, performance capabilities rise and *standards* become the dominant concern. As far as the

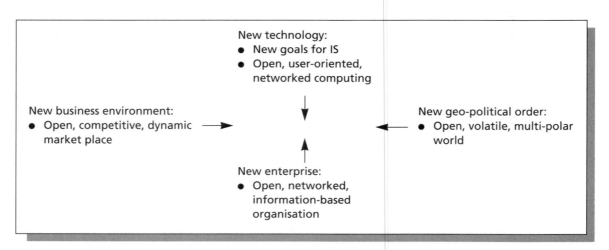

**Fig 8.8 ◆ Four forces for openness**

use and management of IS is concerned there have been three critical moves as a result of this paradigm shift. These moves are:

- From personal to work group computing
- From island systems to integrated systems
- From internal to enterprise computing

These changes and their enabling technologies are shown in Figure 8.9.

So the technology dimension of the paradigm shift builds in layers. The people teams are enabled by a range of technical moves towards more flexible, open ways to network media, systems and people. This changes the business team approach from a design for *accountability* which was appropriate when the organisation needed to focus on *control*, to the design for *commitment* necessary when the organisation needs to gain *accomplishments*. This move from 'stand-alone' humans to high-performance teams challenges the existing business approach and demands the technology-driven re-engineering of those approaches. Competitive advantage may have been the buzzword of the 1980s but re-engineering for empowered teams is the concern of the 1990s.

The integration of people into teams can be built upon by the increasing integration of systems. These integrated systems permit the organisation to change into an integrated organisation. The integrated systems allow the integration of business processes to increase the effectiveness of the organisation's provision of a coherent unified view of itself to its customers. The gradual move away from arbitrary and divisive distinctions between voice, data and images and the growth in open standards allows technology to build the integrated organisation that can then become the *extended* organisation.

Technology has now moved beyond the era of simply seeking to lock in customers and beyond simple EDI links with suppliers into an era of strategic *alliances* that are *supported* by IS. Examples of this are everywhere: banks have to collaborate

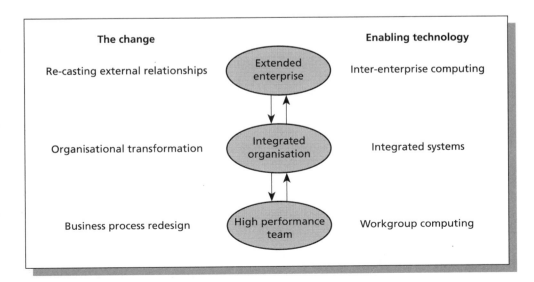

| The change | | Enabling technology |
|---|---|---|
| Re-casting external relationships | Extended enterprise | Inter-enterprise computing |
| Organisational transformation | Integrated organisation | Integrated systems |
| Business process redesign | High performance team | Workgroup computing |

**Fig 8.9 ◆ IS critical changes and enabling technologies**

275

on new ATM networks, hotel chains must collaborate on reservation systems, the international aerospace industry is highly competitive with development and supply costs measured in millions of dollars and so it must operate by using world-wide collaborative partnerships. This increase in regional, national and global alliances complicates the nature of business process redesign but creates the extended enterprise that recasts its external relationships by using inter-enterprise computing, a trend again driven by standards and probably begun by the humble fax technology. It is possible to identify seven key drivers to the information, information systems, and information technology paradigm shift, they are:

- *Productivity of knowledge and service workers*: IS is needed to automate this area in order to achieve productivity gains of any significant size. Such productivity gains can be from either lower costs or higher performance and IS permits the development of new high performance work models.

- *Quality*: product and service quality programmes are increasingly information-based and *not* production-based. The key issues are consistency and predictability and these are ensured by the employee motivation, supplier involvement and performance measurement enabled by IS. Countless works focus upon the issue of quality and total quality management.

- *Responsiveness*: it is now essential for any business to respond fast. The new global markets demand that organisations become far less time and space dependant. The time lag between opportunity and action is the key to opportunistic strategies – 'better never than late' sums up the costs of missing the opportunity time. Stalk (1988) focuses particularly upon this key driver and claims it is time (and related responsiveness) that is the key to competition in the 1990s.

- *Globalisation*: this key driver is often associated with mergers, acquisitions and alliances that are responses to the *world economy* created by the removal of national shelters for inefficiency. The alternatives of either operating from 'home' and treating overseas as sales and service colonies for standard products with the resulting economies of scale and undifferentiated goods versus tailoring to local conditions with the resulting duplication of effort and resources can now be replaced by a third approach which is to treat the world as the marketplace. The organisation may manage regionally and locally as always, but these 'regions' are independent of physical restraints and it is advances in production and communication technologies that support this globalisation.

- *Outsourcing*: there is growing concern to focus upon the key areas of business, those of key value-adding capability and hence a refusal to dilute the management attention given to these areas. The technical infrastructures that support the extended enterprise's links to its customers and suppliers also support the move to outsourcing. Organisations 'stick to their knitting' and, rather than seeking self-sufficiency, go for *streamlining* with key suppliers, alliance partners, support organisations, etc. Many organisations restructure themselves into a 'shamrock' organisation, where a core of qualified professionals, technicians and managers are the focus of the resources since they represent how the organisation competes. They have the role of developing strategy, analysing problems, planning, and communicating. This core is *flanked* by outsourced key services and a flexible labour force. This shamrock organisation is illustrated in

Figure 8.10. The use of part-time, temporary workers and the outsourced key services demands a far greater reliance upon IS to manage this more complex relationship web.

- *Alliances*: these often occur between organisations that previously had nothing in common. The extended enterprise takes many forms, from research consortia to shop–bank link-ups. The role of technology in these alliances is ambivalent. Whilst technology supports enterprise-level collaborative work just as it does individual and work group level collaboration, the constraints of technical 'Berlin walls' are being felt far longer than the survival of the actual wall!

- *Social and environmental responsibilities*: the 'me now' selfishness of the 1980s has driven a backlash leading to a significant rise in social awareness making the 1990s the 'decency' decade. The organisational rise of empowerment and autonomy demands respect for the individual and these individuals now demand a stake in the success of the organisation and appropriate tools in order to help achieve it.

The first wave of the information revolution has tended to automate existing processes. It is not just that this was limited, it has also frozen the structure and approach of the business. The thrust of process redesign is to unfreeze this frozen structure and so un-pick the departmentalisation of thirty years ago that is now inappropriate and replace it with structures and methods that are suitable to the fast-paced, customer-focused business environment of the 1990s.

The frozen, inappropriate departmentalism creates tremendous fragmentation and specialisation that creates expense and yet is inimical to good customer service by being slow, error prone and incapable of change as market situations alter. Therefore BPR initiatives are undertaken *simultaneously* to lower costs and improve customer service in order to create dramatically improved competitive health. The specific aims in BPR, as reported by Kelly (1996), are as shown in Figure 8.11 grouped as cost or service objectives.

The drive to use IS in such process redesign obviously has a significant impact upon the organisational type, the types of staff needed, the appropriateness of training and reward systems and the necessary management roles. This last issue is particularly critical with the move towards flatter organisations and is discussed in Chapter 11.

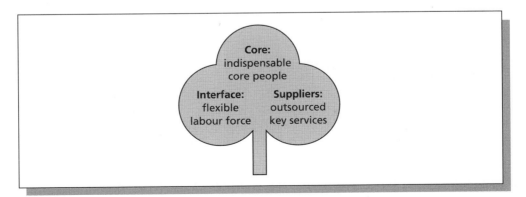

**Fig 8.10 ◆ The shamrock organisation**
(after Handy)

BPR is, obviously, an approach to organisational improvement and is closely related to, but distinct from, a number of other organisational improvement techniques. Most closely related are the notions of Total Quality Management (TQM), collaborative working, multi-skilling, organisational delayering and organisational learning. The issue of collaborative working is discussed in Chapter 10, multi-skilling in Chapter 11 and organisational learning in Section 8.7. That leaves just delayering and TQM to be touched upon here.

TQM is an incremental bottom-up approach to bringing about process improvements where those engaged in a process are highly involved in identifying improvements in a continual and incremental manner. BPR is related to this notion in the sense that the organisational awareness of the value of taking a process view of itself is often established through TQM. In fact, Johansson *et al.* (1993) argue that TQM is a necessary pre-requisite to successful BPR. TQM and BPR are also similar in their recognition of the necessity to make deep cultural changes not just superficial ones, and to build in performance measurement and benchmarking as an inherent aspect of a process in order to be able to track future process performance.

The two techniques are fundamentally different however in two important ways, the involvement of those from inside the process and the scope of their activity. BPR is a top-down process that may not engage staff participation until *after* a broad design is conceived, although commitment to the purpose of BPR is very necessary at all stages. The greatest difference between the two, however, is in their scope. BPR is radical and revolutionary and whilst needed fairly regularly (in

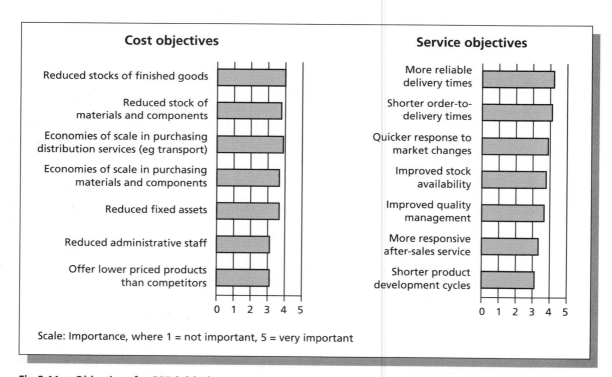

Scale: Importance, where 1 = not important, 5 = very important

**Fig 8.11 ◆ Objectives for BPR initiatives**
(adapted by permission of *Computer Weekly* from Information Service, 18 January 1996)

theory anyway) it is *not* a continuous evolution. TQM, by contrast, is continuous change over time and is focused *within* the framework of existing processes. BPR and TQM are by no means mutually exclusive, although when combined there may be a danger that TQM acts as a displacement activity for BPR and 'soaks up' all organisational energy. Despite that danger, BPR may be effectively used at specific points within an overall TQM framework, being used, as Zairi and Sinclair (1995) suggest, to 'kick start' TQM. It has already been noted that TQM may act as the organisational learning path to BPR.

The relationship between BPR and delayering is more straightforward. Delayering is the removal of layers of management made unnecessary by the use of approaches that 'amplify management capabilities'. These techniques may include the use of IS-enabled links but are not exclusive to technology-based ones and BPR is one such amplification technique. The 'well designed' process resulting from a BPR initiative 'manages itself'. There is no need for the close management supervision of decision making nor for the complex matrix management approaches needed to enable teams to operate within outmoded process arrangements. This 'clean up' makes delayering possible.

### 8.5.2 ◆ The 'classics' of business re-engineering

The terms business engineering, business re-engineering and business process redesign have all become familiar from press and journal articles. Whilst the successful examples are still relatively rare, 'tales told' are beginning to emerge that show that in the right circumstances IS can offer the chance to transform the business completely. The emphasis shifts from:

- This process *is* this.... it *needs* this

to:

- This process *can* be this because of IS

Perhaps the risks are still too high (anecdotal evidence puts the number of *failed* BPR initiatives at anything from 70 per cent to 85 per cent) for any but the most courageous, or the most desperate, though organisations that survive the current recession will consider the risks worthwhile.

Despite all the work many organisations have put in to ensure that IS supports business activities, many of them have been disappointed in the return on their IS investments. Hammer (1990) amongst an emerging school of writers suggests that the problem is often the design of the work itself and that there may be over 40 per cent gains in quality, cost reduction and time compression from the 'new' business that results from business re-engineering. To illustrate this point the two most commonly quoted examples of successful business process redesign are Mutual Benefit Life (MBL) and Ford, which are described in Figure 8.12.

Despite being one of the 'classic' successes of business process redesign, MBL filed for the limited trading status defined by America's 'Chapter 11' – a situation that arose because of problems with their funds management side, in particular the exposure to real estate loans rather than the areas addressed by their redesign initiative. This does not invalidate MBL as an example of business process redesign and the benefits that can be gained. Rather it illustrates that operational excellence does not guarantee survival!

| Mutual Benefit Life (MBL) | MBL completely *re-engineered* their insurance applications processing by taking a radical approach that was enabled by IS. This meant moving from a situation where 5 departments, 19 specialists, 30 internal checks, 7 different computer systems, 225 administrative staff and many months of elapsed time were required to issue a life insurance policy to a situation that only required 1 case manager, 1 computer system, only 100 administrative staff and 1 day of elapsed time to issue a policy (and more being issued at that). This was done by sweeping away specialisation and the fragmentation of the task and replacing it with IS-empowered single-person decision making. Since this redesign crossed many department boundaries, senior management resolution of disputes was vital to the success of the redesign process. |
|---|---|
| Ford | In the early 1980s Ford put their accounts payable sections under scrutiny in order to save costs. Management aimed to reduce the existing head count of 500 by 20 per cent. This seemed a reasonable goal until they looked across at Mazda who operated with only five people rather than the 400 Ford planned implying that Ford's accounts payable section was five times the size it should be. Nothing to do with Japanese culture either!! |
| | Analysis of the existing system showed that the major problem was with the work required on purchase order/receipt document/invoice mismatches. Rather than *dealing* with these mismatches Ford *stopped* them happening. They did this by initiating and storing orders on an on-line database, with no physical copies going to anyone. When the goods come in, someone checks the database, if they match, okay, if not they are simply sent back. |
| | The old process required the accounting department to match 14 data items; the new process needed only 3, a part number, the unit of measure, and a supplier code, and all of this matching is done automatically by the computer system whereupon it automatically prepares the cheque, which accounts payable sends to the vendor. There are no invoices in the new system since Ford told vendors not to send them. Ford gained two major benefits, a 75 per cent reduction in head count and financial information that is significantly more accurate. Ford had completely *re-engineered* their accounts payable. |

Fig 8.12 ◆ Classic cases of business process redesign

## 8.5.3 ◆ What is involved in BPR?

Business re-engineering is not the universal business panacea that journalistic and consultant's hype sometimes suggests. It is, however, clearly a valuable addition to the corporate armoury and, if used carefully, it can take organisations into a new realm of competitive effectiveness. However, redesign of *individual* processes will always have a limited impact unless it is implemented as part of a wider view of the organisation as a whole and that '*wider*' view must take root into the corporate culture. This is the difference between *business* re-engineering and *process* re-engineering since the first takes this wider perspective whilst the second is far more focused.

The experiences and comments of those organisations who have engaged in business redesign suggest that such redesign is more likely to succeed when stretch targets are used, since this is not about incremental moves but about major changes and so traditional step-by-step approaches are inappropriate (although Vowler

(1995) reports that many firms in reality 'aimed low and hit low'). Business redesign requires holistic and creative thinking about how the organisation satisfies and delivers value to its customers and cannot be meticulously planned in advance or executed in small, hesitant and cautious steps. Re-engineering is an all-or-nothing decision of high risk and uncertainty.

After the initial hype surrounding the potential benefits offered by BPR the mid-1990s have brought a number of cooler-headed assessments of it. There have been only a few stories of outstanding success and a large number of stories of failures; see for instance, Hayward (1995) for an estimate that only 1 per cent of BPR initiatives succeed. We can set aside the fact that many activities are misleadingly called BPR; staff or cost cutting programmes are not BPR unless they are tied to the rethinking and redesigning mentioned earlier. If it is not BR then failing at it tells us nothing about BPR. We can also set aside those who question that BPR is anything other than, as quoted in Davenport and Stoddard (1994), 'any project you want to get funded' since if there is nothing special about BPR we cannot draw any coherent conclusions about it. We can also set aside the fact that it may be so inherently risky that only those organisations already failing undertake it since there are examples of successful firms (*see* for instance Smith (1996) for the example of N&P) undertaking BPR. Even setting aside all these factors there are still a large number of failures. Kotter (1995) identified what he saw as the eight key mistakes that organisations engaged in BPR make, They are:

1  Not establishing a great enough sense of urgency.
2  Not creating a powerful enough guiding coalition.
3  Lacking a vision.
4  Under-communicating the vision by a factor of ten.
5  Not removing obstacles to the new vision.
6  Not systematically planning for and creating short-term wins.
7  Declaring victory too soon.
8  Not anchoring changes in the corporation's culture.

Re-engineering identifies the essential elements of a core business process right across the organisation and sometimes beyond its boundaries. The new process design is based upon the necessary sequence of necessary events. To do this often needs cross-functional IS. Although this is a paradigm shift, it is still perception-based and so a conceptual, cultural issue since someone must define *necessary*.

Business redesign emerged as an issue during the 1980s when writers began advocating the removal of department-based systems in order to facilitate cross-divisional data flows. It was suggested that organisations must remove the legacy of 25 years of IS developments since these hampered their activities for the new decade. Customers demand, at least the *illusion* of, a totally personalised service, 'a huge leap backward to the days of the corner shop'. The new business environment means that intermediaries within the organisation as well as between businesses are obsolete since they come *between* the customer and the supplier. The organisation needs to create centres of *total* information about accounts, orders, shipments, etc and the only way to do this is to re-engineer the *whole* business process. IS has a critical role to play in this since, by definition, re-engineering will involve the co-ordination of organisational and technological change:

- Efficiency was the price of staying in business in the 1960s
- Effectiveness was the price of staying in business in the 1970s
- Competitiveness was the price of staying in business in the 1980s
- Adaptability is the price of staying in business in the 1990s

Process redesign is a way of achieving the simultaneous goals of cost savings; speedier service; and improved quality, which are the competitive necessities of the 1990s. It is *not* just reorganisation by another name, since it means re-aligning support services with *essential* business processes to lead to radical benefits in customer service; product development; production; and revenue generation.

Just which of these desirable ends matters *most* to any given organisation may vary. Ascari *et al.* (1995) found that certain factors are common to all BPR initiatives. Common features are:

- the need for IT solutions tailored to fit the business
- the focus on processes
- the intent to use a pilot project approach
- the need for top management commitment
- the need for the communication of plans

The importance of other factors however, varied by whether the organisation was competitively successful or was in a crisis situation. Features strongly sought by those in a competitive crisis were:

- the need for a refocusing on the customer
- the need to create coherent incentive programmes
- an emphasis on training
- the redefinition of jobs
- the need for cross-functional teams
- the move towards empowerment

Organisations at crisis point do *not* emphasise the need for adaptability. By contrast, firms who are already successful reverse this situation and deem the need for adaptability to be more important than the six features listed above. It may be that since they *are* successful they must already be addressing those six features, at least partially, and firms *in* crisis may be in crisis because of a neglect of those features. If that is so, then it would seem that adaptability is the future-oriented feature, whilst the others are competitive maintenance issues.

Tapscott and Caston's (1993) work on the Paradigm Shift has an important message for IS strategy planning. They criticise the 'project bias' of creating strategy plans as an *event* with a start and an end. The technology paradigm shift they discuss *must* mean that changes are needed in the process of developing an IS strategy. Their suggestion is illustrated in Figure 8.13.

A number of early 1990s surveys are finding that there is an inverse relationship between the existence of formal, separate IS plans and the effective contribution of IS. There is still a need for plans for managing the technology, how to manage with the technology is the province of all management. Tapscott and Caston suggest the

| | The IS strategic project | Continuous learning action |
|---|---|---|
| Relationship to business strategy | Separate or tenuously linked | Part of business strategy |
| Ownership | The IS function | The business function |
| Process | Planning event | Continuous learning |
| Domain | Internal | Integrated internal and external |
| Structure | Reflects organisation chart | Based on client/service model |
| Information class | Data processing | Multi-media information processing |
| Time frame to results | Long cycle | Quick hits |

**Fig 8.13 ◆ Paradigm shift impact upon IS strategy planning**
(adapted from Tapscott and Caston)

use of a set of principles to provide the direct statement of what the organisation regards as *good practice,* and that these should be accompanied by some brief rationale and a list of implications. They give an instance of this as where consistency of service is needed and so there is a 'principle' of standardisation. Once these principles are established existing approaches can be checked against them.

Creating a view of how to do the radical redesign is proving less tractable than writing encouraging papers! British Telecom do claim to have a methodology (which involves CSFs) for process design, including the automating of it. It may be that increasingly organisations will turn to techniques such as ends-means analysis or similarly focused derivatives given the obvious suitability for process redesign. Melliou and Wilson (1995) identify seven steps that must be undertaken in a BPR initiative. They are:

1 Develop a vision
2 Identify performance gaps
3 Identify processes
4 Define process performance requirements
5 Identify IT capabilities
6 Measure performance achievements
7 Design a prototype

Davenport (1993) suggests a similarly staged approach:

1 Identify the process for innovation
2 Identify the change levers
3 Develop the process vision
4 Understand the existing processes
5 Design and prototype the new process

Davenport does not separate the notion of vision and it seems implicit in his work that the *entire* approach creates vision as the organisation concentrates on the most *critical* processes, and creates a 'vision' of how they should be, and in doing this they challenge *all* the old assumptions about work flows, job definitions, management procedures and organisational structures; and all the, often implicit, rules must be tested for validity. The organisation will need to focus upon *outcomes* rather than *tasks* and use IS to empower one person to achieve that outcome. Whilst the redesign may demand an entirely new IS infrastructure the process is even more about change management. Sections 8.5.4, 8.5.5 and 8.5.6 give a summary of what is necessary as conceived by Davenport, look more closely at the sort of tools and techniques that may be used in BPR, explore the role of IS and finally look at the all important people issues of BPR.

### Identify the process for innovation

In identifying the *major* processes a debate ranges over how many there are. Many writers suggest that there are really only two:

- Managing the product line
- Managing the order cycle

whereas others feel that there are actually three or four core business processes but that some business activities lie outside these. British Telecom list five processes:

- Manage the business
- Manage people and work
- Serve the customers
- Run the network
- Support the business

At the far extreme, IBM during the 1980s felt they had at least 140 (though they now work on the basis that they have only 18). At the same time the organisation needs to decide upon the process *boundaries* since they will be by no means clear. They are then in a position to assess the strategic significance of each process and judge its 'health'.

### Identify the change levers

The major enablers of the business process changes are information, and so IS, and the culture and structure of the organisation. IS is a key enabler *and* a key constraint. Mutual Benefit Life demonstrates by its benefits and its problems just how IS forms part of the problem and the business solution. In order to 're-engineer' an organisation needs to overcome the enormous inertia generated by their traditional, departmentally focused IS which expects to automate *existing* business processes, and in a piecemeal way at that.

Whilst there has been much disappointment when using IS to chase competitive advantage, IS *does* give any organisation the potential to manage globally, instantly and correctly and it is innovation in the use of information that drives the redesign of work. Information allows and supports performance monitoring and integration both within and between processes. Equally, human skills drive the process redesign and team structures that assist and do not hinder the necessary changes needed. These enablers must be considered *early* in the process redesign since some view of what mechanisms can be used will, of course, shape the nature of the changes considered.

### Develop the process vision

Developing the process vision is about generating a view of how the process could be. This is obviously shaped by the perceptions that developed during stage two and also the vision must be consistent with the strategic direction of the organisation. The concepts of strategic "fit", the alignment of the 7 Ss (strategy; structure; style; systems; skills; staff and super-ordinate goals) apply here and are perhaps even more important than when considering less radical actions. True understanding and sharing of the vision can only occur if it is consistent with all these aspects of the organisation, and without a vision to act as the motivator the processes are usually just simplified (potentially very useful) rather than re-thought (possibly crucial). So even when changes intend radically to alter the business the change must happen in a *managed* way.

### Understand the existing processes

Understanding the existing processes is not as simple as it might at first seem but is none the less important since such understanding will help communication amongst the cross-disciplinary teams. Creating documentation for the current process allows the stages to the necessary change to be identified. Understanding the problems inherent in the existing business processes should ensure they are not repeated. Not all advocates of BPR are convinced of the need to consider *existing* processes. However the likelihood of overall success diminishes if the real organisation (as seen through its existing processes) is ignored.

Since the existing gives a baseline for improvement measurements this understanding means that resultant benefits can be measured. If cost justification figures get progressively more difficult as the organisation moves from automating for efficiency, through supporting for effectiveness, to searching for competitive advantage, then the calculations may seem *impossible* when transforming the way the organisation does business. It is meaningless to separate out elements of an IS investment when the benefits will be far more (or less) than financial. Separating long-term from short-term benefits may be one way to keep flexibility when dealing with such uncertainty, but even that distinction may be meaningless given the increasing speed of change.

Appropriate techniques for this stage can be drawn from any traditional process defining approach such as flow charts or cost build-up charts; techniques are further discussed in Section 8.5.5.

### Design and prototype the new process

This stage brings the organisation to the point of designing the replacement process. Having established a vision of what processes are to be transformed and into what, the mechanics of it all have to be defined. Success in this stage hinges upon the *creativity* of the team of people who use the data gathered during the earlier stages in order to create the designs of the new process. It is then necessary to implement the new design, probably through early attempts to prototype it. One of the key issues in process redesign is the importance of the most senior levels of management in resolving the inevitable inter-section disputes. With the amount of cultural changes that may be needed as a result of the redesign, it is vital that they are handled carefully if they are not to destroy the implementation. Care must be taken either *explicitly* to manage cultural change or consciously to refuse to invest in any re-engineering project where the risk of failure from an unmanaged cultural resistance is high. This and other human issues are further discussed in Section 8.5.6.

## 8.5.4 ◆ Tools and techniques

Given the amount of management attention that has been devoted to the notion of BPR it is not surprising that a number of tools and techniques (both human and computer-based) have emerged to support it. Tools that support BPR can conveniently be categorised into two sets: those that help *analyse* and *model* the business from a process perspective, and those that help plan the workflow of the business. Any or all of these tools may be supported in software. Relatively few works on BPR have considered the types of techniques to be used within it, but exceptions include Obolensky (1994), Johansson *et al.* (1993) and Classe (1994) all of which give extended coverage of manual or automated tools to support BPR. It should be noted that the current concern is to automate the techniques used in order to gain benefits such as those summarised by Classe (1994) as:

- A computerised model can easily be updated as understanding evolves, without losing legibility
- The tool may provide cross-referencing and completeness checking
- The tool may carry out quantitative analysis too complex to be achieved by hand
- Diagrams can be printed out in an organised and presentable form
- Once the processes are complete, they can be made available on-line as a quality aid
- The model built within the tool can provide the basis for the specification, or automatic generation, of a workflow or application system to support the process
- Some tools help with process prioritisation or project evaluation

Despite these benefits of automation most of the initial process modelling attempts will be manual ones as few of the automated tools help with the creative aspects of generating new visions. The tools provide support for the detail, but such rigour can be distracting during the early steps of BPR. There are also dangers that, if computerised, a process model will be accorded the status of fact far too soon. Therefore the most effective role for automated tools seems to be as a way of *quickly* generating 'pictures' of alternatives plus the provision of detailed reference materials once choices have been made.

Moving on from the advantages and disadvantages created by automating BPR's support techniques, just what techniques might be used to analyse and model the business process? Many of these will be those used in any other business analysis activity and therefore might include SWOT, BCG Matrix, 5-Forces, Value Chain and System, Ends-Means, Critical Success Factors and so on. Obolensky (1994) describes a large number of such techniques that could be used in BPR, including not only those listed here but also a host of others.

The purpose of many specifically BPR-related techniques is to decide what are 'core' processes (ie those contributing to value), where their *logical* boundaries should lie and how they are *related* to other processes. Note that the word 'decide' rather than 'identify' was used with respect to core processes. Just what is a core process is a construct of the organisation, it is a result of what the organisation 'chooses' to see as crucial, what it sees groupings and relationships to be. Core processes are not an objective reality, they are an interpretation. Techniques therefore may both explore possible interpretations and document agreed perceptions. Various types of process mapping are used in just this way, worked on collaboratively they surface assumptions about what *does* happen and what *should* happen with respect to the given process. A popular tool is the data flow diagram (DFD), illustrated in Figure 8.14 in the international definition (IDEF) form of its conventions, which maps process delineations with respect to their inputs, controls, outputs and mechanisms.

The disadvantages associated with using such specifically data-driven approaches to process mapping, for instance a DFD, are that these approaches make it difficult to break away from considerations of *existing* data and documents and they do not represent people and their roles at all. In favour of using DFDs is their ability to represent process detail in levels; this matches the need in BPR to consider a broad picture for as long as necessary *before* moving into details within a given process area.

Techniques to support workflow planning and design seek to ensure a good match between peoples activities and detailed process designs. Whilst discussed here with respect to BPR, ideas of workflow planning also relate to office automation initiatives and to organisational restructuring into flatter, team-based arrangements. This latter relates as closely to Computer Supported Collaborative Work (CSCW) as it does to workflow planning, see Chapter 10 for a discussion of CSCW and groupware.

Two distinct types of workflow can be distinguished. The logic of where efficiency and quality improvements come from is quite different in each. One type

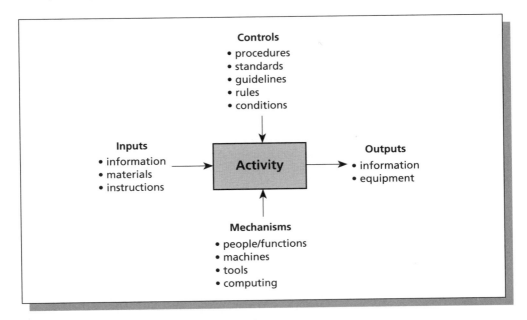

**Fig 8.14 ◆ Data flow diagram: IDEF conventions**

focuses upon planning what *should* be done, what Miers (1994) calls back-office, heads down workflow; the other focuses upon planning what *support* is needed, what Miers calls front-office, heads-up workflow.

Heads-down workflow planning rigorously defines the nature of the process activity and usually goes on to automate the provision of a continuous routing flow of tightly specified tasks. In this type of workflow it is believed that efficiency is improved by removing time-lags and wasteful repetitions, quality is improved through enforcing conformance to defined standards. When BPR initiatives are accused of de-humanising tasks it is this workflow philosophy that is being challenged and heads-down workflow planning is in stark contrast to the notion of empowerment often associated with heads-up workflow planning.

Heads-up workflow planning is activity planning for the organisations customer-facing and knowledge workers. In this form, the analysis concentrates on considering the various paths events might take and the different consequences actions may have. The design philosophy is to provide a single-point widely informed decision-making team that is customer focused. Efficiency is improved through the reduction in the numbers of staff and stages needed to take a *full* decision, quality is improved by extensively informing that decision.

Given these two quite different philosophies it is not surprising that quite different forms of IS have developed to support them. The efforts of document management systems and office automation most closely match to heads-down workflow philosophies whereas CSCW/groupware efforts more closely match heads-up workflow planning.

## 8.5.5 ◆ BPR and the role of IS

The previous section has mentioned that computer-based tools may be used to support BPR initiatives. However this is not the only aspect of the relationship between BPR initiatives and the nature of IS. This relationship can be looked at in three ways. In the way that technology makes it *possible* to free process designs from the constraints associated with physical information stores and carriers (people, documents, time and place, etc). Secondly, in the role that IS may take in the process by which organisational change is managed. And thirdly, in the change that IS must accommodate within itself to be effective in the post-BPR organisation.

The potential competitive and organisational impacts of IS have been much discussed in Chapters 5 and 6, and in the earlier sections of this chapter. Venkatraman (1994) points out that BPR forms the meeting place of the capacity that IS has to give efficiency gains and to enhance capabilities. This is, in effect, the technological result of IS and shows the general sense of what is possible from the exploitation of information technologies. In many cases it is only such technology-based solutions that will make the logical process designs feasible.

Technology is essential for successful BPR but IS is much more than technology. In the context of this text, IS is all the arrangements (people, procedures, structures, relationships, accountabilities, priorities, etc) by which an organisation's information technologies are delivered and managed. For this reason, IS is an organisational issue, emerging through a set of people.

What role should IS play in the *process* of process redesign? It seems clear from a multitude of sources, see for instance Benjamin and Levinson (1993), Vowler (1994), Martinez (1995), Moreton (1995) and Ovans (1995), that despite the key role of technology the effective role for IS is *not* to lead BPR initiatives. The nature of the relationship that IS should take probably alters as BPR progresses. Figure 8.15 illustrates Martinez' (1995) suggestion of how that role changes.

IS must show a number of characteristics, all of which are organisational rather than technological in their orientation. For effective BPR, IS must contribute its special skills and therefore be:

- a provider of cross-functional perspectives that encourage a 'big picture' vision and mitigate against 'turf wars'
- a facilitator of ownership of BPR initiatives by others
- a communicator, in business understandable language, of the business possibilities offered by the 'invisible' capabilities of technology
- a provider of skills in the management of large and complex projects
- capable of the speedy provision of the software systems needed to embody the 'new' process vision

To satisfy this last role characteristic IS may have to make significant alterations to its systems delivery paradigm. The short-term situation may require IS to explore ways in which to provide temporary 'fixes' to the inevitable mismatch between old systems and new processes. In the longer term, IS will need to reassess the perception it has of existing systems. IS must adopt approaches within which such legacy systems can serve as a boost up into the fast provision of solutions to continually changing requirements. This is in contrast to the common pre-BPR situation where either it is not noticed when existing systems fall out of step with business processes or, if noticed, it is believed that they must be totally discarded and replaced. Such systems adaptability, probably achieved through a flexible basket of acquisition methods (*see* Chapter 12), including at least outsourcing, user self-development, standard packaged solutions, stores of systems components, rapid prototyping and so on, will be necessary for post-BPR to allow IS to service the need for the fast provision of non-wasteful reuse-capable business-relevant systems. However during a BPR initiative the symbolic power of visibly 'throwing out the old' may be important to represent the extent of the change in the nature of the organisation.

| Re-engineering area | Business leaders' role | Information systems' role |
| --- | --- | --- |
| Overall accountability and leadership | Leadership | Support |
| Business vision | Leadership | Support |
| Re-engineering plan of attack | Partnership | Partnership |
| Technology expertise | Support | Leadership |
| Project management expertise | Support | Leadership |
| Business change management expertise | Leadership | Support |
| Business re-engineering idea generation | Partnership | Partnership |
| Business process analysis | Partnership | Partnership |
| Business model design | Partnership | Partnership |
| Business model implementation | Partnership | Partnership |

**Fig 8.15 ◆ Role of IS by different aspects of BPR**
(after Martinez)

Post-BPR IS will itself have been redesigned and the logical groupings will, of course, emerge as a result of the organisation's choices but it is likely that much of the front-line service activities will be devolved *into* the business to face the customer more directly. Heads-up workflow planning for IS translates as IS devolved *into* the teams that manage processes, intensely supported so that they are equipped to take informed IS decisions. What might conveniently be thought of as 'the IT department' back-office aspects of IS split into strategic infrastructure decision making (another field for heads-up workflow planning) and the operation of the large-scale transaction processing systems such as order processing, the payroll, scheduling, operating the network, etc. This area is a candidate for heads-down workflow planning to streamline and standardise, and frequently to automate IS tasks.

## 8.5.6 ◆ BPR and people issues

It should never be forgotten that BPR is about change, and radical change at that. Change management stands or falls on people issues and this is very much true of BPR initiatives. There are a number of people-related paradoxes inherent to BPR:

- BPR must be top-down to address radical redesign, yet seeks to create improved bottom-up performance

- BPR is likely to be a 'forced march' so that it overcomes resistance, and yet it requires significant co-operation

- BPR will need to reduce redundant management layers (and hence cut staff numbers), and yet requires universal management commitment

- BPR is associated with heads-down workflow planning to create more automation driven people, yet BPR is also been associated with heads-up workflow planning to create fewer less automation driven people.

The high failure rate in BPR initiatives must result, at least in part, from the failure to resolve these paradoxes. Strassmann (1995) provides a strong argument *against* radical redesign (BPR) and *for* incremental process improvements (TQM and the like) founded primarily on the fact that the philosophies of BPR are likely to damage irreparably the *human* capital of the organisation, and that the net result of BPR's brutality and disconnection from the actual organisation is to weaken not strengthen most firms. He argues that BPR 'may leave an organisation in a crippled condition', since it is a: 'drastic cure from which a patient may never fully recover because of demoralisation'.

The route, therefore, to effective BPR must hinge on achieving its aims of reduced costs and improved service *without* demoralising or otherwise destroying the capabilities of the remaining people. It may be germane here to remember (from Section 8.5.3) that when already successful firms undertake BPR they focus primarily on increasing adaptability whereas firms in a competitive crisis when undertaking BPR seek a large number of objectives and do *not* emphasise the seeking of adaptability. The point is that it may be more feasible to obtain large-scale commitment to adaptability than to a large number of different objectives, many of them directly focused on cost cutting. Achievement of adaptability occurs from the ability to accommodate continuous change. This capability comes only when throughout the organisation there is both the willingness and the ability to take personal charge of identifying and acquiring necessary skills. Terms such as openness, trust and honesty about self and others are much applied to this notion, the 'newly' designed processes and the consequent new organisational relationships all require them. As Strassmann (1995) suggests:

> When you want to perform surgery on management overhead, do not do it in a dark room with a machete. First you must gain acceptance from those who know how to make the organization work well. Second you must elicit their cooperation in telling you where the cutting will do the least damage. Third, employees must be willing to share with you insights about where the removal of an existing business process will improve customer service.

In BPR it is intended that *everything* is up for challenge and could change, yet it is often forgotten that *everything* does change. What Hendry (1995) refers to in this context as the 'dynamic balance of the organisation' (the interaction between values, motivations, incentives, tasks, structures and so on) needs to be re-established. A key aspect to this is that the redesign process that creates significantly different criteria of process performance must be matched by a redesigning of the incentive and reward arrangements.

# 8.6 ◆ ORGANISATIONAL LEARNING

Chapter 1 discussed a number of different notions of strategy and noted the growing interest in the view of strategy as an unfolding process by which judgements are made and actions taken rather than perceiving strategy simply as a product. In other words, strategy is a construct not a phenomenon. This view casts strategy as a distributed web of decision making ↔ action interactions and not a 'simple' matter of designing a blueprint that *others* implement. As part of this shift of interest, concern moves from seeking to understand how discrete planning teams should design a strategy (the formal-rational analytical planning perspective) to seeking to understand how strategy comes about in organisations from an interpretive, learning perspective. This later perspective sees planning as an infrastructure within which learning can occur, as in Shell's pioneering work with Scenarios (*see* Chapter 2). A key objective, as discussed in Section 8.5.3, that *already* successful firms have for BPR is to gain adaptability. The reason for this is to cope with change and if the sections of this chapter have shown anything it is that change is now continual. Perceiving strategy only as a discrete design activity will paralyse responses, but perceiving strategy as a continual unfolding, learning activity accommodates continual change.

At one time, the key distinction for IS to grasp was that data    information and so its efforts should be directed to understanding what *made* information and so provide data appropriately presented, in a timely fashion, to those it had relevance for. Over time it also became apparent that there was another key distinction, information    knowledge and IS should direct its efforts to understanding what *made* knowledge and so support the exercise of experience and judgement. However, continual change can only be accommodated by an ability to *generate* knowledge as needed. This ability is what is meant by organisational learning, the ability to:

- identify what knowledge is needed
- have the capacity to create that knowledge

So learning is to knowledge what education is to training. Just as education equips people to be capable of *self*-training, learning equips people to be capable of knowledge creation.

This last distinction implies moving beyond solving specific problems to addressing problem solvers' skills, approaches and attitudes. What is usually referred to as 'the Learning Organisation' is one which believes that learning is the critical variable in its ability to cope with continuous change (*see* Dixon (1994) for a large number of definitions of organisational learning). Learning, in this sense, is thus a condition of permanently striving after attributes such as those identified by Senge (1990) who argues that these 'five disciplines' are those things that a learning organisation must continually develop. These he defines as:

- *Personal mastery*: a personal capacity to create results and an environment which encourages others to develop themselves towards the goals they choose.
- *Mental models*: reflecting on, clarifying and improving internal pictures of the world and understanding how they shape actions and decisions.
- *Shared vision*: building group commitment to a vision of the future and the guiding practices for moving towards it.
- *Team learning*: conversational and collective thinking skills so that groups can reliably develop capabilities greater than the sum of the individual member's talents.
- *Systems thinking*: a way of thinking about, describing and understanding the forces and inter-relationships shaping the behaviour of systems so that systems change can be more effective and in tune with larger processes.

Senge, in presenting these 'five disciplines', is drawing upon a large body of theoretical underpinning in systems theory and systems thinking. There are a number of aspects to systems thinking:

- A consideration of the relationship between events and the underlying pattern behind them rather than just at individual events.
- Recognising that systems are a working *whole* and the whole system must be dealt with rather than just symptoms or no improvement will be made.
- Appreciating that language is not describing an objective reality that is outside ourselves.
- Appreciating that language is a *process* through which groups *explore* and *create new realities*.
- Accommodating the realisation that, since each individual 'makes sense' of their world and acts on the basis of the sense made, there is no objectively 'correct' reality, and there exist multiple interpretations and therefore multiple realities.
- And seeing that it is a negotiation process (conducted through using language) which 'selects' which view of reality to use for a particular purpose.

For a deeper consideration of systems thinking see, for example, Jackson (1991) and Skyttner (1996). Note that systems thinking has been criticised for many of these base assumptions: that organisations are purposeful, that what is an 'improvement' is incontestable, and that individuals will act responsibly.

Individual learning is the pursuit of Senge's five disciplines. Argyris and Schon (1978) note that *'individual learning is a necessary but insufficient condition for organizational learning'*. Individual learning depends on social context and so is essentially what has been described as systems thinking; for instance Dixon (1994) defines the essence of individual learning to be:

- we interpret what we experience in the world
- we each create our own unique interpretations
- the meaning we create mediates our actions

This seems to re-present the tenets of systems thinking.

Organisational learning is a more complex notion bringing in, as it does, the notion of team operation. Just as BPR was associated with a number of paradoxes or tensions so too is organisational learning. These tensions are well described in Garrett (1995) in terms of the need to deal with six dilemmas, these being illustrated in Figure 8.16.

A useful way of thinking about organisational learning is to draw upon the idea that meaning is an interpretation; individuals and groups create what Dixon (1994) calls 'meaning structures'. These can be thought of as being in three forms. The first are those meanings we create and 'keep' private, intentionally or because we have no way of articulating them. The second set of meaning structures are those that we are willing and able to share and so are accessible in a group context, although the group may not be able to 'see' a particular interpretation. This set of meanings are dynamic since the act of accessing and talking about our conclusions, motives, rationales, assumptions, etc changes them. The final set of meaning structures are the collective meaning interpretations that form a collective set of shared norms, strategies, beliefs, values, assumptions, etc. These are usually unspoken and unchallenged and yet are often fostered through induction, training or other socialisation programmes. The relationship between the three sets of meaning structures is shown in Figure 8.17.

| Dilemma | Reconciliation |
|---|---|
| • Universal truth versus particular instance? | • Central guidelines with local adaptations and discretions. |
| • Display emotions? Affective neutral versus affective relationships. | • We need to control our expressions so that we also express when we control. |
| • How far to get involved. Specific versus diffuse? | • By integrating specific aspects of the person we can build stronger affiliations. |
| • Group collectivism versus self individulalism? | • Give clear group objectives that need individual initiative and accountability to succeed. |
| • Work for our status (achieved) or is it given (ascribed)? | • Respect what people are so we can better take advantage of what they do. |
| • Do we organise with past, present or future orientation? | • Need clear plans leading from current competences to our new vision. |

**Fig 8.16 ◆ Six dilemmas of organisational learning**
(after Garrett)

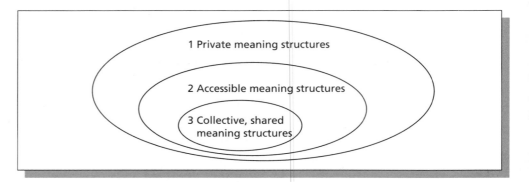

**Fig 8.17 ◆ Organisational meaning structures**
(adapted by permission of McGraw-Hill from *The Organisational Learning Cycle* by N. Dixon (1994) p. 37)

The intent of many of the tools and techniques given in the literature of organisational learning, see for example Senge, Kleiner Roberts, Ross and Smith. (1994), is
to move as much from (1) to (2) as possible, doing this by making people more
*aware* of how they are interpreting their world, less embarrassed and more skilled
in discussing their interpretations and therefore making more of their private
meaning structures accessible to others. Other techniques aim to move as much as
possible from (3) to (2), doing this by making groups more aware of what tacit
assumptions are built into their behaviour and equipped to structurally accommodate and actively welcome challenge.

The notion of organisational learning carries with it a number of implications for
the IS management domain. Firstly it is a body of beliefs about desirable and effective management behaviour and IS people would form just one instance of its
application. Secondly IS people may form important seeding points because of
their (presumed) 'special' systems-related attributes; an awareness of the importance of systems thinking and the need for a holistic perspective, an ability to
challenge tacit assumptions in a non-destructive way and so on.

The third implication is that as notions of what strategy *is* change, this change
must be reflected in a changed view of what IS strategy is. As strategy is perceived
as a *process* whereby decisions emerge from an incremental reflection and critique
of values and opportunities so must the IS strategy emerge also. In the exercising of
judgements the *effect* of the particular decision is being considered, this effect being
how the IS decision will be interpreted as well as how it will alter the overall
system; such interpretations being made and effects felt possibly far distant in time
and place. IS activities are *not* how a business strategy is 'implemented', they are
part of the tapestry of decisions that *make* the organisation. Nor can corporate
groups design an IS strategy that others implement, though such groups can work
to facilitate the negotiation of shared understanding of overall goals. IS strategists
are not an elite group, they are every manager who makes an IS-related decision.

The fourth and final implication for IS of this organisational learning view is that
in the process of reflecting and judging to take an IS resource allocation decision
just *what* should be considered of value has shifted. IS can serve the process of capturing and amplifying learning capabilities and these have the key *value*. This type
of value is, as yet, very poorly described by the value judging techniques discussed

in Chapter 7. Those techniques tend to assume that it is the provision of information, occasionally knowledge but almost never learning, that is of greatest value. They also assume that choices are exercised *before* strategy is selected; the notion of emergent strategy and organisational learning make continuous choices *as* strategy.

None of these implications for IS management are yet well understood. There is little exploration in methods or literature (however see Walsham (1993) for one exception) of how to target IS activities to support organisational learning or how to take a learning perspective onto IS. However, given the promise that the notion of 'the learning organisation' holds for providing a change-capable organisation that is also 'humanistic' in its engagements, no doubt this situation will change during the late 1990s.

**References and further reading**

Alter, A. (1992) *Information Systems: a management perspective*, Addison-Wesley.

Anon. (1993) Sabre at the Competitive Edge, *Computer Weekly*, 25 Feb.

Argyris, C. and Schon, D. (1978) *Organisational Learning*, Addison-Wesley.

Ascari, A., Rock, M. and Dutta, S. (1995) Reengineering Organisational Change, *European Management Journal*, Vol 13 No 1 pp. 1–30.

Banker, R.D. and Kauffman, R. J. (1988) *Strategic Contributions of IT: an Empirical Study of ATM Networks*, Proceedings of the Ninth International Conference on Information Systems, Minneapolis pp. 141–50.

BCC (1988) Bank Counts the Cost of IT Disaster, *Business Computing and Communications*, Mar.

Benjamin, R. and Levinson, E. (1993) A Framework for Managing IT-enabled Change, *Sloan Management Review*, Summer pp. 23–33.

Brown, L. and Pattison, H. (1995) Information Technology and Telecommunications: Impacts on Strategic Alliance Formation and Management, *Management Decision*, Vol 33 No 4 pp. 41–51.

Cash, J.I. and Kronsynski, B.R. (1985) IS Redraws Competitive Boundaries, *Harvard Business Review*, Mar-Apr pp. 134–85.

Cashmore, C. and Lyall, R. (1991) *Business Information: Systems and Strategies*, Prentice-Hall.

Ciborra, C.U. (1992) From Thinking to Tinkering: The Grassroots of Strategic Information Systems, *The Information Society*, Vol 8 pp. 297–309.

Classe, A. (1994) *Software Tools for Re-engineering*, Business Intelligence.

Clemons, E.K. and Kimbrough, S.O. (1986) *IS, Telecommunications and their Effects on Industrial Organisations*, Proceedings of the Seventh Conference on IS, San Diego Dec 15–17 pp. 99–108.

Clemons, E.K. and Row, M. (1988) McKesson Drug Company: a case study of Economost: a Strategic Information System, *Journal of Management Information Systems*, 5:1 Summer pp. 36–50.

Cliff, V. (1992) Re-engineering Becomes the CEO's Policy at Mutual Benefit Life, *Journal of Strategic Information Systems*, Vol 1 No 2 pp. 102–4.

Cooper, K.P. and Kaplan, R.S. (1988) Measure Costs Right: Make the Right Decisions, *Harvard Business Review*, Sept-Oct pp. 96–103.

Coyne, K.P. (1986) Sustainable Competitive Advantage: what it is, what it isn't, *Business Horizons*, Jan-Feb pp. 54–61.

Davenport, T.H. (1993) *Process Innovation: Re-engineering Work through Information Technology*, Harvard Business School Press.

Davenport, T.H. and Short, J.E. (1990) The New Industrial Engineering, *Sloan Management Review*, Summer pp. 11–27.

Davenport, T. and Stoddard, D. (1994) Reengineering: Business Change of Mythic Proportions? *MIS Quarterly*, June pp. 121–7.

Davis, G.B. and Olson, M.H. (1985) *Management Information Systems: Conceptual Foundations, Structure and Development*, McGraw-Hill.

Dixon, N. (1994) *The Organizational Learning Cycle*, McGraw-Hill.

Earl, M.J. (1989) *Management Strategies for Information Technology*, Prentice-Hall.

Feeny, D. (1989) The Essential Element of Effective IT Strategies in Proceedings of Developing A Businesss-Led IT Strategy, *Computer Weekly Management Programme*, 28 Nov p. 1.

Flynn, D.J. (1992) *Information Systems Requirements: Determination and Analysis*, McGraw-Hill.

Frenzell, C.W. (1992) *Management of Information Technology*, Boyd and Fraser.

Garrett, B. (Ed.) (1995) *Developing Strategic Thought*, McGraw-Hill.

Green-Armytage, J. (Ed) (1995) The Place of IT in Corporate Transformation, *Computer Weekly*, 16 Feb p. 18.

Hammer, M. (1990) Re-Engineering Work: Don't Automate, Obliterate, *Harvard Business Review*, July-Aug pp. 104–12.

Handy, C. (1991) *The Age of Unreason* (2nd edn), Century Business.

Harris, C.L. (1985) Information Power: How Companies are Using New Technologies to Gain a Competitive Edge, *Business Week*, 14 Oct pp. 108–14.

Harvey, D. (1989) Blowing IT Open to the Customer, *Computer Weekly*, 23 Nov p 16.

Hayward, D. (1995) Facing the Firing Squad, *Computing*, 2 Nov pp. 36–7.

Heller, R. (1991) The Only Certainty is That Nothing is Certain, *Unix Systems*, July pp. 32–4.

Hendry, J. (1995) Process Reengineering and the Dynamic Balance of the Organisation, *European Management Journal*, Vol 13 No 1 pp. 52–7.

Huff, S.L. and Beattie (1985) Strategic Versus Competitive Information Systems, *Business Quarterly*, Winter.

*IT Matters* (1992) No 8, Summer.

Ives, B. and Learmonth, G.P. (1984) The Information System as a Competitive Weapon, *Communications of the ACM*, Vol 27 No 12 pp. 1193–201.

Jackson, M. (1991) *Systems Methodology for the Management Sciences*, Plenum.

Johansson, H., McHugh, P., Pendlebury, A. and Wheeler, W. (1993) *Business Process Reengineering: Breakpoint Strategies for Market Dominance*, Wiley.

Keen, P.G.W. (1991) *Shaping the Future: Business Design through Information Technology*, Harvard Business Press.

Kelly, S. (Ed.) (1996) Information Service, *Computer Weekly*, 18 Jan p. 16.

Kotter, J. (1995) Leading Change: Why Transformation Efforts Fail, *Harvard Business Review*, Mar-Apr pp. 59–67.

Lamb, J. (1992) Can Model IT Help in Transforming Business? *Computer Weekly*, 13 Feb pp. 28–9.

Lansman, G. (1984) Banking on Innovation, *Datamation*, 15 Aug.

Lederer, A.L. and Sethi, V. (1988) The Implementation of Strategic Information Systems Planning Methodologies, *MIS Quarterly*, Sept pp. 445–61.

McFarlan, E.W., McKenney, J.L. and Pyburn, P. (1983) The Information Archipelago – plotting a course, *Harvard Business Review*, Jan-Feb pp. 145–56.

Martin, E.W., Dehayes, D.W., Hoffer, J.A. and Perkins, W.C. (1991) *Managing Information Technology: What Managers Need to Know*, Macmillan.

Martinez, E. (1995) Successful Reengineering Demands IS/Business Partnerships, *Sloan Management Review*, Summer pp. 51–60.

Mensching, J.R. and Adams, D.A. (1991) *Managing an Information System*, Prentice-Hall.

Meiklejohn, I. (1989) New Forms for a New Age, *Management Today*, May pp. 163–6.

Melliou, M. and Wilson, T. (1995) Business Process Redesign and the UK Insurance Industry, *International Journal of Information Management*, Vol 15 No 3 pp. 181–98.

Miers, D. (1994) Use of Tools and Technology Within A BPR Initiative, in Coulson Thomas, C. (Ed.) *Business Process Re-engineering: Myth and Reality*, Kogan Page.

Moreton, R. (1995) Transforming the Organisation: The contribution of the information systems function, *Journal of Strategic Information Systems*, Vol 4 No 2 pp. 149–63.

Moriarty, R.T. and Swartz, G.S. (1989) Automation to Boost Sales and Marketing, *Harvard Business Review*, Jan-Feb pp. 100–8.

Neo, B.S. (1988) Factors Facilitating the Use of Information Technology for Competitive Advantage: An Exploratory Study, *Information and Management*, Vol 15 pp. 199–201.

Nidumolu, S. (1995) Interorganizational Information Systems and the Structure and Climate of Seller-Buyer Relationships, *Information and Management*, Vol 28 pp. 89–105.

Noorderhaven, N. (1995) *Strategic Decision Making*, Addison-Wesley.

Obolensky, N. (1994) *Practical Business Re-engineering: Tools and Techniques for Achieving Effective Change*, Kogan Page.

O'Brien, B. (1992) *Demands and Decisions: Briefings on Issues in Information Technology Strategy*, Prentice-Hall.

Ovans, A. (1995) Should You Take the Reengineering Risk? *Datamation*, 15 Sept pp. 38–44.

Palmer, C. (1988) Using IT for Competitive Advantage at Thomson Holidays, *Long Range Planning*, Vol 21 No 12 pp. 26–9.

Pearn, M., Roderick, C. and Mulrooney, C. (1995) *Learning Organizations in Practice*, McGraw-Hill.

Porter, M.E. (1985) *Competitive Advantage: Creating and Sustaining Superior Performance*, Free Press.

Porter, M.E. and Millar, V.E. (1985) How Information gives you Competitive Advantage. *Harvard Business Review*, July-Aug pp. 149–60.

Rackoff, N., Wiseman, C., and Ullrich, W. (1985) Information Systems for Competitive Advantage: Implementation of a planning process, *MIS Quarterly*, Dec pp. 285–94.

Rayport, J. and Sviokla, J. (1995) Exploiting the Virtual Value Chain, *Harvard Business Review*, Nov-Dec pp. 75–85.

Reid, M. (1995) Survey of Retailing: Stores of Value, *Economist*, 4 Mar.

Robson, W. (1996) *Changing the Name of the Game: How Changing the Metaphor for Business could Alter IS Management Priorities*, in Proceedings of The Future for Information Systems, First Annual Conference, UKAIS, 10–12 Apr, Cranfield.

Senge, P. (1990) *The Fifth Discipline*, Currency Doubleday.

Senge, P., Kleiner, A., Roberts, C., Ross, R. and Smith, B. (1994) *The Fifth Discipline Fieldbook*, Currency Doubleday

Skyttner, L. (1996) *General Systems Theory: An Introduction*, Macmillan.

Silk, D.J. (1991) *Planning IT: Creating an Information Management Strategy*, Butterworth-Heinemann.

Smith, A. and Medley, D. (1987) *Information Resource Management*, South-Western.

Smith, S. (1996) Rules of Engagement, *Computer Weekly*, 14 Mar pp. 36–7.

Stalk, G. (1988) Time – The Next Source of Competitive Advantage, *Harvard Business Review*, July-Aug pp. 41–51.

Strassmann, P. (1995) *The Politics of Information Management*, Information Economics Press.

Tapscott, D. and Caston, A. (1993) *Paradigm Shift: the New Promise of Information Technology*, McGraw-Hill.

Teece, D. J. (1987) *The Competitive Challenge*, Ballinger Publishing Co.

Unicom (1995) *The Role of IT in BPR: Enabler versus Dictator*, 28–9 March, London.

Venkatraman, N. (1994) IT-Enabled Business Transformation: From Automation to Business Scope Redefinition, *Sloan Management Review*, Winter pp. 73–87.

Vitale, M.R. (1986) The Growing Risks of Information Systems Success, *MIS Quarterly*, Dec pp. 327–34.

Vowler, J. (1994) IT Departments hold the key to business re-engineering, *Computer Weekly*, 27 Oct p. 4.

Vowler, J. (1995) BPR Projects Fail to Deliver. *Computer Weekly*, 22 Jun p. 28.

Walsham, G. (1993) *Interpreting Information Systems in Organizations*. Wiley.

Ward, J.M. (1988) Information Planning for Strategic Advantage, *Journal of Information Technology*, Sept pp. 169–77.

Ward, J. and Griffiths, P. (1996) *Strategic Planning for Information Systems* (2nd edn), Wiley.

Wiseman, C. and MacMillan, I. (1988) Creating Competitive Weapons from Information Systems, *Journal of Business Strategy*, Vol 6 No 2 pp. 42–9.

Zairi, M. and Sinclair, D. (1995) Business Process Re-engineering and Process Management, *Management Decision*, Vol 33 No 3 pp. 3–16.

Zmud, R.W., Boynton, A.C. and Jacobs, G.C. (1986) The Information Economy: A New Perspective for Effective IS Management, *Database*, Vol 18 Part 2 pp. 17–23.

# PART 3

# Information systems strategy choices

The process of strategic planning generates a business strategy. This strategy then serves as a 'peg in the ground' from which functional strategies develop. Functional strategies can be deve-loped to align with, or to have an impact on and so alter the position of that peg. Hence, from that position, the process of IS strategic planning is going to generate the IS strategy. Again the organisation is putting a 'peg in the ground' so that the *process* of getting this far can move from centre stage. The IS strategy forms a benchmark against which policy choices and decisions can be judged. This part is going to discuss four major areas of strategy choice. Each of these is going to involve a range of *potentially* suitable actions. The IS strategy gives a 'template' against which to test the implications of a given decision. For example, there are a number of ways that it is possible to organise the IS function and each of these has a range of possible advantages and disadvantages associated with it. It is only possible to define the *appropriate* balance point (the 'best' makes no sense in this context) between those opposing forces with reference to the chosen IS strategy. It is a truism to say that strategy dictates policy but it is a truism that is too often forgotten. This part discusses some of the policy decisions that emerge as an organisation formulates an IS strategy. Figure A (on p. 300) shows the relationship between an IS Strategy and IS Policies. ▶

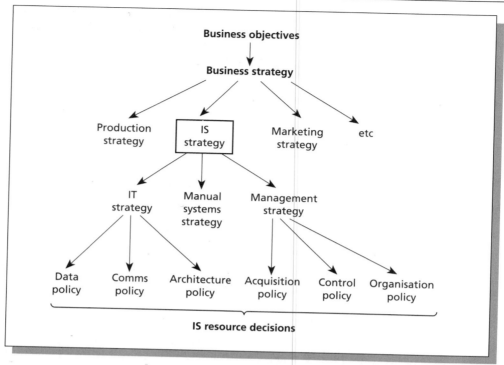

**Fig A ◆ IS strategy/policy relationship**

The IS strategy, however formulated, now exists as a framework for the IS *tactics*. The five chapters of this part cover five areas of major concern when implementing an IS strategy. Each chapter serves as an introduction to that area of concern by briefly outlining some of the alternative approaches along with the advantages and disadvantages frequently associated with each alternative. This will allow the approach that offers the most 'appropriate' interpretation of the IS strategy to be selected. When we choose between alternatives we, however unconsciously, attach a *weighting* to each of the potential advantages and disadvantages of our alternatives. The IS strategy defines, for those able to read and understand it, the weight to be attached to each factor. For example, an IS strategy that is about tight management controls will heavily weight advantages and disadvantages that relate to control and, obviously, these weightings can be either negative or positive. Such a strategy may attach light weightings to issues of a softer nature.

Whilst the choice of issues to include is to some extent arbitrary, I selected those relating to the business concerns of structure, management, and use of IS resources rather than the technical concerns of IT operations. The emphasis of previous parts has been upon how business and IS strategies are selected. The specifics of an IS strategy unfold through decisions about a number of issues and it is these issues that following chapters consider. Whilst chapters appear in a linear fashion, in reality all issues must be addressed in *parallel*, since they interact in complex ways. Retain a large, centralised IS resource and the decision to undertake major in-house development work is already half made. Go down the 'packages only' route and certain roles for IS management are mapped out. The issues of these chapters are not *only* implementation concerns since current and future choices under each heading will affect the *selection* process. It is, of course, the organisation's position on these issues that is assessed as part of the strategy formulation process.

### Key issues in the management of IS

There have been countless management surveys done by academics and practitioners seeking to capture the essential, key, issues in the management of information systems. A list of some of the better known works is given below and the categories of issues identified by three of them are shown in Figure B. Dixon and John (1989) strongly emphasise that there is a difference between the management of the technology of IS and the management of its use. Hunt (1990) is a UK writer who considers that the key issues arise from the business needs, the technology trends and the barriers that exist to use technology successfully to meet business needs. Hunt places the blame for the failure to use IS effectively upon senior management's reluctance to take responsibility for IS as a critical business element. Neiderman *et al.* (1991) provide not only a survey of key issues but data on trends in those issues since they build upon data from earlier surveys.

The chapters in this part focus upon the managerial, rather than the technical,

| Dixon and John (1989) categorise key issues as: | Silk (1990) identifies and ranks the top twenty issues in the management of IS as: | Hunt (1990) lists key difficulties as: |
|---|---|---|
| 1 Management and organisation<br>2 Hybrid partnerships<br>3 Managing the infrastructure<br>4 Macro-financial and planning issues | 1 The impact of IS on users<br>2 Security of information<br>3 The need for an information strategy<br>4 Justifying the cost of new systems<br>5 Managing the IS function and IS development<br>6 Defining requirements adequately<br>7 Integration of data and databases<br>8 Ensuring systems meet manager's requirements<br>9 Standards; flexibility; being locked in<br>10 Back-up and reliability of vital systems<br>11 Changing data into useful management information<br>12 Keeping informed about IT developments<br>13 Problem of updating large systems<br>14 Judging when to get into new technology<br>15 Involvement of senior managers; political factors<br>16 The attitude of IT professionals<br>17 Getting tangible business advantage from IS<br>18 Complying with legal and audit requirements<br>19 Distraction of staff and PCs<br>20 Assessing expert systems | 1 Business-led use of IS<br>2 Value for money from IS<br>3 Open systems<br>4 Standards<br>5 Choice of solutions<br>6 Third party supply |

**Fig B ◆ Key issues in the management of IS**

Neiderman, Brancheau and Wetherbe (1991) compare key issues uncovered in four surveys over the decade:

| Issue name | 1980 | 1983 | 1986 | 1989 |
|---|---|---|---|---|
| Information architecture | NR | NR | 8 | 1 |
| Data resource | 4 | 9 | 7 | 2 |
| Strategic planning | 1 | 1 | 1 | 3 |
| IS human resources | 7 | 8 | 12 | 4 |
| Organisational learning | 8 | 6 | 3 | 5 |
| Technology infrastructure | NR | NR | NR | 6 |
| IS organisation alignment | 9 | 7 | 5 | 7 |
| Competitive advantage | NR | NR | 2 | 8 |
| Software development | 13 | 4 | 13 | 9 |
| Telecommunication systems | 3 | 13 | 11 | 10 |
| IS role and contribution | NR | 15 | 4 | 11 |
| Electronic data interchange | NR | NR | 14 | 12 |
| Distributed systems | NR | NR | NR | 13 |
| CASE technology | NR | NR | NR | 14 |
| Applications portfolio | NR | 10 | 16 | 15 |
| IS effectiveness measurement | 2 | 5 | 9 | 16 |
| Executive/decision support | 5 | 10 | NR | 17 |
| End-user computing | 11 | 2 | 6 | 18 |
| Security and control | 12 | 14 | 18 | 19 |
| Disaster recovery | NR | NR | NR | 20 |
| Organisational structure | 18 | NR | NR | 21 |
| Technology islands | NR | 3 | 10 | 22 |
| Global systems | NR | NR | NR | 23 |
| Image technology | NR | NR | NR | 24 |
| IS asset accounting | NR | NR | NR | 25 |

**Fig B ◆ Key issues in the management of IS (continued)**

aspects of managing information systems; for instance it is *outside* the scope of this book to consider how distributed processing *works* but it is *within* its scope to consider implications for the nature of corporate and personal IS use and management. The specific topic choices are, to some extent, validated by the work of a number of writers, including Clark (1992), that indicates that these form the critical agenda for the management of information systems.

**References and further reading**

Benjamin, R.I. and Blunt, J. (1992) Critical IT Issues: The Next Ten Years, *Sloan Management Review*, Summer pp. 7–19.

Caudle, S.L., Gorr, W.L. and Newcomer, K.E. (1991) Key Information Systems Management Issues for the Public Sector, *MIS Quarterly*, June pp. 170–88.

Clark, T.D. (1992) Corporate Systems Management: An overview and Research Perspective, *Communications of the ACM*, Vol 35 No 2 pp. 61–75.

Dixon, P.J. and John, D.A. (1989) Technology Issues facing Corporate Management in the 1990s, *MIS Quarterly*, Sept pp. 247–55.

Galliers, B. (1992) Information Technology – Management's Boon or Bane? *Journal of Strategic*

*Information Systems*, Vol 1 No 2 pp. 50–4.

Gray, P. (1993) Putting the Future of IT in Balance, *Computing*, 21 Jan.

Grindley, K. (1992) Information Systems Issues Facing Senior Executives: The Culture Gap, *Journal of Strategic Information Systems*, Vol 1 No 2 pp. 57–62.

Harvey, D. (1989) Crystal Ball Offers a Dark Message, *Computer Weekly*, 7 Dec p. 9.

Hunt, G.E. (1990) Challenge of the 1990s: Harmonizing Business and Technology for Commercial Advantage, *Journal of Information Technology*, No 5 pp. 105–9.

Neiderman, F., Brancheau, J.C. and Wetherbe, J.C. (1991) Information Systems Management Issues for the 1990s, *MIS Quarterly*, Dec pp. 474–99.

Rockart, J.F. and Hofman, J.D. (1992) Systems Delivery: Evolving New Strategies, *Sloan Management Review*, Summer pp. 7–19.

Silk, D.J. (1990) Current Issues in Information Management – Update, *International Journal of Information Management*, No 10 pp. 178–81.

# CHAPTER 9

# IS resource management

This chapter will consider three specific themes in IS resource management. These are:

- *What IS will do*: This will relate to the nature of its interactions with its wider community. What roles, tasks and responsibilities IS is charged with. For want of a better phrase I have called this the *role* of the IS function.

- *Where IS will be*: This is the business' perspective of the IS resource and will relate to the location or siting, both physically and managerially, of IS within the enterprise. For want of a better phrase, I call this the *location* of IS.

- *How IS will be arranged*: This will relate to organising those people who we can consider IS professionals. How they are grouped, what responsibilities they have, and what management channels apply to them determines the structure of the IS function. For want of a better phrase, I have called this the *organisation* of IS.

These three areas are important aspects of IS management, but they are not the only issues about which IS resource decisions must be taken. These three have been grouped together here because they all reflect concerns of managing what might once have been referred to as the 'DP Dept' or, more recently, as the 'IT Dept'. As the organisational exploitation of IS has become more complex a number of other issues have grown in significance, and these therefore have been given a chapter in their own right. For that reason, although the nature of the people of IS, the IS profession and its managerial representation are also critical themes in the organising of IS, those themes are considered in Chapter 10. Similarly the IS resource management issues associated with IS that is more directly user-controlled, and the *specifics* of providing IS services and ensuring that they are securely, legally and ethically managed, also get chapters of their own.

## 9.1 ◆ THE ROLE OF IS

The *role* of the IS resource become ever more complex, a fact that has required an expansion of the organisational and structural possibilities for filling that role. The 'components' of the IS resource and therefore the elements whose location, control, and operation must be managed are indicated by the contents of the countless seminars aimed at those who manage an IS resource. To give just one example, the coverage list for an Infotech seminar in November 1992 included:

- IS strategy planning
- Business area analysis
- Supporting business systems development
- Architecture management
- Distributed computing
- Migration and conversion strategy
- Repository/dictionary administration
- Information centre and end-user computing
- Development centre administration
- Quality assurance
- Re-engineering the IS Function

To judge from this list, the IS resource effectively constitutes a business in its own right and managing it involves many of the concerns that managing any enterprise would include. Indeed Cash *et al.* (1992) use 'the business IT' analogy in pulling together their discussion of IS resource management. They discuss IS resources as a business with customers that must be competed for, distribution channels that must be managed and products that must be developed and manufactured. The commercialising of IS is discussed in Section 9.2.3 and the expanded IS management role is considered more fully in Chapter 10.

What role does IS take? The earlier chapters of this text have discussed the shift in its role from provider of business support to provider of business support plus enabler of organisational transformation (*see* Chapter 8). It was also mentioned that IS will have had to 're-engineer itself' as part of that shift. There is, however, significant confusion over just how critical to business success the IS function itself actually is. Green-Armytage (1995) reports on a survey of IS managers that indicates that, whilst they are currently split about equally on whether IS has a strategic or support role, only a quarter expect IS still to be cast in a support role within two years. However, Saran (1996) shows that this view of IS' strategic role is not held universally. IS *managers* may see IS as having that critical role, but the perception by business managers is of IS still firmly in an *efficiency support role*.

There is no doubt that the *role* has changed over time, whether this means that IS is strategic or not can be left as a matter of personal judgement. The evolving roles, changing relationships between IS and its users, and likely structures are shown in Figure 9.1. The structures referred to in this figure will be further discussed in Section 9.2.

One way of categorising or naming the IS resource is to focus upon this IS/user community relationship as Sullivan-Trainor (1989) has done when he suggested that five models for IS structures can be defined. These are:

- *The service model.* This formalises the interaction between IS and its user community into a service obligation. This model is very appealing to organisations who feel that they are still 'catching up' on IS management issues.
- *The partnership model.* This breaks down the functional lines of the service model in order to develop close alignment between IS and its business user community.

| IS role | Relationship | Structure |
|---|---|---|
| Do it to them | IS group sets the rules | 'Traditional' approach |
| Do it for them | Service orientation | Database driven |
| Do it with them | Bridges and partnerships | Functional project groups |
| Help them do it themselves | Influence rather than control | Information centres and decision support |
| Maintain their information warehouse | Bridge between information providers ↔ information users | Externally focused |

**Fig 9.1 ◆ Evolving IS/user relationships**

- *The vendor model.* Any version where IS seeks to market itself and sell its services to its user community. Organisations that are concerned about value to the business from IS are attracted to this model.
- *The expansion model.* A model that has IS creating a flexible architecture that will support common systems to accommodate a user community's growing set of IS issues. This model is attractive to large and growing organisations.
- *The strategic advantage model.* Where the identification between IS and its user community is so close that competitive products are jointly developed.

Whichever model is adopted it is made real through the pattern of decisions taken, what Strassmann (1995) calls its governance principles. These statements about *how* IS will be managed equate to the notion of 'acceptable means' used throughout this text in the definition of strategy as ends + means. Such principles guide how IS works, being overarching statements of values against which actions can be tested for conformance. Such principles are articulated through the IS resource management policies that shape just what the IS/user community relationship is. Strassmann provides examples of policies for the set of issues that collectively define the role of IS in the organisation. Examples are given for:

- Responsibilities of IS managers
- Responsibilities of operating managers
- Responsibilities of planning and finance
- Care for customers of internal IS
- Systems design
- Personnel development
- Technology acquisition
- Configuration management
- Data management
- Decentralisation
- Risk management
- Contracting out
- Reuse
- Telecommunications
- Technology advancement
- Security

With both location and internal organisation (*see* Sections 9.2 and 9.3) it is possible to separate the 'operations' of an IS function, the development, operation and maintenance of management information systems, from its administrative activities, planning, budgeting and personal management. In other words, IS has its *own* value chain. However, the current reality for IS is more complex than that; rather than a simple two-way split, IS actually covers a number of roles, each of which may have a different location. The roles include IS service buying and IS service provision (both of these may be to internal or external groups, or both), with the service provision role further split into service delivery and service support. These separate roles are shown in Figure 9.2 which represents *logical* activities and not departments or sections. All the tasks could be done by one group (or even a single individual) or each task could be distributed over a number of business areas. However, local authorities have already *physically* separated these elements (as we see in Section 9.2.3) in preparation for compulsory competitive tendering.

Amongst the roles of the IS function that may need to be differentially structured are the provision and management of:

- *IS infrastructure (operation and administration)*. This demands that organisational backbone services are delivered in a reliable and cost effective way to ensure quality service. Capacity planning is a major concern, but IS must also ensure security by back-ups, access control, error detection and archiving. This role covers network management but also database management and provision of shared services such as E-mail and collaborative work systems. All this needs to de-emphasise the technical issues (often very complex) and re-emphasise the service aspects (often surprisingly similar).

- *Long term R&D*. Long-term directions need to be given attention and separated from today's concerns. The IS strategy should not be *generated* solely by the IS department but IS management will obviously form part of the team which does formulate it. IS policy decisions will be the province of IS. R&D into technology directions must enable the technical advisor role of IS to be realistic and innovative in appreciating the business potential but coverage of technology trends is outside the scope of this book.

- *Facilitating end-user computing*. The user support role of IS is about persuasion rather than dictation and the need to enable users to conceptualise problems, to select the appropriate technology, to design an acceptable solution and then to implement it. This means a consultancy role for IS but background education, focused training and ongoing support are all elements of this role.

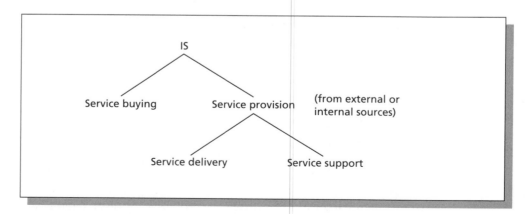

**Fig 9.2 ◆ The logical service roles of IS resource management**

There is a constant dilemma for the management of IS: loosen the reins entirely and the danger is anarchy, impose totally rigid rules and remove the chance of appropriate business responses. There is continuous debate about whether IS structures should *mirror* organisation structures or does IS always need a *different* approach. If it is to mirror the organisation then, obviously, IS would be devolved if the organisation is devolved. However, this is not the only factor and so an organisation may elect to create a data centre even in a devolved organisation. There may be a spectrum of selection approaches, including:

- Centralised – no scope for local divisions
- Close head office control
- Helping hand approach – advises rather than dictates
- Arm's length approach – leaves groups to own devices

There are two powerful reasons why IS should be treated differently from other organisational structural elements, and hence to argue against mirroring organisational structural devolution:

- Systems take longer, and cost more, to change than business structures
- Too much autonomy may mean the organisation can never re-organise its overall business later

It is this structural complication that makes the degree of match between potential partners such a crucial issue in mergers and acquisitions, see for instance McKiernan and Merali (1995) and Hayward (1996). It is certainly difficult to change business structures but IS infrastructures can take even longer.

## 9.2 ◆ THE LOCATION OF IS

Running in parallel with the issue of the internal organisation of IS, to be discussed in Section 9.3, is the issue of its location, that is where it is sited. What once would have been solely a discussion about the relative merits of centralised versus decentralised siting has now become a debate about what to *keep* centralised and what style of decentralisation to use for which element of the rest. There have been powerful pressures for decentralisation, pointing out the extent to which it makes organisational sense and so doubting whether there should be any centrally provided services at all. Conflicting with the strong pressures to decentralise have been equally strong pressures for organisation-wide capabilities and cross-functional integration. Organisations engaged in re-thinking their business structures frequently find that a very devolved IS forms a barrier to new approaches even though it is IS itself that provides the powerful tools that permit new business methods. The necessity for commonly agreed principles that will support autonomy without permitting chaos makes an 'appropriate' IS location vital. The way to decide upon an appropriate location for elements of IS is to test them against the IS strategy that defines the goals for IS. It is useful to make distinctions among three types of siting:

- *(Re-)Centralised*: One single-access function: IS provides one single service, with single-access provision.

- *Decentralised*:  Lots of single-access functions: IS being a number of smaller single-site, single-access centres, a collection of 'mini' DP departments.
- *Devolved*:  Geographically and managerially dispersed: IS is a web of lateral linkages plus a significant degree of end-user control over:
  (i) Processing
  (ii) Application systems development and environment

It is *devolved* IS that is the 'true' opposite of centralised service and not decentralised as much of the IS literature may imply. Decentralised IS can create repetitions of all the same attributes (other than scale issues) held by centralised IS. It is with a devolved location that there are the greatest differences in management control and authority as well as in physical location. Distinctions between centralised and decentralised IS can be hard to identify, devolved IS however can be hard to recognise *as* IS at all.

Any of these three siting arrangements are possible and typically organisations 'add' facets of each category as technology complexities permit and as the business needs demand. As with the internal organisation of IS, location selections should be consistent with the stage of maturity of the technology that it aims to provide/support and with the business' priorities. Understanding the advantages and disadvantages of each location alternative allows the appropriate siting pattern to be built. The organisational 'fit' determines the weight applied to each advantage or disadvantage with reference to the *goals* for IS.

Three further 'special' siting alternatives are possible, all of which can be considered as forms of *super-centralisation*. These special arrangements involve:

- Converting the IS function to a profit centre
- Converting the IS function to a separate company
- Outsourcing some or all of the IS function

The debate about centralised versus devolved technology provision is a long running one. A decade ago King (1983) suggested that IS siting involved three aspects:

- *Location*: The physical siting of the kit; this is clearly far less of an issue now given the price/performance ratio.
- *Control*: The organisational level at which decision making takes place; when this is centrally located the senior levels of management make *all* IS decisions.
- *Structure*: The responsibility for systems can be centralised into the IS function or devolved to the user community.

Despite many reminders that IS location involves more than hardware siting, until recently the major debate has been about the technical facets of IS, that is where the machines should be. As technical issues have been 'solved' the debate has shifted to being about management aspects, that is where should the co-ordination and control be sited. The growing complexity means that any organisation must now consider which *component* of IS to locate where. In other words, what to decentralise, how, and to what extent.

The benefits and drawbacks typically associated with the centralised and non-centralised (encompassing any of the combinations of decentralised and devolved forms) are discussed in this section whilst the process of matching IS location (and IS organisation) to business need will be discussed in Section 9.4.

## 9.2.1 ◆ Centralised IS location

A centrally located IS provision may be a continuation of *always* having been centralised or may be a re-grouping in response to pressures for cost savings. The centralised approach to locating IS is effective at gaining, or re-gaining, *control* over IS. The technology and systems infrastructure can be efficiently and effectively provided and there should be few problems of data format and security or software compatibility. With one agency in control there should be no confusion over responsibilities and it will have the power to impose standards that ensure that all related parts of the business are able to interface successfully. Despite frequently being used to *reduce* costs, the bureaucracy and inflexibility often associated with centralised IS can cause costs to escalate uncontrollably. The early centralised 'law' (Grosch's Law) stated that computing power was proportional to the square of the cost of the processor and indicated that there *are* economies of scale inherent in centralised IS location. Radical changes in cost/performance ratios have challenged this 'law' and so there may be other, more effective, routes to a cost-effective IS infrastructure. Centralised location can lead to confusing the issues of co-ordination (for instance in building the infrastructure) with those of control and ownership, *see* Section 9.4.3. A centrally located IS may also be correlated with IS making a low contribution to the business since it may be preoccupied with the complexities of its own internal concerns and so be out of touch with business priorities and so not able to respond to them.

### Benefits of centralised siting and control

Centralisation gives a number of benefits and there are still many instances when the organisation will find that the strategic direction of IS gives these advantages a significant weighting. Such advantages include:

- Greater control over the operation of the IS resources including systems production, database access integrity and security.

- Providing an efficiency approach to systems development that allows the centralised resource to build expertise in productivity methods. Sophisticated support tools can be justified and growth in services can be accommodated by only small increases in *total* IS size.

- The reduced duplication of effort, resources and expertise means that economies of scale can be reaped and there are overall organisational cost savings.

- The centralised IS function should have the capacity to handle large and complex projects. They can maintain a pool of well experienced staff and shared resources and hence can be successful at major in-house developments of any sort.

- By centralising the IS resource there is less potential for incompatibilities in systems and, more importantly, data since standardisation is, almost by definition, part of a centralised IS provision.

- The larger more varied IS function will generally find it easier to recruit and manage specialist staff, particularly when they are in a shortage. The 'interesting' work environment that is available to IS staff allows skilled people to be retained and kept well motivated. It is also easy to absorb and train incoming staff.

- The central provision of an IS service supports the cross-department systems associated with business process redesign since this central provision provides an umbrella for all business processes. This is a benefit of the *holistic* perception rather than the physical location and so there may be other routes to gaining this advantage.

### Drawbacks of centralised IS services

The benefits of centralised service provision are balanced by a number of drawbacks, these include:

- The IS function is divorced from the 'coal face' of the business and by being removed from the real business arena it can be equally divorced from the concerns and priorities of it. Since it is often difficult for the isolated, fortress-based IS staff to relate to the real work of the business (and, of course, *vice versa*) hostilities may emerge.

- This arrangement gives little scope for personal attention to any individual group. The span of responsibility of the IS function makes it a mass market provider rather than a personal service one and this can easily lead to true *business* priorities being ignored.

- There can be some areas where there are dis-economies of scale. For example back-up costs may be unnecessarily high. Since the service is away from the *action* it has to adopt a range of general policies for its behaviour that in specific instances may be inappropriate. There is less chance to adopt tailored responses to actual needs.

- With a single service provider, access, particularly at peak times, can be slowed. In general, the more centralised the service the more difficult capacity planning is. The large numbers of users of the service makes for large differences between peak and trough demand levels. Therefore centralised services are often associated with the use of penalties and inducements to even out this loading. The trend towards interactive, on-demand, processing exacerbates this problem. In the classic, single host machine instance of centralised IS, when the processor is out of action the entire organisation's processing capability is halted. Whilst this problem is partially offset by remote processing capabilities (intelligent terminals for instance) these must be of a limited nature. This 'all eggs in one basket' approach needs the basket to be reliable!

- If user accounting systems are used, and they often are with this approach which views the users as *outside* customers, there can be a danger of unfairness unless appropriate charging mechanisms are used.

- The communication costs can be very high since the distances between host and client can be great. Reliability of data communication technologies is reducing this cost.

## Scenario for centralised siting and control

A centralised location seems to work well when IS resources are very costly and their use is relatively limited. Whilst the siting should always be consistent with the corporate shape, as it will be if it relates to the IS strategy (we saw throughout Part 2 that these two must be consistent), there are circumstances under which it is most likely that centralised siting and control would be appropriate. So, for most organisations, this is the list of situations for retaining or restoring a centralised location. This list indicates some of what the data centre remains responsible for.

- *System for senior management*: If the system is for use by senior management, for instance an EIS, then it will usually be complex, drawing upon sensitive information, and be politically sensitive in its development and application. For these reasons it will tend to need corporate control.

- *Service common across business units*: If the particular facet of the IS service is common to the whole of the organisation, or even threads across a number of business units, then it is most appropriate for its siting and control to be centralised. The classic examples of this are payroll services, network services and common accounting services.

- *Business unit is very small*: If the particular business function is very small it may be impractical for it to develop and manage its own IS service. In these days of downsizing and cost/performance improvements this instance is very rare unless a small unit needs very complex processing capability.

- *Integration is vital*: If a total integration of the data is vital, and there are technical complications inherent in achieving this, then central siting and management is appropriate. This is another situation that occurs far more rarely in these days of greater understanding of the integration of technologies.

- *Response time is not critical*: If the particular service is such that speed of response is not a business requirement (as opposed to a preference) then the efficiency cost advantages of centralised siting and control may be appropriate.

- *Consistency with IS objectives*: Where the goals of IS are related to efficiency then centralised siting and control should be used unless specific circumstances over-rule this and indicate decentralisation.

Increasingly the complexities of IS infrastructure building force a centralised provision as the only method of ensuring the necessary integration.

## Re-centralising the IS location

Centralisation offers advantages of co-ordination, improves the prospects for standardisation and integration, helps the monitoring of costs and performance, makes it relatively easy to re-allocate staff and also eases some security problems. It also reduces the chance that one sub-system will be optimised at the expense of the organisational system (sub-optimisation). The current demand by management for better IS cost effectiveness and by IS staff for a professional career structure, the ever-increasing security threats and systems complexity and the need to integrate business data to support business restructuring, point towards central control, co-ordination and standardisation and are powerful drivers towards re-centralisation.

The trend to consolidate previously separate data centres into larger centres, or the move from classic decentralisation as a proliferation of mini-DP departments into a centralised IS provider, is a powerful one. The improvement in communication technologies makes the physical location of processing power no longer a major issue and across the world data centres are closing. Multi-national corporations move from one data centre in each nation to just one or two world wide, whilst national organisations move from many regional data centres to a single national one. The drive towards consolidation is made possible by ever more powerful mainframes and the reduction in the number of data centres (mainframe sites) has come about not from downsizing, *see* Chapter 12, and decentralisation as was predicted at end of 1980s, but from consolidation. For instance, in the UK during 1992, Prudential Assurance and Whitbread each closed one of two data centres, the Inland Revenue closed five of their ten data centres whilst American Express closed five of their six world-wide data centres. Factors pointing towards re-grouping elements of the IS resource are illustrated in Figure 9.3.

Cost is usually the overriding *motive* for consolidating IS, made *possible* by a clearer view of what needs to be devolved for effective responsiveness and what is meaninglessly 'scattered'. Where there is no value in the scattering then it can just be consolidated for cost effectiveness and savings can be made on everything from staff levels to software licence fees. Gains from re-centralisation include:

- Greater information control since they are data management centres plus a high level of network control by coupling voice and data applications; indeed Carlyle (1990a) suggests that consolidation moves IS into *primarily* a network management role that is driven by the convergence of data and voice technologies. Consolidation will mean the loss of cover for change management and disaster recovery that comes from duplicated de-centralised provision; such cover must now go to outside contract arrangements, further altering the IS role.

| Business factors | Technical factors |
| --- | --- |
| Major pressure to reduce costs | Poor service delivery record |
| Data centre does commodity system developments that are not strategically important | High degree of technical complexity and variety in hardware and software platforms that can benefit from common environments |
| Business activities need a more robust level of IS provision than the current infrastructure can provide | Need to develop common management practices and standards |
| Need to concentrate on core business functions and IS is not one of them | Weak IS infrastructure that is under-resourced |
| | Inability to attract and retain appropriate staff skills |
| | Organisation is too small to handle service demands |
| | Need to defer major cost jumps in hardware/space/staff, etc |

**Fig 9.3 ◆ Factors influencing re-centralisation**
(after Carlyle)

- More concentrated resources can obtain high calibre IS professionals. However, a drawback of this move is the fear of job losses amongst IS staff and the need to increase the skill level of the retained staff. This makes IS staff an elite group who will need to be nurtured by their organisation. Carlyle suggests they may earn 2½ times the salary of staff in more fragmented IS locations. This can be good for the IS staff but may not always be good for the organisation!

- Ability to exploit competitive opportunities because of leverage from economies of scale when handling millions of transactions per week. The consolidated IS lowers IS costs, IS cost savings lower business costs and lower business costs can give leverage by raising competitive barriers since new entrants immediately require significant scale operations in order to cost compete.

Re-centralisation will create what Carlyle (1990b) calls super-centres, where a super-centre is a utility serving an entire organisation and a good utility is about high volume, low costs and quality service. This need to increase volume without lowering quality and so lower unit costs to the advantage of the organisation requires the centralised service to choose the most economically advantageous physical location (regionally, nationally or globally depending upon the scale of the re-centralisation) and to automate as much as possible. Since the super-centre will deal with large volumes of transactions the emphasis must be to aim for a depopulated 'lights out' operation, and any IS activities that require flexibility more than performance will be devolved to the periphery and not be the responsibility of the centre. Some aspects of such a utility service are illustrated in Figure 9.4.

The emphasis upon the automation of the mechanics of how IS provides services turns IS inwards upon itself, after decades of IS being the driver of automation of other business areas. The eventual logical conclusion of this trend is the 'lights out' IS resource just as the unmanned factory is the logical conclusion of production automation.

Consolidation has proved to be the progression route for mainframe data centres, with Carlyle's findings showing that over half of companies *able* to consolidate (that is, with two or more data centres) intended to do so. They gave the potential reductions in costs as their primary motive, which they equally weighted across hardware, software and staff saving though they also anticipated communication

| Data repositories: | Technology to gather knowledge for the development of key applications into a central warehouse of information. Another name for such a super-centre is an information warehouse |
| --- | --- |
| Network management software: | Brings management of voice and data links under one central point of control |
| Multi-partitioned mainframe operating systems: | Allow one machine to perform as many functions, but still only needing one software licence |
| Automated storage: | Automates the management of tape storage repositories |
| Automated console response software: | Monitors and responds to systems messages in order to maximise systems availability whilst running a lights-out operation |

**Fig 9.4 ◆ Definitions relating to consolidated IS**

expenses and environmental and accommodation savings. Mergers and acquisitions are probably a contributory factor to this trend but the tough economic conditions of the early 1990s must be the prime motivator. John Holland the General Manager of International Data Centre Operations for the Bank of America believes IS standardisation is the critical success factor in consolidating since such consolidation is made possible by standard applications and compatible platforms.

Organisations that had *already* consolidated their data centres found that the savings were much as they had forecast, except in the area of communication costs which did not fall as much as expected. The Bank of America closed its data centre in Hong Kong by consolidating into one based in Croydon and made savings of *more* than the target of $1 million a month. US Steel consolidated two data centres into one super-centre, and this cut the required staff by 25 per cent and saved them $5 million.

The art of successfully centralising into super-centres is to balance the integration and economics consolidation offers with the innovation and differentiation devolution offers. What is the responsibility of the super data-centre and what is outside its province is a constantly shifting balance but transaction processing and the corporate data stores plus the technical vehicles for querying it always are whilst user tools to perform that querying rarely are. The *complementary* pairing for IS location seems to be that it combines *more* centralised data centres plus *more* devolved end-user computing.

Super-centres can easily adapt to operating as profit centres or to providing an IS service to outsiders since collectively all the 'little bits' of excess capacity from decentralised centres may give a meaningful amount that can be sold on. Consolidation of services so that a single super-centre serves more than one organisation is increasingly popular. Super-centre consolidation blurs into the outsourcing of IS services favoured by many organisations *see* Chapter 12 and so super-centre issues are not only an issue for very large organisations.

### 9.2.2 ◆ Non-centralised IS locations

This section considers the nature of the two non-centralised forms of IS location. They are then grouped together in order to discuss their advantages and disadvantages. This is done to avoid repetition and so improve clarity. Many of the issues in which devolved and decentralised offer advantages and disadvantages differ in the degree to which they disperse location, authority, accountability and control. In addition it is rare to find devolved IS without other forms as well, devolved IS locations appearing as a complex *set* of location alternatives used simultaneously. Such mixed approaches appear to be the contemporary 'norm' and are what Edwards *et al.*, writing in Galliers and Baker (1994), seem to call the federal approach and which they argue is the most 'effective and stable' in accommodating continuous change in the business. Issues in matching IS resources to the business community will be further discussed in Section 9.4.

#### Decentralised IS location

The proliferation of multiple IS departments brings IS *geographically* closer to the user community but perhaps no nearer in culture or understanding. Decentralisation has some powerful advantages. Since it can be much closer to the grass roots of the business, IS has a better chance of motivating and involving users and, by distributing the involvement, the logic is that users will act in a responsible way because they are responsible (and in control, and accountable)! Decentralisation focuses less on IS costs and more on user effectiveness. Local IS staff are *part* of the business. More business-relevant systems should be created since, with fewer, more generalist, IS staff who have less chance of being distracted, business needs are the systems drivers rather than technical *interest*. In addition, simpler systems may result and 'small is beautiful' and 'simple engineering is good engineering'! Whilst these points give some benefits over the centralised location of IS, there are drawbacks; primarily what is achieved is many groups all having the same problems so that the main disadvantage is one of duplication-driven higher costs plus staff isolation in the mini-IS sections. Since IS delivers its services in much the same way there is little difficulty in changing from centralised to decentralised provision (as American Express did several times during the 1980s). The cyclical swing between prioritising the control of centralised location and the flexibility of this decentralised location happens perhaps every five to eight years. The ease with which the change can be made makes it clear that nothing is very radically different between them.

The decentralisation of IS resources may be one side of this continually flipping coin or be a stage in a *progression* towards devolved locations. Currently there are strong pressures to lower IS resource costs; there is a growing IS literacy within the entire user community, and there is phenomenal growth in end-user computing. All of this suggests that *decentralisation* cannot effectively provide the balanced complement to the high degree of standardisation associated with centralised IS. Highly centralised IS tends to discourage creativity since IS's fear of chaos if standards are relaxed is a major inhibitor to the high risk, high pay-off application. It would seem that the necessary complement to centralised IS must be *devolved* IS that will transfer authority and responsibility to where IS and the business interface, so that business-relevant innovations can emerge and be delivered from the combination.

In decentralised IS there is a geographic dispersion of some of the range of IS services. This proliferates the IS function. Each mini-DP department gains some advantages of greater responsiveness and flexibility but also causes higher aggregated costs because of the inherent duplication but other than that the situation remains essentially the same for systems development, computer operations, software maintenance, telecommunications and technical support. Decentralisation, by its very nature, may mean that these services are more focused but internally they may be organised in very much the same way as centralised service provision. Hussain and Hussain (1992) provide a brief but clear explanation of the data storage alternatives to be considered when dealing with distributed processing.

## Devolved IS location

The distinction between decentralised IS and devolved IS is of the degree of dispersion of control and authority. This is perhaps the structural name for the collected set of activities that include departmental computing and all forms of user self-managed computing. The advantages and disadvantages of a devolved IS location flow from this dispersal of control. Devolution adds to the technical dispersion inherent in distributed computing but replaces the central IS control with organisation-wide co-operation and co-ordination in order to gain integration.

There is still a need for automated support of activities in a devolved environment. Rather than striving for the 'lights out' operation of centralised data centres, the thrust of automation should be at systems safety. Devolved IS leads to a dangerous potential confusion over who will be responsible for the, perhaps unglamorous, housekeeping aspects of IS; devolution must be about who is accountable for the system in all respects. Since the devolved location leads to a risk that the business of system protection falls as no one's responsibility the answer is to automate them as far as possible. The other area to automate as much as possible is the management of the network backbone itself. Software updates, capacity loading adjustments, etc can be added to basic system and data hygiene housekeeping. The costs incurred in such housekeeping may be lower since the devolution means users have a direct, vested interest in cost effectiveness.

Devolution would seem to be an option favoured by organisations that have a good claim to understanding the appropriate role of IS to a competitive business. Merrill Lynch in 1990 announced their intention to devolve 12 000 IS staff to their business units. This is notable for two reasons, one that they are one of America's largest IS organisations and two that they are one of the classic stories of using IS *right*, that is to 'gain a competitive advantage' from their Cash Management Account (CMA) service as described in Chapter 8. When their competitors began to catch up by the end of the 1980s they assessed their next move and so this is the considered response of a major, innovative, successful exploiter of IS to the need to exploit IS more effectively for the 1990s.

Decentralisation and distributed computing tend to create *islands of technology* whereas devolution puts the resources where they are *business* needed and the main driver for devolution has been the need to get IS closer to the business, its customers. The 'central' IS disappears and is replaced by a utility service that provides the *organisation-level needs* such as network facilities, corporate planning systems, and support for the process of establishing standards and principles for IS procedures. Some central co-ordination and planning will remain.

Devolution has been highly correlated with IS significantly contributing to the business and has been supported by five thrusts:

- *Downsizing trends in processing power*: Powerful desktop computers make local access to any nature of system a technical reality. *See* Chapter 12 for more coverage of downsizing.

- *Growth of standards*: Particularly in the area of networking, these allow 'plug and go' capabilities that therefore demand far fewer IS specialist skills.

- *Greater IS awareness*: Amongst all managers there is greater interest in using and managing IS to the business' advantage.

- *The need to match organisational unit autonomy*: Including supporting business decoupling to enable divestment programmes.

- *The drive to manage costs*: In enlightened organisations this is not only to cut them (often only with the result of weakening the organisation and IS) but to make them *appropriate* (that is, lower than the long-term gains). Devolution places costs where gains can be judged against business productivity (*see* Chapter 7 for more coverage of IS costs).

## Benefits of non-centralised IS functions

Associated with non-centralised IS locations are a range of advantages:

- The data recording of business events can happen much closer to that event. The risk of errors in understanding is lowered and systems are far more likely to be used and less likely to be resisted – they are the user's 'own' systems after all.

- In devolved computing the end-user gains more autonomy to match this greater involvement. The business areas should feel that the higher costs are acceptable in recompense for the higher business responsiveness.

- Departmental computing may lower the overall data communication costs and since systems are generally less complex they may be easier to manage and control.

- The focused nature of the service can allow effort and resources to be targeted appropriately. For instance, back-up costs will be at a necessary level since they can reflect the actual needs.

- Development of IS should be more integrated with the business. This advantage is observable in all variants but IS is most reactive to business needs when fully devolved. (It is not the service provision that constrains the drive for organisational integration although fragmentary services do not help.) IS will be physically and emotionally closer to the users and so should be more sensitive to requirements and more likely to develop correctly in line with them leading to high levels of systems satisfaction and also to be within the department's budget.

- The more devolved the IS resource is the more it can increase the user communities' perception of cost/benefit trade-offs. When the user community is IS (as in devolved service provision) then sensitivity to business benefit concerns should be high. End-users are able to develop a direct appreciation of their own cost/benefit balance. The more devolved the IS provision is the less likely it is to include user charging mechanisms (obviously since most of IS becomes part of the business area's budget) except for certain centrally provided servicing on a task basis. So cost/benefit appraisals become more effective.

## Disadvantages with non-centralised IS resource

Although there has been an irreversible trend towards devolution of some aspects of IS there are some disadvantages apparent when an organisation moves away from using a single access service provider. These include:

- The more devolved the IS provision is the likelier it is that there will be higher aggregated costs. The potential (perhaps inevitable) duplication and the impossibility of using resource demand smoothing techniques ensures this. Whilst costs to any one user group may be lower, those born by the *entire* organisation are higher. The higher costs may bring in relatively greater gains and so there still may be a favourable cost/benefit balance. Unfortunately, the more devolved the service the more 'hidden' are the true total costs. Ignorance of the costs is a powerful driver away from devolution.

- Devolved services run far higher risks of future incompatibilities. Perhaps the most critical incompatibilities are not in the technical infrastructures, but in the information and human resource infrastructures. The more independent each IS activity is, the higher this risk is and so, where integration now (or in the future) is 'mission critical', then decentralisation carries a heavy negative weighting.

- The devolved approaches face limits when dealing with complexity. Their smaller size tends to mean less in-house expertise is available and therefore less sophistication can be tackled. This is exacerbated by the chicken-and-egg situation with packaged software – the organisation buys a package because of lack of skills; but they lack the skills to choose the package well, no in-house expertise is built up and so no options exist next time. Obviously, as the quality of off-the-shelf solutions vastly improved throughout the 1980s, this disadvantage weighs less and less for most organisations. Core business systems, however, are far less likely to be package acquisitions and, therefore, the issue of how far the development of them can be devolved needs to be addressed as does the issue of the long-term IS provision capabilities which devolution may reduce.

- The career paths for specialists can be severely limited. The devolved nature of IS services demands generalists able to deal with a range of issues; breadth rather than depth. When specialists are needed they must be expensively bought-in and can be hard to obtain quickly enough, and will be transient, even if on the staff, and so of uncertain loyalties. This is going to be more of a problem with the increase in 'shamrock' organisations who have only a small core of technical staff and a shifting population of all others.

- The duplication of operations implies *inherent* inefficiency. If everything is not centralised then there must be some degree of duplication. The more devolved the IS resource is the greater is the degree of duplication and inferred inefficiency. This added cost will be a significant disadvantage if it is not balanced by a gain from greater effectiveness. The drive for effectiveness and competitiveness during the late 1980s pushed aside concerns with this inefficiency, focusing only on discovering IS opportunities and so, of course, re-cast the balance point between the advantages and disadvantages such that this was not a *relevant* factor.

- The process of devolving may develop inter-staff hostilities unless the change is well managed. Staff within a reduced central IS utility may resent and hence hinder IS 'upstarts' at the periphery.

These disadvantages, coupled with the advantages of centralised siting are the determinants of what to keep centralised (or occasionally, to re-centralise). As always, reference to the IS strategy is needed in order to establish the policy. As was demonstrated for IS strategies (*see* Chapter 6), a range of approaches will be needed. They should differ, at least, by the maturity of the organisation's use and management of the specific technology and by the business importance of the element of the applications portfolio. Payroll services have a support segment business importance, and hence perhaps a scarce resource IS strategy. In this classic example, centralised service provision can be used as a way of implementing a scarce resource strategy because of the following four factors:

- The cost saving benefits of centralised provision
- The lack of significant data communication needs to drive the costs up
- The need for tight control
- The lack of need for business responsiveness

Bacon (1990) suggested that there are eight principles to the successful use of non-centralised (he calls it systems decentralisation) IS provision:

- *Decentralisation is supported from the very top.* Not necessarily originating from the top but supported via the allocation of the necessary resources to make it successful. Bacon points out that this is a key success principle of any IS policy.

- *Responsibility and authority for IS is specifically delegated and assigned to the appropriate management.* In accordance with general management principles that authority and responsibility should be closely linked. Autonomy of IS activities is explicitly linked to responsibility for compliance with IS standards.

- *Decentralisation is co-ordinated and controlled in a formalised manner.* The principle is that strong reporting for reasons of feedback is needed for effective autonomy. Without clear guidelines energy is dissipated in uncertainty, with clear guidelines energy is channelled into operating within them. In order to control without stifling, true consensus guidelines must be developed.

- *Top-level co-ordination committees.* Often the co-ordination and control is formalised via a senior management steering group. Such groups appear to be more common with decentralisation rather than less common.

- *Corporate retention of key functions and activities.* Certain activities will remain centralised even in generally devolved locations. These include communications network management, data administration, IS strategy and policy support, disaster recovery, financial applications systems and payroll/personnel systems.

- *Compliance with agreed systems standards is strictly audited throughout the organisation.* This may be a matter for job descriptions, job appraisals or even job dismissals for non-compliance. Internal auditors may form the policing arm.

- *The decentralised decision is made on a business unit by business unit, function by function, system by system basis.* There are many possible criteria for choice, obviously the economic ones but also on the basis of size of unit, organisational impact of a given system and the skills required and available.

- *The central IS provider influences the devolved elements by persuasion and example, rather than coercion.* Whilst this seems contradictory to the principle of strict auditing, it is important that planning and control and developing the standards go ahead in a team spirit; indeed devolution is about the team culture.

With devolved IS locations the main danger is that the organisation cannot get a *unified* view of itself or its business and these are vital requirements for effectively competing in the global markets of the 1990s (*see* Chapter 8). It would seem that some part of IS *must* be centrally located in order to support the notions of business process redesign and organisational learning discussed in Chapter 8. There is still a need for guiding principles of some sort in the most devolved location. The issues in striking this balance are explored in Section 9.4.

### Scenario for non-centralised siting and control

As with centralisation there are circumstances that make some version of non-centralised siting and control appropriate. That is, these are the situations that indicate that the data centre is not the most appropriate provider of the service, and either departmental or end-user computing will be:

- *Requirement for speed and flexibility*: When both fast and responsive provision of a service is *required* (as opposed to preferred) then decentralisation is the most appropriate method of delivering the service. This is the most frequent driver of moves away from centralisation but it should be an IS strategy defined requirement; for instance, an IS strategy of scarce resourcing for larger applications does not indicate this since it would only attach to those applications deemed of low business importance, or at appropriate stages of the IS maturity continuum.

- *Unique service*: Where the service is unique to one part of the organisation then it should be sited and controlled within that section. Where the organisation is a conglomerate of autonomous business units as was common during the 1980s, this is a common rationale for keeping the separate service provisions. As the 1990s bring about a re-concentration upon core competencies and main business, this as a driver for decentralisation should decline in importance. As organisations re-shape themselves around core products or core activities so the siting and control of IS services must be re-assessed.

- *Consistency with IS objectives*: Where the goals are related to effectiveness then this is a clear indicator that de-centralisation is appropriate unless circumstances explicitly overrule with a judgement in favour of centralising. Where the IS goals relate to competitiveness there is a far less clear indicator and the other pointers should be used to decide.

In general, devolved use is indicated where resource costs are relatively low but use is relatively high and varied.

Simply because the managerial dimensions of the devolved IS locations are so very difficult there is a danger that organisations will assume that the technical issues are trivial. This is far from true and whilst the managerial concerns may be more difficult to address, the technical aspects of distributed processing are far from easy. Distributed processing is a difficult notion, and encompasses a number of complex technologies, some of which are defined in Figure 9.5, drawn from Massey (1991).

## 9.2.3 ◆ Commercialising the IS function

There is a trend, brought about by organisational frustrations with the ivory tower lack of realism of IS, consciously to take steps to commercialise the IS function. This applies primarily to the data centre utility and may take many different forms such as establishing an IS Profit Centre or launching the IS utility as a separate company. Setting up IS to contract its services, either on a break-even or a profit basis, intends to get IS to be more business aware by having to act as a business itself. By creating customers, contracts, deadlines, after-care needs and so on the organisation hopes for a more responsive service and greater value for money. This approach matches the free market IS strategy since the organisation's own IS company (or profit centre) can compete with those of others as a separate company. This may happen when the organisation believes that its IS capabilities are significant and yet not fully exploited by themselves. Conversely, commercialising may be chosen to educate a user community considered too unaware of IS contributions and so not effectively judging the cost/benefit balance. In either instance this emphasis can provide a way of forcing IS to be customer responsive in a commercial way and so is usually associated with service level agreements of some type.

| | |
|---|---|
| *Co-operative processing:* | The allocation of tasks within an application to the processor type best suited to them. Mainframes for storing corporate data; PCs for local manipulation and graphical displays. |
| *Client/server computing:* | Dividing applications between the client processor (usually a desktop PC) and the server processor. Part of the application is kept on the server but local processing is done by the client. |
| *Distributed database:* | The actual data stores are not all in one place, they are spread across a number of machines at a number of sites. These machines can be from different suppliers and the access tools make the distribution transparent to the users. |
| *File server:* | The forerunner of the database server discussed below, it sends entire files across from server to client. |
| *Database server:* | This may be either hardware or software. When it is hardware it is any store of corporate data that can be accessed by client processors. When it is software it is the systems software that handles the transfer of data in response to client processor's data queries. Servicing data requests rather than file requests (as done by a file server) lessens traffic on the network and so improves response times. |
| *Downsizing:* | Moving computer systems from mainframe hosts to smaller processors that may be minis, workstations or LAN-based PCs and normally forming part of a client/server network. The term can also be applied to lowering total staff numbers or removing levels of management. The intention with both meanings is to save costs and make the organisation more responsive. |
| *Upsizing:* | Arriving at client/server processing from the other direction from downsizing. It can be just as beneficial to link standalone PC applications into a connected whole as to distribute from the host mainframe. |
| *Distributed processing:* | This involves aspects of the issues defined above. It is the end result of moving from proprietary host processing to networked computing. |

**Fig 9.5 ◆ Definitions of distributed processing terms**
(after Massey)

This is an appealing location alternative to those of management who believe that IS *can* be drawn apart from the rest of business activities in order to see what it costs and so manage it better. Such management is subscribing to what O'Brien (1992) calls the 'myth of can measure it, can manage it'. This may be a myth, as O'Brien believes, but it is one much subscribed to. However, this commercialising logic significantly changes the perceived and actual roles of IS within the organisation; it can become extremely divorced from the business and from the inherent purpose of supporting the organisation to the maximum benefit of the whole. Imposing a need to recover costs and make margin clouds that purpose and, even more seriously for many 1990s organisations, it offers no premium on the efforts to integrate.

Commercialising IS means that, to some extent, IS will be in competition with other potential service providers and so IS must woo its customers. The flip side of the outsourcing coin considered in Chapter 12 is that internal IS must sell itself as better/cheaper than the competition. This is obviously *doubly* true if the organisation is seeking to sell IS services to others. IS staff have not traditionally had to understand marketing (except how to develop marketing systems) and the notion of a competitive stance, a product portfolio, being subject to five competitive forces, etc, are still alien concepts when applied *to* IS rather than *by* IS to others! Commercialising the IS department demands it acquire a whole range of skills, IS must run a business as well as responding to a business. The organisations in the forefront of the struggle to commercialise have been the public sector ones as they come to terms with compulsory competitive tendering (CCT).

Compulsory competitive tendering means that at least 80 per cent of local authorities' IS work must be put out to tender. To do this needs IS organised around two divisions, a client unit to purchase IS services plus a contractor unit that can tender as a supplier of IS services in competition with other suppliers. Watkins (1992) found 50 per cent of councils felt that their IS functions lacked commercial realism, 60 per cent felt that they had insufficient project management skills, and, although many attempt to monitor costs, 30–40 per cent are wrong. Given these problems they are ill-equipped to deal with CCT and to compete with outside providers. Presumably outside sources do hold these skills or they would be out of business!

Many lessons can be learnt from the separation of these two roles since the 'supplier unit' may be the outsourced provider prevalent in many firms, whereas the client unit may represent a combination of a central element that steers and co-ordinates direction plus devolved elements that identify grass roots needs. Many organisations retain only a client unit; for instance cost savings were sought by Customs and Excise from a similar separation that was part of a drive towards core business concentration with efficiency savings made on all other activities.

When an IS function must become more commercial, then it wakes up to business issues and just like any other business it needs:

- A clearly defined mission and objectives understood and accepted by all
- Clear leadership from someone who understands its business environment
- Acceptance that it is customers who determine a business' future
- A competitive edge to keep customers faithful and happy with the service
- An honest view of strengths and weaknesses
- Identification of competition and knowledge of the basis of competition.

As with any other business there are primarily three ways to compete, striving to be the lowest-cost producer to the entire market, striving to differentiate its products or services from that of competitors within the entire market, or doing one of these in serving a niche market. So IS must provide the same standard of service more cheaply than others could, or a better service for the same price or it must concentrate on one or other of these for certain IS services. IS *must* move from being simply reactive to being proactive in designing a balance in their product mix. As in any other business the competitive blend of product, price, place and promotion must be struck. So products of high quality, reliable cost and delivery must be offered. To do this the IS function has to understand marketing and so understand its buyers, their buying criteria, and hence adopt appropriate promotional messages. IS has a value chain, therefore IS management needs to understand its own versions of inbound logistics, production, outbound logistics, sales and service. Only then can it effectively judge the role that automation can beneficially play in improving this value chain for the wishes of the business community, just as was discussed in Chapter 5. Dearden (1987) talks of the IS functions of some large organisations being effectively separate software houses. In some cases this situation has arisen from the development in-house of significant systems skills. In other instances they have bought-in software houses to form divisions of the parent company.

Commercialising IS may mean IS becomes the core competence. American Airlines, long quoted as a 'classic' of competitive advantage from IS, is now finding that IS *is* their core business. Whether it makes good commercial sense to shift focus from passenger services to serving other passenger service providers, given the uncertain state of the markets, only time will tell. There is a continuum of commercialised alternative locations, and, at any point, IS may be acting as the sole supplier, as a preferred supplier, or be in full competition with outsiders:

| Profit centre supplying only to in-house | → | Profit centre selling excess to outsiders | → | Separate organisation providing service on a contract basis – outsourcing |
|---|---|---|---|---|

Clearly commercialising IS resource management is all about the ability to:

- *Sell* services rather than merely provide them
- *Price* services rather than merely recover costs
- *Forecast* service trend rather than supply to voiced demands
- *Contract* service quality rather than supporting service use

Most styles of commercialising IS intend to transfer the locus of authority to users supported by outside specialists (software and hardware suppliers) in the hope that quality will be higher whilst costs are lower. There is some danger that in a commercial climate it can be hard to distinguish between what is most profitable for IS and what is most beneficial to the organisation in the long term. Similarly it can be difficult for IS to carry through what is necessary, even if perhaps uncomfortable.

## 9.2.4 ◆ Outsourced IS

This option is often closely related to downsizing and/or divesting to concentrate upon core business competencies and so the management logic can come from lowering costs, reducing the dilution of management attention, or to cover temporary skills gaps. There is a growing tendency for organisations to focus, not upon how to structure their IS function but to question whether they should have one at all. The management logic being: if their core business is *not* IS should they manage outsource deals with others rather than do something they don't do well?

For those organisations that conclude that they are not in the IS business the appropriate siting location may be somewhere else! The cost pressures of the early 1990s have raised the profile of this particular extreme of IS siting. This far extreme of centralised IS location (centralised because it is serving not only all divisions of one company but across several companies) is obviously a location alternative but it sits more firmly as an issue of service acquisition, and given this its chance of success depends primarily upon the provider chosen and the relationships (contracted and informal) negotiated, and for these reasons outsourcing is discussed in Chapter 12.

Outsourcing impacts significantly upon the IS functional structure, but also upon the nature of the IS manager (*see* Chapter 10) and the strategy for acquisition of services (*see* Chapter 12). The IS function ceases to be a service provider itself, but becomes a manager of the service provision contracts. An organisation will still need a core strategy team and a process for effectively monitoring service suppliers' performance. The strategy teams look at 'bulk' contract leverage and integration issues.

# 9.3 ◆ THE ORGANISATION OF IS

This is the internal structure of IS, wherever it is physically or managerially sited. We saw in Part 1 that strategic management has passed through a number of stages, we saw in Part 2 that IS strategic planning had similarly evolved through a number of stages. It is not, therefore, at all surprising that IS resource structures have also passed through a number of stages. These stages have been made *possible* by emerging technologies and been made *necessary* by emerging organisational dissatisfactions with the cost/performance trade-off associated with IS. During the early stages of this evolutionary process a stage would roughly equate to a decade, but the pace of change has accelerated in this area as in so many others, and so there have been four evolutions in the past decade.

Organisational structures for IS have appeared in generations as is typically associated with computer technologies. Unlike such technologies, however, none of these are generations of *obsolescence* since organisations can, and frequently do, incorporate a mixture of the generations. Whilst past approaches to organising the IS resource are still used, different names are now given to some of the features, and to the visible elements of the IS resource itself.

A taxonomy of the generations of organisation structures for the IS resource, and when they first emerged, is given below (note that these are of those elements forming the IS 'profession' to be discussed in Chapter 10):

- 'Traditional' approach          1960s
- Database driven                   1970s
- Functional project groups    1980s early
- Information Centres             1980s middle
- Decision support                 1980s late
- Externally focused               1990s early

Remember that all of these can co-exist within one organisation. The variety may be sought to maximise the advantages and to minimise the disadvantages of each. Each of these six approaches to organising the IS function is appropriate to certain circumstances and situations whilst being inappropriate for others. The choice must be made with *reference* to the IS strategy. Chapter 6 demonstrated that a *set* of IS strategies will be needed and those different technologies and different elements of the applications portfolio need differing IS strategies. It should be obvious, therefore, that different structural approaches may need to cater for these differences.

## 9.3.1 ◆ 'Traditional' IS function

It is rather a misnomer to use the term IS in this instance. This is the data processing department or computer section. Its attitudes pre-date any focus upon the outcome of the technology. The traditional model has a fairly rigid structure that kept the tasks associated with developing, maintaining and operating systems quite separate (Figure 9.6). Each of these areas would have quite different objectives, management styles and structures, and distinct career paths, since they demanded different skills.

Operations staff would have to work shifts in an attempt to maximise the utilisation and therefore the payback from these enormously expensive resources and because no installation of any size could ever function without attention. Operations staff would include any number of associated media management staff and systems programmers, who then, as now, are seen as 'techie weirdos'. Since system development is so divorced from operations, large amounts of system 'tweaking' need to go on.

Data preparation activities are very significant where operations are largely batch oriented. Data preparation is always important but in environments where processing is dispersed the significance is *concealed* (often to the detriment of data security, *see* Chapter 13). The large, powerful group of data preparation staff, usually the largest within the department, would also include the batch control and audit people.

The systems development section was a group made up of 'traditional' systems analysts; business analysis went on elsewhere if it happened at all! Analysis and design were separate and this led to many communication problems and to little consideration of the overall objectives of the development in hand. This is the structure that concentrates upon detail irrespective of relevance and is one that forces documentation to be a 'forest for the trees' problem. This development group might

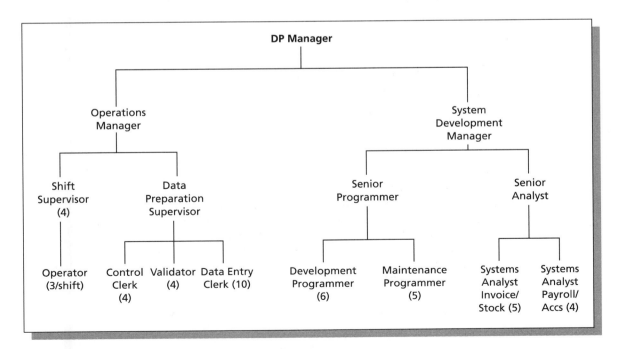

**Fig 9.6 ◆ 'Traditional' IS functions organisation chart**

hold the responsibility for system maintenance but, if separated, maintenance was (as it still frequently is) regarded as a punishment detail. As more and more systems were developed, without any productivity aids, with little structuring and no formal methodology, and generally without documentation standards, then maintenance eats up more and more of the development 'budget' of staff time. This structure is mainly associated with an era of almost total in-house developments, hence the numbers of programmers on the organisation chart.

This type of structure still exists. Where it has been retained, or created anew, it is more normally referred to as a data centre (*see* Figure 9.7), to distinguish it from an information centre (discussed later in this section), and now has a number of internal structural alternatives. This is the element of the total IS function that is responsible for common or centralised service acquisition/provision/support as discussed in Section 9.2.

In the days of the traditional DP structure the reporting line was often through another function. For two reasons this other function would frequently be finance as shown in Figure 9.8. Firstly, financial recording systems, with their large volumes of data but predictable timings and well-defined rules, made ideal candidates for early ventures into computerisation. Secondly, with an expensive resource, the location in finance facilitated the keeping of tight financial control. In this era it is extremely unlikely that any member of the senior management team would hold any specific responsibility for computing, never mind IS or information.

It should, however, be remembered that many other aspects of modern *enlightened* management were not a feature of the 1960s (for example, there was normally no Human Resource Director either) and the nature and capabilities of the technology drove many of the features of this structure. In an era of batch techniques the

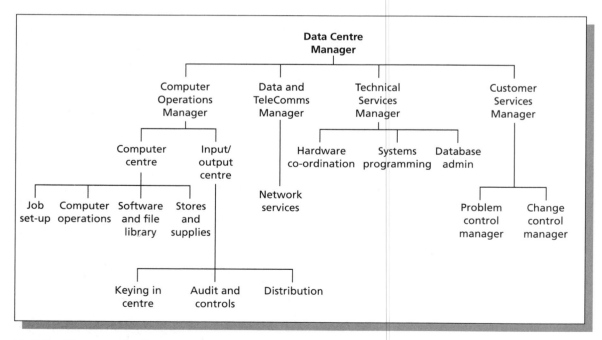

**Fig 9.7 ◆ Structure of a data centre**

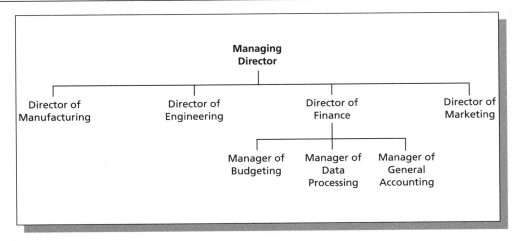

**Fig 9.8◆ DP reporting structure**

efficiency bias was very appropriate. In an era of unreliable computing, grouping together the hard to come by, constantly needed staff, made good sense. The same organising logic still applies regarding many emerging technologies. Before the days of interactive computing, a concentration upon the technical, rather than the behavioural, was quite acceptable and before the days of off-the-shelf software, job demarcations allowed scarce skills to go a long way by augmenting themselves by using relatively cheap and available 'coders'.

This structure, then, worked well in the era of centralised batch-operated systems but, over time, a number of increasingly serious disadvantages emerged that made the structure unsuitable for many of today's prevailing circumstances. This structure continues to work well when the volume of work justifies it and when the organisation's stage of maturity of use and management of IS means that standards are highly valued and everyone, particularly the user community, is conscious of the dangers inherent in the 'ivory tower' approach and therefore puts energy into avoiding the pitfalls. However, with today's wider possibilities, both technical and managerial, other structures can be adopted. Data centres aim to cater for the remaining circumstances where some version of the 'traditional' structure is suitable but will tend to suffer the same advantages and disadvantages as the traditional approach. The early 1990s concern with 'rightsizing' (that is the allocation of activities to IS resource location and arrangement on the basis of their particular processing and control needs) was in recognition of the 'new' opportunities opened up to 'choose' IS organisation arrangements. Some activities are sensibly treated with the structural specialism and efficiency of the Data Centre (those where computational scale, technical complexity, data volume, etc are a feature); some activities are sensibly treated with the structural adaptability and business interactions of externally focused arrangements (those where speed of creation, unpredictability, short 'shelf life', etc are a feature). Rightsizing is the notion of *choosing* and recognising the various values rather than automatically moving to a particular arrangement.

The greatest strength of this or any other IS function-based approach is the specialisation it supports. Within the separate teams the shared job interests will work to increase the skill level. The necessity of any project to move between teams makes standardisation essential (which can certainly be beneficial) but will also generate bureaucracies and slow system developments. Each team is distinct and increasingly divorced from the ultimate consumer – the end user. The 'follow-on' structures have been adopted as responses to one or a number of the disadvantages associated with the traditional DP Department. Briefly, these disadvantages are:

- *Application backlogs*. In this environment the systems life cycle is always prolonged, even with today's data centres it is slow. With the traditional DP department new developments could take years and even amendments to existing systems could take months. Inevitably user dissatisfaction grows.

- *Proscribed systems*. The separation of functions generated the perception that the DP department 'knew best' and led them to deliver their view of the needed system. The heavy emphasis upon the technical vehicle guaranteed that design decisions favoured technical interest or 'elegance' rather than usability.

- *Inflexible systems*. A frozen, formal, specification must be produced for coding teams that are divorced from the user community. These users must request, define, agree and then wait anything up to years for the arrival of the system. Even if the needs were well understood at the start they have, inevitably, moved on. In practice, requirements are rarely that well understood in advance, and so many disagreements occur over the interpretation of requirements. At best, this structure efficiently delivers snap-shot systems, at worst it doesn't deliver at all! Most frequently, it delivers, late, a badly automated version of the current system.

- *Heavy clerical overheads*. The huge demands for data preparation staff place a large clerical burden upon the IS resource. Besides this there is the clerical job of attempting to document creaky and unwieldy systems. With the appearance of more distributed IS resource structures, data preparation has been dispersed throughout the organisation but it has proved one of the most intractable areas to automate. In most organisations, therefore, newer structures merely 'hide' rather than remove this burden. Systems documentation, however, is increasingly automatically generated as a by-product of the development process. Perhaps document imaging and increased electronic links will finally address its removal.

- *Expensive maintenance*. This structure is associated with little or no use of productivity tools, or methodologies for effective systems development, and so there is a steady production of much unmanageable COBOL code that no one, not even the author, can easily maintain.

This 'traditional' approach has been described in some detail for two reasons. The first of these is that 'modern' data centres share many of the characteristics of this approach and so care must be taken not to also share its problems. Secondly, the 'newer' structures for organising the IS function have evolved to deal with one or more of the *problems* of the traditional structure. The growing awareness of the limitations of the structure coupled with an awareness that software and hardware changes permit new structures drives the move to those new approaches. Simultaneously, the need for the new approaches drives software and hardware changes.

$$\begin{array}{ccc} \text{Structural} & \longrightarrow & \text{Technology} \\ \text{alternatives} & \longleftarrow & \text{changes} \end{array}$$

### 9.3.2 ◆ Database-driven structure

This structure organises the IS resource around the needs of data storage. Data is removed from applications and that allows a regrouping of development staff into data analysis and design, and systems development. The main advantage of this structure is that it facilitates user access to data, under the control and/or direction of database administrators. As users take responsibility for more data entry, data preparation staff are devolved to the user departments, perhaps to be grouped in with other departmental clerical functions. Some data entry becomes invisible, or at least no longer the 'fault' of the IS function. As this drift continues it often seems that there is an equal replacement with data communication staff to support the distribution of the system. This can be regarded as a poor exchange given the relative employment costs of communications staff and data entry clerks! However, by making data independent of applications and designing data stores in a consistent way, systems arrive quicker and are more flexible. Grouping IS staff around data areas means that IS begins to communicate with its user community in those terms and there are the beginnings of a focus upon information *requirements* concerns (these must be addressed to define data structures). As users become increasingly involved, at least to the extent of being asked their data requirements, there is the first glimmering of users building IS awareness and skills. The contemporary form of this arrangement is the 'data warehouse' concerned with exploiting opportunities for innovative 'data mining' into very large scale stores. This form of arrangement is needed to support extensive use of executive information systems with their demands for fast data analysis. It is groups arranged in this form that are most likely to explore the organisational use of 'new' data paradigms such as object-based.

### 9.3.3 ◆ Functional project groups

The next generation of IS organisations to emerge combines analysts and programmers into business function-based project groupings, for instance the financial systems team and the production systems team. This is the first recognition of the business *purpose* of IS since it is the first instance of structuring the IS function around *demand* issues rather than *supply* mechanisms. The 'traditional' and data-driven structures group the IS staff by IS *internal* concerns with how the systems will be provided rather than why/to whom they will be for. The business groups are encouraged to build strong ties with their user community. Sometimes, as a further development, they are physically devolved into that user community creating departmental or divisional IS. When they have been so distributed, what remains is a small IS department concerned with the corporate databases and the infrastructure of hardware and software. This remnant is the corporate data centre. Since the functional project teams are focused upon system development and maintenance, operations will continue in the 'traditional' mould. (*See* Figure 9.9.)

Functional project teams are a form of matrix management and hence have all the difficulties associated with such ambiguous structures. Functional project groups can make it difficult to determine reporting responsibilities and career progression paths. Is the member of personnel's IS team a personnel person or an IS person? Does it in fact matter? It is this grouping of IS staff by business functions that, whilst it encouraged more business relevant systems during the 1980s, has also done much to build 'Chinese walls' between business areas. So it has led to barriers

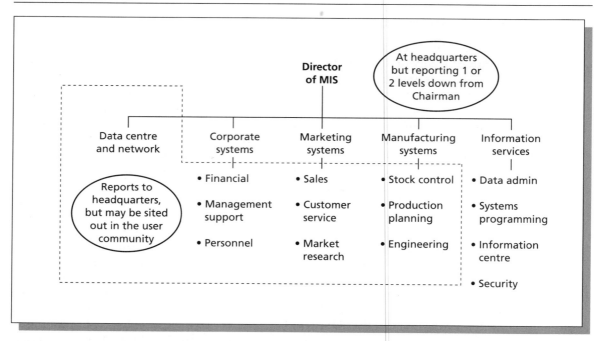

**Fig 9.9 ◆ Functional project group structure**

to the full information interchange so necessary to the business process clarification of the 1990s. Each team will have interpreted business events in different ways and so the island systems handle similar data items differently. An additional problem with this approach is that the uneven workloads may lead to marketing systems being developed for the sake of keeping that project team busy whilst other teams must postpone important developments because of heavy work loads.

This approach, however, did much to get users involved and doing things for themselves and, simultaneously, built far more business awareness (even if in limited areas) into the IS staff. Again the main advantage of this approach is the specialisation it supports, but this time it is a user-biased specialism. IS finally learns some of the language and concerns of its user community and the frustratingly slow learning period of each development is eased. The good relationships that can evolve are positive gains and lead to significant skills transfers.

These two-way skills transfers and exchanges led to major developments in hybrid management and user-controlled computing as discussed in Chapters 10 and 11. Both of these are important enough to form the thrust of chapters in their own right. The two-way skills transfer facilitated by functional project groups provided the *foundations* for the developments in user-controlled computing. Simultaneously, these developments made the next two structures *necessary*.

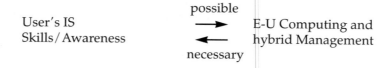

### 9.3.4 ◆ Information centres and decision support

In 1981 IBM marketed the notion of an information centre. Though the idea had been earlier mooted by a number of other firms (including ICL who called it a support centre which is probably a better title), IBM marketed the idea first. This way of organising one part of the IS resource is so widely used to support user-controlled computing that it will be discussed in some detail in Chapter 11. The detailed discussion of information centres is left until that chapter because, whilst user-controlled computing can *exist* without an information centre, an information centre has no *purpose* without such user-controlled computing.

Decision support oriented structures are very closely related to information centres. Decision support arrangements organise the IS function to support management decision making by users though not necessarily with those users controlling the nature of the systems. The IS function is no longer responsible only for the transaction processing systems of DP but for the MIS of *effective* IS use and management. The people within the IS resource are grouped to match the decisions being made by the enterprise itself. Often this will involve breaking down some of the barriers created by the functional project teams and their island systems! (*See* Figure 9.10.)

Both of these structures *aim* to support and encourage the developments of user-controlled computing and hybrid management and both of these developments *demand* the existence of IS resource arrangements such as these.

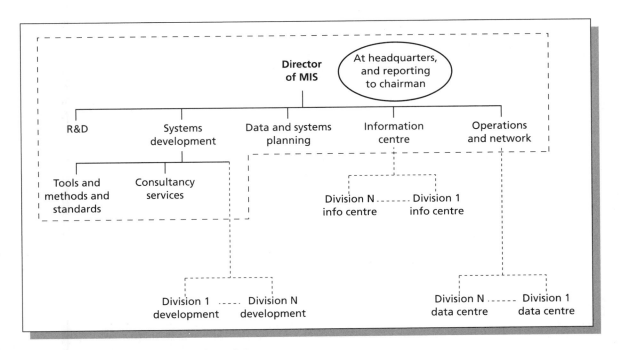

**Fig 9.10 ◆ User-oriented organisation of IS**

### 9.3.5 ◆ Externally focused

As we saw in Part 2, the competitive position of an organisation is essentially an *external* issue. This latest generation of IS structure focuses upon its environment and looks outside itself. This external orientation is through two aspects as illustrated in Figure 9.11. The function is structured around customer service lines to satisfy the business organisation that is the *immediate* environment of IS. IS groups reach service agreements with the user community and these 'contractual' agreements therefore define both IS' *obligations* and the business' perceptions of *value*. Service level agreements will be discussed in more detail in Chapter 12 since they form the fundamental tool in ensuring IS quality when IS provision is the responsibility of an outside agency. The second theme in external orientation is that IS must be externally focused in the same way that all of the organisation must be externally focused upon its 'true' *customers* (those of the organisation). This negates any perception that there is just a simplistic customer/supplier relationship between IS and the business community. IS often is the business and so there will be a two-way impact relationship: the wider business environment must affect IS and IS will affect the nature of business. The structure of IS must be consistent with the structure of the business and so groupings relate to the competitive issues of the enterprise and the business importance of the systems portfolio (*see* Chapters 5 and 6).

All the 'newer' structure arrangements are essentially about devolving autonomy to obtain shorter application development cycles, less prescriptive and more flexible systems that support effective business management in a more cost effective manner. In other words they address the disadvantages of the 'traditional' approach. They do this by distributing some aspects of the systems and their associated responsibilities for development, or acquisition, operation and control and maintenance. The IS resource, it is increasingly apparent, is not one homogeneous thing. The inherent variety therefore requires that different elements be structured in different ways to reflect their different focus.

The 'traditional' structure grouped staff by an IS function (it should be easy to recognise this since staff are grouped by job title) so all the analysts are collected together as are all the operations staff. But the nature of IS projects requires a mix of job titles collected into an IS *team*. So an organisation may adopt a project struc-

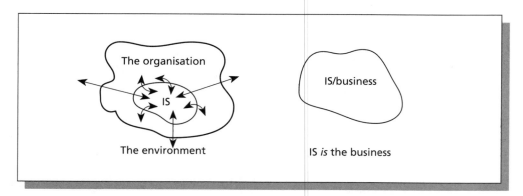

**Fig 9.11 ◆ Externally focused IS – the two aspects of the 'environment' for IS**

ture as the preferred way to make a mix of specialists collectively responsible for 'financial systems' or whatever. The problems then are that expensive and scarce skills cannot always be used efficiently, for instance perhaps the current project needs few network skills so the network specialist is under-employed. Since projects vary widely, the team membership can be very unstable. This instability can be managed by using externals around a core team of project managers but this approach does encourage either IS generalists or business specialism rather than IS specialism. Such encouragement can be to the detriment of the organisation's long-term needs, for instance structuring the IS resource by IS function eases the future process of developing standards and improves career paths.

Matrix management came about by superimposing project teams onto an underlying functional grouping. This added complexity and the 'two masters' problem. Conflict of interests between the two masters may arise where the functional manager wants efficient staff use, whilst the project manager wants project completion. The IS specialist areas are constantly shifting, for instance systems security is now a recognised area of expertise, which it was not in the past; similarly small system popularity coupled with automated application generation has merged the roles of analyst and programmer. So functional groups are complex and shifting, but project groups are also complex and shifting. They may be formed around the nature of the product, for instance office automation systems, or the destination of the project, for instance marketing. These teams may be based within the IS function or out in the user community.

It should be obvious that 'messiness' is inherent in 1990s IS structures, they are ill-defined and certainly going to change frequently. Zmud (1984) sums up the alternatives available and carefully works through the design alternatives for the internal structure of an IS resource. He identifies three different choices available for its management structure, two choices for the management process and two choices for the management co-ordination. IS may be structured on a functional basis as with the 'traditional' structure, on a product basis or on a matrix basis (as already discussed). The management processes of the IS resource may be either organic with high staff discretion and low task rules or mechanistic with low staff discretion and high task rules. The co-ordination within the IS resource may be either of a formal nature, well suited to predictable situations, or of an informal nature, well suited to handle uncertainty. From this 3:2:2 pattern of available alternatives, Zmud gives suggestions for the appropriate combination of structure, process and co-ordination arrangements for six example IS activities. These suggestions are illustrated in Figure 9.12.

Whatever structural alternative is selected it should be consistent with the stage of IS management maturity of the technology that it aims to support. For example, groupings identified as appropriate when the IS service must be organised to support management controls are unlikely to be appropriate to support the integration phase. Similarly, the business' *priorities* must be reflected in the IS structures; the early 1990s recession demanded an IS organised into cost-cutting teams and more and more of the IS resource became the responsibility of *other* organisations as outsource deals were used to reduce costs and make them more predictable. The appropriateness of any potential structure must be tested against the IS strategy since that defines the goals for IS and hence defines the objectives of the structural

*Choice continuum applies to:*

| Structure | Process | Co-ordination |
|-----------|---------|---------------|
| Functional | Mechanistic | Formal |
| Product | Organic | Informal |
| Matrix | | |

*Design suggestions are for:*

| IS Activity | Structure | Process | Co-ordination |
|-------------|-----------|---------|---------------|
| Systems development | Functional | Mechanistic, some organic | Informal, some formal |
| Technical services | Product, some functional | Mechanistic | Informal |
| Information centre | Functional/product | Organic | Informal |
| R&D | Product | Organic | Informal |
| Planning | Functional, some product | Organic | Informal (internal) Formal (external) |
| Administration | Function | Mechanistic | Formal |

**Fig 9.12 ◆ IS resource design alternatives**
(after Zmud)

choice. Tapscott and Caston (1993) point out that the 'new' IS (illustrated in Figure 9.13 on p. 337) is about business process re-aligning, open computing and an 'aligned' IS function. The selection of a *structure* for the IS resource is vital when engaged in business process redesign.

## 9.4 ◆ MATCHING IS RESOURCE TO BUSINESS COMMUNITY

Given the complex range of location and organisation possibilities, it is no surprise that it is a complex and uncertain matter to make choices about managing the IS resource. It is over simplistic to ask whether centralised or decentralised IS is *best*, and it is over-simplistic to ask whether traditional or externally focused arrangements are *best*, the choice is about:

- Is the IS resource in tune with the corporate strategy?
- Is the IS resource in tune with the organisational 'shape'?
- Is this element of the IS resource to be inward looking (focused upon managing the technology)?
- Is this element of the IS resource to be externally oriented (focused upon helping business plan the use of that technology)?

None of these questions indicate that IS should exactly mimic the functional business units, but rather that it should be *consistent* with them. The difficulty in having a goal that the IS resource should be consistent with the business community is the difficulty of knowing just what consistency means, never mind how to achieve it.

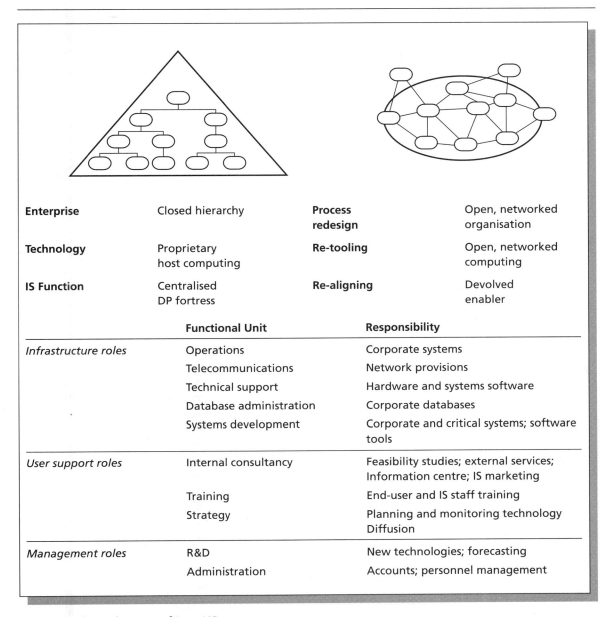

| Enterprise | Closed hierarchy | Process redesign | Open, networked organisation |
|---|---|---|---|
| Technology | Proprietary host computing | Re-tooling | Open, networked computing |
| IS Function | Centralised DP fortress | Re-aligning | Devolved enabler |

| | Functional Unit | Responsibility |
|---|---|---|
| *Infrastructure roles* | Operations | Corporate systems |
| | Telecommunications | Network provisions |
| | Technical support | Hardware and systems software |
| | Database administration | Corporate databases |
| | Systems development | Corporate and critical systems; software tools |
| *User support roles* | Internal consultancy | Feasibility studies; external services; Information centre; IS marketing |
| | Training | End-user and IS staff training |
| | Strategy | Planning and monitoring technology Diffusion |
| *Management roles* | R&D | New technologies; forecasting |
| | Administration | Accounts; personnel management |

**Fig 9.13 ◆ Three elements of 'new' IS**
(after Tapscott and Caston)

A decision must be taken on what aspect, or aspects, of the organisation the IS resource will be 'matched' to. Will it be the *structure* of the organisation that is taken as the reference point (the focus of most of the literature to date and of this section)? However, one implication of the emergence of various forms of new organisational thinking explored in Chapter 8 is that there may be other, more useful, ways of viewing any situation. Perhaps the IS resource location and structure choices should be made with reference to, for instance:

- The organisation's *risk attitude*: organisations that are risk averse may be well matched by formalised arrangements more centrally located.
- The organisation's *change capability*: those organisations that have espoused the notions of the 'learning organisation' may be well matched by extremely devolved arrangements.

Similarly other aspects of the organisation could be used, for example its product line, the *type* of IS services it focuses on (all transaction processing systems, lots of decision support tools or whatever), the degree of coherence in the company culture, etc, etc. Any, or all, of these aspects may be 'matched' to. Chapter 8, of course, also implies that the IS resource management approaches are part of the creation process of the organisation. The IS resource shapes the business community just as the nature of the technology shapes the organisation, *see* for instance Leijer (1989). The conflicting pressures towards each IS resource location possibility as seen from the pressure to match to control issues are illustrated in Figure 9.14.

In most organisations (and in much IS literature) any discussion of *how* to organise the IS resource is inextricably rolled up with the discussion of *where* to locate it. The reason for this is that the logical distinctions between the siting and control and groupings explored in this chapter so far are inevitably messily confused 'on the ground'. In such discussions the term 'centralised' is used to symbolise a whole ethos of IS provision that encompasses all aspects of its relationships and responsibilities. The organisation therefore 'sees' the IS resource arrangement primarily in terms of where it is located.

Harrington (1991) presents an interesting perspective upon the issue of the IS function's location. He suggests that it is a 'conventional perception' that the IS function must manifest itself as an IS *department*. He suggests that it is this conven-

| Pressure for devolved control | Pressure for centralised control |
|---|---|
| Availability of relatively low cost technology that permits user-developed applications where previously centralised servicing was needed, this opens up applications to the user. | Technical competence of research is needed and since resources are all in one location can specialise and develop expertise in a way not economically feasible when decentralised. |
| Backlog of development work and centralised resources can no longer meet the increasing demand or is unresponsive to such demand. | Central body control over data accessibility, integrity, and security is necessary. |
| Direct control over operation increases experience and confidence to develop, implement, and maintain own systems more quickly and easily than centralised. | May be comparatively cheaper when the cost of communications and staff recruitment and training for the alternatives are considered. |
| Local control of resources is a symbol of local competence in the ability to manage one's own affairs. | Information resources easier to control and so facilitates shared knowledge. |
| Maintaining dispersed computing resources lessens the risk of total systems failure and so the susceptibility to natural and human hazards is lessened. | Dispersing equipment and resources may increase or decrease costs depending upon resources deployed. |

Fig 9.14 ◆ Pressures for location alternatives

tional perception of IS that drives the continuing divide between business and IS and the continuing survival of a separate IS provision. Perhaps it is the difficulty in changing such perceptions that drives the yo-yo of changing location and it is an interesting survival of such perceptions that insists that centralisation is for cost saving and decentralisation is for greater flexibility and so effectiveness. This is based upon Grosch's Law (1953) which demonstrates that there are real economies in large-scale IS – thus providing a powerful force in favour of centralisation in organisations that seek to make cost savings. However, more recent work by Mendelson (1987) has demonstrated that this does not hold true when PCs are considered. This means that centralisation = economies of scale may be a conventional perception rather than a 'truth'. The implication of this is that the selection process can recognise the straight line and consider issues *other* than economies. A range of issues that might influence the structural design were presented by Burch *et al.* (1983) and these influencing factors are shown in Figure 9.15. The nature, use and management of user-controlled computing is covered in Chapter 10.

Dearden (1987) is exploring the reality of this perception when he challenges the myths surrounding the dangers of devolution. He argues that the 'single integrated system is best' perception does not stand up to scrutiny of its value in terms of the real need for shared on-line data. This would seem to argue against centralisation and for devolution. Further, it argues for *total* devolution and Dearden is very persuasive about the demise of the internal IS function. He argues that all management logic favours devolution and this powerful logic could only be overturned when perceived economies of scale were even more powerful, and this is no longer the case. While Dearden does not use the term 'outsourcing' (preferring to refer to software companies) his work points that way. The conventional perception of devolution equating to flexibility may be as ill-founded as price per MIPS economies of scale perceptions. The difficulty of cross-divisional transfers that business process redesign often encounters in very devolved environments highlights the dangers of Chinese wall systems frequently created under such conditions.

| Centralised structure | Hybrid structure | Distributed structure |
|---|---|---|
| Local | ← Organisational nature → | Multinational |
| Single product | ← → | Multiproducts |
| Similar operations | ← → | Diverse operations |
| Small organisations | ← Organisational size → | Large organisation |
| Monolithic organisation | ← Organisational structure → | Organisation with well-defined subunits |
| Centralised management philosophy | Management style ← → | Decentralised management philosophy |
| Autocratic approach | ← → | Motivation approach |
| Theory X | ← → | Theory Y |

**Fig 9.15 ◆ Influential factors in structural design**
(adapted by permission from Burch *et al.*)

There is no simple choice to be made on IS management arrangements and nor can most organisations simply adopt one or the other, rather they must now select a complex mix of approaches, chosen so that the location choices (centre ↔ periphery, as summarised in Figure 9.16) relate to the benefit of economy versus the benefit of responsiveness, and the chosen internal organisation accentuates that. The choice needs to balance autocracy with anarchy. In reality, the balance between the two extremes of centralised and devolved is a political and not a rational one. Awareness of the 'sensible' stance does not mean it will happen! Excessive use of either end of the continuum produces a nightmarish mismatch to the organisational structure. The culture and history of the organisation must be matched for there to be strategic 'fit'. Organisations frequently need decentralisation within a framework of principles and guidelines, and this is easier said than done!

So what decisions are taken? There seems to be universal agreement that there is no instance of any form in its 'pure' state, see for example Edwards *et al* in Galliers and Baker (1994), Kelly (1996), Behrsin (1994) and Morison in Gray *et al.* (1994). Three examples of decisions taken are given in Figure 9.17. There is as yet little work done to explore just why and from what background such decisions emerge. One exception is from Brown and Magill (1994) who investigate what combination of features of organisational history (both IS and business-based) lead to particular IS resource arrangements. They also reinforce the point made earlier in this section that no choice alternative is *always good* or *always bad*. Their findings imply that it is the combination and interaction of factors that lead to particular IS resource management decisions occurring. Their findings also imply that it is the interplay between them that makes for an IS resource that is either well matched or mismatched to the organisation.

|  | Benefits | Difficulties/problems |
|---|---|---|
| *Centralised* | Ability to achieve and control consistent strategy | Failure to achieve response to local conditions |
|  | Co-ordination of activities | Difficulties in developing general management capabilities |
|  | Simpler control systems | |
|  | Allocation of resources facilitated | Cumbersome and costly central overhead |
|  | Speedier strategic decision making | |
| *Non-centralised* | Rapid response to specific or local problems | Definition of split of operational and strategic responsibilities |
|  | Improved motivation/commitment | Failure to devolve power of decision making resulting in lengthly referral processes and delayed decisions |
|  | Factorises decision making when complexity is too great to be dealt with at apex of organisation | |
|  |  | Frustrated management |
|  |  | Complicated control procedures |

Fig 9.16 ◆ Centralisation *v* non-centralisation

January 1992: County councils not to devolve IS to districts because of the wasteful duplication and potential for confusion. Smaller groups could not cope with the move to competitive tendering. This is in condemnation of the trend for many districts to take control of their own IS destinies from their county councils. Districts have shown classic customer ignorance: 'it is only taking place because districts want to have more control'. The problem of standards was highlighted in the Cooper and Lybrand Deloitte report.

The Information Technology arm of the Post Office, called iT, is a business in its own right, with its own managing director. Provides, as a commercial IT supplier, the technology infrastructure for the four core businesses of the Post Office. But it also has to contribute to provide strategy advice. So iT manages the database and the networks and assists the Business Systems Managers of the Post Office businesses to develop their IS plans. The profit centre approach forced the IS staff to address customer satisfaction issues and forced the Business Systems Managers to learn how to express their needs. So IS copes with real commercial issues, such as value for money, customer focus and total quality. And has to ask questions such as:

- who is my customer?
- who benefits if I suggest an enhancement?

The AA is an illustration of the centralised control of IS functions; since the business has a corporate centre, an IS data centre forms part of that, spending £1 million per week on IT. However business and IS strategies are the province of the business units. This corporate data centre provides the corporate software house, and competes with outsiders as well. The in-house software must be able to beat the open market on price, quality and speed or be disbanded. This data centre has some significant advantages: it does not need a sales force, it can have a simpler tendering process, and it has an intimate knowledge of the business already. These advantages should mean that it is able to beat all comers.

**Fig 9.17 ◆ IS resource management arrangements actually chosen**

The complexities of current IS demands means that most organisations will adopt a mixture of arrangements, *see* Morison in Gray (1994) and Edwards *et al.* in Galliers and Baker (1994). They will accommodate a mix of decentralised groups and several shifting and differentially shaped central groups internally arranged to provide various services, for example one group to manage the infrastructure operations, another responsible for a strategic review, yet another for vendor contract management, and so on. The findings of Brown and Magill (1994) were also that hybrid arrangements are now the norm. This hybrid mixture is often called a federal arrangement, as by Edwards *et al.* and by Behrsin (1994). Any combination that includes any significant element of 'true' devolved IS (that is where autonomy is distributed) can be thought of as federal since power is not being exercised from the centre outwards, but rather in *combination* between a federation of local and central governance groups. The notion of rightsizing of the early 1990s was primarily concerned with the choice of IS infrastructural platform scale (the late 1980s being the first time *real* choice of different scale platforms became possible). This has given way to a concern with what Behrsin calls 'right powering' as real alternatives in IS governance becomes possible and Chapter 11 explores the issues of overall organisational management of direct IS governance by IS non-professionals. Trimmer (1993) for instance, despite being entitled 'Downsizing' and providing extensive coverage of technological infrastructural issues, surfaces a large number of 'right powering' concerns such as in security or in the notion of the systems 'proprietor'.

One final point about choosing IS resource arrangements is that the complexity of issues to be considered when deciding the location of IS means that it will often become appropriate to *move* IS, particularly as there is a tendency for organisations to yo-yo between centralised and decentralised provision. As well as the organisational and managerial discontinuities this will lead to, the implication is that the IS resource *physically* moves. Given that the IS resource provides the IT infrastructure for the organisation, moving it is no small problem. This is such a major issue that specialist IS relocation companies exist to oversee the whole event. Relocation management may be one of the services provided by outsourcing agencies. The news reported in Kelly (1996) of the split up of the IS function at the National Westminster Bank, formerly the largest IS function in the UK, into a mixture of teams with different accountabilities brings home the uncertainties, the timing and strategic difficulties of changing IS resource groupings. Generally the approaches revolve around all-at-once or phased moves but whilst a move *away* from the centre readily lends itself to moving in stages, a move *towards* the centre is more likely to be the higher-stress, all-in-one-go option. Relocation may be a choice to deal with the need to make significant cost savings in the central data centre.

### 9.4.1 ◆ Symptoms of structural fit

If an organisation does adopt an *appropriate* location then such a structure should offer the following benefits, namely it will:

- Enable rapid development of systems
- Ensure that the IS function and the business operations work in harmony
- Enable IS to provide a tailored service to the user community
- Be cost effective
- Support the developments of technology infrastructures
- Minimise redundancy or oversights of developments
- Link IS success to business success and so link staff goals and rewards to business success
- Allow the business community, who understand the changes needed, to have an optimised participation in the change of IS services
- Enable the organisation to pursue leading-edge or centrally planned IS strategies
- Allow IS human resource management
- Encourage the user-driven construction of software from reusable 'parts'
- Enable the assessment of IS costs/business gains

Throughout his book O'Brien (1992) raises some thought-provoking and unusual ways to consider issues associated with the formulation of IS strategies. One important point that he makes is that the selection of any particular way to *organise* the IS function will pre-determine the nature of many of the IS *decisions*. The IS structure is not only a matter of implementing an IS strategy; IS structure creates the organisational environment that fosters a particular IS-Business interaction. The nature of that interaction fundamentally shapes perceptions of the opportunities to exploit IS. When sections of the business must compete for a share of the IS budget quite different decisions are made than when market forces are allowed to prevail totally. The choice of organisation for the IS-Business interaction is a meta-strategic issue since it shapes the strategy. Whatever approach is selected it should form a coherent *whole*. O'Brien suggests that there are six items to get right when selecting an IS location:

- Regard the relationship between IS and the business as the environment that affects *all* other decisions and so is a strategic decision is its own right
- Regard this environment as a whole which must have underlying principles; it must not be a piecemeal creation
- Determine the underlying principles as part of the IS strategy: all detail should flow naturally from these
- Consider the two extremes of IS, that is mirroring the business organisation with the IS organisation, or adopting a separatist pseudo (or actual) commercial approach to IS services
- Do not let the environment 'emerge' – select it, otherwise it will be incoherent and inconsistent
- Ensure the environment for IS-Business interaction is consistent with other facets of the IS strategy and its implementation.

## 9.4.2 ◆ Symptoms of structural misfit

When an IS structure is inappropriate for the organisation, its strategies or IS goals, there are a number of typically associated symptoms. The signs that there is a mismatch are:

- *Continual conflict*: When there is continuous and ongoing conflicts between IS and its user community over the roles, responsibilities and control authority for some or all aspects of the IS service provision then this is likely to be an indicator that the currently adopted structure is inappropriate.
- *Continual complaints about IS*: When there are continual complaints from the other two elements of the MIS triad (*see* Chapter 3) about the performance of IS then this is an obvious symptom of structural mismatch. The user community may complain about slow IS responses whilst senior management may complain about high cost/low business gain. Not only is this a symptom of structural mismatch but also of communication problems, what Grindley (1992) calls the 'culture gap'.
- *Competitive decline*: When the organisation is completely disadvantaged it may be because the IS service provision is so structured that it *cannot* respond to competitive thrusts.
- *Lack of interest in IS*: This is not a situation of conflict. When all is quiet within the organisation because of senior management and user community disinterest in (or ignorance of) IS opportunities it may be because IS structures have throttled all healthy interest – IS is off the debate agenda. This symptom is unlikely to be spotted except when IS service is tightly controlled by the centralised IS department.
- *Skills problems*: If the availability and location of IS skills is a cause for complaint then it is probable that the IS service structures do not gather the people necessary or locate them where they are needed. A classic symptom of this is an IS structure that has many structured programmes in the centralised service and

yet needed developments at the business interface are under-resourced with end-user development facilitators and network expertise.

- *High staff turnover*: This symptom can mean many things (and may not always be a problem, for instance when skills demands are changing) but one cause is the professional dissatisfaction resulting from inappropriate structures generating conflicts and not generating successes.

- *Gaps and overlaps*: Where there is significant overlapping, or redundant, developments and yet large business gaps this is a clear symptom of poor match between IS goals and IS structures.

This situation is unlikely to happen all at once. One of the capabilities that IS must embody is that of being able to monitor the effectiveness of its 'fit' with the organisation. It can be very difficult to notice a gradual deterioration from a previous good match. It is even more difficult to notice that there has *never* been a good fit. It may be possible to identify danger signs, and therefore presumably improve the fit. These three layers of *cumulative* danger signs, or 'stages of descent', Vowler (1996) identifies as:

- When the IS function has an arm's length relationship with the business. Visible when IS has to compete with external providers for IS service to business-based IS service buyers. The relationship will be entirely formal and monitored through rigid service level agreements. The nature of this stage is such that it barriers communication.

- When relationships become strained. Visible through increasing battles over IS costs; outsourcing is used as a threat and a culture of blame pervades both communities (and they very much are two groups with objectives that differ).

- When relationships break down completely. Visible through major project failures, business managers aggressively looking for alternative sources of IS services, proclaiming they receive no support from IS and IS senior management is deposed.

It is hoped that by consciously formulating IS strategy that specific IS resource management decisions will match business strategy (*see* Chapters 6 and 7), and that by understanding the nature of user-controlled IS (*see* Chapter 11) and the complexity of service provision (*see* Chapter 12) then these 'stages of descent' will never happen.

## 9.4.3 ◆ Ownership of data controversy

Very closely related to the issue of where the components of the IS function should be sited and who should control them is the issue of how the organisation perceives 'ownership of data'. How is the responsibility for, and authority over, data within the organisation viewed?

There are real data ownership problems associated with both ends of the location continuum. With centralised locations the value of data is well recognised, it is guarded, protected, but often to the detriment of accessibility. However, business runs on information not data. Devolved locations by contrast have their own problems. Some sense of responsibility must exist and yet that responsibility must be to furthering the wider applicability of information use not personal power issues.

Data is a corporate and not a parochial asset. Central IS may be the guardian of data security and integrity but that does not mean draconian restrictions on data use. Devolved IS has an obligation to ensure that data guidelines are adhered to for the greater competitive 'safety' of all. The commonest analogies in this area are to the rules of the road. No one owns the road – all are made safe in their use of the road system by virtue of the rules that are adhered to.

Ownership of data is often the last battleground for an embittered IS that feels it is fighting devolution. It may feel that any significant role it had has been eroded and so fight on the dubious ground that it must own corporate data. This is a non-sense – even with devolved IS siting, the IS strategy development, the IS infrastructure management, and IS consultancy are more important than ever and are properly the role of corporate IS.

Regardless of where IS is located, perceptions of ownership may be an issue. The centralised structures of IS services will tend to lead to a situation where that IS service sees itself as the 'owner' of all the organisation's data as it is responsible for its servicing. The non-centralised structures will, conversely, tend to lead to a situation where individual business units consider they 'own' their own section of the data as illustrated in Figure 9.18.

Both of these situations are detrimental to a more desirable view of data as a corporate resource out of which corporate information can be crafted, and hence these default situations must be addressed in order to gain or retain information as a corporate asset. If data is caught in what Dance (1994) calls 'Data Pools' that are created by the shape of the organisation structure, then only if there is the adoption of what Christoff (1990) calls 'stewardship' rather than ownership will data be able to flow out of the constraints formed by these pools.

Whilst the devolved view brings data ownership into the business which is desirable, it fragments the data, which is not desirable and particularly acts as a barrier to the initiatives of co-ordinating and integrating information along the value chain. The critical distinction made between computer (or technology) management and information management comes into play here. During the computer management stages, the organisation has a technical focus upon the vehicle and not the product, this makes it most unlikely that information *can* be viewed as a *resource*. Once the critical divide has been crossed the focus shifts towards the product and away from the vehicle. So during computer management (stages 1, 2 and 3

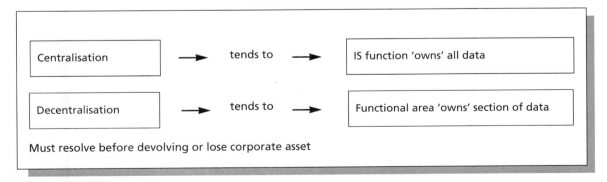

**Fig 9.18 ◆ Ownership of data**

on Nolan's model, *see* Section 5.6.1) IS or business functions can, and do, own data but during more advanced, information management, stages this view is most inappropriate since, as the name implies, the organisation needs to manage, not own, data in order to gain the corporate resource, information. Of course, this point about appreciating that operating for local goals (data ownership) will often be to the detriment of the whole (information use) is precisely the point that systems thinking and the notion of the learning organisation address (*see* Section 8.6).

### 9.4.4 ◆ Related issues

Related to the issue of structure and siting alternatives for the IS *resource* is the notion of charging (or otherwise) for IS *services*. Internal charging, also known as chargeback, transfer pricing, or cost recovery, is explored in Chapter 12 since it obviously relates to the overhead and direct costs in acquiring systems resources. The charging techniques, management issues for consideration, and the objectives of the charging systems relate to the IS structure and siting since different elements of IS, located under a different control regime, must be accorded differential treatment.

An additional, closely related issue is that of measuring IS service performance. An evaluation of the appropriateness of the IS structures is very much part of the process of implementing (and indeed generating) the IS strategy. Such IS assessment measures might include measures of:

- Performance metrics (such as network down-time)
- Development productivity metrics (such as speed of development)
- User satisfaction metrics (such as perceived contribution to business)
- User support metrics (such as hot line response times)
- Organisational health metrics (such as responsiveness to further change)

Sometimes the drive towards organising as a service entity is going to be contradicted by service concerns since it can be very difficult to find where service is needed, judge its quality, and provide it in a very devolved environment. Performance measurement was considered more fully in Chapter 7 and service assessment will be considered more fully in Chapter 12.

**References and further reading**

Ahituv, N. and Neumann, S. (1990) *Principles of Information Systems for Management* (3rd edn), W.C. Brown.

Ahituv, N., Neumann, S. and Sviran, M. (1989) Factors Affecting the Policy for Distributing Computer Resources, *MIS Quarterly*, Dec pp. 389–96.

Angell, I.O. and Smithson, S. (1991) *Information Systems Management: Opportunities and Risks*, Macmillan.

Anon. (1992) County Councils Receive IT Vote, *Computing*, 13 Feb.

Aylott, B. (1993) Managing Distributed Systems, *IT Matters*, No 9 Winter, pp. 14–16.

Bacon, C.J. (1990) Organizational Principles of Systems Decentralization, *Journal of Information Technology*, No 5 pp. 84–93.

Behrsin, M. (1994) *Reshaping IT for Business Flexibility*, McGraw-Hill.

Brown, C. and Magill, S. (1994) Alignment of the IS Functions with the Enterprise: Towards a Model of Antecedents, *MIS Quarterly*, Dec pp. 377–403.

Burch, Strater and Grudnitski (1983) *Information Systems: Theory and Practice*, Wiley.

Carlyle, R. (1990a) The Tomorrow Organisation, *Datamation*, 1 Feb pp. 22–9.

Carlyle, R. (1990b) Why Consolidation Makes Sense, *Datamation*, 15 Apr pp. 24–9.

Cash, J., McFarlan, F., McKenney, J. and Applegate, L. (1992) *Corporate Information Systems Management* (2nd edn), Irwin.

Cerullo, M.J. and Cerullo, V. (1989) Approaches to Organising Computer Facilities, *Information Age*, Vol II No 3 pp. 165–70.

Christoff, K. (1990) *Managing the Information Center*, Scott Foresman/Little Brown.

Clark, T.D. (1992) Corporate Systems Management: An Overview and Research Perspective, *Communications of the ACM*, Vol 35 No 2 pp. 61–75.

Dance, S. (1994) *Inforpreneurs, The Hidden People Who Drive Strategic Information Systems*, Macmillan.

Davis, D.B. (1990) IS Automates for Data Center Survival, *Datamation*, Vol 36 No 22 pp. 95–8.

Dearden, J. (1987) The Withering Away of the IS Organisation, *Sloan Management Review*, Summer.

Earl, M.J. (1989) *Management Strategies for Information Technology*, Prentice-Hall.

Edwards, B., Earl, M. and Feeny, D. (1994) Any Way Out of the Labyrinth for Managing Information Systems, in Galliers, R. and Baker, B. (1994) *Strategic Information Management*, Butterworth-Heinemann.

Fay, J. (1993) On the Road Again, *Personal Computer Magazine*, Jan pp. 137–45.

Galliers, R. and Baker, B. (1994) *Strategic Information Management*, Butterworth-Heinemann.

Gray, P., King, W., McLean, E. and Watson, H. (Eds.) (1994) *Management of Information Systems*, Dryden Press.

Green-Armytage, J. (Ed.) (1995) The Place of IT in Corporate Transformation, *Computer Weekly*, 16 Feb p. 18.

Grindley, K. (1992) Information Systems Issues Facing Senior Executives: The Culture Gap, *Journal of Strategic Information Systems*, Vol 1 No 2 pp. 57–62.

Grosch, H.R.J. (1972) High Speed Arithmetic: The Digital Computer as a Research Tool, *Journal of Opt Society America*, Apr pp. 306–10.

Harrington, J. (1991) *Organisational Structure and IT*, Prentice-Hall.

Hayward, D. (1995) Facing the Firing Squad, *Computing*, 2 Nov pp. 36–7.

Hayward, D. (1996) Rough Justice? *Computing*, 8 Aug pp. 22–3.

Hussain, D.S. and Hussain, K.M. (1992) *Information Management: Organisation, Management and Control of Computer Processing*, Prentice-Hall.

Jones, R. (1989) Time to Change the Culture for Information Systems Departments, *Information and Software Technology*, Vol 31 No 2 pp. 99–104.

Kelly, S. (1996) Doing the Splits, *Computer Weekly*, 22 Feb p. 16.

King, J.L. (1983) Centralised versus Decentralised Computing: Organisational Considerations and Management Options, *Computing Surveys*, Vol 15 No 4 pp. 319–49.

La Belle, A. and Nyce, H.E. (1987) Whither the IT Organisation, *Sloan Management Review*, Summer.

Lemming, A. (1990) Creating a Business-oriented IT Department, *Journal of Information Technology*, Vol 5 pp. 175–7.

Leijer, R. (1989) Matching Computer-Based Information Systems with Organizational Structures, *MIS Quarterly*, Vol 12 No 4 pp. 537–49.

Lodahl, T.M. and Redditt, K.L. (1989) Aiming IS at Business Targets, *Datamation*, 15 Feb.

McKiernan, P. and Merali, Y. (1995) Integrating Information Systems after a Merger, *Long Range Planning*, Vol 28 No 4 pp. 54–62.

Maglitta, J. and Mehler, M. (1992) The New Centralisation, *Computerworld*, 27 Apr pp. 85–7.

Martin, D. (1992) Discovering that Less Means More, *Computing*, 26 Mar.

Massey, J. (1991) Together Forever, *Personal Computer Magazine*, Feb pp. 64–71.

Meikljohn, I. (1989) New Forms for a New Age, *Management Today*, May pp. 163–6.

Mendelson, H. (1987) Economies of Scale in Computing: Grosh's Law Revisited, *Communications of the ACM*, Vol 30 No 12 pp. 1066–72.

Nonnenberg, K. (1990) The Changing Role of Support Providers in the Data Center, *Datacenter Manager*, Vol 2 Sep/Oct pp. 14–15.

O'Brien, B. (1992) *Demands and Decisions: Briefing on Issues in Information Technology Strategy*, Prentice-Hall.

O'Brien, J.A. and Morgan, J.N. (1991) A Multi-dimensional Model of Information Resource Management, *Information Resources Management*, Vol 2 No 2 pp. 2–12.

Parker, C.M. (1990) Developing an Information Systems Architecture: Changing How Data Resource Managers Think about Systems Planning, *Data Resource Management*, Vol 1 pp. 5–11.

Peters ,T.J. and Waterman, R.H. (1982) *In Search of Excellence*, Harper and Row.

Radding, A. (1991) Improve It or Loose It, *Computerworld*, Vol 25 No 19 pp. 71–4.

Ring, T. (1991) The Balance of Power, *Which Computer?* Vol 14 No 2 pp. 42–52.

Saran, C. (1996) Muddle at the top over IT's role, *PC Week*, 4 June p. 4.

Silk, D.J. (1991) *Planning IT: Creating an Information Management Strategy*, Butterworth-Heinemann.

Strassmann, P. (1995) *The Politics of Information Management*, Information Economics Press.

Sullivan-Trainor, M. (1989) Changing the Fixtures in the House that IS Built, *Computerworld*, 24 July pp. 51–60.

Tapscott, D. and Caston, A. (1993) *Paradigm Shift: The New Promise of Information Technology*, McGraw-Hill.

Trimmer, D. (1993) *Downsizing: Strategies for Success in the Modern Computer World*, Addison-Wesley.

von Simpson, E.M. (1990) The 'Centrally Decentralised IS Organisation, *Harvard Business Review*, July-Aug pp. 158–62.

Vowler, J. (1993) IT Success Flies in the Face of American Airlines' Losses, *Computer Weekly*, 25 Feb p. 2.

Vowler, J. (1996) In the Ring of Confidence, *Computer Weekly*, 9 May p. 24.

Watkins, S. (1992) Council IT Arms Short of Muscle, *Computing*, 9 July.

Zmud, R.W. (1984) Design Alternatives for Organising Information Systems Activities, *MIS Quarterly*, Vol 8 No 2 pp. 79–93.

# CHAPTER 10

# IS management and the IS profession

As with IS resource structures and arrangements, organisations adopt many alternative approaches to who to make responsible for IS management and in this chapter the variety of IS management styles are explored. In Chapter 6 some pointers to management style were given by conducting a systems portfolio analysis. In this chapter these alternatives and possible reporting hierarchies are explored further. Similarly, the convergence of disparate technologies mentioned in previous chapters is now considered from the perspective of its association of activity, technology, and management role and title.

The focus of this chapter is upon the 'IS Manager' with a discussion of changes in experience, education, required skills, responsibilities, and loyalty profiles and how these changes relate to approaches to IS resource structure, siting, user-controlled computing and the nature of the IS profession. The variety of roles and titles of an 'IS Manager' in a 'mature' organisation are therefore explored along with key issues and tasks facing such a manager. Once the organisational structure of IS has evolved to the point that it encompasses the multiple forms discussed in Chapter 9, what will IS management involve, who will be involved in it? This chapter looks at two key IS management dimensions:

- The role and nature of IS management
- The key IS management issues and tasks

The nature of IS management is very tightly related to the topics of the previous and next chapters since the structure and location of IS and the organisational response to the alternatives posed by user-controlled computing significantly affect the nature of IS management.

The increasingly external focus of the IS resource creates an additional issue, that of 'hybrid managers'. What this term might mean is discussed in some detail since readers of this text will often be destined to become part of such management developments. Some definitions and examples of hybrid management are provided. Such hybrid *managers* must be contrasted with hybrid *users* and 'traditional' DP management. Whilst readers on first degree programmes are likely to find themselves, at least initially, categorised as either hybrid users or members of an IT management team, in other words single dimension managers, those on postgraduate or post-experience programmes may quickly become part of hybrid management developments.

Some of the potential advantages and problems associated with hybrid management are explored along with a discussion of approaches to developing hybrid managers considered from the perspective of the organisation and of the individual. This discussion includes considering the problems of developing multiple skill strands. The final section of this chapter will discuss just what all this means for any notion of an IS profession

## 10.1 ◆ THE ROLE AND NATURE OF IS MANAGERS

In today's world of organisational dependence upon IS it is certain that the most senior IS manager is at a position in the management hierarchy far higher than would ever have been held by a 'DP Manager' of old. The significance of information, and hence issues relating to information systems and information services, is now so widely recognised that many organisations recognise the value of an Information, or Information Systems, Director. Kelly (1996) indicates that, whilst in 1995 only just over one third of organisations (37 per cent) had the most senior IS responsibility at Board-level, by 2000 half will have Board-level IS representation. The integration of information issues with all aspects of business can be fully achieved only when information issues are debated as part of the mainstream business agenda and *not* just at a specialist, technical level under a distinct 'add on' agenda item. Conversely, it is equally certain that the IS service manager is wrestling with ever-increasing technical complexities, Green-Armytage (1995). The rank and title of the senior information job will have changed and it is increasingly rare for organisations to perceive IS as reporting directly through other support functions, since IS cuts across the entire business to form the glue holding the organisation together. Figure 10.1 shows a possible placing of the IS Director. In the US this same managerial function is usually referred to as the Chief Information Officer (CIO). However, despite this independent status Financial Directors may still take a strong hand in making IS decisions, *see* Bradbury (1995).

With the changing role and concerns of the IS function comes a comparable set of changes in IS *management*. The traditional DP Manager has disappeared, replaced by a complex *set* of managers. The IS function is still 'managed' but the nature of that management has radically altered over the past decade. The convergence of technologies means that corporate information systems require someone responsible for a wider range of technical issues as the distinction between computing, factory automation, telecommunications and office automation blurs. Data centre management will be complemented by many other managers responsible for information centres and departmental, work group and personal IS.

The IS Director must take a role that is more concerned with information and information systems strategy than with information technology minutiae. The IS Director may actually hold a title such as Information Manager, Information Services Manager, Information Director, etc, but to avoid confusion in this section the term IS Director is taken to mean the most senior manager with specific *information* responsibility. The experience, educational background and skills profile of such an IS Director has evolved, in parallel with the generations of organisational structures for IS, from the technical bias of such a manager of the 1950s. The findings of a number of surveys, for instance Hershey and Eatman (1990), clearly show

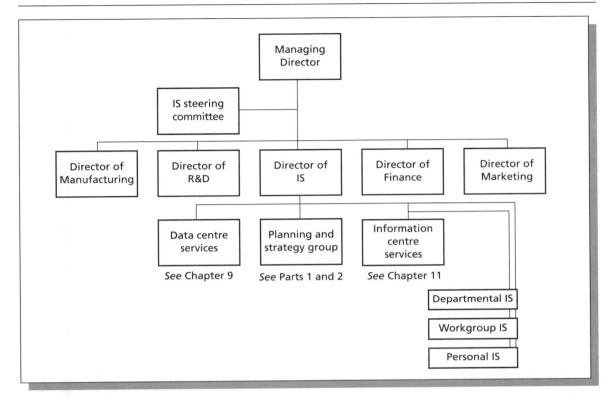

**Fig 10.1 ◆ Reporting hierarchy of IS director**

that the given title is largely irrelevant to what the senior IS Manager does and is responsible for, though just as clearly the title matters to the person holding it! The sort of person needed to fill these shoes can be seen from Figure 10.2.

The evolution of IS management is driven by the recognition of information as a company-wide asset and hence the management of information becomes the job of *every* manager whilst the management of IS is a pan-organisational issue. The increasingly external focus of IS *demands* the existence of business-literate IS managers, sometimes considered to be the hybrid manager. It is the business acumen of such hybrid managers that ensures the existence of business-consistent IS strategies that can be implemented effectively. It is no longer appropriate for an IS Director to be solely a computer specialist if it ever was (though managers of some services responsible for certain aspects of operational management may be). This evolution is shown in Figure 10.3.

This IS Director will co-ordinate the activities of the technically skilled managers responsible for infrastructure elements plus the hybrid skilled managers involved in line management roles. The IS Director is therefore fundamentally involved in mainstream business activities *using* different managers with different management styles as different business demands dictate. Figures 10.1 and 10.2 indicate just some of the complexity of the *visible* aspects of IS that such an IS Director may be responsible for. The fact that some of the services indicated may be supplied by *external* service providers drives another critical demand for hybrid managers. The

The IS Director will establish policies, standards and procedures for information, information systems, and information services even when elements are geographically and functionally distributed. They will collaborate with other senior managers to ensure the most effective use of information. Although the IS Director will provide central management, he or she must be prepared to share power with managers and supervisors who control information at functional levels. The distribution of information technology and control depends upon the culture and structure of the specific section of the organisation. The IS Director will continue to integrate technology to meet business and information needs of both senior managers and users. Towards this end, the Director should direct the necessary educational and training activities to maintain a state-of-the-art posture. For example, current information concerning user-controlled computing, software management, telecommunications, electronic filing, and information resource management should be provided to decision makers at all levels within the organisation.

The IS Director must maintain a broad corporate perspective and a leadership role to manage information as an organisational resource. To establish the importance of the IS Director's position, users and managers regard information as a valuable corporate resource to be managed as an integrated entity. In addition, the IS Director will have some duties common to directors of traditional data processing or computer centres and such areas of responsibility include personnel practices, salary matters, administration of hardware resources, and selection criteria for application software development. The IS Director must ensure that the centralised information services function provides consulting services to the operating divisions and functions as appropriate, that is information experts should be available to educate and answer queries.

The IS Director will contribute part of their knowledge to the professional society as well as to society as a whole. Active participation in professional bodies will be required and should entail more than just paying membership fees or attending an occasional meeting. The chosen Director will offer service at the local, regional, or national levels of these organisations and should speak to professional and community groups about topics of current interest within the discipline. Other forms of public service such as guest teaching at local schools and universities or serving on industry advisory committees to provide information will be an integral part of the role.

**Fig 10.2 ◆ Section of a possible job description for an IS director**

new era of complex service acquisition discussed in Chapter 12 demands a far clearer view of overall direction, informed allocation of resources and evaluation of alternatives. When most technical services are provided under contract arrangements, the organisation no longer holds technical skills at a premium, rather it becomes negotiation and conflict resolution skills that are required. Vowler (1995) would also argue that it is necessary for the IS Director to be a diplomat in balancing the satisfaction of the parochial concerns of one business department against the organisational overall benefit.

There are contradictory tensions pulling at the IS management role. One pull is towards the need for a more business literate, less technology biased IS Director. The current perception of the required skills for such an IS manager is:

- A good business manager
- A realist
- Able to resist technological distractions
- Able to see through to bottom line implications

This skills list appears to define the Finance Director rather than the IS one! Perhaps that is why IS often reports through finance? The information content of

| Attribute | 1950s | 1960s | 1970s | 1980s | 1990s |
|---|---|---|---|---|---|
| Experience | Programming | Programming/ analysis | Programming/ analysis/project management | Analysis/project management/ system development | Line management |
| Educational background | School mathematics | Technical first degree | First degree/ higher degree | Higher degree | Business higher degree |
| Technical skills | Batch systems | Batch/on-line systems | Enough to talk to staff | Hands-on of application software | Varied application experience |
| Organisational skills | Super-clerk | Report generator | Change agent | Leader | Visionary |
| Reporting hierarchy | To finance | To finance | To member of board | To Chairman of board | To corporate board |
| Loyalties | To computer | To computer department | To organisation as a whole | To organisation/ professional body | To corporate group |

Fig 10.3 ◆ Evolving nature of IS management

products and services is *competitively* crucial to some organisations, primarily those whose information intensity is high, for instance airlines and financial service companies, or *operationally* crucial for those organisations engaged in restructuring their business processes. These factors lead an organisation to create an *Information Director* in recognition of the *business/information* dimension. Such a director may emerge from the IS function's management or from line functions of the organisation. An interesting trend is highlighted by the KMPG/Impact research reported by Palmer (1992) that emphasises the role of marketing experience rather than IS technical experience in appreciating a strategic role for IS. This seems to back up the anecdotal shift to business targeting; not financial systems, not competitive advantage but better customer relationship systems. Interestingly, running counter to many current assumptions that generalist backgrounds are most useful, the same survey found that the effective IS Director, as measured as one that had a good relationship with the Chief Executive, may have spent most of their career within IS.

However, as IS increasingly becomes embedded within business processes it becomes the case that dealing with IS is dealing with the business. The drive for lower IS costs puts more service provision out to contract arrangements. The trend towards networked systems distributes IS across the entire business. All these trends act to place IS control into the hands of *every* manager, so is the separate IS Director needed when every director is, in some part, an IS Director? Indeed, already many profit-generating divisions feel anger at the Board level inclusion of an entirely service function; after all there is no Canteen Services Director. This anger can be deflected by quoting instances such as American Airlines, where that service function became the profit-generating division, and by pointing to the business process combined, rather than functionally divided, perception of organisations. Of course, many would pick up on this last point as an argument *against* the existence of a Board-level IS Director since such an appointment perpetuates destructive functional distinction. A final argument against the presence of an IS-specific director is that IS is *too* important to 'delegate' in this way, see Martin *et al.* (1995). After the mid-1980s rush to create IS Directors (known as CIOs in the USA) it looked as if this debate had ended with the resolution to dispense with their services. In the USA it was joked that CIO stood for 'career is over'. However that may have been a short-term response to recessionary times. With the mid-1990s it seems to be that such jobs are on the increase, see Dataview (1995) and Robertson (1996), perhaps recognising the importance that organisational level co-ordinated IS has for competitive survival.

A technological pull countering the business pull is that infrastructures are currently very difficult to manage and their managers need strong technical skills and such skills command a high value. These factors lead an organisation to create an Information *Technology* Director to reward, and hence retain, scarce and valuable *technical* skills. However, as any given technology becomes more reliable and simpler to use, apply and manage, will the IT Director disappear just as the IS Director might?

An IS Director will be responsible for overseeing the *implementation* of the IS strategic plan and be one of the team that *develops* it (see Parts 1 and 2 for a discussion of ways and means of developing an IS strategy). However, when we recognise the hierarchy inherent in the system of strategies discussed in Chapter 4 there must be a distinction between IS and IT managers. IS managers are employed for what they are responsible for whereas IT managers have by far the more technical responsibilities and so are employed for what they know.

Given the organisational and technical changes in the nature and management of IS there are now three IS management concerns (these three concerns will be explored further in Section 10.2):

| | |
|---|---|
| • Manage the technology | Operational |
| • Manage the use of information systems | Tactical |
| • Manage information | Strategic |

Since the levels of these tasks roughly equate to a conventional view of the levels of management we can see that there is a commensurate need for three levels of IS management. The literature that solely talks of elevating *the* IS manager is misrepresenting the picture. A truer picture is that the IS management role has broadened and fleshed-out to include a full spectrum of managerial levels and, as with conventional management theory, this spectrum recognises differences in the management demands and decisions at each level.

Despite the differences between them, both IS and IT managers are often criticised for operating *outside* the normal business styles of the organisation. Whilst this criticism may be valid, it is equally true that IS reality may not be the same reality as operating for the rest of the organisation. For IS the pace of change may be twice as fast as in other business areas, as is the rate of obsolescence of hardware, software and operating procedures. This pace of change and obsolescence makes write-off periods and planning horizons unpredictable and often meaningless. IS, and even more so IT, managers continually face the real likelihood of being entirely wrong in their predictions of technology trends.

All managers will change in the light of the impact of IS upon office activities. So far this has been most noticeable in small organisations where managers routinely perform many tasks traditionally handled by a secretary. There is now, however, a matching trend in larger organisations towards an extensive use of electronic mailing services plus a growing desire to interact directly with management information systems to make speed and flexibility gains and to remove 'filtering' influences. Obviously, this trend changes the role of the manager; however the role of the secretaries that remain alters even more, they increasingly become true assistants, supporting core activities rather than merely doing clerical tasks. No doubt the increase in personal diary and time management systems will continue this trend.

IS developments, particularly in business redesign, mean there will be relatively fewer managers since each can achieve more, but all the remaining managers must change, they must add to their business skills some technological capability. Some will go beyond that and become a hybrid manager, able to steer the direction the business/IS partnership may take.

> *A new type of information systems professional is required. One who is not only comfortable with change, but who has the skills that make such change possible.*
>
> Scott Morton, MIT Sloan Management School.

This new type of IS professional overlaps with the new type of general manager generated by the developments in user-controlled computing to create the need for, and availability of, the hybrid manager to be discussed in Section 10.3. The technological capabilities that they may hold are discussed in O'Brien (1995). Figure 10.4 makes some distinctions between general managers and technical specialists.

So at the one end of the spectrum small and personally focused systems drive IT literacy whilst, at the other extreme, increasing sophistication in simulation, sensitivity and risk analysis systems ensures that managers are 'IS empowered' decision managers. These decision makers must become hybrid users, naturally having an understanding of their business arena, but also competent in using the technology

| Attitudes and values | Technical specialists | General managers |
| --- | --- | --- |
| Goals | Member of profession with transferable skills | Focus on present employer |
| | Applying latest technology | Getting job done |
| | Solving problem in elegant ways | Cheap, simple, workable solution |
| | Agent of change | Reluctant to change for change sake |
| Time horizons | Long-term projects | Dependable results immediately |
| | No need for immediate feedback | Used to continual performance monitoring |
| Interpersonal | Problem-oriented | People-oriented |
| | Systems thinker | Get things done through people |
| Formality of organisational structure | More freedom of action | Works through formal organisational structure |
| | Few formal rules and hierarchy | High premium placed on hierarchy |
| | Project-oriented, non-hierarchical | |
| | Works directly with people and bypasses chain of command | |

**Fig 10.4 ◆ Technical specialists *v* general managers**

required. The decision making manager has much in common with the 'jack of all trades' from the smaller firm even when part of a huge multinational and, to succeed in this arena, managers must be both systems fluent and capable of both human management and evaluation of alternatives. The flatter organisation has no need of the many levels of data filtration and presentation managers. Tapscott and Caston (1993) suggest that IS management is actually not just about management, but rather about leadership. They suggest that the only way that an organisation can effectively change from being a closed hierarchical one serviced by an IS function that is also closed (and technology vehicle focused) into being an open, networked organisation served by open IS is to be *led* into and through that change. The leadership dimension of IS management they suggest is not only the 'lead from the very top' of old-style charismatic leaders but the involved, part of the team leadership that can emerge from any level of an organisation's hierarchy.

## 10.2 ◆ KEY IS MANAGEMENT ISSUES AND TASKS

IS management has become a complex activity and the issues and tasks involved are being defined by a number of organisational and technical changes. The key issues were first identified in the introduction to Part 3 and can be summarised, as by Fried (1995), as being the need for:

- People focus – rather than placing technological concerns to centre stage.
- Cost effectiveness – and to be *seen* to be cost effective by way of demonstrable business value.
- Information dispersal – and to relinquish inappropriate control mechanisms that reduce information use.
- Business process redesign – the real embodiment of technology-enabled change.
- Reporting relationships – that place IS into the business and *not* at an 'ivory tower' distance.

The most significant change is that IS can no longer be viewed as a single homogenous area with a single, middle level, manager responsible for it. The distinction between IS buying and IS provision has led to selection and acquisition, the IS *buying*, increasingly becoming a line management responsibility assisted by IS consultants who may be internal or external to the organisation. IS *provision*, in turn, sub-divides into two areas, IS *delivery* and IS *support*, both of which may be covered by internal or external arrangements.

### 10.2.1 ◆ Allocating IS management tasks

The distinctions made above separate the use of IS from the management of the infrastructures it requires. As line management takes responsibility for the use of information this directs IS to manage the technology that will enable all types of data to feed into this information use. This is analogous to the distinction between a council Highways Department which manages the road network and road users, including both professional and private drivers, all of whom operate within 'safety' rules to be discussed in Chapter 11, who require the road network. The

| IS Function | Line business unit |
| --- | --- |
| Strategic planning for IS | Tactical planning for applications |
| Physical systems design and development (or joint procurement) | Business analysis and logical systems design |
| Training and consulting | End-user computing developments |
| Telecommunications network management | Local data centre management |
| Manage across whole organisation | Manage for local organisation |
| Develop and manage shared and feeder databases | Develop and manage local and application databases |
| Provide IS professionals to business units | Provide business managers to IS unit |

**Fig 10.5 ◆ Non-contingent distribution of IS management tasks**

Highways Department must acknowledge traffic requirements in its planning and provision and, similarly, drivers can only travel where and at what speed road conditions permit.

Whilst there has been a steady transfer of IS management tasks to line management from 'traditional' IS management, the detailed allocation of tasks between the two is not always easy. Figure 10.5 illustrates a simple view of the separation of tasks.

Boynton *et al.* (1992) provide a more sophisticated, contingency model for allocating IS management tasks. They model the allocation of IS *responsibilities* and are careful to distinguish these from the structure and location of the physical resources as discussed in Chapter 9. They suggest that there are five generic IS management tasks, which they list as:

- *Setting strategic direction*: Facilitating the planning of the IS strategy(ies).
- *Establishing infrastructure systems*: For data, network highways, standards and shared applications.
- *Scanning emerging technologies*: Including all aspects of R&D. Such forecasting is vital if the organisation is not to find its IS strategy rendered obsolete.
- *Transferring technology*: Where technology is the knowledge of how to do things and so the transfer is the learning from others how to do things. This knowledge of how to do things must be diffused throughout the organisation.
- *Developing business systems*: The planning, 'building' and running of applications, including all acquisition approaches.

Boynton, Jacobs and Zmud further suggest that for *each* of these five generic tasks organisations should distinguish the 'container from its contents', that is the *what* from the *how*. For instance, separate the task of defining the format of strategy documents from defining the strategy itself, and separate the specification of development methods from developments.

Such separation of the logical *what* from the physical *how*, whilst in tune with two decades of research into systems development methods, seems difficult for organisations to accept when applied to management tasks! Who should be given the

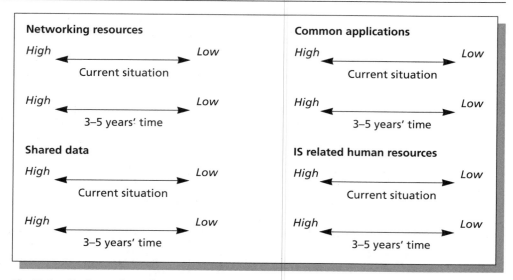

**Fig 10.6 ◆ Horizontal requirements indicators**
(adapted from whose Responsibility is IS Management? by Boynton et al., *Sloan Management Review* (1992) pp. 32–8. © 1992 by Sloan Management Review Association. All rights reserved)

responsibility for each of these five (or ten) task sets Boynton *et al.* suggest is contingent upon the organisation's position with respect to four factors. These key factors are the organisation's need for:

- *Networking resources*: To exchange information internally or with the external world
- *Shared data elements*: To share common data internally or with the external world
- *Common applications*: Systems common across the organisation
- *Specialised human resources*: IS-related specialised personnel

The methodology by which the task allocation can be made requires the organisation to chart its current, and future, requirements for these four factors, shown in Figure 10.6, as either high or low. Boynton, Jacobs and Zmud call this a horizontal requirements indicator. The main purpose of this charting process is to focus attention upon where to allocate responsibility for the five (ten) tasks, although for most organisations only one or two will be critical. An example allocation might be that IS will define development standards, business units will be responsible for developments themselves, the Board is to define the strategy content format, whilst the definition of the IS strategies themselves is to be the joint responsibility of IS and each business unit.

## 10.2.2 ◆ Strategic IS management

Since Chapter 12 will look at aspects of IS buying in more detail, this chapter primarily considers IS provision, that is the tasks involved in managing the technology, not its use, plus the overall co-ordination tasks.

Hussain and Hussain (1992) describe IS as a business within a business with a structure akin to a manufacturing business. This is a more detailed discussion of the ideas of Cash *et al.* (1992) discussed in Section 9.2.3. Their illustration is shown in Figure 10.7 and fits the emphasis of this chapter since it concentrates upon the IS *provision* role. Note that the comparison assumes the internal development of systems but the analogy works equally well if package acquisition and outsourced arrangements are included. After all, many manufacturing concerns sub-contract specialist tasks or buy-in standard components in order to concentrate upon core business areas.

When IS is perceived as having a full company structure then many IS tasks become obvious. Since information is the product then the users (line management) must take responsibility for choosing and using this product. Additionally, IS marketing becomes necessary; this involves IS establishing what the market needs are, that is what information is needed at what cost, and through what availability channels, and then IS must ensure that it can supply to this market demand. Promotion is only one part of marketing, customer service and product to market design are equally important elements. It is no great surprise then that much IS literature now predicts that senior IS management of the future will often have a marketing rather than a technical background. A predicted alternative is to have a *personnel* background given the increasing human and communication dimensions to IS management.

The likening of IS to a complete business is not particularly new and more than a decade ago Nolan (1982) referred to the IS Steering Committee as akin to the Board of Directors of a business. In very few instances will a business not have a management hierarchy with some management committee forming its apex. The issue of

| Manufacturing business | IS business |
|---|---|
| Product planning | Information systems planning |
| Facilities planning | Infrastructure configuration planning |
| Market research | IS demand forecasting |
| Product research | Technology scanning |
| Market development | User education |
| Product design | Application design |
| Problem analysis | Business analysis |
| Tooling | Programming |
| Production scheduling | Job scheduling |
| Production | Computing and operations |
| Production control | Production/operations control |
| Stock control | Supplies inventory |
| Quality control | Quality control |
| Consumer survey | User satisfaction survey |
| Consumer services liaison | User liaison |
| Personnel management | Personnel management |
| Administration | Administration |
| Product for sale | Information (whether sold or provided as an overhead service) |
| Product line strategy | Applications development strategy |
| Product cost strategy | Applications project estimation |
| Pricing policy | Charge policy |

**Fig 10.7 ◆ IS as a manufacturing concern**
(adapted by permmission of Prentice-Hall, a division of Simon & Schuster from *Information Management: Organisation Management and Control of Computer Processing* by Hussain and Hussin)

IS steering committees is picked up and considered in some detail by Ward and Griffiths (1996) who identify them as being charged with:

- ensuring top management involvement in IS planning
- ensuring the fit between IS and business strategy
- improving communication with top and middle management
- changing user attitudes to IT.

This seems to mean that they are single-handedly (if a committee can be said to be single-handed!) charged with creating effective IS management. After all, these points would serve as a useful definition of effective IS. However, perhaps because of the blandness of their purpose, they are frequently perceived to be a failure. Ward and Griffiths cite many criticising comments:

- wrong people/too many people attend; the right do not attend
- wrong terms of reference
- discuss the wrong things
- meet too infrequently/too often
- make too many/not enough decisions
- do not understand the real issues
- are too remote from reality

Ward and Griffiths conclude that the key issue with IS steering committees is as much the *way* they operate as *what* they do. The implication one can draw from their comments is that, as with all committees, the selection of process is one that must be done carefully in a way that matches the demands of the particular situation. The IS steering committee for a given organisation must have a membership, terms of reference, frequency and a procedural style tailored to the circumstances of the organisation.

The most senior IS management level has not always recognised the business structure requirement. IS management may move through an *evolutionary* development, with the leadership types focusing upon different key concerns at different phases. Possible phases are:

- *Delivery*: During this phase the IS manager is primarily concerned with matters that are internal to the IS function, that is with delivery of the IS services. In line with this emphasis, an appointed manager is likely to have a proven record of dealing *efficiently* with operating the function.

- *Re-orientation*: This phase moves the IS management concerns outwards from the IS function. During this phase the priority tasks are to exploit IS for competitive advantage and to ensure that the IS strategy is consistent with the business strategy (see Part 2). This phase is usually initiated by creating a management position *above* the existing IS manager, that is an IS Director. This position is usually filled by a senior manager drawn from within the organisation but outside IS.

- *Re-organisation*: During this third phase the IS Director's key concern is to manage the relationships between the IS function and the rest of the organisation. The rest of the organisation is not a single entity but a complex set of groups, each having differing degrees of user-controlled computing, data complexity, and strategic dependence upon IS. To manage this organisational complexity the IS function must be re-organised and a key task is to provide expanded education for both business and technology staff.

These three IS management phases can be summarised as in Figure 10.8 and it is clear that IS management has stratified into the operational, tactical and strategic management levels.

So strategic IS management deals with issues related to policy, people, control, evaluation, cost, investment, and organisation leaving the more detailed concerns of technology, applications and implementation to the tactical/operational level. The objectives of IS management at the respective levels is to:

- Manage information                         Strategic
- Manage the use of information systems       Tactical
- Manage the technology                       Operational

Those responsible for strategic IS management, be they an IS Steering Committee or a single IS director, will be responsible for three key issues, which are:

- *Direction setting*: An IS strategy must be developed and maintained that determines the direction of the organisation's use and management of IS by channels, even if often limiting the initiation of projects towards the organisational goals. This defined direction reconciles the conflicting demands upon the organisation's finite IS resources and indeed rations resources between IS and other business commitments.

- *Co-ordination*: Since IS is similar to a manufacturing business which has much to be gained by having reusable standard elements combined in an innovative way so IS should aim for reusability and commonality of IS components to avoid redundancy and valueless differences. The co-ordination task may also encompass IS structuring and staffing.

- *Support*: Business and not technology units will be responsible for IS use, but they will be supported by the technology units that will provide the resource infrastructures and advise and assist on problem solving. This IS management task may also include auditing to ensure that the co-ordination and direction setting is proving effective.

|  | Delivery | Re-orientation | Re-organisation |
|---|---|---|---|
| The focus of the IS Director | Within IS | Into the business | Interfaces |
| Their priority concern | Credibility | Strategy | Relationships |
| Who provides the leadership | The Board | The function | Coalition |

Fig 10.8 ◆ Three phases of IS management

The last of these issues relates to the networked organisation having complex interfaces that forms the base structural assumption to much business process design work.

Griffiths (1992), reporting on a Kobler Unit survey, found that such strategic IS responsibility could lie with one or four groups:

- IS Director                         48 per cent
- MD or Chief Executive       34 per cent
- Finance Director                  6 per cent
- Business Unit Directors       12 per cent

The survey findings indicate that there are a range of advantages and disadvantages to the four alternatives, as summarised in Figure 10.9.

As the job description included in Section 10.1 indicated, IS management tasks include establishing policies, standards and procedures for information, information systems, and information services even when elements are geographically and/or functionally distributed. Collaboration with other senior managers must be supported to ensure effective use of information and to integrate technology with business needs. Such collaboration and integration requires IS-directed educational and training activities.

|  | Advantages | Disadvantages |
|---|---|---|
| *Finance Director* | Leads to good cost control and co-ordination across units with all other related costs, such as training, being well integrated. | Does not always provide best value for money and, with insufficient time dedicated to IS concerns, there is a danger of lost opportunities. |
| *IS Director* | The degree of technical expertise should lead to accurate systems being adopted using sound technology. | IS is often not completely linked to business and, since human and organisational issues are overlooked, there can be an information overload. |
| *Business unit directors* | Applications will be directly linked to the business and user friendly systems will be adopted by a process of continuous development. | Systems are not co-ordinated and incompatibilities and duplication in data inputs and formats can result from systems that often have to re-invent the wheel. |
| *The Board* | There is a clear strategic direction to IS and *major* problems are tackled. | There is little concern with logistical details and that means that systems are often not *fully* exploited and infrastructure (high technical complexity) systems may be weak. |

**Fig 10.9 ◆ IS responsibility alternatives**
(after Griffiths)

## 10.2.3 ◆ Operational IS management

Likening IS to a complete manufacturing business showed that it will involve different levels of management. The issues and tasks associated with managing information as an organisational resource form the strategic level of management. Tactical IS management equates to managing the business-appropriate use of information systems and this increasingly, and properly, falls as a responsibility of line managers so that IS tasks are fully integrated into their portfolio of general management activities. What remains are those issues and tasks associated with managing the *technology* itself, that is the operational management of IS provision including both delivery and support. It is this 'branch' of IS that is usually implied in any discussion of IS resources or IS resource management. (*See* Figure 10.10.)

Management of service provision is the operational level of IS management and at its heart are three key principles:

- Separate innovation from production
- Manage the technology not its use
- Integrate all types of data.

### Separate innovation from production

This separation requires differing management emphases, perhaps by different management units, to achieve the goals of each. Production must have an efficiency bias where all *routine* activities should be automated since they are not likely to add value, whereas innovation requires speculative, and potentially wasteful, experimentation. Technology scanning is important to avoid technology strategies being made obsolete by unexpected technology changes but also innovative uses of technology should be nurtured. IS operational management must accept that it is increasingly line managers who take responsibility for the justification of applications since they are the ones in a position to judge the *value,* though they need IS assistance to estimate the *costs*. The production process is one that must be about efficiency, about quality and about engineering. There is a danger that production can seem almost pedestrian in contrast to the *ideas* generation of technology innovation. In many organisations 'traditional' IS operations have dramatically shrunk or disappeared altogether in the wake of the move towards third party packages and services.

| General | For products, services and standards |
|---|---|
| Plan | Define and describe |
| Train and consult for effective use | Acquire and maintain |
| Account for use of services | Control quality and integrity |
| | Organise and make accessible |
| | Protect and secure |
| | Recover/restore and upgrade |
| | Determine obsolescence and dispose |

**Fig 10.10 ◆ Possible IS resource management tasks**

What is involved in IS operational management will vary by the stage of maturity of the use and management of any technology. Following a four-stage model of maturity in the style of Nolan's work, then operational management may involve:

- *Stage 1*: Concerned with R&D and projects running as pilot schemes and at this stage is not primarily involved with return on investment assessment issues.
- *Stage 2*: IS management during this stage is concerned with tasks relating to experimentation to increase organisational awareness.
- *Stage 3*: With this stage IS management becomes involved with initiating management controls. Such tasks are necessary to ensure efficient use.
- *Stage 4*: With this stage, management issues relate to the mature use of fully appropriate management controls.

Stages 1 and 2 are almost entirely concerned with innovation to be effective (doing the right things) perhaps at the expense of production efficiency (doing things right). Having discovered innovative and effective uses during Stages 1 and 2 then Stages 3 and 4 are about establishing and maintaining operational efficiency. As technology emergence of Stages 1 and 2 moves into the technology diffusion and dependence of Stages 3 and 4, new management issues and tasks emerge. Indeed, different management units may be required as long as the second key principle of service provision is ensured, that of managing technology not its use.

## Manage the technology not its use

Whilst some levels of IS management have become less technology driven, operational IS management still retains a distinctive technical role. IS can be likened to the functions of marketing, production, and finance. However, given its responsibility for information flows, it is unlike those other functions in that it cuts across the entire organisation. Managing the *technology* means developing, maintaining, co-ordinating and controlling the infrastructure backbones of communication networks, data centres and application standards. The use of the specific applications that call upon these infrastructure resources is the responsibility of the business units, who may need to appoint service buyers to liaise with the account managers within IS who still 'front' IS to the customer.

IS operational management needs to cost allocate, or chargeback in some way (discussed in Chapter 12), for the technology resources used; this maintains the distinction between the management of technology and the management of its use and permits IS, and its customers, to judge the provided service levels and assess the degree of customer satisfaction. Systems providers, whether inside or outside the organisation, often see themselves as having a relationship with the systems users that ends with the *delivery* of the system. This is not, however, usually the perception of the service users. Users generally look for an *ongoing* service to support their business goals, and therefore seek a commitment from IS to provide a continuing, defined and measurable level of service. This can be done through a service level agreement (SLA) which is a user definition of the products and services to be provided.

A service level agreement is a written agreement, typically fairly brief, but including a description of the service, service goal measurements and the procedures to be followed when the service is unsatisfactory. Most importantly, a service level agreement binds both the users and providers of the service and can equally apply to outside vendors and suppliers. Service level agreements can therefore be integrated into performance appraisal and reward systems since rewards can directly attach to success measures defined within the SLA. There is a danger however, that the SLA will undesirably act to create a ceiling of service performance. Fried (1995) argues very forcefully that the Chief Information Officer – this is an American text and so uses this term for the IS Director – should develop a team that continually strives for customer 'delight'. He defines this delight as being the *exceeding* of expectations. Although Fried does not explicitly discuss this with respect to SLAs, the implication is that the terms of the SLA can only set the customer *expectations*; true customer satisfaction will only be achieved if they are exceeded. To increase service satisfaction, IS operational management needs to look to other, non-IS, service providers for examples of good practice. For instance, supermarkets provide express checkouts to prevent customers who are buying a few items having to wait behind queues of full trolleys. In the same way IS may be able to provide a quick response queue for small service requests. Proactive IS management does not make user complaints the primary tool for identifying service provision problems.

IS resources are always finite so there must be some method of balancing conflicting requests for infrastructure access from different groups. When business management is fully IS autonomous it can decide if it is willing to pay the IS 'price' for access (however such a price is declared and/or recovered). When business management is *not* fully IS autonomous, a higher decision making level must resolve the conflicts between operational demands made by different areas of business management. In either instance, the accurate forecast of resource costs must be provided and it is resource planning that does this. IS operational management is very much about resource planning, often referred to as capacity planning, though it must be far more than simply performance monitoring or 'straight-line' extrapolations forward to future demands. Resource planning is the assessment of the different resource demands made by alternative potential activities. These sensitive cost implication estimates support *informed* value judgements.

Software to automate the modelling of the sensitivity analysis of different resource/demand scenarios can identify the organisational optimum trade-off between increased benefit and increased resource costs. Similarly, such capacity planning modelling allows the operational IS activities to be finely tuned for the optimum trade-off between increased costs and increased business performance. Poor resource planning can lead to either:

- Premature hardware/software replacement:   Costs the organisation money
- Delayed hardware/software replacement:   Costs the organisation computer performance

Whilst the first is an obvious problem the second is equally as significant. If a competitive advantage can be loosely defined as either an increase in business revenue or a decrease in operating costs, then computer performance can directly increase the first, and help to significantly decrease the second. Resource planning must use good technology forecasts to predict accurately the life cycle of hardware and software and then chart positions on these life cycles to build budget plans from these positions. In particular, hardware life spans must be realistically recorded, otherwise any calculations of lease terms and write-offs will be inaccurate. Note that end-user computing applications must be predicted and catered for in resource plans. However this is extremely difficult since, by their very nature, they are unpredictable (few users are able to articulate accurately *in advance* how they will use IS) and almost secretive. Application plans may be kept secret, even when possible to articulate, in those circumstances when user-controlled computing emerges as a result of alienation between IS and its business community (*see* Section 9.4.2).

Resource planning is often very closely linked to two other IS operational management issues, service charging and service and performance monitoring, all discussed in Chapter 12. Indeed, the same base data can be used for all three purposes.

## Integrate all types of data

Different types of data have traditionally been the province of different functions. Automating the handling of different data types has also traditionally taken different paths but over the last decade real data integration has been needed and partially achieved. The previously disparate technologies and the data types they have typically been responsible for are illustrated in Figure 10.11.

These technologies have all become integrated not just across the physical levels of commonality of equipment and communication methods but also at the deeper level of sharing a common data infrastructure architecture. This integration is illustrated in Figure 10.12. The merging referred to can, of course, happen by degrees. For instance 'factory automation' is itself a set of islands of technology. If 'DP' and/or 'Communications' are used to provide bridges between, say, design technologies and production technologies then the level of integration achieved can be called computer integrated manufacturing (CIM). However when a fuller integration is achieved it would need to be called something such as IS-enabled organisation (perhaps the intent of BPR, *see* Chapter 8) to reflect the fact that no one aspect, for instance manufacturing, is technologically separated.

In some organisations other data-related technologies are being integrated into this set, for instance those of business *library* services. Since this, like other facets of IS, provides business *information* and shares many technology systems, moving it under the single IS umbrella offers the many advantages of *integration*. In other organisations the 'personal' technologies of diaries, time planners and similar once totally paper based but now increasingly digitally stored aspects are being integrated. The integration of these four (or five or six) technologies does not do away with the need for some technology specifics, and even more technically specialist staff, but rather it co-ordinates the business-beneficial sharing of data under a common umbrella. Even more strongly it brings home the fact that *anything* that relates to information (which is much of organisational life) is a matter of IS concern.

| Technology | Typical data type |
|---|---|
| Data processing | Mainly numerical or structured textual data |
| Communications | Transitory, mainly voice data |
| Office automation | Large volume, unstructured textual data |
| Factory automation | Design and control data |

**Fig 10.11 ◆ Traditional data technologies**

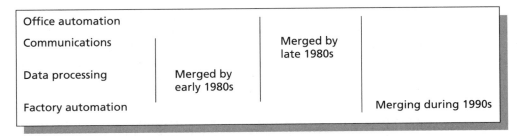

**Fig 10.12 ◆ Integration of automation technologies**

The IS role in aiding communication makes IS management about any aspect of moving data around the organisation. Clearly such data must be sufficiently accurate but there is a danger that IS pride will lead to expensive data accuracy sought beyond the level that business needs dictate. Since many organisations are now information and IS dependant, IS management must be able to guarantee that data, and the support for using it, will always be available whenever, and wherever, it is needed. Time and place must not be constraints. Open system architectures play a significant role here, although 'open' systems *can* mean proprietary hardware and systems as long as all interface and communicate (*see* Chapter 12 for a fuller discussion of this).

In addition, operational IS management will have some activities in common with the operational management of other functions. Like all other departments, IS management must plan the department's activities, prepare and manage its budgets, schedule and monitor tasks and appoint, train and assess staff. Personnel matters can be particularly difficult given the large skills range and task variety within an IS function. Not surprisingly, the nature of the tasks and issues involved in IS operational management varies with the size and complexity of the IS function. A small IS function with a small budget, few staff and a small and simple applications portfolio faces mainly *technical* rather that truly managerial issues. Conversely, a large IS function with a large budget and staff organised in complex ways and with an extensive portfolio of large and complex applications will contain many technical specialists to perform many of the operational tasks. For this reason, its IS management must primarily concentrate upon *management* issues and tasks.

## 10.3 ◆ HYBRID MANAGEMENT

This management description is not just another term to describe the users engaged in the user-controlled computing as will be discussed in Chapter 11. A clear distinction exists between hybrid *users* and hybrid *managers* and this distinction is one of emphasis and purpose. Hybrid users are the people involved in user-controlled computing, they combine a degree of technical competence (perhaps defined by notions such as the end-user continuum of Chapter 11) with, of course, the business literacy required to fulfil their primary role. Hybrid managers, as opposed to managers who are hybrid users, require this business literacy and technical competency plus a third dimension. This third item is the organisational astuteness that allows a manager to make business-appropriate IS use and management decisions that enhance or set business directions as well as follow them. It is fairly well recognised that hybrid users can be *trained* whereas the more sophisticated development of hybrid managers is problematic, perhaps requiring inbuilt talent and personal qualities, but *can* be encouraged or discouraged. For this reason undergraduate study can generally produce only hybrid users whilst postgraduate and post-experience study can support the development of hybrid managers.

The notion of hybrid management is an essentially British one and a significant amount of work on the concept of hybrid management has been done by Earl (1989) and the British Computer Society (1990, as reported in *Computing*, 31 January 1991). Earl provided the initial working definition of hybrid managers that has been subsequently adopted by other works. The BCS has done much to define the benefits gained by having such managers and a great deal of work on outlining initiatives to develop and train managers who would meet Earl's definition. Skyrme and Earl (1990) defined the required characteristics of a hybrid manager and these are summarised in Figure 10.13. The critical success factors from this table of skills, competencies and traits are undoubtedly personality and motivation. The job titles of hybrid managers can vary enormously and generally reflect little of the multi-dimension nature of their role. They tend to retain titles that relate to just one dimension, *either* business or IS, on an almost accidental basis. The given title rarely reflects the breadth of activities they are involved in, or the status that they may hold, but then the mobile nature of their posts makes naming them difficult. This variety, and the ill-defined nature of their roles, can make it extremely difficult for an organisation to know whether they have any hybrid managers (equally so for someone to know if they are one themselves). The table of attributes can be used as benchmarks against which to assess whether a manager is already a hybrid manager, to select candidate hybrid managers or identify skills gaps when developing them, all from a self or organisational perspective.

Hybrid managers are a high risk, high cost, people infrastructure that enables the organisational integration of IS and business. This integration ensures both business-consistent IS and IS-exploitative business and so hybrid managers straddle two, previously disparate, disciplines. No amount of communication, or translation bridges, between the two separate disciplines can achieve the same degree of integration. Whilst there is no theoretical reason why hybrid managers cannot be drawn from any discipline, experience seems to show that it proves easier to add IS 'technical' knowledge to a base of business awareness than to inculcate IS technicians with a broader, organisational vision. The primary benefits of hybrid managers are that they create 'islands' of true business/IS understanding; these islands then provide the catalyst that leads to an *organisational* hybridisation. Even from the earliest stages of hybridisation programmes, organisational gains in flexibility and effectiveness are reported.

Since developing hybrid managers (or any form of management development) is a costly and uncertain exercise it can be a problem notion in recessionary times. The long-term benefits, rather than short-term gains, of such a development programme can look easy to 'trim' out of recession-hit budgets. And yet, paradoxically, it is precisely this type of people infrastructure that supports the cross-boundary, radical re-works typically associated with business process redesign to enable significant future cost savings. Medd (1991) sums it up and shows that the business redesign focus of the 1990s demands the hybrid manager who is, not narrowly specialist, but capable of seeing the broad picture and the

| Business knowledge | General business knowledge about the organisation's goals providing a global view |
|---|---|
| Organisation-specific knowledge | Culture<br>Structure<br>Processes<br>Key people and their motivation |
| IS knowledge/ experience | Experience of project managing IS applications in the organisation's business<br>Awareness of existing/potential applications in the organisation's business<br>Knowledge of who can provide expertise on specific technologies |
| Interpersonal skills | Unusual set of interests<br>Can influence top management<br>Can relate to the 'broad picture'<br>Can develop co-operative relationships with large numbers of people inside and outside the organisation<br>Develop team work<br>Sensitive to personal needs<br>Can motivate specialists/subordinates/peers |
| Communication skills | Value information sensing<br>Good listening skills<br>Good at informal communication<br>Responsive |
| Cognitive capabilities | Above-average intelligence<br>Moderately analytical<br>Strongly intuitive<br>Good problem solving skills |
| Personality traits and behaviour | People oriented<br>Development and change focus<br>Outgoing<br>Commitment and integrity<br>Energy and enthusiasm |

**Fig 10.13 ◆ Characteristics of hybrid managers**
(adapted from *Hybrid Managers: What should you do*? by Skyrme and Earl, British Computer Society (1990), p. 3)

opportunities present in this total view. O'Connor and Smallman (1995) conclude that hybrid managers will be critical to the survival of the IS function into the next decade. The continuing devolution of many IS areas requires a hybrid manager to manage the 'new' IS and indeed even the act of assessing the relative merits of different paths to devolution, and judging what *not* to devolve requires the skills as defined to be of a hybrid manager.

Whilst there is a general agreement as to the value in hybrid managers as the people element that ensures effective use of the inanimate elements of IS, there remain two central themes associated with employing such management types, these are:

- Understanding the *problems* inherent in this 'new' management type in order to minimise them

- Understanding approaches to *developing* such managers

The following sections look at these two issues, along with what hybrid management may mean from the inside, that is from the perspective of aspiring or actual hybrid managers.

O'Brien (1995) argues that it is not sufficient merely to define hybrid managers as being those who have technological capabilities as there are distinctly different *levels* of capability. He illustrates this with respect to two illustrations, one of which is given in Figure 10.14. O'Brien points out that Level D capability is unlikely to be needed of a hybrid manager but organisations can include many different *combinations* of Levels A, B and C, *all* of which can be called 'technologically capable'. It is the specific nature of this mixture that must be considered, not the general statement.

It may be that all this focus upon the newly named hybrid manager is misplaced. Not misplaced in the valuing of broad personal qualities and skills, but in the coining of a new name for this skill set. The developments, referred to under the heading of hybrid management, may actually be defining the varieties of managers that can effectively compete, indeed survive, in business in the 1990s. These then can come in three varieties: the general manager who must understand IS well enough to articulate IS requirements and to direct IS projects successfully; the IS professional who is able to succeed in making a transition to management by understanding business and how it functions, this manager has ceased to be merely a technical specialist; and the IS function's manager, who must present and sell IS to the business world. There has always been a recognition of the value of a broad business education, which used to mean an arts background plus management training in business line functions. Perhaps the hybrid management

| How much do you know about distributed database? | |
|---|---|
| Level A: | 'Though computer-literate, I am not really sure when a database counts as distributed and when not. I use the term, if at all, loosely and perhaps sometimes incorrectly.' |
| Level B: | 'I know the essential points that determine what is a distributed database and what is not. This helps me to grasp, though without knowing much of the detail, why it is that distributed database is quite an advanced, and hence sometimes risky, technology. That is as far as my knowledge goes.' |
| Level C: | 'I understand, in outline not detail, the key concepts in distributed database: horizontal fragmentation, vertical fragmentation, replication, distributed updating etc. This means that I can make a reasonable judgement whether any given distributed database I come across is a relatively simple or relatively complex case.' |
| Level D: | 'I have designed the technical part of a distributed database system. Also, I could explain in detail the relative merits of the routing optimisation features in the rival software products DB2 and Oracle.' |

**Fig 10.14 ◆ Different levels of technological capability**
(adapted from *Information Management Decisions* by O'Brien (1995) Pitman Publishing)

developments are simply recognising the impact of IS on business life and so the 'valuable generalist' must now be a technology generalist. For the sake of clarity the name Hybrid Manager will continue to be used as a label for the 'modern' manager who, for reasons of the dispersal of IS throughout an organisation, must be an IS manager when managing *anything*.

## 10.3.1 ◆ Problems associated with hybrid management

Whilst hybrid managers are of undoubted value to an organisation there are a number of potentially problematic issues associated with the concept that must be acknowledged and effectively handled if expensive hybridisation programmes are to achieve their full potential. These issues are:

- *Hybrids challenge*: It is often the specific role of a hybrid manager to challenge existing assumptions about how information is used and managed. Unless these challenges are well directed they can be destructive rather than constructive. Internal challenges are *always* hard to manage.

- *The need to re-assess budgets*: There are many dimensions to this issue: the need to re-assess training and education budgets; the difficulties of maintaining a separate 'hybrid manager's development budget'; plus the issue of establishing investment budget appraisal approaches that appropriately recognise the contributions of such managers.

- *Dislocation*: Hybrid managers, and programmes to develop them, lead to significant times of dislocation, particularly when transfer programmes are used as a management development method. At the time of an initial crossover between general management and IS, or IS and general management, even if this crossover is *conceptual* rather than *physical*, problems may result.

- *Perceptions of unfairness*: Hybrid managers face organisations with a difficult balancing act, between *encouraging* innovative ideas that may 'appear' undeliverable and so lead to perceptions of unfairness, against the danger of *discouraging*, and hence quashing, innovation.

- *Skills loss*: Since the IS function often experiences a critical skills *shortage* there may be an equally critical, if short-term, apparent skills *loss* resulting from any transfer of managers from IS units to line activities. This problem is usually more perceived than real.

- *Reward structures*: It may be difficult to identify, administer and appraise appropriate reward structures that adequately reflect the long-term benefits and combination achievements of hybrid managers. Further, the necessary differences in reward structures can be a source of discontent.

- *Poaching*: Since hybrid managers are a valuable staff group there is a high risk of them being head-hunted by other organisations. This risk often drives the nature of the reward structures and exacerbates discontent from other staff. Such poaching may be from other organisations, or be 'self poaching', that is hybrid managers have precisely the entrepreneurial skills needed in successful start-up managers and so they may establish their *own* organisations.

- *Fear by superiors*: As with all 'fast track' newcomers, immediate superiors may fear the hybrid manager, as can single function contemporaries. Such fears can be exacerbated by the corporate, rather than functional, loyalty base of hybrid managers, plus the fact that these hybrids are frequently championed by far more senior managers.

- *Early damage*: As soon as an organisation considers the notion of hybrid management, whether explicitly or implicitly, then it is likely continually to place candidate managers into high-risk arenas. Such constant risk exposure means that hybrid managers face a higher chance of failure. A high failure rate can lead to organisational damage to the perceived status or value of either hybrid management in general, or the specific individual. It can also lead to personal damage from lost confidence and courage.

- *Time horizons*: Hybrid managers shorten the time horizons of projects they are involved with. This is because both the process of developing hybrid managers and the way the organisation is likely to use them probably involves transfers every 12–18 months. The problematic issue is that many people or technology infrastructure decisions have far longer time horizons, perhaps three to five years, by which time the originating hybrid manager is elsewhere. The timing differences can cause hybrid managers to be dangerously divorced from the effect of their decisions.

- *Recruitment policies*: There is normally a need to adjust recruitment policies if seeking to 'buy in' hybrid managers, or at least the candidates for such roles. It can be very difficult to judge conflicting values and selection criteria in such a complex area.

- *Loyalties*: Hybrid managers are likely to develop a different loyalty allegiance than their contemporary, single function, manager. The hybrid manager may have limited loyalty to any given unit since IS innovations may, at any time, alter the nature of that unit, or indeed remove the reason for its existence. Group loyalty can be hard to develop and maintain until managers are in senior positions and this fact would tend to support the view that hybrid management is about senior management.

- *Assessment*: The organisation's 'conventional' method of management appraisal may be inappropriate for a management type that is, almost by definition, risk seeking. Since challenges are rarely comfortable, appraisal of those that challenge is notoriously difficult.

The IS specialist manager whose development emphasised the skills of precision, project management, and service delivery to meet the defined needs of others is not an ideal candidate for hybrid management roles. Because of this, the IS function may develop two career paths; where this happens, it is unlikely that both paths will hold the same status and so effective management of career aspirations is needed to avoid loss of technical expertise.

## 10.3.2 ◆ Approaches to developing hybrid managers

Debate about hybrid management began in the mid-1980s. Initially, whilst the concept was unfamiliar, the debate centred around definitions, and identifying the potential benefits and possible problems associated with hybrid managers. With greater familiarity, the emphasis during the 1990s has shifted to discussion and debate about how best to create, acquire, develop and use the hybrid manager.

There are a number of possible strategies to build the hybrid management infra-structure. These include a range of *complementary* approaches such as:

- *Recruitment*: It is possible, though probably expensive, to recruit partially developed hybrid managers directly. This approach is of uncertain value since the candidate hybrid manager may have demonstrated success only in a different arena, and may not yet have any demonstrable successes to claim; any claims may be hard to substantiate and, in any case, organisational astuteness may be non-transferable.

- *Training and education*: An obvious approach is to train and educate likely hybrid managers in 'missing' skills. The difficulty in identifying likely hybrid managers, and the difficulty in articulating what *is* missing, has made this a problematic and so far unpopular strategy. Existing organisational training and education provision to develop hybrid users or to increase the organisational awareness of technical specialists can be used. These may include in-house or external short courses, seminars or academic programmes, but may do little to develop the additional, third dimension of the hybrid manager.

- *Cross-fertilisation*: Rather than consciously training hybrid managers, an alternative approach is to involve all, or some, managers in crossover work to allow hybrid managers to *emerge*. Consciously expanding the participation in organisation-wide committees might be included here.

- *Transfers*: An approach that takes cross-fertilisation a stage further is to formalise it via management transfer programmes. Here again, the intention, and the hope, is for hybrid managers to emerge. The difference between cross-fertilisation and transfers may be simply one of timescales. When a move is for days or weeks it is a cross-fertilisation activity, whereas if it is for months or years then it is a job rotation, or secondment, as part of a transfer programme.

- *Encouragement*: A less formal approach than either transfer programmes or cross-fertilisation is to adopt an encouraging stance to all non-traditional involvement, either by line managers in IS suggestions and decisions, or by IS managers in business (not IS support to business) suggestions and decisions.

Each of these suggestions has its own advocates and its strengths and weaknesses. It must be stressed that these approaches are frequently used in combination and are frequently the by-product of other intentions. It is very difficult to decide how best to develop hybrid managers when it is even difficult to know if/where they currently exist within the organisation. Esso uses job rotations, Lucas uses a combination of education and training while British Airways combines the two approaches. The first generation of very high profile hybrid managers is being followed by ever-increasing numbers of IS senior executives who are managers more than IS technicians. However, the anecdotes still seem to show that such people 'emerge' and the anecdotes give little guidance on how to turn the technical manager into the politically astute director. The critical success factor in producing hybrid managers does not seem to be education, or training initiatives, although both can contribute to success, but seems to depend upon giving 'real' business responsibilities to forge the necessary perceptiveness. Of course, giving these 'real' responsibilities as a learning process generates risks, however there are consultancy firms who will provide support during such 'baptism by fire' development of hybrid managers, and one such is described in Kavanagh (1995).

As mentioned before, Earl (1989) provided an early definition of hybrid managers and the BCS (1990) has done much to outline initiatives to develop and train managers who met Earl's definition. The BCS is one of the strongest advocates of hybrid managers in the UK, estimating that the UK needed to produce 10 000 such managers by 1995 and suggests that by the year 2000 a full 30 per cent of British managers will need to be hybrid managers. Perhaps the view of the BCS may not be free from bias since they are validating training programmes and part-time MBA qualifications which they wish to promote as the vehicles for producing hybrid managers. It also allows them 'legitimately' to open a door to far larger numbers of BCS members!

Education programmes do exist, and most add technology options to business areas since that seems the most comfortable assimilation and meets the academic principle of context before content. However, technologist courses do increasingly encompass business literacy issues. As yet, few programmes truly integrate from both disciplines. Such academic programmes may provide hybrid user qualifications but it remains *essential* to add specific organisational awareness to the general base education in order to produce a hybrid manager.

So far, only Esso has articulated any concrete way of assessing the *success* of hybridisation programmes. Esso uses three metrics:

- How many new projects are running to time and budget
- What financial benefits are gained from these projects
- How do internal operating costs compare with competitors' costs

Together these three metrics measure the *efficiency* of a given project plus the *effectiveness* of the organisation at selecting a portfolio of appropriate projects, that is those that lower costs and increase revenue and so offer business grounded benefits. Esso report that 90 per cent of projects are now on time and to budget rather than the 60 per cent before their hybridisation programme. However, these improvements may only indicate part of the benefits of hybrid managers. Additional value comes from the fact that they can act as catalysts for breaking the whole organisation out of any IS/business unit data jealousy so that information can be perceived as a *real* corporate resource. So not only will selected projects be more effectively managed, but this second point should mean that the projects that are selected will improve overall organisational performance. They are less likely to be chosen to optimise a local issue at the expense of *overall* opportunities.

It is claimed that the hybrid manager breaks away from the 'techie' introvert role of the IS specialist and therefore is more likely to be able to challenge the status quo. To develop people who have the personal skills to question existing practice plus the technical understanding to appreciate when they are being 'fobbed off' is difficult. However the very nature of the debate about hybrid management may perpetuate outdated orthodoxy. The literature on hybrid management may fuel a view of business as containing two discrete elements, business and IS. This two-theme view runs counter to the, more productive, view of business management as a *single* job that needs a portfolio of skills that includes leadership, people management, decision making and tool using. However, the term has provided a convenient, business legitimate, way for IS Directors to describe themselves that emphasises their 'towards the business' focus.

### 10.3.3 ◆ From the perspective of a hybrid manager

Most of the discussion about hybrid management inevitably takes the organisation's perspective but there is, of course, another side to the coin. Since many of the readers of this book are destined to be hybrid managers, how do things look from that perspective?

The candidate hybrid manager must obviously have the attributes of a hybrid user, that is they must have a degree of technical competence and a degree of business literacy. The precise nature of these skills will vary for each individual and may focus upon any areas of business, but the IS elements are likely to be broad in scope (it may be hybrid managers that define the areas of current IS concern). In addition to hybrid user attributes, the hybrid manager must hold a range of personal rather than technical qualities. In order to be an effective hybrid, a manager must be:

- *Comfortable with conflict and change*: It can be difficult to show, and even assess for yourself, the degree of comfort you feel with conflict and change and demonstrate that this is channelled into *productive* interests, rather than destructive change for change's sake.

- *Commitment and drive*: To be effective hybrid managers cannot operate within a '9 to 5' boundary, and it is vital that high levels of personal commitment and a refusal to even think 'it's not my problem' are both present. This commitment replaces the more identifiable, but more limited, business area loyalty of the single function manager. Unfocused commitment can be difficult to demonstrate and most hybrid managers must have a well-placed sponsor. This sponsor can champion the cause, and so smooth the path, of a hybrid manager. Because a sponsor is needed, good social and interpersonal skills are vital. Such personal skills are both developed by, and needed for, the mobile world of hybrid management.

- *Luck*: Much IS literature, particularly that of strategic IS for competitive advantage, quotes examples of hybrid managers. Most of these stories show that the managers referenced were, to some extent, luckily placed at some point in their career. Whilst luck is a vital ingredient of hybrid management, it may be another differentiation between the hybrid user and the hybrid manager, in that the latter *make* their own luck.

For the manager who has business literacy, technical competence and organisational astuteness there are some significant career benefits. Barnatt (1996) concludes that it is 'those with the best technical, software and data handling skills who will become tomorrow's corporate executives'. There can be undoubted personal satisfaction, but also significant financial reward since, after experiencing some initial job location problems, a hybrid manager is a valuable asset and so very employable. Debate about the employability of hybrid managers emerged as soon as the notion itself did. No doubt some early hybrid managers encountered the Japanese syndrome of 'not bred by *our* organisation' that made moving from one organisation to another very difficult. The recession-hit early 1990s increased the value placed upon certainty, and so head-hunting *proven* managers seemed a safer route to hybrid management than developing untried candidates. To counter this career gain however, the early 1990s made development routes for the hybrid manager much tougher as organisations reduced education and training initiatives. Despite this, the organisational turbulence of the first half of the decade, plus the drive to use IS to create profitable businesses, has given the self-developed hybrid manager greater opportunities to demonstrate their achievements. (The same competitive conditions laid to rest any debate about whether general managers need to be IS literate – all managers must be, to some extent, hybrid users.)

To balance the potential benefits there are, of course, a number of problems associated with being a hybrid manager. These need to be dealt with, but it is probable that, by definition, a hybrid manager cannot choose whether to be one or not! The problems and uncertainties of being a hybrid manager are:

- *Risk of failure*: Any hybrid manager is going to be costly to the organisation and usually engaged in high-risk areas of business activities. The higher *chance* of failure is exacerbated by a perceived higher *cost* to any failure. Hybrid managers are high profile and so are their failures, as well as their successes.

- *Stress*: Since the hybrid manager operates in high-risk business areas, in unfamiliar roles, with uncertain and ill-defined objectives and with some dislocation from single-dimension management colleagues, stress levels are inevitably going to be high. The effective, long-term hybrid manager must be emotionally stable.

- *Transference problems*: Given the weight of evidence that indicates that hybrid managers need organisational astuteness and the fact that this needs to be *assimilated* in some way, there are questions about just how transferable are the skills of the hybrid manager.

- *Uncertain career path*: Since much of the literature on hybrid management quotes instances only of the *accidental* development of senior hybrid managers there are few role models or signposted career paths to follow. With few pointers to how, and in what business area, should the intended hybrid manager gain their early experience it is hard to know how best to accumulate evidence of managerial worth.

- *Personal disruption*: The personal disruption experienced by the hybrid manager proceeding through transfer and crossover programmes will be high. However, some hybrid management development strategies do *not* lead to such great personal disruptions and, equally, there are other management career paths that do.

- *Identifying and obtaining training*: Most hybrid managers will experience difficulties in identifying the gaps in their skills set and even *more* difficulty in finding the most appropriate ways of plugging them. General management development is a notoriously difficult training area whilst *technical* training is just that and hence is rarely sufficiently multi-dimensional to develop an understanding of relevance and implications, rather than technique.

Finally, the hybrid manager must work out how to give continuous and 'appropriate' weight to the three parallel themes of hybrid management, which are:

- *Business awareness*, both in the general sense and specific to the current business arena

- *Management style and competence*, both in procedural and interpersonal ways

- *Technical competence*, initially, to keep current and for 'future watching'.

## 10.4 ◆ IS AS A PROFESSION

Not everyone who engages in the IS profession is destined for, or interested in, hybrid management in the sense described in Section 10.3. This chapter has constantly shown that IS is not homogenous; the IS profession now involves roles that are varied and subject to continual change. The paradigm shift discussed in Section 8.5.1 has created three streams within the IS profession as it forms one instance of the shamrock organisation of Figure 8.10 (*see* p. 277), the IS equivalents of which are shown in Figure 10.15.

The core of indispensable people are going to be those who are 'the organisation'. These can conveniently be thought of as the hybrid managers as discussed in Section 10.3. They are those responsible for IS, for the formulation and direction of IS strategy and therefore for managing the *way* the organisation exploits IS. The discussions of hybrid management as a 'new' phenomenon tend to focus on the fact that significant technological skills are now required of the contemporary manager. However what makes these hybrids *core* to their organisation, and may actually be what is 'new' about them as forms of IS management, is their possession of organisational astuteness as discussed in Section 10.3. The notion of the core is based not on tasks performed but on personal qualities and capabilities.

Whilst those of the core may be responsible for the overall direction of IS it is *delivered* through two other groups, the IS specialists and the external service providers. This latter group includes those who provide the outsourced services and those who provide the packaged solutions both discussed in Chapter 12. This group may also include those providing consultancy skills and development support, also discussed in Chapter 12. The IS specialists are all those who provide the internal IS expertise, both technical and managerial.

There are no hard boundaries between any of these three groups. IS specialists are often neither exactly in-house nor exactly external (contract-based employment

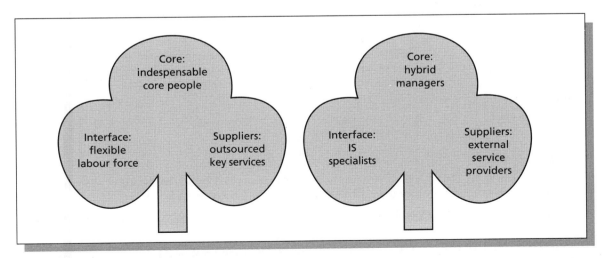

**Fig 10.15 ◆ The shamrock organisation of IS**
(after Handy)

| Position | Brief description |
|---|---|
| CIO | • Most senior executive responsible for information technology across the whole organisation. |
| MIS director | • Responsible for the day-to-day operations of all aspects of IS for the whole organisation. |
| IS executive | • Responsible for the day-to-day operations of all aspects of IS in one division, plant, or unit of the business; usually a general manager of that business unit, not the central IS group. |
| IS planning manager | • Analyses business and develops an architecture for the hardware and software to support systems in the future; may also forecast technology trends. |
| Manager of emerging technologies | • Evaluates new technologies, fosters experimental projects to test new technologies in the organisation, consults with users on appropriate application of new technologies, and approves new technologies for use in the organisation. |
| Development manager | • Co-ordinates all new systems development projects, allocates systems analysts and project managers to projects, schedules development work. |
| Manager of E-UC C or information centre | • Oversees the operation of computer hot line and user help-desks; training on user development tools and fourth-generation languages; and personal computer installation and support. |
| Maintenance manager | • Co-ordinates all systems maintenance projects, allocates systems analysts and project managers to projects, schedules maintenance work; depending on organisation structure, development and maintenance manager may be one person or several people responsible for different segments of the business. |
| Operations manager | • Supervises the day-to-day operations of data centres and possibly also data entry, data network, computer file library, and systems hardware and software maintenance staff; schedules computer jobs, manages downtime, and plans computer systems capacity. |
| Programming manager | • Co-ordinates all applications programming efforts; allocates and organises staff into project teams, acquires tools and languages to improve programmer productivity. |
| Telecommunications manager | • Co-ordinates the installation and operation of the corporate data and voice network. |
| Systems programming manager | • Responsible for support and maintenance of systems software (operating systems, utilities, programming language compilers, etc); interacts with vendors to install updates and request changes, may overlap duties with Telecommunications Manager and Database Administrator. |
| Data administrator | • Plans databases and co-ordinates the use of data management software. |
| Project manager | • Supervisor of analysts and programmers working on the development or maintenance of application system. |
| Manager of EDP auditing or QA | • Co-ordinates activities that set standards and checks compliance with standards to improve the quality and accuracy of systems. |
| Computer security manager | • Develops procedures and policies and installs and monitors software to ensure the authorised use of computing resources |

**Fig 10.16 ◆ IS management positions annotated to indicate core/interface boundary**
(adapted from *Managing Information Techology* (2nd edn), Martin *et al.*, © 1994, by permission of Prentice Hall Inc. Upper Saddle River, NJ)

being common). Organisational changes may result in IS specialists becoming 'core' or those of the core may move outside the organisation and yet still be providing services to it. In order to illustrate where the boundary between the core and interface lobes may lie the table in Figure 10.16 shows a list of management positions drawn from Martin *et al.* (1994) annotated with a dashed line to indicate where that boundary could fall for an organisation for whom IS is important but not competitively crucial. Those who *report* to these positions may also be in the interface lobe but are very likely to form the supplier set. One difficulty for the aspirations of the IS professionals, and one of the reasons why they may seek the organisational relevance of being hybrid managers, is that of perceptions of personal attributes. Since being 'core' depends on personal capability rather than tasks the continuing perception that IS people do not have the 'right' organisational awareness (see the report in *Computing* (1995), Vowler (1995), Boyle (1995) and Mansell-Lewis (1995)) always casts IS into the interface or supplier lobes.

The technical aspects of the skills of those engaged in the IS profession may need to change fast but there are enduring themes of business awareness, the capacity to acquire technical skills as needed and the capability to identify what skill is needed when. The demand for those who hold these competencies is generally very high. The level of demand reached a peak of 5 000 IT jobs advertised per quarter in the late 1980s. The demand was hit by the recessionary pressures of the early 1990s, falling to about 1 000 jobs advertised per quarter. However, with the mid-1990s reawakening of concern with IS-enabled business demand is again strong, approaching 2 000 jobs advertised per quarter and rising. The level of demand for IS professionals remains higher than for most other commercial roles (job statistics are drawn from Green-Armytage (1995a)).

In summary, the IS profession is well placed in terms of being employed but poorly placed in terms of organisational career progression. Salaries will be high for those who can acquire, continually update and sell as a service commodity, the *appropriate* competence. Prospects for those who wish to form an organisational core are poor, the perception of IS people as lacking organisational astuteness mitigates against this. The trend towards IS devolution makes it impossible for many to pursue IS managerial career prospects from *within* IS, see Briggs (1996), and so the IS profession may be the last one to choose from which to seek IS management positions.

However, the uncertainty of contract work, the low managerial prospects of interface staff, the poor senior management prospects for core staff are offset by high demand, high salaries or 'fast-track' prospects for those able to identify and exploit the 'correct' lobe for them.

**References and further reading**

BCS Case for Hybrid Managers (1991) *Computing*, 31 Jan p. 38.

Barnatt, C. (1996) *Management Strategy and Information Technologies*, International Thomson Press.

Boyle, B. (1995) Why IT and Business Managers Must Talk, *Computer Weekly*, 10 Aug p. 26.

Boynton, A., Jacobs, G. and Zmud, R (1992) Whose Responsibility is IT Management? *Sloan Management Review*, Summer pp. 32–8.

Bradbury (1995) Planning for A Change, *PC Week*, 7 Mar pp. 8–9.

Bray, P. (1993) A New Type of Manager, *Computing*, 14 Jan pp. 30–1.

Briggs, P. (1996) Business Units Restrict Careers of IT Personnel, *Computing*, 27 June p. 41.

Broadbent, M., Lloyd, P., Hansell, A. and Dampney, C. (1992) Roles, Responsibilities and Requirements for Managing Information Management, *International Journal of Information Management*, Vol 12 No 1 pp. 21–8.

Cane, A. (1992) Shared Vision of IT, *Financial Times*, 14 May.

Cash, J., McFarlan, F., McKenney, J. and Applegate, L. (1992) *Corporate Information Systems Management* (2nd edn), Irwin.

Computing (1995) Rift Deepens Between IS and Business, *Computing*, 22 June, p. 1.

Craver, D. (1990) Training the Hybrids in their Own Image, *Computer Weekly*, 5 Apr p. 16.

Currie, W. (1995) *Management Strategy for IS: An International Perspective*, Pitman Publishing.

Dataview (1995) Top Jobs Bounce Back, *Computer Weekly*, 11 May p. 1.

Devine, M. (1990) Turning Boffins into Hybrids, *The Times*, 15 Mar.

Earl, M.J. (1989) *Management Strategies for Information Technology*, Prentice Hall.

EDP Analyser (1986) Organising for the 1990s, *EDP Analyser*, Dec Vol 24 No 12.

Frenzel, C.W. (1992) *Management of Information Technology*, Boyd and Fraser.

Fried, L. (1995) *Managing Information Technology in Turbulent Times*, Wiley-QED.

Green-Armytage, J. (1995a) Advertisements for IT Jobs, *Computer Weekly*, 11 May p. 18.

Green-Armytage, J. (1995b) Fantastic Voyage, *Computer Weekly*, 18 May pp. 32–3.

Griffiths, C. (1992) Responsibility for IT – A Grey Area of Management, in *Proceedings of Evaluating and Managing the IT Investment*, Unicom Seminars.

Hamilton, S. (1992) Board Games, *Computing*, 10 Sept pp. 16–19.

Harvey, D. (1990) Technology-Mixed Breed: Mixed Blessings? *Director*, Vol 43 No 14 Aug p. 82.

Harvey, D. and Kavanagh, J. (1992) *Business Benefits and IT: The Hybrid Skills Connection.*, Business Intelligence.

Hershey, G. and Eatman, J. (1990) Why IS Execs Feel Left Out of Big Decisions, *Datamation*, 15 May pp. 97–9.

Hussain, D.S. and Hussain, K.M. (1992) *Information Management: Organisation, Management and Control of Computer Processing*, Prentice-Hall.

Jarvenpaa, S. and Ives, B. (1991) Executive Involvement and Participation in the Management of Information Technology, *MIS Quarterly*, June pp. 205–27.

Kavanagh, J. (Ed.) (1995) Hybrid IT Managers Required for the City, *Computer Weekly*, 4 May p. 52.

Kelly, S. (1996) IT Moves Closer to the Board, *Computer Weekly*, 1 Feb p. 14.

Mansell-Lewis, E. (1995) Programming for Change, *Computing*, 13 July p. 39.

Martin, B., Batchelder, G., Newcomb, J. and Rockart, J (1995) The End of Delegation? Information Technology and the CEO, *Harvard Business Review*, Sept-Oct pp. 161–72.

Martin, E., DeHayes, D., Hogger, J. and Perkins, W. (1994) *Managing Information Technology: What Managers Need to Know*, MacMillan.

Medd, K. (1991) I Manage: Therefore I am an IT Manager, *Infomatics*, Feb, pp. 43–6.

Nolan, R. L. (1982) Managing Information Systems by Committee, *Harvard Business Review*, July-Aug, pp. 72–9.

O'Brien, B. (1992) *Demands and Decisions: Briefings on Issues in Information Technology Strategy*, Prentice-Hall.

O'Brien, B. (1995) *Information Management Decisions: Briefings and Critical Thinking*, Pitman Publishing.

O'Brien, J.A. and Morgan, J.N. (1991) A Multi-Dimensional Model of Information Resource Management, *Information Resource Management Journal*, Vol 2 No 2, pp. 2–12.

O'Connor, G. and Smallman, C. (1995) The Hybrid Manager: A Review, *Management Decision*, Vol 33 No 7 p. 19–28.

Palmer, C. (1990) From Potential to Reality, *British Computer Society Report*.

Palmer, C. (1992) An IT World in Turmoil, *IT Matters*, Summer pp. 5–8.

Robertson, C. (1996) Senior recruitment rise shows promise, *Computing*, 25 Jan p. 33.

Skyrme, D.J. and Earl, M.J. (1990) Hybrid Managers: What Should You Do?, *British Computer Society Report*.

Tapscott, D. and Caston, A (1993) *Paradigm Shift: The New Promise of Information Technology*, McGraw-Hill.

Vowler, J. (1995) The Director as Diplomat, *Computer Weekly*, 8 Jun p. 30.

Ward, J. and Griffiths, P. (1996) *Strategic Planning for Information Systems* (2nd edn), Wiley.

# CHAPTER 11

# Managing user-controlled computing

The two previous chapters of this section have considered several important aspects of an organisation's IS resource: where it may be located, its activities organised and the possible nature of its IS professionals and senior management. Some of the disadvantages of the 'traditional' IS function were introduced in Chapter 9 and many of those difficulties remain intractable. For example, despite a theoretical awareness of its importance, communication between IS professionals and the wider organisational community is often flawed. Backlogs of development requests remain long despite the efforts to automate the 'software factory' as discussed in Chapter 9. There have been a number of simultaneous responses to the limitations of 'traditional' IS. One response, that of improved development approaches, has already been mentioned in Chapter 9, which also discussed alternative forms of IS organisation. Chapter 10 has explained hybrid managers as those capable of bridging communication divides. Another possible response is to 'offload' the intractable difficulties of IS by outsourcing some or all IS activities, and outsourcing will be discussed in Chapter 12. This chapter will discuss one more response to the same perception of IS difficulties, the response in this case being that of individuals 'taking' (sometimes unilaterally, sometimes in an encouraged way, sometimes in an enforced way) control of their own IS needs. This user control, often called end-user computing, represents computing by, and for, decision makers.

This chapter will also consider why such user-controlled computing generates managerial concerns quite distinct from IS by 'professionals' – though it must be noted that there is no longer, if there ever was, a sharp dividing line between these two classes. These distinct concerns lead to user-controlled computing being managed in distinct ways and this chapter also discusses how the directing and supporting of user-controlled computing can be handled. The notions of BPR, workflow planning and organisational learning discussed in Chapter 8 relate to user-controlled computing in complex ways and some of these, in particular the notions of team-based computing, will also be discussed.

Throughout this chapter the term user-controlled computing (U-CC) is used rather than the more common, but ambiguous, term 'end-user computing'. 'Traditional' IS arrangements have always had their 'end-users' who act as *customers* of systems and services. However, the main thrust of user-controlled computing is just that, user-controlled systems are not directly controlled by the IS professionals. Therefore, to highlight this critical distinction of who is holding the responsibility and authority and to avoid the possibility of confusion with the 'traditional' data processing notion of end-users an alternative phrase, user-controlled, has been chosen.

## 11.1 ◆ WHAT IS USER-CONTROLLED COMPUTING?

For many organisations, the response to the IS problems outlined above has been to choose to redirect, or to allow the drift of, IS responsibility and authority *away* from IS departments and *into* user-controlled computing. Despite recognising the need for this move and hence the need for structures and approaches that help users to help themselves, the actual resource allocations (remember the discussion in Chapter 1 of emergent versus intended strategies) frequently remain firmly in the hands of the IS department.

Not *all* user-controlled computing involves development work but much of it will. When U-CC involves developing systems then this is referred to as user application development (UAD). U-CC and UAD should result in reduced time delays in systems life cycles and make the achieved systems more 'in tune' with the business needs since there is a reduction in communication problems. McNurlin and Sprague (1989) sum it up as:

> End-user computing is the direct, hands-on use of computers by end users – not indirect use through systems professionals or the data processing staff ... a subset of end-user computing is end-user programming. Here, end users create procedures that they store and use over and over.

The management logic behind user-controlled computing is that IS is too important to leave totally to computing professionals. To reflect its importance there needs to be some way of providing IS education, training, support and knowledge, though the IS function has often been either unwilling or unable to transfer skills across. The existence of U-CC does *not* suggest that IS professionals cease to exist, but rather that U-CC can take on a complementary role.

User-controlled computing has moved through a number of stages; it was initially about persuasion, about getting nervous managers to use a PC, to tempt them with gorgeous graphics and seductive software to overcome their fears of a technology they did not customarily deal with directly. Then it became about what and how to control and harness the PC anarchy and reduce the time and money waste associated with the gorgeous graphics and seductive software. Currently it is fundamentally about how to *balance* U-CC costs and benefits for the competitive benefit of the business. This should all sound very familiar – Nolan's stages of growth model discussed in Chapter 5 suggested the concerns associated with any new technology will *vary* by the stage of maturity of the use and management of that technology. However, irrespective of the stage of maturity there are a number of technological aspects to what user-controlled computing does, include:

- *Corporate information management and retrieval*: To manage the modern deluge of data using DBMS packages that offer query languages and report generators and to use them on personal, departmental, corporate or external databases. Similarly, personal information management (PIM) software helps to manage oneself, and executive information systems (EIS) help to handle strategic information.

- *Personal Information Management (PIMs)*: Where personal productivity is enhanced along with the ability to communicate across groups, divisions, organisations and externally.

- *Decision support*: Users can build analytical models of their business area and use the tools available to create interactive analysis of alternatives to better inform their decisions.

- *User application development*: With the growth in tools that allow rapid development cycles, then developing systems, or altering existing ones, becomes relatively easy. The user can be the developer without being an IS-professional.

One of the most significant factors about U-CC has been its phenomenal growth rate. Indeed it is not the technical or application complexities that have driven the often fearful organisational reactions to it but rather its unbridled proliferation. It is the most rapidly growing sector of IS use, with up to 75 per cent of an organisation's total IS workload coming under the heading of user-controlled computing, and this starting from minute proportions a decade ago. Why has user-controlled computing grown from accounting for less than 25 per cent of IS budgets in the early 1980s to probably accounting for 75–90 per cent of them during the 1990s? This rapid growth is due to the *accumulated* weight of a number of factors that include:

- The development history of IS structures built a reservoir of users prepared for, and capable of, taking some form of technical plunge.

- The frustrations of the long applications backlog generated a pool of go-it-alone users eager to respond to this visible backlog.

- The development of a critical mass of end-user software development tools, both micro and mainframe based, provided easy access to IS solutions.

- The spread of good cost/performance ratio micros stimulated economic interest in user development of applications and reduced the focus on machine efficient applications.

- The general increase in computer literacy in the working population due to the spread of on-line systems has made computers an acceptable way of life at work and at home.

An explosion in software targeted at the collaborative work process is further fuelling the growth in user-controlled computing. Developments in electronic mail, joint word-processing, scheduling and project management software may give even more users their first *real* reason to be involved in IS.

In addition, it is perceived that there are a number of advantages to any organisation that has *managed* user-controlled computing, in that it:

- *Liberates a scarce resource*: Specialist IS skills can be used in areas that demand them.

- *Reduces development backlog*: This is, at least, dispersed. There is some evidence that the reduction may be temporary with three drivers of an increased backlog as U-CC becomes established: increased IS awareness leads to more requests, U-CC developments increase in sophistication to the point where corporate IS must be involved, and user perceptions are that the list will be shorter and so they make more requests.

- *Reduces time lag*: The delay between a business need being identified and an IS solution being available is reduced. It avoids the 'invisible queue' syndrome of business innovations that never get proposed since the innovator knows they would have to wait too long for the system for it to be worth the bother of suggesting it.

- *Suits task culture*: As organisations move from method based to task based, that is they move from prescribing how things must be done to what needs to be *achieved*, U-CC has a good cultural 'fit'. User-controlled computing accommodates the expansion of decision-maker autonomy in the 'flatter' organisations of the 1990s.

- *Encourages innovation*: It is business managers who tend to conceive of innovative uses of IS. U-CC tends to have less bureaucracy than corporate IS (less not none) and this lessening encourages innovation. This development of an innovative culture may generate yet more ideas and requests going to the corporate IS function!

The dramatic rise in the amount of user-controlled computing, at all levels of an organisation, has opened up many opportunities, but policies for managing it effectively must be constructed with reference to the overall organisational goals for IS if these opportunities are to be realised. The benefits discussed above can be summarised as producing an increase in an individual's performance, which creates the *potential* for enhanced organisational efficiency and effectiveness.

From the organisational perspective there is, inevitably, a downside to user-controlled computing. A number of concerns are expressed about its dangers, there are:

- *Duplication and waste*: Since many people are likely to identify the same needs and use their autonomy to address them, this, at least, *implies* that the organisation is accepting a measure of duplication and waste. Many aspects of the management of U-CC are concerned with identifying and reducing this waste.

- *Increased costs*: Just because the processing power ordinarily used by user-controlled computing is cheap does not mean that U-CC itself is cheap. Estimates put the support costs of end-user computing at four times the purchase price of the necessary hardware and software, per year – as Fawcett (1996) points out, too expensive to own! The absolute amount of IS activity increases as well as the relative unit cost. This increase in absolute and relative costs will happen whether user-controlled computing is offering any business gain or not! Costs can further escalate from inappropriate uses, for instance where senior managers spend extensive amounts of time developing systems that do not need their particular expertise.

- *Data integrity concerns*: There are generally concerns about the integrity of corporate data once it is being used by U-CC systems. These fears of lost accuracy can be somewhat alleviated by technical solutions, such as read-only access mechanisms. However, many U-CC applications revolve around the data manipulation of corporate data and concerns about the validity of such manipulations must be allayed.

- *Questionable quality systems*: Many user-controlled computing systems may be of lower absolute 'quality' than corporate ones. They may include bugs, have poor (or no) documentation, have no security and control mechanisms and make no provision for archiving and back-ups. The clear danger is that business decisions may be being made from very shaky foundations. As Manchester (1995) says 'Anybody can throw a TV dinner into a microwave but it takes an expert to prepare a proper meal.'

Care must be taken when stating that user-controlled computing systems are of poorer quality. Issues of quality are not clear cut and 'fitness for purpose' and 'value for money' are going to be a prime concern. A user-controlled computing system may not require extensive documentation or inappropriate controls if it is an almost disposable system. Though *enough* accuracy must be built in, the meaning of 'enough' may be that it will permit information sharing: in today's business world it is the fear of incompatibilities preventing future sharing that is the biggest concern with user-controlled computing. Simply defining standards for hardware and software does *not* overcome this danger, for example data names and meanings may vary from one user-developed system to another. The drive to information 'warehousing' is making this the most important disadvantage associated with user-controlled computing.

# 11.2 ◆ DESCRIPTIVE MODELS OF USER-CONTROLLED COMPUTING

Before moving on to discuss ways in which user-controlled computing may be managed it will be useful to introduce a number of the ways that such computing has been modelled. Managing U-CC is essentially about making trade-offs and achieving a 'suitable' balance between opposing tensions. The advice is generally in a contingent form informed by organisational nature and technological issues, but also by the nature of the organisation's instance of U-CC.

It is fairly straightforward to identify the consumers of a delivered computer system; these are the operators of an MIS, the sales order entry clerks for instance, whose sole or main job is to operate a system. These consumers, or end-users, can be distinguished from the creators of the systems. These developers are the IS professionals whose sole or main role is to develop systems. For many years this two-category descriptor of consumer/creator served to describe all who were involved with IS. It did not preclude user involvement in systems developments, in the sense that the creators sought their requirements and preferences when making the development decisions. What this two-horse race does preclude is a description that adequately covers the salesman who creates his own spreadsheet model to calculate commission rates against discounts given. Creating systems is *not* his main role and yet he is the creator here. It is no longer very helpful to describe just user and supplier roles when considering people's involvement with IS.

## 11.2.1 ◆ Described by skill and job content

A more useful way to describe those involved in systems is by their technology competence and the nature of their job content. Rockart and Flannery (1983) offered a six-level continuum for classifying all those involved with IS and this is shown in Figure 11.1. Although this continuum classifies all *users*, not all classes represent *user-controlled computing*, since class 1 and class 6 are our old friends the consumer/creator extremes. Despite being rather broader than just U-CC, this description of all involved with IS allows different support needs to be identified and provided. The six classes are:

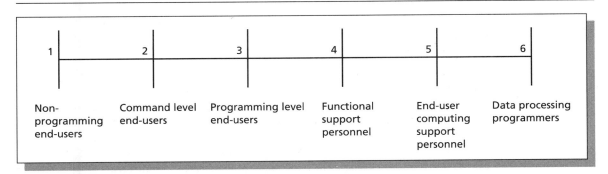

**Fig 11.1 ◆ End-user computing continuum**
(after Rockart and Flannery)

1 *Non-programming end-user*: The 'traditional' user of IS. These are the operators of the systems developed by others. This category is the sales order entry clerk whose support needs are very focused, specific system training and fault fixing, time efficient support.

2 *Command-level end-users*: These are the users of a 'raw' package, which they will often do along with operating pre-written systems. This class of user has some knowledge of the application package, perhaps enough to use it to integrate data from several sources or to write DBMS *ad hoc* queries. This user requires development support and training and is willing to learn enough to enhance the performance of their day-to-day job, be it in personnel, marketing, or whatever.

3 *Programming level end-users*: These are sometimes called 'power users' since they can create systems for their own use. They develop their own applications, some of which are eventually used by others. This is the accountant who knows far more about the spreadsheet than the IS department does. This user needs methodology support and training.

4 *Functional support personnel*: These are the functional project groups of Chapter 9. They are the decentralised IS groups who routinely develop systems for use in that one business area. This user class provides support and training but only on the systems they develop and need specialist training and support themselves. A class 3 user would see themselves as an accountant *using* IS, whereas a class 4 user would see themselves as IS people *developing* accounting systems.

5 *End-user support personnel*: These exist solely to support others. They can be targeted at helping any/all of class 1, 2 or 3 in their IS tasks. This category of user is almost never going to develop systems for use by others. They require complex training and support themselves since there is a need to train the trainers and support the supporters. In addition, they may provide some aspects of training and support to class 4 users or even class 6 users.

6 *Data processing programmers*: These are the 'true' developers. They have a lot in common with classes 3 and 4 since they will need to encompass the depth of class 3 and the breadth of class 4. These are typically less business aware than class 4, they are likely to be more concerned with, and hence more skilful at, infrastructure issues such as:

- Capacity planning
- Development tools and methodologies

- Standards and connectivity
- Network management and efficiency.

  This user is very rarely self-taught as class 3 might be. This class represents the staffing of the data centre.

One of the most powerful features of classifying IS relationships in this way is that the given descriptions permit *movement*, and so:

- Class 1 may move to class 2: When they discover the need to do a little more
- Class 2 may move to class 3: With time, practice and inclination
- Class 3 may fall back to class 2: With the advent of new software
- Classes 4, 5 and 6 may transfer: As resource demands dictate.

## 11.2.2 ◆ Described by control discretion

An alternate way of describing the nature of user-controlled computing is to look, not at job *content* and technology *skill*, but at the level of user *autonomy*. Four levels of this can be defined:

- *Level A – No discernible user autonomy*: This is the system operator again since the IS function has responsibility for, and authority over, the system. The user is in a 'take it or leave it' relationship with the system.
- *Level B – User input but not control*: This level of user may specify the required system so, in that sense, is responsible for its nature but the IS function remains responsible for developing and maintaining it.
- *Level C – User selection and operation*: This level of user is the first that can be considered to be engaged in U-CC since the responsibility extends to the full selection and use of the system (may be through choice and use of an application package). The operational authority and responsibility are in the user's hands.
- *Level D – User development*: This level of user holds total control over the development as well as the operation of the system.

Only levels C and D would normally be regarded as user-controlled computing. There is a very useful analogy to transport types that is frequently used to explain these differences, it is:

| Transport type | Level of end-user |
|---|---|
| Train | A |
| Taxi | B |
| Self-drive car | C |
| Self-build car | D |

When taking a train, customers *collectively* have an impact, but individually must go by the route and at the time dictated by the company. By taking a taxi, a customer can select the precise start and end point and time of the journey but not *how* the driver will achieve it, the taxi driver is free to decide upon the detail of the route and the speed of travel! When self-driving a car, one can choose when, where and how to make the journey. Building (or servicing and maintaining) the car as well gives total independence and one can go when, where, how and in what style one chooses.

This transport analogy is useful since it highlights two important issues associated with user-controlled computing. Firstly, there must be a concern for standards. It is standards that provide the highway code, or the rule of the road, applicable to the taxi and the self-drive car. It is standards that provide the MOT of the taxi, self-drive and self-build car. It is immediately obvious that a different set of rules pertains to the 'selection and use only' level of U-CC than the 'develop and operate and maintain' level of it. The issues are, as in transport, that of certifying roadworthiness of the vehicle (quality of development) and of policing the safety of the driving (use of the application).

The second issue highlighted by this transport analogy is the difference between on-road and off-road driving. Public highway driving requires rules for the safety of *others*, whereas off-road driving requires safety only for *oneself*. Similarly, truly personal end-user computing may require much looser 'rules' than multi-user or workgroup end-user computing. Corporate systems are in a curious position: When they operate on the road, they need even more controls, however when they operate alone, and so in a protected mode (on rail tracks), they perhaps need fewer controls and these are special and specific. The 'rules of the road', in other words the managerial controls, need to vary by degree of user autonomy and the scope of the reliance upon the system.

## 11.2.3 ◆ Described by maturity stage

An important development of Nolan's stages of growth model (*see* Section 5.6.1) was proposed by Huff, Munro and Martin (1988) when they suggested that similar stages of maturity are gone through by the 'new' technology of user-controlled computing. Their model categorises, not the users of U-CC, but the processes of growth in user-controlled computing. This model is an important one since it leads to considering the differing issues in managing U-CC and its *growth*. Huff *et al.* suggest that user-controlled computing becomes more sophisticated over time, and suggest that the maturity of the applications that are the tangible output of it form the main measure of this maturity. This maturity of applications can be best judged by looking at the nature of their integration. Unlike Nolan's model, that of Huff *et al.* has five stages, and these are:

1 *Isolation*: There is little or no exchange of data between applications. Only pockets of U-CC activity produce applications that are best thought of as learning rather than business tools. Organisational dependence on them is low.

2 *Stand-alone*: The applications remain 'islands' with no integration, these stand-alone applications are more critical to the performance of the job. This dependence is restricted, however, to just the individual's immediate area. The islands proliferate to the point where many businesses depend upon sequences of such applications but the data is being re-keyed at each point.

3 *Manual integration*: During this stage the U-CC developments require significant exchanges of data but this is achieved by *manual intervention*. Links may be by physical transfer of disks or the logical transfer of files over networks or

between accounts. The need for this integration, even though not automated, forces the issues of standards and development discipline to the attention of those managers responsible for, and engaged in, U-CC.

4 *Automated integration*: The focus shifts to *automating* the transfer of data, and integration is considered even during the application's design. The burden of manual intervention for every download or data exchange is lifted by the automation of the connections. This is the dawning of true integrated systems but ones that still require user knowledge of location and structure of the required data.

5 *Distributed integration*: The distinctions of location and structure disappear at this stage since the applications can be written without having to navigate to the required data. Irrespective of the physical distribution of data it can be accessed as if it was in a central warehouse store (*see* Section 11.5).

These five stages are summarised in Figure 11.2.

## 11.2.4 ◆ Described by three key variables

Although assessing user skills, U-CC maturity or levels of control is important. Cotterman and Kumar (1989) suggest that *understanding* user-controlled computing is actually more complex. They develop a user cube as a way of classifying users according to three key factors; this cube is shown in Figure 11.3. These factors are:

- *Operation*: Of the hardware or software, including the manual tasks associated with the system. The writers clearly distinguish between use, which implies operation plus consumption of the final product, and that which is solely operation.

- *Development*: The performance of any or all aspects of systems development by whatever means, including traditional methods, prototyping or package purchase.

- *Control*: Over IS resources with decision making authority to obtain and use any element of the system.

Cotterman and Kumar place operation along the x-axis, development along the y-axis and control along the z-axis of a cubic model of user-controlled computing where all three axes represent a continuum of possible values. Although this gives an infinite variety of potential classes, in general, the eight corners are enough to

| Stage | Characteristics |
|---|---|
| Isolation | Little or no exchange of data |
| Stand-alone | Data is re-keyed or not exchanged |
| Manual Integration | Manual controlled electronic exchanges, disk or file exchanges |
| Automated Integration | Automated exchanges are designed into applications |
| Distributed Integration | Physical location of data is irrelevant as network not end-users handles navigation |

**Fig 11.2 ◆ User-controlled computing stages of application's maturity**
(after Huff *et al.*)

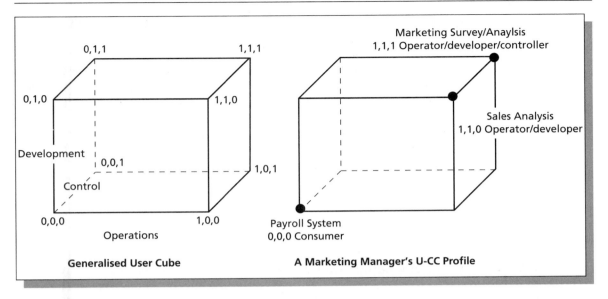

**Fig 11.3 ◆ User cubes**
(adapted by permission of the Association of Computing Machinery from User Cube: A Taxonony of End Users by Cotterman and Kumar (1989), *Communications of the ACM*, Vol 32, No 11. Copyright © 1990 ACM)

give eight representative types of users. These types are summarised in Figure 11.4. The pure consumer of a system developed and controlled by IS professionals is at 0,0,0 whereas 'full' U-CC would be at 1,1,1.

Since the eight states *are* different, they provide a way of identifying and so developing management strategies for U-CC that reflect each of these distinct states. Thus policies for data integrity, risk assessment, standards and procedures, training, procurement, documentation, application controls, etc, should all *differ* depending upon the actual class. The example user's profile, illustrated in Figure 11.3, shows how this more detailed end-user classification system could be used to highlight the different roles that need to be managed in different ways.

| XYZ | User classification |
| --- | --- |
| 0 0 0 | User-consumer |
| 1 0 0 | User-operator |
| 0 1 0 | User-developer |
| 0 0 1 | User-controller |
| 1 1 0 | User-operator/developer |
| 0 1 1 | User-developer/controller |
| 1 0 1 | User-operator/controller |
| 1 1 1 | User-operator/developer/controller |

**Fig 11.4 ◆ Types of end-users**
(adapted by permission of the Association of Computing Machinery from User Cube: A Taxonony of End Users by Cotterman and Kumar (1989), *Communications of the ACM*, Vol 32, No 11. Copyright © 1990 ACM)

## 11.3 ◆ APPROACHES TO DIRECTING USER-CONTROLLED COMPUTING

The descriptive models presented in Section 11.2 are only useful if they assist in some way to make user-controlled computing effective. Whilst contemporary technologies are making U-CC ever easier, they don't, of themselves, make it effective. For U-CC to be organisationally effective, successful managerial decisions on achieving the balance between freedom (to gain the innovations and other advantages) and anarchy (creating incompatibilities and other disadvantages) must be taken. Since the overall resource consumptions of U-CC are very large U-CC must be managed to ensure that the beneficial results are similarly substantial.

This issue of trade-offs to achieve balance was summed up by Munro *et al.* (1987) as being choices made on two management variables:

- The rate of expansion of U-CC activities
- The level of control over U-CC activities

The rate of expansion can be managed by making information easier or harder to get; hardware and software easier or harder to get; more or less support available; or altering the costs borne by the user community. The level of control can be managed by determining the extent of the restrictions on free selection of hardware and software products; the policies on micro/mainframe use; the restrictions on free access to data; the restrictions on the acquisition process. The Munro *et al.* two-variables matrix is illustrated in Figure 11.5. The expansion/control framework for assessing strategies and their evolution acknowledges that access to the tools that are the fundamental basis of U-CC may be one of the most significant determinants of growth. Frustrations caused by the unpredictable supply of hardware, software, network services, etc can most effectively hold back growth.

A fast rate of expansion is concerned with seeking most of the *advantages* of end-user computing whilst strong control is concerned with getting least of the *disadvantages*. Munro *et al.* suggest that high expansion and high control is the 'mature' management strategy, combining as it does the best of both worlds. This matrix can be used in association with models of organisational objectives and culture

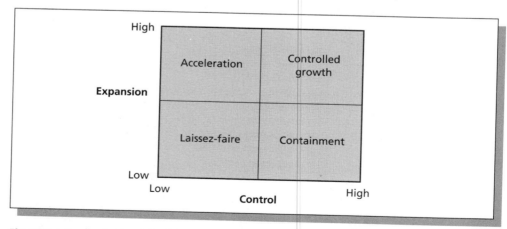

**Fig 11.5 ◆ Expansion/control matrix for user-controlled computing**
(adapted by permission of M.E. Sharpe Inc. from Expansion and Control of End-User Computing by Munro *et al.*, *Journal of Management Information Systems*, Vol 4 No 3 (1987) p. 9)

to evaluate options for managing U-CC, for instance low control approaches are unlikely to be adopted by risk-averse organisations whereas high expansion approaches would suit risk-seeker organisations. An organisation uses control and expansion tactics to manage the pace and direction of U-CC. The four possibilities are:

- *Laissez-faire*: This approach is the 'opening position' for most organisations; their interest in U-CC is low and there is no attempt to either expand or control the direction of user-controlled computing.

- *Acceleration*: Organisations adopting this approach have decided to provide abundant resources but little setting of a direction for U-CC. The management logic is to allow every individual the freedom to make the decisions they deem 'best'.

- *Controlled growth*: This approach enables U-CC to grow rapidly but in a carefully controlled environment. Sufficient resources are provided to ensure growth and appropriate controls ensure that this growth is in line with organisational requirements. Establishing *sufficient* and *appropriate* is the constant management dilemma.

- *Containment*: This 'slowly and carefully' approach to U-CC is to ensure that the organisation feels its way along a very precise and clearly defined channel of user activities.

O'Brien (1996) argues that there are not, in fact, four possible approaches but only three since, he suggests, setting low controls on U-CC will be to 'abstain from any attempt to influence the rate of expansion'. However it is perfectly feasible for an organisation to abstain from directing the *nature* of U-CC activities (ie low control) whilst simultaneously seeking to increase the *volume* of U-CC activities (ie high expansion).

Any organisation adopting a completely *laissez-faire* or draconian tight control approach to U-CC is unlikely to be *effectively* managing it. Completely restricted use stifles experimentation and innovation; indeed Arkush (1986) defines innovation as 'creatively managing ... by experimenting and taking risks' and yet unguided uses might be detrimental to the organisation by leading to harmful waste and even more harmful incompatibilities, although Strassman (1995) urges firms to remember that 'whoever governs least, governs best' and that all interventions drive up costs. The appropriate balance must be struck and the definition of *appropriate* can only be derived by reference to the goals as stated in the IS strategy, and the current situation, defined, for instance, by the stage of maturity. Revisiting the five stages of growth provided by Huff *et al.*, (1988) shows how the management approach *may* differ by stage:

1 *Isolation*: Organisations typically adopt a *laissez-faire* approach and make no attempt to support or control U-CC. Consequently there is effectively no organisational U-CC planning, control, training or support. Towards the end of this stage an embryonic Information Centre (IC) may emerge (see section 11.4 for discussion of what an IC is).

2 *Stand-alone*: During this stage organisations tend to promote the role of the IC by advertising the support and training it has to offer. Simultaneously the IC begins to formulate the procedures for evaluating, acquiring and, to a lesser extent, standardising user hardware and software. The IC begins to move from a reactive to *proactive* stance.

3 *Manual integration*: This stage represents greater *formalising of goals* for U-CC. There is greater IC involvement in audits and evaluations to assess organisa-

tional benefits from the cumulatively significant U-CC investments. After two stages of being 'IS mavericks' the IC must now begin to work closely with corporate IS to facilitate systems integration.

4 *Automated integration*: *Management* of U-CC data becomes the dominant issue and the IC often takes on the role of formulating and implementing policies for data access and data security.

5 *Distributed integration*: The IC staff are *business analysts* as well as software support staff. The IC itself may be distributed to strengthen the business awareness. The necessary and appropriate policies on developments, data access, planning justifications are all integrated into the 'normal' work environment.

As the maturity of U-CC increases so the information centre takes a more prominent role. Some of the issues relating to information centres are discussed in Section 11.4.

Gerrity and Rockart (1986) were amongst the first to give names to generic management strategies for user-controlled computing (*see* Figure 11.6). As with Porter's business strategy, Parsons' overall IS strategy (that has now come to be regarded as corporate IS) is a list that represents the essential logic of a number of alternatives that may be chosen or a description of what has emerged.

1 *Maintaining the IS monopoly* ensures there is almost no U-CC and so it is hardly a strategy for managing it! In theory this could be a managerial response, and it is often tried during the early stages of user-controlled computing. In practice, however, where IS becomes too recalcitrant it is IS that will be altered, not U-CC.

2 *Laissez-faire*, or 'do nothing', is neither to encourage nor discourage U-CC. Again, this is a common management stance in the early stages of U-CC, but becomes rarer later on because of the following problems:

● The variety of software tools makes it unrealistic for users to select the 'best' for their circumstances.

● User needs may be driven by immediate problems to the detriment of overall or long-term opportunities or threats.

● There are *intrinsic* inefficiencies in leaving users to 'learn for themselves'.

● The inevitable lack of standards means inevitable inefficiencies and 'networking' U-CC applications more difficult than is necessary.

● The transition of an application from a U-CC one to a corporate one is extremely difficult.

3 *Support through an information centre* collects a group, or groups, of staff *removed* from the corporate IS groups and gives these support staff the responsibility for

● Maintain the IS monopoly
● Laissez-faire
● Support through an information centre
● Managed free economy

**Fig 11.6 ◆ Generic management strategies for user-controlled computing**

responding to user needs. The nature of information centres has evolved, increasingly being de-centralised to the user community, see Section 11.4. Despite such distributions, the information centre may remain inherently *reactive* giving rise to a number of problems, such as:

- IC staff may hold extensive software/hardware skills but may lack business knowledge.
- ICs may please no one; their operation may be at odds with corporate IS and yet not be reflective of user needs.
- ICs may not be able to support all of the main U-CC technologies: communications networking, personal computing, office automation systems.

4 *Managed free economy* takes a more sophisticated approach to obtaining a *balance* between the two equally important but sometimes contradictory forces within U-CC:

- The user need for *freedom* to define their information needs
- The user need for *direction setting* that will guide development and provide an infrastructure

Gerrity and Rockart felt that there are five attributes of a managed free economy approach to U-CC, which are:

- A *stated* U-CC strategy; that has been devised by senior management, including senior IS management, that specifies the role of U-CC in achieving the business aims and the roles of all concerned.
- A user/IS working partnership that can *constantly* strike the 'best' balance.
- An active targeting of organisationally critical user applications.
- An integrated user support approach from a single, centralised, IC organisation.
- An emphasis upon education; to achieve all the first four attributes needs a real commitment to creating an IS skilled and empowered user community.

Given these five attributes the biggest difference between this and the support through an information centre is the shift from reactive to proactive. The same issue of offering classifications of possibilities is covered by Clark (1992), who discards any suggestion of maintaining the IS monopoly and describes three possible strategies for managing U-CC as:

- *User autonomy*: Where the users are fully responsible for purchases, developments, budgets and support. This definition roughly equates to that of Gerrity and Rockart's laissez-faire approach.
- *User partnership*: Where some responsibilities are shared, for instance the setting of budgets, but purchases must be to corporate guidelines and support and advice is available. This definition roughly equates to that of Gerrity and Rockart's Information Centre approach.
- *Central control*: Where IS controls the budgets and the purchases and developments are joint ventures that are significantly supported by IS. This definition roughly equates to Gerrity and Rockart's managed free economy.

The generic strategies listed by both Gerrity and Rockart (1986) and Clark (1992) are general descriptions of how U-CC may be directed. Such direction is essentially responding to the perceived risks associated with U-CC whilst wishing to retain the advantages. Alavi and Weiss (1986) summarised the organisational risks associated with U-CC and identified what effective U-CC management must therefore achieve as:

- *User-controlled computing may solve the wrong problem.* Since users are not analysts they may incorrectly define the problem, indeed there is a tendency for U-CC to alleviate symptoms rather than address root problems. Support and management structures need to deal with the issue of problem solving.

- *Waste.* User-controlled computing runs the risk of wasting IS resources and user time, and, in short, the organisation's resources. Waste can only be defined as such resources being used for no gain; management and support structures must ensure that gains are made.

- *Development risks.* Even when the correct problem is being addressed an incorrect solution may be used. U-CC is notorious for not involving error checking and testing. Management and support structures must therefore ensure *appropriate* levels of accuracy.

- *Incompatibility.* Even when the right problem is efficiently and accurately solved there is still a risk from the potential incompatibility of different solutions created within the same problem area. Support and management structures must identify whether compatibility is critical and, if it is, ensure that it happens.

The existence of these risks is not an argument for *eradicating* U-CC to remove all risk, since that would stifle development. It is, however an argument for being *aware* of, and *managing,* those risks. Figure 11.7 illustrates some of the specific managerial and technological responses that might achieve an effective trade-off between a given risk and stifling user activities.

Weber (1986) reminds us that the planning and control issues associated with end-user computing are frequently exactly those wrestled with and, if not solved, at least coherently addressed for corporate systems. These issues are:

- System development issues of choosing which systems to develop and how and by whom.

- Operational issues of the 'mundane', or at least daily, sort, such as back-ups, security, capacity planning, legal issues, etc. All these operational issues are less formal, more hidden, and therefore more concerned with U-CC.

- Hardware and software issues: Primarily these are of standardisation, acquisition approaches, legality, upgrades and the organisational rationale for purchases.

- Training and support issues related to U-CC. The support and training approaches for corporate systems are a well considered area; U-CC is fast catching up, and with increasing research into the various support mechanisms, especially the information centre.

- Behavioural issues have to be addressed, such as an individual's reluctance to become involved in U-CC, or their reluctance to be realistic about its capabilities, and somehow U-CC needs to develop ways to identify and promote the organisationally important applications. Corporate IS has been tackling this issue for decades.

- The major managerial challenge of user-controlled computing is how to transfer the lessons learnt from corporate IS to U-CC *without* transferring its inflexibility.

| | User application life cycle stage | Organisational risk | Control mechanisms |
|---|---|---|---|
| **Analysis** | *Analysis of user tools* | Ineffective use of monetary resources | Cost/benefit analysis |
| | | Incompatible user tools | Hardware/software standards |
| | | Threats to data security and integrity | Policy for user access to corporate data |
| | *Analysis of user application* | Over-analysis and insufficient search for the solution | Providing user training in problem solving and modelling |
| | | Solving the wrong problem | Involve analyst in the design process for review |
| **Design** | *Conceptual design of user applications* | Applying the wrong model | Technical training Reviews |
| | | Mismatch between the tools and applications | Policy for technical reviews |
| | *Development of user application* | Little or no documentation | Enforce documentation standards Include documentation in development process |
| | | Lack of extensive testing | Testing/validation standards User training in application quality assurance |
| | | Lack of validation and quality assurance | Analyst/auditor 'walk through' Auditor reviews |
| | | Redundant development effort | User training in modelling application development Common development library |
| | | Inefficient expenditure of non-IS personnel time | Management policy for limits on allocation of non-IS personnel time Support from analyst |
| **Implementation** | *Operation of user application* | Threat to data integrity | Input data validation routines User training in data integrity issues |
| | | Taxing the mainframe computer resources | Management policy on the role of U-CC Integrating U-CC and IS planning Control of U-CC growth through budgets and internal charging |
| | | Threats to security | Access control via passwords Physical access control (restricted areas) Standards for back-ups |
| | *Maintenance* | Failure to document and test modification | Maintenance review by analyst |
| | | Failure to upgrade the application | Periodic system review by user analyst |

**Fig 11.7 ◆ U-CC risks and potential control mechanisms**
(adapted with permission of M.E. Sharpe Inc. from Managing Risks Associated with End-User Computing by Alavi and Weiss, *Journal of Management Information Systems*, Vol 2 No 3 (1986) p. 19)

There is, unfortunately, a basic dichotomy in these planning and control issues; avoiding problems requires the existence of checks, controls and policing mechanisms whilst being innovative requires freedom to experiment. In addition to that basic problem is the issue of 'traditional' IS's fears of U-CC. Many 'DP' staff act as if users were dumb and behave angrily if users get 'uppity'. IS arguments against user-controlled computing are that:

- U-CC can lead to systems' fragmentation and so will have a negative effect on the culture of the organisation. In reality, perhaps IS staff are more likely to be out of tune with the business, its goals and needs!

- IS is needed to integrate. This is probably true for integrating, for instance, order processing with sales, but for most organisations that level of integration has now been achieved; the remaining integration of data is essentially an organisational rather than a technical issue.

- Users are dumb. This is only true if they have only got access to dumb terminals and users can take responsibility for local computing if they have got local processing and software capability.

- Users are not software designers. This is probably true but they do not need to be in the conventional sense given the availability of automated software tools.

- Users are not strategists. Some users are not but some, of course, will be, and if they are not, who is? When this argument is proffered by IS it generally means that IS does not wish users to select hardware platforms. A useful heuristic with such infrastructure concerns is: Business sets the goals, IS maintains the tools.

So to sum up, directing U-CC is about achieving balance and making trade-offs. The *way* in which U-CC is directed is, as defined by Galletta and Hufnagel (1992):

> *A set of statements, reflecting an organisation's strategy for user-directed computing, that identifies the responsibilities of both information systems personnel and users, limits the range of acceptable choices and establishes specific control practices to be followed by all users who perform their own data processing and system development tasks.*

Any number of variations of responses to the issues of U-CC are possible, for instance some common responses are as illustrated in Figure 11.8.

| Issue | Response |
| --- | --- |
| Hardware selection and maintenance | The IS staff select the *types* of hardware that can be purchased and maintain it |
| Software selection | The IS staff select the *types* of user tools that can be purchased and support them |
| Training | The IS staff provide training for users on the selected software and hardware |
| Data availability | Users control their own data, and share it using local area networks. Corporate data can be accessed under guidance of IS staff |
| Data security | Corporate data access limited to user's needs and 'read only' |
| Systems development | IS staff help users with analysis and design where necessary and ongoing development support through help lines |

Fig 11.8 ◆ Common response to user-controlled computing issues

There are, of course, many factors that will influence just what type of U-CC policy (the managerial choice on how the trade-offs are to be made) an organisation is likely to have. Galletta and Hufnagel (1992) have developed a contingency model, illustrated in Figure 11.9, that provides a framework of predictors of the expected formality of the process of developing the U-CC policy, its comprehensiveness and degree of restrictiveness, and suggests that both of these will affect the degree of compliance with the stated policy. Examples of their findings are that where formal, well-structured planning efforts exist, and interest in U-CC is high, and maturity of U-CC is low, then the formality of the process of policy setting and the comprehensiveness of the resulting policy will be high. Increasing the formality of the policy setting process increases the comprehensiveness of the policy itself but not necessarily its restrictiveness. Increasing the degree of comprehensiveness of the policy increases the chance of compliance with it.

## 11.4 ◆ INFORMATION CENTRES AND USER SUPPORT

The earlier sections of this chapter have shown that there are organisational benefits to be had from user-controlled computing but there are also many risks associated with poorly managing it. User support seeks to ensure that the advantages are realised whilst the risks are minimised. There is no doubt that, whilst there are other approaches to supporting and managing U-CC, the most commonly adopted one is the information centre (IC). An information centre is an organisational construct that exists to support the development and operation of the personal or small group systems generated by U-CC. The phrase *information centre* was first used by IBM in

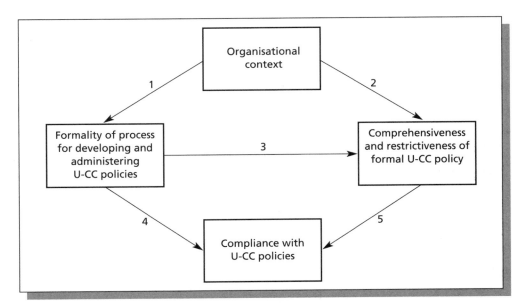

**Fig 11.9 ◆ Relationship between organisational and user variables**
(adapted from A Model End-User Computing Policy by Galletta and Hufnagel, *Information and Management*, Vol 22 No 1, p. 2 © 1992, with kind permission of Elsevier Science NL)

the mid-1970s (though support centres had been used by a number of organisations even earlier) to describe the structure complementary to the corporate IS service provision that is currently known as the data centre or IS department. IBM created the first information centre, as Carr (1987) said, to provide:

> *a portion of the information systems development resource organised and dedicated to support the users of IS services in activities such as report generation and modification, data manipulation and analysis, spontaneous enquiries, etc. The fundamental premise underlying an IC is that if proper education, technical support, usable tools, data availability, and convenient access to the systems are provided, users may directly and rapidly... and willingly... satisfy a part of their business area requirements that depend on the IS environment.*

Like user-controlled computing, an IC *can* exist in a totally mainframe environment but is more frequently associated with the technology changes of downsizing and growth in PC use to which it is the structural parallel.

The information centre concept has been defined in many different ways. It is taken here to be the organisational *opposite* to the data centre. So whereas the data centre may be decentralised but is *probably* centralised, the information centre may be centralised but is *probably* decentralised (not devolved since it is a service rather than a line activity). The data centre handles mass volume data processing transactions, hence its name, whilst the information centre transfers skills and access awareness in order to improve information use and management, hence its name. Data centres support the processing by IS professionals that is meant by 'indirect use of IS' whilst information centres help people become/continue to be *direct* users of IS. Information centres may represent the organisation's commitment to U-CC and provide the advice and support mechanisms that aim to ensure that user-controlled computing is *effective*. Some evidence exists, see Guimaraes and Igbaria (1994), that ICs significantly increase an organisation's chance of successful results from U-CC.

It is possible, however, to view information centres in a rather different light. An information centre may develop, implement and police the 'appropriate' controls that form the 'highway code' of E-UC applications and the quality assurance procedures that form their 'MOT test'. So rather than representing a commitment to support and encouragement they may be agents of control by IS departments and so be *colonies* of the data centre rather that complementary to it. In fact White and Christy (1987) defined an IC in terms of serving the IS department by *controlling* U-CC.

If Gerrity and Rockart's (1986) work is acknowledged then the 'classic' view of the information centre as a purely support mechanism must be augmented by proactive elements that direct user-controlled computing activities. Direction can sit uncomfortably with a stated aim of support, though this largely depends upon interpretation of the word *support*. Some implementations of an IC take it to mean helping those engaged in U-CC, whilst others take it to mean helping the *organisation* get the best out of U-CC's potential.

So just what does an information centre do? In essence most ICs provide:

- Hardware support
- Software support
- People support

The specifics of the services they provide to give this support are very varied, and examples of what they might do are given in Figure 11.10. U-CC may create a situation where every manager now has two systems they intend to get around developing, rather than the previous highly visible and aggregated list of twenty systems waiting for IS to develop them. However, the business 'coal face' is now setting its own priorities. Given the user's new direct responsibility for managing their own development priorities an additional key service the IC should provide is to equip users with the skills needed for this role.

Some writers view it as part of the role of an information centre to actually provide applications, others specifically exclude it from IC services. Dr Alan Solomon, a PC guru, whilst Chairman of the IBM PC Users Group gave his views on this as:

> *The role of the information centre is to help users help themselves. It is not to develop applications. If the information centre develops applications, then it has to support them. That is a trap to be avoided.*

The fact that information centres usually work in such a way that support to any one individual or work group is provided only in short bursts encourages a concentration upon small system's development. This keeps U-CC targeted where it is generally most beneficial and working in the most appropriate way. It also encourages prototype development methods that have modification stages that reflect the stages when help has been sought from the IC.

The issue of systems *suitable* for user-controlled computing is an important one and one fundamental task of the IC is continually to assess just where the boundary of suitability lies. Procedures for judging those boundaries vary in style – from informal self-judging processes where the IC identifies, but does not police, particular rules of guidance through to rigidly bureaucratic approvals processes enforcing ridged demarcation. Figure 11.11 illustrates the characteristics likely to be found either side of this boundary.

The more uncertain are the requirements and the more simple to use are the tools, the more the application is likely to be a candidate for U-CC. These applications are business complex and technology simple. The more clear are the requirements and the more complex are the hardware and data environments, the more an application is likely to be a candidate for professional IS. These applications are business simple and technology complex.

| Basic services | 'Extra' services |
| --- | --- |
| Computer literacy education | Development of communication software |
| Training on U-CC tools | Data administration |
| Application consultancy including data access | Installing and testing new product releases |
| Security support | Maintenance of PC hardware |
| Help centre and help-line service | Project management for U-CC developments |
| Hardware/software products evaluation | Quality assurance for U-CC developments |
| Hardware/software products standards | Prototype development for users |
| Hardware/software products support | Executive Information System management |
| Hardware/software sharing | Forming and administering user groups |

Fig 11.10 ◆ Two levels of information centre services

| Typical characteristics of applications and development process | |
| --- | --- |
| **Suitable candidates for user-controlled computing** | **Suitable candidates for corporate IS** |
| *Application characteristics:* <br>• One-off enquiries to pre-stored data <br>• Simple reports retrieving pre-stored data and using end-user oriented tools <br>• Business sensitivity testing (What-If? analysis) using high-level tools <br>• Applications that can be developed using application generators or other high-level tools | *Application characteristics:* <br>• High volume transaction processing or applications that will be in place for a long time <br>• Applications that span several departments or organisational units <br>• Applications that will change data values stored in corporate data stores <br>• Applications that require use of procedural languages |
| *Development process characteristics:* <br>• To identify application requirements needs user to be directly involved in the development process <br>• System is self-documenting, or 'disposable' requiring no documentation <br>• Application development time will be short and is suitable for user-oriented tools. <br>• Development by end-users is permitted <br>• Organisational guidelines appropriate to the application exist | *Development process characteristics:* <br>• Formal specifications are needed in advance <br>• Extensive documentation is needed <br>• Development process is long |

Fig 11.11 ◆ Defining user-controlled computing *v* corporate IS applications

Having determined that an application is a candidate for U-CC is not to imply that there will not be involvement by IS professionals, or vice versa. Figure 11.12 graphically illustrates a possible spread of involvements by the two groups described by the four key tasks of IS use and management: development, operational maintenance, use and managerial control. The roles and responsibilities for a personal information system (PIS), resulting from user-controlled computing, will be rather different to those of a corporate information system (CIS), resulting from computing by IS professionals. Such roles might be:

**Development**: The PIS might be developed primarily by the eventual user, though there will be an input by the IS professionals either directly through advice and support or indirectly in the setting of 'rules'. The CIS might have some design involvement by users as regards their requirements and objectives but it will be developed by the IS professionals.

**Operation and Maintenance** The nature of this, which includes such activities as taking back-ups, preparing documentation, change management, etc for PIS, is exactly as development. For a CIS, however, it is rare for there to be any user involvement.

**Use**: PIS is used entirely by users, of course, whereas CIS is used mainly by users but also partially by IS professionals for checking, testing and during emergencies.

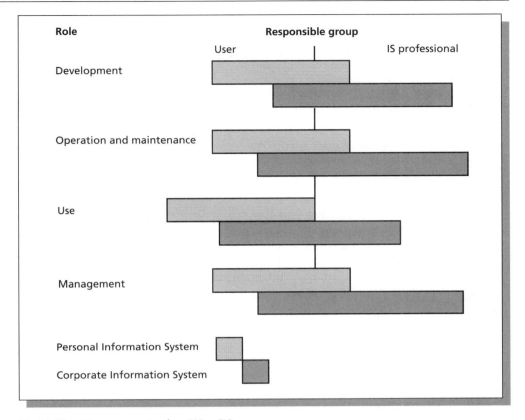

**Fig 11.12 ◆ Management roles: PIS v CIS**

| **Managerial** : **Control** | This is the responsibility and authority and with a PIS is held mainly by the users with some involvement by IS professionals. The situation is reversed for CIS with managerial control mainly held by IS though authorisation of expenditure may be a user function. |
| --- | --- |

If the stages of growth hypothesis that produced models of IS evolution such as those discussed in Chapter 5 is accepted then, given that the IC is a support device, it should evolve as the thing it is supporting evolves. This does not mean that the organisation ceases to include any beginners at IS use, but rather that the *organisational* maturity of the use and management of a particular emerging technology, in this instance end-user computing and information centres, has increased. Publications about information centres would seem to bear out the stage hypothesis. Articles published from 1980–5 tend to provide definitions and descriptions of information centres as if these can be provided in a once and for all way. However, articles published from 1985–90 tend to discuss the *evolving* role of an information centre and question whether it will eventually cease to exist as it develops user skills to the level where it is no longer required. Current publications cover a wider spectrum, from specific journals dedicated to the mechanics of managing an information centre to 'general' papers, not specifically discussing the information centre but assuming that user-controlled computing and its corresponding support mechanisms will form an integral part of the use and management of information, information systems and information services. This spectrum of coverage presumably represents the dawning of the maturity stage, where the chronology of the stages has been:

- Early 1980s   Initiation
- Mid 1980s   Contagion
- Late 1980s   Formalisation
- Early 1990s   Maturity   Less need to *debate* ICs since they have settled into a *balanced* role where they fill one part of the complex IS whole

Magal, Carr and Watson (1988) explore the idea that an information centre passes through different stages of maturity and that at each stage its critical success factors may vary. They develop a stages of growth model specifically adapted to the information centre where the original Nolan 4-stage model is adapted by using benchmark variables appropriate to an information centre. It is interesting to note that Magal, Carr and Watson acknowledge the empirical weakness of the original stage hypothesis and yet go on to use it anyway! Their research showed that the fundamental critical success factors of an IC's service are:

- Quality of information centre support services
- Facilitation of end-user computing
- Commitment to information centre concept
- Role clarity
- Co-ordination of end-user computing

This list ranks the critical success factors in order of importance. The CSFs are not all equally important but the ranking does *not* alter throughout the stages. However, the *way* in which each critical success factor is met may vary with the stage.

The evolving information centre moves through encouraging the *growth* of user-controlled computing, to encouraging *quality* user-controlled computing, to encouraging *self-sufficient* user-controlled computing, and hence to encourage *effective* user-controlled computing. Service for service sake is gradually replaced by service for the business' sake. However, even accepting a stage of maturity hypothesis there remains a continual debate as to whether information centres are a temporary thing needed to support the early stages of U-CC, or a necessary element of an IS service that deals with the rich range of IS possibilities. In the latter case the information centre becomes the *visible* face of IS with the data centre as the 'engine' behind it to generate and maintain the *data* that information centres help people access for themselves.

### 11.4.1 ◆ Problems associated with information centres

Many of the problems associated with an information centre come from the tensions inherent in the four-dimensional relationship it has with U-CC, that is to simultaneously promote, control, support and manage end-user computing. This leads to a constant dilemma for IC staff, and that is whether to *help* or to *do*. It can be difficult to resist the temptation to 'take over' a failing user project, particularly if deemed organisationally 'worthy'. Since ICs are frequently over-stretched, particularly in their early days, they may lose sight of their skills transfer purpose in the efficiency drive to 'take it away and fix it'. The control role can make it doubly difficult to differentiate between helpfulness (by encouraging experimentation) and keeping order (by policing the control rules). It is often difficult to be proactive, it is hard to identify what users *should* be doing when the scarce information centre resources are bogged down in helping them with what they are doing *now*.

Normally information centres can adequately support only a limited range of tools, although in fact any one user or user group is likely to be able to handle only a sub-set of this range. This limited tool set makes it inevitable that U-CC is never using the 'perfect' tool for the job, even if one could be defined. This may be a problem when the implied inefficiencies of users developing mailing systems in spreadsheets (or data manipulation in their favourite word processor) are aggregated across the entire organisation. The slower the information centre is to respond to new software needs the greater this problem is, but the information centre may support hundreds of user developers committed to a given tool set. The number and dispersion of these user developers may make it very difficult to upgrade or change the tool set; the inertia to overcome is significantly greater than with corporate IS and the additional, even if short-term, training and support costs make an upgrade or change to a major standard something that needs careful benefit appraisal. And so, despite the image of reactionary corporate IS and dynamic U-CC, it may be that user-controlled computing must be the more conservative. Corporate IS can move into leading edge technologies and approaches far more readily than numerous, scattered business users who are only developers as a secondary activity.

Whilst support and promotion call for experimentation, control may not, and to be *seen* to be effective the information centre may wish to constrain any excesses with U-CC. Information centres can *institutionalise* the existence of personal data kingdoms by helping users create them and thus an information centre can run counter to the 'information is a corporate resource' ethos that many organisations seek to develop. On the other hand, information centres provide a measure of co-ordination, control and standardisation of end-user computing through establishing policies; the procedures that implement them; the education of users in the value of the policies; plus the subsequent policing of the compliance with them and this role of the IC as a control mechanism may run counter to the very ethos of U-CC which is about *creativity*.

Issues of whether to chargeback the costs of IC services are a particularly thorny problem. Chapter 12 provides a fuller discussion of IS service chargeback but charging for services is often used as a behaviour modification technique, either by its presence or absence. The information centre's support role in its early stages argues *against* chargeback whereas the support role in its later stages argues *for* chargeback. The information centre's control role always argues for charging being managed as a tool to apply to activities to be discouraged, including U-CC itself, or encouraged, including a particular style of end-user computing, and hence removing from U-CC its declared autonomy.

The information centre may take many forms but they all assume that non-traditional development methods will be used to access or manipulate data that already exists and is maintained by the corporate systems that lie *outside* the province of U-CC and hence the information centre. The nature of user-controlled computing puts little emphasis upon data *entry* and much more upon data *manipulation* and therefore ICs are similarly slanted. The constant advent of new user software and hardware defines much of the IC's role, that of either doing or supporting the evaluation, selection, installation, maintenance and training on such tools. Change is an essential ingredient of user-controlled computing and hence the information centre world.

U-CC may lead to one person taking upon themselves the responsibility for producing a system but then the business almost imperceptibly becomes reliant upon it and when it is a *set* of people doing this the problem is exacerbated. This unwitting business reliance is one of the risks of user-controlled computing and the related danger associated with an information centre is that of providing enough knowledge to be dangerous but not enough to be safe. If the IC's skills transfer service addresses only *software*-related skills then U-CC risks are increased since users have software development skills without the education to see the dangers in having an organisation reliant upon a chain of secret systems.

Precisely the same type of problems exist with the accuracy of user-developed systems; the information centre increases U-CC risks if it equips users with the ability to create systems without the ability to create *accurate* ones. The information centre must carefully balance the danger of over-burdening user systems with documentation and testing requirements with the danger of jeopardising business performance with unsafe, inaccurate or inappropriate systems. When this balance is misjudged then end-user computing will be policed by Kewney's (1992) 'network nazis' who use the management of the network, often the province of the information centre, to regain IS's 'lost' control and hence lost status. This imbalance means that the information centre is too heavily weighting its control role and this may destroy its support and skills transfer role. The danger is that this turns out 'network zombies'; it is vital to *effective* user-controlled computing that the information centre empowers users with the skill and freedom to *decide* on IS issues for themselves.

### 11.4.2 ◆ Relationships between U-CC / IC / IS

Once an information centre has been established it adds to the web of IS-related relationships. In 'traditional' IS there are frequently problems of communication, where IS is seen by end-users as theoretical, out of touch, uninterested in business needs and problems and over-keen to change for change's sake. Similar communication problems with user-controlled computing may lead to users being seen by IS as woolly minded about their requirements, stick in the mud about the procedures of the business whilst constantly changing their minds over their IS wants and yet blaming IS for all costs and problems caused by such decision changes. Senior management feeling frustrated by the lack of results from both groups and the seriousness of these communication problems may create educational programmes, steering committees to mediate, or even ombudsmen to arbitrate between the different groups. Senior management may see user-controlled computing as an unexploded bomb with the information centre as the bomb disposal unit or the unit that will light the fuse. Conversely, senior management may feel IS has been an expensive act of faith that has not come off and so user-controlled computing is the road to salvation with the information centre as the providers of this salvation or one more obstacle on the road to it depending upon their risk attitude.

The corporate IS group may feel all the frequently documented fear and resistance to a perceived loss of power, control and influence felt by any organisational function considering itself under threat. The popular image of IS professionals as young, dynamic, hungry for, and adaptable to, change may be inaccurate when the function is well established and staffed with personnel who have spent their working lives developing systems in essentially the same way. That these systems have often radically changed the working practices of others has often by-passed the IS department itself. It may be that this resistance and fear is only one side of a three-way mistrustful relationship. Corporate IS sees user-controlled computing as dangerous. The users see the IC as either unsympathetic when they have problems or too draconian in their policing of control policies and, if affiliated to corporate IS, over technically oriented. The IC staff see IS as out of touch, ivory tower dwellers and users as unruly children. IS may fear that their mystique will be 'exposed' by the openness of the information centre since ICs can be seen as encouraging users to put awkward questions to IS. User-controlled computing data access crosses business unit boundaries and therefore this often creates further relationship tensions.

User-controlled computing may be a response to an already poor business and IS relationship. The information centre may be part of the IS department reporting to the IS manager or part of a business unit reporting to a business manager. Although information centres that evolve from IS in an attempt to control U-CC are significantly different to information centres that evolve from business units seeking to maximise U-CC, both grow out of dissent. The information centre may *aim* to be neutral territory, but its physical location, affiliations, reporting structure, and charging arrangements all may generate barriers between itself , IS staff and users. In addition, the level of staffing and what services the information centre offers affects relationships, the number of staff alters both continuity and speed of response, whilst insisting on the right of approving application developments may lead to more resentments than if simply supporting them.

One of the difficulties specific to an information centre is that it can be seen to be the generator of system performance degradation issues *actually* caused by a lack of performance awareness within user-controlled computing. Information centres may not hold the technical skills necessary to predict fully the performance effect of a user's actions either. IC staff are recruited for their ability to help people and communicate, they are rarely going to hold the knowledge of all technical ramifications, though, with increasingly complex solutions, nor do IS staff. The lack of performance awareness means that user developments, even when guided by IC staff, may perform badly and to the detriment of others. For instance, both user developers and the information centre staff deal with *logical* data models and modelling tools but their systems access the *physical* data stores. The potential performance problems inherent in this dislocation can be eased by using software that provides estimates of the time taken for a given query to run. Since this could be anything from minutes to hours the software indicates when an application is moving outside the province of user-controlled computing and the information centre. Estimation software of this type has been used at Volvo to good effect in easing performance problems.

A complementary approach to performance problems is to ensure that the education provided by the information centre includes coverage of how the actions of one person affects the life of others; effective user-controlled computing is about good *neighbourliness* as well as good IS hygiene and should not grind the network to a halt by running huge queries when major production runs are due. Standalone PCs may hide some performance problems but user developers still need assistance to appreciate and therefore decide upon IS effects to establish fully the *costs* as well as the benefits of what they intend to do. It is perfectly appropriate for both sides of this equation to include skills building for *future* work as long as both the costs and benefits associated with such speculative investments are honestly assessed.

As the information centre increases in importance users engaged in U-CC often see only the IC staff and hence blame them for all frustrations with technology, the machine breakdowns, software recalcitrance, etc. At the most extreme, the information centre may be seen as *outsiders*, as agents of the hardware/software vendors they define as *standards* and negotiate with. Most information centres perceive this view as a problem and attempt to overcome it by increasing the amount and effectiveness of the communication channels they use. A few, however, view this divide as a good thing in itself, akin to the commercial customer/supplier relationship where the customer gets good service by being on the outside, as opposed to the bureaucratic relationship where the lack of outsider accountability can lead to poor quality. This second perception leads to a focus upon professionalism, service levels, and giving value for money. The growing attention being given to the *type* of staff suitable for user support roles and how adequately to support these supporters (*see* Whitehouse (1995) and Section 11.4.4 for more on this) are both in response to the need to improve the relationships between all concerned with U-CC. Similarly work on Service Level Agreements (SLAs) can, amongst other benefits (*see* Chapter 12), improve relationships by clarifying what the support expectations can reasonably be.

Most users want specialist advice to be available and yet, as they become aware of the implications of their actions, they want to choose priorities and decide trade-off positions for themselves so that their business gains set the goals for IS use and management. The relationship between the IC and the user cannot be merely a customer/supplier one since there is a skills transfer role to complicate matters. The information centre, at least in the latter stages of its development, will usually focus on the management rather than the support of user-controlled computing and therefore it is not simply a supplier of services that users 'buy' but rather an attempt to create and maintain a self-drive culture that is organisationally 'safe' and 'encouraged' to be moving in an appropriate direction. The need to *manage* may be a factor of success, but clearly user *satisfaction* will significantly influence IC/user relationships and the two may be contradictory.

Organisational relationships can be viewed from either a support or an agency perspective. The information centre may be seen as primarily a vehicle for encouraging/supporting/enhancing/proliferating user-controlled computing, the word selected reflects the viewpoint of the speaker; in this instance the relationship between the IC and IS may be strained. Conversely, the information centre may be seen to act primarily as a vehicle for controlling/containing user-controlled computing, again the word chosen will reflect the perspective of the speaker; in this instance the relationships between the IC and the users engaged in user-controlled computing may be strained.

The agency perspective on IC/IS/user relationships has been briefly mentioned already. This theory describes two bodies in any activity, the dependant body, known as the *principal*, which must appoint *agents* to perform the tasks it cannot.

Both parties to this contract incur costs *beyond* the costs that are inherent in doing a given task. The principal incurs costs from the various incentives and checking actions that it must use to monitor and direct the activities of its agent (to ensure that the task is carried out in the way they want). The principal bears a further cost, known as the residual loss, from the inevitable discrepancy between the principal's intentions of what should happen and the agent's actual behaviour. The agent incurs additional costs, known as bonding costs, from having to reassure the principal of both its good faith and good behaviour. Perceptions of the U-CC/IC/IS relationships depend upon the view of the information centre, either as an agent and colony of IS or as promoter and supporter of U-CC. When IS utters phrases such as 'if you can't beat them, join them' then it would seem that the agency view of the relationships is an appropriate one!

### 11.4.3 ◆ Measuring information centre success

Much of the discussion of information centres has a 'hidden agenda' and, since ICs exists solely as an adjunct to user-controlled computing, it is actually U-CC rather than the role, use and management of an information centre that is being discussed. It is only appropriate to discuss ICs with reference to their effectiveness at reducing the organisational disadvantages associated with U-CC and maximising the potential organisational benefits of it. Evaluating ICs will be on their ability to ensure that user-controlled computing creates:

- Active and effective business exploitation of IS potential
- Cleared or *appropriate* application backlogs
- Fast small system development

Frequently information centres are set up because of management's fear of U-CC, that it is too dangerous, or too expensive, or too slow to take off, or too difficult to manage. As maturity increases, information centres reach the point when they become expensive and at that point it becomes desirable or necessary to assess the benefits gained for that expense. At this stage there is a need to identify appropriate metrics for judging the information centre's success or failure. Hoopes (1990) tabulates five possible approaches to evaluating information centre success and these are shown in Figure 11.13.

Measuring user satisfaction may be an evaluation technique employed to judge the information centre's success. Not surprisingly, since achieving user satisfaction and measuring the degree of this achievement are very important. Bergeron *et al.* (1990) report upon findings that identify the effect upon user satisfaction of six aspects of running an IC, these findings are summarised in Figure 11.14. The first three factors are positively correlated to user satisfaction with the information centre, that is user satisfaction goes *up* when there is an increase in any or all of these three factors. The second group of items is negatively correlated to user satisfaction, that is user satisfaction goes *down* when there is an increase in these factors. The research of Bergeron *et al.* concludes that the information centre with the greatest chance of satisfying its users is small but well organised, offers diverse services but supports only a small set of software tools to access a single corporate database.

Since the information centre exists as a *service* provider, levels of service provided must be assessed. Such assessment may be of the quantity and variety of

| Evaluation approach | Measurement technique |
|---|---|
| Cost/benefit analysis | Return on Investment |
| Using simple measures | Use by users perhaps by logging calls for help, numbers of people calling into the IC, number of training classes, and the number of applications developed; increase in hardware and software use; IC staff productivity measures. |
| Chargeback | Account for training, equipment use, and consulting for instance on a flat fee or per hour charge. |
| Impact upon organisation | Goals of IC as indicated by its strategic plan and organisation are closely allied; critical success factors; improved customer service; number of managers using the IC. |
| User-assisted measurements | Quality measures such as how good hardware and software products are; user satisfaction questionnaires; decrease in timesharing costs; number of staff reductions versus rise in U-CC numbers. |

**Fig 11.13 ◆ Approaches to evaluating ICs**
(adapted from Information Center Evaluation by Hoopes in *Proceedings of the 23rd Annual Hawaii International Conference on Systems Sciences*, Vol IV (1990), p. 217 © 1990, IEEE)

services offered or, generally more valuable, of how effective services provided are. Since an information centre provides its services as part of *managing* user-controlled computing the effectiveness of the IC's services may include user satisfaction measures but may also require some judgement of the *effectiveness* of such computing itself.

An information centre has a four-dimension relationship with user-controlled computing that simultaneously includes:

- Promotion
- Control
- Support
- Management.

Given this variety of roles it is likely that there must be commensurate variety in the factors measured and the measurement techniques used. How the success of an IC is measured depends upon which of the four dimensions is being considered, and by who. An information centre successful at *controlling* U-CC may not be an

| Potential influences of user satisfaction | Correlation |
|---|---|
| The proximity of the IC to the user premises | + |
| The number of different services offered by the IC | + |
| The proportion of IS budget allocated to the IC | + |
| The size of the IC staff | − |
| The number of software tools supported by the IC | − |
| The number of corporate databases made available to users | − |

**Fig 11.14 ◆ Correlation of user satisfaction and IC factors**
(after Bergeron *et al.*)

information centre successful at *promoting* it. Measuring the success of an information centre may be very difficult since some would argue that the only really successful IC is one that has 'skills transferred' itself out of existence and, since ICs are the management mechanism to promote, control, support *and* manage user-controlled computing, evaluation of each role may be different and contradictory.

### 11.4.4 ◆ Help-desks and direct user support

One important service provided by most information centres is a user help-desk. This may be a face to face contact or, more usually, a telephone line or some combination of these two. A help-desk aims to ensure that expensive user-controlled computing resources, including the users themselves, are as productive as possible for as much of the time as possible. The customer focus that is so much a factor in so many organisations has also 'spilled over' into a greater awareness of how *internal* customers must be responded to. The help-desk is where this response occurs. It has been suggested that any information centre that supports 200 or more users should operate a continuously staffed help-desk. Of course, help-desks are not only a feature of user-controlled computing and information centres but are also a routine part of the IS department's support of users of systems developed by IS professionals; however the nature of the questions and the scope of the difficulties dealt with will significantly differ. Both information centre and IS department help-desks can take various forms, they can be:

- *Unskilled*: Where staff simply record and route calls onwards to the appropriate member of the IS or IC staff. This style of help-desk is useful for large organisations where large numbers of queries need to be dealt with whilst keeping the lines of communication open.
- *Skilled*: Where staff on the help-desk aim to actually answer a majority of the user's queries, the 80 per cent of queries that form the top twenty questions with the remaining 20 per cent transferred to the relevant expert, as with an unskilled help-desk.
- *Expert*: Where staff endeavour to support all user problems and deal with all queries.

Given that there are three types of help-desks each with quite different skill levels it is important to clearly define the responsibilities of a specific information centre's help-desk so that management intentions and user expectations are aligned. The specific choice must be made by recognising what users *do* not just what technology they *use*.

With all types of help-desks, automating as much of the drudgery as possible and drawing management information from the operational systems is the key to cost effective running. The automating of help-desk services forms part of two parallel trends. The first is to reduce information centre costs by making a few staff go a long way and providing clear cost justifications of the remaining costs. The second trend is to track development activities and progress to re-combine islands of U-CC activities as part of business process redesign. Interestingly help-desk software began as a peculiarly British phenomenon, perhaps because generally American information centres reached the maturity point of having to cost justify their services rather earlier than British ones did and before any such software could be available. Help-desk software is now a mainstream business application; by the middle of 1995 there were nearly 150 help-desk packages available.

Help-desk data tracks what requests for help have come in and this provides one input to the process of planning the use of information centre and user-controlled computing resources. The information centre can meaningfully discover what type of questions are asked by users and make some estimates of why. Feedback from the help-desk data can drive proactive information centre education and training programmes, since knowing the type, frequency and origin of calls highlights who should be offered training and at what level. Additionally, the help-desk data should form one input to the process of selecting U-CC standards since it indicates what software and hardware generates proportionately the greatest problems.

The information centre help-desk may act as a filtering device for support queries that will ultimately be dealt with by *experts*. These experts may be within the information centre, within the organisation's IS department or outside, associated with the software or hardware vendor. Until recently the purchaser of hardware or software has generally been able to access a telephone line help-desk; however as ever more complex combinations of hardware and software become associated with U-CC that free service is being replaced by a service that must be purchased. When vendor help-desk services are a purchased commodity it becomes more important that internal help-desks effectively support routine queries and effectively act as liaison bodies to those expensive external help-desks.

Help-desks are not the only source of direct user support. In the majority of instances troubled users will probably turn to informal 'guru' support from colleagues. Many organisations are troubled by this situation. The volume of hidden costs such unmanaged support accounts for, well over 50 per cent of total support cost (*see* Green-Armytage (1995)), is just one problem in the use of guru support. Others, Mellor (1995b) suggests, are:

- the unofficial guru's own work suffers
- gurus tend to be localised so solutions to common problems are not made known to everyone
- nor are *internal* help-desks the only source

At the same time as many organisations are strengthening their information centre help-desk many large information centres transfer their help-desk services to outside agencies. These are outsource service providers (*see* Chapter 12) who specialise, not in a single product or even a set of them, but in analysing data on repeated requests in order to establish a 'top twenty' of user problems. These help-desks then provide the inter-personal communication skills to ask questions effectively, and either answer them, if they fall within that top twenty, or pass them to the appropriate experts, another instance of the 80/20 rule. An example of such outsourced help-desks is that the IBM PS hardware range and AMEX card queries are both handled by the same help-desk agency.

Despite the attractions of external help-desk support for complex environments (*see* Black (1995), Goodwin (1995) and many others), there is a growing tendency to use help-desk automation, as discussed above, to evaluate the internal provision of direct user support. This trend is fuelled by some lack of faith in the effectiveness of external provision (*see* Robertson and Briggs (1996)), but also a wish to *capture* the lessons learnt by direct user support into broader aspects of directing U-CC, such as education and training programmes. Therefore, to some extent help-desk software and help-desk outsourcing can be seen as *alternative* solutions to providing direct user support.

## 11.5 ◆ GROUP-BASED USER COMPUTING

Some of the early structural arrangements for corporate IS created the very Chinese walls between business areas that current IS activities are so much hampered by. Similarly, many of the early instances of user-controlled computing, whilst doing much to improve personal productivity, also did much to *isolate* decision makers. As the technology to support U-CC and the organisational awareness of U-CC progresses there is greater interest in exploiting group-based user tools. The emergence of the new organisational forms discussed in Chapter 8, most of which are team based, often across multiple organisations, is also driving this interest. The 'real world' of business decisions is rarely characterised by individuals taking solitary decisions supported by completely individualistic information. This is especially true as hierarchies become less significant than network forms of organisation. As Kyng (1991) observed:

> Work is fundamentally social. Most activity, and certainly its meaning, arises in a context of co-operation.

This notion of groups employing technology to support their work is described by a large number of ill-defined terms. Labels that are used, more or less synonomously, include:

Computer supported cooperative work (CSCW)
Groupware
Workgroup computing
Computer-augmented teamwork
Collaborative systems
and so on

This area is too new for clear definitions to have emerged, but in general phrases such as groupware and workgroup computing are used when the focus is upon the *technology* whereas a term such as CSCW is used when the focus is upon how teams *work*. Section 11.5.2 will explore some of the tools used to support groups along with the issues associated with them. For the purpose of clarity, this section will use the term CSCW, a phrase usually taken to be the most all-encompassing name for this phenomenon.

### 11.5.1 ◆ What is CSCW?

CSCW represents a combination of technology and organisational arrangements that are what Johansen in Bostrom *et al.* (1992) calls a 'new perspective on computing and telecommunications'. The newness of the perspective lies in the focus being as much on interactions as on tasks. This perspective also concerns bringing technology to the user's domain without making any excessive demands that humans behave in ways to suit the technology. CSCW also adds capabilities to teams that are not possible in the real, physical world. Examples of new possibilities are the simultaneous alteration of a single document by several people across dispersed locations.

Given its complexity, to help to understand CSCW it is helpful to explicitly categorise its features. Wilson in Scrivener (1994) suggests that its technology includes:

- communication systems
- shared workspace facilities
- shared information facilities
- group activity support facilities

He also suggests four categories for its human components:

- individual aspects
- organisational aspects
- group work design aspects
- group dynamic aspects

Of course, separating technical from human issues may perpetrate an over-emphasis on technological issues that IS is so often criticised for.

One frequent misconception of CSCW is to take the 'co-operative' to mean total agreement and shared values and to assume that only when such social smooth-ness is present can CSCW be present. However, CSCW, just as 'traditional' (ie non-CSCW supported) group work, is associated with varying degrees of collab-oration. Collaboration can lie between spontaneous and coerced and between total and specific task based. It may be helpful, when considering CSCW, to think about different forms of group working, for instance:

*Independent* – decisions taken with no interactions with other decision makers.
*Communication* – independent decision making taken while exchanging status information and decision results.
*Co-ordination* – as communication, plus the exchange of decision rationale along with some mutual understanding regarding goals, both shared and independent.
*Collaboration* – joint decisions taken with mutual understanding regarding goals, both shared and independent.

Clearly each of these four different types of group work calls for different types of technological support, *see* Section 11.5.2.

CSCW technologies are by no means plain sailing. The benefits sought from it relate to moving ever closer to the attributes of the 'virtual organisation' in which people skills can be called upon irrespective of physical constraints of time or place (and even of who is the primary employer). According to a PA Consulting Group survey, as reported by Kavanagh (1995), the top six benefits sought from CSCW in advance are:

- shared information
- better communication
- shared resources
- team working
- shared files
- easier to contribute

The reality, as shown by the same survey, is that the top six benefits *actually* achieved by CSCW initiatives are:

- more efficiency
- shared information
- shared resources
- shared files
- better communication
- more productivity

These benefits then are the results of the move, as the jargon has it, 'from personal to interpersonal computing'. However, the actual gains are ones that relate more to *access* than to attitude and are gains that may cost a great deal to achieve. For instance, Davison (1994) argues that returns on investment of 180 per cent are achievable for service industries, but manufacturing organisations will need to be selective if they are to reap rewards greater than the high costs involved. As is frequently the case with emerging technologies it is simply the lack of knowledge of them that creates the greatest difficulties. Groups underestimate the cultural shift that information sharing requires. The dramatic pace of change in the technology elements make infrastructure management extremely complex and it is often just not possible to build up CSCW incrementally. Unless a critical mass, of say access to document databases, is possible no use at all is productive. Similarly, unless everyone is willing and able to use group scheduling or even straightforward E-mail systems then paper duplicates must be used alongside electronic versions, largely negating potential benefits.

One of the most complex issues associated with CSCW is its entanglement with other IS management issues. As already noted, it is closely related to, and is often considered as an evolution from, U-CC. The notion of CSCW is also related to a number of technology infrastructure issues (*see* Chapter 12). The nature of a chosen infrastructure – open or proprietary, client-server, host-based or peer-to-peer – will significantly influence the *styles* of CSCW realistically possible. Perhaps the thing most closely interconnected with CSCW is that of Business Process Re-engineering (BPR) and its associated issue of workflow planning and workflow systems as discussed in Chapter 8. As Wallace (1994) points out, most workgroup support applications are developed from some form of process analysis and modelling, just as BPR initiatives are. Both BPR and CSCW seek to fundamentally re-shape the organisation. Both are *not* more-of-the-same support, which U-CC can be. Both require a radical thinking about what technology may make possible that would have no physical or manual equivalent.

## 11.5.2 ◆ Groupware systems

As indicated earlier, when we focus on groupware as an aspect of CSCW then we are essentially taking a technological stance. Groupware is a phrase used when discussing specific applications that, alongside the behavioural issues of how teams work, make up CSCW. Such applications can take many forms and can support many aspects of group interactions. To help select the type of groupware application required for a given situation we have available a number of different ways to categorise such tools. Three ways of describing groupware are given here. We could consider them in terms of where in space and time they offer group support, what application structure paradigm they are based upon, or in terms of organisational levels and degrees of interaction.

The first framework for considering groupware applications is to consider that support for teams can be related to time and place. It is virtually 'conventional' to consider groups by their degree of geographic and time dispersal. For instance, the matrix in Figure 11.15 from Johansen in Bostrom (1992) places groupware applications according to the different/same place–different/same time interactions. Obviously many applications offer support in more than one segment.

As with other classification methods this matrix offers a useful heuristic to assist in making choices about the type of groupware to adopt. An organisation that is geographically dispersed though within one time zone and working conventional office hours should emphasise place rather than time (although time-independent communication, such as E-mail, can always be useful). Alternatively, organisations that have more informal working structures, so that availability is unpredictable, may gain more from time displacement applications.

An alternative way of classifying groupware applications is to focus on whether they are directed at storage (database driven) or communication (E-mail driven). Groups that must make decisions with reference to recorded data or organisations that are concerned to create an 'organisational memory' (perhaps they suffer high staff turnover) may be more interested in database-driven groupware. Groups that

|  | Same time | Different time |
|---|---|---|
| **Same place** | *Need*   *Face-to-face meetings*<br><br>e.g.   Copyboards<br>PC projectors<br>Facilitation services<br>Group decision rooms<br>Polling systems | *Need*   *Administrative filing and filtering*<br><br>e.g.   Shared files<br>Shift work<br>Kiosks<br>Team rooms<br>Group displays |
| **Different place** | *Need*   *Cross-distance meetings*<br><br>e.g.   Conference calls<br>Graphics and audio<br>Screen sharing<br>Video teleconferencing<br>Spontaneous meetings | *Need*   *Ongoing co-ordination*<br><br>e.g.   Group writing<br>Computer conferencing<br>Conversational structuring<br>Forms management<br>Group voice mail |

**Fig 11.15 ◆ Group needs and groupware systems**
(after Johansen and reprinted from *Computer Augmented Teamwork: A Guided Tour* by Bostrom *et al.* (1992) p. 8)

work on the transmittal of status and opinion information may more appropriately favour communication-based groupware. An example of the difference between these two is that 'the world-wide web' is a data storage-driven instance, whilst E-mail is obviously an instance of communication-driven groupware.

A third approach to describing groupware alternatives is to consider the degree of group interactivity they support. An example of this approach is that of Holtham given in Mellor (1995a) who categorises groupware by the organisational level and degree of interactivity they support. A summary of this is given in Figure 11.16.

These three are just examples of the many ways of classifying groupware. The purpose of each classification system is two-fold. Firstly to give a framework for selecting where the greatest support potential lies, since each classification system offers a way of considering the group situation with respect to available applications. Secondly, as a framework for considering what issues might arise in the adoption of any given application. For instance, an organisation could use the categorisation summarised in Figure 11.16 to consider the degree of interactivity that particular groups can culturally accommodate. Equally they may use Holtham's categorisation to highlight the fact that the implementation of, for example, group calendaring, will require a great deal of attention given to making teams comfortable with high interactivity (the 'public' viewing of individual time commitments).

Groupware is not only about software applications. The term also encompasses what are often more specifically referred to as meeting systems. Such systems must also address architectural issues of room layout and facilitator roles along with the software aspects of electronic whiteboards, voting systems and the like.

High degree of team inter-activity:

- Group decision support
- Workflow
- Collaborative writing

Medium degree of team inter-activity:

- Shared insight
- Discussion
- Conferencing
- Scheduling
- Mail
- Messaging
- Resource sharing

Low degree of team inter-activity:

- EIS
- Project/status reporting
- Database access

Fig 11.16 ◆ Groupware applications by degree of team interactivity and organisational level (after Holtham in Mellor)

Central to many instances of groupware, and to all those based on a data storage paradigm, is the notion of *large* stores of data. These are often referred to as information (or data) warehouses. This name captures the essential logic of what they are: containers of data gathered from *all* over the organisation available for a wide variety of uses to be made by group (or individual) accesses. The cultural issues of information sharing have already been touched on, data warehousing has such culture related difficulties and it is also technologically complex. Querying from these very large data stores from across distributed networks could be excruciatingly slow unless a careful choice of storage paradigm is made. Data warehouses, therefore, are associated with using specialist data storage and retrieval techniques such as on-line analytical processing (OLAP). In OLAP the data storage principles of multi-dimensional analysis of data from disparate sources are employed to permit *ad hoc* user analysis without intervention by IS professionals.

The groupware applications most likely to draw upon the technologies of OLAP and the data warehouse are those conventionally referred to as executive (now enterprise) information systems (EIS). Indeed these systems are often synonymous with OLAP. OLAP and data warehousing are likely to be the terms used when the focus is upon issues of storage, searching and retrieval from large data stores without performance degradation. However we are likely to use the term EIS when the focus is primarily upon decisions to be taken from the presented data, on the proactive issue of alerting decision makers to business issues, and on interface concerns of information needs and presentation.

## 11.6 ◆ SUMMARY AND CONCLUSIONS

This chapter has explored a number of issues associated with information systems when they are the responsibility of the business rather than the IS professional. Such issues revolve around a number of tensions and the trade-offs that must be made to achieve balance between these tensions. The essential issue is one of balancing freedom to innovate against counter-productive anarchy. If user-controlled computing is mismanaged into anarchy it may create individual information kingdoms that are socially and technologically incompatible with both the individual kingdoms of others involved in U-CC and with the corporate IS provision. If user-controlled computing is mismanaged into rigidity it may create an IS-stagnant organisation that fails to take advantage of the potential to enhance *every* individual's productivity.

Developments in location and arrangement alternatives for corporate IS have sought to address the flexibility limitations in IS and its ability to communicate with its user community. It is paradoxical that these same developments have created a technological and skill situation that enables users to 'take over' the role of IS. It is equally paradoxical that the emergence of U-CC sought to *increase* organisational flexibility and nimbleness with respect to IS and yet extensive U-CC often acts as a barrier to the current IS frontier of group-based computing. And of course for U-CC to be effective it must usually be characterised by *standards*. Freedom (a central notion of U-CC) almost always *limits* ultimate flexibility when situations change.

The organisational issues generated by a history of U-CC can be a barrier to creating an information warehouse. Current systems do not inter-operate and people are very reluctant to give up their personal systems and databases. Highly decentralised organisations have most trouble in this area since decision making autonomy is ingrained. High levels of trust need to be established; this tends to be obvious when sharing with outside agencies but is equally true of internal sharing. Information sharing, particularly outside the organisation, is an important aspect of business process re-engineering and is the IS perspective on the strategic alliances discussed in Chapter 1. Staff may resist information sharing initiatives when they feel the need to increase personal value to the organisation by controlling some key data or system. These private goals can be very much at odds with the corporate goals! The existence of many group or collaborative work technologies runs counter to the individualistic ethos of the first generation of U-CC.

As organisations are forced to look at making decisions faster (and better) to survive stronger competition they seek to increase the skills base involved in making those decisions. Individuals alone may not be effective, collaboration is necessary. This collaboration is helped by E-mail, electronic meetings and other instances of CSCW. Many of the instances of re-engineering discussed in Chapter 8 were achieved by using groupware to develop *teams*. Not all collaboration must be on the grand scale of BPR, but all need some critical mass to achieve productivity. No organisation will find major investments in CSCW software of infrastructure platforms worthwhile without commensurate organisational intent to operate through teams. In the case of CSCW technologies we would expect, as with any emerging technology, the stage model to apply. If so, early promotion will proceed through infectious contagion (many organisations are currently at this point) into strict management control with the need to *demonstrate* the monetary gains to be achieved and finally through to a mature seeking of a broad basket of benefits from a mature business tool.

Increasingly the management of user-controlled computing is a fundamental part of business management. It is just as much part of IS management as managing the corporate IS provision. The management of information sharing and group working ventures is becoming just as fundamental. Often, however, any collaboration demanding systems must be associated with centralised management, for organisational rather than technical reasons. It is typical now to find U-CC being viewed as the conservative barrier to the new approaches of CSCW. This is precisely how corporate IS was viewed a decade ago at the birth of user-controlled computing.

**References and further reading**

Alavi, M., Nelson, R.R. and Weiss, I. (1988) Strategies for End-User Computing: an Integrative Framework, *Journal of Management Information Systems*, Winter.

Alavi, M. and Weiss, I. (1986) Managing the Risks Associated with End-User Computing, *Journal of Management Information Systems*, Vol 2 No 3 pp. 5–20.

Amoroso, D.L. and Brancheau (1990) Using the Expansion-Control Framework for Measuring Management Action in Support of Emerging Technologies, in *Proceedings of 23rd Annual Hawaii International Conference on Systems Sciences*, Vol IV, IEEE Computer Society Press.

Arkush, E. (1992) Beyond End-User Computing: Managing in the Third Era, *Journal of Information Systems Management*, Spring pp. 58–60.

Bartram, P. and Youett, C. (1993) *The Groupware Report '93*, Policy Publications.

Bergeron, F., Rivard, S. and De Serre, L. (1990) Investigating the Support Role of the Information Center, *MIS Quarterly*, Sept pp. 246–60.

Black, G. (1995) Simplify End-User Computing: Outsource It, *Datamation*, 15 Sept pp. 67–9.

Bostrom, R., Watson, R. and Kinney, S. (1992) *Computer Augmented Teamwork: A Guided Tour*, Chapman and Hall.

Carr, H. H. (1987) Information Centers: The IBM Model *v* Practice, *MIS Quarterly*, Sept Pt III pp. 325–38.

Christoff, K. (1990) *Managing the Information Center*, Little Brown.

Clark, T. (1992) Corporate Systems Management: An Overview and Research Perspective, *Communications of the ACM*, Feb pp. 60–75.

Classe, A. (1995) Call and Response, *Computer Weekly*, 5 Oct p. 62.

Codd, E., Codd, S. and Salley, S. (1993) *Providing OLAP (On-Line Analytical Processing) to User-Analysts: An IT Mandate*, E.F. Codd and Associates.

Cooper, D. (1995) How to be a Good Service, *Computer Weekly*, 27 Apr, p. 28.

Cotterman, W.W. and Kumar, K. (1989) User Cube: A Taxonomy of End Users, *Communications of the ACM*, Vol 32 No 11 pp. 1313–20.

Couldwell, C. (1994) Undercover Agents, *Computer Weekly*, 25 Apr pp. 30–1.

Davison, C. (1994) Share Issues, *Computer Weekly*, 30 June pp. 30–1.

Dennis, A.R., George, J.F., Jessup, L.M., Nunamaker, J.F. and Vogel, D.R. (1988) Information Technology to Support Electronic Meetings, *MIS Quarterly*, Dec pp. 590–624.

Fawcett, N. (1996) PCs Too Expensive to Own, *Computer Weekly*, 11 July p. 6.

Galliers, R. and Bates, B. (1994) *Strategic Information Management*, Butterworth-Heinemann.

Galletta, D.F. and Hufnagel, E.M. (1992) A Model of End-User Computing Policy, *Information and Management*, Vol 22 No 1 pp. 1–18.

Gerrity, T.P. and Rockart J.F. (1986) End-User Computing: Are You a Leader or a Laggard? Sloan Management Review, Summer pp. 25–34.

Goodwin C. (1995) Where to Turn for Help, *Computer Weekly*, 18 May p. 46.

Grohowski, R., McGoff, C., Vogel, D., Martz B and Nunamaker, J. (1990) Implementing Electronic Meetings Systems at IBM: Lessons Learned and Success Factors, *MIS Quarterly*, Dec pp. 368–83.

Guimaraes, T. and Igbaria, M. (1994) Exploring the Relationship between IS Success and Company Performance, *Information and Management*, Vol 26 pp. 133–41.

Henderson, J.C. and Treacy, M.E. (1986) Managing End-User Computing for Competitive Advantage, *Sloan Management Review*, Winter pp. 3–14.

Hoopes, J.E. (1990) Information Center Evaluation, in *Proceedings of 23rd Annual International Conference on Systems Sciences* Vol IV, IEEE Computer Society Press.

Huff, S.L., Munro, M.C. and Martin, B.H. (1988) Growth Stages of End-User Computing, *Communications of the ACM*, Vol 31 No 5 pp. 542–50.

Kavanagh, J. (1995) Managers Slammed for Ignoring Business Needs, *Computer Weekly*, 29 June p. 54.

Kewney, G. (1992) Network Nazis, *PC Magazine*, Apr p. 41.

Klepper, R. (1990) An Agency Theory Perspective on Information Centers, in *Proceedings of 23rd Annual Hawaii International Conference on Systems Sciences* Vol IV, IEEE Computer Society Press.

Kyng, M. (1991) Designing for Co-operation: Co-operating in Design, *Communications of the ACM*, Dec.

Leitheiser, R.L. and Wetherbe, J.C. (1986) Service Support Levels: An Organised Approach to End-User Computing, *MIS Quarterly*, Dec pp. 337–49.

Leitheiser, R.L. and Wetherbe, J.C. (1991) A Comparison of Perceptions about Information Center Success, *Information and Management*, Vol 21 pp. 7–17.

McNurlin, B.C. and Sprague, R.H. (1989) *Information Systems Management in Practice* (2nd edn), Prentice-Hall.

Magal, S.R., Carr, H.H. and Watson, H.J. (1988) Critical Success Factors for Information Center Managers, *MIS Quarterly*, Sept pp. 412–25.

Manchester, P. (1995) Power to the People, *PC Week*, 14 Mar pp. 10–11.

Meiklejohn, I., Matthews, J. and Batram, P. (Eds.) (1993) *The Groupware Report '93*, Business Intelligence.

Mellor, C. (1995a) Groupware Machines Roll On, *PC Week*, 11 Apr pp. 36–7.

Mellor, C. (1995b) Symptoms of Shadow IT, *PC Week*, 19 Sept pp. 8–9.

Milne, J. (1996) Into Another Dimension, *Computing*, 25 Apr pp. 30–1.

Munro, M.C., Huff, S.L. and Moore, G. (1987) Expansion and Control of End-User Computing, *Journal of Management Information Systems*, Vol 4 No 3 pp. 5–27.

O'Brien, B. (1996) *Information Management Decisions: Briefings and Critical Thinking*, Pitman Publishing.

O'Brien, J.A. (1993) *Management Information Systems: A Managerial End-User Perspective* (2nd edn), Irwin.

Palvia, P. (1991) On End-User Computing Productivity: Results of controlled experiments, *Information and Management*, Vol 21 pp. 217–24.

Rainer, R. and Watson, H. (1995) What Does it Take for Successful Executive Information Systems? *Decision Support Systems*, Vol 14 pp. 147–56.

Raymont, P. (1994) *IT Infrastructure*, Blackwell.

Rivard, S. and Huff, S.L. (1988) Factors of Success for End-User Computing, *Communications of the ACM*, Vol 31 No 5 pp. 552–61.

Robertson, C. and Briggs, P. (1996) IT Managers Lack Faith in External Help Desks, *Computing*, 18 July p. 31.

Rockart, J.F. and Flannery, L.S. (1983) The Management of End-User Computing, *Communications of the ACM*, Vol 26 No 10 pp. 776–84.

Scrivener, S. (Ed.) (1994) *Computer-Supported Cooperative Work: The Multimedia and Networking Paradigm*, Avebury Technical.

Strassman, P. (1995) *The Politics of Information Systems*, Information Economics Press.

Wallace, S. (1994) Working Smarter, *Byte*, July pp. 100–1.

Weber, R. (1986) Planning and Control Issues in End-User Computing, *The Australian Computer Journal*, Vol 18 No 4 pp. 159–65.

White, C.E. and Christy, D.P. (1987) The Information Centre Concept: A Normative Model and a Study of Six Installations, *MIS Quarterly*, Dec pp. 450–8.

Whitehouse, B. (1995) Economics of the IT kind, *PC Week*, 30 Apr pp. 8–9.

# CHAPTER 12

# Selection and acquisition

This penultimate chapter of the IS strategy choices section of this text considers acquisition-related issues. Part 1 looked at the nature and development of business strategies, Part 2 looked at the nature and development of IS strategies and here in Part 3 we are considering some of the elements that turn the conceptual strategy into the reality of IS decisions. The IS strategy is made real through how IS is arranged and located, how it 'sits' within the organisational structure, how it is managed and staffed, and how it relates to its business community and to non-IS professionals. The most direct and unequivocal aspect of how an IS strategy is implemented, or emerges, is as the pattern of choices made in acquiring software, hardware and human resource elements of IS activities. The management concerns during the procurement process define the content of this chapter.

This chapter will describe not only the procurement process itself, with some associated scoring and ranking techniques and procurement guidelines, but also some of the current pressures acting upon the selection alternatives. These issues include:

- The impact of generalised packaged software, both upon the selection process and upon the organisation.

- The notions of downsizing and open systems that form the technological parallel to the organisational issue of new organisational forms as discussed in Chapter 8 and of user-controlled and group-based computing as discussed in Chapter 11.

- The external provision of IS elements, often referred to as outsourcing, that relates closely to the resource structures described in Chapter 9 and the IS management features discussed in Chapter 10.

The essence of choice in this chapter is of allocating resources in ways considered most beneficial. Given the complexity of forms of contemporary IS that have been discussed in the preceding three chapters, it should be clear that there is not *one* body making IS choices but rather a *network* of groups making various acquisition choices. The *logical* relationships of these various groups are shown in Figure 12.1. It should be noted that physical groups may be involved in more than one logical role. The issues discussed in this chapter touch on *all* of these groups and therefore the different forms of 'payment' for acquisitions – be it to an external agency or through an internal transfer system – are addressed. Within this chapter we are obviously primarily concerned with the service *buying* aspect of the IS buying/IS delivery distinction inherent throughout the preceding three chapters.

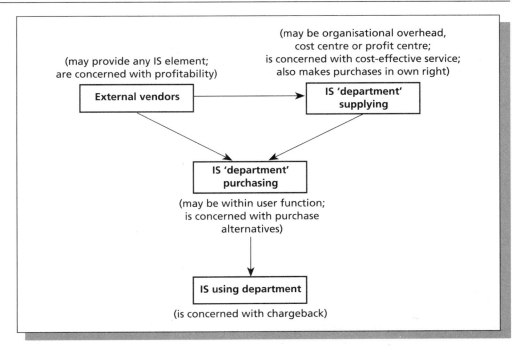

**Fig 12.1 ◆ IS service cost transfers**

As the opening of Part 3 pointed out, all these strategy implementation issues interact. The choice of IS organisation and structure significantly influences the selection alternatives available and, perhaps even more significantly, selection alternatives drive the nature of the IS organisation, structure and management. Very devolved IS is unlikely to be able to undertake to provide major IS elements from in-house expertise, whilst the long-term transfer of IS elements to external providers shapes the nature of internal IS management. Cutting across all of these *specific* factors are three major management responsibilities to get the 'best' from IS investments. These responsibilities are:

- Senior management *must* recognise the potential for gain in any acquisition and therefore acknowledge the importance of the procurement process by taking an active or, at least, supportive role. Senior management commitment is particularly vital during the *first* acquisition of a particular IS element and, though such a commitment becomes less vital as the acquisition becomes more 'routine', the procurement process never declines in importance.

- During the acquisition process it is important to review and re-review the relationship to the business and IS strategies to verify that the method of selection is, and remains, in step with long-term goals as well as with short-term requirements and expediencies. Implicit in this is the need to involve *all* affected groups in the selection process, and staff from both the technical and the business domains should be driving towards the same objective.

- The implications of any sensitive applications must be fully assessed as part of the procurement process. It will frequently be *business* sensitivity rather than technical or economical factors that place any rigid constraints upon the procurement process.

This is an appropriate point to make a brief digression to look at change control since it is the degree of business sensitivity that will largely determine the appropriateness of a changeover strategy. Figure 12.2 illustrates the four basic changeover approaches in broadly ascending order of 'risk' and descending order of generating additional running costs. Depending upon the *nature* of the sensitivity a particular approach will be chosen. Clearly where continuity of service is *vital* then parallel running is likely to be a better changeover method than the stop/start approach. Similarly, if the given system element depends upon others then a phased changeover reduces risk. All of these approaches trade-off risk against additional expense in a balancing act determined by the business importance of implementation problems or cost saving. In many highly publicised systems failures, the London Ambulance System to name just one, it has been considered too expensive to do anything other than a direct changeover. This 'big bang' approach finds popularity because it can *force* commitment and also does not generate the additional costs associated with parallel systems or create the planning complexities of pilot initiatives.

The changeover approach should be determined *before* the acquisition is made, and early in the selection process, since the choice of conversion strategy will influence other choices to be made. Conversely, there may be some feature of the project that pre-determines the nature of the changeover in which case this constraint should obviously be recognised early in the procurement process in order to accommodate it. Currently a major concern in IS management is to ensure that systems can accommodate the dates from the year 2000. Such date-specific deadlines are likely to require 'big bang' changeovers with no possibility of parallel or pilot running.

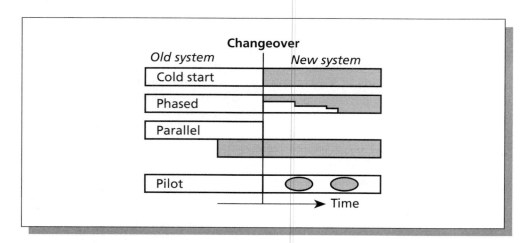

**Fig 12.2 ◆ Four basic changeover approaches**

# 12.1 ◆ THE PROCUREMENT PROCESS

As we saw in Chapters 9 and 10, the logical distinction between IS service buying and IS service provision is increasingly sharp because, where once all IS provision was the province of the internal DP Department, there is now a large set of alternative providers. This distinction is all the clearer because there are changes in *both* elements. IS service buying has increasingly moved to being the responsibility of the business manager. The procurement process becomes the responsibility of the end consumer of information whilst their IS *supplier* may be an in-house service facility or a collection of external agencies. However, every business activity sits within a value chain of other activities and so even the in-house IS section must buy in component building blocks to build the service they will pass along to their customers. Changes in both IS service buying and IS service provision mean that both the user manager and the IS manager must engage in the procurement process and manage suppliers. The re-emergence of internal charging as an area of concern is largely the result of the growing recognition of this supplier/consumer relationship even *within* the organisation.

The strategy formulation process develops a picture of requirements that is based upon business issues and priorities. The picture of priorities developed by the IS strategy now gives the basis for selection between alternatives since, to make an effective selection, an organisation must know what it wants to do and define its goals clearly. The much misunderstood relationship between demand and supply, or needs and capabilities, is explored in O'Brien (1992) but at some point selection requires the identification of a prioritised set of needs. Prioritising may, of course, be conscious or unconscious, spoken and shared, or individualistic and untested, but it represents the *actual* IS strategy. Prioritising may be on a two-way basis, separating:

- Mandatory features
- Desirable features

Using these categories, any alternative *without* the mandatory characteristics goes no further in the selection process. For example, if there is a *fixed* budget figure then it is a mandatory characteristic that the selection candidate be below that figure. Alternatively, a three-way divide may be used to give a greater degree of precision to the process; this divide could separate:

- *Must-do features*: these are the things about the selection that are non-negotiable. Without these features a candidate is not even in the running.

- *Should-do features*: without these features it is *unlikely* that a selection would be made but they may form the basis of a beneficial trade-off.

- *Nice-to-do features*: these are the enhancements and frills, those things that, all other items being equal, might tip the balance in favour of a particular candidate.

To be able to define, assess and classify requirements requires *knowledge* and one critical success factor for the procurement process is to have adequate knowledge. This means that an organisation must invest in enough IS competence, internally or externally, to be able to explore its needs and priorities and to rank and judge alternatives. The procurement process, of course, inherently carries within it the risk of making poor selections. Only management time and attention can reduce selection risk and so, as well as firstly knowing *what* to do and secondly having access to enough *knowledge* to do it, the third feature of effective selection is being prepared to spend an amount of *time* appropriate to the significance of the acquisition.

IS service buying *must* involve some selection process. Such selection will *usually* involve some form of scoring and ranking technique (Information Economics as described in Chapter 7 was just such a technique). No matter how formal or informal is the application of the method of selecting between alternatives, the general principles are:

1  Select the criteria for making the choice
2  Associate weights to each criteria
3  Score acquisition alternatives in terms of how they satisfy each criteria
4  Calculate a candidate's rating by multiplying each score by the weight and then sum to a total
5  Select the one with the highest score!

Spreadsheet models (and the self-creation of one is talked through in Stott (1993)) exist to automate this process and they certainly take some tedium out of the calculation stage. However, the *difficult* and critical steps are the first ones of developing and weighting a criteria list and identifying suitable benchmarks and benchmark tests to provide attribute scores. The choice of benchmarking methods must be taken with care; many vendors optimise activities simply to suit benchmark processes rather than *realistic* use. If benchmarks are to be used (and they are common for large scale and/mid-range activities and for specific components of desktop systems) then they should be as customised to the intended *actual* use as possible. Figure 12.3 shows a possible selection tree for choosing among three candidates for a small office automation project. Not all branches of the tree have been completed but already it is possible to see that it will include tangible elements, such as speed and capacity, that can be objectively measured plus other, softer, elements, such as flexibility and ease of use, that require value judgements.

The weighted ranking process means that each preference becomes one attribute which is weighted against the other characteristics at the same level of detail; all features at the same level of detail adding up to 100 per cent. Once the relative weightings have been identified then a method of scoring the candidates for their possession of that attribute must be chosen. Score tables, such as where between 0 and 10 marks are awarded for each attribute, are useful. Generally 0 is awarded when the feature is not present at all, 1 if it is very poor and 10 if it is extremely good. These score tables can rate the objectively measurable items, such as processor speed, with the highest speed possible scoring 10 whilst the lowest scores 0 and such tangible items are appropriately the subject of benchmark tests. The same scoring table can also accommodate intangible features by using the numerical table to translate the *qualitative* judgements of 'very good', 'average', 'poor', etc into *quantitative* values to be used in the candidate ranking calculations. In the example illustrated in Figure 12.3, hardware items are deemed to be worth 20 per cent of the overall system, with output devices such as printers accounting for 50 per cent of that importance and so on across the selection tree. In this instance, scoring highly on hardware tests contributes less to the overall rating than scoring highly on software tests will. Figure 12.4 illustrates part of the score calculation process.

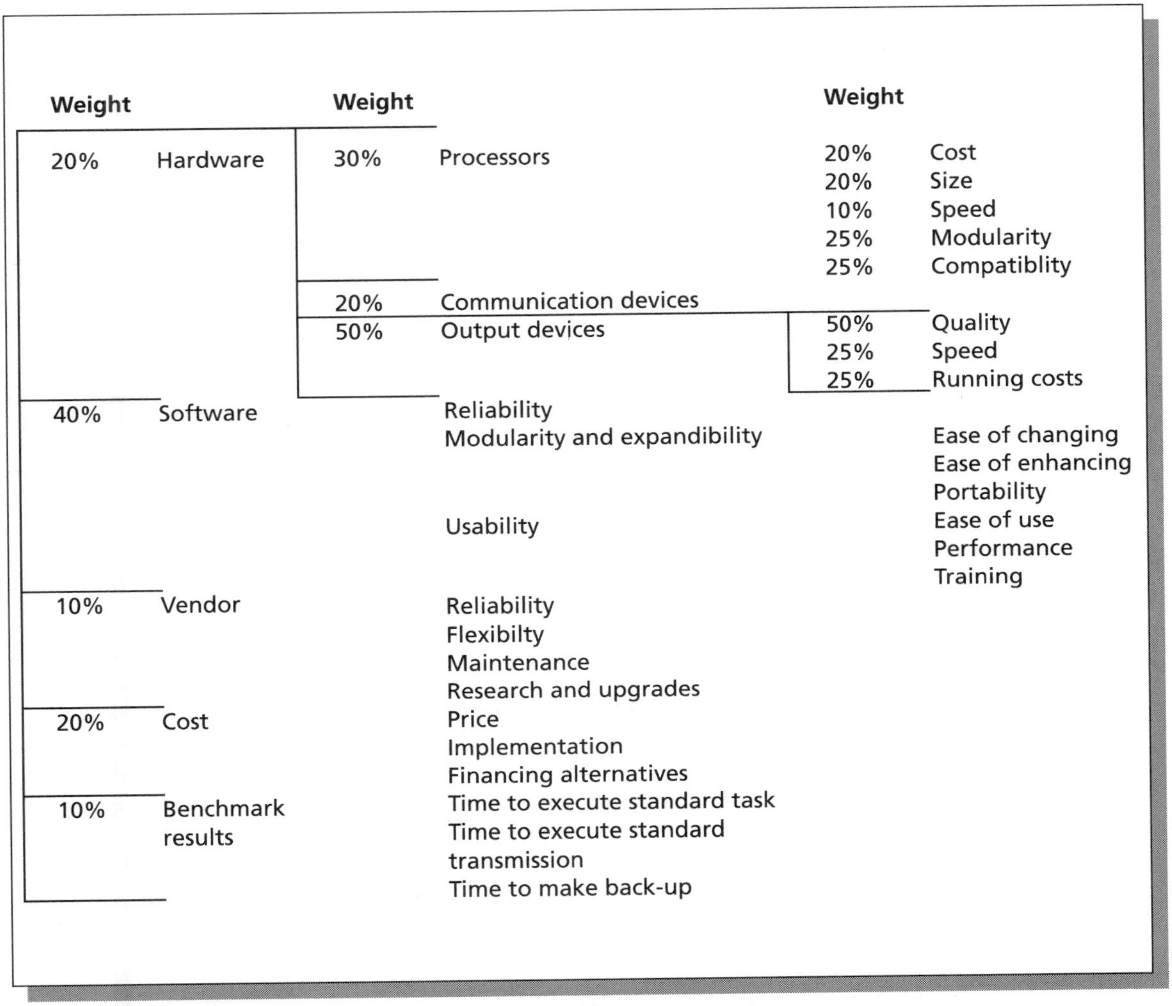

| Weight | | Weight | | Weight | |
|---|---|---|---|---|---|
| 20% | Hardware | 30% | Processors | 20%<br>20%<br>10%<br>25%<br>25% | Cost<br>Size<br>Speed<br>Modularity<br>Compatiblity |
| | | 20% | Communication devices | | |
| | | 50% | Output devices | 50%<br>25%<br>25% | Quality<br>Speed<br>Running costs |
| 40% | Software | | Reliability<br>Modularity and expandibility | | Ease of changing<br>Ease of enhancing<br>Portability |
| | | | Usability | | Ease of use<br>Performance<br>Training |
| 10% | Vendor | | Reliability<br>Flexibilty<br>Maintenance<br>Research and upgrades | | |
| 20% | Cost | | Price<br>Implementation<br>Financing alternatives | | |
| 10% | Benchmark<br>results | | Time to execute standard task<br>Time to execute standard<br>transmission<br>Time to make back-up | | |

**Fig 12.3 ◆ Partial weighted selection tree for small office automation project**

The criteria list defines the set of *characteristics* that the selection candidate should have; it is this set of characteristics that someone within the organisation must be prepared to prioritise according to the must do/should do/nice to do separation mentioned earlier. The ranking process draws the key criteria from the IS goal set and then judges candidates against these criteria to generate the scores and hence the candidates' rank. The intention in a weighted ranking selection process is two-fold. Firstly it is to give some illusion of objectivity to the process. Secondly, the intention is to break down the complexity of the proposed solutions into their con-stituent parts so that it becomes manageable to compare one solution that is simple to use but limited in capabilities with an alternative that offers more but in less friendly wrappings. In other words, a method of comparing chalk and cheese! If the 'best' score does not cause the candidate to be selected then there has been a covert, 'hidden', agenda that has distorted the *overt* process so that the weighted

**Printer speed score table**

| | | | |
|---|---|---|---|
| less than 3 pages per minute | 1 | 7 pages per minute | 6 |
| 3 pages per minute | 2 | 8 pages per minute | 7 |
| 4 pages per minute | 3 | 9 pages per minute | 8 |
| 5 pages per minute | 4 | 10 pages per minute | 9 |
| 6 pages per minute | 5 | more than 10 pages per minute | 10 |

Printer speed weighting is 20 per cent × 50 per cent × 25 per cent = 0.025 the multiplier for each score
Note: in this instance above a certain speed faster printing does not merit awarding a higher score

**Printer quality score table**

| | | | |
|---|---|---|---|
| Unreadable | 0 | | |
| Very very poor | 1 | Good | 7 |
| Very poor | 2 | Very good | 8 |
| Poor | 3 | Very very good | 9 |
| Adequate | 5 | Excellent | 10 |

Printer quality weighting is 20 per cent × 50 per cent × 50 per cent = 0.05 the multiplier for each score
Note: in this instance not every numeral is used

**Candidate scores**

| | Candidate A | Candidate B | Candidate C |
|---|---|---|---|
| Printer speed score | 2 | 5 | 8 |
| Multiplied by 0.025 weighting | 0.05 | 0.125 | 0.2 |
| Printer quality score | 10 | 8 | 7 |
| Multiplied by 0.05 weighting | 0.5 | 0.4 | 0.35 |
| *Contribution to overall rating* | 0.55 | 0.525 | 0.55 |

Note: in this instance printers A and C score the same and hence printer running costs could be the determining attribute

**Fig 12.4 ◆ Example system scores**

criteria do *not* truthfully represent the values to the selector. Usually this is because some valued characteristic is seen as private and so not publicly weighted and scored. Examples of such private criteria may include the 'friendliness' (or otherwise) of the supplier or the perceived political knock-on implications of a selection.

Effective selection can be a problem when there are differing criteria lists. Often one group must *test* alternatives for another group to make the decision, or decisions must be ratified by yet another group. In such cases it is vital that all are using the *same* perceptions of the *same* criteria list, perhaps what Davenport *et al.* (1989) call the IT management principles. These, of course, relate to the IS strategies and set the value parameters for the selection process. Davenport *et al.* distinguish clichés like 'data is an asset' that do *not* help in selection since candidates cannot be scored as achieving more or less of it, from the helpful principle that gives something for candidates to be scored against. Davenport *et al.* suggest that to be of help during selection the attribute must be contradictable and as examples of this point they quote:

> *We are committed to a single vendor environment.*
> *We will select the best technology for each business situation, regardless of vendor.*

The organisation's set of principles then inform and guide all groups involved in the business of weighting selection criteria. For most selection activities there are far too many products for it to be feasible to evaluate them *all* and so the organisation's IT principles should be used to generate some key criteria that can speedily be checked to sift and shorten the candidate list.

Some items that might appear on the criteria list are fairly obvious, for instance those relating to the *cost* of IS elements; however others are far less clear since they capture some perception of service. In fact the trade-off between one factor and another, that is the relative weighting they are given, is particularly complex in the area of services. Weighting between included-in-purchase, third-party, all-in-one or charged-for-individual-pieces maintenance contracts is a case in point. Software has traditionally come with support included and so the *quality* of it was the only candidate attribute to score. Now with software vendors limiting such free support, by time or type, the *amount* and *type* of support needs to be scored. (Third party support for software to cater for the difficulties arising from the complex integration of elements is a growing feature of external IS service provision.) Allied to the notion of judging the value of various forms of service is the need to judge the value of any *additional* incentives offered in association with a particular IS element. Examples include: consultancy and training included with acquisitions; software or installation 'bundled' with hardware and so on. A similar important but 'soft' issue is to require a judgement of the quality of the supplier as well as their product. Suppliers can be judged on their reputation, financial strength, size, conformance with any quality accreditation agencies, etc.

It is possible to synthesise a number of general selection guideline points that should influence attribute weighting and the scores given against the attributes. These guidelines are:

- Any selection decision motivated primarily by a desire to gain hardware economy is usually wrong.
- Software not hardware should drive almost all IS selection decisions; see Behrsin (1994) who describes how to determine prioritised needs, with the selection rhythm being:

  Business need
  $\longrightarrow$ Application software
  $\longrightarrow$ System software
  $\longrightarrow$ Hardware

  Failure to follow this route leads to a danger of becoming blinded with science and of a 'right tent, wrong desert' solution being selected.
- Software generally has a longer life than the hardware on which it runs; some software applications still running were designed and first written in the early 1960s; the organisation's data, however, has greater longevity than either.
- The choice of an architecture is more important and enduring than the choice of a particular piece of kit.
- The IS function should not be migrated from one hardware architecture to another without some very good reason. This means compatibility with current architecture will probably score highly and compatibility with a variety of options will score most highly of all.

- Connecting two or more vendors' components is generally difficult unless the components were designed to fit together (or produced to a well-defined standard).

- Connecting kit from different vendors is usually technically *feasible*, whether it is *desirable* or not depends upon the trade-off between the benefits and the added complexity.

- A 4GL should be used for software development unless a good argument exists for using a lower-level language since it is one possible definition of a 4GL that it delivers a ten-fold productivity improvement over 3GL developments.

- With the widespread use of high productivity development tools, the critical requirements when implementing a selection shift from the developers to the users who define the goals.

- Information requirements can never be fully defined in advance and so the selection must be capable of continual adaptation and growth. Flexibility matters more, and so should score more highly, than 'correctness'.

- Avoid pioneering unless good business justifications for doing so exist and normally consideration of the current client base should form part of the selection process. Seeing is believing when it comes to IT capabilities.

These guidelines can be summed up as don't change without reason and when change is needed keep it simple and go for flexibility wherever possible. Above all, work from business *problem* through software and hardware to a *solution* and do not look for ways to choose the most elegant solution irrespective of the actual problem.

Figure 12.5 gives a schematic of the selection process showing the acquisition elements in two logical groupings, broadly the software and the hardware. Since external provision forms an alternative in *each* block there is a third logical element,

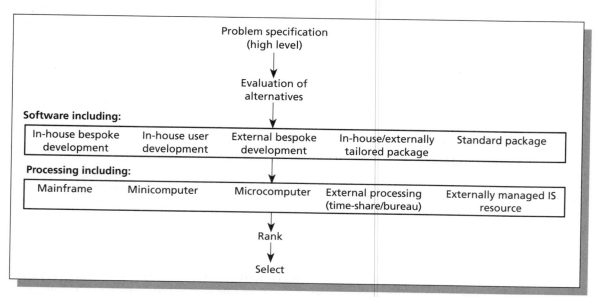

Fig 12.5 ◆ Schematic of the selection process

that of external provision of services. These three acquisition elements, software, hardware and services, and their associated concerns, are considered in Sections 12.2, 12.3 and 12.4.

### 12.1.1 ◆ The role of rules, standards and open systems

Who will *perform* the ranking and selecting, that is who will set the terms of the procurement process, varies with the organisation. Taylor and Tucker (1989) argue very strongly for a centralised procurement process quoting the advantages of cost savings through specialist and therefore skilled and effective buyers and also the greater co-ordination of activities. They suggest that central procurement can gain significant discounts and other concessions from vendors, avoid legal hazards, decrease the risk and increase the certainty and smooth the whole acquisition process by removing fragmented and devolved buying. They also argue that the advantages of such centralised procurement can be obtained no matter how decentralised the organisation is and give a description of a way to implement such a method into a decentralised organisation. This is an interesting account of how a centralised service process can be 'sold' in an environment of devolved decision making and, whilst the full service seems to have taken five years to put in place, the 'carrot' approach worked well for this group of eight data centres and shows itself an effective competitor to the 'stick' approach of rigid procurement rules.

By contrast, a *PC Week* (May 1993) editorial points out that whilst the freedom of devolved purchasing *may* lead to an 'unkempt IT garden – where no one in the organisation can remember what has been planted and what is likely to sprout next spring' it has also led to an appreciation of the flexibility gained by breaking away from the old autocracy of the DP department. Such flexibility is worth retaining but not at the expense of anarchy. Despite increasing involvement in IS by IS non-professionals it is overwhelmingly those IS professionals that are the ones ultimately deciding on IS acquisitions. Less than 20 per cent of acquisitions will involve non-IS professionals and this is standard across a variety of types of acquisitions, see Green-Armytage (1994). Interestingly the one exception to this is with printers whose acquisition is by non-IS professionals in 30 per cent of instances; perhaps this is a technically simple acquisition which will be *directly* used by non-professionals.

Clegg (1995) identifies the limitations for business advances resulting from IS professionals having a stranglehold on the IS acquisition process. He caricatures the damaging attitudes that unfortunately may prevail within procurement groups. These are the:

- *Wimp* who avoids confronting issues with suppliers and so is 'sold' IS elements.
- *Technofreak* who jumps on every bandwagon irrespective of business relevance.
- *Technoflop* who whilst responsible for procurement rules is technically incompetent to determine organisational suitability and so is driven only by financial considerations.
- *Soft touch* who is only concerned with how smoothly the procurement process runs and so selects IS elements from suppliers who are 'easy' to deal with irrespective of the real suitability of their products.
- *Big picture* merchant who selects IS elements on the basis of how the supplier may be useful to other procurement activities irrespective of suitability for a given need.

Clegg argues that only when procurement groups take an *advisory* rather than *rule setting* stance will a sensible balance between flexibility and anarchy be struck.

Public bodies have particularly difficult times with procurement. On the one hand they are constrained to lengthy and tedious tendering processes that make them unable to negotiate fast deals with suppliers to save money and yet on the other they face auditor criticism when they spend highly. For instance, Lambeth Council was publicly criticised for purchasing an upgrade option that, it transpired, implementation plans did not warrant. It is not only *national* governments that set limits to the freedom of the procurement process, the European Community (EC) also sets rules limiting public procurement, for example that large contracts must be notified through the EC's Official Journal and not merely advertised locally. In general, public procurement is a painfully lengthy business for both the buyer and the vendor and this pain strongly motivates a buying approach to reduce costs, not just in the purchase, but in the purchase *process*. One such a reduced cost approach, an extreme of centralised procurement, is group buying or purchasing co-operatives. Such ventures are now emerging amongst the new National Health Service Trusts where hospitals are able to establish volume leverage even from a structure whose buying power is very devolved. Buyer and seller gain when the voluminous documentation and detailed tender specifications can be produced once and reused throughout the buying group. This method of IS acquisition is particularly significant to the IS industry as the UK NHS is currently the largest employer in Europe.

Many organisations find that they are now in the position of relying upon discrete islands of technology created by their large number of incompatible systems. These systems are discrete because, when they were first developed, either it was not envisaged that there would be any *need* to be integrated or the high cost of integrating them would not have been justified by the resulting business benefits. However, the current IS environment with its requirement to leverage business process gains from information sharing means that there is a real *need* for systems to share data. The 1980s were characterised by a steady devolution of IS responsibility and authority and so the 1990s are, inevitably, going to be characterised by the struggle to rationalise and integrate the IS results of that devolved decision making. The importance of integrating previously disparate IS activities will, obviously, vary from organisation to organisation. However, it is likely to be critical in those many organisations who, as in the case of Chase Manhattan reported in Moad (1994), are reorganising to strengthen the focus on customer service. There are various *degrees* of integration and there are various responses to pursuing the desired level of integration. One response is to institute *organisational* procurement standards, as discussed above; a second response is to choose to use IS elements that adhere to *generally* agreed standards. In order to create the *effect* of IS being 'one single system' it is necessary to adopt *standards* since it is only through operating standards that the multi-vendor, variety approach sites created during the 1980s can work co-operatively as needed in the 1990s. *Open systems* is the term given to the framework of IS standards that allow a building block approach to creating IS solutions. *Proprietary* approaches are the opposites of open systems since they, by definition, do not work to publicly available standards, but deal with each IS activity in a vendor-chosen *ad hoc* way. It must be noted, however, that proprietary does not mean that components cannot be added. Open systems standardise IS components and so these components can then be guaranteed to combine in ways to suit the given organisation. This IS building block approach *should* give three benefits:

- Portability
- Scalability
- Inter-operability.

McCormack (1994) would add a fourth necessary characteristic for an open system, that of user portability from a common look and feel.

Open systems is the phrase generally given to the use of technologies that conform to a set of standards that are in the public domain. That is, the standards are published so that *anyone* can use them, with the obvious hope that *everyone* will use them. This is akin to the electricity supply standard that means that a householder can use electrical appliances supplied by any vendor and yet confidently expect the appliance to work with the same power network. Interestingly, in this analogy the power supplier is both a vendor (of the power supply) *and* the standards defining body. So it is with open systems and there are frequent cases where a particular vendor, often, but not always, the first or largest supplier of the technology, defines the *de facto* standard for a technology. A vendor practice can only become a *de facto* standard if it is possible for other vendors to adopt that practice. This standard then gives the consumer freedom of vendor choice when buying the particular technology, and potentially the greater competition means lower costs. Interestingly it can often be that there are lower costs to be had by following the market leader 'closed' proprietary supplier. For instance, software applications to run under Windows 95 (a closed system) are more readily available and often cheaper than applications to run under Unix (an open system). 'Allowing' vendors to define standards by a process of market emergence alone is often impractical so the International Standards Organisation (ISO) works to define standards for providing a common IS service, and that model is Open Systems Interconnection (OSI).

Open systems are fundamentally about connectivity. Proprietary approaches had few drawbacks when putting an isolated application in place and the vendor chosen approach could be most effective but, for most organisations, stand alone applications are no longer adequate. Modern business use of IS depends, not upon systems, but upon combining and integrating data to gain a 'sum greater than parts' advantage. That advantage can only be gained if the technology helps, rather than hinders, business integration and that requires systems connectivity and hence the definition of standards that can be used freely by all and are not 'owned' and private. Public domain standards, at least in theory, allow all vendors' components to be used together. Unfortunately, public standards have inherent difficulties when compared to private standards. If a vendor wishes, they can relatively easily and quickly ensure that everything they produce will work together since every element is under their own control. To reach agreement between *all* vendors is a lengthy process and tends to take either a lowest common denominator approach giving a subset of capabilities or to be dominated by the most technically advanced giving a proprietary approach by another name! The essence of pursuing open systems is of making trade-offs, these trade-offs being between initially higher costs (from both the act of changing and the increased complexity) and hoped-for future lower costs when future changes are needed and between guarantees of future potential for portability, scalability and inter-operability (if a really 'open' system is chosen) and reduced functionality *now*.

In the context of selection and acquisition, open systems probably defines the objectives of the IS architecture where these objectives become the *mandatory* attributes of selection candidates, that is that they can operate with other IS elements existing now and planned for the future. Open systems is the name given to the hope that local freedom will not generate anarchy since its defined and implemented standards should provide the degree of co-ordination needed. Unfortunately, open systems standards definitions and implementation are still at an early stage. This stage is similar to the early railway stage of everyone creating trains that will run on rails, but the actual implementation of the railway may lead to two or three rail types and all sorts of distances apart. Within any one rail company's region there is no problem and journeys run smoothly, until reaching the border with another company. Selecting within one vendor's implementation of open systems will generate few problems, until reaching the border with another vendor's implementation of open systems.

Open systems apply at *all* architecture sizes from desktop machines to mainframes. The very use of the phrase 'desktop computing' in preference to a phrase such as 'PC-based computing' (a name describing a proprietary standard) illustrates this. Any organisation should find that they are able to employ various levels of local intelligence, from dumb terminals through to full computing nodes, and, under open systems, the IBM PC and the Apple Macintosh are both viable architectures to provide this local intelligence.

The concerns of business re-engineering parallel the issues of open systems and, just as user-controlled computing is the organisational parallel to the technology of downsizing, so open systems is the *technological* parallel to the *organisational* issue of process design. Only the ability, at any time, to link in new IS architecture elements with certainty of co-operating with existing ones will support the redesign of processes and the development of new products and services. This is where portability and scalability as necessary attributes of open systems come in. The ability to move business solutions from one architecture to another, and up and down the size scale, is fundamental to the needs of open systems supported process redesign.

Before the days of a common electricity supplier, 'appliances' were built, in situ, by specialists to work with the particular circumstances and the householder had only to supply the requests and the money. With the existence of the common power supply grid the householder must choose and 'install' the television, the stereo and the fridge, and if the fridge creates interference on the stereo it is the householder who must resolve the integration problems. The only alternative is to employ an interior designer as a specialist in making appliances work together. Open systems pose just the same problems: where once discrete applications were created in situ by the vendor specialists who ensured that they would work in the particular circumstances, they are now plug-in appliances and any mutual interference must be resolved by the user. The only alternative is to employ an integration specialist, the IS interior designer. As choice increases, choosing becomes more complex, and open systems is about providing choice and hence, as with moving towards the use of packaged software, the critical skill becomes that of selection rather than development. A fundamental shift in the perception of IS acquisitions drives the importance of open systems. IS acquisition is recognisably a *continuous* and not a one-off process. Open systems make it explicitly possible for this to be the case.

## 12.1.2 ◆ Definitions associated with open systems

The following are a useful set of definitions, amended from Keen (1991), of the terms frequently encountered when discussing standards and open systems.

- *Architecture*: The technical blueprint for the corporate resource that can be shared by many users and services. This blueprint is of how things fit together and so must concern itself with standards (just as house plans concern themselves with building regulations). The opposite of architecture is to select every element on a project by project basis. The need for devices such as bridges and gateways to permit integration would never arise with common architectures.

- *Interface*: Many aspects of standards relate to defining interfaces, where an interface allows two dissimilar architecture elements to work together. Only when the interface specification is very *precise* can pieces *reliably* fit together. The definition of the RS232C interface allows processors to work with printers, any brand of processor to any brand of printer as long as both use the same interface rules.

- *Open systems*: These are vendor-independent systems, though can be achieved from a proprietary or *vendor-specific* system if the proprietary element is treated as a base line by enough other vendors. If everyone operates to the proprietary rules then that generates an open system. (The RS232C was a Radio Shack proprietary standard that became 'open' through the extent of conformity to it.) OSI is the international blueprint for open systems, though the blueprint is not fully implemented yet.

- *Open system interconnection (OSI)*: Gives a framework of interface definitions with the intention of giving individual vendors freedom over internal features provided interface rules are met so that system elements fit together. The interfaces may be at the physical level, as the RS232C interface, or at the logical, message level.

- *Systems network architecture (SNA)*: The IBM proprietary version of OSI, in that IBM's telecommunications architecture gives *one de facto* standard and many other vendors target SNA compliance.

- *Standards*: These are the voluntary agreements reached in the interest of being able to connect system elements – agreements to all use the same railway track width. The committees involved, including American National Standards Institute (ANSI), International Standards Organisation (ISO) and Consultative Committee for International Telephony and Telegraph (CCITT), are committees and so are usually slower to agree standards than the markets need them to be and so many of the widely complied-with standards are *de facto*, or market force set, rather than committee defined standards.

- *UNIX*: Frequently talked about as the system software of open systems since it is intended to be highly portable across many hardware platforms. The number of variants available challenges this perception and, whilst available for everything from microcomputers to mainframes, it is most closely associated with the mini-computer and the super-microcomputer. It is, however, growing in popularity and downsizing trends will increase that.

## 12.2 ◆ ACQUISITION OF SOFTWARE

This is the element of a system that users interact with and, since it is the bit that determines what they can achieve, clearly its acquisition is very important. Hardware and software acquisition decisions both revolve primarily around the choice of the *channel* of supply. Whilst for hardware this means which external source to use, for software it means the choice between various internal as well as external approaches to management of the development process. Such options lie along a continuum of possibilities and Figure 12.6 shows this continuum and that there is no sharp divide between internal and external developments and only options 1a, 1b, 4 and 5 can be unambiguously defined.

If the selection rhythm has determined the software before selecting hardware (or at least as *part* of the choice) then the entire development spectrum should be available. However, if a specific hardware choice has already been made, or existing kit must be used, then that constraint may mean that only options 1, 2 and 4 are possible.

Irrespective of whether the ultimate *development* is to be in-house or not, internal expertise is needed to establish *requirements*. It is the nature of these requirements, which capture the principles laid down by the IS strategy perhaps in terms of the need for compatibility, integration, communication, etc, that determine which of the acquisition routes are *most* appropriate. It should be obvious that the requirements must include any constraints on the selection *process*, for instance a weighting in favour of one type of process such as the use of contractors or standard packages.

It is not within the scope of this text to discuss the specifics of the many methods by which in-house developers, or even external development teams, may create a system. Large numbers of excellent texts both describe the principles of a specific method and the techniques it uses whilst other, equally important texts consider the choice of method for the given situation. Here we are concerned with the choice of process involving the trade-off of control against cost, the flexibility and controllability of teams within the organisation against the shorter time scales, lower costs and higher certainty potentially offered by outside agencies. This section will look briefly at the two extreme categories of in-house developments versus packaged, or shrink wrapped, solutions. There has been a continual drift from the first to the second but, despite that drift, there is still a real choice to be made. As Vowler (1995) points out 'the buy versus build dilemma has been with us for decades, and never quite disappears'.

| In-house development | | | | | | External development | |
|---|---|---|---|---|---|---|---|
| 1a | 1b | 2 | 3a | 3b | 3c | 4 | 5 |
| In-house systems and application software | In-house user application development | Contract staff working in-house | Vendor system tailored by in-house staff | Vendor system contractor tailored | Vendor system vendor tailored | Vendor bespoke turnkey solution | Standard package |

Fig 12.6 ◆ Software acquisition continuum

## 12.2.1 ◆ In-house development

It would be extraordinary if the major units of system software, the operating system and network management software, were to be developed in-house but the many system and network *utilities* that are required because of specific combinations of requirements most frequently are. In-house development work may generate the system software add-ons that keep a particular infrastructure running, though such 'middleware' can increasingly be bought in. Very large data centres, or organisations with very specific needs, may be forced to be exceptions to this rule, in which case they will generally exhibit the characteristics of a software house.

However, when application software is considered the situation is very different, and many organisations do choose to develop their own systems. The larger the IS section, and the more centralised it is, the more likely it is to develop large-scale systems. Very centralised IS functions take on many of the attributes of external bodies and developments by them share many of the attributes of development types (3) and (4) in Figure 12.6 except that the inevitable margin over costs is retained *within* the corporation rather than draining to an outside body.

Software development approaches have moved away from the rigid 'signing-off' of requirements that cast these requirements in stone over lengthy delivery time scales. Modern software development projects contain inherent uncertainties because of their need to retain flexibility in an environment of fast-changing requirements. This *inherent* uncertainty can cause runaway projects that generate costs far in excess of the potential benefits and, what is more important for many organisations, the delays mean that IS-supported competitive opportunities are lost. To avoid such runaways, in-house development work demands:

- *effective* project control using contemporary project management approaches
- software *production* attitudes and tools

The need for effective project control is obvious but will be difficult to achieve until software is production engineered rather than individually crafted. A production engineering focus creates the software *factory* and will recognise the benefits of making products that, wherever possible, contain re-usable standard components. The interest in object-based development approaches is precisely to gain *reusable* components. Such use of standard sub-assemblies frees effort to be expended where it gives benefits, in the system's value added features, rather than draining it away for non-essentials. The building of standard components and assembling them into systems can be well supported by technology tools. Components could be sourced from external vendors, internal re-cycling or purpose developments with all elements assembled *quickly* to suit the current need. Software development as a production process rather than as a craft will improve the productivity of all software development teams but recognition of this, and the employment of production tools and techniques, has generally been pioneered by the software houses. Those whose competitive *livelihood* is the developing of software for others have more readily recognised that the production of software creates their product whereas in-house teams have tended to retain a 'craftsman', hand-built attitude to software development.

There has been a steady trend *away* from large-scale in-house staff development teams. The poor reliability history, the perceived lack of skilled project management and the difficulty of retaining skilled teams in a fast-changing technology environment are all factors driving this trend. One result of this is that user application development, as considered in Chapter 11, is the commonest form of in-house work for most organisations. Frequently those projects unsuitable for user development simply move to external providers. Figure 12.7 suggests a possible process for selecting the software development path.

Many organisations are now forced to *justify* the in-house development decision where once it was the default. This change may happen even *during* large projects, for example Bournemouth District Council who had chosen in-house development of their community-charge system (and sold it on to other councils) opted in 1992 for a packaged solution for the replacement council-tax system. The £550 000 purchase price of the package was judged to be cheaper than internal development and the time scale to be more manageable. Figure 12.8 illustrates an example of the possible cost differential of in-house development against buying a package. Somewhat bucking this cost-driven trend is the much publicised Hong Kong and Shanghai Bank's approach to IT. This bank feels that IT *is* banking and hence the close fit offered by successful internal developments is deemed essential to business success and packages are rarely used despite the *apparent* cost savings.

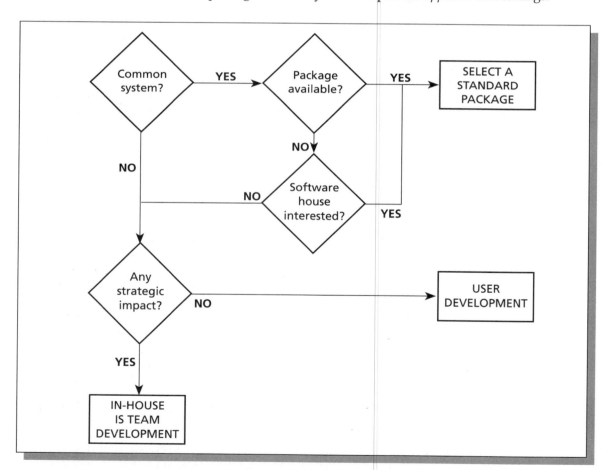

**Fig 12.7 ◆ Process of choosing the software acquisition approach**

| Development activity | In-house development | Purchased standard package |
|---|---|---|
| Initial feasibility analysis | £100 000 | £100 000 |
| Requirements definition | £250 000 | £200 000 |
| Detailed system design | £100 000 | – N/A – |
| Coding and module testing | £200 000 | – N/A – |
| System testing | £130 000 | £100 000 |
| Documentation and manual procedures | £120 000 | £25 000 |
| Installation, data preparation and changeover | £100 000 | £150 000 |
| Purchase price | – N/A – | £100 000 |
| **Total** | **£1 000 000** | **£675 000** |

Fig 12.8 ◆ Tabulation of example costs: in-house *v* package

As a result of the trend towards user application development and purchased packages, much in-house work will be on the maintenance and enhancement of *existing* systems, often on the re-engineering of such existing systems with little on truly new developments. Pre-existing systems are popularly referred to as legacy systems with a connotation that they are worthless millstones to be replaced in as timely a manner as possible. The greater the volume of past in-house developments the more effort the maintenance of such legacy systems consumes. The current trend towards packaged solutions generally diminishes the maintenance backlog though the long-term effect of extensive user development activities upon maintenance pressures is uncertain. Packages, of course, also generate many of the negative aspects that are usually implied by the term 'legacy systems'. 'Old' application packages can create just as much inflexibility as 'old' bespoke software.

## 12.2.2 ◆ Use of standard packages

This is the preferred software acquisition source for such a large, and growing, number of organisations, that this section considers it in some detail. Firstly though it should be noted that this section is not just, or even primarily, referring to PC-based packages. Though the PC platform has encouraged the use of standard applications such packages feature on *all* hardware architectures, for instance a popular word processing package, Uniplex, runs on mid-range Unix architectures.

More and more businesses have grown to depend upon IS, particularly in their common business areas, and yet many of them are lacking in-house IS expertise, and to resolve this conflict they have turned to standard, packaged solutions. In 1985 perhaps only one third of organisations used packaged solutions, now that would be something like 95 per cent, and across a wide range of application areas. Business methods are *not* as varied as most organisations assume and most standard packages are well equipped to cater for the small number of business-valid differences. Packages are, by definition, pre-developed, although many firms are able to provide inputs into the development process. Because they are pre-developed they must aim at a 'wide' market, though this market may represent only single figure sales for the expensive packages, and target this wide market by working to sound common business practices. Adopting these sound practices is to the advantage of most organisations, particularly in application areas of low strategic significance. With the computerising of the small firm anything *other* than packaged solutions is generally unthinkable. Figure 12.9 illustrates just some of the benefits offered by packages over bespoke developments.

The basic returns for time and money will usually favour a package. The purchase or licence cost of the package, whilst perhaps high, is *certain*, unlike the development cost of in-house software. For example, the licence for a personnel management package for a mid-range computer may cost £39 per month; the equivalent in-house development cost might be around £50 000–£75 000 but final costs would be unknown and the development duration would be uncertain. However, whilst the up-front costs of buying a package are *relatively* low, in-house costs should be set against their long-term skills-building value. When a package is purchased all the development learning has been retained by the package vendor.

The requirements analysis stage of package acquisition is every bit as demanding as it is for in-house developments but, once selected, the *delivery* of the solution can be very fast. This fact generates enormous appeal to organisations struggling with lengthy IS backlogs. This 'speedy' process is assisted by the fact that the generalised nature of most packages includes modular designs, user hooks to other packages, in-house developed software, and customisable parameters defining the detailed features of the system. For example, an invoicing package allows for changes in screen layout, discount percentages, payment periods and report formats. In addition, whilst the quality of the documentation provided with packages may *seem* poor, it is likely to be of a far higher standard than that generated by in-house technical teams. Standard packages are the work of software houses who must sell to customers and good product presentation is hence, for them, *competitively* critical. Software houses, unlike internal teams, will usually employ authoring as well as technical expertise. Software firms may result from the *commercialising* of internal IS sections, the ones of the purchasing organisation or those of others, and Chapter 9 discussed this extreme instance of IS structure and location.

Support for a package may vary in quality but is generally provided as part of the purchase price, however there is a move by large software firms to charge different fees for different levels of support. Training gains from the wider usage of the software since, whilst it may be less focused upon the organisation, it should be cheaper and more readily available. Packaged training materials are available for most popular packages.

In the acquisition of packages the effort and skill required shifts from the *development* of the software into the *selection* of the package, a rather different development cycle to that with bespoke development. Also, since most packages can be adapted,

---

- Rapid availability
- Sound business procedures
- Known and verifiable quality
- Low up-front and overall costs
- Inspectable documentation
- Available maintenance
- Continual research and updates
- Varied support and training

**Fig 12.9 ◆ Advantages offered by standard packages**

a number of acquisition paths exist and must be chosen between. The identified and prioritised requirements mentioned earlier in this chapter must be matched against something that already exists and the purchaser needs to map where the gaps are and decide upon a process for managing the capability 'holes'. Figure 12.10 illustrates the different strategies for dealing with the inevitable mismatch between business needs and package capabilities, though ordinarily no package should be purchased where the match is less than about 80 per cent.

It is not always wisest to modify the package. Since ownership of the software copyright is held by the vendor, their withdrawal of licensed software can negate expensive customisation work. Vendor updating and enhancing of packages whilst normally beneficial may mean that new updates also negate past custom work, perhaps to the point that an entire system, built upon an old edition and dependant upon features that no longer exist, becomes obsolete. Many vendors support only a limited number of previous generations of their package and so upgrades are, effectively, mandatory. It is for this reason, as well as for financial reasons, that vendor updating is not always beneficial. An OTR survey reported in Green-Armytage (1995) shows that many organisations regard this updating (with its subsequent withdrawal of support for older versions) to constitute an upgrade 'trap' that 75 per cent felt generates no financial benefits. OTR estimated that over five years it cost £2 500 per workstation to upgrade existing standard software packages. This is one area in which bespoke applications can score with lower costs than packages.

It is not only the potential for lost 'systems' that questions the sense of customising (where customising is distinct from the in-built adaptability of the package

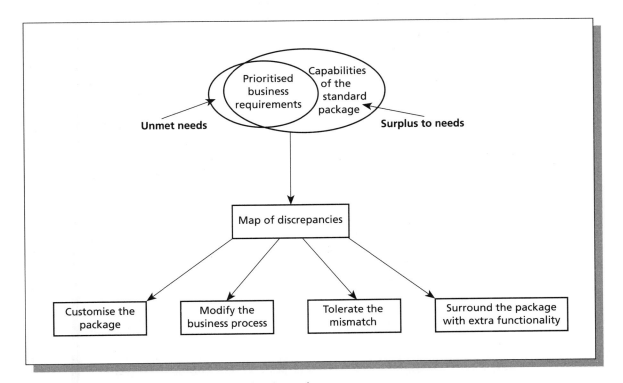

Fig 12.10 ◆ Strategies for capabilities/needs mismatch

itself), a good package uses good methods and the business will benefit from changing working practices that are unconsidered oddities rather than value adding procedures. It may be that the cost argument simply favours tolerating a minor mismatch between the package and the working practices or, alternatively, that the organisation can bridge across or surround the package with additional in-house applications to avoid modifying it.

Before embarking upon the process of purchasing a standard package, or defining a 'packages preferred' policy for software acquisition, there are a number of management factors to consider. The issue of adapting the organisation to someone else's view of how the business process should be performed has already been mentioned, though this is a less contentious issue now than in the early days of packages. Firstly, a far larger number of solutions are likely to be available giving greater choice and so a greater chance of obtaining a good fit. Secondly, the sharper focus upon business operations and the distinction between *core* processes and *support* activities has reduced the 'always done it that way' mentality. The discipline of imposing standard, low cost, methods on support activities is widely recognised as an advantage.

For those with a free choice between in-house development and packaged solutions then the selection of a package will generally be on a cost and time gained basis. It should be noted however that increasingly this is *not* a free choice since it may be impossible to do anything but buy a package if earlier decisions have removed the in-house development teams. Downsizing, discussed in Section 12.3.2, is another trend that favours the use of packages. To implement the policy of moving platforms generally requires the time advantages inherent in using packages. The policy of downsizing itself has probably been motivated by potential cost saving and the use of packages is certainly characterised by fixed costs as well as increased flexibility. The move towards open systems, as discussed in Section 12.1.1, will also favour the use of packages since greater vendor independence generates greater competition and so package costs should fall making them yet more attractive.

For some elements of the systems portfolio cost saving should be the primary selection consideration. A scarce resource generic IS strategy is likely to apply to those systems of relatively low business importance, perhaps those categorised as being in the support or factory segments of the McFarlan and McKenney (1983) strategic importance grid described in Section 5.3.3. To judge the cost *savings* the costs must be accurately compared, even though savings generally accrue from the coding element of the development cycle rather than from business analysis activities. Figure 12.8 tabulated one example of such savings. For most organisations the further the application area is from the 'core' business the more likely it is that cost is the driving motivation of the selection of a package, and conversely, the closer the application is to the core of the business then the likelier it is to be a candidate for in-house development. The business complexity and the smaller market size have meant that vertically integrated applications are the least likely to be catered for with a packaged solution.

Packages offer lower costs and an earlier return on investment than in-house or vendor bespoke developments do, perhaps 15 per cent faster and 45 per cent cheaper, but these gains need to be assessed *realistically*. An extreme illustration of the potential savings is quoted by Schlender (1989) when he gives the instance of Lotus Development Corporation spending $7 million to develop Lotus 1-2-3 version 3, with an additional $15 million on its testing and quality control; it currently sells in the UK for about £300; clearly the huge volume sales can be to the advantage of the purchaser. Customising the package to include user routines, whoever does the actual tailoring work, causes costs additional to the package purchase price. Such alteration is always slower and more expensive than anticipated, especially if it is done in-house, since the internal team will be working with someone else's material. Items such as converting files to the required format can be technically difficult and surprisingly slow whereas in-house developments usually work with the existing formats. File conversion problems decline when data is *already* maintained by a package and as *standard* data formats emerge and the import and export routines within packages improve. In-house developments rarely use either.

To balance the lower development costs there *may* be higher operational costs. It is possible that the 'lowest common denominator' approach adopted by a package generates more inefficiencies than in-house developments that can be optimised for a given environment. It is equally likely, however, that a package will be *more* efficient in anything but the most esoteric environment since one of the features of a package is the vendor's ability to do large-scale testing and amending. Using packages as development tools may generate higher than necessary maintenance costs. Vowler (1994) cautions that the use of low-cost visual environments aimed at the user developer, for instance the capabilities of Windows spreadsheets, 'hides' the code logic. This concealment ultimately causes high overall IS costs despite the very low initial package cost.

A final additional cost is that of training, not, of course, a cost exclusive to packages and indeed it is an overlooked additional cost for in-house work as well! Training requires a sum of money over and above the purchase price but it may be a smaller one than if in-house software was used since standard packages breed standard training courses. Along with training, support will also be standardised and in the UK we may suffer from support at a distance. However, the point about packaged, as opposed to in-house, software is that if the style of the software, its documentation or its support seems inappropriate then an alternative vendor will be chosen. Not all packages are equal and supplier reliability and long-term intentions may be important. Section 12.4 considers issues associated with vendor selection and management.

We have already mentioned that acquiring a package may not result from a free choice. If a 'packages preferred' route is chosen then the organisation is creating a 'no in-house skills' set-up that pre-determines future choices. The current in-house development projects are the training grounds for future development skills. Unless this acquisition represents a minor and trivial part of the overall development portfolio then electing to use a package is a long-term decision. However, to balance the long-term nature of the decision, it is probably *opening* out later choices on interfacing, migrating and integration. In many instances the *same* package can be purchased for a wide range of hardware and system software architectures and when these are likely to alter, as is the case for organisations embarking upon downsizing initiatives and open systems migrations, then selecting an appropriate package *now* may ease moves *later*. An argument *against* taking a long-term view when selecting between packages is that an organisation should not use complex, lengthy and hence expensive selection processes that focus upon long-term needs when buying packages for fast-changing business areas. The organisation should establish a fast, and cheap, selection process for the package and concentrate only upon the more readily identifiable current needs. This cheaper selection process makes it justifiable to write off the purchased package fairly quickly, perhaps after three years, and start again with a newer, more capable package which is once again more suitable for current needs.

One significant feature of the acquisition of packaged software solutions is that it shifts the critical acquisition skills from development to requirements specification, from the 'computing' skills of system design and programming to the 'business' skills of prioritising and selecting. Therefore a significant management issue is that selecting a package does not necessarily require the specialist IS function to be the *major* player. Even when IS is to be involved they take one set of roles rather than control most of the process as they do with internal developments other than user-controlled computing applications. Departmental distributed computing and standard packaged solutions are mutually fuelling drives and Figure 12.11 shows one possible task split.

Since any software will require maintenance it must, of course, be established who will be responsible for the package's maintenance and where amendments will fit within any maintenance agreement. If in-house modifications have been made it must be clear who owns the rights to the source code of these. Since the cost of maintenance can easily equal the original purchase price it may be that an even *more* generalised solution, such as an application generator rather than an application package, may be justified. Since vendors rarely supply source code then this could be lodged with what is called an escrow agent (a third party agreed on by both) so that the purchasing organisation is assured of an alternative source of support should the original supplier cease trading.

Many of the managerial factors described in this section weigh heavily in favour of packaged solutions. The inherent time lag before a particular business process is supported by a package remains the most powerful force against. The organisation doing something for the *first* time will not, of course, have access to a package. The market forces must allow time for a software vendor to identify the market need, design and build the package and then it is obviously a 'mass' market commodity.

| Task | Responsible body | |
|------|-----------------|---|
| Acquiring resources | Business unit | |
| Defining requirements | Business unit | |
| Implementing system | Business unit | |
| Managing acquisition process | Corporate IS unit | |
| Assuring technical quality | Corporate IS unit | |
| Negotiating contract | Corporate IS unit | |
| Modification of package | Corporate IS unit and/or package vendor | |
| Maintaining system | Corporate IS unit and/or package vendor | |
| Nurturing the team | | Joint |
| Selection of package | | Joint |

Fig 12.11 ◆ Possible task split during acquisition of packaged software

Custom in-house development will remain associated with striving for a competitive gain in a core business area. Such striving is, by definition, about innovation whilst, also by definition, a package would be accessible to all. The process of selecting the software acquisition method was illustrated in Figure 12.7 and the nature of that decision tree means that there are three ideal-use scenarios indicating the selection of packaged solutions:

- A set of well-integrated applications for a relatively small organisation willing to take the package without any changes. This may equally apply to a smallish division of a larger group and is even more strongly indicated where a set of such applications can be sourced from a single vendor.

- An application *not* critical to the business' mainline activities that has a well defined and relatively simple interface to other sections of the organisation's applications portfolio.

- A complex application needing technical expertise in an area in which the organisation does not feel it can gain any significant competitive advantage. If the technical expertise is of low competitive value then the cost of developing such expertise cannot be justified, at least for this area alone.

Packages may be selected not simply as *individual* entities and there are two combination situations to consider. The first is that of using standardised approaches. An organisation may elect to take all its packages from the same supplier to get a common interface that should increase user productivity, and perhaps lower the costs of purchase, training and support. Using standard packages should offer economies of scale in licensing copies and the ability to provide better support and training and increase staff mobility throughout the organisation. However, people and politics issues as well as more concrete factors, such as any differences in languages and accounting laws across international groups, may require compromises. The 'not invented here' problem inherent in selecting a package in preference to in-house developments is *doubled* when a section of the business must use a standard package that it has not even chosen. This notion of 'rules' in the acquisition process was discussed in Section 12.1.

There are four different approaches to defining the degree of freedom business areas can have when selecting packages:

- *Total freedom*: this approach lets all business areas select their personally preferred package and can lead to chaos, with no one knowing what to purchase, high installation, training and support costs and, of greater business significance, potentially enormous future costs from lost integration opportunities. However, each business area can select a package that closely matches their needs without any compromise.

- *Data exchange*: this approach allows individual areas to buy whatever package they wish providing it will support data exchanges with other packages and systems as necessary.

- *Short list:* with this approach some standards-setting body within the organisation defines a short list of acceptable packages and the individual area may choose from that list only.

- *Fixed standards:* with this approach a standards body defines *the* permissible package and so the individual business area can have 'any colour they want as long as it is black'.

All but the first of these approaches raises the issue of *who* will define and police the standards used. The last of the four approaches by using a single package throughout the organisation offers many cost advantages but may increase hardware costs since the chosen standard may be a more powerful and processor 'hungry' package than individual areas need, or it may reduce effectiveness by taking a compromised, lowest common denominator, approach to application requirements.

The second package group consideration is that of buying an integrated package or a suite of packages rather than making package by package decisions. Cost advantages, guaranteed compatibility and uniformity assisted ease of use are the advantages offered by both integrated packages and package suites. As Figure 12.12 shows, sales of most PC-based individual and integrated packages are losing ground to sales of package suites indicating the popularity of such grouped selections. These suites, either from a single vendor or for a single environment, offer advantages of compatibility and uniformity by adopting a single user interface, such as *from* Microsoft or *for* Microsoft Windows, the popular PC graphical user interface.

---

*Application areas with increasing volume sales:*

- Package suites (eg Office 95)

- Project management software (eg EasyProject

- Database engines (eg Access)

- Integrated office applications (eg Works)

*Application areas with declining volume sales:*

- Spreadsheets (eg Excel)

- Wordprocessors (eg Word)

- Accounts packages (eg Sage)

- Presentation graphics (eg Powerpoint)

Note: The increased volume of sales of suites packages during the 1990s has been many hundreds of percent whilst the increased sales of project management applications will have been less than 100 percent and increased sales of integrated applications may have only been single figure increases. The low increase and the net decline in stand-alone application packages reflects both that markets are mature (growth opportunities being therefore limited) and the loss of sales to suites.

---

Fig 12.12 ◆ Changing pattern of packaged software sales volumes during the 1990s

## 12.3 ◆ ACQUISITION OF HARDWARE

In discussing the acquisition of hardware there are essentially two key issues, the source of supply and the nature of the hardware *platforms*. This section will briefly consider hardware selling channels and, at slightly more length, the notion of downsizing. The concepts of open systems, whilst relating very much to hardware choices, have already been discussed in Section 12.1.1.

### 12.3.1 ◆ Hardware source channels

With the minor exception of microcomputer assembly, *all* hardware will be acquired externally and the *size* of the platform will largely define the scope and nature of the acquisition channels that are available. Figure 12.13 summarises the available hardware source channels.

Mainframe computers come primarily from their manufacturers, although there is a growing trade by third party vendors and in second-hand equipment causing the second-hand markets to flourish, both in direct purchases from the first user and from specialist re-conditioners. Mensching and Adams (1991) argue that the second hand market provides a valid source of equipment since such kit will generally have been replaced because of technical *obsolescence* rather than physical *deterioration*. When buying second-hand computers the critical issue is, not the age of the hardware, but rather the condition of it, as with used cars! If the requirements of any maintenance agreements have been met then the second-hand market offers a very cost effective source of mature technologies. Savings of 20 per cent to 50 per cent on new prices can be had. Other advantages include the immediate availability of the machine and the ability to obtain an addition to existing equipment if it is no longer produced. By buying second-hand hardware the purchase risk moves from the uncertainty of the technology to the uncertainty of the condition and, rather as second-hand cars, certain makes and models will retain more market attractiveness than others by 'holding their price'. There are various sources of buying and selling guidance on hardware 'book prices', one such being the Econocom Guide to the Data Processing Market that can be used as a reference aid by both sellers and buyers. Downsizing initiatives as discussed in Section 12.3.2 may mean that fairly new mainframe and minicomputers are disposed of, and these offer attractive deals to those organisations upsizing or consolidating, or simply replacing elderly equipment. Obviously it is not *only* mainframes that can be bought second-hand but a relatively high price and long shelf life are necessary for a stable second-hand market. This source of supply is sufficiently reputable for many manufacturers to offer an authorised channel; see Mills (1995). Computer auctions are rather less reputable, but are growing in importance. For large organisations they are a quick and relatively cheap way of disposing of unwanted equipment. For smaller organisations and personal buyers they can be a very effective source of bargains.

| Mainframe | Manufacturer<br>Third party specialist | |
| --- | --- | --- |
| Minicomputer | Manufacturer<br>Value added resellers | However,<br>*all* sizes of<br>hardware |
| Microcomputers | 'Traditional' manufacturer's sales teams<br>Value added resellers (VARs)<br>High street shops<br>Computer supermarkets<br>Direct mail order<br>In-house component assembly | may be<br>bought<br>second-hand |

**Fig 12.13 ◆ Sources of hardware**

Minicomputers have essentially similar sources of supply to mainframes but at the smallest end of the hardware size scale there are far *more* choices to make than simply of brand and whether to buy new or second-hand. For microcomputers there are many sources of supply leading to some difficult channel decisions. Figure 12.14 illustrates the findings of a 1995 Romtec survey into sources of supply. These microcomputer sources include:

- *Manufacturer's dealers:* if the client is large enough then the option to buy direct from the manufacturer may be available. The manufacturer's sales team may then develop a long-term relationship with the client that will, theoretically, allow very specifically tailored solutions to be designed by the technically knowledgeable sales team. For the organisation in the position to be a major account for the manufacturer, the possibility of a tailored service plus the greater maintenance and spares reliability may outweigh the generally higher cost than direct mail order buying and the narrower, more biased focus than the value added resellers. As multi-vendor environments become the norm, the lack of integration support offered by single vendor's agents becomes a more critical problem.

- *Value added resellers (VARs):* these dealers will generally be geared to selling, and supporting, a small range of products. By definition, VARs add a margin to the basic cost of hardware to cover their provision of 'services'. This provision may include selecting a total solution consisting of hardware, software and networking arrangements through to installation and training. In the past, dealers have added their margin uniformly, however recently the *itemising* of available services has become prevalent allowing an organisation to make a pick and mix selection of business-beneficial features. VARs still appeal to organisations that must integrate system elements for microcomputer-based business-critical systems when the value offered by the integration expertise of VARs is worth their higher per PC cost. The trend towards itemised services applies to other channels of supply and to software as well as hardware although hardware maintenance is perhaps more visibly a feature of the purchase contract. The greater the business importance of the system, and the greater its degree of specialism, the more likely it is

| Channel | Number | % | Revenue (£m) | % |
|---|---|---|---|---|
| Value added reseller | 8 965 | 44 | 14 019.5 | 43 |
| Dealer | 5 610 | 27 | 7 405.9 | 22 |
| Corporate dealer | 470 | 2 | 1 467.2 | 4 |
| Retailer | 2 675 | 13 | 3 712.6 | 11 |
| Direct mail order | 1 200 | 6 | 2 562.6 | 8 |
| System integrator | 820 | 4 | 1 509.6 | 5 |
| Distributor | 815 | 4 | 2 250.3 | 7 |
| Total | 2 055 | 100 | 32 927.7 | 100 |
| | | | Revenues at annual rate | |

**Fig 12.14 ◆ European hardware channels**
(adapted with permission of *Computer Weekly*, based on information from Romtec, 1995)

for the channel of supply to be a VAR. As the desktop computer industry has matured there have been three stages of evolution regarding buyers' attitudes to VARs, which have been:

1  Ignorance  buyer feels they need the VARs
2  Confidence  buyer rejects the VARs in favour of direct buying
3  Understanding buyer appreciates the benefits of the VARs

All VARs should be skilled at defining PC-based business solutions. A buyer *may* possess such skills, in which case the VARs offer them little, or the buyer may have IS expertise in *other* areas, in which case 'leaving it to the experts' may be business beneficial, and potentially cheaper when *all* factors are considered. This channel is regarded as being under threat by both the direct sellers and the high street retailers. However, many users continue to regard the 'value added' element as worth paying for.

- *High street shops:* as microcomputers become commodity items similar to televisions and fridges so they are sold in the same way as other consumer products. Such channels cater primarily for the home or small business market and this market is an expanding one, including as it does many instances of hardware for the home-based worker discussed in Section 12.4.1. The so called SoHo (Small Office, Home Office) market accounted for only 17 per cent of PCs in 1994 but 28 per cent of them in 1995, see Dataview (1996). Although high street retailers offer only limited expertise, they usually offer the opportunity to see and try the hardware before buying it. Such stores rarely offer much variety and obviously *never* anything out of the main stream.

- *Computer supermarkets:* This acquisition channel is enormously popular in America and 1991 saw the opening of the first computer supermarket in the UK. Such supermarkets are targeted at mass population centres such as London and Glasgow. As with high street stores, they are unlikely to cater for the large organisation but they seek to offer the scale of choice of the direct channel combined with an element of personal service, plus the opportunity to view products before purchase. Whilst fairly common in America, computer supermarkets are still rare enough in the UK to offer a source of supply to only a few organisations and are more a reflection of the growth of home computing. This type of retail outlet may be moving beyond personal sales, as Murphy (1995) reports that only the largest organisations exclude purchasing through this channel.

- *Direct mail order:* The greatest change in the source of supply has been away from VARs and to direct mail order and yet it is the computer supermarket and the high street store that are the direct competitors to the mail order channel. Manufacturer's agents and VARs offer such different deals that they may be more conveniently regarded as complementary channels. There has been significant growth in the direct channel, according to *Computer Weekly* figures from 14 per cent of the UK microcomputer unit sales in 1990 to 29 per cent of this market in 1991. This growth indicates that desktop computers are now viewed as a price-critical commodity item. Where price *is* the critical selection criteria then the direct channel is likely to be the preferred source since it can be 15 per cent to 25 per cent cheaper than VAR sources. This channel appeals when an organisation needs to provide mass coverage or where internal expertise is high so that 'off the page'

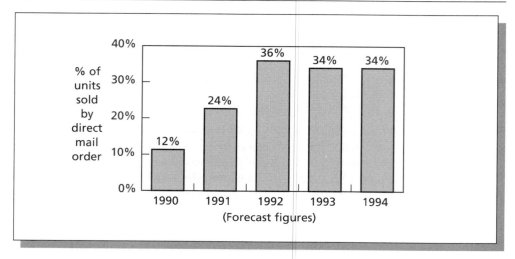

**Fig 12.15 ◆ Direct mail order of PCs in the UK**
(adapted by permission of *Computer Weekly*, based on information from Romtec 1993)

selections are cost effective. The danger exists of the chosen supplier defaulting or ceasing to trade. If long-term arrangements are needed then vendor selection is as important as hardware selection but if a 'hit and run' buy is appropriate then the cost is critical. As PCs become more business critical one of two things may happen. The organisation may develop extensive *internal* expertise so that it can effectively select all hardware, software and networking elements for itself and this extends the use of the direct channel. Alternatively, the increased business importance may make the stability of the supplier relationship equally critical and so the organisation returns to the fold of the VARs. The findings of a Romtec survey, illustrated in Figure 12.15, would seem to support this point and their forecasts indicate that the direct mail order hardware channel has reached its peak.

- *In-house kit building:* an option that some organisations have flirted with is to buy in components such as motherboards, monitors, disk drives, etc and assemble them themselves. Plummeting hardware prices have made this acquisition source unattractive except where very specific or peculiar configurations are needed.

The essence of selecting a channel of supply is one of balancing 'extra' services such as integration into a total solution, needs analysis and purchase advice against lowest costs, greater variety of products and maximum vendor independence. A key part of the acquisition process is for an organisation to understand the supplier expectations it has and choose a channel that matches. In that way satisfaction with the supply process will be maximised. Figure 12.16 illustrates levels of supplier satisfaction.

## 12.3.2 ◆ Downsizing

The second key aspect in hardware selection is that of the scale of the hardware platform. What is usually referred to as downsizing is the current stage of a very long-term trend, that of developing smaller and hence more distributable hardware bases for software systems. What is discussed here as downsizing is the *technical* parallel to the *organisational* issue of user-controlled computing (U-CC).

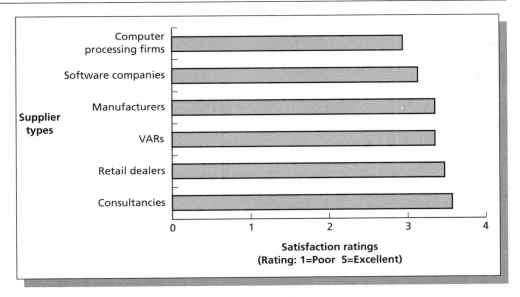

**Fig 12.16 ◆ Levels of user satisfaction with supply channels**
(reproduced by permission of *Computer Weekly*, based on Quality of IT Suppliers Survey 1994, Kew Associates)

Obviously microcomputers can, and do, form part of a purely corporate IS environment and, equally obviously, U-CC can, and does, exist in a purely mainframe centralised processing environment. However, it is more *likely* that the choice to distribute processing power represented by downsizing be driven by greater user autonomy caused by U-CC and, in turn, the greater flexibility offered by networked PC applications over mainframe systems will encourage the growth of end-user computing. Whichever of the two trends is the *driving* force, there *has* been a significant move towards using smaller processing platforms to the point that new developments are just as likely to be based on desktop platforms as on midrange or mainframe architectures.

If a jargon term can be said to have a definition then, 'correctly', downsizing is the creation of systems on a smaller platform than before. Although the term is used very loosely, it essentially implies the *migration* of a system or a set of systems from a mainframe or minicomputer to a minicomputer or PC network. However, *new*, small platform-based applications are also given this name. By implication, a significant degree of networking and processing distribution is included in the term. Edelstein (1992) gives a very clear explanation of the difference between what he calls personal mainframe computing (what Chapter 11 called corporate computing) and client-server networks. The term *rightsizing* is best defined as being the process of choosing between platforms, that is the process of selecting the correct or most *appropriate* hardware platform for the given business application.

Downsizing applies across all business and systems areas, for example even BBC sports coverage is affected when there is a change from a minicomputer being used to generate on-screen graphics to using a PC network, (Ringshaw, 1993). Perhaps the most interesting point here is the news worthiness of this move attesting to what, some argue, is the fashion factor, rather than any really revolutionary development.

Such fashion changes tend to be self-fulfilling, for instance printer sellers *assume* downsizing moves and hence target their products accordingly, and then printer price and availability, in turn, influence the viability of platform choices.

The downsizing trend is also paralleling the greater focusing upon *value* for money as considered in Chapter 7, with the greater perceived value of smaller environments motivating the downsizing. Cost savings are generated by price/performance ratio gains on smaller machines from the reduction in buying and operating costs. The downsized application moves into the mass market for equipment and away from the expensive paraphernalia of the big machines. However, cost is not always the strongest motivation. Tim Hopkins, European MIS Manager for Pepsi Cola, feels that downsized applications generally give staff more room to manoeuvre, to the advantage of the organisation, suggesting that:

*the empowered user is a happy user, and therefore a productive one.*

This means that downsizing is culturally in line with the business trend towards the flatter, leaner organisation. This issue of downsizing producing a 'better' IS product is more difficult to assess than whether it creates a *cheaper* IS product. Perhaps because of that inherent difficulty it is on the reality of cost savings that downsizing has been extensively challenged. As Figure 12.17 shows there are many advantages and possible gains from downsizing but potentially there are also a number of disadvantages and losses. To make the platform *decision* implied by rightsizing then the reality of the advantages must be tested and the costs implied by the disadvantages must be assessed.

Downsizing is not necessarily an all-or-nothing decision and a PC network is often used to provide a friendly front-end access to existing, or legacy, systems. This semi-downsizing creates easier-to-use technology and offers faster integration of new systems into a whole in the future. Many of the gains from *total* downsizing will come in the future since it is generally easier to introduce new systems onto

| Possible advantages of downsizing | Possible disadvantages of downsizing |
|---|---|
| • Greater user control and power | • Weakened central control |
| • Increased flexibility | • Hidden costs |
| • Decentralised costs | • Increased user skill demands |
| • Lower costs | • Increases user workload |
| • Improved responsiveness | • Large initial capital outlay |
| • Encourages purchased systems | • Staff resistance |
| • Reduces IS workload | • Skills shortfall |
| • Encourages innovation | • User management distraction |
| • Eases and speeds integration | • Database disintegration |
| • Business responsiveness | • Discourages common systems |
| • Moves to open systems | • Encourages parochialism |
| • Faster system development | • Fragments strategic direction |
|  | • Disruption to business |
|  | • Technical complexity |

Fig 12.17 ◆ Potential advantages and disadvantages of downsizing

the smaller platform since downsized systems are likely to be inherently modular. In addition, so many packages are available in the PC world that downsized environments can more readily use pre-developed software and even where in-house development takes place the evidence indicates that coding is faster for PCs than for mainframes. There are, however, many implementation and operational concerns with the greater distribution of processing power. Such distributed approaches are still immature and so things go wrong more frequently than in the mature and stable world of centralised processing, be it mainframe or minicomputer based. It is extremely difficult to maintain versions, data and security to the same degree and so viruses and illegal software are more frequently a problem of the PC and client-server world than the mainframe one. The nature of the environment can lead to many incompatible solutions because of the pressure for fast and dirty solutions and the process of change can cause tension between IS and business areas if the downsizing decision has come from the business drivers and not from IS.

The potential for cost saving and increased user controls (an indirect version of the same thing perhaps) are generally given as the critical advantages. Generally, the larger the scale of hardware, the higher the associated costs, especially the operational overheads. This is the factor that drove the trend towards minicomputers throughout the 1960s and 1970s and so downsizing is not a particularly new trend. In the early days of downsized applications significant cost savings were quoted and figures, such as those by Schifreen (1991) summarised in Figure 12.18, were given as irrefutable proof of the cost advantage, and indeed the 'business benefits' claimed for downsizing were all in terms of freedom from IS costs. Similarly, Bass, amongst the most often quoted UK instance of downsizing, switched from a mainframe to a LAN-based environment across their 98 UK sites and invested £35 000 in a PC-based system to identify which pubs it is beneficial to sell, having estimated that a comparable mainframe-based system would cost £8 million.

As downsizing initiatives have become increasingly common, the extent of the true cost savings have been doubted and it would seem that the 'proof' offered by the early examples is perhaps not as clear cut as it appears. Disputes over the *real* costs of PC networks lie at the heart of this debate with one camp, such as the IBM consultancy Xephon, claiming that, over five years, networked PCs actually cost between £9 400 and £15 500 a year to operate whilst mainframe terminals breed

| Running Costs: DEC VAX | | | | Running Costs: PC Network | |
|---|---|---|---|---|---|
| Hardware | £9 518 | Sale Price of Old | £98 000 | Hardware | £710 |
| Software | £607 | | | Software | £154 |
| External services | £3 687 | Purchase Price of New | | External services | not needed |
| Operational staff | £8 500 | Hardware | £73 000 | Operational staff | not needed |
| Total per month | £21 949 | Software | £90 000 | Total per month | £864 |
| **Total per year** | £263 388 | | | **Total per year** | £10 638 |

The cost of the new hardware was less than the re-sale price of the old and the yearly running costs apparently fell from £263 388 to £10 368

**Fig 12.18 ◆ Cost comparison: minicomputer *v* 50 networked PCs**
(adapted from Schifreen)

only between £5 282 and £5 973 a year in operating costs. This 'PC costs are very high' view is challenged by many proponents of downsizing, such as Moor Stephens Technology Group, who suggest a much lower figure of £4 800 per PC per year in operating costs. KPMG feel that the cost of running a desktop system when all hidden costs are included is around £5 914 per year per station. Since it is almost impossible to *actually* identify the total of such costs it is difficult to gain much insight on this matter.

Accurate assessment of the realistic costs in the more distributed downsized environment is only now emerging since so many cost components are hidden. There are two aspects to the underestimated downsizing costs, the true *operating* cost plus the cost of *migration*. There *are* still high operating costs in the new environment even though Schifreen's figures, shown in Figure 12.18, would deny them. There are increased costs in some areas when developing on smaller, more distributed platforms. Such areas include broader training needs and increased help-desk demands as changes in the application platforms require changes in the *type* of support offered. Support must be provided in a more flexible and distributed form to match the new, more distributed, environment; and downsizing costs are increased when the full cost of support by such things as the local expert is included. The situation implied by Schifreen's figures is of self-supporting networks but the reality is that supporting networks is a *costly* exercise, not primarily in physical terms but in administration terms. Figure 12.19 indicates a more realistic assessment of where network costs lie. Because of the cost breakdown illustrated in that figure, effective use of networks demands effective network management.

Other high cost areas come about because of the greater security problems and increased communication costs inherent in distributed environments. This section is concerned with downsizing as a hardware trend but it is not *only* processors and peripherals that are cheaper in the smaller environment, so too are systems and applications software. But these lower costs are only in *comparison* to those for

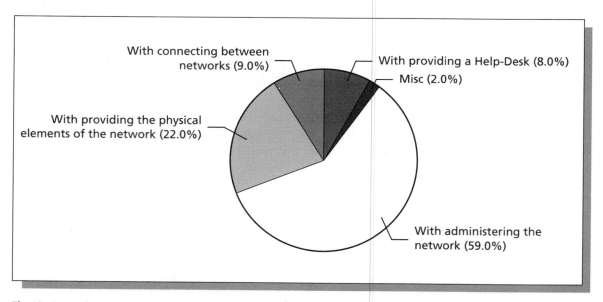

With connecting between networks (9.0%)

With providing a Help-Desk (8.0%)

Misc (2.0%)

With providing the physical elements of the network (22.0%)

With administering the network (59.0%)

**Fig 12.19 ◆ Where do the costs associated with providing networks lie?**

larger platforms and they are still *expensive* and staying so despite falling hardware prices. And finally, as well as the hidden operating costs, there is the hidden cost of actually making the migration. These costs arise from needs definition activities, new training needs, redundancies amongst existing staff, recruitment of new staff and the physical re-organisation and extensive re-cabling, etc. It should not be forgotten however that, despite the overlooked and hidden costs of downsizing, there is generally still going to be a two-fold to five-fold return on the total investment. Simpson (1995) suggests that expensive *systems* will be replaced by expensive *operation*. It will be speed in making future changes that is the real gain.

The growing appreciation of the true costs inherent in downsizing means that currently, whilst cost savings are still identified, business gains are trumpeted as the critical advantage; for instance Parceline's £3.7 million downsizing project took from two mainframes to 37 UNIX machines distributed to serve 31 depots and took just seven months to complete and boosted business performance by £10 million, winning the *Computer Weekly* title of IT Champion of the Year award for Chris Ogg its hybrid manager (*see* Chapter 11) leader.

### Rightsizing

The process of choosing the most *appropriate* IS architecture is called rightsizing. In a client/server environment this usually means the choice of platform to act as the server to the client PC, where this server may be a mainframe (that is, central processing), a minicomputer or another microcomputer. Even given the resolution of the debate about potential cost saving from downsizing there are still instances when the decision will be made to remain with the current hardware platform or even 'upsize'. There can be something of a resurgence in mainframe acquisitions to act as the server in client/server relationships. Additionally, for organisations that *must* maintain large single databases, banks and airlines for instance, mainframe applications are the best position for the data stores. However, even in such cases, the desktop PC will almost certainly be providing the access points.

There is now a range of processing hardware alternatives available and the advantage and disadvantages of each in any given instance should provide a way of making the business-driven rightsizing decision. This decision may be made on a case by case basis, or as a single, overall, infrastructure policy decision as discussed earlier. Case by case decisions are likely to prevail where the IS emphasis is on cost saving whereas the overall policy decision is likely to result from an integration-focused IS strategy.

Centralised processing versus distributed processing was discussed in Chapter 9 as the *location* of the IS resource and here it has been described as an acquisition issue but in both instances a key concern is to resolve the ownership of data issue. This debate must be resolved before downsizing since with greater distribution of *processing* comes a greater distribution of *data* and cross network data sharing can be both technically and culturally difficult. User groups may feel some reluctance to 'give away' data that their business area has incurred costs in maintaining and the IS technical staff may favour keeping islands of data as a last ditch attempt to 'divide and rule' as they see IS power slipping away. Only careful planning and effective change management can overcome these problems.

The decision to change platforms must obviously be taken carefully, when it is an acquisition principle that potential savings on *hardware* should not be the ruling motive. However, moving when *other* organisational changes are required does make sense, as does moving an obsolete application or to seek the greater availability of packaged software. Figure 12.20 shows a table of suggestions of how to go about making the hardware platform decision. It is worth remembering that developing new applications on small-scale hardware does not necessarily render existing applications obsolete. It may be that many new developments are addressing problems that are only now proving amenable to computerising. What may now be used as the platform for a highly interactive user decision supporting system relates little to that for large-scale transaction processing systems, especially those with automated or semi-automated data capture.

The issue of rightsizing is not just about whether to move from the mainframe to a PC network. The movement decision may be from a mainframe to a minicomputer, from a minicomputer to the PC or equally from a PC network to a minicomputer or mainframe. Some of these changes are traditional ones, for instance the migration from a minicomputer to a mainframe is an accustomed one since organisations have always expected that when their current hardware creaks at the seams too much then they will move to a larger machine (though as yet the move upwards from PC networks is rare). The unfamiliar territory is to move down the size scale when the rightsizing decision is to downsize. Figure 12.21 shows some do's and don'ts when engaged in making this move.

A final note about an important aspect of hardware acquisition and especially when alterations in the hardware architecture are made. This aspect is of legacy systems. Whilst a legacy is a beneficial thing in lay terms in an IS management sense it represents the problems caused by *past* acquisitions that no longer fully match *current* needs. Open systems discussed in Section 12.1.1 and downsizing discussed in Section 12.3.2 both imply that new approaches make old systems

---

1  Weigh up all financial considerations, including estimating hidden costs, to establish whether the costs will really be lower.

2  Consider the degree of match between organisational structure and processing structure. The decentralisation of downsizing must be appropriate to the shape of the organisation.

3  Identify the importance of security; if it is vital then distributed processing could prove costly.

4  Establish the necessity for certainty of data availability since PC-based systems still lag behind mainframe ones in terms of reliability.

5  Assess the volume of data to be processed and stored since mainframe systems are better suited to large-scale processing than are PCs.

6  Establish the significance of open systems initiatives to the information strategy since downsized developments readily accommodate non-proprietary equipment and therefore encourage data sharing with partners.

7  Weigh up the pioneering spirit within the organisation since downsizing is the new, and therefore more risky, use of technology platforms; it will not suit the risk-averse organisation.

8  Assess the need for information processing stability since where this is critical the timing of migrations must be carefully managed.

---

**Fig 12.20 ◆ How to make the rightsize decision**
(adapted by permission from Thinking Small by Lewis (1992), first published in *Computing*)

| | |
|---|---|
| **Do** | Ensure that downsizing is part of the strategic IS direction |
| **Do** | Be rigorous in cost comparisons |
| **Don't** | Believe all that vendors promise about seamless multi-vendor integration |
| **Do** | Migrate gradually unless software is identical for both platforms (unlikely) |
| **Don't** | Start with important systems, practise first |
| **Do** | Check that bespoke mainframe applications *can* be re-developed |
| **Do** | Establish the future role of the mainframe: Is it to be obsolete or a super-server? |
| **Do** | Acknowledge the people factor for users to ensure user dedication and senior management support |
| **Do** | Acknowledge the people factor for IS staff, carefully integrate the existing staff but acquire new with the newly required skills |
| **Do** | Iron out maintenance issues in the new multi-vendor environment |
| **Don't** | Overlook implementation details such as office accommodation or re-wiring |
| **Do** | Plan adequate security measures before migration |
| **Do** | Maintain funds for inevitable configuration changes |
| **Do** | Take independent advice during planning and implementation of downsizing |

**Fig 12.21 ◆ The process of migrating to a smaller platform**
(adapted by permission for Thinking Small by Lewis (1992), first published in *Computing*)

obsolete. In some cases this is true, see for instance the case of Yale Security Products reported in Gilbert (1996). In these instances the issue with legacy systems is how to keep enough processing and human resources working to permit the phasing out and replacement with new systems. This is frequently a case of transfer of responsibility to an external agency to 'free up' internal time and skills for the 'new' versions. The cost lies in maintaining two architecture and skills setups. In others, however, the existing systems embody business processes that are still valid. In such cases the legacy systems are a 'bonus'. The addition of more useful front ends, improved integration links, or migration to a different platform is indicated. In these instances the issue with legacy systems is how to separate desirable from obsolete sections of applications or how to enable the existing hardware to interface with newer desktop technologies. The cost lies in providing application 'wrappings' and architectural 'glue'.

## 12.4 ◆ EXTERNAL ACQUISITION OF IS SERVICES

This chapter has looked at some of the issues associated with acquiring software and hardware. However, there is a third IS acquisition category, that of IS services where IS services are deemed to encompass both of the first two categories and, in addition, to include some measure of managerial control over them. IS services, the provision of overall solutions, can obviously be provided on an internal basis since that is the usual role of the IS resource; however, such services can also be provided by external bodies. The name currently applied to such external service acquisition is *outsourcing*, meaning the purchasing, from outside the organisation, of the IS services needed to perform business functions. Tapscott and Caston (1993) see outsourcing as an extreme form of the centralised IS structure described in Chapter 9. Rather than one IS structure serving many *divisions*, one IS structure serves many *organisations*. The issues associated with outsourcing may blur into those associated with commercialising the IS resource, in that the internal function may become 'external' when it operates as a profit centre; however it is true outsourcing that is considered here.

Outsourcing is the term used to encompass three quite different levels of external provision of IS services (Berkshire County Council refers to outsourcing as 'externalising' IS services). These levels relate to the extent to which the management of IS, rather than the technology components of it, have been transferred to an external body. It should be noted that the names are not at all precisely used and the term outsourcing may mean any one, or all, of these three levels which may also be called contracting out – or even opting out!

- *Time-share vendors:* These provide on-line access to an external processing capability that is usually charged for on a time-used basis. Such arrangements may merely provide for the host processing capability onto which the purchaser must load software. Alternatively the client may be purchasing access to the application. The storage space required may be shared or private. This style of provision of the 'pure' technology gives a degree of flexibility allowing *ad hoc*, but processor intensive, jobs to be economically feasible. Such needs were very common in the early days of computing but have become rarer as price/performance ratios have altered. This style of outsourcing is now used primarily as a short-term capacity smoothing facility or as a disaster recovery approach. The split responsibility between processing security and application security leads to fears of data change and unauthorised access. The main remaining use is for 'high tech' science parks and the like, that are home to the number-crunching small scientific businesses. Overall this form of contract will tend to be expensive and gives little advantage to the purchaser in the difficult area of IS management, though it may ease IS provision costs when such provision must be very uneven and during times of upgrading or location changes.

- *Service bureaux:* These provide an entirely external service that is charged by time or by the application task. Rather than merely accessing some processing capability, as with time-share arrangements, a complete task is contracted out. What is contracted for is usually only a discrete, finite and often small, element of overall IS, for example the payroll processing from paper or electronic time sheets. Again, this type of service may be held on a retainer basis as a security back-up. The specialist and focused nature of this type of service allows the bureau to be cost effective at the tasks it does since the mass coverage allows up-to-date efficiency-oriented facilities ideal for routine processing work. The specific nature of tasks done by service bureaux tend to make them slow to respond to change and so this style of contracting out is a poor choice where fast-changing data is involved. It is also difficult to build any additional value from the data resources although the task focus means that, once the initial service agreement has been reached, bureaux require very little internal management effort. Both time-share vendors and service bureaux can provide the sort of technical expertise that can be difficult to retain in-house but they do little to address management skills shortages.

- *Facilities management (FM):* This may be the semi-external management of IS provision. In the physical sense all the IS elements may remain (or be created from scratch) within the client's premises but their management and operation become the responsibility of the contracted body. Facilities management contracts provide for management expertise as well as technical skills. FM deals are the legally binding equivalent of an internal service level agreement. Both specify what service will be received but significantly differ in that, unlike when internal IS fails to deliver, with an FM contract legal redress is possible. For most organisations it is this *certainty* of delivery that makes facilities management attractive. The vendor management service may experience a greater problem in staying technically up-to-date than bureaux and time-share vendors (especially since hardware, and software may remain owned by the service purchaser) but FM contracts can offer far more flexibility with no loss of access to the information resource. Facilities management deals are increasingly appropriate for stable IS activities in those areas that have long been automated so that accurate internal versus external cost comparisons can be made. FM can also be appealing for those areas of high technology uncertainty since it offers a form of risk *transfer*. The service *provider* must accommodate unforeseen changes or difficulties in maintaining service levels.

These three arrangements are all forms of external contract for services and lie along a continuum representing the degree of transfer of management responsibility for IS. Figure 12.22 summarises the features of this outsourcing continuum. The generic term 'outsourcing' offers a convenient single word for the entire set (though many writers use the phrase facilities management interchangeably with it) but clearly the precise point upon the continuum of any given arrangement will generate some important differences related to the degree of management responsibility retained.

| | Time-share processing vendor | | Service provider (bureau) | | Full facilities management |
|---|---|---|---|---|---|
| | Continuum along which an infinite variety of arrangements may lie | | | | |
| | ⇐ | | | | ⇒ |
| **Degree of retained management responsibility** | Almost all (only processing shifts – management as before) | ⇐ | Moderate | ⇒ | Almost none (only contract management and perhaps strategy management retained) |
| **Relationship with service provider** | Product purchasing | ⇐ | Service purchasing | ⇒ | Partnership |
| **Probable contract duration** | Short-term (including transitional cover , eg disaster recovery) | ⇐ | Medium-term | ⇒ | Long-term |
| **Probable contract focus** | Operational tasks | ⇐ | | ⇒ | Strategic services |
| **Rationale for contract** | Cost savings | ⇐ | Service quality Access to task expertise | ⇒ | Process quality Access to management expertise |

Fig 12.22 ◆ Outsourcing arrangements lie along a continuum retained/divested management responsibility

Classically, facilities management contracts have involved handing over the management of large-scale, traditional DP operations. Outsourcing arrangements have widened and now may encompass networking, development projects, user support, or indeed any aspect of IS operation or management. One notable new trend is to outsource microcomputer management; this has become a candidate for external contracts as the PC becomes more business important; PC services may be offered by providers of other IS services, such as Hoskyns and EDS, or may be offered by specific PC FM specialists. Outsourcing is now such a popular and common route that *Computer Weekly* has a regular column, FM Watch, devoted specifically to news about FM deals. There is little indication that outsourcing is likely to decline in importance, and, on the contrary, moves such as Compulsive Competitive Tendering for local authorities will drive further outsourcing development.

The management logic behind outsourcing is that the *best* level of service will be obtained when such service is provided by those whose business is dedicated to provision of that service. Many organisations have their staff canteens run by catering providers and suggest that many facets of IS can be treated in the same way. Perhaps the growth in outsourcing is also fuelled by an underlying lack of faith in the internal providers.

Overall then, outsourcing is a growth industry, a 1996 Kew survey indicating that UK organisations have increased the spending on outsourcing from £698.4m in 1994 to just over £1bn in 1995. Kew predict a further 50 per cent rise in 1996 to £1.5bn. However, research by IDC, summarised in Figure 12.23, suggests that this growth is not even and, not surprisingly, in areas where IS is long established there will be greater competition amongst vendors and hence better deals to be had.

The external provision of services is a further development along the same theme as the external development of software (package purchase) where each organisation concentrates upon its *core* competence. In recognition of the need to reflect core competencies, the nature of the organisation and the business importance of the IS element will be the two factors determining the suitability of any outsourcing arrangement. If the core competence is the provision of IS service, then IS should obviously be kept in-house, but if an organisation's core competence is actually the innovative use of *information*, then outsourcing may be appropriate. There are problems associated with the outsourcing of IS services and care should be exercised since it may be that only by retaining direct control over key IS areas can control over the organisation's strategic direction be ensured.

| No growth | Hardware maintenance<br>Operations consultancy/training | Mature market, services already mainly externally provided |
|---|---|---|
| Medium growth | Systems software/utility support<br>Operations management services<br>Environmental services | Some outsourcing, usually split 60/40 in favour of internal service provision |
| High growth | Network management services<br>Disaster recovery | Immature market although disaster recovery already 75 per cent outsourced |

**Fig 12.23 ◆ Outsourcing market growth**
(Source: IDC)

A general principle for outsourcing is to *retain* control over core activities. There is, however, a degree of confusion over the phrase 'core activities' and the related idea of 'strategic' outsourcing. Alexander and Young (1996) identify four ways in which the phrase core activities is used. Organisations use it to describe:

- Activities traditionally performed internally with long-standing precedent;
- Activities critical to business performance;
- Activities creating current of potential;
- Activities that will drive the future growth, innovation or rejuvenation of the enterprise.

The phrase 'strategic outsourcing' is also used in two different ways. Firstly it may refer to the fact that outsource contracts are constructed within an overall policy framework, this is the meaning used by Willocks *et al.* (1995). By this meaning strategic outsourcing is implied to be 'better' than *ad hoc* outsourcing since it forms part of some wider direction setting. A second meaning of strategic outsourcing is a willingness to outsource core activities as defined by *any* of the four interpretations listed above. The word strategic is used to describe the heightened risk associated with outsourcing activities with any of the attributes these four senses of the phrase imply.

One of the key arguments *for* outsourcing is that when specialists perform a task they are able do it better, where *better* is defined as more service for less cost. A key question must therefore be: *Are* the IS costs associated with external provision less than those generated by internal providers? Organisations embarking upon outsourcing contracts are likely to find that the actual costs are significantly higher than the expected costs and a 1994 Romtec survey indicates that only just over half (57 per cent) of outsourced deals actually achieve any cost savings.

Cost gains may be illusory and so, if it is critical to lower overall costs, outsourcing may not deliver to expectations. The FM contract must, obviously, be profitable to the provider and one of the reasons why the *provision* of FM services is seen as a lucrative and high growth area is that such good profits can be made; these good profits are directly at the 'expense' of the purchaser. KPMG suggest that, because most FM deals are structured around initially fixed costs that then rise in line with the Retail Price Index, the purchaser is disadvantaged since, in many areas of IS, real prices are falling. KPMG also suggest that an outsourcing arrangement that accounts for £1.21 million over five years would, more realistically, generate only £0.73 million in real IS costs. KPMG intend to produce an index of IS costs, arguing that it is only from such an index that the *effective* comparison of internal and external costs can be based; they also suggest that outsourcing contracts would then be re-structured, probably with higher initial costs than are currently quoted, but the more realistic structure would be to the long-term benefit of the client. Where development work is a feature of the outsourcing arrangement many organisations will find that overall costs do not fall. Indeed development costs may rise given that, in this staff intensive area of IS activity, development costs become the cost of the staff plus the margin for profit. In addition, if a change of staff location is needed then the costs incurred in the move can exceed any cost savings to be made (staff problems associated with outsourcing are considered in more detail in Section 12.4.2).

It should be noted however that, even when overall costs are not as low as expected, it may still be that the *certainty* of the fixed price contract remains appealing. Many organisations find it useful to manage IS expenditure by translating many capital expenditure areas into operating expenses, giving greater flexibility despite following a different set of perceptions than those discussed in Chapter 7.

Outsourcing *clients* are inevitably at the mercy of any quality problems within the vendor. One extreme example of this came in June 1993 when an American government regulatory body, the Federal Deposit Insurance Corp (FDIC), wrote a letter to customers of NCR's outsourcing services warning them that weaknesses in data security and production controls were 'serious and may adversely affect' services by NCR. Fears about poor security arrangements would seem to be real. In return, outsourcing *vendors* are at the mercy of the many organisations who are gathering free consultancy. The organisation, in seeking to lower IS costs, contacts an outsourcing provider who then submits a bid for efficient FM services. This bid may then become, not an FM contract, but the blueprint for improved internal efficiency. Using free consultancy in this way may be deliberate or, more frequently, arise out of a genuine ignorance of any alternative IS operating possibilities meaning that the 'simple' suggestions made by the vendor look internally manageable. A further consultancy related issue is that it is increasingly the case that the major IS strategy consultancies are advising a move towards outsourcing of IS activities when they are also the major suppliers of FM services. For instance, in April 1992 Arthur Anderson advised the Stock Exchange to outsource their IS operations, and then were awarded the contract to do so!

Whilst some outsourcing arrangements are short-term capacity smoothing contracts, it is the long-term agreement, anything between five and ten years, that is increasingly an FM feature. A PA Consulting survey, reported in Green-Armytage (1995), indicates that typical outsourcing contracts are getting longer and larger in scale. PA Consulting feel that this indicates growing confidence in outsourcing; equally, however, it could reflect the fact that arranging the contract is a locus of costs and so organisations are seeking the 'economic order quantity' with respect to outsourcing. Lengthy contracts can be a grave problem given that IS needs can only be predicted over a relatively short time scale. Unless the outsourcing contract is flexible, or easily ended, expensive long-term mistakes are likely to be made. For instance, one US company had to pay a $10 million penalty clause to free itself from a no longer appropriate outsourcing contract. It is not just the unnecessary cost resulting from the penalty clauses that is a problem, what are even more significant for the organisation caught in this way are the lost competitive IS opportunities that cannot be exploited because it is impossible to change the way IS is being used. Contract re-negotiation costs are a significant hidden cost to outsourcing since, even when the initial contract provides for restructuring, someone must *manage* that process.

One of the biggest problems that results from transferring IS skills to an external body is the difficulty of regaining them when necessary. If the external acquisition of software through buying packages de-skills internal development staff and makes future internal development work impractical, de-skilling IS management and operation has even wider implications for future actions. IS costs at the start of an outsourcing arrangement may fall but, since the buyer may be locked in, the costs can then escalate. Even with contracts that do not impose high penalty clauses, there are significant switching costs in making a change of IS management and these switching costs provide an effective barrier to change. Some organisations overcome this danger by frequently changing FM vendors; others by having multiple small-scale FM deals, each for one element of IS services. The difficulty with both these approaches is that the internal management effort is very great, and the potential for total service provision disappearing between the vendor cracks is very high.

Baker (1990) explores three statements that highlight some of the problems inherent in outsourcing.

1 *Facilities management is a partnership:* This statement is often used to sell FM deals, by the FM vendor and by those internal staff who wish to promote the arrangement. It must be recognised that outsourcing creates a customer/supplier relationship with both sides having conflicting goals; this conflict can best be acknowledged and managed through a completely unambiguous contract that covers performance, productivity and accountability expectations, this is *not* a partnership.

2 *Facilities management provides a total solution:* It may do, but there are many IS related activities that should not go to externals; outsourcing should not be a cop out but a use of specialism and so internally someone must remain capable of defining and allocating roles. Extensive outsourcing will leave the internal IS department as the co-ordinator of strategic IS directions, the negotiator of FM deals and the quality control watchdogs. Since cost saving is the often quoted reason for outsourcing it is important not to overlook that there is a cost incurred in managing the contract. Willocks *et al.* (1995) found, in fact, that selective outsourcing was more likely to prove successful than total outsourcing.

3 *We are a specialised supplier of facilities management to your industry:* Although a degree of specialism is often a good thing, being an FM supplier is a specialism and so further sub-division will rarely be effective. Small is not beautiful when provision of fixed service level is needed and, although big may not necessarily equal best, a certain vendor size is needed to maintain stability. FM suppliers may not know a given business very well but scale gives a certain degree of future proofing.

Despite the many cost and effort advantages, the potential problems associated with outsourcing have led many organisations to decline to make use of external service providers. Figure 12.24 illustrates the types of fears that led UK organisations to reject the notion of outsourcing during the early 1990s when it was still a relatively recent and untried phenomenon. Many of these fears are justified. Outsourcing is *not* a panacea for IS difficulties. Organisations who have poor current IS management are unlikely to hold the managerial skills necessary to negotiate, select and manage beneficial outsourcing arrangements. Collins (1995) reports on the PA Consulting survey that indicates that outsourcing customers must push for innovations, co-ordinate the activities of various suppliers and understand just what service has been supplied. None of these are trivial tasks, and are likely to be just the skills gaps that have contributed to weak pre-outsourcing IS management.

| Potential problems with outsourcing: | How likely to be reason for rejecting outsourcing |
|---|---|
| Dependance on FM company | 71% |
| Price may rise uncontrollably in the future | 64% |
| FM company's lack of understanding of our business | 54% |
| Loss of control of IT/IS services/direction/strategy | 52% |
| Loss of in-house expertise | 48% |
| No cost reduction in real terms | 45% |
| Loss of security of data | 22% |

Fig 12.24 ◆ Fears that keep organisations away from outsourcing

## 12.4.1 ◆ Managing outsourcing arrangements

Despite the fears discussed above, given the popularity of outsourcing, discussed earlier, in most instances the acquisition decision is not outsourcing or not-outsourcing but rather what and how to outsource. Managing outsourcing arrangements can conveniently be thought of as three elements: determine what (if anything) to outsource, manage the contract negotiation, manage the relationship.

Buck-Lew (1992), Putrus (1992) and Lacity and Hirschheim (1993) and a host of others all offer suggested ways of deciding whether, and what, to outsource. All approaches depend upon the assessment of the business importance of the IS element as the key determinant of the outsourcing decision. Lacity and Hirschheim also confirm, from their research into the experiences of thirteen organisations, that the majority of outsourcing literature has distorted the true costs and benefits of contracting out. Where piecemeal outsourcing is used this can maximise IS flexibility by 'cherry picking' the best that outsourcing has to offer and, additionally perhaps, revitalise the internal IS provision by making them aware of competitors. When making the outsourcing decision the organisation must trade off its own:

- In-depth knowledge of the *organisation*
- Built at own cost but then retained in-house

against the outsource vendor's:

- In-depth knowledge of the specifics of the *problem*
- Acquired at the purchaser's cost and retained by the vendor.

However making this decision on a *continuous* basis gives the potential for the most beneficial trade-off. Selecting the areas appropriate for outsourcing contracts returns to the need to distinguish truly *strategic* IS, those things upon which business success is founded, from non-strategic IS. Most would agree that such strategically important systems are poor candidates for outsourcing. Since FM deals quite clearly separate IS *provision* from IS *use* then they can reduce the costs associated with the non-strategic IS and simultaneously allow the strategic IS elements to be given the organisation's full attention.

The general wisdom in selecting *what* to outsource is that strategic areas should not be, commodity services should be. However as Lacity *et al.* (1995) identify this is not quite as simple as it appears. They advocate posing five questions of every IS activity to determine whether the provider should be inside or outside the organisation. These questions are:

1 *Is this system truly strategic?* Strategic *functions* are not necessarily supported by strategic systems. Complexity does not make something strategic.
2 *Are we certain that our IT requirements won't change?* If not then internal or short-term external arrangements are necessary.
3 *Even if a system is a commodity, can it be broken off?* Complex interfaces make a given element impossible to separate. This then makes outsourcing impractical.
4 *Could the internal IT department provide this system more efficiently than an outside provider could?* Only instituting a 'bidding' culture that encourages internal providers to use best practice can determine this.
5 *Do we have the knowledge to outsource an unfamiliar or emerging technology?* A firm cannot manage what it does not understand so *before* outsourcing, skills must be recruited.

The whole area of acquisition of software, hardware and services has boiled down to a consideration of the choice between internal and external provision, where a number of factors must be weighed up. These factors include:

- *Management calibre:* Different acquisition paths make different demands upon management skills. The organisation's management styles, culture, and capabilities form the essential backdrop for the appropriateness of any route.

- *Staff calibre:* It is probable that skills shortages in technical, business awareness, project management or contract negotiation will significantly limit alternatives. As will the degree of staff commitment.

- *Long-term position:* The potential consequences of long-term management, staff and resource transfers along with the de-skilling of internal staff in favour of giving the value added expertise enhancements to the external organisation must be considered.

- *Cost effectiveness:* The possible sharing of costs to the advantage of both parties can be offset against the inherent conflict of interest in the customer-supplier relationship.

- *Commonality:* Since no-one should seek to re-invent the wheel, the degree of commonality of requirements should significantly affect the decision.

This issue of 'when, what and how' to outsource is summed up in Figure 12.25. This illustrates the advice of Ascom Timeplex, as reported in Classe (1996), on how to determine these issues in an organisationally specific way.

Having determined what to outsource, the focus of managerial concern must shift to that of contract negotiation. Schrodel (1992) offers some advice, summarised in Figure 12.26, for dealing with outsourcing fears and problems at the contract negotiation stage. Section 12.4.3 in discussing vendor management will look more closely at issues of *negotiation*.

Deciding what to outsource and then negotiating a suitable contract is not the end of the story. The relationship then needs to be *managed*. Just how this relationship will be handled will depend upon how it is perceived. Basically external providers can be

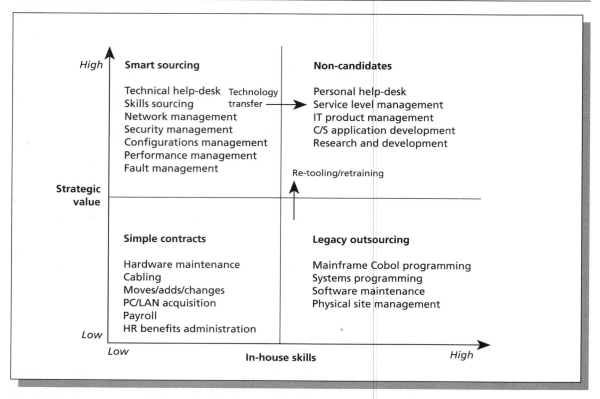

**Fig 12.25 ◆ Determining what and how to outsource**
(adapted by permission of Computer Weekly, based on information from Ascon Timeplex, 1996)

considered as 'partners' or as 'suppliers'. These two views influence the degree of formality in the process of managing outsourcing. Where vendors are seen as suppliers only then the primary management devices will be penalty clauses and forced compliance with contracted agreements. Where vendors are seen as partners (and these two are just extremes along a continuum of relationship in which the same parties may take different views at different times and for different service elements) then the primary management devices will be informal communication and negotiated flexibility. Figure 12.27, from Willocks and Ju Choi (1995), illustrates how these two new points may differ.

Whether management is through contractual obligation or through seeking a cultural fit it requires time, effort and knowledge on the part of those receiving the service. Most of the 'horror stories' of failed and expensive IS outsourcing have resulted from falling between these two stools. Either tight, well targeted and continually measured service contracts are needed *or* extensive exploration is needed to discover partners who are a close cultural fit. In this second case successful service should matter as much to both sides, for instance the host organisation may be a critical reference site for the other. Given the rarity of such a close fit, more and more organisations are recognising that outsourcing must be primarily a service *contract*-based relationship.

| Fear/problem | Suggested response |
|---|---|
| Difficulty of maintaining performance service levels | Include in contract measures of:<br>• Availability (uptime percentage)<br>• Quality (response time, time to initiation, percentage of work completed to schedule)<br>• Response to requests for new services and capabilities<br>• Keeping current in software and hardware<br>Set sliding scale penalties for size and frequency of failing to meet parameters |
| Inappropriate contract time scale | Five years is typically long enough for gaining benefits without making contract onerous<br>Make contract term shorter if major architectural change is expected |
| Difficulty of protecting software entitlement | Software payment must cover where the software is run, usually by making extra licence payment at start and end of outsourcing contract, unless the vendor already holds a licence |
| Loss of copyright on own software run by vendor | Explicit contract clauses must cover:<br>• Ownership of software<br>• Its security<br>• Its confidentiality |
| Loss of copyright on software vendor develops as part of outsourcing | Make explicit in the contract, before development, the trade-off between value of the product, its exclusivity and cost of development, leading to copyright held by either:<br>• Outsource client<br>• Outsource vendor<br>• Jointly |
| Difficulty of transferring to a new vendor | To avoid becoming dependant upon IS elements to which this vendor has the exclusive rights the outsource client should use only that which:<br>• they own<br>• have rights to<br>• is publicly available<br>• easily replaced |
| Difficulty of grouping/ separating IS applications or functions | Separate contracts for logically separate services, such as data centre management from local equipment support, to increase flexibility<br>Closely connected services should be covered in one contract to increase service quality |
| Impossibility of regaining original in-house staff | Outsourcing contracts should not prevent the re-hiring of staff at contract end but outsourcing should be viewed as a semi-permanent decision and do not plan to re-gain staff |

**Fig 12.26 ◆ Managing outsourcing problems** (after Schrodel)

| | Supplier | Partner |
|---|---|---|
| *Focus* | Control through contract | Results through partnership |
| *Time-scale* | Short-term | Long-term |
| *Criticality of relationship* | Low | High |
| *'Mind-set'* | 'Contract Out' | 'Strategic Alliance' |

**Fig 12.27 ◆ Two different views of external providers**
(adapted from Co-operative Partnerships and 'Total' IT Outsourcing by Willocks and Ju Choi, *European Management Journal*, Vol 13 No 1, © 1995, with kind permission from Elsevier Science Ltd)

## 12.4.2 ◆ Managing vendors

In many large organisations, and all public bodies, publicised requests for tenders form part of the procurement process and the logical start point of a relationship with the potential vendor. Mensching and Adams (1991) suggest that such a request for tender be constructed to give much detail. Figure 12.28 shows the sections they suggest such a request could contain.

| Section | Contents |
| --- | --- |
| Introduction | Reason for request for tender<br>Organisation name<br>Contact person<br>Dates, when bids due, of evaluation and of required product delivery |
| Organisation background | History and future expectations of the organisation<br>Present and planned hardware and software configuration |
| Requirements | Details of mandatory and desirable features<br>Summary checklist |
| The form of proposal | Format in which the tender must be submitted |
| Evaluation criteria | Methods of evaluating the submitted bids |

**Fig 12.28 ◆ Suggested elements of a request for tender**
(adapted from *Managing an Information System* by Mensching and Adams, © 1991, by permission of Prentice-Hall Inc. Upper Saddle River, NJ)

When sending out requests to tender, enough of the anticipated requirements must be specified for each solution to be valid and yet the requirements should not be so rigidly constrained that innovative solutions to the problem would be disbarred. Once the invitations to tender have been issued, and subsequent tenders received, the management of vendors moves into negotiating a deal. During the negotiation stage the balance of power may lie with the buyer but the experience all lies with the seller. Ring (1992) lists some negotiation techniques used by Paul Middleton of the Leeds Permanent Building Society to redress the experience imbalance. Four of these negotiation techniques are summarised in Figure 12.29.

Much of the vendor relationship relates to the contractual arrangements, and the legal framework for these is considered in Chapter 13. However, not all of managing a vendor hinges upon the legality of the contract. Negotiation skills and the partnership arrangements are also important. Before entering negotiations the organisation needs to pre-determine those factors that are the most important and distinguish these from the areas in which compromise is possible. For instance, compatibility is usually an unshiftable requirement whereas the precise number of hours of training to be provided is negotiable.

| Wooden legionnaires | Since salesmen cannot resist checking the visitors' book, arrange meetings with vendor's prime competition immediately before vendor meetings. |
| Last bite | When the deal is almost concluded, go for one last concession when the fear of losing a 'certain' sale is strongest. |
| Knife and fork | Get detailed cost breakdowns. Use the breakdowns to get price improvements on individual elements. These can aggregate into major cost reductions, and at least will show up illogical price structures and so make vendor feel vulnerable. |
| Cherry picking | Threaten to buy elements from the cheapest vendor of each service component. Each vendor therefore risks selling only components on which it has the lowest margin. |

**Fig 12.29 ◆ Negotiation techniques used by Middleton of Leeds Permanent Building Society**
(adapted by permission from Just Good Friends by Ring (1992a), first published in *Computing*)

Vendors can provide *more* than the IS product itself since wrapped around this product are all manner of technical and advisory services. As long as the degree of bias is acknowledged, vendors act as valuable 'free' consultants providing, for example, technical specifications and integration data. The wider the range of products a vendor sells, then the greater are the chances that they will be able to provide total solutions, including taking responsibility for integration problems.

Reynolds (1995), amongst others, offers advice for effective vendor negotiations. This advice is tabulated in Figure 12.30. Consultants can provide some of the expertise needed during this process, but then they themselves are also vendors well used to selling their services so the organisation should beware! All advisors are clear that a critical success factor is to allow *time* in the procurement process adequately to manage the vendor negotiations so that procurement impatience never leads the organisation into signing the vendor's standard contract. The use of the vendor's standard contract is generally a dangerous thing since the vendor is usually selling while the buyer is *not* always buying. This imbalance in experience levels means that the vendor has had a great deal of practice at creating the contract most advantageous to them and most purchasers would be wise to consider whether the guarantee, warranty and penalty clauses need re-negotiating.

So far, this section has focused upon the adversarial aspects of managing vendors, but increasingly the buyer/vendor relationship is discussed as a partnership. Such discussion may be as a result of IS fashion, sometimes may be the vendor seeking an additional edge or may be a real change in the relationship. Partnerships are complex and, in fact, the adversarial relationship may be the simplest one; at least there is no illusion in it. Alex Wallace of Littlewoods doubts that discussion of partnership results from really changed relationships, he feels that:

*When suppliers talk about partnerships, I know they intend to rip me off.*

*When suppliers talk about strategic partnerships, I know that they intend to rip me off for a long time.*

1   Allow at least three months for negotiating a final contract.

2   Use the services of a qualified expert in the law, finance and negotiation of IS acquisitions.

3   Do *not* proceed with serious negotiations until the vendor representative with final approval authority is present.

4   Never sign the standard contract.

5   Establish a contract that is a service level agreement (SLA) with the vendor whilst the balance of power is with the purchaser.

6   Ensure that the SLA establishes the penalties for any failure to deliver to specification and so can be an objective, rather than an emotional, tool. Service levels should reflect data about IS good practice obtained from all available sources.

7   Be willing to halt negotiations to improve a position since sales staff are generally more eager to sell than an organisation is to buy.

8   Ensure that original agreements, contracts and all subsequent discussion are formally documented, all oral promises must be written into the contract.

9   If a 'best price' is claimed, include the right to a rebate if it is subsequently discovered that a better price is offered elsewhere.

10  Avoid package deals where individual components are not required.

11  Require the vendor to provide regular statistics on delivery of any service elements, and then spot verify these from time to time in order to action any deviations from the SLA.

12  Periodically invite new suppliers to tender for the activities performed by the current vendor. Use the resulting data to advantageously change the SLA.

**Fig 12.30 ◆ Vendor negotiation advice**
(after Reynolds)

Implicit in this statement is the difficult resolution of long-term vendor complacency against long-term vendor familiarity. Since a vendor's familiarity with an organisation's business, problems and technology is likely to be a high scoring characteristic of a candidate solution then 'preferred suppliers' naturally emerge, and are often formalised into contractual agreements for lowered prices and job guarantees. Countering this valuable feature is that long-term vendors may well become complacent and so drift into not *working* to retain the guaranteed contract, after all they are the preferred supplier. There is no easy answer to balancing these two other than clear, non-subjective service quality agreements that are rigorously adhered to, by both parties.

As outsource arrangements increase in popularity then supplier management becomes more important. It should not be forgotten that user departments have always had to manage vendors, the vendor was the DP Department and the buyer had to live with the 'standard contract'. It has only been with the distribution of technological capability called downsizing and the organisational change called end-user computing that has given user sections a taste of buyer power to balance the frustrations. What is different is that now it is the turn of the IS section to manage supplier relations as it takes on the role of the manager of outsourcing arrangements. The parallel trends of downsizing, end-user computing and outsourcing increasingly leaves the in-house IS unit responsible for strategy and policy issues and with procuring and managing the external contracts. IS becomes a broker to negotiate the 'best' IS deals, and such a role is not at all straightforward since quality in the provision of a service is notoriously difficult to agree upon. The IS unit should guard against becoming closer to the service vendor than the service consumer.

## 12.4.3 ◆ Human issues in outsourcing

Many of the potential problems with outsourcing can be avoided by carefully deciding which IS services can appropriately be contracted out and which cannot. Other problems, however, can only be avoided by an effective implementation of that decision and one such is the potential staff problem when transferring IS management and operation to an external body. In March 1992 the TSB's IS staff voted to strike over plans to outsource the management of business networks. The staff concerned were quoted as feeling they were being treated 'like pieces of furniture that the bank can buy and sell as it pleases'. Whilst outsourcing contracts may make provision for some staff to be retained, either on secondment to the FM company or as full transfers to them, the cost saving intention of outsourcing means the aggregate staff figures will generally be lower. Employment law requires that the transferred staff be moved on the same, or better, terms and conditions as prevailed from their original employer, but having had the benefit of any redundancy pay-off. Clearly this staff cost can be a major drain, and an additional cost in the outsourcing agreement, either borne by the purchaser or the vendor. It is most likely that, of any staff made redundant by the outsourcing arrangements, a disproportionately high number will be IS management since the FM contract significantly reduces IS management requirements.

For many years it has been local and central government employees that have felt the greatest fear of outsourcing. Compulsory competitive tendering generates a climate in which outsource deals flourish, and yet FM vendor organisations are probably cultural opposites to the council IT department. These two facts lead to major, but not necessarily adverse, change being experienced by transplanted staff. For most employees it is the forcing element of the transfer that generates the unrest. Some council's staff (Birmingham 1989, Oxford 1992) volunteer to make the move rather than wait to be pushed, even promoting the outsourcing arrangement, perhaps to get over the waiting around for it to happen. Early FM deals generally retained the old internal staff on reasonably generous rates, because they held the organisational-specific knowledge. This staff security increased the attractiveness of outsource contracts to councils, and other employers, making staff unions accept the change, and often only pension rights have been a sticking point because of the scale of the civil service pensions. However, in June 1993 Telecom Capita, a major FM provider, planned the redundancies of staff only four months after transferring them in an FM deal with Kent County Council. Until recently the critical IS skills shortage has meant that IS staff are in high demand. If staff security is eroded then councils in particular may re-assess their attitude to FM contracts and perhaps, when the currently explosive growth in outsourcing contracts slows or declines, then staff fears will be re-awakened.

Staff, however, often find the growth potential, greater variety and greater business focus of some outsourcing jobs very appealing, and working for an FM vendor is actually popular with staff once the transition has been made. To an IS staff person, the FM vendor organisation can offer wide and interesting career paths and almost a return to the traditionally sized IS section with all its scope for specialism. This variety of career path is unlikely to be offered by the slimmed-down IS provision internal to most organisations. The FM supplier's core business is IS and hence resources flow into new developments and advances in a way that can give interesting and rewarding career opportunities. Instead of IS staff being treated as a necessary overhead, they become the organisation's critical asset. Not all outsourcing jobs are equally appealing however, and some roles can be very unpopular, for instance the unglamorous mainframe maintenance tasks, or the limited future horizons offered by contracts to support existing systems and platforms whilst new replacements are being developed.

Currently, although FM contracts are being arranged to lower IS costs, the overall shortage of IS skills means that most IS staff can expect to be retained or re-directed by the FM vendor company. This overall skills shortage also means that staff problems are primarily generated by poor change management, and often by contract negotiation leaks before the outsourcing arrangements are made. Once the outsourcing contract is confirmed, and staff become the responsibility of the new provider of IS services, relations will generally improve; after all, most major FM vendors have enormous experience at staff management.

Staff working conditions are not the only people issues in outsourcing. Hendry (1995) presents a discussion of the value of the informal, human links within an organisation and argues that outsourcing dramatically alters the informal structure of an organisation within which *humans* operate. This disturbance is problematic itself since outsourcing will reduce the degree of shared understanding between various groups and hence their ability to communicate. Outsourcing will also place people as 'outside' the organisation and this reduces the extent to which they are motivated by the well-being of that organisation. These difficulties are, Hendry argues, the hidden costs of outsourcing (and perhaps hidden costs of some of the new organisational forms discussed in Chapter 8) and may offset the advantages of outsourcing in ways illustrated in Figure 12.31. Such changes must be recognised and factored in to ensure both short-term effectiveness, which may press for outsourcing, and long-term effectiveness, which may argue for maintaining the organisational 'community'.

## 12.5 ◆ CONTRACT STAFF AND CONSULTANTS

One form of external acquisition that cuts across all the selection categories is the use of contract and consulting staff. Consultants and contractors are external to the organisation but are working very directly for a specific client and the difference between the two terms is often only one of status! The key point here is that the management *control* remains in-house whilst the actual tasks are performed on a sub-contract basis. This sub-contracting gives the host organisation the advantage of being able to smooth out skill and staffing level spikes. Although such staff are technically outsiders they work very closely with the organisation, usually physically within it, and so they are far more accountable than any 'true' outsider. Money is traded for the contractor's time and, whilst the rate is usually higher than awarded for internal staff appointments, training is not required and expensive skills need not be kept idle giving a workload buffer. Often the contractors work long-term for the given organisation in which case little difference can be detected.

| Benefits | Costs |
|---|---|
| *Cost and efficiency savings* <br> from:      reduced overhead, <br>            self-dependency, <br>            visibility | *Reduced learning capability* <br> from:      high stress levels, <br>            poor information flows |
| *Operational flexibility* <br> of:      contracts vs employment | *Reduced robustness* <br> from:      limited slack, <br>            limited scope for informal adjustment |
| *Financial flexibility* <br> from:      lower fixed cost base | |
| *Short-term responsiveness* <br> through: market awareness, <br>             autonomy of contractors | *Reduced long-term responsiveness* <br> through: reduced scope of awareness |
| *Control* <br> through: financial and contractual visibility | *Reduced co-ordination ability* <br> through: lack of informal information flows |
| *Focus on core activities* | *Damage to core competencies* |

**Fig 12.31 ◆ People issues in outsourcing**
(adapted from Culture, Community, Networks: the Hidden Costs of Outsourcing by Hendry, *European Management Journal*, Vol 13 No 2, © 1995, with kind permission from Elsevier Science Ltd)

As the use of contract staff to even out resource loads becomes ever more popular, the two key issues to be dealt with are:

- Managing the bureaucracy
- Managing the selection process

Since consultants and contractors *are* external to the organisation, the relationship with them needs a stronger, and more formal, framework than is normally applied to internal staff. This framework must recognise that there are conflicting goals in this relationship. The welfare of internal staff is directly linked to their employer's welfare, but the welfare of contract staff is more ambiguously related to the welfare of the contract buyer. This formal IS relationship will have a clear emphasis upon contracts (*see* Chapter 13) and reports and documentation. The shift of emphasis may allow the organisation to exist with much less reliance on technical skills, which are provided by the contractor, but the formality demands a high level of managerial skill to cope with identifying and resolving the inherent conflicts of interest. The fact that organisations must take responsibility for *their* consultants is not always recognised. As Bird (1994) points out, consultants are frequently used, not to contribute skills but to provide a scapegoat or a legitimating device for internal decisions.

Across all IS areas the use of consultants and contractors is important. Three simultaneous trends have contributed to this importance. The first trend is the rise of the 'shamrock' organisation where only core strategy setting and technology infrastructures are the responsibility of internal staff. This promotes the extensive use of *external* consultants and contractors to provide all remaining services. The

| External consultants and contractors | Internal consultants and contractors |
|---|---|
| Maintaining full-time internal consultants and contractors is too expensive | External consultants' and contractors' fees are too high |
| They are ideal for short-term, one-off projects | They offer a quick turnaround to solution delivery |
| They understand the IS problem | They understand the organisation's culture, politics, structure, and objectives |
| External staff provide an objective opinion freed from internal politics | Internal staff provide a valuable counterweight to outside opinion. |

Fig 12.32 ◆ Key features of internal and external consultants and contractors
(after Arnondse et al.)

second trend is the increasing complexity of IS use and management and the fast pace of technology change, both meaning that few organisations can have all, or even most, required IS skills available in-house. This again encourages the use of *external* consultants. The third trend is the commercialising of the IS resource requiring the organisation to manage the division between IS provision and IS buying. This commercialising means that the IS staff become *internal* IS consultants or IS contractors as the user area sub-contracts expertise from the IS function.

The popularity of consultants has been dented somewhat by debates over two issues. Firstly over the real benefits gained for the costs incurred, and secondly over the quality of their achievements. Government use of consultants has been particularly extensive and particularly costly. For example, a 1994 Cabinet Office Report identifies Government spending on IT consultants as £508m between 1992 and 1993, all to save just £12.2m. Commercial use of consultancies is also challenged on the basis of cost effectiveness with continual stories of failed projects and of high prices charged for ill-experienced trainees. Consulting firms are naturally worried about their poor reputation and solutions such as contractor/consultant certification, *see* Jack (1996), are being explored.

Despite these difficulties IS consultants and contractors remain significant providers of IS human resources. Just what skills are needed from them? Well there are some differences if they are truly *external* consultants or part of a growing band of internal consultants. Figure 12.32 illustrates what Arnondse *et al.* (1988) suggest are the key differences between these two types of consultants.

Just what precise role consultants will be called upon to take will depend upon how IS is internally perceived. Arnondse *et al.* (1988) also offer a chart of how IS consultancy roles may differ, this chart is shown in Figure 12.33.

So far in this section consultants and contractors have been discussed as physically based *within* the organisation whilst they are engaged by it. However there are many instances where this is not the case. Increasingly contract staff employed on clearly defined tasks may be located anywhere in the world. Some countries in fact (notably India) have specialised in providing contract programming skills. This trend in the use of offshore contracting may have begun to save costs but continues because the existence of CSCW tools (*see* Chapter 11) facilitates multinational teams. Virtual links allow the necessary skills to be sourced and managed irrespective of physical location.

| Internal role | Technology | Consultant's attitude |
| --- | --- | --- |
| IS as chauffeur to the user | DP batch systems | Tell me where to go and I will take you there but I will not teach you to drive as the car is too complex |
| IS as high priest | MIS on-line systems on dumb terminals | I am the guard of what mere mortals operating the terminals cannot hope to understand |
| IS as coach | Interactive on-line systems on intelligent terminals | I will teach *real* IS players IS skills and techniques and then stand in the background when they use them. |

**Fig 12.33 ◆ Consulting roles – three generations of IS management**
(after Arnondse *et al.*)

Such distance management is not used just for contract programming teams in India but it also enables a growing trend throughout UK organisations, that of *teleworking*. Teleworking is not always the province of freelance external staff. Working from, or at, home is increasingly an option for permanent employees. So what is teleworking? The term is used to describe work that is conducted at premises other than those of the employer. It is usually facilitated by the use of telecommunications, though not necessarily particularly high-tech instances, a fax and a phone may be all that is necessary. Like many of the IS management issues discussed in this text, teleworking is another aspect of the new organisational form discussed in Chapter 8. It is still arguable just which roles can be considered as candidates for teleworking – the debate revolving around just how much personal contact may be necessary. Bray (1994) argues that if interfacing with people represents more than 15 per cent of time then there is little point to teleworking. In Milne (1995) however it is argued that any office worker can be remotely based. Perhaps the resolution of these conflicting views is that the term teleworking means different things to different people. 'Pure' teleworking in the sense of working exclusively at home is relatively rare. Electronically supported mobile and mixed working modes are increasingly common. By making physical presence a *flexible* commitment many of the negative aspects of teleworking, such as social isolation and task negotiation, are removed. The term now most frequently used to describe working arrangements that do not necessarily demand a physical presence is the *virtual organisation*.

For the virtual organisation to be an effective component of, or substitute for, physical forms of human resource location then new forms of management are needed. The current situation is that most firms have yet to come to terms with staffing as a *concept* rather than a physical actuality. IS staff resources sourced remotely are an early instance of a growing trend.

## 12.6 ◆ ACQUISITION PAYMENT ALTERNATIVES

Having selected a particular alternative, and supposing it is for acquisition from outside the organisation, then the appropriate financing method must be chosen. The available alternatives are for the outright purchase of the IS element or some form of 'temporary' purchase, in other words renting and leasing. Each of these financing options has its own advantages and disadvantages but the full range is not normally associated with every IS element. For instance, some software may only be available to rent whilst low-cost hardware items may only be available for outright purchase.

## 12.6.1 ◆ Outright purchase

When the particular IS element is to be kept for its entire life then outright purchase generally offers overall cost savings. The high up-front expenditure is rewarded by the *freedom* of ownership. The IS element is fully owned and can be used or disposed of in any way the organisation sees fit and there may be some residual value since, even at the end of its life for one organisation, it can be of use to another, and may be sold as second-hand equipment. As well as the freedom of ownership, that is the right to modify in required ways, outright purchase also transfers all the *costs* and *risks* of ownership. The responsibility of maintenance and insurance and all the risks of obsolescence are 'bought' along with the IS element. The risks inherent in ownership may make outright purchase a poor financing option during a time of technology flux since, during such a time, it is difficult to be certain of the operating life of the IS product.

Given the capital intensity of this financing alternative, outright purchase is a difficult proposition when a significant number of IS elements must be bought together, perhaps by a company or division start-up or when making major infrastructure changes. Extensive outright purchasing is also difficult to reflect in the organisation's asset valuations given the significant fall in real terms of many IS element costs. Despite the capital and accounting difficulties, for IS elements associated with a degree of certainty that all selection criteria are being met, this is the *simplest* acquisition payment method.

## 12.6.2 ◆ 'Temporary' purchase

Rather than an outright purchase, a *temporary* arrangement may be made, either directly with the vendor, or through a third party. The charges associated with temporary purchases are generally more flexible than when making an outright purchase, particularly since the organisation usually need only make a small initial outlay and the lease and rental payments are completely allowable against tax liabilities. However, most temporary purchases are for a *fixed* duration and there may be high penalties for early termination if the organisation finds that its needs change. These penalties mean that fixed-term temporary purchase arrangements are a poor choice during times of internal organisational flux. The vendor, who is still the owner, retains *most* of the risk of ownership, though the actual extent retained or transferred depends upon the variety of temporary purchase. Despite transferring some risks the purchasing organisation may find that an upgrade route is difficult and, with ownership held elsewhere, development investments can be difficult to protect.

Temporary purchases come in three varieties, straightforward or operating-leasing, purchase-leasing and renting, with each having distinct advantages within the overall flexibility advantage offered by temporary over outright purchase. In much literature all *three* forms are generically called leasing. Each one of these three usually requires that the maintenance and insurance of the IS component be covered by the client or, where it is provided by the vendor, it will be charged as an additional item.

### Straightforward, or operating, lease

With an operating lease the IS element is financed by being the subject of a payment contract running over three, four or five years, and with or without significant advance payments. The precise financing arrangements can vary widely and, therefore, extensive 'shopping around' can be to an organisation's advantage. The straightforward, or operating, lease leaves the vendor as the owner of the IS element, hardware or software, at the end of the lease period, and in this respect is closely akin to renting, apart from the length of the agreement. The lease vendor makes a margin out of the residual value of the equipment at the end of the lease term and so, with the ownership being held by the lease vendor, their permission is required before alterations, upgrades, etc are made and these may be difficult to obtain if they wish to protect their investment. Bayles (1989) identifies four clear incentives to leasing:

1. Leasing is cheap and requires less internal expertise to recover the residual values than purchasing does
2. Leasing is flexible and therefore responsive to change and the need for upgrades
3. Leasing is VAT efficient and so is attractive to financial sector companies
4. Leasing releases capital funds for use in other investment areas

Leasing has mainly been applied to hardware elements, and generally to cost justify the effort in setting up the lease, on a threshold value of about £15 000. However, software leasing is growing in two directions, with the leasing of software itself and with the allowing of licence arrangements to cover the software on leased and rented hardware.

Despite the potential profitability of leasing arrangements, 1990 saw the spectacular bankruptcy of a major IS leasing company. Atlantic Leasing's demise bought home to many leaseholders the degree of dependence they have upon the stability of the actual owner of the IS element upon which they are making themselves business reliant. Many leases are appealing because of their provision of negotiable upgrade options for the future, but these obviously rely upon the lease's vendor being in operation to negotiate with in the future.

### Purchase-lease

This type of lease is also referred to as a finance-lease since it is a way of instalment financing the eventual purchase of an IS element. With this style of financing the lease holder has a *right* to ownership at the end of the lease, this ownership being by virtue of the payments already made, or upon payment of some pre-agreed additional sum. Examples of such agreements are Hewlett-Packard's finance-leases that, over two to five years, enable the purchase of Hewlett-Packard equipment. For instance, the purchase-lease for a £15 000 piece of equipment would require lease payments of £1 400 per quarter for 12 quarters, and at the end of the three year period the leaseholder can either continue to lease at a peppercorn rent, or may keep 95 per cent of the resale value if disposed of. This type of purchase-option lease is very commonly available, and even on small value items, so much so that consumer computing magazines such as *PC Plus* carry advertisements quoting lease arrangements. One instance is Technomatic (1993), who quote finance-lease arrangements over two to five years, and Figure 12.34 shows the quarterly repayments they quoted in March 1993. Note that these quarterly sums are *repayments* and not merely operating costs.

|  | 2 years | 3 years | 4 years | 5 years |
|---|---|---|---|---|
| Quarterly per £1 000 | £140 | £105 | £88 | £77 |

Minimum order £999 before VAT. At lease end item can be purchased at token value

**Fig 12.34 ◆ Technomatic leasing finance: typical repayments as at 9 October 1992**

The cost of the purchase-lease payments is generally calculated as the outright purchase price, plus the predicted interest, plus a profit element, so obviously finance-leases must be somewhat more expensive than an operating lease but do give the organisation the residual value of the equipment to offset against the higher cost. Of more significance to most organisations is that the finance-lease contract can provide the *right* to ownership at contract end, and this right gives some freedom to modify the leased IS equipment. Figure 12.35 illustrates a comparison between costs typically associated with the two different types of lease.

| Lease period | £1 per £1000 per month | | Cost per month on £5000 capital cost | |
|---|---|---|---|---|
|  | *Purchase-lease* | *Lease* | *Purchase-lease* | *Lease* |
| 3 years | £40.08 | £38.92 | £200.40 | £194.60 |
| 4 years | £33.28 | £32.04 | £166.40 | £160.20 |
| 5 years | £29.60 | £28.29 | £148.00 | £141.45 |

**Fig 12.35 ◆ Comparison of costs: operating-lease v finance-lease**

Leasing has applied mainly to hardware elements and, in many instances, to cost justify the effort in setting up the lease over a threshold value of about £15 000. However, as software becomes the IS high-cost item, software leasing is of growing importance in two areas, the leasing of the software itself and the permitting of software licence arrangements to cover the software installed on leased and rented hardware. The difficulty with software is that it has virtually no residual value at the expiry of the lease. Software is then, more reasonably, the subject of a financing lease and, although so far such leases are rare in the UK, they are fairly common in America, as Hamilton (1990) describes. The potential benefits in software leasing are summarised in Figure 12.36.

## Renting

Renting IS elements involves making relatively short-term temporary purchase arrangements. This option is generally the most expensive of the financing alternatives but the rental times can be as little as one month, although three months is a more typical contract length. The shorter the rental term, the more expensive is the overall purchase since *payment* must be made in return for increased *flexibility*. For instance, the rental payments on a £4 017 workstation would be £236 per month for a one year contract, but would rise to £331 per month when the contract runs for only six months.

| Benefits to purchaser | Benefits to vendor |
|---|---|
| ● All those of general leasing <br> ● Makes software price increases more palatable <br> ● Provides a better match to actual software and services received | ● Encourages customers to buy more software <br> ● Provides sales force with effective new selling tool <br> ● Receives cash up-front without discounts <br> ● Allows software to be bundled with services and training |

Fig 12.36 ◆ Potential advantages to software leasing

Figure 12.37 gives a table of average rental costs and such rents are typically about 10–12 per cent per year of the capital cost of the equipment although it is possible to make rental financing arrangements where some, perhaps 40 per cent, of the rental payments can be set against the purchase price of the equipment. Rental arrangements offer the same tax advantages as leasing since the rental payments can be fully set against tax liabilities.

Renting is an option useful to cover demand peaks and to test out possible configurations before an outright or lease purchase. The main advantage to rental agreements is that their short-term nature allows the most up-to-date technology to be consistently used. Open-ended rentals allow either side to cancel at any time whereas contract renting arrangements have a minimum term and penalty clauses for early termination.

The main drawback to rental arrangements, however, is the high overall cost and the specific limitations on use that are often a feature of the rental agreements. For example, rental agreements may include usage clauses that specify the upper limits of hardware utilisation, being perhaps:

- 176 hours per month
- 8 hours per day
- 22 days per month

These may be a significant problem since such usage clauses can be operationally crippling. A further problem associated with the renting of hardware is the issue of software licensing. If the hardware rental is a short-term one, perhaps only for three months, its *true* cost skyrockets if software must be purchased, even for this short time, in order to remain within the law. In response to this issue it has

| Capital cost (£) | Rental period (months) | Cost per month (£) | Annual cost (£) | Actual cost (Excluding 10% as maintenance cost) |
|---|---|---|---|---|
| £5,000 | 3 months <br> 6 months <br> 12 months <br> 24 months | £505 <br> £379 <br> £316 <br> £264 | £6060 <br> £4548 <br> £3792 <br> £3168 | £5454 <br> £4093 <br> £3413 <br> £2851 |

Fig 12.37 ◆ Hypothetical rental costs

become possible to make software rental arrangements, typically at about 10 per cent of the full retail price for each month's use, and, in the wake of this arrangement, rented 'bundles' that include a PC, appropriate software, plus a printer, have become popular, although certainty of virus-free safety remains very important.

Choosing the purchase option revolves around the balancing of the risks inherent in the three considerations of:

- flexibility      responsiveness to organisational change
- obsolescence    responsiveness to technology change
- costs            cost of capital availability

Figure 12.38 illustrates the position of the main financing alternatives with respect to these three factors.

In most instances, only the availability of capital can fully determine a given organisation's optimum choice, but flexibility in operation is becoming a less critical factor in the acquisition of IS elements for which the term of use is predictable, and given that technologies increasingly will offer inbuilt flexibility of:

- storage options
- processing options
- modularity of applications
- flexibility of data formats

As the rate of technology and organisational change increases the more critical factor becomes the degree of risk of obsolescence associated with the financing alternative. This leads to leasing and renting becoming attractive options because of the high risk of technology obsolescence associated with making an outright purchase. Figure 12.39 illustrates why temporary options may be used even for small-scale purchases. When additional power is needed but it is known that a

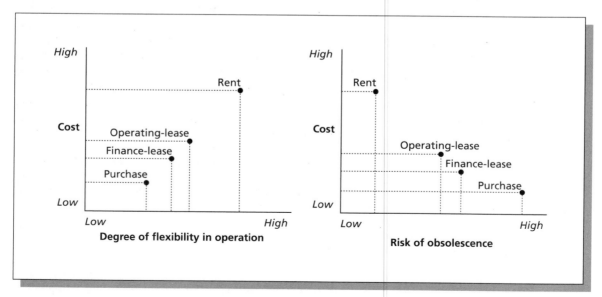

**Fig 12.38 ◆ Comparison between financing alternatives**

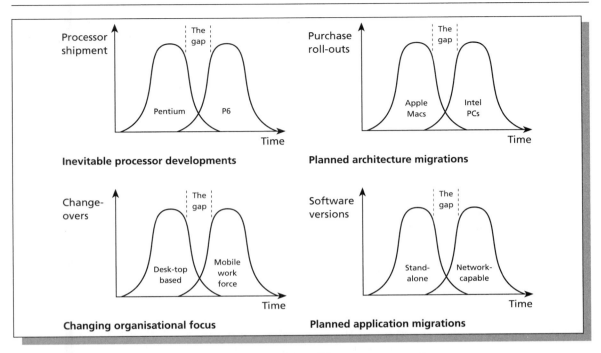

**Fig 12.39 ◆ Example instances where leasing is useful to fill temporary capacity gaps**

purchase would have only a short shelf life a temporary purchase arrangement can usefully bridge a capacity gap. Either of the lease routes offers a good compromise of cost against low obsolescence risk.

Since cost must *always* be one significant factor when selecting the financing option there are a range of ways of calculating which is the cost advantageous method. A break-even point calculation gives a method for quickly, though roughly, estimating the number of months the particular acquisition needs to be in use for it to reach its purchase break-even point. Figure 12.40 shows an example break-even calculation. If the acquisition in this example has an expected life of less than forty months then leasing is indicated, by the cost variable at least, whereas if the expected life is over forty months then, similarly, an outright purchase is indicated. Such ready reckoner techniques take no account of the utility value of the capital expended, or of the flexibility/obsolescence risk trade-off.

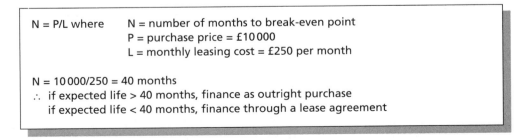

$N = P/L$ where     $N$ = number of months to break-even point
$P$ = purchase price = £10 000
$L$ = monthly leasing cost = £250 per month

$N = 10 000/250 = 40$ months
∴ if expected life > 40 months, finance as outright purchase
if expected life < 40 months, finance through a lease agreement

**Fig 12.40 ◆ An example break-even point calculation**

NAL = C − L    where  C =   present value of ownership cost after tax
                          L =   present value of cost of leasing after tax over
                                same period, including consideration of lease
                                length and payments, depreciation and re-sale
                                value if retained (£5 000)

Calculate  C = P − (A + B)

P = purchase price (£10 000)
A = depreciation value of tax benefits over expected period of use (£4 000)
B = present value of predicted sale price at end of expected life (£2 000)

C = £10 000 − (£4 000 + £2 000) =  £4 000
∴ NAL = £4 000 − £5 000 = −£1 000

If NAL > 0 then cost optimum alternative is leasing
If NAL < 0 then outright purchase is cost indicated
∴ NAL < 0 so cost advantage suggests finance through outright purchase

**Fig 12.41 ◆ An example net advantage to leasing calculation**

Calculating the net advantage to leasing (NAL) offers a more complex, but more realistic, assessment of the relative cost advantage of the alternatives since it builds in a recognition of the value of money over time. This style of calculation allows an organisation to establish whether there is an over-time advantage to leasing (*see* Figure 12.41). Again it is the cost advantage that is being indicated since the softer issues of *risk* of ownership versus *freedom* of ownership cannot be captured in such calculations.

## 12.7 ◆ IS COST RECOVERY

IS cost recovery through internal cost transfers is the last link in the IS financial chain; the justified project becomes an investment into selected IS elements, financed in the appropriate way, and there only remains the issue of which section of the organisation is to be responsible for the IS costs incurred. Increasingly, initial costs are the direct responsibility of the user function and, as many aspects of IS use and management are now devolved to the user area, so the user area bears the associated costs. However, there will still be a number of IS services provided to user areas by some form of IS section. These services include, amongst other shared services, the operation of the information centre to support the smaller user-controlled computing systems, technical, procurement and strategy advice, and the operation and management of the technology infrastructure that enables the entire web of IS use. There should be no fundamental difference in premise between charging for internal IS provision and charging for any other shared service, except perhaps the high cost incurred. Nor should there be any difference from paying an *external* body for the provision of the IS service, except perhaps the complex nature of charging systems.

Internal IS cost recovery, also called charging, chargeout or chargeback, is the notion of recovering from business areas IS-associated costs. The objectives when doing so may include the intention to:

- *Improve financial control for IS and user departments:* The logic being that charging encourages both areas to try to gain all the benefits possible for the, now clearly identified, costs. Shifting the IS/user relationship into that of a 'full' supplier/customer relationship through the cost transfer mechanisms gives a greater service delivery emphasis. The improved financial control then flows through to future justification and selection processes because cost transfer must be supported by accurate service costing and such accurate costings are a fundamental element of any cost-benefit appraisal. Awareness of the charges incurred for particular services, provided that the charging system is appropriate, ultimately leads to a more informed position when judging system cost effectiveness and so gives a good base measure for justifications for future decisions. The use of IS cost transfers often forms a preliminary stage to any decision to outsource IS services to allow *true* cost comparisons to be made. Charging systems may also be used as a complement to outsource agreements to allow internal IS providers to compete with external bodies for service contracts.

- *Encourage judicious use of IS:* As with improved financial control, this depends upon the use of an *appropriate* charging system that permits the user to judge what discretionary services are available and what they will cost. In such an environment, the user is the best judge of the value gained for the costs incurred. Related to this objective is the use of the charging systems as a behaviour modification method, to cost subsidise or cost penalise certain elements of IS to encourage or discourage use. This may be the same process as a telephone company's use of lower off-peak charges to even out service loadings or it may be a process to make safety and security services subsidised to encourage the use of IS elements for which there may be little direct and visible value. In these instances, charging aims to provide incentives rather than to recover costs.

- *Improve the morale and motivation of IS staff and users:* Through internal charging's increased focus upon the supplier/customer relationship, by placing a concrete value upon the services delivered by IS staff, a strong customer services mentality can be encouraged to the advantage of IS quality. User staff should become more eager to appreciate, at least, the cost implication of the IS choices they make. Such motivational effects of internal charging should be treated with care since the strong customer/supplier footing can also increase the 'us and them' isolation of IS unless an effective market research, in the sense of research to understand the client's world, programme is in place.

There are dangers in using cost transfer systems as behaviour modification mechanisms unless the *full* impact of the altered behaviour has been assessed. For instance, rather than advantageously smoothed resource loads, it may actually be *detrimental* to the organisation to discourage prime-time IS use. Off-peak IS use may generate high overtime costs whilst reducing the support offered to the organisation's customers during peak-times, both leading to a less advantageous IS cost-benefit position. Charging must be part of overall cost management.

The costs incurred by an IS section can be treated in a number of ways. At the simplest level, they can be treated as a general, shared overhead that must be covered as part of the overall business operating costs. Clearly, with this treatment, IS costs are neither assigned nor recovered from any specific business area and there is *no* internal charging. Once the organisation moves away from this simple treatment of

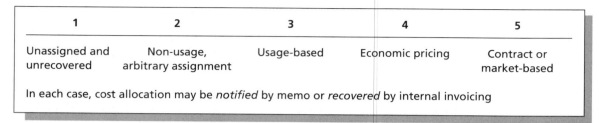

| 1 | 2 | 3 | 4 | 5 |
|---|---|---|---|---|
| Unassigned and unrecovered | Non-usage, arbitrary assignment | Usage-based | Economic pricing | Contract or market-based |

In each case, cost allocation may be *notified* by memo or *recovered* by internal invoicing

Fig 12.42 ◆ Continuum of IS cost recovery techniques

IS as a shared overhead then a particular IS cost recovery mechanism must be chosen. Figure 12.42 shows the charging methods along a continuum of their potential impact upon IS-related behaviour.

Each method must then be implemented through the use of appropriate calculation measures and can form a 'real' charge levied through internal invoicing or can form a memo advice. The choice of levied charge or memo notification depends largely upon the degree of emphasis upon cost recovery or upon the provision of better IS information. Since stage one of the continuum is the absence of IS cost recovery there is no need to describe its features! The *other* four internal charging methods are:

2 *Non-usage allocation:* The break-even IS cost recovery is done on the basis of some non-usage measure such as the size of the department, the number of terminals it has or a ratio to revenue. The logic of this method is that user areas pay according to their *ability* to pay. This approach aims to recover *all* the organisation's incurred IS costs and the allocation may be calculated at the end of the accounting period or predicted before it, in which case various types of end-of-period adjustments will be made to deal with the inevitable difference between predicted and actual costs. Whilst offering some measure of fairness, this method gives the charge payer little sense of influencing IS costs and so little incentive to lower them. The simplicity of the approach is appealing but, like unallocated overheads, can lead to IS costs escalating as IS is perceived as a 'free' service since the user area has already paid, or will pay, for it irrespective of individual use levels.

3 *Usage-based allocation:* This second cost *recovery* strategy is one that seeks to be fair through the logic of user areas paying according to their IS use. This approach suffers from two main problems. The first is that usage-based charging can *discourage* use even when such use would be to the overall benefit of the organisation. The second problem is that additional IS overheads are created since time recording systems are required to chargeback for development effort used; job accounting software is needed to chargeout processing and storage used; and indirect costs must be identified, categorised and allocated. As with non-usage allocation, *all* IS costs are to be recovered to the break-even point, although this method is often used in combination with level one or two; for instance, only development and processing costs are charged for on a usage basis whereas the indirect IS costs are treated as a shared overhead. The initial approach to implementing this method is generally to record 'use' in IS terms and units such as CPU cycles, disk accesses, lines of code developed, etc, and so the user is faced with a completely incomprehensible bill. However the cost allocation system will

usually evolve to one on a user task basis, such as invoices processed and printed, database query reports generated, electronic mail messages transmitted, etc, so that the cost units are such that users can recognise what they have 'spent'. Since IS costs are generally finally set *after* the event it can still be difficult for users to control their IS expenditure or make informed IS decisions.

4 *Economic pricing:* This method can be very similar to the usage-based allocation, in that IS services performed are recorded and charged for; however the *amount* charged for each item is now a *price* rather than a *cost* allocation. In other words, subsidies below cost or margins above cost can be used to encourage or discourage the use of certain services and so favour cheaper technologies or organisationally desirable actions. This behaviour modification can lead to lower IS costs or to increased IS effectiveness. Once IS costs are distinguished from IS pricing then the decision must be made whether IS should be a cost centre, recovering all or part of incurred costs to a more or less break-even point, or whether it should be a profit centre, having its own value adding chain that creates a margin over costs. IS cost centres can suffer from having little incentive to be productive but profit centres can suffer from having little incentive to support the business' objectives when there is a sharp focus upon the IS section's bottom-line profit figures. Figure 12.43 illustrates some of the key advantages of each approach. It should be remembered that, for most organisations, the provision of IS service is a business support function rather than a core business competence, in which case, structuring IS as a profit centre to gain business awareness is a useful method as long as minor IS service 'losses' do not discourage organisationally profitable uses of IS. Internal recovery of IS costs is a form of internal accounting that can lead to more informed decision making, it is not a way of making 'real' money.

| IS as cost centre | IS as profit centre |
|---|---|
| Promotes interactive planning | Easy to understand |
| Forces managers to manage variances | Promotes business management |
| May lead to beneficial conflict | Eases external comparisons |
| Forces decision making | Establishes financial rigour |
| Re-enforces the SLA and capacity planning process | Allows outside sale of IS services. |

**Fig 12.43 ◆ Advantages compared: IS as cost centre *v* IS as profit centre**

5 *Contract or market pricing:* This method moves away from the 'after the event' approaches described until now since contract-based pricing recovers IS costs (or profits since, like the economic pricing method, it must be decided whether to operate IS as a cost centre or a profit centre) by a negotiated contract covering a fixed service for a fixed fee. User areas are obviously more able to plan with this method than with any of the others since they have agreed the contracts, and so know the cost, *in advance*. This method demands that IS be able to cost activities and services accurately and then adequately deliver them to contract, cost and price and is therefore likely to be associated with IS structured as a profit centre. Both sides are equally bound to the contract and will meet penalties for failure to comply with its clauses. This means that if user areas over, or under, use IS

services then they are penalised just as much as IS will be if it fails to deliver the agreed quality. Despite its many advantages, this charging method can lead to functional, rather than organisational, optimisation. The approach is frequently associated with a free market generic IS strategy since comparisons with potential external providers are a significant force in agreeing the contract pricing. It may also be adopted as a precursor, or compliment to, outsourcing arrangements.

Before any decision to employ internal charging can be made, much less deciding what type of charging system to use, a number of issues must be considered. These include:

- The IS function must be of reasonable size and maturity as a prerequisite of internal charging. Users should not normally be charged before the IS function can identify performance standards and workload levels. Very-small-scale IS services would be relatively immaterial to decision making and hence probably best treated as a general overhead.

- The nature of the organisation has a major impact upon the relevance and type of internal charging. The more cost conscious the organisation is, and the more frequently cost is the main IS deciding factor, the more likely it is that internal charging would match the corporate culture and therefore can be successfully implemented.

- It is essential that all appropriate usage statistics can be measured and automatically reported by standard means since accurate costing will require time and processing recording software, even when the charging unit is task based. IS charges must be calculated in IS units, and this software adds a charge of its own.

Moving from a cost centre, whose chargeback systems are motivated by the need to recover IS costs, to a profit centre that needs to charge internally to generate a margin over costs, is going to complicate the loyalty held within the IS service unit. Where IS is a significant corporate expertise that is sold to outside organisations then the IS profit centre may be perfectly appropriate and successful. Profitable IS is, however, a more limited horizon than is the organisationally profitable *use* of IS. Inevitably, the business importance of IS sets the framework for the internal charging policy decision and Earl (1989) relates the IS operating principles to the strategic importance matrix categories as described in McFarlan *et al.* (1983) and discussed in Chapter 5. Earl defines four IS operating principles; these are IS operating as:

- Service centre that forms an overhead charge
- Cost centre that recovers only costs incurred
- Profit centre that adds a margin to costs
- Hybrid arrangement containing features of the previous three

Earl then suggests that there is an optimum match between operating principle and McFarlan *et al.* matrix segment where:

- Service centres match the turnaround segment
- Cost centres match the factory segment
- Profit centres match the support segment
- Hybrids match the strategic segment

| Fair | Perceived by those charging and those being charged. |
|------|------|
| Complete | Calculations include all IS resources. |
| Understandable | Charging algorithm uses comprehensible language for meaningful service units. |
| Equitable | Method makes same charge for same service in non-discriminatory way showing clear relationship between costs and benefits. |
| Reproducible | Same calculation gives same answer. |
| Discretion | Users must be able to exercise discretion as to use of IS element. |
| Administrable | Cost of chargeback *systems* should not outweigh gains from internal charging. Such gains are clarification of IS costs, greater sensitivity to IS benefits and improved cost effectiveness of IS. |
| Above margins | Recognises marginal costs and marginal utility and so uses simple measures to gain maximum advantage for minimum outlay. |

**Fig 12.44 ◆ Principles of 'good' charging systems**

Figure 12.44 lists the principles of a 'good' charging system and many writers, including Frenzel (1992) and O'Brien (1992), provide detailed descriptions of internal chargeback approaches and methods that would satisfy these principles.

Successful internal charging must always be seen as 'fair' by those paying the charge and this seems to be the most critical charging system success factor. For this to be the case, there should be a reasonably direct relationship between usage and cost and those incurring costs should have some control over the level incurred. Unless there is this direct relationship, charging becomes an expensive internal accounting process offering few gains, rather than a valuable technique able to improve IS cost-benefit appraisals.

It is increasingly difficult to deal with charging for distributed and integrated IS elements, such as client-server networks and corporate databases, that form the corporate infrastructure and still adhere to the principles of good charging methods. Charging for these infrastructure items on any usage basis may violate many of the principles of 'good' charging systems in that individual users have no control over costs, and indeed may face charges incurred for performing IS activities, such as data updates, that generate benefit elsewhere in the organisation. Very commercialised charging systems tend to work *against* information integration. Information centres, with their role of promoting and supporting user-controlled computing, obviously have particular charging problems.

Figure 12.45 illustrates the complex relationship between the computing environment and the type of charging systems likely to be appropriate to it, as modelled by McKinnon and Kallman (1987). For the sake of clarity the original model's third axis, the development of the CIO, has been omitted. This leaves the four categories of strategic importance, as defined in McFarlan *et al.* (1983), as the *x*-axis categories and the six stages of MIS maturity, as defined by Nolan (1979), as the *y*-axis categories. Both of these analysis measures were discussed in Chapter 5.

The charging systems indicated as being appropriate for the different environments are:

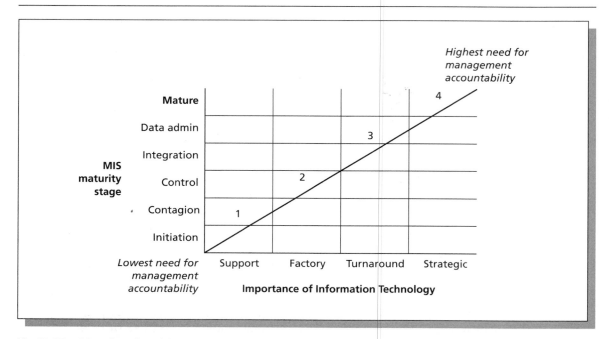

**Fig 12.45 ◆ Mapping charging systems to environment**
(adapted from McKinnon and Kallman (1987) by special permission of MIS Quarterly)

1 *Allocation chargeback*: Suitable for the support segment and during the initiation stage. Charging prices are set to educate high-level users about IS costs and method uses 'soft-money' charges such as memo pricing. Similar to (2) in Figure 12.42.

2 *Average cost chargeback*: Suitable for factory segment and during control stage. Prices are based upon past usage and costs and this creates cost fluctuations that are beyond the user's control. The user is charged 'hard-money' through internal invoicing.

3 *Standard cost chargeback*: Suitable for turnaround segment and during integration stage. Future costs are fixed to give users more control in budgeting and tracking IS costs. This, and the previous system, are similar to (3) in Figure 12.42.

4 *Flexible price chargeback*: Suitable for strategic segment and mature stage. Prices are set to influence resource consumption and maximise benefits at low levels of management. Similar to (4) in Figure 12.42.

The notion of chargeback and the design of effective charging systems remains important despite the 1970s image that such charging often has. A 1996 Forrester Research survey, reported in Bicknell (1996), shows that 87 per cent of organisations have charging systems of some sort, a primary purpose for these systems being to modify users' behaviour. However 44 per cent of users found the actual chargeback systems useless. Charging systems seem to mitigate *against* creating the very climate of business ownership of IS choices they seek to create.

**References and further reading**

Alexander, M. and Young, D. (1996) Strategic Outsourcing, *Long Range Planning*, Vol 29 No 1 pp. 116–19.

Allen, B. (1987) Make Information Services Pay its Way, *Harvard Business Review*, Jan-Feb pp. 57–63.

Angell, I.O. and Smithson, S. (1991) *Information Systems Management: Opportunities and Risks*, Macmillan.

Anon (1993) Dispute over findings of Downsizing Report, *PC Week*, 23 Mar p. 2.

Anon (1993) PC View, *PC Week*, 4 May p. 6.

Arnondse, D.M., Ouellette, L.P. and Whalen, J.D. (1988) *Consulting Skills for Information Professionals*, Dow Jones Irwin.

Aryanpur, S. (1989) Bridging a Gap in the Leasing Game? *Computer Weekly*, 7 Dec p. 26.

Baker, C. (1990) Facilities Management: Some Home Truths, *Computer Weekly*, 28 June.

Barnatt, C. (1996) *Management Strategy and Information Technology*, International Thomson Business Press.

Bayles Jaq (1989) Lease it Out, Guv, *Corporate Computing*, Sept-Oct pp. 16–18.

Behrsin, M. (1994) *Reshaping IT for Business Flexibility: IT Architecture as a Common Language for Dealing with Change*, IBM McGraw-Hill.

Bergeron, F. (1986) Factors Influencing the Use of DP Chargeback, *MIS Quarterly*, Sept pp. 224–37.

Bicknell, D. (1996) Internal Charges Come Under Fire, *Computer Weekly*, 4 Apr, pp. 19–20.

Bird, J. (1994) Are You Being Served? *Management Today*, Sept pp. 70–2.

Black, G. (1991) Recession Speeds Shift to Packages, *Software Management*, Mar pp. 6–7.

Blackstaff, M. (1994) IT Leasing, *Computer Bulletin*, Sept pp. 19–21.

Bray, P. (1994) PC Perspective, *Computing*, 1 Dec p. 16.

Buck-Lew, M. (1992) To Outsource or Not? *International Journal of Information Management*, Vol 12 pp. 3–20.

Choudhury, N., Sircar, S. and Ras, K.V. (1986) Chargeout of Information Systems Services, *Journal of Systems Management*, Sept pp. 16–24.

Classe, A. (1996) Hired Hands, *Computer Weekly*, 20 June pp. 78–9.

Clegg, B. (1995) You Pays Your Money and…, *PC Week*, 7 Nov p. 14.

Collins, T. (1990) Funeral at the Cumberland, *Computer Weekly* 24 May, pp. 24–5.

Collins, T. (1995) Why The Truth Could Hurt FM Suppliers, *Computer Weekly*, 5 Oct p. 16.

Dataview (1996) SoHo Markets Gain Share, *Computer Weekly*, 18 Jan p. 1.

Davenport, T.H., Hammer, M. and Metsisto, T. J. (1989) How Executives Can Shape Their Company's Information Systems, *Harvard Business Review*, Mar-Apr pp. 130–4.

Delaney, E. (1995) Strategy Consultants – Do They Add Value?, *Long Range Planning*, Vol 28 No 6 pp. 99–106.

Earl, M.J. (1989) *Management Strategies for Information Technology*, Prentice-Hall.

Edelstein, H.A. (1992) Lions, Tigers, and Downsizing, *Database Programming and Design*, Mar pp. 39–45.

Evans, D. (1993) District Auditor Slams Lambeth Buying Policy, *Computer Weekly*, 27 May p. 2.

Evans, J. (1992) Stock Exchange Faces Flak Over FM Decision, *Computing*, 23 Apr, p. 6.

Evans, J. (1992) Maverick Bank Chief Sets out Midland Plan, *Computing*, 11 June p. 6.

Fawcett, N. (Ed.) (1993) Direct Pressure Puts CompuAdd on the Line, *Computer Weekly*, 8 July p. 17.

Frenzel, C. W. (1992) *Management of Information Technology*, Boyd & Fraser.

Fried, L. (1995) *Managing Information Technology in Turbulent Times*, Wiley-QED.

Galliers, R. and Baker, B. (1994) *Strategic Information Management*, Butterworth-Heinemann.

Gilbert, M. (1996) Legacy? Its a Wrap, *Computing*, 11 Jan pp. 24–5.

Goodwin, C. (1995) Standard Life, *Computing*, 26 Jan pp. 32–3.

Green-Armytage, J. (Ed.) (1994) IT Purchasing: Who Recommends Suppliers, *Computer Weekly*, 24 Nov p. 18.

Green-Armytage, J. (Ed.) (1995) IT Outsourcing, *Computer Weekly*, 23 Mar p. 20.

Green-Armytage, J. (1995a) Caught in the upgrade trap, *Computer Weekly*, 3 Aug p. 5.

Green-Armytage, J. (Ed.) (1995b) Indirect Channels in Main European Countries, *Computer Weekly*, 7 Dec p. 24.

Green, P. (1991) Saving Even More, *Software Management*, Feb p. 12.

Hamilton, D. (1990) Can Leasing Software Save You Money? *Datamation*, 15 May pp. 47–50.

Hamilton, S. (1992) Welcome Release, *Computing*, 5 Mar pp. 24–7.

Hamilton, S. (1992) All Change, *Computing*, 11 June pp. 22–3.

Handy, C. (1995) Trust and the Virtual Organization, *Harvard Business Review*, May-June pp. 40–2.

Hendry, J. (1995) Culture, Community, Networks: The Hidden Cost of Outsourcing, *European Management Journal*, Vol 13 No 2 June pp. 193–200.

Holland, I. (1991) Charged Under Section, *Network*, July pp. 8–15.

Hufnagel, E.M. and Birnberg, J.G. (1989) Perceived Chargeback System Fairness in Decentralised Organisations, *MIS Quarterly*, Dec pp. 415–30.

Jack, T. (1996) Eye to Eye Contract, *PC Magazine*, Sept p. N23.

Jones, K. (1989) Safe Haven in Escrow's Nest, *Computer Weekly*, 9 Nov p. 24.

Keen, P.G.W. (1991) *Shaping the Future: Business Design Through Information Technology*, Harvard Business School Press.

Lacity, M.C. and Hirschheim, R. (1993) *Information Systems Outsourcing: Myths, Metaphors and Realities*, Wiley.

Lacity, M., Willocks, L. and Feeny, D. (1995) IT Outsourcing: Maximise Flexibility and Control, *Harvard Business Review*, May-June pp. 84–93.

Lewis, J. (1992) Thinking Small, *Computing*, 2 Apr pp. 20–1.

Lucas, H.C., Walton, E.J. and Ginzberg, M.J. (1988) Implementing Packaged Software, *MIS Quarterly*, Vol 12 Part 4 pp. 537–49.

McCormack, A. (1994) What is an Open System?, *Computing*, 1 Sept p. 32.

McCrone, J. (1993) Software Sagas, *Computing*, 14 Jan pp. 16–18.

McFarlan, F.W. and McKenney, J.L. (1983) *Corporate Information Systems Management*, Irwin.

McFarlan, F.W., McKenney, J.L. and Pyburn, P. (1983) The Information Archipelago – plotting a course, *Harvard Business Review*, Jan-Feb pp. 145–56.

McFarlan, F. and Nolan, R. (1995) How to Manage an IT Outsourcing Alliance, *Sloan Management Review*, Winter pp. 9–22.

McKinnon, W.P. and Kallman, E.A. (1987) Mapping Chargeback Systems to Organisational Environments, *MIS Quarterly*, Mar pp. 4–20.

Manchester, P. (1993) Businesses See First Signs of End to Make or Buy Dilemma, *PC Week*, 1 June, pp. 14–15.

Mangoletsi, P. (1994) Paying the Rent, *PC Week*, 14 June pp. 8–11.

Massey, J. (1989) Debit Where Debit's Due, *Network*, May pp. 58–64.

Mensching, J.R. and Adams, D.A. (1991) *Managing an Information System*, Prentice-Hall.

Mills, J. (1995) Any Old Iron, *Computing*, 15 June pp. 36–7.

Milne, J. (1995) Break for the Borders, *Computing*, 16 Mar, p. 42.

Moad, J. (1994) At Last! Standards then Stick, *Datamation*, 1 Oct pp. 60–2.

Morris, P. (1993) Computing to Lease, *Personal Computer Magazine*, June pp.147–51.

Murphy, J. (1995) Working on the Chain Gang, *Computer Weekly*, 20 July pp. 28–9.

Nissen, R. (1996) Teleworking and the Virtual Organization, *Computing and Control Engineering Journal*, Vol 7 No 1 pp. 11–15.

Nolan, R.L. (1979) Managing the Crisis in Data Processing, *Harvard Business Review*, Mar-Apr pp. 115–126.

O'Brien, B. (1992) *Demands and Decisions: Briefings on Issues in Information Technology Strategy*, Prentice-Hall.

O'Brien, B. (1995) *Information Management Decisions: Briefings and Critical Thinking*, Pitman Publishing.

PC Futures (1993) Boomtime Ahead for Outsourcing IT Market, *PC Week*, 25 May p. 40.

PC Futures (1993a) Application Sales are Seriously Under Threat, *PC Week*, 29 June p. 56.

Peppard, J. (Ed.) (1993) *IT Strategy for Business*, Pitman Publishing.

Putrus, R.S. (1992) Outsourcing Analysis and Justification Using AHP, *Information Strategy: The Executives Journal*, Vol 9 Part 1 pp. 31–6.

Raymont, P. (1994) *IT Infrastructure*, NCC Blackwell.

Remenyi, D., Money, A. and Twite, A. (1991) *A Guide to Measuring and Managing IT Benefits*, NCC Blackwell.

Reynolds, G.W. (1995) *Information Systems for Managers* (3rd edn), West Publishing.

Ring, T. (1992) Just Good Friends, *Computing*, 9 Apr pp. 20–3.

Ring, T. (1992) Change for the Better, *Computing*, 4 June pp. 34–5.

Ringshaw, G. (1993) The Mainframe's Last Gasp, *Computer Weekly*, 8 July pp. 28–9.

Schifreen, R. (1991) Downsizing Cuts Costs, *Software Management*, Sept pp. 1–3.

Schlender, B.R. (1989) How to Break the Software Logjam, *Fortune*, 25 Sept pp. 72–6.

Schrodel, J. (1992) Avoid a Faustian Bargain, *Computer Weekly*, 13 Feb p. 22.

Simpson, D. (1995) Downsizing: Pull the Plug Slowly, *Datamation*, 1 July pp. 34–7.

Snell, T. (1993) Industry Split over Downsizing, *Computing*, 1 July p. 10.

Stott, D. (1993) Weighing Up the Odds, *PC Direct*, Feb pp. 268–71.

Tapscott, D. and Caston, A. (1993) *Paradigm Shift: The New Promise of Information Technology*, McGraw-Hill.

Taylor, J.R. and Tucker, C.C. (1989) Reducing Data Processing Costs Through Centralised Procurement, *MIS Quarterly*, Vol 13 Part 4 pp. 486–99.

US Bureau (1993) Regulator Exposes Data Security Failings at NCR, *Computer Weekly*, 17 June p. 14.

Vowler, J. (1993) Users Want Salesman's Promises in Stone, *Computer Weekly*, 3 June p. 4.

Vowler, J. (Ed.) (1994) Cheap Packages Could Hit Client-Server Users, *Computer Weekly*, 4 Aug p. 16.

Vowler, J. (1995) Buy Now, Pay Later?, *Computer Weekly*, 9 Nov p. 24.

Warren, L. (1996) Piece IT Together, *Computer Weekly*, 16 May pp. 36–7.

Willocks, L., Fitzgerald, G. and Feeny, D. (1995) Outsourcing IT: The Strategic Implications, *Long Range Planning*, Vol 28 No 5 pp. 59–70.

Willocks, L. and Ju Choi, C. (1995) Co-operative Partnerships and 'Total' IT Outsourcing: From Contractual Obligation to Strategic Alliance?, *European Management Journal*, Vol 13 No 1 p. 67–78.

Woollacott, E. (1993) The Hidden Costs of FM, *Computer Weekly*, 20 May p. 36.

# CHAPTER 13

# Responsible IS management

In this final chapter a number of issues associated with ensuring that IS is managed in a 'safe' manner are addressed. Safe IS is that which is:

- Organisationally 'safe', that is secure;
- Socially 'safe', that is ethical;
- Judicially 'safe', that is legal.

These three concerns of IS security, IS ethics and IS law overlap. There are often legal and moral obligations regarding the security of information and its storage, processing and retrieval. The current IS legislative framework codifies a social view of what is right, ie IS ethics. Maintaining IS security may pose legal and ethical dilemmas. And so on in complex inter-relationships. Each of these three areas is the province of whole professions and it is beyond the scope of this text to cover them fully. This chapter however will outline the main managerial issues associated with each area.

## 13.1 ◆ MANAGING IS SECURITY

IS security management is about viewing and managing risks in terms of the causes, effects, and therefore costs, of a loss of security. A security breach can be defined as:

> *The failure of elements of a computer based information system to perform the function or provide the service(s) for which it was intended.*

Such failure can be in terms of the loss of any, or all, of:

- availability
- integrity
- confidentiality

From this definition develops the notion that organisations need to *manage* the risk exposure of every IS element. This management will be considered in terms of balancing the costs resulting from a breach of security with the costs resulting from security enhancing measures. Such a balance is illustrated in Figure 13.1 and the focus of this section is to identify this *optimum* balance of the hard cash costs of security measures against the procedural costs of lowered flexibility. *Any* change in

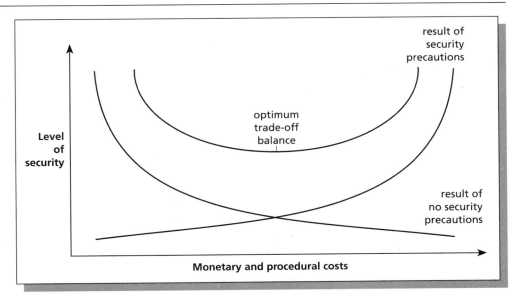

**Fig 13.1 ◆ The security cost balancing act**

the relative importance of elements of the information systems portfolio or the business or operational environment will require a review of the risk management approach since the implications will 'ripple through' to change the optimum balance point and so managing IS security is a continuing process.

It has become impossible, and largely irrelevant, to question whether most organisations could continue to exist after a major breach of security, it is only a question of how long before they would have to cease trading. Davis and Olson (1985) produced estimates of survival times and these are shown in Figure 13.2.

A 1990 MSA survey findings suggest that 24 to 72 hours represents the maximum operating time after a major disaster. The latter estimate is of shorter operating times than those suggested by Davis and Olson, indicating, naturally enough, that most companies were more reliant upon IS in 1990 than they were in 1985. MSA quote ASDA as believing that:

> *If we lost both computer rooms, the company would be dead.*

The cost of *having* security is relatively clear in advance whereas the cost of not having security can be hard to define, even when break-downs occur, although a 1994 survey, reported in Yazel (1994), suggests that UK losses are around £1.2 billion a year. Risk *management* is the attempt to reduce these losses. A systematic approach to risk management will allow IS security to be managed in a way that acknowledges the vulnerability and sensitivity of the organisation's systems, and the data they contain, but also the feasibility and costs, in social, financial, and technical terms, of the risk handling controls and counter measures. No system can be made completely secure and still be *used*. Systematic management allows counter measures to be chosen and implemented not on an *ad hoc* basis but in a planned and managed way. Too *many* counter measures wastes money and flexibility, just as surely as too *few* do through the reduced IS capability. Many of the

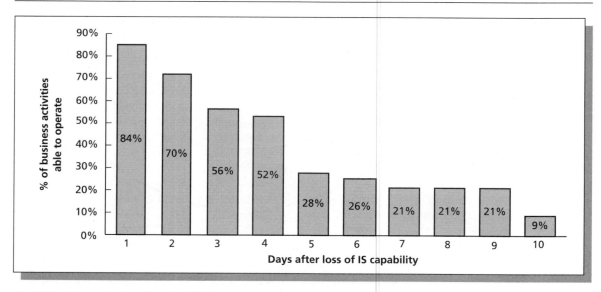

**Fig 13.2 ◆ Organisational survival following a security breach**
(adapted by permission of McGraw-Hill from *Management Information Systems* by Davis and Olson (1985))

security management methodologies use primarily *qualitative* analysis, although the more formal methodologies try to use *quantification* wherever possible.

There are a number of risk management methodologies available. Probably the most widely used one is the government-approved method produced by the CCTA, Risk Analysis and Management Methodology (CRAMM). This follows a systematic pattern of risk identification, analysis and subsequent listing of recommended counter measures. CRAMM is well supported by software to automate the management process and it has defined links into the government-approved development method SSADM. Questionnaires are used to gather data about IS assets and potential threats and CRAMM software makes risk handling recommendations. Despite the popularity of this comprehensive approach, it suffers from being rather time consuming. RiskPAC is an American PC-based risk management package, MARION is a French equivalent and Structured Risk Analysis (SRA) is yet another UK methodology. All these methods use approaches that are broadly similar to those used by CRAMM and all model threats and consequences in order to calculate the severity of the risk and hence to balance this against the cost of any potential counter measures.

Whichever specific methodology is followed, the systematic management of IS security boils down to four distinct stages:

1 *Risk identification*: During which stage the organisation seeks to identify all the risks to which they are potentially exposed.
2 *Risk analysis*: During which stage the organisation must quantify the probability and expected frequency of occurrence of each identified risk and also assess the likely severity of the consequences.
3 *Risk handling*: Having identified and analysed the risk exposure pattern the organisation can then proceed to select the controls and counter measures to reach the optimum security net cost position.

4 *Disaster recovery*: Since no security management process can be absolute, contingency planning for recovery from disasters should run in parallel to the other three stages so that a recovery plan exists and is continually monitored, reviewed and tested.

## 13.1.1 ◆ Risk identification

The first step in a systematic management of security is to identify 'all' the risks that a particular system, set of systems, function, or organisation is vulnerable to. To do this fully needs two things, a fairly detailed working knowledge of the given organisation plus an appreciation of likely vulnerability areas. The second part of this jigsaw, the understanding of likely risk, can reasonably be done by external advisors, but the first part, the identification of the specific threats, is probably best done by internal staff or internal consultants. External advisors bring the wider awareness, whilst the internal staff bring the depth of organisational understanding but both instances raise the question of 'who guards the guards?'

Full risk identification typically requires initial brainstorming sessions and subsequent categorisation to lead forward into a systematic analysis of the risks and is about finding *weak* spots, an organised process of identifying:

• Source of potential threats

• Assets which are vulnerable to loss

• Locations of these risks

Threat category checklists try to ensure that, during this exploratory stage, potential threats: are not overlooked. One useful awareness-raising matrix is illustrated in Figure 13.3 in which the axes act as reminders that there are categories of *types* of threats, physical and logical; deliberate and accidental.

Organisations should recognise that not *all* threats are the result of deliberate, human, abuse of physical IS elements. Accidental risks include such items as floods, fires and smoke damage, human errors that cause damage to data, and

| Threat intent | | Physical | | Logical |
|---|---|---|---|---|
| Accidental | eg | Machine failure<br>Power failure<br>Lightening<br>Flood<br>Fire | eg | User error<br>Software bug<br>Configuration fault |
| Deliberate | eg | Theft<br>Sabotage | eg | Viruses<br>Piracy<br>Fraud<br>Hacking |

Threatened element

**Fig 13.3 ◆ Threat identification checklist**

system crashes. Deliberate abuse includes such things as theft, fraud, malicious damage, or industrial action. In this category, the least common tends to be the most sensational and hence attract the most attention. Therefore, whilst hackers and major bank frauds are *relatively* rare, they are frequently discussed. Virus infections are certainly high profile, but may cause little physical damage, their main impact being upon confidence in IS. Figure 13.4 shows the relative importance of some of these types of threats, as reported by Lambeth (1996). Theft has always been a big problem in big organisations, this is because tracking the location of data, software and equipment is complicated by size. An ever more IS literate society makes data, software and equipment more saleable, and so more stealable, whilst electronic funds transfer systems make money more accessible and so more vulnerable.

An alternative threat identification method is to consider threats systematically by the vulnerability of:

- specific asset
- generic risk.

When assessing risks a specific asset may be exposed to items such as the communication networks, the data and storage media, the hardware and software, the documentation, or the staff skills, the question being posed is:

*What can happen to this particular asset?*

For example, according to Satya (1988), network vulnerabilities might include:

- Radiation destroying data transmissions, either deliberately or accidentally
- Wire taps into the messages, either actively as modifications of the message stream, or passively as the interception of messages
- Crosstalk leading to noisy communication channels
- Hardware failures at the sender, receiver, or in some element of the communication route. Hardware failures always lead to software failures.
- Software failure in any element of initiating, controlling or receiving messages. It is software that maintains access controls so if software fails a major security loss results.

Threats are not only to the 'high-tech' elements of IS; for instance fax machines and other, less fashionable, office automation elements are subject to all forms of risk. In one instance of concern over such assets, the Malaysian government implemented strict rules on access to fax machines for fear that indiscriminate use of a fax machine (less secure than traditional postal communications) might lead to the leakage of sensitive data.

As an alternative to concentrating upon a specific asset, a generic *threat* may be the focus, where dangers such as natural disasters, the physical environment, theft, breakdown, internal or external sabotage, are all the subject of a different question, that of:

*How are we vulnerable to this type of risk?*

For instance, one category much assessed is the physical environment of the IS equipment, and the potential threats to power supplies, air conditioning, vibration,

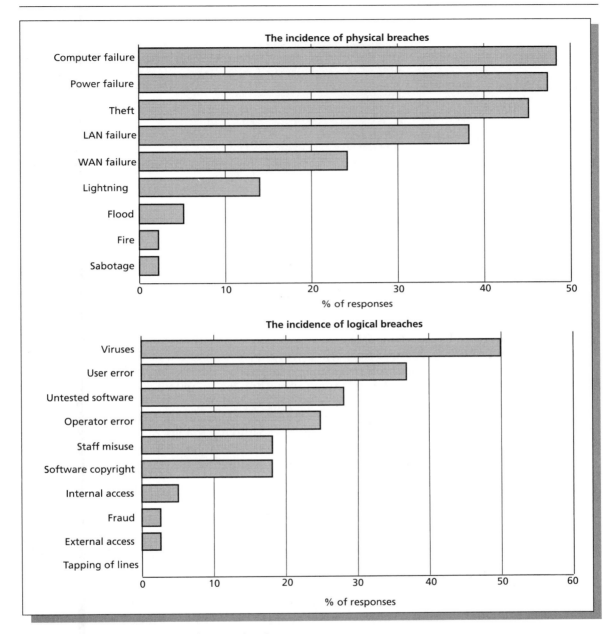

**Fig 13.4 ◆ Relative importance of IS security threats**
(adapted by permission of *Computer Weekly*, based on information from the National Computing Centre, 1996)

subsidence, or access to the protection systems themselves, could be listed. Such threats could also include reduced power levels, water damage from sprinkler systems, or heat and dust damage caused by inappropriate machinery locations.

Fire is an ever-present threat, not just to IS but to many business operations and it is essential to ensure that this risk is kept to a minimum since every instance of a fire is liable to lead to significant IS, particularly physical, damage. If the damage is

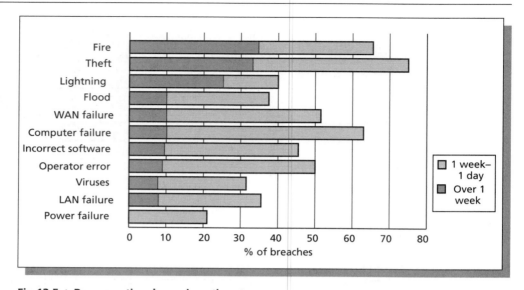

**Fig 13.5 ◆ Recovery time by various threats**
(adapted by permission of *Computer Weekly*, based on information from the National Computing Centre, 1996)

not done by the flames themselves, then it can be done by the associated smoke and fumes. Even more frustratingly, an enormous amount of IS damage is done by the water and chemicals used to control fires. In one American instance, a middle-sized fire in a public telecommunications hub led to up to three weeks' loss of data connections. The experience forced many organisations to construct networks that could be routed through alternative central exchanges. In fact, as Lambeth (1996) reports, recovery from fire damage is most likely to take over a week to recover from. This is in contrast to power failures that can generally be recovered from in less than a week. Figure 13.5 illustrates the differential recovery times for various threats as reported in Lambeth (1996).

The reasons that fires are a significant threat to IS include:

- Computer rooms are often filled with combustible materials like paper and cardboard boxes.

- Fires in computer equipment are often difficult to fight because hardware components, wiring and magnetic tapes, emit dense toxic fumes which force personnel from the vicinity.

- For reasons of access control most computer rooms have only one or at most two exits. With heavy smoke or dense fumes this can be a serious hazard to staff.

- Fire fighting systems can cause secondary damage through flooding, or be a possible hazard to personnel if chemicals are used.

- Fire can cause the complete destruction of data files, programs and documentation. Consequential losses from this can be immeasurable.

- Although desktop computers do not require air conditioning, many larger processing locations do. Air conditioning ducts can spread fire, heat and smoke from room to room even though the rooms are independently fire-resistant.

- Computer areas commonly have floor and ceiling grids in which fire can develop and spread. The most dangerous are those which have combustible material in their construction, and those which are not fire-stopped and so allow fire to spread over partitions and walls.

- The switchgear associated with the power supplies to the computer equipment is a perpetual source of fire risks. Plastic sheathed cables, although slow burning or self extinguishing, give off corrosive and toxic fumes when ignited.

Many potential threats result from a *weakness* of some sort in one, or all areas, of:

- manufacture
- maintenance
- design
- user education and training
- operating procedures.

Security breaches resulting from a weakness indicate that some reduction in the threat can result from the removal of the weakness. In recognition of the weakness implications, one method of threat identification is to use, what Americans call, tiger teams. Tiger teams are individuals or squads of security experts that set out *deliberately* to break into systems, steal, modify or destroy software, data or equipment, in other words to highlight the organisation's vulnerability areas. Tiger teams, because they deliberately set out to expose an organisation's staff, systems, and procedures to criticism, raise many ethical doubts, and, in any case, they can generally only highlight vulnerability to *deliberate* abuse.

### Hacking

Hacking strikes fear into many organisations, most of which perceive themselves at risk from malicious and criminally minded external attackers. In fact, most hacking, ie accessing areas to which one is not authorised, is done by internal staff rather than external attackers, see for instance Alexander (1995), Lynch (1994) and Atkins (1991) for some examples that illustrate this. Hacking simply refers to the attempted, or successful, unauthorised entry to a system and, no doubt, much is prompted by curiosity rather than criminal intent. However, once into the system, the unauthorised user may do anything. Hackers' activities can range from theft and siphoning off funds to the modification of R&D results, the planting of a virus, or the alteration of data. During the last general election a Labour MP accused the Conservative Party of hacking into his computer system and thereby stealing Labour Party secrets. The vulnerability to system hacking will largely depend upon:

- *Personnel*: Physical and procedural protection on access can be breached at any element of the network.

- *Size of network*: The larger the network, the larger the risk potential. Single building links can be tightly secure whilst international networks are unlikely to be.

- *Quality of data transmission*: The higher the value of the data being transmitted, the higher the risk of threats succeeding since the value obtained by deliberate abuse justifies the abuser expending money and effort.

The legal aspects of hacking are considered more fully in Section 13.3.

### Viruses

In 1992 a survey by S&S International found that 61 per cent of the over 1 000 organisations investigated had experienced a virus infection. Even more notably, 28 per cent of those infections had taken place in the *month* before the survey. The IBM consultancy, Xephon, now estimates that over half of reported mainframe disasters are virus infections, although this should be kept in perspective since crime is the most costly disaster. Education establishments are particularly vulnerable to viruses and CHEST estimates that 4 per cent of their software purchases in 1991 were on virus protection programs, as distinct from only 0.5 per cent of software spending in 1989. It is not only educational establishments that are vulnerable to infections, indeed all organisations find it hard to persuade staff not to bring in rogue software; such rogue software is not only associated with virus problems, but also with legal problems. Irrespective of the originating motive, viruses are *created* as a form of *deliberate* abuse, the intentional creating of a software bug, although sometimes any software bug is called a virus. Unfortunately viruses are most frequently *spread* as an example of *accidental* abuse through an ignorance of the danger.

The decline in hacking incidents and the rise in virus variety and infections may indicate that IS-related criminal tendencies, as opposed to criminal tendencies that merely exploit IS to make a monetary gain, prefer the lower detection rates associated with virus creation. One difficulty for most organisations is to assess the reality of the virus threat. There has been a great deal of media hype surrounding this risk. Virus occurrences are growing, probably because more desktop computing means more disk use and hence more disk exchanges and so more virus infections. Although PC-based viruses generally receive the greatest attention, it is not only PCs that suffer from viruses, mainframes do too. Mainframes are inherently multi-user machines and often create environments with vastly distributed access points. One of the most famous virus infections attacked a mainframe-based network at IBM during Christmas 1987 when the network was brought to a standstill because of the loading of a chain-letter Christmas card. Mainframe environments are particularly vulnerable to the event bomb style of virus, where the running, or withholding, of a particular program triggers the virus and these are used for IS-driven blackmail.

The nuisance value of virus infections causes high prevention costs, but many viruses do little *overt* damage and, once the virus is removed from a machine, it is back to normal. However, system disruption, lost IS confidence and data damage caused by user's panic reactions all do generate serious costs. In the case of viruses, prevention may not be better than a cure, since sensible back-up and recovery procedures are an appropriate response to a large number of risks and may be more cost effective than expensive preventative measures undertaken solely in response to a single threat.

## 13.1.2 ◆ Risk analysis

Once threats have been as fully identified as possible, their potential *impact* can be analysed. If the risk identification stage is a form of brainstorming, then the risk analysis stage is a more structured process, although often in a *qualitative*, rather than narrowly *quantitative*, manner. The analysis must assess the expected loss caused by a particular threat, where:

Expected loss = Potential loss × Frequency of loss

Analysis of the potential impact – that is, for each risk identified, the probability of occurrence and likely severity of consequences – therefore requires two stages. The first stage assesses the business costs arising from the breach of security and this assessment should include, at least rough, financial estimates even for the conceptual costs such as loss of goodwill and damage to user expectations. There are a number of issues associated with defining the potential loss resulting from a breach of security and the next section looks at these in more detail.

Some monetary or other value metric of the lost business, confidence, morale, equipment, etc must be used to quantify the effect of the threat *if* it happens; to this is then added the estimated *chance* of it happening and so the second stage of risk analysis is to estimate the frequency of occurrence of any breach of security through the probability of attack and probability of the attack succeeding. (Note that 'attack' in this context refers to any breach of security, not necessarily a deliberate, human abuse.) These estimates can be drawn from:

- Actuary tables
- Empirical evidence
- Reasoned estimates.

It is, as yet, difficult to predict reliably the chance of a particular IS threat occurring or succeeding; the use and management of IS changes too quickly for past data to build into accurate probability charts. In any case, because of fear of damage to business reputations, *reported* successful attacks almost certainly represent only a tiny minority of *actual* successful attacks. However, by using relative measures, such as very high, high, medium, etc, and assigning each relative measure a numerical value, such as 90 per cent, 70 per cent, 50 per cent, etc, an approximation can be calculated. The use of these approximations is more effective than attempting to build in spurious and misleading accuracy. Figure 13.6 shows some frequency calculations using such probability approximations.

The product of cost and frequency gives the expected annual loss exposure for each threat:

$$\begin{matrix} \text{Cost} & \times & \text{Frequency} & = \text{Annual loss exposure} \\ \text{(from consequences)} & & \text{(from estimates)} \end{matrix}$$

These loss exposures can be tabulated in a number of ways, and Figure 13.7 shows one example 'ready reckoner' annual loss exposure (ALE) table. Such a table must be developed to a scale relevant to the threat pattern under analysis.

| Threat | Probability of attack | | × Probability of success | | = Frequency |
|---|---|---|---|---|---|
| Incorrect data entry | Very high | 90% | Medium | 50% | 45% |
| Fire | Medium | 50% | High | 70% | 35% |
| Hacking | Low | 20% | Medium | 50% | 10% |

Note: Risk reduction discussed in Section 13.1.3 may reduce probability of attack or probability of success in order to reduce frequency; may also reduce resultant costs to reduce loss overall

**Fig 13.6 ◆ Threat frequency calculations**

| Loss | Frequency (Probability of attack × probability of success) Mean-time between events | | | | | | |
|---|---|---|---|---|---|---|---|
| | 300 years | 30 years | 3 years | 100 days | 10 days | 1 day | 1/10 day |
| £10 | | | | | £300 | £3 000 | £30 000 |
| £100 | | | | £300 | £3 000 | £30 000 | £300.000 |
| £1 000 | | | £300 | £3 000 | £30 000 | £300.000 | £3 000 000 |
| £10 000 | | £300 | £3 000 | £30 000 | £300.000 | £3 000 000 | £30 000 000 |
| £100 000 | £300 | £3 000 | £30 000 | £300.000 | £3 000 000 | £30 000 000 | |
| £1 000 000 | £3 000 | £30 000 | £300.000 | £3 000 000 | £30 000 000 | | |
| £10 000 000 | £30 000 | £300.000 | £3 000 000 | £30 000 000 | | | |

Fig 13.7 ◆ Annual loss exposure 'ready reckoner'

This table then allows the *true* annual exposure to be calculated. For example, a power reduction that causes £100 of consequent loss each time it occurs and, perhaps because of faulty cabling, happens once a day somewhere throughout the building, therefore has an annual loss exposure of £30 000. The ALE quantifies the threat severity and, by understanding the *severity*, allows a cost effective set of counter measures to be implemented, that is ones whose annual costs are less than £30 000.

The quantification of the ALE table in hard monetary terms may not be easy, in which case a qualitative ranking chart, the threat *severity* matrix, can be used. This uses a simple relative, and frequently logarithmic, scale to represent the magnitude of the consequent losses and their probability of occurrence. Figure 13.8 shows a partially completed threat severity matrix. Risks that happen often are on the extreme right and events that happen rarely are on the extreme left whilst the cost of the event is read top to bottom. Risk handling, discussed in Section 13.1.3, will generally concentrate upon two categories, those that happen frequently, since counter measures are likely to give a high net return, plus the absolute catastrophes, however infrequent, since they would lead to a business close-down.

Risk analysis establishes one side of the optimum balance point between the cost of loss and the cost of security measures. Risk handling, will identify possible counter measures and then select from them the right set for that optimum trade-off. The classic response to low frequency, but high potential cost, threats is insurance and so the chosen controls and counter measures that make up an organisation's security policy will generally be targeted at those events with a high frequency even though a low cost.

Effective risk analysis requires an appreciation of the true magnitude of losses resulting from each threat if it was to happen, and that is difficult. Effective risk management also requires a realistic appraisal of the likelihood of the threat becoming reality. Research by Loch *et al.* (1992) indicates that many organisations are oddly blind, not to the threats themselves, or to their potential costs, but to the likelihood of the event happening to their organisation.

| | | Rating of frequency | | | | |
|---|---|---|---|---|---|---|
| | | 1 | 2 | 3 | 4 | 5 |
| Severity rating of probable loss | 1 | | | Virus infection | | Incorrect data entry |
| | 2 | | | Theft | Transmission loss | Power interruption |
| | 3 | | | Storm | | |
| | 4 | | Fire | | | |
| | 5 | Earthquake | | | | |

Note: Probabilities are as for Fig 13.7

**Fig 13.8 ◆ An example threat severity matrix**

## Loss

When analysing IS risks some method of quantifying the losses resulting from a loss of security must be found. A number of IS elements are subject to losses that must be rated in some way. These IS elements include:

- *Hardware*: The loss of this is relatively easy to value and these elements are often insured, indeed insurance may be a requirement of any lease or rental agreement. These items can be valued at their replacement cost plus an additional sum representing the cost of repeating the procurement process.

- *Data and information*: This is the most serious loss, and the hardest to quantify. The total loss of sales data would leave an organisation ignorant about its debtors, at most times representing perhaps 20 per cent of turnover. Production data losses equally can halt the operation of the organisation. Partial loss can, of course, be less damaging to the overall ability to trade but recovery costs depend upon the recovery precautions.

- *Software*: The main complication when valuing software loss is that the intrinsic value, or cost of replacement, of the software bears no relation to the original cost of development. To add further complications, the loss of software leads to the loss of processing capability and so that factor must be included in the software loss quantification.

- *Processing capability*: The length of the disruption is the key variable in determining the value of this loss. Defining time bands appropriate to the organisation allows costs to be calculated for each band and they will vary widely. Complex real time systems may generate huge costs after only a few seconds whereas low dependency organisations may only need to ensure periodic processing.

- *Staff*: Perhaps the most frequently overlooked cost is of a loss of key staff. The loss may be significant either for their knowledge *about* something, or their competence to *do* something. The cost of lost staff, whether lost because of head-hunters, accidents or industrial action, constantly changes depending upon what such staff are involved in, and so this part of the consequent loss calculation must be frequently re-done.
- *Funds*: Since 'money is money is money' the amount of funds likely to be lost depends upon the type of business. Accidental or fraudulent losses need to be broken into bands relating to different types of security breaches so that fund losses can be quantified. Anecdotes suggest that frauds often follow accidental mis-moves of cash that are undetected.

All the losses consequent upon a breach of IS security relate to the value adding attributes of information and the three categories of such losses are:

- *Availability loss*: The loss of security destroys, fully or partially, the organisation's ability to access data and information.
- *Integrity/accuracy failure*: The loss of security destroys the organisation's ability to trust their data or worse to have data of uncertain accuracy.
- *Confidentiality/security loss*: The loss of security destroys the organisation's exclusive ownership of their data and hence leads to a loss of the power and trust conferred by data ownership. Again, the worst case is of uncertainty of disclosure.

The first step in assessing the magnitude of the loss resulting from the security breach is to consider the *primary* consequences of the loss of security. These primary consequences are those things that follow directly, and usually immediately, upon the security breakdown. Individual, both threat and organisation-specific, metrics must be developed but some examples of primary consequences are given in Figure 13.9.

---

**Direct loss examples:**

- Interruption of processing in the long or short-term
- Corruption of data records, this often includes back-up material and the worst case is where corruption is undetected or of uncertain extent
- Destruction of storage media
- Running of unauthorised software, at best this clogs-up networks and reduces processing capabilities, at worst systems are destroyed and funds are misdirected
- Disclosure of sensitive information
- Removal of equipment, data or software; and such theft or pirating can be hard to recognise
- Loss of accounting or other records, at best this will impair historical analyses, at worst it will mean the standstill of cash receipts.

---

Fig 13.9 ◆ Primary consequences of a loss of security

Not all business losses are the *direct* result of the security breach. An equally important part of the loss calculation is the secondary or consequent loss. The consequent losses are those things that follow from the *primary* consequences, rather than from the breach of security itself. The relationships between the loss of security, the primary consequences and the secondary consequences are shown in Figure 13.10. What is not shown in that figure is that many primary losses lead to similar secondary losses and, no matter how different the security risks, if the losses are the same then the costs are the same. This similarity is very significant to risk handling decisions, given that the cost of risk avoidance is likely to differ widely despite the comparable consequent losses.

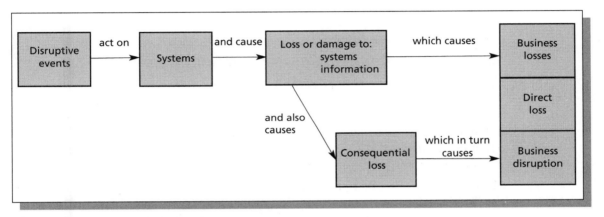

**Fig 13.10 ◆ Losses resulting from a loss of security**

If primary consequences can be hard to quantify, it gets even more difficult to assess the value of the secondary consequences. Consequent losses tend to be even more costly than the direct losses and, since they are business costs, they generally emerge over a long time. It is rarely practical to attach detailed monetary values to secondary consequences, rather qualitative ratings are used. Figure 13.11 gives some examples of possible secondary losses.

The total loss magnitude of a breach of security is the sum of the primary and secondary consequences and so, if the primary consequences can be minimised, and that is the intent with good disaster recovery, discussed in Section 13.1.4, then there is a *double* gain. This is because, if the primary loses are reduced, then the secondary losses are further minimised. For example, if a software fault corrupts data the potential loss magnitude could be extensive. However, effective back-up and restore procedures will minimise the primary loss and, because of those minimal inaccuracies and delays, the consequent loss is also reduced.

### 13.1.3 ◆ Risk handling

Threat identification and analysis is done to select risk handling strategies offering the best net effectiveness, that is maintaining the desired optimum balance. Risk handling is the application of controls and counter measures appropriate to the risk, according to time, money and other constraints. The previous steps of:

---

**Consequent loss examples:**

- Lost production
- Delayed deliveries
- Cash flow problems
- Loss of customer goodwill
- Inaccurate accounting and tax statements
- Meaningless, inaccurate, or untimely management information
- Penalties from breach of statutory obligations
- Inability to continue system function
- Loss of competitive position
- Inability to continue business.

---

**Fig 13.11 ◆ Secondary consequences of a loss of security**

1 Listing potential threats
2 Quantifying the loss consequent upon successful threats
3 Determining the ALE or some other measure of probability and severity of occurrence

are valuable steps but only as a means to an end. The purpose is to identify the 'best' method of handling the risk, where best is defined as the cost effective management of potential losses of security. There are four generic strategies for risk handling:

- *Risk avoidance*: If the threat is such that it is possible to avoid it then the organisation *can* take steps to totally avoid it. This may mean siting systems away from dangerous areas, placing sensitive data entry operations in well-screened areas, deciding against decentralisation, altering methods of working or dispensing with the security-threatening feature, such as basement computer rooms.

- *Risk retention*: If the net losses are such that an organisation can bear the expected loss, without undue embarrassment, then they may adopt a 'grin and bear it' strategy. This approach is generally applied to risks with low associated costs because the consequences are minor. The 'true' costs may depend upon the utility value of capital, in which case the *annual* loss exposure may be an overly aggregated measure. For most organisations it is easier to find ten instances of £1 000 during the year than it is to find one instance of £10 000. However, the true total exposure is often overlooked and risk retention may be an inadvertently chosen security strategy.

- *Risk reduction*: This is the commonest risk handling strategy for obvious reasons: it is very difficult to *avoid* a threat fully, and it is often inappropriate to ignore it and so risk reduction is a suitable compromise. Risk reduction is the policy of introducing controls and counter measures to reduce the likelihood of occurrence and/or reduce the losses consequent upon the breach of security. The portfolio of controls and counter measures is only economically effective if it produces a reduction in the ALE greater than the annual increase in cost (of all types) resulting from the implementation of the measures. All counter measures add costs to:

— Development
— Operation
— Maintenance
— Flexibility.

So, to calculate net effectiveness, the risk reduction equation balances the full costs of primary and secondary consequences against the full costs of security measures. Since the organisation is seeking to minimise the sum of the additional costs and the negative predicted costs the key question is:

*To what degree will the risk be reduced?*

• *Risk transfer*: This fourth risk handling strategy passes over the costs resulting from a breach of security to a third party, typically this means insurance policies, maintenance contracts, or standby arrangements held on retainer agreements. Note that the excess clause of any insurance policy, and the operating and servicing rules within maintenance agreements, define the extent to which a degree of risk is retained. Such retained risk may then be subject to a risk avoidance strategy.

Identifying a risk management portfolio is about selecting a mixed set of risk handling strategies dependant upon the systematic application of risk identification and analysis. To do this the organisation usually lists risks in *descending* order of ALE to provide some priority to the consideration of counter measures. However, potential disasters are treated as a high priority item. This prioritised list allows efforts to be concentrated to give the best net position. Most organisations will use risk avoidance and risk transfer for total calamities, risk retention for threats with very low consequent losses, often irrespective of frequency unless possible controls are very cheap and do not impair flexibility, and then a mixture of risk reduction and risk transfer for the remaining threats.

Increasingly, IS security must be seen as a strategic issue and an organisation should invest in security insofar as the money spent contributes to overall IS goals. If the result of the losses prevented or reduced is greater than the security cost then there is a net *contribution* to profits. Recognition of this fact may overcome some of the negative image associated with security expenditures. When following this line of reasoning, it is important to note the law of diminishing returns. This means that the higher the *current* level of security, the more the next step will cost. It is the net *balance* that must be the constant focus, to question, not only what measures *could* be used, but what measures *should* be used.

Smith (1993) explores this law of diminishing returns as applied to PC security measures, and he concludes that, not only does it get more expensive to take the security level up a notch, but additional security measures have a *detrimental* effect on overall utility. Smith suggests how the list of all possible defences can be filtered to ensure that a beneficial, rather than detrimental, set is used. Such filters are best based upon 'hard' issues that can be determined by an objective test, instances include:

- *Interconnectivity of the PC to other PCs*: Where he suggests three categories, stand alone PC, PC connected to data server, PC connected to program server. The greater the interconnectivity, the greater the threat.
- *Number of users*: Many PCs are a shared resource and the more sharing of access the greater the risk.

These filters objectively remove those measures offering *no* benefit. The remaining options should then be prioritised to the point at which marginal utility reaches zero. It is the 'soft' issues, such as corporate culture, that determine the utility threshold. Indeed, since effective computer security is largely about motivating staff, the corporate culture and style will always have a significant impact upon the selection of an optimum risk management strategy set and the appropriateness of potential controls and counter measures.

When the control or counter measure introduces additional risks of its own then the risk cost-benefit appraisal used must be rigorous. Cheap measures applied broadly are generally more net effective than expensive measures narrowly applied, for example using relatively cheap password verification on all systems is more effective than using expensive signature verification on a few. Risk reduction applies equally to the unglamorous, but significant, field of internal errors and minor frauds, as it does to the high profile field of IS crimes, still blessedly fairly rare.

Risk transfer, usually through insurance, is appropriate for high-cost low-probability threats and where full recovery is impossible. Insurance spreads the cost of such high-cost low-frequency events over time and over many organisations. The biggest problems associated with such a strategy are the choice of insurance type, and the fact that insurers generally demand some threat-reduction procedures before underwriting the risk. Equipment insurance is relatively straightforward, but it is insurance on data and secondary losses that is really needed to transfer the *risk*, otherwise the organisation stops trading but the liquidators can recover the equipment replacement costs from the insurers! Equipment insurance premiums are frequently about 1 per cent of the sum insured if the equipment is maintained, 6 per cent if it is not. Consequent loss insurance is offered by Lloyds, but only if risk management policies are sound, including making standby arrangements. Both loss of gross revenue and increased operating costs can be reimbursed and insurance can even cover lost business opportunities resulting from lost R&D data.

A security *policy* defines the level of security that matches the value of what is to be protected and the expense and inconvenience of the protection measures. Such policies document the result of the risk identification and analysis followed by the chosen risk handling strategies. Saunders (1989) suggests the policy document covers, at least:

- *The information to be protected*: since the nature of the information will determine its internal sensitivity and its external attractiveness
- *The value of the information*: since this quantifies the potential losses
- *Access to the information*: since this defines who is authorised to view, modify, upload or down-load data
- *Recovery of the information*: since this defines how the lost or damaged data can be restored and subsequently used

Security policy documents will normally include tables explaining the risk handling strategy for each of the threats considered. A sample security policy table is shown in Figure 13.12.

### Controls and counter measures

Risk handling strategies are *implemented* through controls and counter measures. The choice of the set that cost effectively avoids, reduces, or transfers the risk impact is obviously a critical aspect of risk management. Controls and counter measures, equally obviously, relate primarily to avoidance *and* reduction strategies.

| Risk | Potential loss | Probability | Counter measure | Cost |
|------|----------------|-------------|-----------------|------|
| Computer room destroyed by fire | Processing capability for production scheduling, payroll, order processing Replacement of equipment Site reconstruction | Low | Ensure back-up Maintain fall-back systems Insure Use fire precautions | £30 000 |
| Complete loss of records | Unable to bill customers Production line stoppage within four days Unable to continue trading within four weeks | Action mandatory | Ensure remote copies of all vital files Insure against consequential loss during recovery | £10 000 |
| Theft of information of use to competitors | Erosion of market position Estimated saving to competitor of £100 000 | Low | Strict control of access to vital files Personnel vetting | Impose system for user authentication Tighten recruitment procedures |
| Illegal use of processing capability | Slightly increased processing costs Possible adverse affect on own processing | Low | Spot checks | No action: low risk/small loss outweighed by staff morale considerations |
| Checklist shows *what* is at risk but worded by *how*, allows actions to be clear | In sequence by priority of effort | Policy must explain the threat range used. Relative probabilities are preferred to spurious absolute ones | If there are too many entries, then defined risk was not specific enough | Each action needs to have corresponding costs identified |

**Fig 13.12 ◆ An example risk-handling table**

Security measures and controls must be considered in terms of the net costs arising from their adoption *and* the potential new, or increased, risks resulting from this adoption.

There are essentially two types of controls. The general counter measures that are introduced to reduce the threats to all IS activities within the organisation; an example general control is the universal use of log-in user identification. The second type of counter measures are the application controls designed to protect one specific area from threats. To a large extent, application controls are a sub-set of general controls and, for most organisations, a number of general measures are applied to all IS areas with additional precautions taken for particular areas. Any weakness in general controls could lead to loss of security in any system and so the cost of these measures should be seen as 'shared' across all protected areas, rather like insurance.

Controls and counter measures are not a single homogenous set. To produce the result of 'good' security the various threats must be countered by layers of controls targeted at different aspects of IS use and management. The precise nature of the instances of each control layer will depend upon the nature of the organisation, the value of its information and the nature of its IS environment. In the case of the IS, the determining factors are:

- *Hardware platform*: This influences type and *amount* of controls available
- *Degree of distribution*: This influences the emphasis of the controls needed
- *Integration of the infrastructure*: This influences the nature of the threats exposed to

Any change in this IS environment means that the security implications ripple through all the control layers. For instance a downsizing initiative certainly alters the hardware platform, and probably alters the degree of distribution and the degree of integration. This therefore demands that the net position on controls and counter measures be re-assessed.

Even within each control *layer* there are different intentions associated with each specific measure. They may be intended to prevent, detect, or reduce the impact of the anticipated threats. Figure 13.13 illustrates the relationship between the control stages and Figure 13.14 indicates where these controls lie in relationship to the business losses experienced as a result of a loss of security (first illustrated in Figure 13.10). These three stages apply to most layers of control. For example, authorisation software may attempt to prevent unauthorised use, but also records

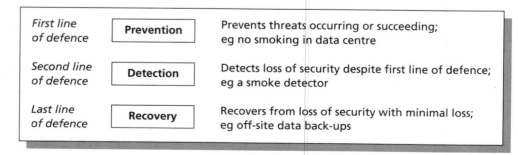

**Fig 13.13 ◆ Three stages of controls and counter measures**

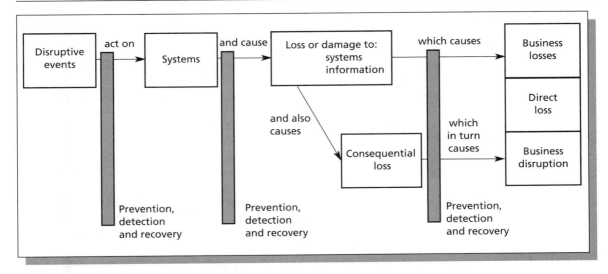

**Fig 13.14 ◆ Controls block the effects of threats**

aborted log-ins in an attempt to *detect* attacks in progress and then uses second-stage encryption to *minimise* the damage caused by the illegal system entry.

The main objective when selecting controls and counter measures, and therefore defining the security policy, is to create a balanced situation between risk costs and control costs. Trouble results when organisations do *not* effectively balance threats with controls and counter measures. Figure 13.15 shows how the levels of controls and security measures applied to some IS elements are strong whereas for others they are weak. This would not be a problem if it were not that the areas of weak controls are areas, such as user-controlled computing, of high risk. Unless threat and controls are matched level for level then the security policy is ineffective.

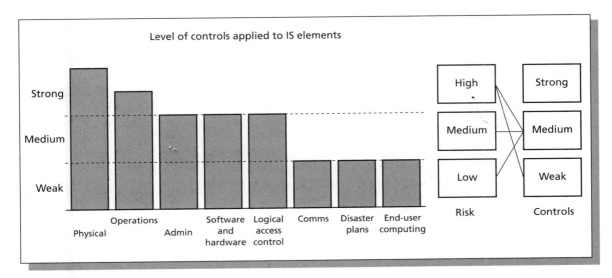

**Fig 13.15 ◆ Level of controls not matched to levels of threats**

Measures to counter IS threats do not always require IS-related actions. For example, the work of Courtney (1989) indicates that IS-related crime is closely related to wage levels and therefore adjustment of pay rates might form a cost-effective risk-reduction measure. Rather more than 80 per cent of the theft by computer was contributed by employees in the bottom 40 per cent of the wage scale. This separation of risk and counter measure raises the thorny problem of who is to select the set of threat-averting actions. In this example, the IS section may take the responsibility for maintaining IS security, and yet is unlikely to be free to take the responsibility for wage rates. This makes it clear that IS security is an organisation-wide strategic issue and one that requires senior management involvement.

As with threats the counter measures chosen may be either *logical* or *physical*. Logical controls are the measures taken to ensure that development, data integrity and operations continue smoothly. Such controls could include data reconciliation, data dictionaries (which are a good way to implement a whole series of data controls in one go), usage logs, development and testing standards, change management rules, fault logging systems, job control software, or access logging. One of the commonest, most trusted, and frequently inadequate, logical control measures is the use of user ID and password systems to restrict system access. These logical controls may protect data by ensuring that it cannot be got at, or that, when it is got at, it is meaningless. Physical security measures are what generates most cost, least effectiveness and most resentment and therefore their use should be carefully assessed. Their purpose is to minimise the risk of unauthorised access that might then lead to accidental or deliberate:

- Disclosure of information
- Modification or destruction of data, software or equipment
- Unauthorised use of IS capabilities
- Theft of data, software or equipment

Physical security controls could include the use of security staff, surveillance systems, locks, key cards, and other access tokens. These measures filter the physical access to the use of IS elements. A simple example is the equipment location decision since it is unwise to leave unsecured access equipment near public areas or to have important processing centres in physically threatened locations such as basements (floods) or near outside walls (eavesdropping).

When selecting a set of counter measures, organisations exhibit a tendency to prefer the physical over the logical. It should also be recognised that, as processing capabilities get ever more portable, they get ever more vulnerable, and whilst in hardware terms they may become a low-cost commodity item that you can lock and insure like a bicycle, the software they hold is less replaceable and the data is every bit as valuable as that stored anywhere. The rest of this section looks at some logical and physical controls and counter measures in rather more detail.

## Operating standards

It seems to be true that an organisation always pays for standards either it pays in the present for *developing* them, or pays in the future for *not* having them. Standards provide the framework within which IS can effectively and safely function. Standards offer two benefits:

- Rationalisation of practices to aid communication and management, and simplify education and training.
- Compatibility of software, hardware, data, staff and communication channels offering potential portability of all these. This, therefore, is an instance where controls also generate threats, for instance standard interface and access mechanisms help staff to access unauthorised areas.

Despite generating threats in some areas operating standards offer benefits to:

- Project management: since the who/what/when are defined
- Developments: since approaches can be structured and production oriented rather than craft and 'Sinatra syndrome' biased
- Operations: both the logical procedures and the physical actions become clearer and less error prone through ambiguity
- Quality and documentation: these can be improved by the use of the *appropriate* standards

The maintenance of standards is a full responsibility in its own right, and one that leads to a definition of the minimum performance standards so that 'loss of security' can be more easily measured.

## Segregation of responsibilities

A traditional security control is to ensure that there are no instances where *one* individual is solely responsible for setting, implementing and policing controls and, at the same time, responsible for the use of the systems. The use of a number of people, all responsible for some part of IS controls or operations, allows each to act as a check upon another. Since no employee is performing *all* the steps in a single transaction, the others involved in the transaction can monitor for accidents and crime. The logical grouping of IS activities might be:

- systems development
- managing input media
- operating the system
- management of documentation and file archives
- distribution of output.

Where possible, to segregate responsibilities fully, no one person should cross these task boundaries. Associated with this type of security control is the use of rotation of duties and unannounced audits. This type of counter measure rather belongs to the 'staff are not trustworthy' style of management, and can be culturally inappropriate for objectives-driven modern management approaches. Hinde (1993), however, analyses the film Jurassic Park as a perfect example of an IS disaster that happens precisely because responsibilities were not segregated! Clearly the nature of some IS developments, for instance user-controlled computing, does not lend itself to such measures and a more effective staff-based counter-measure is to establish a climate of honesty and motivate all staff to be personally involved in maintaining IS security by being alert to security-threatening situations.

## Network security measures

The first step in selecting network security measures is to produce a diagram that indicates the potential access points; this is because security can only be as good as the security on these access nodes. The diagram of the physical facilities of the network also helps the organisation in its capacity planning and so operational costs saved may 'pay' for the network security measures. Any network activity involves three elements:

- The initiating terminal
- The receiving terminal
- The transmission channel

For adequate network security there must be safety measures at initiating and receiving terminals, and during data transmission. Such measures may include the use of:

- Handshake: This is a predetermined signal that must be received from a valid terminal
- Dial-back modems that call the presumed user at a predetermined number
- User IDs and passwords that validate the person operating the initiating or receiving terminal
- Encryption of transmission data to protect the data during transit or to cover the instances when other measures fail or are circumvented.

It should be remembered that prevention, detection and recovery are all security measure goals and each of these three should be provided for each of the three network elements.

## Passwords

A method frequently used to reduce the threat of internal and external hacking, and indeed to reduce the chance of accidental damage, is the implementation of password security. There are three dimensions to the use of password systems:

- Individual user identities, in which case the password is private and 'proves' that person's identity
- Group access, in which case the password 'proves' membership of that group and all members of the group must have access to the password
- Using passwords as the 'key' to unscramble encrypted data stores

In any instance, who will select the password, and how, is of primary importance.

Passwords can be generated in two ways. They can be created, automatically, by the password system and this has the advantage of forcing regular password changes and the use of non-word passwords. Non-word passwords are undoubtedly safer than guessable dictionary words and names, *unless* their confusing form leads them to be written down. To reduce the chance of users recording the password, and thereby compromising security, automatically generated passwords do tend to be short. The alternative to the system-generated password is the user-selected password. These have the advantage of being personally memorable and therefore do not need to be physically recorded, their disadvantage is that most users select readily guessable words, and are then reluctant to change them. One major ($10 million plus) network virus attack was made possible by the hacker accessing password protected systems, and a file of only 400 words gave enough variety to break through the log-in sequences encountered. Apparently the top four passwords in the UK are 'Fred', 'God', 'Pass', and 'Genius'. The chance of guessed passwords is reduced if they are not a word at all, but use alpha-numeric sequences; these can be personally memorable *linked* words, like 'green3paint'; and they are *never* written down.

Since *detection*, and not only prevention, is an objective of security controls, then the password system must maintain a log of the number of failed password entries. Multiple password entries can mean that the password-setting system is inappropriate and the *legitimate* user is forced to try several times, in this instance the organisation should review its password-setting process.

Passwords are only as good as the management of them and therefore all staff must be educated to appreciate the security dangers in 'lending' passwords, in recording them, or otherwise disclosing them. Furthermore system users should be encouraged to only type in passwords when their actions are not overlooked. Passwords are administered by software systems, and so any damage to software can reduce the effectiveness of the password safety and so *further* compromise security. This means that the costs of counter measures taken to protect software will also act to protect password systems and therefore these costs are 'shared'.

### Data encryption

On network systems the communication channel is often the weakest link and therefore the data travelling over it may be encrypted. Similarly, when data storage media are stolen, if the data they contain is scrambled it is worthless and then, when systems are illegally accessed, encryption protects the data asset. On all systems the files in which passwords are stored must be encrypted and often the encryption techniques *themselves* must be protected. The three instances for which the use of encryption is indicated are:

- Transmission of data from one point to another: Communication encryption
- Protection of passwords or keys used to restrict access or usage privileges: Password encryption, key encryption
- Storage of data in databases and files: File encryption

Encryption techniques turn clear, human-readable material into cipher text in an unintelligible form and, by doing this, encryption serves three security principles:

1 *Identification*: Helps to identify authorised senders and receivers
2 *Control*: Helps to prevent alteration of messages
3 *Privacy*: Helps to protect from eavesdropping.

Over a network, encryption may be applied in two ways: firstly as end-to-end encryption, in which only the initiating and ultimately receiving terminal need deal with ciphering and deciphering scrambled data. The more secure, but slower, alternative is link-to-link encryption in which, at each stage of the data transmission, data is unscrambled and re-scrambled before onward transmission. Encryption methods are outside the scope of this text except to note that *deciphering* requires authorisation and so the encryption becomes only as good as the protection given to the key to unscramble it. Related to encryption is the notion of *hiding* data, and many software systems allow files, or elements within the file set, not to be displayed. Whilst these settings are often easily reversed, such measures are cheap, in purchase and procedural terms, and therefore may have a high net effectiveness.

### Anti-virus security

In all forms of IS management there is a general need for anti-virus security measures. These are, inevitably, in stages, with the stages being:

- To prevent the virus infection, if possible, by using virus monitoring systems
- To detect the infection, as early as possible, by using storage media scanning systems and thereby reduce the clean-up costs and the severity of the consequent losses
- To remove the effects of the infection, as fast and as cheaply as possible, by using good back-up procedures to speed up the recovery process

Measures that protect systems from illegal access obviously act to prevent deliberate virus infections. However, deliberate virus infections are rare in comparison to *inadvertent* infections resulting from authorised staff using *unauthorised* disks and software. Education programmes are the most effective measure to counter these inadvertent actions since 'good housekeeping' not only reduces the danger of virus infection, but also the dangers from many other breaches of security, and forms a foundation for adequate recovery procedures.

### Fire detection and prevention

An appraisal of the risks and costs of fires shows that costs are high whilst the likelihood is not low. Since both costs and frequency are high then it follows that it will be cost effective to employ a large number of security measures. Such measures might include the restriction on unauthorised access to reduce the risk of arson, but more usually will include the use of general fire prevention and detection systems.

It should be noted that *all* computers, even desktop machines, are particularly vulnerable to smoke and fume damage and from water and chemical fire extinguisher systems. Figure 13.16 shows various pollutants, including a smoke particle, in comparison to disk head clearances. The trend towards desktop computing generates the need to assess fire prevention and detection mechanisms throughout the organisation and not just in the computer room. During this assessment the effect that 'cheaper', pollutant causing, extinguisher systems may have on distributed data storage must be considered. The information created from the data is valuable irrespective of the location of its storage and so PCs bring the demand for the expensive, pollutant free, fire precautions of the data centre to the general office.

Chosen security measures will usually reduce overall productivity since they usually reduce flexibility and the speed of information access. For this reason it is important to ensure that the selected set of threat counter measures reduce, avoid or transfer the identified risks in a cost effective manner since:

- A set that is too heavy wastes money and needlessly reduces flexibility
- A set that is too light leaves an unacceptable level of risk

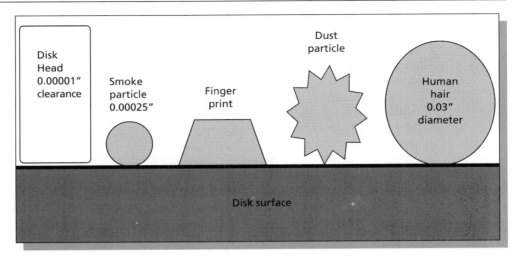

**Fig 13.16 ◆ The potential effects of pollutants on data storage media**

The organisation must remember that *all* changes to the IS environment mean that the optimum set of counter measures must be reassessed Whilst seeking a cost effective balance in security measures, a number of legislative requirements may override purely cost-driven decisions. For example, the Data Protection Act of 1984 makes data security a legal *requirement* and, in theory, the Data Protection Office could enforce security measures. The Companies Act of 1985 also requires security and audit procedures to be adequate to 'permit detection of any attempt to falsify such information'.

## 13.1.4 ◆ Contingency planning and disaster recovery

The fourth, and final, element of the systematic process of IS security management assumes that *total* risk avoidance is impractical or impossible, and therefore that an organisation must plan how to deal with, and recover from, the *inevitable* security break-downs. Such planning is called contingency planning and includes plans for the interim methods of working that will allow the organisation to *survive* the disaster and the longer-term processes that will allow the organisation to *recover* from the disaster. The first stage is to cope with the disaster itself by ensuring safety, minimising damage and enabling a return to work. The second stage is to minimise the consequent effects of the disaster. Terms associated with these stages are:

- *Downtime*: Length of time before operations are partly or wholly functioning
- *Standby or fall-back*: Keeping the business going through key systems until 'normality' can be resumed
- *Re-instatement*: Subsequently updating systems with all data generated during down-time

Certainly risk management seeks prevention where possible, but it must plan for disasters, following the old adage of:

*Hope for the best, and prepare for the worst.*

Disaster recovery must always be catered for in readiness for any failure in risk prevention and indeed a risk reduction strategy explicitly recognises that there will be a residual probability of loss of security. For some instances, when the risk consequences are low, it is not true that prevention is better than cure and so recovery *alone* may be an adequate risk handling strategy.

Not surprisingly, a 1990 MSA survey concluded that the sophistication of an organisation's disaster recovery efforts was related to the degree to which IT was deemed critical to their business. Where reliance was seen as total, then elaborate recovery provisions, including preparing to base IS in the car park by using pre-fabricated buildings and sub-car park cabling, were made. The *degree* of such reliance is difficult to be certain of with so many organisations not only reliant upon IS for operational efficiency but for operational practicality. Despite the name 'disaster' recovery, and that publicity is generally concerned with responses to terrorist bombings, fires, flood, and earthquakes, much of contingency planning provides for less dramatic causes of a loss of security. Business losses consequent upon lost data from a disk crash are just as thoroughly losses as if it was a flood that caused the data loss. With the IS-dependant organisation a major machine breakdown can be the 'disaster'. Much of the contingency planning process is hampered by the fear of embarrassment associated with disaster recovery, so much so that one recovery service provider advertises as offering 'fast, effective and discreet support in a crisis', where presumably the discretion is as important as the effective service! However, the volume of natural and deliberate disasters that have occurred during the 1990s has done much to put contingency planning on the strategic agenda.

For most organisations the first step in contingency planning is to classify systems and applications in order of their necessity to business operation. This classification allows the organisation to draw up a 'timetable of importance' that shows when each element of IS *must* be functioning again for the business to survive. This timetable then allows efforts to be channelled in the most productive way. The *standby* element of the plan will often only cover the business-*critical* systems, but the *recovery* plan must cover all aspects of IS use and management. The timetable should be based on business importance, and not technical difficulty, and generally looks rather like Figure 13.2, but with system descriptions attached. Such descriptions identify just what aspects of functionality are needed and when. A 1995 survey, reported in Green-Armytage (1995), found that for 78 per cent of firms systems availability was paramount to business activities and was very important for 10 per cent more (despite this, only just over half had any explicit strategies for ensuring systems availability). As Figure 13.2 illustrated, there can be plateaux in the recovery process and there will be a group of IS business operating elements that must be functioning 'immediately', perhaps within one day, but there will be others for which the recovery time can be a few days, three or four perhaps, then a further set for which a week or so is available, and then the remainder to be dealt with 'at leisure'. For convenience, the timetable of importance is drawn up assuming a total lack of operating ability in any given function.

Since contingency planning is part of the *strategic* management of IS it cannot be divorced from other management aspects of IS use and must be considered concurrently with other strategy selection and implementation issues. There is a clear distinction between traditional DP disaster recovery, primarily ensuring machine room re-building, and the current need to plan for the maintenance of *business continuity*. The adequacy of data availability, and not the functioning of the mainframe site, is the single most important success factor in maintaining business continuity after an IS disaster and therefore data back-ups form a fundamental cornerstone of any recovery process. Despite their importance, back-ups are frequently not taken, when they are taken never tested, and even when tested frequently not safely stored.

Many contingency plans deal only with a subset of IS elements, often only the mainframe-based systems, and so few plans can really be defined as 'business continuity' plans. One cause of this lack is that the planning process is left to the IS specialist who is not in a position to judge the *real* business timetables. Something like 80 per cent of disaster recovery plans will fail when first tested, and this is usually because of the lack of awareness of the business interdependencies. Nor is it only ignorance of *internal* dependencies that reduces the effectiveness of recovery plans. Increased electronic trading and just-in-time business activities make one organisation vulnerable to disasters experienced by those up-stream, and down-stream, of the value chain.

There are two major, and inter-related, problems in disaster planning. These are the difficulties in staying up to date with the disaster types, and the difficulty in staying up to date with the business' timetable of importance. The state of business continuity/disaster recovery planning in the UK is fairly poor, and it is probable that the majority of organisations will have either no plans at all, or plans that are significantly out of date, untested or limited in scope. This situation is illustrated in Figure 13.17.

Merry (1992) quotes research that found that 84 per cent of the organisations surveyed claimed to have a disaster recovery plan, but only 64 per cent could claim to have an *office* recovery plan. It is only such office recovery plans that will include desktop computers, telephone and network connections, and other distributed computing related facilities. The office, rather than the computer room, is now the site of much business-critical computing. This shift in location is something that many disaster recovery, and disaster prevention, strategies continue to ignore. For instance, around 90 per cent of mainframes are protected by uninterruptable power supplies (UPSs) but only 6 per cent of LANs are. It took the April 1992 IRA bombing of the City of London to highlight, for many organisations, the value of the data they had stored on their desktop machines. The machines themselves are ever cheaper, but the systems and data they contain are ever more valuable as more 'real' business operations are based upon them.

| Probability that organisation will have: | | Probability that organisation (with initially tested & effective plan) will follow up initial testing: | |
| --- | --- | --- | --- |
| ● No business continuity plan at all | 40% | ● Never | 15% |
| ● Vague/unrealistic plan | 15% | ● Within 1-2 years | 15% |
| ● Untested plan | 20% | ● Within 6 months to a year | 30% |
| ● Tested & effective plan | 25% | ● Within past 6 months | 40% |

Fig 13.17 ◆ Profile of UK business continuity/disaster recovery planning

If the business is not kept running in the short-term then long-term recovery will be irrelevant, therefore immediate standby arrangements are critical to the organisation's chances of disaster survival and to the overall costs incurred. The types of standby arrangements include:

- *Hot site facilities*: Where everything to enable IS operation is already installed. These sites allow almost instantaneous business operation, provided that data back-ups are available

- *Cold site facilities*: Where an equipped but empty data centre is available. These sites are general purpose and therefore cheaper to retain than hot sites, but make it slower to get business operations running since there is the need to install business appropriate features in them *after* the disaster.

- *Portable facilities*: Where 'hot', or 'cold', provision is made from portable vehicles, or semi-portable pre-fabricated buildings. These are a popular option since they can readily be shared.

Each must be associated with ensuring that the data 'raw material' is available for the recovered systems. Electronic journaling is the regular electronic transfer of mirror sets of data for just this purpose.

It was not only *perceptions* of value that were changed by the 1992 wave of terrorist disasters. They also changed the nature of the required 'hot site' recovery, from the provision of mainframes, to a guaranteed provision of PCs with network management software provision and appropriate software pre-installed. Mutual, reciprocal standby arrangements are a successful strategy for divisions within the same group but rarely work between independent organisations because the still-operating partner may be reluctant to free up capability or, again as major disasters have shown, they may be affected themselves. Major disasters will always be a problem for standby arrangements when many service subscribers are 'hit' all at once. Whichever standby arrangement is made, modern disaster recovery will require the provision of a communication hub since large numbers of staff are now dependant upon portable, and handheld, computing using modems to create a 'virtual' organisation in which they operate.

Although many organisations have trouble in determining how to establish contingency plans, Bolton (1992) quotes Lloyds as saying that it is *self-evident* what organisations should do in planning for disasters. Lloyds regard this 'self-evident' list as mandatory before they are prepared to underwrite any insurance, they therefore require:

- First-line physical defences and detectors
- Off-site back-up for data, software and documentation
- Standby hardware if appropriate
- Thorough and reliable maintenance contracts
- Rules for software development and acceptance
- Good personnel procedures

Contingency planning cannot be something that is added 'after the fact', and so *all* IS development approaches, including the full gamut of acquisition approaches, must provide for recovery points. For instance, IS elements can be 'parcelled up' into black boxes with identified inputs that, following a security break-down, could be gathered by alternate means, even manually. This modularity then allows any still-operating IS elements to function as fully as possible. Disaster recovery needs put pressure upon an organisation to modularise, downsize and outsource, or, at the very least, use easily replaced software packages for non-critical applications. Contingency planning must give careful consideration to the likely nature of any standby facilities and their potential effect upon applications. Effective disaster recovery has planned, in advance, how to deal with any incompatibilities and, again, there is a pressure to use industry standard, building block, IS components to reduce the scale of the possible incompatibilities.

During the standby phase many security control and counter measure features are likely to be missing, inadequate or simply different, either because operations are at a standby site at a different location, or because human stress levels are high. This means that a critical part of contingency planning is to identify the further threats that emerge as a result of the disaster recovery process itself. For example, manual data gathering may be more error-prone than automatic data capture, and the use of a shared standby site increases the threat of unauthorised data access. Even during this time of dislocation, legally required data security, software licensing and audit procedures must be maintained. The Maxwell organisation was raided by FAST to uncover software copyright violations shortly after the disappearance of Robert Maxwell and whilst the organisation was in turmoil.

Disaster recovery planning must arrange appropriate security measures for all the off-site elements since the contingency plan is likely to call for the extensive use of off-site storage, and it is particularly vital that the plan itself is protected. Many disaster recovery attempts have been wrecked because all copies of the disaster plan went up in flames in the 'disaster', or equally because the keys to the, sensibly used, fireproof safes were incinerated because they were, not so sensibly, stored in ordinary desks.

By its very nature the recovery plan document will be specific to an organisation. Most will first address standby planning, where the emphasis is upon the obtaining of an alternative interim method of operation, and then recovery planning, where the emphasis is upon how to recover fully from the loss of security, or the standby position. Hill (1992) gives a detailed description of the ten sections he feels a disaster recovery document should contain, and these are given in Figure 13.18. Hill's work, therefore, provides a useful framework for the deliverable resulting from contingency planning.

It is not just equipment, or even software and data, that is lost in most disasters. Generally a disaster will involve the buildings and the staff as well and so disaster plans must identify the key people, who to contact under what circumstances, where items are safely stored, what insurance arrangements there are and, in short, how to manage the situation. Whatever the plan encompasses, the *process* of contingency

- **Introduction and index:** Including a brief description and summary of the manual, how it is structured, who holds copies of the plan, version numbers, a thorough index, how to use the plan, etc.

- **Definition of a computer disaster:** Provided here is an exact definition of what, to the organisation, a disaster is, for example a loss of service or loss of revenue. Also included in this chapter should be the organisation's policy on disaster planning. The document should define *levels* of disasters since there will be different recovery strategies for different types of disaster. It should be sufficient to identify five different levels, where level one could be a small, on-site fire causing little damage or interruption, whilst level five would be the worst-case scenario, a major fire destroying the whole data area.

- **Assumptions:** Plans will be based on assumptions and these need to be explained. For example, one assumption may be that a standby recovery operations centre will support, for a specified time, all applications identified as critical, and that all key personnel will be available. These assumptions should be tested regularly.

- **Disaster exclusions:** There may be certain types of disaster, due to their magnitude, which the manual is unable to cater for, one example might be a nuclear holocaust. Even so, exclusions should be listed so there is no doubt what disasters the plan does cover.

- **Inventories:** This section or chapter will itemise all software and hardware, including data and voice communications equipment, which is covered by the disaster recovery manual. Also included should be staff organisation charts, floor plans, wiring diagrams, entrance and exit routes, etc. Service levels should also be inventoried and this section will identify and list, not only the organisation's critical applications, but also state when services will start following recovery. Availability of standby systems, contractual agreements and commitments, and supply of replacement equipment should also be highlighted. If the organisation needs to satisfy any statutory requirements, a relative section should appear here.

- **Emergency budgets:** This chapter or section should detail how urgent cash flows will be generated during an invocation. Special budget codes should be identified, in advance, with adequate audit trails for post-disaster analysis and cross-referencing to those responsible for claiming from the insurance company.

- **Invocation:** This section will detail how the alarm is raised and the plan invoked. There may be several methods of raising the alarm and contacting key personnel depending upon the disaster scenario being planned for. Disaster management teams must be defined and included here should be the organisational structure of all recovery teams, presented to an appropriate level of detail and outlining all respective team action plans. These could be supported or represented by a flowchart showing the logical sequence of activities, interdependencies, timings and checkpoints.

- **Logistics:** Without adequate logistics planning there is a high degree of risk that the disaster recovery plan will fail. Examples of logistical planning will include sections on transport, staffing, supplies such as media, communications, access and security arrangements, services, etc.

- **Maintenance and testing:** Defining how the plan will be tested and maintained. Particularly important to any organisation operating in a dynamic IS environment where constant changes are made to hardware, software and product range. All change control documentation, maintenance schedules, test results, etc should be shown.

- **Appendices:** The area in which to file copies of:
  - Insurance policies
  - Any third-party standby service contracts
  - Vendor agreements
  - Any important or useful correspondence
  - Results from risk analysis
  - Business impact reviews and post-test mortems.

**Fig 13.18 ◆ Suggested structure for the disaster planning document**
(after Hill)

planning must provide for regular testing, monitoring and updating of the plan. This ensures it works to the current, rather than some past, timetable of business importance. Only in this way will it enable the maintenance of business continuity.

# 13.2 ◆ IS MANAGEMENT AND ETHICS

Section 13.1 has considered how IS management can ensure that IS is organisationally safe. IS security is about maintaining IS availability, integrity and confidentiality. In Section 13.3 the legal responsibilities of IS management will be explored. Responsible IS management is however more than just security or law. It is also a matter of ethics. IS ethics are not, however, *separate* from those issues of security and law. As will be seen in Section 13.3, specific legislation, such as the Computer Misuse Act, criminalises certain behaviour. This makes certain instances of IS use into criminal acts and is it 'right' to create a new type of criminal? As discussed in Section 13.1, many banks and financial bodies are reluctant to publicise security breaches for fear of losing public confidence. Is it 'right' to mislead other organisations and the public in this way, and what obligations do these firms have to avoid such events in the first place? These questions are *related* to IS security and IS laws but they are primarily issues of IS ethics.

This brief section will introduce various ethical frameworks used to judge the 'right' way to behave in IS management situations. It will also introduce some of the ethical questions specifically generated by IS. This section is brief, not because the notion of IS ethics is unimportant or even straightforward. It is brief because the ethical dimension of IS management is relatively unexplored. Increasingly organisations systematically address the security and legal issues associated with their IS management. Few have begun to deal systematically with ethical issues. These ethical dilemmas of IS are dilemmas because determining what to do cannot be made just with reference to IS security, IS law or even IS profitability. Effective IS management contributes to achieving personally, organisationally or socially desirable values. Difficulties arise when there are too *many* such values, all estimable and yet contradictory. Ethical IS management must *consciously* addresses the trade-offs inherent in conflicts of values and ensure a *socially* responsible balance.

## 13.2.1 ◆ Ethical frameworks

Ethics is a branch of philosophy (so it is sometimes referred to as moral philosophy) that deals with the principles of right and wrong. It is concerned with considering and informing the choices that people make. Ethics, of course, apply in all walks of life and not just business or IS management decisions. However, the complexity of contemporary commerce and the way that IS continually generates new situations does pose some 'special' problems. Responsible IS management requires sensitivity to ethical issues. The difficulty therefore is that there can be no one clear view of what good or bad decisions are. This is where ethical theories come in.

As already indicated, ethical theories are frameworks of beliefs that serve to inform behaviour. Unfortunately there are a number of ethical theories and 'good' behaviour as defined by one may not match 'good' as defined by another. These frameworks can be thought of as belonging to one of two camps concerned primarily with either:

- the fundamental morality of behaviour
- the consequences of behaviour

The first of these ethical theories (often called deontologism or kantianism) is that there are basic and unarguable instances of right and wrong. For instance, theft, deceit, inequality and so on are *always* wrong. By this framework ethical IS management must *never* use IS to mislead or differentiate. This type of ethical framework has an individualistic stance. The notion of protecting employees is an instance of what is considered 'right' by this viewpoint. This type of view allows there to be a *logically* accepted 'good' act argued from first principles of basic morality.

The second type of ethical framework, that of consequentialism (sometimes referred to as teleological or utilitarianism), is concerned primarily with the social *effects* of behaviour. Ethical behaviour is that which maximises the overall benefit to society. In this instance it is harder to *logically* argue what is a 'good' decision. Current behaviour is not determined from first principles but from *anticipated* and estimated *overall* effects. This is the 'ends justify the means' viewpoint. However the nature of that 'end' must be ascertained.

Whether an ethical framework is based around fundamental principles or consequences there is a need to determine what are the agreed principles of right and wrong or the adjudged 'good' effects. It is convenient to consider these, as in Watson and Pitt (1993), as drawing upon either a sense of rights or justice. Theories of rights frameworks judge acts 'good' if they do not contravene certain fundamental human rights (essentially individualistic in nature and so again employee rights are an instance). Cavanagh *et al.* (1981) suggest that there a five such basic rights:

- the right to free consent
- the right to privacy
- the right to freedom of conscience
- the right to free speech
- the right to due process

IS management decisions may directly relate to all of these, for example automated systems may compromise individual ability to express consent directly. Some concerns, such as with IS and privacy, become codified as legal responses, such as the Data Protection Act to be discussed in Section 13.3.

Rather than focus on an individual's rights the justice of the overall situation can be considered. By this, the first principles or the consequential effect would be that equity, fairness, and impartiality are achieved. Again IS management decisions relate to each of these, for example access to information may empower or disenfranchise certain groups. Again, some concerns, such as those with IS and inequality, are codified as laws, such as those of fair trading.

So various frameworks exist by which the human and social quality of IS management decisions can be judged. Ethical IS management is that by which such 'quality' decisions result. This does not happen by chance. IS ethical concerns must be explicitly addressed. This can be done by articulating an IS management code of practice, either an organisation-specific one or more likely from one of the IS professional bodies such as the British Computer Society (BCS) or the Association of Computing Machines (ACM). This code of practice is the *chosen* ethical framework and then needs *real* adherence to it.

## 13.2.2 ◆ IS issues that pose ethical dilemmas

The essential difficulty with each of the various ethical frameworks is how to apply them to IS! Deontologism (the working from moral first principles) is likely to define good IS decisions in terms of *individual* good, whilst utilitarianism (the working from overall effects) is likely to define good in terms of the *common* good. Problematically, one may be at the expense of the other. For example current developments in international communications via the Internet may increase an individual's right to free speech and yet may simultaneously decrease the collective ability to protect the weak (from pornography, character defamation, religious, gender and racial intolerance, etc). Given this conflict, how should ethical IS management respond? All areas of collective human activity, government, law, education, etc, have had to address (and re-address as social beliefs evolve) how the tensions between these two will be handled. IS management is just coming to grips with this difficulty.

A number of writers, in attempting to create a sensitivity to IS ethical issues, have offered ways to highlight different types of ethical issues that are 'special' to IS. See for instance Mason (1986), LaChat (1986) and Watson and Pitt (1993). They seek to help focus upon a code of conduct that coherently covers IS ethical concerns associated with each category. It must be noted that a key point about IS is that it frequently generates new and unforeseen tensions. One of the most commonly used categories by which IS ethical questions are considered is by using Mason's acronym PAPA. The four key IS-generated concerns Mason argues are:

1  *Privacy*: IS may pose questions regarding disclosures about a person and their interactions. The common good may push towards using IS capabilities to uncover socially damaging situations (eg patterns in data stores that indicate criminal activities) whilst the individual good may push against such use. How this is currently codified as law will be discussed further in Section 13.3.1.
2  *Accuracy*: IS may pose questions with respect to achieving informational accuracy and redress from inaccuracy. IS capabilities can be used to process more information than it is humanly possible to check. Decision making on the basis of stored data may facilitate speed of action (potentially 'good') at the expense of occasional errors. Each error, however rare (though in fact increasingly likely given the volume of data and its reuse for unanticipated purposes), represents a potential for individual wrong (erroneous credit rejection for instance) or social damage (draconian community charges because of inaccurate council income calculations).
3  *Property*: IS may pose questions with regard to ownership of information and its transfer channels. Is technological advancement appropriately an ownable asset (as in patents) or a social commitment (as in public health). The net result of an organisation's IS activities is a store of data about its interactions with others, for

instance customers, suppliers and employees. Who has the rights of ownership and how can communal ownership be mediated in a morally just way? Mason (1986) quotes the example of the overstocking of common grazing land as an example where unregulated individual responses destroyed the asset for all. Are information communication channels similarly vulnerable?

4 *Access*: IS may pose questions with respect to access to information and techno-logical capability. This is perhaps the most stark tension in IS *management*. So often exploitation of IS capability directly disenfranchises one organisational group whilst at the same time it may strengthen another. More broadly, if IS lit-eracy is a *fundamental* requirement then to what extent does society have *rights* to 'free' training and access?

These four categories, along with the unresolved ethical issues associated with replicating human attributes (for instance through artificial intelligence and robot-ics), can conveniently be used to structure an organisational code of ethical IS conduct. To do that positions with respect to dilemmas such as the following must be decided:

• A switchboard supervisor who has received complaints about an operator has the technological capability to listen in on conversations to monitor service. Should this be acceptable or not?

• A manager under competitive pressure is considering a new application of IS that will eliminate five people's jobs. These five will not be able to find similar jobs elsewhere. Should this be acceptable or not?

• A planned new IS use will (legally) support decisions about sales discounts with customer history analysis. The volume of data used means that it cannot be manually verified for accuracy. Should this be acceptable or not?

• An organisation is intending to produce an electronic catalogue of products from which customers will make orders. It is both technically feasible and currently legal to include subliminal advertising into the catalogue software (*see* Jones (1995) to promote 'special offers' and the like. Should this be acceptable or not?

• An organisation is considering a commitment to teleworking (*see* Chapter 12). Even though the organisation would supply all equipment this would mean that only candidates who had suitable home situations (space, quiet, security for the equipment, confidentiality from others, etc) could be recruited. Should this be acceptable or not?

• Given the current legal framework (*see* Section 13.3) many organisations circu-late formal instructions against software piracy. An organisation is intending to send round such instruction even though it knows that it will be difficult for areas to meet budget targets without *some* use of illicit software. Should this be acceptable or not?

The need for more than *ad hoc* individual rectitude in IS management is increas-ingly recognised. Most initiatives to date, for example the 1993 ACM Code of Conduct for IS professionals, address personal responsibility with respect to sys-tems design. Growing attention is given to the issue of IS intrusion and the morals of intellectual property rights. As yet there is very little in the way of broader con-cerns about how IS is deployed and used.

## 13.3 ◆ MANAGING IS AND THE LAW

All organisations have a legal obligation regarding information and its storage, processing, and retrieval. This obligation and the additional issue of the impact that IS can have on the nature of crime and its detection are the focus of this section. Since organisations have a responsibility for the security of management information systems and their products, managers involved with these systems must be aware of the legal issues and current legislative framework. No corporate or personal use of information systems exists outside this framework, and particularly at the strategic planning stage, the current and impending legal climate must be considered.

It is not just what the national situation is with regard to relevant laws that must be considered. As IS creates a globalisation of business so IS relevant legislation must be considered on an international scale. Some initiatives, such as the Computer Misuse Act discussed in Section 13.3.5, have attempted to address the situation where criminal acts are initiated, or felt, in countries other than the UK. Similarly the EC directives are generally attempting to create a harmonisation of laws across the member states, see London (1994). It is not simply a matter of adopting the most stringent versions of the copyright laws of the countries operated in (if such a concept could be identified) since the organisation must also stay competitive. There remains a great deal of confusion around international rules for privacy, intellectual property, trading rules and criminal misuse.

This section will concentrate upon the 'big four' legal issues of confidentiality and privacy; copyright and software protection; contractual obligations; and IS and crime. There are a number of other related legal issues. Examples include the legal requirements for document management; early disposal of potentially damaging records is obviously illegal but over-long retention of records, or the existence of back-ups, can 'trip up' an organisation. American presidential security advisor, Oliver North, found that back-up tapes of damaging Iran-Contra memos existed, and therefore could form evidence. The need to maintain legally required copies may mean retaining paper duplicates of electronic data systems (EDI for instance) or, worse, that new systems must be record-compatible with old systems to facilitate retrieval when legally required. This can lock an organisation into backward-compatibility driven limited systems or long-term expensive maintenance of obsolete systems merely to comply with legal record access rules. Record management forces IS to be concerned with the long-term fate of the information generated, and this fate in terms of, not just how, but why, where, and for how long. This section will also look at, though in less detail, issues associated with the maintenance of legally required working conditions.

### 13.3.1 ◆ Confidentiality and privacy

One of the most complicated and challenging obligations in IS management is that of resolving the conflicting tension of privacy and accessibility. The legislative pattern is such that all those responsible for the use and management of IS are also responsible for resolving this tension. *Privacy* is an individual's right to determine for themselves what about them is communicated to others. *Confidentiality*, by contrast, is an organisation's right to determine what will be communicated about commercially held information that is not about people, for instance, sales data, R&D findings, profitability figures. In layman's terms we think of privacy as a personal, social right, whereas confidentiality is a commercial demand but it must be stressed that these distinctions are ones of custom and usage rather than legal validity.

Since maintaining privacy and confidentiality is in contradiction to the need to interact socially through the disclosure of information then it is extremely difficult to assess to what degree an individual's interests are best served by allowing them to limit data access. The transfer of some data is inevitable, and desirable, in any of the myriad of interactions between individuals, and between individuals and organisations. The concept of privacy is a difficult one and in the UK there is no general right to privacy, only limited rights obtained through a number of laws that define specific aspects of privacy, and so the laws relating to contract, confidence, defamation, trespass and copyright may all indirectly provide some redress for any perceived loss of privacy. Personal data protection must be a balance of

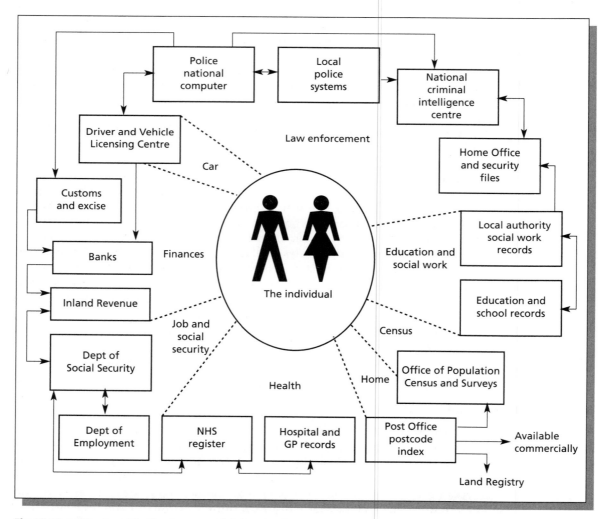

**Fig 13.19 ◆ Direct and indirect personal data transfers**

interests between the individual and society and the legal framework is the current way that authority regulates that balance. Figure 13.19 illustrates just some of the IS-supported data transfers that modern interactions involve. Governments who pass laws have a greater interest in invading privacy than in protecting it, as Flaherty (1989) found:

> It cannot be emphasised too strongly that the incentives for the government and the bureaucracy are in the direction of invading, or at least ignoring or neglecting, privacy interests rather than protecting them. Most measures that are perceived as 'necessary' to cope with a societal problem involve surveillance through data collection.

There is a wide variation in what people regard as 'private' information concerning themselves. These variations exist between one individual and another, between different sections of society and different countries. Clearly then 'privateness' is not an attribute of data itself because the same data can be considered private in one context and public information in another. Therefore the important concern must be what the data is going to be used for.

Despite growing concerns about privacy, some would argue that it is often in a person's best interests to reveal rather than withhold private information. For example, credit could not be provided if borrowers were unwilling to release the relevant personal information to allow their credit worthiness to be assessed, and fair decisions concerning personal taxation could not be made if lawful personal data was not provided by the appropriate people. The anxiety about the issue of firearms licences to 'unsuitable' individuals could be addressed by insisting that *all* forms of personal data be electronically available for such purposes. It should be remembered that there are aspects of privacy that have no immediate connection with the handling of personal data through information systems, for example intrusion into the home, powers of entry and search, and embarrassing publicity in the media and, on the other hand, there are aspects of data protection, such as accuracy, that have no connection with privacy.

Whatever the privacy debate, privacy protection is very important, and is likely to become more so as developments such as PINs, smart cards, the new Police National Computer, document image processing, etc, mean that new classes of data and actions must be considered to effectively ensure the privacy of individuals. Hussain and Hussain (1992) describe two currently important privacy issues:

- *Fair use*: The concept of data privacy that would only allow data to be used in support of the organisation's specific business mission. This would require an organisation to seek an individual's permission before passing personal data on to others. Data use is complex; it seems legitimate to use personal data for marketing purposes, perhaps to direct advertising efforts. However, once such personal data is gathered it describes individuals in ways that can have less savoury use, such as for political harassment, or to allow criminals to identify lucrative (or soft touch) targets.

- *Gate keeping*: The restricted access to services, privileges, benefits or opportunities on the basis of certain data values. Some gate keeping seems inevitable, and acceptable; entry to a university permitted by certain A Level points is one such example and a point scoring system for credit provision is another. However, the same principle can be used to keep out 'trouble makers', and then the central issue becomes: *whose* definition of trouble maker?

The Serious Fraud Squad (SFO) and the London Stock Exchange authorities received supposedly confidential data from the Inland Revenue's computerised files in the 1993 Asil Nadir (Poly Peck) affair. This raises a political debate about whether crime reporting takes precedence over the current Data Protection Act or does maintaining privacy carry the higher importance. If criminals are to be reported then law enforcement agencies need new guidelines on the lawful process of doing so.

In the UK the role of government with respect to privacy has traditionally been a less pressing concern than the commercial uses of personal data. There are privacy fears surrounding the potential national ID card, and the civil liberty dangers inherent in the inter-linking of disparate state data stores. Despite this, however, most legislation (and most fears) are targeted at personal data on people as *consumers; see* for instance Warren (1995) and Evans (1995).

Other unresolved privacy concerns remain. Since the UK's only specific legislation in this area is a *data* protection act and not a *privacy* protection act it does little to address issues such as employee privacy and the Act offers no guidance about how the capabilities of technology should, rather than could, be used to monitor staff performance.

Data accuracy is obviously a requirement of data processing, but only to the degree needed for the *given* application. Privacy questions arise when the original application, commercially unconcerned with accuracy, passes on data to an application that needs *greater* accuracy. Many life styling databases are built upon data gathered in a casual, almost incidental way and this data is not validated for accuracy but is then used as the basis for customer decisions. For instance, TRN Information Service, typical of many American data wholesalers, gathers data from thousands of companies, they then organise and store this data into credit histories to provide 24 000 subscribers with 35 million credit reports a year. TRN receive 350 000 complaints a year leading to 100 000 changes to inaccurate data. Press reports would indicate that:

- Probably     20 per cent     of credit rating data is inaccurate
- Perhaps      40 per cent     of marketing data is inaccurate
- And even     10 per cent     of police data is inaccurate.

## Data Protection Act 1984

Legislative controls may formalise the requirement to manage IS responsibly but laws do not *initiate* that requirement. Whilst the confidentiality of manually stored data has been partially protected in law for many years, providing for the protection of electronically stored data is a more recent phenomenon.

The Data Protection Act 1984 is the UK response to the need for privacy protection legislation. This Act gives individuals rights about what may be stored and processed about them on computer or other automatic data processing medium, for example microfiche; it further gives them rights to examine that information, challenge it, if appropriate have it amended or deleted where necessary and, in some cases, to claim compensation for damages caused. The Act also places certain obligations upon the data user in that they must register their data use with the Data Protection Register, and implement good practice regarding the usage and disclosure of information held. Figure 13.20 sums up the data users' responsibilities and the data subjects' rights as defined by the Data Protection Act.

| Responsibilities of the data user | Rights of the data subject |
|---|---|
| • Adhere to the eight data protection principles<br>• Register data use to validate adherence to the data protection principles | • Establish what personal data is stored by sending a Subject Access Request<br>• Ensure stored data is accurate and correctly collected, stored or used<br>• Can complain to Data Protection Registrar<br>• Claim compensation through court actions |

**Fig 13.20 ◆ Data protection rights and responsibilities**

Concern over data privacy was not the only driver of data protection legislation, of equal significance was the Council of Europe's concern over transborder data reliability. The Council of Europe Convention sought:

> ... To secure in the territory of each party state for every individual ... respects for his rights and fundamental freedom, and in particular, his privacy with regard to the automatic processing of personal data relating to him.

If the UK did not pass data protection laws then other countries, with such legislation, would forbid data transfers to and from the UK to the detriment of multinational trading. Subsequent EC directives, in seeking harmonisation across member states, extends protection to *all* data held. This includes paper-based stores of personal data. Perhaps the major pressure was not *public* pressure but commercial *trade* pressure. These two drivers explain the apparent contradictions in the European Council Directive intended to harmonise data protection laws throughout the community.

- Article 1(1) Member States shall ensure, in accordance with the Directive, the protection of the privacy of individuals in relation to the processing of personal data contained in data files
- Article 1(2) Member States shall neither restrict nor prohibit the free flow of personal data between Member States for reasons to do with the protection afforded under Article 1 (1)

These two articles mean that the free flow of data does not, in itself, compromise privacy and therefore members cannot use privacy as an excuse against cross-border data flows.

The Data Protection Act 1984, using terms defined in Figure 13.21, is founded upon the concept of organisations taking responsibility for eight data protection *principles*. These are:

1 The information to be contained in personal data shall be obtained, and personal data shall be processed, fairly and lawfully
2 Personal data shall be held only for one or more specified and lawful purposes
3 Personal data held for any purpose or purposes shall not be used or disclosed in any manner incompatible with that purpose or those purposes
4 Personal data held for any purpose or purposes shall be adequate, relevant and not excessive in relation to that purpose or those purposes
5 Personal data shall be accurate and, where necessary, kept up to date

6 Personal data held for any purpose or purposes shall not be kept for longer than is necessary for that purpose or those purposes

7 An individual shall be entitled:

- At reasonable intervals and without undue delay or expense:
  i To be informed by any data user whether he holds personal data of which that individual is the subject
  ii To access any such data held by a data user
- Where appropriate, to have such data corrected or erased

8 Appropriate security measures shall be taken against unauthorised access to, or alteration, disclosure or destruction of, personal data and against accidental loss or destruction of personal data

A fundamental feature of the Data Protection Act is the requirement for virtually all data users and computer bureaux to register. The concept of near universal registration is intended to enable the Registrar, who is the central figure for the implementation and enforcement of the Act, to regulate the uses of personal data in the UK.

The Act states that any user who holds personal data must, unless all the data falls into one of the exempt categories described later in Figure 13.23, apply for registration. From the information supplied on this application, the details will appear in the data user's register entry available for public viewing. This publicly available entry gives:

| | |
|---|---|
| **Data** | Within the context of this Act data is defined as 'information recorded in a form that can be processed by equipment operating automatically in response to instructions given for that purpose'. |
| **Personal data** | This is defined as 'information relating to a living individual who can be identified from that information'. Therefore, data about organisations falls outside the definition. The act is solely concerned with natural, and not legal, persons. |
| **Information** | This is defined as 'factual information' relating to individuals, for instance names, addresses, ages, income, marital status, etc. The Act also includes 'expressions of opinion' as information but does not include statements of the intentions of the data user. Distinguishing between opinions and intentions is not always easy. It is important to note that word processors, when used solely for preparing the text of documents, are not covered by the Act. |
| **Data subject** | A data subject is simply an 'individual who is the subject of personal data'. |
| **Data user/ computer bureaux** | The act covers both data users and computer bureaux. A data user is 'one who holds personal data, that is the data forms part of a collection which has been processed, or is intended to be processed, and the 'user' controls the contents of the use of data'. A Computer Bureaux is defined as a 'person providing a service in respect of data' by holding other people's data and processing it at another person's instructions. |
| **Processing** | In the context of the Act processing is defined as 'amending, augmenting, deleting, re-arranging or extracting information'. |

Fig 13.21 ◆ Terms used in the Data Protection Act 1984

- The data user's name and address
- The purpose for which the personal data is held
- Details of the personal data held
- The sources from which the personal data may be obtained
- The people to whom the personal data may be disclosed
- The overseas countries to which the personal data may be transferred

Once a data user has registered under the Act they must adhere to the data protection principles. If the data user fails to adhere to any of these principles the Registrar can take action against them. The Registrar has a range of enforcement powers to ensure that:

- Data users and computer bureaux comply with the data protection principles
- Data users and computer bureaux operate within the terms of their registration entry

Failure to comply with any of the principles is not in *itself* an offence, nor does it give grounds for any civil rights of action. The offences under the Act may arise from facts or circumstances that are in themselves breaches of the principles; Figure 13.22 gives a summary of these offences.

Serious offences, which would include the unregistered holding of data, failure to comply with an enforcement notice and knowingly or recklessly operating outside the terms of the register entry, raise the issue of the powers of the 'Court'. Such serious offences can be tried by the Crown Court or the Magistrates Court. For these to be criminal offences there must be criminal intent, so they must have been done knowingly or recklessly. There is an unlimited fine when found guilty by the Crown Court and if found guilty by the Magistrates Court there is a statutory maximum fine. The remaining offences, including the failure to ensure that a register entry contains a user's current address, are dealt with by the Magistrates court, where there is a maximum fine, currently set at Level 5, or £5 000. The court can order computer-held personal data to be forfeited, destroyed or erased.

---

1  Failure to register when keeping computerised personal data.

2  Giving false information to the Registrar.

3  Holding personal data for a purpose other than the specified purpose or purposes described.

4  Failure to inform the Registrar of your current address.

5  Disclosure of information by a computer bureaux without the authority of the person for whom the service is being provided.

6  Obtaining (to be held by the data user) personal data or information to be contained in such data from a source other than as specified.

7  Disclosing personal data held by the data user to any country or territory outside the UK other than one named or described in the entry.

8  Failure to comply with notices issued by the Registrar.

**Fig 13.22 ◆ Offences under the Data Protection Act 1984**

As well as the power to serve the previously mentioned notices, the Registrar also has powers of entry and inspection. To exercise these powers, the Registrar must have reasonable grounds of suspicion that an offence under the Data Protection Act is taking place, and he must apply to a circuit judge for a warrant to enter and search for evidence. This facility can also be used if the Registrar suspects that a contravention of any of the eight Data Protection Principles is occurring. The Registrar will not *automatically* be issued with a warrant; he must first satisfy the judge that:

1 There are reasonable grounds
2 He has already given seven days written notice to the occupier
3 He has had access denied at a reasonable time
4 The occupant has been notified of the application for a warrant and been given a chance to be heard

The Office of the Data Protection Registrar has produced a set of eight clearly written guidelines on the data protection legislation. These have the same relationship to the Data Protection Act as the Highway Code has to the various traffic and driving laws, that is they explain how *to behave* in such a way as to abide by the eight principles of the Act. The guidelines themselves are *not* the law, being essentially simplifications of it, but they help organisations avoid the criminal penalties and civil remedies that may result from failure to comply with the law since they remove the *ignorance* of the law.

### Rights of data subjects

One of the main purposes of the Act is to give data subjects the right to find out whether, and if so what, information is held on computers about them and to have it corrected or erased if necessary. The Act allows a data user to charge the data subject, up to £10, for the administration of providing the information. If the data user has more than one data registration the data subject can be charged £10 for each access. However, many organisations do not charge at all, or charge a reduced amount. Whilst lower charges are generally welcome, some data subjects may be discouraged from making access requests because of the charge uncertainty. Data users must provide the requested information within forty days of receiving the request and they must provide the information as it stood when the request was made. The only amendments allowed are the 'normal' and routine amendments or deletions. If the data user refuses to provide the requested information then the data subject can either complain to the Registrar or ask the court to order the user to comply with the request.

Data subjects have the right to compensation if they suffer damage from inaccurately held data or inadequate data security systems. However, data users may have a defence if they can prove that they had taken reasonable care in the circumstances to ensure data accuracy.

The Data Protection Act contains a number of exemption clauses. These exemptions are tabulated in Figure 13.23. If personal data falls within one of the total exemptions categories then:

• The data need not be registered

• The individual has no right of subject access

• The Registrar has no power under the Act. However, a court may require inspection if it is claimed that the data should not be exempt.

| Total exemptions | Non-disclosure exemptions | Subject access exemptions |
|---|---|---|
| • Data held only in connection with personal, family or household affairs or for recreational use<br><br>• Data used only for preparing the text of documents (in *effect* an exemption though not strictly in this category)<br><br>• Personal data held solely for calculating wages and pensions, keeping accounts, or keeping records of purchases and sales for accounting purposes<br><br>• Information that the law requires to be made publicly available such as company share registers<br><br>• Data held by unincorporated sports or recreational clubs (if members do not object)<br><br>• Data used for distributing articles or information to data subjects through mailing lists, if the data subject has consented<br><br>• National security data | • Disclosure to the data subject or with consent<br><br>• Disclosure to employees or agents<br><br>• Prevention of crime, injury or damage to health<br><br>• National security<br><br>• Disclosures for legal and taxation purposes<br><br>• Emergency disclosures | • Prevention of crime, and taxation purposes<br><br>• Judicial appointments<br><br>• Legal professional privilege<br><br>• Statistical or research data<br><br>• Back-up data<br><br>• Data relating to credit references, as this is covered by the Consumer Credit Act 1974<br><br>• Data incriminating the data user |

### Modification of the Right to Subject Access

The Act allows in certain instances for the right of subject access to be *modified*; these modifications apply to:

• Health data
• Social work data
• Disclosures prohibited by law
• Data held by financial regulatory bodies

**Fig 13.23 ◆ Exemptions from the Data Protection Act 1984**

In the case of total exemptions there is no requirement for registration. However, in the case of non-disclosure exemptions then the data must still be registered; it is not however an offence to disclose the information even though the person to whom it is disclosed is not described in the register in the disclosures section. In the final instance of subject access exemptions, then when these apply:

- The subject has no right of access
- The Registrar or Courts cannot give access
- Unless exempt, the data must still be registered and is subject to the other powers of the Registrar and courts

Of interest amongst the instances of exemptions is the case of the BT debt collector who was sacked for a breach of the Data Protection Act when he hacked into BT's database of defaulting payers in an attempt to improve his employer's debt control practices. His sacking was overturned at an industrial tribunal; presumably the data fell under the classification of 'solely for accounting purposes'!

### Cost to an organisation

There are a number of practical steps that an organisation should take to ensure their compliance with the Data Protection Act. Whilst these form the foundations of good data handling practice they inevitably add costs to the organisation's use and management of IS. The first section of this chapter considered the systematic management of IS security, and this is a legal requirement of the Data Protection Act. The Act talks of Computer Bureaux in many instances, that is to recognise that these bureaux have data security responsibilities even when they are not the ultimate data user. Bureaux are not the only bodies required to be concerned with data security and conventional data users have a responsibility to maintain adequate security over the data they process.

Developing the organisation's policies and procedures relating to the Data Protection Act is the first move towards demonstrating that the organisation is taking its responsibilities and duties seriously. These policies and procedures should be subject to periodic review to ensure that the automatic processing of personal data does not conflict with the principles of the Data Protection Act. Management needs to impress on staff that they, as well as the company, are individually liable to conviction under the Act if found guilty of knowingly or recklessly contravening its provisions. This includes ensuring the correct *disposal* of information; the Registrar highlighted an incident where a member of the public found a printout near a rubbish tip, the data user was warned for unauthorised disclosure and required to renew their disposal practices.

In another example of unauthorised disclosure, the siting of a terminal in a department store meant that personal data was entered on the screen in full view of other customers, the data subject complained and the data user was prosecuted and required to rearrange their terminals. These examples indicate the need to invest in staff training and awareness campaigns to show how such innocuous incidents can, under the Act, create serious consequences. Certainly the organisation must provide staff with training in how they need to respond to the demands of the Data Protection Act, and this could include the use of leaflets, hand-outs, letters, notices, briefings, videos, training sessions, etc. Training is expensive, but as ignorance of the law is not accepted as a defence, it is an important aspect of compliance.

Such data protection 'housekeeping' measures as money spent on training and improved data management procedures will aid an organisation's defence in potential civil actions by demonstrating that 'reasonable care' was taken to comply with the Act. A sensible further precaution is to extend public liability insurance to cover any civil action that may arise. The most immediate impact of the subject access provisions is that it requires organisations to be much more open about the information they hold and their assessment of employees.

Registration is the first problem encountered by many organisations since the registration form is broad and somewhat vague, and potentially creates the following expensive situations:

1  Registration when not required
2  Broad-based registrations in order to avoid potential prosecutions
3  Multiple registration to deter subject access

The £75 fee is not the only cost of registration; organisations covered by the Act need to undertake systems and procedures audits to register correctly, but most must also develop systems and controls to ensure that any *subsequent* changes to registration are identified and the Registrar informed. This is necessary to ensure that the offence of 'knowing or recklessly using ... data other than as described in the register entry' is avoided. The cost of these audits in large organisations will be very high and, in large or small organisations, the expertise to undertake such audits may not exist, meaning that consultants will have to be called in. In an attempt to reduce the costs (or recognising a market opportunity) the NCC have produced a software package to store and print registration forms.

Additional staff costs are a tangible cost of the Act, for instance many large organisations employ Data Protection Controllers where the main responsibilities of such controllers are to:

1  Be the focus for any queries relating to the Act
2  Provide education and training as necessary
3  Submit new or amended registration requests
4  Complete annual audit of data holdings
5  Conduct periodic monitoring of Data Protection Act access requests and queries

More intangible than the cost of additional staff or additional training courses is the cost of the effort required to implement procedures and processes to ensure that the data is well protected, is totally accurate and is accessible to the data subject upon request. These procedures and processes may result in the organisation making significant changes to the way they operate and significant capital investments. Such costs are obviously ongoing ones but may generate benefits well beyond the avoidance of non-compliance fines and penalties. The financial costs of complying with the Act can be high. Changes imposed on the credit information industry have, they claim, cost £ billions in incurred bad debts on top of £ millions in software changes; however these figures are certainly open to dispute.

Other costs inherent in the Data Protection Act may include the image that a customer develops of an organisation based upon access to what was designed as *internal* data. This data may have *commercially* adequate accuracy and yet still be deemed inaccurate by the data subject, who may also be adversely influenced by the speed of providing the requested information.

### Privacy concerns despite the Data Protection Act

There are a number of potential problems inherent in the Data Protection Act. The significance of each of them will depend upon an individual's perception of the privacy debate. A major issue with the Act is that an individual is effectively powerless to prevent a disclosure of information regarding them if the data user is registered and the disclosure is covered in the registration. Similarly, many regard the Representation of the People (Amendment) Regulations (1990), which force Electoral Registrars to sell the register to anyone who places an order, as compromising privacy and the Data Protection Act since it transfers personal information, legitimately obtained, but which an individual may not wish to be distributed. Perhaps of more minor concern is that the Act's privacy coverage is limited to:

- Individuals only and not companies
- No rights for the deceased which may cause distress to relatives

The Act is intended to be largely self-policing, the hope being that data subjects, through the exercise of their right of access, will be the main instrument of monitoring data users to ensure the quality of data. This monitoring has been of only limited effectiveness for several reasons, including:

- The information provided in the public register is very broad, which means that potential enquirers have difficulty ascertaining what data different organisations are holding and processing, and, in the case of multiple registrations, the correlation between them. This vagueness can be compounded by difficulties in actually finding a register to examine.
- The mechanism as provided for subject access is somewhat unwieldy to operate and susceptible to poor results.
- If a subject access reveals errors, there are further problems with the right to compensation, unlike the Consumer Credit Act 1974 where compensation is awarded; under the terms of the Data Protection Act 1984, the subject needs to go to court in order to get compensation.

The Act also raises concerns for the data user. The provision of subject access levies a cost on the data user and some are concerned that the £10 maximum fee does not cover the full cost incurred in obtaining and disclosing the necessary information whilst others are concerned that the frequency of reasonable access is not defined. The vagueness and complexity of some sections of the Act cause registration problems for data users, for instance what is the status of a bookseller's list that contains book titles and book sales figures; if the author were identifiable by any other information then the list would be classed as personal data, although, at first inspection, it does not seem to be. The restrictions that registration place upon data usage and disclosure can also restrict business innovation since, if the usage or disclosure was not originally planned for, then alterations must be made to the registration *before* the new data use can be made. This may cause operational problems, and, although registrations in the post are judged acceptable, there is always the possibility of a refusal meaning that the innovative data use is in breach of the law.

Despite the many potential problems, the Act is increasing in significance; a good indicator is that the complaints rise annually whilst the Data Protection Office is, with experience, becoming more adept at dealing with them, complaint resolutions times being:

| | |
|---|---|
| 36 per cent | 3 months |
| 67 per cent | within 6 months |
| 9 per cent | longer than 1 year |

During 1992 the Data Protection Office received 2 700 complaints, and 60 per cent of these complaints related in some way to credit checking and the Office has had a number of successes with improving the data protection procedures of the credit agencies. In one instance the tribunal decided that the search procedures used by CCN Systems, a major credit reference agency, were unfair and credit checking can no longer use the data subject's address as the key search item around which to build a credit history. To comply with the eight data protection principles they must use name only.

The Data Protection Act is not the only piece of legislation that confers data responsibilities and rights; the Companies Act makes organisations responsible for the security of company statements and the Consumer Credit Act 1974 allows the data subject to see their credit reference data. The Data Protection Registrar is particularly concerned with the data protection processes of the credit checking agencies and draws the attention of data subjects to the addresses of the four main credit checking agencies, and reminds them that, by sending £1, the Consumer Credit Act provides for any data subject to obtain a copy of their credit reference file. In fact, since the Consumer Credit Act 1974 allows for the data subject to have access to all credit reference data held, irrespective of storage media or processing intent, then there is no need for Data Protection Act provision of access rights and so this data type forms one of the access exemptions.

## 13.3.2 ◆ Copyright and software protection

This section will consider the laws that ensure an organisation is complying with the ownership rights of others whilst protecting its own 'inventions'. In both these instances it is *intellectual* property protection that is being discussed. There are many facets to intellectual property protection, the main ones being copyright, patents, trademarks and designs. There are some significant differences in law between the protection offered to the different IS elements. Mensching and Adams (1991) suggest that existing laws have catered adequately for protecting ownership rights on hardware developments since hardware devices are usually covered by patent law. However, they feel that the large investment in software is not so adequately protected. Certainly software developers make major investments and their investments must be protected and, if they are not, then many speculative, and hence vulnerable, moves would be halted, to the detriment of the overall IS industry. By contrast, protection that is too draconian will stifle innovation and technology transfer; suppose Newton had patented all acknowledgement of the law of gravity? Confidence, patents and copyright legislation seek to balance these two tensions. The main thrusts of the different legal protections are summarised in Figure 13.24.

The UK Patents Act 1977 protects monopoly rights to inventions. However since it specifically excludes as inventions programs for computers and the presentation of information its relevance to IS is limited. Only those organisations developing new hardware components or physical devices with embedded software can use this form of protection. Similarly, whilst some areas of an organisation may be directly concerned with protecting trademarks, and so need to call upon the Trade Marks Act 1938, it will be rare that IS management falls into this category.

| Method | Protection offered | Item protected | Weakness |
|--------|--------------------|-----------------|----------|
| *Confidence* (American notion of trade secrets) | Protects ideas and methods of implementation | Both hardware and software | Makes development and marketing difficult |
| *Copyright* | Prevents copying of the expression of an idea | Software | Does not protect ideas themselves |
| *Patent* | Right to control a novel product or process (a unique combination may also be protected) | Hardware | With the exception of embedded elements, software not covered |

**Fig 13.24 ◆ Types of legal protection**

### Confidence

Ways of working, plans and interactions are all trade secrets and protection for them is achieved through the law of confidentiality. This protection is created where there is a direct contractual obligation. For example, were a member of the IS function to be aware of their department's plans to develop an innovative use of IS they are duty bound not to disclose this. If employment contracts define confidentiality obligations these are generally upheld in court. If these obligations are not defined it may be necessary to determine the degree of good faith in any disclosure. Once employment ceases, employers cannot unreasonably restrict an employee's right to work. For example, a past employee would be free to use skills, however expensively supported, acquired whilst in employment. Disclosure of knowledge of secret trade processes can be restricted post-employment.

The situation is more complicated in the case of indirect employees. With the growth of the 'shamrock' organisation discussed in Chapter 8, this is of increasing concern. Implied rights of confidence exist only when there is a provable relationship in which it is reasonable and acknowledged to expect confidentiality. Using contracts to define specific confidentiality obligations for consultants, joint-venture partners and the like is strongly advised.

### Copyright

The Copyright, Designs and Patents Act 1988 confirms that software is a 'literary' work for the purpose of copyright. Copyright means that there are a number of actions that only the copyright owner may do, these are:

- To copy the work
- To issue copies of the work to the public (including rental of copies)
- To perform, show, or play the work in public
- To broadcast the work or include it in a cable programme service
- To make an adaptation of the work or do any of the above with an adaptation

Adaptation is obviously a restricted act, and this includes any translation in and out of compilers, de-compilers or different language levels. Source code is clearly copyright but the position for object code is often far less clear, except as an adaptation of the original source code. Activities considered 'fair-dealing', and therefore acceptable, are using the protected material for purposes of research or private study, criticism, review, or news reporting. The Copyright (Computer Programs) Regulations 1992 make permissible some further actions specific to computer programs, such as taking a back-up copy. Semiconductors (chips) are covered by their own special form of the Copyright, Designs and Patents Act 1988. Design Right (Semiconductor Regulations) 1988 came into force on 1 August 1989.

A software licence is the permission to do something normally forbidden by copyright. The licence then moves the concerns into those associated with contract law, to be discussed in Section 13.3.3. The Copyright (Computer Programs) Regulations (1992) place design materials into the same category as source and object code, and that is as literary works for copyright. It should be noted that damages for contravention of copyright are not the full cost of the software development, but rather set to represent a notional lost licence fee, perhaps equivalent to a ten per cent royalty.

Copyright protects only the expression of an idea and not the underlying idea itself. It can be extremely difficult to separate these two concepts and so software copyright raises many issues of the legality of reverse engineering since copyright protects primarily the source code and documentation. It is the extension of this legal notion that has led to the numerous American 'look and feel' copyright cases. The look and feel of software can be judged as part of its expression rather than part of its underlying idea or purpose. If the look and feel are part of the expression, and can be identified, then they are protected by copyright; this concept is explored later in this section.

The law is not the *only* way of protecting software. Where legal protection is considered insufficient then other measures can be taken, many being issues of IS security, discussed in Section 13.1, but may include randomising blocks in the source code to disguise its logic even when the object code is dis-assembled. At the extreme end of user inconvenience is the need for hardware devices to be present for the software to work and, at the other extreme of least user inconvenience, are lower prices to make illegal copies less attractive. Elaborate copy protection on software is declining in popularity since it has often worked against the lawful user more forcefully than the software pirate who simply 'cracked' the copy protect routines. The appropriateness of protection options very much depends upon the scale of operations involved but, besides hardware-based protection systems, software or administrative systems can be used to provide protection. Increasingly the value of intellectual property assets is recognised and IS management may be charged with developing a coherent strategy with respect to managing such assets. Rabino and Enayati (1995) outline offensive as well as defensive ways of addressing intellectual property management. These are illustrated in Figure 13.25.

### Software piracy

There is no *legal* distinction between the breach of copyright of a mass-market product or of a bespoke development but the central concerns do differ. For that reason, software package piracy is discussed as distinct from the copyright on

| Defensive strategies | Offensive strategies |
| --- | --- |
| 1 Identify intellectual property assets and establish asset protection schemes. | 1 Identify indirect barriers to entry in desired international markets in order to establish a proprietary position in as many markets as possible. |
| 2 Define and profile target markets according to pre-established criteria (growth, potential, competitive threats and opportunities, etc.) | 2 Identify direct barriers in desired market and deal with these barriers, for instance with the threat of infringement suits. |
| 3 Identify the appropriate form of legal protection by matching target characteristics with viable asset protection schemes. | |
| 4 Adopt a comprehensive in-house intellectual property policy monitoring trends in legislation and technology. | |

**Fig 13.25 ◆ Example strategies for managing intellectual property assets**
(adapted from Intellectual Property: The Double-Edged Sword by Rabino and Enayati, *Long Range Planning*, Vol 28 No 5, © 1995 with kind permission from Elsevier Science Ltd)

bespoke developments, whether in-house or not. What is described here as 'software piracy' is the clearly detectable copying of commercially available software. It is usually popular PC software that is the subject of this piracy since it is readily copyable and readily saleable, and so many people have access to the skills, equipment and interest necessary to take illegal copies. In software piracy it is *detection* that is the critical issue; in the next section the breach of copyright associated with development work itself is considered where the issue of establishing *similarity* is the critical one. So this section discusses the legal relationship between a software *developer* and the software *user* whilst the next section discusses the legal relationship between one software developer and another.

With the large amount of money invested in software package developments software houses are understandably concerned to protect their investment. The illegal use of packaged software is now so extensive that there are a number of pressure groups (driven by the major software developers) dedicated to reducing the extent of this piracy. The best known UK group is the Federation Against Software Theft (FAST) whilst a world-wide equivalent is the Business Software Alliance (BSA). Both of these groups campaign to tighten laws on software copying and detect and prosecute breaches of the existing law. Despite their efforts the Copyright (Computer Programs) Regulations 1992 extended the software user's rights awarded in the Copyright, Designs and Patents Act 1988 in line with European Community Directive of 1991 (91/250/EEC). This amendment awards three rights to the legitimate software user:

- The right, under certain circumstances, to 'decompile' an existing computer program
- The right to take necessary back-up copies
- The right to copy and adapt, including for error correction

Software sellers cannot lawfully impose software licences that remove either of the first two of these rights. Licences cannot now purport to forbid the use of any means to observe, study, or test the functioning of the system, in order to understand it. However, decompiling is not permitted if the data needed to understand the system is reasonably available or needed for an unlawful infringement. If only a small part of the software is decompiled then this would not have been an infringement under the previous (1988) Act. The necessity to take lawful back-ups is obvious, but such copies must only be retained for safety purposes and not be used to multiply the instances of use. The third right is the least commonly available since software licences can, and often will, override to forbid it although, if not expressly forbidden, errors can be fixed by someone else. Some exceptions apply, but restrictions to the lawfulness of licence terms took affect only after 1 January 1993.

The extent of software piracy is hard to gauge. For instance, the BSA, on the basis of their own annual surveys, claim that software piracy in the UK currently costs the software industry between £300–400 million in lost sales each year. The BSA agree that piracy rates are falling and legally licensed packages represent a growing percentage of the packages in use. The BSA estimated the 1995 UK piracy rates as being approximately 49 per cent, which makes the UK one of only *six* countries worldwide with piracy rates of below 50 per cent. In contrast, the BSA estimate piracy rates in the Russian Federation to be at 98 per cent.

Software piracy seems to come in a number of forms. It can be an international money-maker involving organised rings counterfeiting named brands, such as Microsoft products, including all the packaging, and this clearly involves criminal intent. At the other end of the scale, however, and far more common as Figure 13.26 shows, is the ignorance copying done on an *ad hoc*, personal basis, although this ignorance copying is no less illegal for all that.

With the majority of offenders being the ignorant rather than the deliberately criminal, the activities of FAST and BSA are targeted at making software users *aware*, firstly of the law on copying, and then secondly of their own organisation's situation regarding the software copies it uses. The 'advice' that FAST provides

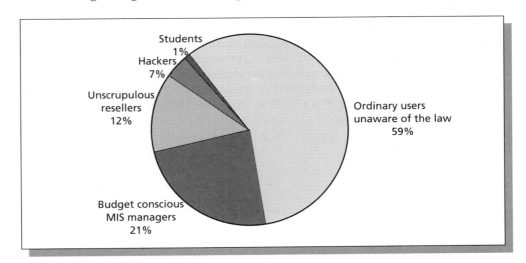

**Fig 13.26 ◆ Offender analysis of 1 100 software piracy investigations: 1992**
(source: Federation Against Software Theft)

falls into two parts, guidelines for software management and guidelines for software use, both illustrated in Figures 13.27a and 13.27b. Much of the lobbying by FAST and BSA plays upon warnings to organisations about the *costs* of being illegal. These *costs* come from fines, the need to purchase the software being run (plus any upgrades produced in the interim) but also from the fact that unacknowledged software makes version control, software support and integration difficult and takes up storage space needed for legitimate software.

---

### SOFTWARE MANAGEMENT CHARTER

**How to set up a software policy to deter theft:**

1 Ensure staff understand the law and its penalties:
   - Circulate a software code of conduct and distribute leaflets, posters and stickers to promote user awareness.

2 Appoint a software auditor:
   - This could be an employee or an external consultant who can conduct an internal audit regularly, collate the information gathered and use it as a basis for monitoring software use

3 Conduct audits and regular unannounced software inspections:
   - Look for software licence documentation or proof of purchase and match with software in use;
   - Ensure upgrades are not used as additional copies;
   - Reallocate software not being used (where the program licence permits);
   - Destroy any illegal copies.

4 Maintain a register of all software bought and its location, in particular make accurate notes of the following:
   - The date and source of software acquisitions, including details of site licences, volume discounts or network version terms;
   - The location and serial number of the hardware on which each copy of the software is installed;
   - The name of the authorised user;
   - The existence and location of back-up copies.

5 Ensure secure storage of original software media:
   - By providing secure storage for original program media you can reduce the risk of software theft and illegal copying.

6 Budget enough and plan ahead to meet future needs:
   - By allocating an adequate software budget urgent requests can be met promptly, thereby eliminating illegal copying encouraged by job requirements.

7 Initiate internal disciplinary procedures for illegal copiers:
   - No organisation can tolerate or condone law-breaking. Employees need to understand that as software theft jeopardises the entire organisation, illegal copiers will be treated with extreme severity.

**Controlling software helps you:**
- Minimise the risk of prosecution
- Make more effective use of software
- Control your hardware and software investment
- Cut the cost of training and support
- Reduce the risk of virus infection
- Protect your company's reputation.

**With legal software you may get:**
- Product guarantees
- User manuals and tutorials
- Telephone support
- Upgrades and updates.

---

**Fig 13.27a ◆ Legal software management**
(source: Federation Against Software Theft)

---

### SOFTWARE USE CODE OF CONDUCT

*Remember*
- Software copying, or using unauthorised software, is asking for trouble. Don't jeopardise your organisation and career
- If you need software, make sure you obtain proper licensed copies
- If you want to make a back-up copy, check the software program licence permits you to do this
- Keep your program media securely (preferably under lock and key) when not in use
- Keep a record of the software resident on your PC
- Unauthorised software may contain viruses which may ruin your programs and your data. They may even contaminate the whole network.

*Don't*
- Don't copy software
- Don't share software with colleagues to make copies
- Don't make additional non-licensed copies if you are using a network
- Don't make copies of your software to take home
- Don't accept 'free' software from colleagues or friends.

**Fig 13.27b ◆ Legal software use**
(source: Federation Against Software Theft)

All of these figures should be treated with caution since they suffer from two problems. Firstly, estimates of the number of pirated copies in existence are open to question, and secondly and more critically, every pirated copy, whilst illegal, does *not* represent a lost sale. BSA and FAST are federations of software vendors and so their pronouncements should be judged accordingly. It is interesting that the anti-piracy pressure groups are not taking action in Eastern Europe even though piracy is far more prevalent there than in Western Europe. The software vendors may recognise the long-term financial advantage of 'locking-in' new users at an early stage of their commercial computing, despite the short-term financial losses caused by the prevalence of pirating.

FAST make much of the fact that illegal software is generally not known about and, if no one knows software is there, clearly it is not needed. A major tool in ensuring the legality of all software used is the software audit. Auditing lets an organisation know what software it has, such knowledge can then be used to synchronise upgrades, versions, and support, target back-ups and recovery after disasters, and monitor access, not just to detect 'criminals' but to log the *usefulness* of all software. The issue of IS asset auditing is of relevance beyond compliance with licenses, see for example the discussion in Chapter 7 of the *value* of IS assets. Many external auditors offer services that combine both such intents. Figure 13.28 gives an example set of such services.

FAST does not provide any discussion of the legality of the vendor's copying restrictions, naturally enough it takes the line of helping organisations to meet such restrictions, and there is no doubt that using software for which a legal entitlement is not held is a crime. Unfortunately it is not always that simple to be sure that all software used is being *legally* used and that is the role of software auditing. Given

**Virus check:**

- By using anti-virus packages, will cleanse systems of all infections. Cost is from £35 a workstation or from £350 per day.

**Asset audit:**

- A complete audit of the hardware or software or both, presented in any format, as a listing, in a spreadsheet or database, on an asset register or other form. This level of service will cost around £75 a workstation or £400 per day. The price will rise if adjustments are to be made to the system.

**Network audit:**

- Anti-virus and recording of all systems details is included in this audit. Servers are defragmented, back-up procedures are checked and parameters can be changed. Systemhouse charge £695 per day for this service and prefer not to work on a per workstation basis because it is hard to tell exactly what needs to be done until the systems have been reviewed. A firm price for the work may not be quoted until an initial assessment has been made.

**Performance audit:**

- This is more of a productivity review than an audit. Systemhouse will check what is on the system and assess its value to the business. Versions and various application's options are explored as well as access rights and the deployment of the operating system. Prices again are towards the top end of the scale.

Fig 13.28 ◆ Levels of Systemhouse system audits

the difficulty of guaranteed legality when licences are so complex, many organisations may feel 'bullied' into corporate membership of FAST to avoid FAST and BSA 'raiding' their premises. It is generally suggested by software *users* that software *vendors* could contribute to increasing the legal use of software by simplifying licence rules and making site licences cheaper and easier to obtain. Most FAST and BSA raids lead to legal actions being taken but these are mostly settled out of court so the licensing rules are never subject to full scrutiny.

### Systems development protection

Software piracy is essentially concerned with the legislation that applies once the pirated copy has been located, it applies to those who have irrefutably copied a piece of software, usually a software package. This section however, looks at the legislative protection of the works of hardware and software developments from other would-be developers, rather than simply users. Since such development protection must apply to bespoke work, Section 13.3.3 considers the related area of contract law.

The central issue in protecting the work of one software developer from the unlawful actions of another developer is to establish whether a protected aspect of the work has been duplicated in breach of copyright under the Copyright, Designs and Patents Act 1988 or the Copyright (Computer Programs) Regulations 1992. Since copyright can protect the expression of an idea but not the idea itself it can be very difficult to assess the fact, or extent, of duplication. Hunt (1993) explains that the decompilation of an existing piece of software to create something else that can work with it is perfectly legal. Inter-operability needs allow decompiling and such decompilation cannot be excluded by the contractual agreements defined in the software licence (if they were contracted after 1 January 1993). Although inter-operability is a legal motive for decompilation this right is limited and cannot result in:

- Using the information obtained for any other purpose
- Extending the activities beyond those strictly necessary for the decompilation
- Supplying the information obtained to any third person except where necessary in connection with achieving the decompilation.
- Using the information to develop, produce or market a program that is substantially similar to the original program.

With the emphasis in law upon ownership when establishing copyright it is necessary for an organisation to recognise the very real difference between internal and external staff, with the default ownership state being:

- Work written by an internal employee in the normal course of their employment, ownership is held by the employer
- Work written by a consultant belongs to the consultant unless the contract assigns the copyright.

Strategic developments, major in-house developments and almost all developments if the organisation is a software house, the need to recognise the value of staff and the potential damages their leaving could cause; the value of these can be protected through sensible and reasonable restriction clauses. The trend towards the shamrock organisation (*see* Chapter 8), and so ever greater use of external staff, makes establishing ownership of copyright very important.

Hart (1988) was amongst the first to question the identity of the owner of the copyright of *computer-generated* works, the possibilities being:

- The creator of the program which generates the work
- The originator of the data upon which the computer operates to generate the work
- The person responsible for running the computer to produce the work
- A combination of any of these

Computer-generated works fall into three categories:

1 Works created *using* a computer: Copyright probably held by the author and not the operator, or the creator of the computer program used as a tool.
2 Works created *by* a computer: Copyright held by the owner of the software.
3 Intermediate works: Where the skill needed to generate the finished product is held jointly by the developer of the software and the user of it. The author of the finished work is the vendor and needs to be covered by contractual agreements.

With so many decision support aids, including expert systems and other intelligent devices and computer-generated graphics, etc, the question of copyright ownership becomes ever more critical.

## 13.3.3 ◆ Contracts

Contract law covers the basic process of negotiation and execution of a legal contract for services. It is this law that ensures an organisation of adequate legal protection whilst making acquisitions (*see* Chapter 12 for more detailed coverage of the acquisition process). Contract law applies to IS in the same manner as it does to any other manifestation of a contractual situation, that the process of striking a legal contract occurs whenever an arrangement is made to provide goods or services in return for payment. Under these circumstances a contract, even if it is an informal one, is formed. (Although verbal promises of performance do form a contract, these should be formally defined in any written contract to give some certainty of enforcement.) A contract must include an exchange of some value and is defined by a two-stage process:

1 The offer of goods or services for specific remuneration; this statement of willingness to deal will expire after a certain time
2 The acceptance of the offered arrangements; agreement to the offered goods or service under the specific terms

The only unique aspect of contracts for elements of information systems is the complex interaction of those elements and therefore the problem in contracts for computer services is mainly one of defining the expectations in unambiguous terms.

The more specific are the written terms of any contract the clearer are the rights and responsibilities of the two contracted parties. The clearer the contract is, the less danger there is of either party defaulting and so leading the other into the need for expensive legal redress. Any contract should define the provisions of the agreement and present the performance requirements in such a way that it is quite clear when they have been breached. A 'good' contract adds, to the clear definition of required performance, a clear indication of the agreed recourse for any breach of this performance. There are two forms of breach of contract:

• *Breach of condition*: Where a *key* element of the contract has been breached, for instance the failure to deliver to specification

• *Breach of warranty*: Where a more minor element of the contract has been breached, for instance the interruption of service or delay in meeting delivery specification.

Breach of condition justifies a cancellation of the contract, breach of warranty does not. After a dissolution of the contract, legally called rescission, any goods or payments exchanged must be returned to each party. For a breach of warranty there may be specific money charges attached to various levels of non-performance. These charges, legally called liquidated damages, are best defined in the contract, otherwise the courts must estimate the impact of the particular contractual failure. When a contract provides coverage of specific contractual points judges generally interpret the terms strictly; where there are no such clauses then they will be implied.

If liquidated damages (the amount, or method of calculating the amount, of damages) are fixed at the contract stage and attached to a particular requirement then, by estimating the damages, there is the implied acceptance that this requirement is not a *condition* clause. That is, where damages can be associated with a particular clause that clause is not one that would entitle the cancellation of the contract.

Indeterminate or innominate clauses are not defined as condition or warranty clauses at the contract stage, but rather acquire their definition at the breach stage. Whilst pragmatically useful, the lack of certainty can make it unclear whether, under a particular set of circumstances, the parties have the right of cancellation.

The computer press is always full of tales of contractual difficulties. In one typical example, given by Bicknell (1992), the Salvage Association was disputing the quality of a bespoke software development by CAP Financial Services whilst CAP was claiming that the bugs in the contracted system were 'in sight of' repair (making them warranty, rather than them condition, terms) and, in any case, the faults were the result of the changes in requirements from the original contract. Because of contractual uncertainties many claims are settled out of court. Contracts apportion risk and care must therefore be taken since, although the difficulties of definition may be peculiar to computing contracts, the contract law is not. The Chartered Institute of Purchase and Supply (CIPS) have published a series of ten model contracts covering hardware supply and installation, buying bespoke software and negotiating licence agreements. The CIPS suggest that *any* contract should clearly define seven areas:

1 Functionality
2 Reliability
3 Performance
4 Portability
5 Maintainability
6 Availability
7 Economy

Reynolds (1992) also suggests seven points that should be included in a contract, this time when it is with a *consultant*. These are:

1 Specify what deliverables will constitute acceptable completion of the assignment
2 Define a time schedule for completing each deliverable
3 Obtain an estimated cost for every deliverable
4 Specify certain daily sums to be deducted from the amount owed if the consultant fails to meet certain time performance limitations
5 Specify the right to terminate at will without prior written notice
6 Require regular written status reports or meetings on a regular and specified basis
7 Clearly identify the responsibilities of both the client and the consultant

With the increased use of consultants the contract should also make provision for retention of copyright since, by default, it resides with the consultant. Time-based contracts can be problematic since they make it financially attractive to 'spin-out' the work, or even, as illustrated by the case described in one news report (*Computing* 8 July 1993), to sabotage the project to maximise earnings. In this instance, a contract programmer was accused of delaying a Dun and Bradstreet development project by several months to continue in the lucrative (£1 000 a week) employment.

The law can address verbal discussions that do not make it into the contract. If such promises are not fulfiled they may be misrepresentations, and either:

• fraudulent

• negligent

• innocent.

If the misrepresentation is made as fraud or recklessly, that is not caring whether they are true or not, then cancellation of the contract is legal and the rescission makes it as if the contract had never been, so the injured party can recover any money already paid out. It is, however, wiser *not* to assume that verbal promises can be taken to legally define contract breaches. Performance claims not substantiated could be a matter of fraud but that is far harder to prove since *pre-contract* representatives are not legally binding. However a 1993 Romtec survey indicates that 87 per cent of the 80 IS users questioned would like to see this situation changed. (The same survey found extensive ignorance about contract liability limitations.) These results are shown in Figure 13.29.

Contracts for IS elements will fall under two different laws. Hardware will be covered by the Sale of Goods Act 1979, as amended by the Sale and Supply of Goods Act 1994 but the supply of bespoke software is covered by the Supply of Goods and Services Act 1982. The position of off-the-shelf software packages is not entirely clear, although the 1996 ruling on the *ICL* v. *St Albans High Court* appeal discussed later indicates that a software package will be covered by the Sale of Goods Act. Even more confused is which Act is applicable when making purchases of 'bundled' IS elements involving both hardware and ready written software, and perhaps including some bespoke customising work. Bainbridge (1993) suggests using the 'predominant purpose of the purchase' as the deciding factor, that is did the buyer consider themselves to be primarily acquiring hardware or software? The Sale and Supply of Goods Act 1994 states (in a section derived from the earlier Sale of Goods Act 1979):

2(1) A contract of sale of goods is a contract by which the seller transfers or agrees to transfer the property in goods to the buyer for a money consideration called the price and that the goods must be of merchantable quality.

So for items that can be defined as 'goods' this Act applies and offers the comprehensive regulation of the contract and that the goods match their description, be fit for the purpose, be of satisfactory quality and the seller has the right to sell. Goods are defined as:

*All personal chattels other than things in action and money.*

The Sale and Supply of Goods Act therefore covers hardware items that may encompass some embedded software and the protection offered by the terms of this Act cannot be excluded or overridden by contractual provisions. The purchase of bespoke software is primarily the purchase of a service (it is certainly a 'thing in

| | No | Yes | Don't know |
|---|---|---|---|
| Should contracts exclude salesmen's pre-sales promises to customers? | 87% | 10% | 3% |
| Would you welcome contractual provision of arbitration process to avoid legal disputes? | 3% | 96% | 1% |

**Fig 13.29 ◆ 1993 survey of opinions on IS contracts**
(source: Romtec)

action' that cannot be touched or moved) and not of goods as defined by the Sale of Goods Act, as amended, and is therefore covered by the less comprehensive Supply of Goods and Services Act 1982.

IS and contracts do produce 'special' difficulties. For example, as Newman (1988) explores, the use of electronic forms of communication can make it unclear *when* an agreement has been reached. Contracts become binding when an offer is accepted. To cater for distance between parties Postal Rules exist that make a contract binding as soon as an acceptance is *sent* through the post. It is unclear as to what electronic forms Postal Rules may apply. Postal Rules do not cover instantaneous forms of communication such as the telephone or telex (nor the couriering of acceptances). A contract acceptance may be sent by E-mail, as is increasingly the case with Internet shopping and electronic trading. It is unclear at what time, and equally importantly under what country's jurisdiction, the contract comes into being.

As well as special difficulties when using IS to *construct* a contract there are many when the contract is *about* IS. For instance the 'provision' of a system may happen before it is actually *usable*. Bull (1995), for example, points out that the Supply of Goods and Services Act 1982 requires 'reasonable' payment to be made by a 'reasonable' time after supply. The complexity of IS projects makes it difficult to establish just when the goods and services are supplied. Unless the contract explicitly addresses the matter, delivery of the hardware, software and documentation may be taken to constitute the delivery of the bulk of the costs even though without testing, training, connections to other systems, etc these have little usable value. As with most instances of potential contract difficulties, be they IS related or not, the management best practice is to have a clear and unambiguous contract. Bull (1995) argues for the inclusion of a payment schedule that identifies at what roll-out stage what proportion of the total payment (and what penalties to impose for lateness of each stage) will be made. Extending this advice, McNevin (1995) identifies ten steps to take to avoid the need for court intervention, These are:

- Set clear parameters for projects
- Avoid long, complicated projects
- Ensure suppliers are adequately qualified and have sufficient resources to carry out projects
- Contracts should either contain a penalty clause or be fixed price
- Get down to the contractual issues at an early stage
- Resolve disputes before they happen by constantly discussing expectations
- Avoid unreal expectations
- Be aware of mutual expectations
- A good contract is something you never look at again
- Avoid 'scope creep' where projects get out of hand

Even following these ten steps an organisation cannot *always* avoid the need for recourse to adjudication. This may not always be the courts. Various alternative forms of dispute resolution and mediation may be used. Sometimes though only contract litigation will deal with the problem. How to prepare for such an eventuality was clearly illustrated in a landmark case on IS contracts in July 1996 when ICL lost its High Court appeal against damages awarded to St Albans District

Council for a faulty Poll Tax system. As Collins (1996) argues, St Albans won because:

- the requirements were specified unequivocally
- it explicitly stated that all systems should meet all legislation, even that not yet enacted
- records were kept of all correspondence and conversations with the supplier
- all the specifications and the invitation to tender were bundled into the contract

This text-book handling of an IS contract did more than demonstrate what the attributes of contract management should be. The legal implications of this case lie in four areas, summarised by Hayward (1996) as:

- In a contract between a supplier and an end user, a liability-limitation clause which has been taken without substantial change from the supplier's standard terms and conditions is subject to the Unfair Contract Terms Act 1977 (UCTA). This means the clause can be tested for 'reasonableness' by a court, even though it was freely accepted by the end user during negotiations. To avoid UCTA applying, suppliers must change these clauses by negotiation.

- When a supplier agrees to supply a system designed to meet requirements set by changing legislation, it accepts the obligation to meet changes demanded by future, unforeseen legislation. Deadlines set by the changing legislation over-ride those in the original contract, unless the supplier renounces the obligation in its contract.

- An application sold as a package can be treated as a good, and is therefore subject to the Sale of Goods Act 1979, as amended by the Sale and Supply of Goods Act 1994 i.e. it must be of satisfactory quality and fit for the purpose supplied. Software produced under a development contract between two parties cannot be treated as a good, but the contract nevertheless contains an unspoken 'implied term' under which the software must be 'reasonably fit for its intended purpose'.

- Local councils have the right to reclaim money lost to their taxpayers through faulty software. ICL had argued that because the inhabitants of St Albans – rather than the council – had suffered the loss in question, the council could not recover any sums.

The fact that software packages could be considered as goods is particularly interesting since the Sale of Goods Act 1974, as amended by the 1994 Act, is quite specific as to the requirements of satisfactory quality. Goods must be satisfactory for all of their usual purposes. Section 14(2B) of the Act states that the quality of goods includes:

> their state and condition and the following (among others) in appropriate cases aspects of the quality of the goods:
>
> (a) fitness for all of the purposes for which goods of the kind in question are commonly supplied,
> (b) appearance and finish,
> (c) freedom from minor defects,
> (d) safety, and
> (e) durability.

By this it becomes possible that software bugs that cause a function normally associated with that style of package (for instance the spellchecker in a wordprocessor) could fall foul of this clause. The Act requires that, if the buyer makes known any particular purpose then the goods must be fit for that purpose. So it is also possible that the purchase of a package for a specific and declared purpose (for example, to work in a particular network environment) that does not, in that context, prove satisfactory would also be a breach.

Almost all business and IS areas will deal with contracts to the extent that software licences are contracts. Most however will engage in more complex contracts for many elements of IS, hardware, software development, and even for IS management services. It should be noted that, other than copyright aspects, conditions made in a software licence that is only readable *after* purchase are unenforceable in law. Since the contract is struck when the goods or service are exchanged for the price then a licence agreement not visible before that time is unlikely to be contractually binding. This means that the status of any term forbidding the taking of a back-up copy is unclear. In any case, if a back-up copy is necessary to the operation of the software then the contract cannot take away that right.

With the increased devolution of the purchasing of the hardware associated with desktop computing, and the increased use of the direct channel of supply, then all business areas need a working knowledge of their rights under the Sale of Goods Act 1979 and the Sale and Supply of Goods Act 1994.

It is particularly necessary to note that the Sale and Supply of Goods Act 1994 makes some important distinctions between consumer and non-consumer buyers. Those new to the responsibility of making IS purchases will find some key differences from the rights they would enjoy as private citizens. When purchasing as a consumer all the terms of the Act are conditions, that is any breach of them gives the buyer the right to rescind the contract, get a refund and claim damges. For a business buyer (a non-consumer) then under a number of situations the terms are warranties instead, that is a breach of terms may not lead the contract to be rescinded, though claims for damages will still be possible. The Act states that its terms will be considered to be warranties and not conditions for non-consumer contracts where

(a) *the breach is so slight that it would be unreasonable for the buyer to reject, and*
(b) *the contract does not show a contrary intention that the terms are to be treated as conditions.*

The business buyer who is more accustomed to purchasing IS goods in a personal capacity should also note that, for non-consumer contracts, it is possible to operate within a contract that specifically excludes particular terms of the Act if it is *reasonable* to do so under the terms of the Unfair Contract Terms Act 1977.

There is one further contract relationship that an organisation may need to engage in, that of issuing or receiving a licence to publish software. Whilst technically this can happen in two ways, through an exclusive licence or the assigning of a copyright which transfers the ownership of the software, there is virtually no difference in practice. The major contractual arrangements will be based around establishing payment terms, either lump sum or royalties based, but such contracts should also cover issues of confidentiality and liability.

### 13.3.4 ◆ Health and safety

Maintaining a safe and healthy work environment is, of course, not *only* a legal requirement; enthusiastic staff are effective staff and poor working conditions do much to destroy morale and motivation, *see* Kavanagh (1994). Given the emphasis of this chapter the concern here is with the legal framework that defines the minimum healthy and safe working environment. Whilst many obvious safety concerns, particularly in computer rooms, such as trailing cables, are well catered for by traditional workplace safety laws, the specific nature of working *with* IS makes new demands upon staff health. This means mainly the issues of defining the nature of 'safe' work with visual display terminals (VDTs) since these are the elements of the technology that the humans must interface with. The VDT is taken to represent the screen, keyboard and all other input or output devices, and the relationship between these elements.

Common sense indicates that a good working environment requires comfortable seats, leg room, regular breaks, an adjustable terminal and good lighting. There are, however, two problems with leaving health and safety maintenance to common sense. The first of these problems is the inevitable early ignorance of the long-term effects of any 'new' industry and its equipment (perhaps this ignorance has been exploited by the prevalence of scare stories in press reporting and advertising). The second problem is that when 'computing' involved only clerks working in specialist data preparation rooms these rooms could be purpose designed (using whatever knowledge of good practice was available at the time) but now the parallel trends of downsizing, distributed processing and user-controlled computing have all placed VDT use in 'unsuitable' places, that is ones that have not been prepared for that purpose and, in any case, must serve *several* purposes.

The use of information technologies has been linked with many health problems. Monitor use has been linked to causing abnormal pregnancy terminations, with causing myopia, with destroying dental fillings and of course with causing eye strain. Not all these links have been proved but monitor safety rules seek to address both health and general environmental concerns about electromagnetic emissions, interference and energy consumption. Keyboard use has been linked to causing carpal tunnel syndrome and to repetitive strain injury (RSI), called Cumulative Trauma Disorder (CDT) in the United States. Keyboards themselves, as opposed to their positioning, are not subject to any ergonomic guidelines or regulations. Despite this, and denials that RSI exists, 'ergonomically' shaped keyboards are made by a number of manufacturers. It is the spatial *relationship* between desk, keyboard, monitor, chair and lighting that is the most likely culprit of the commonest health problems of back and eye strain and head and muscle aches.

The Health and Safety Commission (HSC) is the UK body that must implement the five proposals of the European Directive 90/270/EEC that became the Health and Safety (Display Screen Equipment) Regulations 1992. These regulations apply to all new workstations and to existing ones that are deemed to generate staff health risks. It should be noted that any *major* changes, even to the *software* used on the workstation, makes an existing station count as a new one. The regulations set general objectives for the hardware, software, the environment (lighting, heating, noise), furniture, accessories, peripheral equipment and working practices and health care. The requirements are that employers must:

- Analyse all workstations and take action to remedy any risks which are discovered
- Make sure that workstations satisfy minimum requirements which are set for the display screen, keyboard, desk and chair, working environment and task design and software
- Plan display equipment work so there are breaks and changes of activity
- Provide information and training for display equipment users

For existing, and unmodified, stations organisations had until 31 December 1996 to fully comply with these regulations providing all *immediately* identified risks are removed.

Hall (1992) suggests a number of steps involved in compliance with the regulations:

1 Immediately assessing all workstations
2 Reducing risks
3 Meeting minimum ergonomic standards
4 Planning display screen work
5 Offering eye tests
6 Providing information and training

The HSE estimates that the implementation of these regulations will cost up to £40 million a year, 55 per cent of this on the assessment, risk reduction and minimum ergonomic standards of each workstation and 35 per cent on employer-provided eye tests. Compliance with the regulations is therefore likely to add £40–60 to the cost of equipping a new workstation, figures suggested by Hall and confirmed in Harnett (1993); this represents less than 1 per cent of the overall cost of equipping the workstation and improved productivity may well offset these costs.

It can be difficult to identify equipment that complies with the regulations and British standards exist that can be used, although the law does not make conformance to any standard mandatory; these include BS 5459, covering desks and chairs in detail, and BS 7179 – Ergonomics of design and use of VDTs in offices. Figure 13.30 tabulates the sections of BS 7179 that are of relevance. Equipment purchasers should ensure that equipment conforms to Parts 3 and 4 whilst all organisations should attempt conformance to Parts 2, 5 and 6. Although the International Standards Organisation (ISO) intends to release an international standard, ISO 9241, the British Standard is likely to form the basis of this and so will not be superseded.

---

**Part 2:** Recommendations for the design of office VDU tasks

**Part 3:** Technical specifications for visual displays

**Part 4:** Technical specifications for keyboards

**Part 5:** Specifications for VDU workstations

**Part 6:** A code of practice for the design of VDU work environments

---

**Fig 13.30 ◆ Relevant sections of BS 7179 – Ergonomics of design and use of VDUs**

These regulations apply only to *habitual* users of the technology and therefore mainly address the first of the health and safety problems, in that they provide minimum working conditions for the 'professional' technology user. Except that they *suggest* what is minimum good practice for *all* technology users, they do little to address the second safe use problem. This may matter less than it seems since 'casual' users of devolved computing may often have work patterns that lead to natural breaks whereas 'professional' users, particularly data preparation staff, do not. Any organisation should recognise, however, that working responsibilities change and particular projects may change the nature of staff responsibilities and make them, temporarily or permanently, habitual users of the technology and therefore covered by the regulations. Reid (1993) offers some guidelines to judge when the regulations will apply, that is where most of the following are true:

- There are no practical alternatives to using the VDT to do the job
- There is no choice as to whether to use the equipment
- It needs significant skills in the use of the equipment to do the job
- The equipment is normally used daily for continuous periods of an hour or more at a time
- The job requires the fast transfer of information between the person and the screen
- Performance requirements demand high levels of attention

Whilst compliance is legally required as part of the Health and Safety at Work legislation it is likely that it will be local authority Environmental Health Officers (EHOs) who check and prohibit the use of unsuitable technology where necessary.

### 13.3.5 ◆ Information systems and crime

Much of this chapter has been concerned with civil law, this section, however, is concerned with *criminal* law. Most organisations would consider that privacy is something they must *offer*, copyright is something they *have*, whilst crime is something *done* to them. Information systems offer powerful tools to support the criminally minded but they also generate new crimes. 'Existing' crimes of fraud, theft and damage are covered by the existing legal framework whilst the main legislative vehicle for dealing with the 'new' crimes created by the very existence of IS is the Computer Misuse Act 1990.

For most organisations, computer-assisted theft and fraud are going to be the most significant computer crimes. Under these headings the offences can include, obtaining property or services by deception, false accounting, false company statements, suppression of documents and income tax fraud. It is particularly difficult to charge computer crimes under the deception laws since machines cannot be deceived, this being a human failing. The Audit Commission recognises four types of computer fraud (the survey referred to is the one documented in its 1991 report):

1. Input fraud: Entry of unauthorised instructions, the survey gives 36 examples
2. Data fraud: Alteration of input data, the survey gives 17 examples
3. Output fraud: Suppression of data, the survey gives 14 examples
4. Program fraud: Creating or altering a program to perform a fraudulent act, the survey gives only 6 examples, probably because of difficulty in detection rather than lower frequency

There appears to be an increase in internal theft and fraud of which, according to a 1995 PA Consulting survey, 55 per cent will be computerised. This same survey indicates that computerised fraud and theft costs UK business £5 bn each year, and this figure only covers admitted losses from large organisations. Poor security management (*see* Section 13.1) is often blamed and so too is the 'outsider' culture created by the 'shamrock' organisation in which little inter-personal loyalty is felt. Perhaps computerised crime is another hidden cost of outsourcing as discussed in Section 12.4.3. Yet a further potential cause is the prevalence of an aggressively competitive climate that (at least informally through the 'tales told') advocates that 'anything goes in order to make money'.

Many 'computer' crimes are traditional crimes simply using the computer as a new tool; for instance 'salami slicing' where the computer is set to deposit a small amount of money from every one of a large number of transactions into the criminal's account is a new version of a traditional ledger book crime. Other crimes, such as hacking, viruses or data theft, however, are IS specific. Amongst reported crimes are many incidents of computer-assisted blackmail using viruses, time bombs, etc. In one example, Media Research who produce software used by the record company EMI are suing a freelance programmer, alleging that he planted a time bomb that causes the system to stop periodically. In another example, a freelance employee illicitly installed a commercially available password security package, thereby becoming a hacker, to put a password barrier onto an important system because he claimed he was owed fees. Despite the £36 000 lost business causing the company to cease trading, the judge ruled that this was a 'minor' offence. Possession of computer pornography is also an offence under existing laws. Fears of one crime may lead to a related crime being treated severely, for instance many organisations have made it a sacking offence to run computer games, not because of the misuse of facilities (a crime) but because of the risk of virus infections (only *potentially* a crime).

*Computing* (8 July 1993) report that Chinese authorities take computer-assisted crime very seriously, and in April 1993 they executed Shi Bao, an Agricultural Bank of China employee who embezzled £122 000 by manipulating the bank's computer systems. The UK is rather more lenient and the maximum penalty under the Computer Misuse Act is only five years imprisonment.

One of the most significant of the 'traditional' crimes now directed at IS is that of computer chip theft. A 1996 DTI-sponsored survey found that, whereas in 1994 only 28 per cent of firms had experienced cases of such theft, in 1996 it had nearly doubled to 46 per cent. It is not only user organisations who suffer, manufacturers' delivery vehicles are hijacked and production plants raided. It is the high value/low volume nature of chips and their ready saleability that makes this a problem. In crime terms computer chips have joined tobacco, liquor, cash, etc as vulnerable products.

Carr (1990) doesn't question the *existence* of IS crime, what he, most lucidly, questions is its nature, extent and cost. He challenges both the spurious accuracy of many of the figures quoted and the almost apocryphal basis to the received wisdom. For instance, the CBI 'estimate' of the £400 million cost of computer crime to UK industry seems to be a figure originating at the London Business School but to have gained its credence from repetition rather than from solid foundations. On more certain ground, the Audit Commission conducts a triennial survey into computer fraud and abuse in local authorities and the National Health Service and its findings suggest that, whereas only 16 per cent of fraud cases in 1987 were computer related, by 1990 it was 73 per cent, and 88 per cent by 1994. The Audit Commission reports indicate that such fraud is more likely to be perpetrated by internal staff than by outside hackers and that most reported cases were identified by chance and never *detected* as such. For example, defence IT supplier Ferranti was almost destroyed by a £215 million fraud committed by senior managers of International Signal and Control Group, with which it merged in 1989. The Audit Commission's findings are in line with the received wisdom in this area that 80 per cent of computer crime (and crime in general) is done by insiders committing traditional crimes using the new tools, indicating that the large sums of security expenditures that are targeted at keeping outsiders out might be better re-directed to monitor the activities of *insiders*.

Insurance against computer crime may now be available. In 1992 an American company, Aetna, developed a policy called 'Coverage for Computer and Electronic Network Technology' (Accent) to cover fraud involving systems, wire money transfers, forged faxes, viruses, computer software piracy, toll call fraud, voice-initiated money transfers and service bureau faults. Although it is aimed squarely at American banks, the international nature of these banks means that the insurance cover provided is also international.

Many of the IS-specific crimes come about because modern computer systems, with their dispersed nature, are extremely susceptible to unauthorised access. Bainbridge (1993) offers a nice analogy, likening the modern computer system to the locked filing cabinet that stores valuable data. In the past, this would have been a 'real' filing cabinet locked and stored away in an inaccessible office. However, although the 'cabinet' is still locked, it is now stored in a public place so anyone who finds, or makes, a key to fit the cabinet will be at leisure to look through, alter, or remove the files it contains. Before the Computer Misuse Act 1990 that 'look through' would have been difficult to deal with as a criminal offence, and even copying or making minor amendments would not certainly be criminal. In response to this problem the Computer Misuse Act 1990 created three new offences of unauthorised access (s 1), ulterior intent (s 2) and unauthorised modification (s 3). These sections are described in Figure 13.31. The Computer Misuse Act 1990 also deals with potential loopholes caused by the stateless nature of computer systems. If any of the computers involved in an offence are based in the UK then a UK offence has been committed. If any of the other computers involved are in other countries then there is a double (or multiple) offence committed. It is also possible that the computer hacker has committed a data protection offence if he obtains data not now lawfully registered.

The Computer Misuse Act 1990 formalises the offence of hacking, that is the unauthorised access to computer material, and Figure 13.32 gives a calendar of events leading up to and after its implementation. The stereotypical (external) hacker and virus writer is perceived as young, male, and a computer enthusiast who sees entry to the system, or creation of a virus, in the light of an intellectual challenge. The hacker tolerant argue that, since unauthorised access to some safety critical systems by more malicious criminals or terrorists would be extremely dangerous, the highly publicised entries of 'nuisance' hackers causes all security to be

Section 1 of the Act provides that an offence is committed when:

- A person causes a computer to perform any function with intent to secure access to any program or data held in any computer.
- The access he intends to secure is unauthorised and he knows at the time when he causes the computer to perform the function that this is the case.

Such offences are tried at a magistrates' court and the maximum penalty is six months imprisonment, a fine up to level 5 (currently £5000), or both.

Section 2 of the Act provides that an offence is committed when the 'unauthorised access' of s 1 is with intent:

- To commit a further offence
- To facilitate the commission of a further offence (whether by himself or by some other person).

Such further offence must be a criminal one with a maximum penalty of not less than five years. This ulterior or intent offence carries a maximum penalty of five years, and/or an unlimited fine.

Section 3 of the Act provides that an offence is committed when someone:

- Does any act which causes an unauthorised modification of the contents of any computer
- At the time when the act is done has the requisite intent and the requisite knowledge.

This section covers virus distribution, even if someone else puts the infected disk into the machine. Even if good back-ups reduce the consequences of the action, the offence is still criminal. The use of time bomb style viruses comes under blackmail section of the Theft Act 1968 and, if the modifications result in any physical damage, perhaps to a disk head, then the Criminal Damage Act 1971 will apply.

**Fig 13.31 ◆ The three new offences of the Computer Misuse Act 1990**

tightened against the dangerous. This argument must be treated with extreme care since it would seem to say that the 'pesterer' is valuable if they make organisations fearful of the greater danger. Are such pesterers to be rewarded or prosecuted? Early 1993 saw the arrests of four alleged members of the Association of Really Cruel Viruses (ARCV), an organised virus writing ring, and the arrest of the proprietor of the Virus Clinic, an organisation allegedly selling viruses by mail order. Since the Computer Misuse Act 1990 does not use the word 'virus' it is unclear whether the Act covers the sale or writing of viruses if they are never *used*. The stereotype of the hacker/virus writer may need some updating in the light of these prosecutions; in the first instance ARCV is an *organised* group, and in the second the virus writer is also the director of a company selling anti-virus products with a vested interest in the spread of viruses, or at least the spread of fear of viruses!

Perhaps the most famous case under the Computer Misuse Act (1990) is notable for its precedent setting rather than the level of monies involved. Woods, Strickland and Bedworth (all students) formed the Eight Legged Groove Machine Club, gave themselves Tolkeinesque aliases, such as Gandalf and Cyclone, and contacted each other, not in person, but across bulletin boards. They used simple equipment, for instance a £200 BBC micro, and used swapped passwords to access BT's Packet Switch Stream and the academic network JANET. The damage they caused was valued at £12 000 plus telephone bills of £25 000 in, what the case judge

| June 1990 | Self-styled 'Mad Hacker' Nicholas Whiteley sentenced to four months imprisonment, with a further eight suspended, on charges of criminal damages to computer systems at the Universities of London, Bath and Hull as a result of 'declaring war'; the first to be jailed for a 'hacking' crime. No hacking law at the time. |
|---|---|
| Aug 1990 | Computer Misuse Act came into force. |
| Oct 1990 | Crown dropped charges against Edward Singh, accused of breaking into Ritz Video's systems. |
| Apr 1991 | Ross Perlstone convicted under the new act of hacking into Mercury systems; fined £900. Although not the first to be charged, he was the first to be convicted under the act. |
| July 1991 | Sean Cropp, the first person to be charged under the Act, was acquitted when the judge decided that hacking only takes place when one computer accesses another. |
| June 1992 | Court of Appeal overruled judge in Cropp case. |
| June 1992 | Richard Goulden convicted under Section 3 of the Act but given two-year conditional discharge and a £1 650 fine. His actions cost victim Ampersand typesetters £36 000 in lost business. |
| Mar 1993 | Paul Bedworth acquitted of three conspiracy charges under the Computer Misuse Act on the grounds that, since he was addicted to computing, he could not form the criminal intent necessary to be guilty of conspiracy. |
| May 1993 | Neil Woods and Karl Strickland (co-defendants with Bedworth) each sentenced to six months imprisonment as first to be jailed under the Computer Misuse Act. |
| Dec 1993 | Malcolm Farquarhson jailed for six months as the major offender in a hacking case, yet it was his accomplice who accessed the computer at his request. |
| Nov 1995 | After five years in existence, the Computer Misuse Act 1990 is used against a virus writer for the first time. Christopher Pile, alias the Black Baron, sentenced to 18 months for writing and spreading two computer viruses, Pathogen and Queeg. |

**Fig 13.32 ◆ Computer crime calendar**
(after Lauchlan 1993)

called, 'intellectual joyriding'. The *Mail on Sunday* claimed that Allied Gulf War plans had to be changed as a result of these hackers scrambling weather computer data. The three were charged with conspiracy rather than 'simple' hacking and, since it was a conspiracy charge, criminal intent had to be proved. Bedworth was acquitted when his psychiatrist showed that he was addicted to hacking and so incapable of forming a criminal intent. Strickland and Woods were convicted and given prison sentences of six months, making them the first to be jailed under the Act, illustrated in Figure 13.32.

In addition to the landmark UK hacker cases, perhaps the most famous hacker ever, Kevin Mitnick, is awaiting trial in the US. Generally referred to as 'the most wanted man in cyberspace' by the media, Mitnick's ability to evade capture by manipulation of computer systems has done much to create a frontiersman-like mystique around hacking.

Whilst not an IS *created* crime, the issue of electronic creation, storage and transmission of pornography is none the less a real concern to IS management. Whilst bulletin boards and World Wide Web sites have taken the brunt of the blame, a report by Marshall (1994) estimates that one in twenty commercially used PCs will store pornographic images. There are three acts relevant to this areas, the Obscene Publications Act 1959, the Protection of Children Act 1978 and the Criminal Justice Act 1988. Although it is likely that computer-*simulated* pornography is not covered by these three, the volume and unpleasantness of simulated as well as 'real' computer pornography pose an ethical as well as a legal problem to IS management. Unfortunately this issue, perhaps because there are no software vendors to take a lead, has not been pursued as vigorously as that of software piracy. As with piracy, IS management must take a lead by showing a real (rather than lipservice) commitment to clean up policies. Actually, according to most surveys, IS professionals are those who are most likely to have amassed extensive stores of digital pornography. In most organisations they are the ones who are most likely to have complete freedom of machine use, extensive access rights to communications systems and to be exempt from any checks. The BCS provides guidelines on eradicating pornography stores. These are essentially the same actions that could be taken to irradicate pirated software and therefore can have a *double* benefit. The BCS suggests that IS management should:

- Establish and publicise strong house rules on computer use that forbids employees loading personal software onto machines. This must be backed by a willingness to proceed to disciplinary action if illegal or offensive material is found.

- Conduct routine and random checks of systems. Printing directories and questioning non-registered ones will identify 80 per cent of cases. If concealment is suspected an audit, though expensive, can be used.

- Monitor access to public networks and ban access to UK 0891 numbers.

- Enlist the support of any union policies on sexual harassment and equal opportunities.

- Institute a confidential contact point to which concerned users can report worries. Since the IS support team is considered to be the most likely to be involved in the distribution of computer pornography, the contact should not be an IS professional.

The issue of IS and crime does not end with using computers with criminal intent. Computers also have a significant role to play in preventing, detecting and prosecuting crimes. Cashmore and Lyall (1991) give the example that theft at the retail point of sale is reduced by requiring all cashiers to enter personal identification numbers. Computer fraud can be detected by computer systems, for instance Peter Smith, who embezzled £88 000 from Hackney and Kettering Borough Councils, was caught when it was recognised that fake benefit accounts had been set up using his password. The increasing sophistication of 'cashless' systems reduces cash crimes, just as it raises the dangers of other crimes. The processing capability of on-line banking systems allows the status of accounts to be checked instantaneously meaning frozen accounts can be spotted, so stolen cards cannot be used and credit limits cannot be exceeded. Fast processing allows fast testing of balances against each other, the use of encryption systems and the use of virus scanning software, etc, and all use the number crunching and pattern matching abilities of a computer to detect errors, whether criminal in intent or not. For example, Barclaycard users on unusual spending sprees may find themselves interrogated by store detectives because the credit card company has a knowledge-based system, Fraud 2000, that warns stores about apparently out-of-character purchases by cardholders.

The use of IS *by* police and security services is generally discussed as an area giving rise to ethical concerns, but it is also an area of crime reduction. Systems can be developed to support the work of crime prevention, detection or prosecution. For example, customs officers have developed a computer documentation system that frees them from paper-based documentation so that they have more time for drug detection. The same system stores data on many aspects of drug concealment methods and facilitates data sharing to increase the chance of smuggler detection. Whilst it was designed for drug smuggling methods, its process of listing 'what to look for where' will be expanded to cover all smuggling techniques. In another example of IS improved crime detection, police investigating fraud in shares issues were able to detect multiple-applications using an ICL mainframe-based 'fuzzy logic' system, that can compare different, but similar, names and addresses. Using computer systems means suspects are *cleared* as well as caught, for instance computer-based systems allow car ownership to be checked in seconds whereas with manual systems it took hours.

Since 1991 there has been a national police IS strategy. Police forces are large businesses in their own right, having budgets as large as £200 million, and their 'core competence' is maintaining law and order. As with any business, IS can be used to support that core competence. Inappropriate systems strategies can also hinder police work, just as poor systems strategies hinder business success. Prior to the creation of a national police IS strategy in 1991, Home Office software regulations allowed forces to run incompatible systems. This incompatibility forced the West Midlands Police Authority, when hunting the kidnapper of Stephanie Slater, to have to install an additional 20 terminals able to access the separate systems of the West Yorkshire force. There are two main suppliers of systems conforming to the early 1980s Home Office Large Enquiry System (HOLMES) specification, Bull and McDonnell Douglas, and they cannot communicate on-line, although file transfers are possible. So even though HOLMES is a *standard*, different implementation interpretations barrier compatibility. The difficulties in *practice* of inter-operability from standards-driven approaches have driven a reassessment for the HOLMES2 project. The current IS strategy issues for the police and other emergency services are just those which many large organisations are struggling with: should there be operating unit autonomy or central directing, what role should national standards play, who should control the IS strategy process, should developments be large-scale and delivered by a single supplier (to reduce compatibility difficulties) or standards-led, component based and delivered by continual competition (to reduce lock-in dangers and major project risks)? As with many large organisations it is the potential situation created by past experiences that tends to influence the answers to these questions.

Despite the trend towards ever more use of technology in police work the police themselves are not particularly well equipped or technology literate. For example, Northumbria Police when investigating an allegedly forged betting slip that would have netted £3.8 trillion had to calculate the earnings using the betting shop's calculators, because the police computers were inadequate. *Computing* (1993) contrasts this situation with the Canadian Mounties who, during fraud investigations, all have laptop PCs. A 1993 Home Office report indicated that most police staff are inadequately trained to appreciate the significance of information technology. They miss vital clues and often do not even realise the possible role of computers as evidence-containing devices. The report argues that police must learn to recognise that the computer, at home or at work, often contains the very data they have routinely looked for in diaries and address books.

And finally, computers and crime extends to fictional crime. Computers are well known as the generators of elaborate special effects used in films and television. As Button (1996) discusses, the support of the IS profession is just as essential to the entertainment business as to any other. Software helps to develop plots as well as special effects. At least two software packages, Plots Unlimited and Collaborator, exist to help authors develop crime (and other) plots and the software development teams included crime writers. *Computing* (1992) credit this type of software with the plot of the Kevin Costner film 'Dances with Disk Drives'! Button (1996) also credits MCA's IS strength for another Kevin Costner film, 'Waterworld'. But who holds the copyright?

**References and further reading**

Adler, P. Jr., Parson, C.K. and Zolke, S.B. (1985) Employee Privacy: Legal and Research Developments and Implications for Personnel Administration, *Sloan Management Review*, Vol 26 No 2.

Alexander, M (1995) The Real Security Threat: The Enemy Within, *Datamation*, 15 July pp. 30–3.

Anaokar, M. (1996) Hacked Off About Security? *Computing*, 4 Apr pp. 20–1.

Anon (1993) Law is No Defence Against Ignorance, *Computer Weekly*, 24 June p.17.

Anon (1993) Ten Things You Ought to Know About: Computers and Crime, *Computing*, 8 July p. 60.

Aryanpur S (1993) Credit where Credit's Due, *Computer Weekly*, 15 July pp. 26–7.

Atkins, W. (1991) Jesse James at the Terminal, *Harvard Business Review*, Report 85401.

Audit Commission (1991) *Survey of Computer Fraud and Abuse 1990*, HMSO.

Audit Commission (1994) *Opportunity Makes a Thief*, HMSO.

Bainbridge, D. I. (1993) *Introduction to Computer Law* (2nd edn), Pitman Publishing.

Bailey, J. (1993) *Managing People and Technological Change*, Pitman Publishing.

Barry, F. (1992) Notebook: Risk Analysis and Management, *Computing* 11 June pp. 38–9.

Bawden, D. and Blakeman, K. (1990) *IT Strategies for Information Management*, Butterworth-Heinemann.

Beardson, C. and Whitehouse, D. (1994) *Computers and Society*, Intellect.

Bicknell, D. (1992) CAP Blames User 'Errors' in Software, *Computer Weekly* 13 Feb p. 11.

Birkinshaw, P. (1988) *Freedom of Information: The Law, The Practice and The Ideal*, Weidenfeld and Nicolson.

Black, G. (1991) Recovery or Cover-Up: Are Britain's Corporate Disaster Recovery Plans Sufficient? *Software Management*, Aug pp. 2–4.

Bolton, R. (1992) Take Cover, *Computing*, 23 Apr pp. 22–3.

Bull, G. (1995) 'Acceptance' as a trigger of Payment, *IT Manager's Briefing*, No 37 pp. 4–5.

Bundy, A. and MacQueen, H. (1994) The New Software Copyright Law, *The Computer Journal*, Vol 37 No 2 pp. 78–82.

Button, K. (1996) Tales from Tinsel Town, *Computer Weekly*, 28 Mar p. 38.

Carr, E. (1990) Elemental Issues, *Micro Decision*, June pp. 30–1.

Cashmore, C. and Lyall, R. (1991) *Business Information: Systems and Strategies*, Prentice-Hall.

Cavanagh, G., Mosberg, D. and Velasquez, M. (1981) The Ethics of Organisational Politics, *Academy of Management Review*, Vol 6 No 3 pp. 363–74.

Coleman, A. (1992) *The Legal Protection of Trade Secrets,* Butterworth.

Collins, T. (1996) Gamble of the Century, *Computer Weekly,* 1 Aug pp. 13–4.

Cornwall, H. (1989) *Hackers Handbook IV*, Century Hutchinson Scientific.

Cornwell, R. and Staunton, M. (1985) *Data Protection: Putting the Record Straight*, National Council for Civil Liberties.

Courtney, R.H. Jr. (1989) Proper Assignment of Responsibility for Data Security, *Information Age,* Vol 11 No 2 pp. 83–7.

Data Protection Registrar (1989) *Guidelines* (2nd series), Data Protection Registrar.

Data Protection Registrar (1992) *Eighth Report of the Data Protection Registrar,* HMSO.

Davis, G.B. and Olson, M.H. (1985) *Management Information Systems: Conceptual Foundations, Structure and Development* (2nd edn), McGraw-Hill.

Edwards, C. and Savage, N. (1986) *Information Technology and the Law*, Macmillan.

Elbra, T. (1990) *A Practical Guide to the Computer Misuse Act 1990*, NCC Blackwell.

Evans, D. (1995) Taking Liberties, *Computer Weekly,* 11 May pp. 32–3.

FAST (1992) *Corporate Membership: A Guide For Management*, Federation Against Software Theft.

Flaherty, D. (1989) *Protecting Privacy in Surveillance Societies*, The University of North Carolina Press.

Flynn, D.J. (1992) *Information Systems Requirements: Determination and Analysis*, McGraw-Hill.

Forrester, T. and Morrison, P. (1994) *Computer Ethics: Cautionary Tales and Ethical Dilemmas in Computing* (2nd edn), MIT Press,

Fried, L. (1995) *Managing Information Technology In Turbulent Times*, Wiley-QED.

Green-Armytage, J. (Ed.) (1995) Systems Availability, *Computer Weekly,* 5 Oct p. 24.

Gustoff, M.E. and Sexton, T.J. (1988) Personal Computer Security, *Information Age,* Vol 10 No 4 pp. 195–201.

Hafner, K. and Markoff, J. (1991) *Cyberpunk: Outlaws and Hackers on the Computer Frontier*, Simon and Schuster.

Hall, L. (1992) Safety in Numbers, *Computing,* 30 Apr pp. 26–7.

Harnett, J. (1993) Action Stations, *Computing,* 17 June pp. 38–9.

Hart, R.J. (1988) *Copyright and Computer Generated Works,* Aslib Proceedings, No. 40 pp. 173–81.

Hayward, D. (1996) Rough Justice? *Computing,* 8 Aug pp. 22–3.

Hill, J. (1992) Notebook: DIY Disaster Recovery Manuals, *Computing,* 23 Apr pp. 28–31.

Hinde, S. (1993) Jurassic Park and Computer Disaster Recovery, *Computer Audit Update* Sept pp. 1–6.

Hunt, A. (1993) Notebook: When is Decompiling Legal?, *Computing,* 17 June p. 41.

Hussain, D.S. and Hussain, K.M. (1992) *Information Management: Organisation, Management and Control of Computer Processing*, Prentice-Hall.

Jamieson, R. and Low, C. (1990) Local Area Network Operations: A Security, Control and Audit Perspective, *Journal of Information Technology,* Vol 5 No 2 pp. 63–72.

Johnson, D. (1985) Equal Access to Computing, Computing Expertise and Decision Making about Computers, *Business and Professional Ethics Journal,* Vol 4 No 3 pp. 95–104.

Johnson, D. (1994) *Computer Ethics* (2nd edn), Prentice-Hall.

Jones, P. (Ed.) (1995) Ads to Get Under the Skin, *PC Week,* 17 Oct p. 14.

Kahane, Y., Neuman, S. and Tapiero, C. (1988) Computer Backup Pools, Disaster Recovery and Default Risk, *Communications of the ACM,* Vol 32 No 1 pp. 78–83.

Kavanagh, J. (Ed.) (1994) Health Campaign Aims to Keep Staff Smiling, *Computer Weekly* 6 Jan p. 27.

LaChat, M. (1986) Artificial Intelligence and Ethics: An Exercise in the Moral Imagination, *AI Magazine,* Vol 7 No 2 pp. 70–9.

Lambeth, J. (1996) Time to Get Serious about Data Security, *Computer Weekly,* 21 Mar, p. 4.

Lauchlan, S . (1993) Bedworth Case Puts Law on Trial, *Computing,* 25 Mar p. 7.

Loch, K.D., Carr, H.H. and Warkentin, M.E. (1992) Threats to Information Systems: Today's Reality, Yesterday's Understanding, *MIS Quarterly,* June pp. 173–86.

London, W. (1994) EC Information Security Legislation: Where Now? *The Computer Law and Security Report,* Vol 10 No 5 pp. 226–53.

Lynch, M. (1994) Safety Nets, *Computing,* 3 Nov pp. 32–3.

Marshall, S. (1994) A View to a Thrill?, *PC Week,* 25 Jan pp. 8–9.

Mason, R. (1986) Four Ethical Issues of the Information Age, *MIS Quarterly,* Vol 10 No 1 pp. 5–12.

McNevin, A. (1995) Users Toughen Up and Take Suppliers to Court, *Computing,* 12 Jan p. 8.

Mensching, J.R. and Adams, D.A. (1991) *Managing an Information System*, Prentice- Hall.

Merry, J. (1992) Executive Window, *Infomatics,* Dec pp. 45–8.

Morgan, R. and Steadman, G. (1987) *Computer Contracts* (3rd edn), Longman.

Moscove, S. and Simkin, M. (1989) *Accounting Information Systems*, Wiley.

MSA Business Survey (1990) *Excellence and the IT factor: IT inside Excellent Companies in Britain*, MSA.

Nabarro Nathanson (1994) *A Legal Guide to Innovation*, Prince of Wales Award for Innovation.

NCC (1990) *Data Protection Codes of Practice*, NCC.

Newman, J. (1988) How to Avoid Contracting Troubles, *Communications,* Aug pp. 24–6.

News (1993) High-Earner Duped D&B to Prolong Contract, *Computing,* 8 July p. 3.

PC Direct (1992) Guide to the Law, *PC Direct,* November.

PC Futures (1993) Most UK Firms Fall Down Over Disaster Planning, *PC Week,* 4 May p. 40.

Pernul, G. (1995) Information Systems Security: Scope, State-of-the-Art, and Evaluation Techniques, *International Journal of Information Management,* Vol 15 No 3 pp. 165–80.

Rabino, S. and Enayati, E. (1995) Intellectual Property: The Double-Edged Sword, *Long Range Planning,* Vol 28 No 5 pp. 22–31.

Rahman, A.S. (1992) Stricter Rules on Use of Government Tax, *New Straits Times,* 15 Oct p. 3.

Reid, P. (1993) Safe and Sound, *PC Plus,* Mar pp. 296–97.

Reynolds, G.W. (1992) *Information Systems for Managers* (2nd edn), West Publishing.

Satya, V. (1988) Secure Computer Network Requirements, *Information Age,* Vol 10 No 4 Oct pp. 211–21.

Saunders, G. (1989) Protection Is Better Than Cure, *Computer Weekly,* 22 June pp. 30–1.

Saxby, S. (Ed.) (1990) *Encyclopaedia of Information Technology Law,* Sweet and Maxwell.

Sizer, R. and Clark, J. (1989) Computer Security – A Pragmatic Approach for Managers, *Information Age,* Vol 11 No 6 pp. 88–98.

Sizer, R. (Ed.) (1994) *Security Guidelines In Information Technology for the Professional Practitioner*, BCS.

Smith, M.R. (1989) *Common-sense Computer Security*, McGraw-Hill.

Smith, P. (1993) PC Security: A Model to Determine Appropriate Defences, *Computer Audit,* July pp. 2–7.

Snell, T. (1993) Industry Pushes Pirates Overboard, *Computing,* 10 June p. 9.

Solomon, S. and O'Brien, J. (1990) The Effect of Demographic Factors on Attitudes Toward Software Piracy, *Journal of Computer Information Systems,* Spring pp. 40–6.

Stross, C. (1992) The Information Revolution, *Computer Shopper*, Feb pp. 319–22.

Tapper, C. (1990) *Computer Law,* (4th edn), Longman.

Warren, P. (1995) Private Lives, *Computing,* 26 Jan p. 27.

Warren, P. (1996) Little Brother or Big Brother? *Computing,* 21 Mar pp. 2–3.

Warren, P. (1996) Organising Crime, *Computing,* 18 Apr pp. 26–7.

Wasik, M. (1991) *Crime and the Computer*, Clarendon Press.

Watson, R. and Pitt, L. (1993) Personal Computing Ethics: Beliefs and Behaviour, *International Journal of Information Management,* Vol 13 pp. 287–98.

Yazel, L. (1994) The High Price of Insecurity, *Computing,* 21 Apr p. 23

# AUTHOR INDEX

# GENERAL INDEX